Islamists and the Politics of the Arab Uprisings

Islamists and the Politics of the Arab Uprisings

Governance, Pluralisation and Contention

Edited by Hendrik Kraetzschmar and Paola Rivetti

EDINBURGH
University Press

Edinburgh University Press is one of the leading university presses in the UK. We publish academic books and journals in our selected subject areas across the humanities and social sciences, combining cutting-edge scholarship with high editorial and production values to produce academic works of lasting importance. For more information visit our website: edinburghuniversitypress.com

Edinburgh University Press Ltd
The Tun – Holyrood Road
12 (2f) Jackson's Entry
Edinburgh EH8 8PJ

Typeset in 12/14 Arno and Myriad by
IDSUK (Dataconnection) Ltd, and
printed and bound in Great Britain

A CIP record for this book is available from the British Library

ISBN 978 1 4744 1925 3 (hardback)
ISBN 978 1 4744 1926 0 (paperback)
ISBN 978 1 4744 1927 7 (webready PDF)
ISBN 978 1 4744 1928 4 (epub)

Contents

Abbreviations

ACM	Anti-Capitalist Muslims (Kapitalizmle Mücadele Derneği)
AKP	Adalet ve Kalkınma Partisi (Justice and Development Party)
AP	Authenticity Party (Hizb al-Asala)
AQAP	Al-Qaeda in the Arabian Peninsula (Tanzim al-Qaeda fi Jazirat al-'Arab)
AQI	Al-Qaeda in Iraq (al-Qaeda fi al-'Iraq)
ASU	Arab Socialist Union (al-Ittihad al-Ishtiraki al-'Arabi)
BDP	Building and Development Party (Hizb al-Bina' wa al-Tanmiyya)
CAP	Civilisational Alternative Party (Hizb al-Badil al-Hadari)
CDR	Call for Democratic Reform (Nida' al-Islah al-Dimuqrati)
CEDAW	Convention on the Elimination of all Forms of Discrimination against Women
CHP	Cumhuriyet Halk Partisi (Republican People's Party)
CM	Constitutional Movement (al-Harakat al-Dustouriyya)
CNSFP	Commission for National Security and Foreign Policy
CP	Centre Party (Hizb al-Wasat)
CU	Constitutional Union (al-Ittihad al-Dustouri)
DFK	Democratic Forum of Kuwait (al-Minbar al-Dimuqrati al-Kuwaiti)
DFP	Democratic Front Party (Hizb al-Gabha al-Demuqrati)
DP	Da'wa Party (Hizb al-Da'wa)
EBDA	Egyptian Business Developmental Association
ECP	Egyptian Current Party (Hizb al-Tayyar al-Misri)
ESDP	Egyptian Social Democratic Party (al-Hizb al-Misri al-Dimuqrati al-Ijtma'i)
EU	European Union
FEP	Free Egyptians Party (Hizb al-Misriyeen al-Ahrar)
FJP	Freedom and Justice Party (Hizb al-Hurriyya wa al-'Adala)

FSA	Free Syrian Army
GCC	Gulf Cooperation Council
GDP	Gross domestic product
GPC	General People's Congress (al-Mo'tamar al-Sha'abi al-'Aam)
HP	Homeland Party (Hizb al-Watan)
IAF	Islamic Action Front (Jabhat al-'Amal al-Islami)
IAS	Islamic Action Society (Jam'iyyat al-'Amal al-Islami)
ICM	Islamic Constitutional Movement (al-Harakat al-Dustouriyya al-Islamiyya)
ICP	Iraqi Communist Party (al-Hizb al-Shuyu'i al-'Iraqi)
IFLB	Islamic Front for the Liberation of Bahrain (al-Jabha al-Islamiyya li-Tahrir al-Bahrayn)
IG	Islamic Group (al-Jama'a al-Islamiyya)
IG	Islamic Gathering/Kuwait (al-Tajammu' al-Islami)
IHCHR	Iranian High Council for Human Rights (Settad-e Hoquq-e Bashar)
IMF	International Monetary Fund
INA	Iraqi National Alliance (al-I'tilaf al-Watani al-'Iraqi)
INC	Islamic National Coaliton (al-'Itilaf al-Watani al-Islami)
IP	Independence Party (Hizb al-Istiqlal)
IPG	Islamic Popular Gathering (al-Tajammu' al-Islami al-Sha'abi)
IRGC	Islamic Revolutionary Guard Corps
IS	Islamic State (al-Dawla al-Islamiyya)
ISCI	Islamic Supreme Council of Iraq (al-Majlis al-A'ala al-Islami al-'Iraqi)
ISI	Islamic State of Iraq (al-Dawla al-Islamiyya fi al-'Iraq)
ISIS	Islamic State of Iraq and al-Sham (al-Dawla al-Islamiyya fi al-'Iraq wa al-Sham)
JCO	Justice and Charity Organisation (al-'Adl wa al-Ihsan)
JDY	Justice and Development Youth (Chabibabte al-'Adala wa al-Tanmiyya)
JMP	Joint Meeting Parties (Ahzab al-Liqa' al-Mushtarak)
JP	Justice Party (Hizb al-'Adl)
JPA	Justice and Peace Assembly (Tajammu' al-'Adala wa al-Salam)
KMB	Kuwaiti Muslim Brotherhood (al-Ikhwan al-Muslimun fi al-Kuwait)
LJP	Labour and Justice Platform (Emek ve Adalet Platformu)
LRC	League of Revival and Change (Rabitat al-Nahda wa al-Taghyir)
MB	Muslim Brotherhood (al-Ikhwan al-Muslimun)
MENA	Middle East and North Africa
MSC	Mujahidin Shura Council

MTI	Mouvement de la Tendance Islamique/Islamic Tendency Movement (Harakat al-Ittijah al-Islami)
MUR	Movement of Unity and Reform (Harakat al-Tawhid wa al-Islah)
NAB	National Action Bloc (Kutlat al-'Amal al-Wataniyya)
NATO	North Atlantic Treaty Organisation
NDC	National Dialogue Conference
NDP	National Democratic Party (al-Hizb al-Watani al-Dimuqrati)
NIA	National Islamic Alliance (al-Tahaluf al-Watani al-Islami)
NSF	National Salvation Front (Jabhat al-Inqadh al-Watani)
NUG	National Unity Gathering ('Tajammu' al-Wahda al-Wataniyya)
NWP	New Wafd Party (Hizb al-Wafd al-Jadid)
OMSC	One Million Signature Campaign (Yek Milyun Emza bara-ye Laghv-e Qavanin-e Tab'iz Amiz)
OREMA	Organisation du Renouveau Estudiantin au Maroc/Students Renewal Organisation in Morocco
PAB	Popular Action Bloc (Kutlat al-'Amal al-Sha'abi)
PAM	Party of Authenticity and Modernity (Hizb al-Asala wa al-Mu'assara)
PDCM	Popular Democratic and Constitutional Movement (al-Haraka al-Sha'biyya al-Dustouriyya al-Dimuqratiyya)
PDRY	People's Democratic Republic of Yemen
PJD	Party of Justice and Development (Hizb al-'Adala wa al-Tanmiyya)
PKK	Partiya Karkerên Kurdistanê (Kurdistan Worker's Party)
PL	Party of Light (Hizb al-Nour)
PM	Popular Movement (al-Haraka al-Sha'biyya)
PNPA	Peace and National Partnership Agreement
PPS	Party of Progress and Socialism (Hizb al-Taqqadum wa al-Ishtirakiyya)
PSD	Parti Socialiste Destourien/Socialist Destourian Party (Hizb al-Ishtiraki al-Dustouri)
PU	Party of the Ummah (Hizb al-Ummah)
PUK	Patriotic Union of Kurdistan (Yekîtiya Nishtimane ya Kurdistanê)
PYD	Partiya Yekîtiya Demokrat (Kurdish Democratic Union Party)
RCD	Rassemblement Constitutionnel Démocratique/Constitutional Democracy Rally (Hizb al-Tajammu' al-Dustouri al-Dimuqrati)
RDMP	Reform and Development Misruna Party (Hizb al-Islah wa al-Tanmiyyah – Misruna)
RIHS	Revival of the Islamic Heritage Society (Jam'iyyat Ihya' al-Turath al-Islami)

RNI	Rassemblement National des Indépendants/National Rally of Independents (al-Tajammu' al-Watani lil-Ahrar)
RP	Refah Partisi (Welfare Party)
RTP	Revolution's Tomorrow Party (Hizb Ghad al-Thawra)
SBP	Syrian Baath Party (Hizb al-Ba'ath al-'Arabi al-Ishtiraki)
SCAF	Supreme Council of the Armed Forces
SCC	Supreme Constitutional Court
SCIRI	Supreme Council of the Islamic Revolution in Iraq (al-Majlis al-A'ala li-Thawra al-Islamiyya fi al-'Iraq)
SEP	Strong Egypt Party (Hizb Misr al-Qawiyya)
SG	Salafi Gathering (al-Jam'iyyat al-Salafiyya)
SIG	Salafi Islamic Gathering (al-Tajammu' al-Islami al-Salafi)
SM	Salafi Movement (al-Haraka al-Salafiyya)
SMB	Syrian Muslim Brotherhood (al-Ikhwan al-Muslimun fi Suriyya)
SMF	Social Movement Family
SPAP	Socialist Popular Alliance Party (Hizb al-Tahaluf al-Sha'abi al-Ishtiraki)
SSNP	Syrian Social Nationalist Party (al-Hizb al-Suri al-Qawmi al-Ijtima'i)
TESEV	Turkish Economic and Social Studies Foundation
TWJ	al-Tawhid wa al-Jihad (Monotheism and Jihad)
UAE	United Arab Emirates
UIA	United Iraqi Alliance (al-I'tilaf al-'Iraqi al-Muwahhad)
UK	United Kingdom
UN	United Nations
UNTM	Union National du Travail au Moroc/National Labour Union in Morocco
UP	Ummah Party (Hizb al-Ummah)
US	United States
USFP	Union Socialiste des Forces Populaires/Socialist Union of Popular Forces (al-Ittihad al-Ishtiraki lil-Quwat al-Sha'biyya)
VAT	Value-added tax
VP	Virtue Party (Hizb al-Fadila)
WS	Wilayyat Saina' (Sinai Province)
YAR	Yemen Arab Republic
YPG	Yekîneyên Parastina Gel (People's Protection Units)

Notes on the editors and contributors

Hendrik Kraetzschmar is Associate Professor in the Comparative Politics of the MENA at the University of Leeds, United Kingdom. He has published a number of peer-reviewed journal articles on electoral, associational and party politics in the Middle East and North Africa and is the editor of *Opposition Cooperation in the Arab World: Contentious Politics in Times of Change* (2012) and co-editor of *Democracy and Violence: Global Debates and Local Challenges* (2010).

Paola Rivetti is Assistant Professor in Politics of the Middle East and International Relations at Dublin City University, Ireland. Her research interests focus on the government of societies and polities in the Middle East and North Africa, on political mobilisations and on Iranian domestic politics. She also worked on the movement of people from the region and on precarity in academia and academic freedom. She published on these topics in academic as well as non-academic outlets. In 2017, she received the award of Early-Career Researcher of the Year from the Irish Research Council. She is co-editor of *Continuity and Change before and after the Arab Uprisings: Morocco, Tunisia and Egypt* (2015).

Ibrahim Al-Marashi is Associate Professor of Middle East History at California State University San Marcos, USA. He is the co-author of *Iraq's Armed Forces: An Analytical History* (2008) and *The Modern History of Iraq* (2017).

Souhaïl Belhadj is Researcher at the Center on Conflict, Development and Peacebuilding of the Graduate Institute of International and Development Studies in Geneva, Switzerland. He is the author of the book *La Syrie de Bashar al-Asad: Anatomie d'un régime autoritaire* (2013). His current research is concerned with the political transition process in Syria and Tunisia, with a focus on the re-composition of political institutions, particularly the local government. He started a two-year project entitled 'Tunisia: Security Provision and Local State Authority in a Time of Transition', with the support of the Gerda Henkel Foundation.

Nazlı Çağın Bilgili is Assistant Professor in the Department of International Relations at Istanbul Kultur University, Turkey. She was formerly a post-doctoral researcher in the Arabic, Islamic and Middle Eastern Studies Department at the University of Leeds, United Kingdom. Her research focuses on democratisation and the role of institutional and social Islam in it. She has published articles and book chapters on religiosity and democratisation, and the Alevi minority in Turkey. Her current research examines the political and social role of the Islamic left in Turkey.

Francesco Cavatorta is Associate Professor in the Department of Political Science and Research Fellow at the *Centre Interdisciplinaire de Recherche sur l'Afrique et le Moyen Orient* (CIRAM), Laval University, Quebec, Canada. He is the author and co-author of a number of books, including *Civil Society and Democratization in the Arab world* (2010) and *Politics and Governance in the Middle East and North Africa* (2015), and several journal articles on democratisation, civil society and Islamist movements in North Africa.

Chérine Chams El-Dine is Assistant Professor of Political Science in the Faculty of Economics and Political Science at Cairo University, Egypt. From September 2012 to January 2013 she was a Research Fellow at the German Institute for International and Security Affairs (Stiftung Wissenschaft und Politik) in Berlin. In 2011–12, she held a lectureship in Middle Eastern politics at the Institute of Arab and Islamic Studies, University of Exeter, United Kingdom. Her current research focuses on the resilience of authoritarianism and the democratisation process in the Middle East, including political-business elite connections, civil-military relations and social movements, with special emphasis on Iraq and Egypt.

Katerina Dalacoura is Associate Professor in International Relations at the London School of Economics and Political Science (LSE), London, United Kingdom. In 2015–16, she was British Academy Mid-Career Fellow. Her work has centred on the intersection of Islamism and international human rights norms. She has worked on human rights, democracy and democracy promotion in the Middle East, particularly in the context of Western policies in the region. Her latest research focuses on the role of culture and civilisation in International Relations with special reference to Turkey. Her latest book is *Islamist Terrorism and Democracy in the Middle East* (2011).

Jérôme Drevon is Research Fellow of the Swiss National Science Foundation at the University of Oxford, United Kingdom. His doctoral and post-doctoral research at the universities of Durham and Manchester examined Egyptian Salafi–jihadi groups and networks from their inception to the post-2011 uprising. He has undertaken extensive field research with their leaders and members to comprehend their mobilisation and socialisation processes. Drevon is generally interested in the meso-level study of Islamist movements, political violence and contentious politics. His research was published in numerous academic journals and book chapters, including *Mediterranean Politics* and the *Middle East Journal*.

Vincent Durac lectures in Middle East Politics in University College Dublin, Ireland, and is a Visiting Professor at Bethlehem University. He is co-author (with Francesco Cavatorta) of *Politics and Governance in the Middle East* (2015) and of *Civil Society and Democratization in the Arab World: The Dynamics of Activism* (2011). His work has been published in *Mediterranean Politics*, *Democratization*, the *British Journal of Middle Eastern Studies*, the *Journal of North African Studies* and the *Journal of Contemporary African Studies*.

Laura Ruiz de Elvira Carrascal is Researcher at the French Institut de Recherche pour le Développement (IRD), Paris, France. Her research interests focus on charities and civil society, commitment and social movements, politicisation and political crisis and social policies, namely in Syria and Tunisia. She has published several book chapters and articles in peer-reviewed journals including *Archives de Sciences Sociales des Religions*, *International Journal of Middle East Studies*, *Revista Española de Ciencia Política*, *Maghreb-Machrek* and *A Contrario*. She is also the co-author of *Civil Society and the State in Syria: The Outsourcing of Social Responsibility* (2012).

Melissa Finn is Post-doctoral Researcher at the Balsillie School of International Affairs and the Department of Political Science at the University of Waterloo, Canada. Her work examines how citizenship is made meaningful through activism, refusal and resistance. She investigates how local Arab activists in the Middle East and North Africa and transnational Arab activists in the West chip away at the infrastructure of authoritarian regimes, and at the contours of political engagement among Arab and Muslim youth in Canada.

Courtney Freer is Research Officer at the Kuwait Programme at the London School of Economics and Political Science (LSE), London, United Kingdom. Her research focuses on the domestic politics of the Arab Gulf states, with a particular focus on Islamism and tribalism. Her work has been published in the *International Journal of Middle East Studies* and *Middle Eastern Studies*. She previously worked as Research Assistant at the Brookings Doha Center and as Researcher at the US–Saudi Arabian Business Council.

Angela Joya is Assistant Professor in International Studies at the University of Oregon, USA. Her research focuses on globalisation and neo-liberal reforms in the Middle East and North Africa. She is currently completing her book manuscript on the political economy of Egypt under Mubarak. Her other research explores the relationship between globalisation and forced displacement of refugees and migrants in the region.

Wanda Krause is Assistant Professor at the School of Leadership Studies at Royal Roads University, Canada, and an international consultant. She has fifteen years of experience as a scholar-practitioner leading action research-focused projects, primarily evaluating the impact of women leading political change on civil society in the Middle East through a developmental lens. Her main research areas of focus include women's leadership, community development, organisational development and civil society. In addition to her geographical focus on the Arab Gulf and Egypt, she has several years of experience working on strategic planning and evaluation of various programmes in Canada.

Mohammed Masbah is a political-sociologist whose work centres on Salafism, political Islam, authoritarianism and youth movements, with a focus on North Africa. He is currently Associate Fellow at Chatham House (United Kingdom) and a Post-doctoral Fellow at the Crown Center for Middle East Studies, Brandeis University, USA. Previously, he was a Nonresident scholar at the Carnegie Middle East Center and fellow at the German Institute for International and Security Affairs (Stiftung Wissenschaft und Politik, SWP) in Berlin, Germany.

Alam Saleh is Lecturer in Middle East Politics and International Relations at Lancaster University, United Kingdom. He received his PhD, MA and BA from the School of Politics and International Studies at the University of Leeds. Saleh is a Fellow of the Higher Education Academy and he has previously taught undergraduate and graduate courses on International Relations, Security Studies and Middle East Politics at Durham, Leeds and Bradford Universities. His book, *Ethnic Identity and the State in Iran*, was published by Palgrave Macmillan in 2013. He has published his works in a number of well-ranked, internationally peer-reviewed journals such as the *Middle East Journal, British Journal of Middle Eastern Studies, Iranian Studies* and *National Identities*. Dr Saleh has also been engaged with policy practitioners and external professional bodies such as the UK Ministry of Defence, NGOs and think tanks.

Jillian Schwedler is Professor of Political Science at the City University of New York's Hunter College and the Graduate Center, and Nonresident Senior Fellow of the Rafiq Hariri Center for the Middle East at the Atlantic Council. She is member of the Board of Directors of the Middle East Studies Association of North America. She is member of the editorial committees for the *International Journal of Middle East Studies, Middle East Law and Governance,* and the Middle East Research and Information Project, publishers of the quarterly *Middle East Report.*

Mariz Tadros is Professor in Development Studies and the Power and Popular Politics Cluster Leader at the Institute of Development Studies, University of Sussex, United Kingdom. She has written extensively on democratisation, religion and gender. Her books include: *The Muslim Brotherhood in Contemporary Egypt* (2012), *Copts at the Crossroads* (2013) and *Resistance, Revolt and Gender Justice* (2016).

Truls Hallberg Tønnessen is Research Fellow at the Norwegian Defence Research Establishment. In 2016 he was a visiting scholar at the Center for Security Studies, Georgetown University, Washington, DC. His primary research focus is on jihadi–Salafi insurgent groups in Iraq and Syria. He has published his research in various peer-reviewed journals, including *Perspectives on Terrorism* and *Political Violence and Terrorism.*

Marc Valeri is Senior Lecturer in Political Economy of the Middle East and Director of the Centre for Gulf Studies at the University of Exeter, United Kingdom. He is the author of *Oman: Politics and Society in the Qaboos State* (2009; 2nd edn 2017) and co-editor of *Business Politics in the Middle East* (2013).

Anne Wolf is Research Fellow at Girton College, University of Cambridge, United Kingdom. She has published numerous articles on Tunisia and is the author of *Political Islam in Tunisia: The History of Ennahda* (Oxford University Press, 2017). Her current research focuses on the evolution of the networks of Ben Ali's Constitutional Democratic Rally party and authoritarian resilience after the 2010–11 uprisings.

Luciano Zaccara is Research Assistant Professor in Gulf Politics at the Qatar University, Gulf Studies Center. His research interests are in Iranian politics and foreign policy, Gulf politics, the International Relations in the Persian Gulf and the electoral systems in the MENA. His latest publications include a co-edited book on Iran-GCC relations, a book chapter on Iranian foreign policy and several peer-reviewed articles on Iranian politics and foreign policy, GCC citizenship policies (co-authored), and the foreign policy of the GCC states.

Barbara Zollner is Lecturer of Middle East Politics at the Department of Politics, Birkbeck College in London, United Kingdom. Her academic research focuses on Islamist politics, social movements and political parties in the MENA region. She is author of *The Muslim Brotherhood: Hasan al-Hudaybi and Ideology* (2008). Her recent publications include, among others, 'The Muslim Brotherhood in Transition', in Peter Lintl, Christian Thuselt and Christian Wolff (eds), *Religiöse Bewegungen als politische Akteure* (2016). She also contributes to *Opendemocracy*.

Acknowledgements

This edited volume flows out of a collaborative research project on 'From over-estimation to under-estimation: the trajectory of political Islam in five MENA countries', funded by the Gerda Henkel Foundation and developed between 2012 and 2014 which, in addition to both editors, involved Francesco Cavatorta, Vincent Durac, Alam Saleh and Emanuela Dalmasso. We are grateful to the foundation for supporting the field research that contributed to the publication of this book. Paola Rivetti also acknowledges the support received by the Irish Research Council and the New Horizon Grant Scheme (grant no. REPRO/2015/33) in 2016–17, which made it possible to dedicate time and work to this volume. Both editors are very grateful to the numerous external reviewers for their critical engagement with, and input into the chapter contributions of this volume, and to Edinburgh University Press, and Nicola Ramsey in particular, for guiding us so skilfully through the production of the manuscript. Last but not least, we editors are indebted to all our contributors in helping us bring together such an exciting and insightful account of the diverse trajectories of political Islam in the aftermath of the Arab uprisings. We hope this volume will be useful to colleagues and students who wish to deepen their understanding of the complexity of political Islam.

Chapter 1

Political Islam and the Arab uprisings

Paola Rivetti and Hendrik Kraetzschmar

This book emerges from the observation that much has changed in the field of political Islam following the popular uprisings that rocked the authoritarian *status quo* in the Middle East and North Africa (MENA) in 2010–12, nowadays widely referred to as the Arab uprisings or 'Arab Spring'. Prominent instances of such change include the dramatic rise to (and fall from) power of moderate Islamist political parties/groupings in Egypt and Tunisia – forces that had been violently repressed and/or dismantled by pre-uprising authoritarian regimes – the pluralisation of the field of Islamist political players, including most notably the formation of Salafi parties and their ascent to political prominence in electoral and institutional politics, the escalation of sectarian conflict between the region's Sunni and Shi'a communities, exacerbated by war in Yemen, Syria and Iraq, and the emergence of the jihadi–Salafi organisation al-Dawla al-Islamiyya (Islamic State, IS) which advances formal ruling pretentions over territories in Syria and Iraq, which constitutes a new quality to such groups. All of these developments suggest that a renewed analysis and approach to the study of Islamist political and social actors are needed. While extant pre-uprisings scholarship had already noted part of these dynamics and devoted efforts to their analysis – such as for instance the case of Salafi participation in electoral politics,[1] or the growing relevance of the sectarian variable in MENA politics[2] – it can hardly account for their development in the new environment that the Arab Spring has brought about. A cursory look at the scholarship available on the subject of political Islam post-2011 seems to suggest, in fact, that the uprisings constitute just one phase in the long history of Islamist political and social forces present in the MENA, a history characterised by periods of political opposition, inclusion and co-option by authoritarian leaders.[3]

However, although history may outweigh recent dramatic changes – and although old elites and pre-uprising institutions have remained in place and appear to be functioning in many of the countries that have experienced political turmoil – things will hardly stay the same when it comes to contentious politics and state–society relations.[4] Indeed, as of 2018, the whole region seems in flux both at the international level – with regional powers trying to impose their hegemony over other regional competitors – and at the domestic level, with many countries facing unstable national environments prone to political crisis, authoritarian retrenchment and sessionist tendencies, such as in the case of Iraqi Kurdistan.[5] Moreover, as Gilbert Achcar noted, the mass protests that took place across countries from Morocco to Iran and the Gulf region have instilled an unruly spirit within the MENA public, which is likely to play out in the *longue durée*.[6] Alongside countries such as Egypt, where a military coup brought to power an even more repressive form of authoritarianism than had existed under the erstwhile president Hosni Mubarak, in other contexts such as Morocco and Tunisia, the spirit of the 2011 uprising is still alive in the recurrence of popular protests ever since.[7] In fact, while it is true that in many MENA countries a grim authoritarian cloud has come to overshadow the glaring democratic horizon that brightened up the prospect in 2010–11, it is also true that the uprisings put in motion demands for change that go beyond the limitations imposed by the political elites' definition of what a democratic space for political action ought to look like. The most recent protests in the Rif region of Morocco are significant in this respect, precisely because they take place in a country that is considered to be among the most stable in the whole region, with an authoritarian ruling class that efficiently quells potential political instability through a mixture of reform and repression.[8] While taking levels of contention to an international level, and transcending the boundaries of the nation-state, the pro-independence vote of Iraqi Kurds in September 2017 also represents an example of the popular demands for change put in motion by the uprisings of 2010–12. Indeed, these demands have developed 'a life on their own', overcoming well-established arenas of political action and contention, such as the nation-state.

What then is the regional and domestic impact of the Arab uprisings and their aftermath on Islamist political and social organisations, their behaviour, programmatic development/outlook and their interaction with other domestic and transnational forces? This book is concerned with precisely these questions, epitomised by the concepts of 'governance', 'pluralisation' and 'contestation' spelled out in its title. Including a wide range of country-based case studies and covering countries from Iran in the east – whose 'Green Movement' of 2009–10 was a prelude in many ways to the subsequent Arab uprisings – to Morocco in the far west of the MENA, the book offers a comparative analysis of how Islamist organisations/activists have been affected by and dealt with changes brought about by the uprisings and their longer-term implications. Drawing on original research, the individual chapters present an analysis of political Islam that is underpinned by a rejection of 'exceptionalist' thinking, according to which organised political Islam (that is Islamist political parties, social movements, NGOs and charitable associations) is too peculiar to compare with non-Islamist social and political organisations. Exceptionalism contends that what makes Islamist organisations/actors unique is their ideology – that is, Islamism – which, according to this approach, plays a predominant role in determining their choices and political strategies over 'rational' and interest-driven calculations. It follows, as emphasised by Elizabeth R. Nugent,[9] that scholars have rarely compared Islamist and non-Islamist political and social organisations. One such example is the Sage's *Handbook of Party Politics*, which focuses on a wide range of party ideologies and models from different corners of the planet, yet hardly devotes any attention to Islamist political parties, their experiences and workings.[10]

The lack of serious comparative engagement with Islamist social and political organisations is the result of a scholarly approach in political science that goes back to the 1960s and 1970s, and that tended to overlook Islamism as a meaningful socio-political force. As Frédéric Volpi and Ewan Stein explain,[11] Islamism hardly featured as an analytically relevant factor, as at that time academic debates were dominated by modernisation and class theory. Indeed, wherever considered, Islamism tended to be dismissed as the expression of conservative social forces, historically obsolete and doomed to disappear. This nurtured the perception of Islamism and Islamist organisations as 'exceptional', contributing to their isolation from other social and political players.[12] This treatment of Islamism as a tangential and temporary phenomenon changed only after 9/11, when the dominant approach to its study became the prism of security, radicalism and terrorism, exposing the 'exceptional' propensity of Islam and Islam-inspired politics towards violence and radicalism, as well as their incompatibility with democracy.

Although this volume focuses exclusively on Islamist social and political forces, our contributions aim to facilitate dialogue and interaction with the scholarship that has examined other, non-Islamist political and social organisations in a context of change. Far from downplaying the relevance for Islamists of religion as a moral compass informing policy choices, the volume highlights that the behaviour of Islamist organisations is very similar to that of political parties and socio-political organisations more broadly in contexts of change, be they liberalisation, authoritarian resurgence or regime change. Our analyses and findings expose significant parallels to studies conducted on other, non-religious political and social organisations in changing and (potentially) unstable environments, such as for instance communist parties in Central Asia and Eastern Europe following the collapse of the Soviet Union in 1991. Anna Grzymala-Busse and Pauline Jones Luong examine the post-1991 state-(re) building in post-communist Central Asia and Eastern Europe, locating elite competition at the core of this process.[13] The structural constraints that affected intra-elite contention and consequently party politics in the region – such as access to the competition itself (thanks to the existence of some previous organisational structure upon which elite factions may claim their share of power, ideational and material resources), access to the administration and bureaucratic system and to international business networks and the ability to fit strategic discursive and policy templates – resonate with contexts where Islamist organisations have taken part in the process of institutional bargaining post-uprisings, as well as with settings where countries experienced regime change or where an intra-elite compromise could be found to assure continuity for the ruling authorities.[14]

Similarities revolve not only around context, however, but extend to the choices and behaviours of Islamist organisations/activists too. When it comes to political parties, for instance, contributors to this volume underline that moderate Islamist parties have chosen to respect the political limitations imposed by higher authorities, such as a ruling monarch, in exchange for the possibility of governing and/or participating in institutional politics. As highlighted by the case of the Moroccan Hizb al-'Adala wa al-Tanmiyya (Party of Justice and Development, PJD) and its post-2011 rise to power, or the strategic choice made by the Bahraini Shi'a political society Jam'iyyat al-Wifaq al-Watani al-Islamiyya (Entente – National Accord Islamic Society, henceforth al-Wifaq) at the time of the Pearl Roundabout protest movement in 2012, parties disassociated themselves from the protesters in exchange for continued political inclusion. Mohammed Masbah, who authored the chapter on the PJD in Morocco in this volume, talks about a 'pragmatisation' that underpinned the party's post-2011 choices, a statement that echoes Marc Valeri's examination of the behaviour of al-Wifaq, as well as that of the mainstream Sunni Islamist opposition in Kuwait by Luciano Zaccara, Courtney Freer and Hendrik Kraetzschmar, despite the significant differences that exist in the outcome of the three experiences and the fate of the parties/forces in question.

'Pragmatisation for participation' is similar to the strategy adopted by former communist parties in Eastern Europe during the post-1989 'transition period' in response to both liberal democracy and the market economy. Margit Tavits and Natalia Lekti argue that ex-communist and leftist parties in Central Europe adapted to the free market mantra by promising (and, once in power, carrying through) cuts to public spending in order to survive as credible participants in the new institutional politics and to become viable political choices in the eyes of the electorate.[15] In Hungary, for instance, the former Communist Hungarian Socialist Party (known by its Hungarian acronym, MSzP) was able to shed its pariah status in society at the beginning of the political transition, when it reoriented its economic policies, showing commitment to democracy and the market economy.[16] Once elected, the MSzP government implemented a stabilisation package that cut spending for social welfare and accelerated privatisation.[17] In post-1989 Poland as well, the transformed former communist ruling party – Social Democracy of the Republic of Poland (known by its Polish acronym SdRP) – remained a discredited political force, whose local party offices were often robbed or attacked, and local members assaulted. Again, as with the MSzP in Hungary, its political fortunes changed, however, once it committed programmatically to market-economic principles and reforms.[18] While a monarch imposing the rules of the game was absent in Eastern Europe, former communist parties were fighting for political inclusion and electoral success, by abiding by the limitations of a post-1989 political agenda pillared around capitalism and liberal democracy, avoiding appeals to nostalgia and socialist ideology, and actively engaging in tough and aggressive anti-welfare economic reforms.[19] As Tavits and Lekti put it, these parties needed to show that their leaders were capable managers, rather than obsolete ideologues.[20] In order to stand any chance of success in a changing political and economic environment, they pragmatically abided by the new rules of the game.

However, far from homogenising the trajectories of Islamist political parties and organisations in the region, the volume also explores cases in which political and social actors decided not to obey extant structural limitations, choosing exclusion from the formal political sphere instead. The chapter by Barbara Zollner on Egypt, for instance, highlights how strategic and rational calculations may motivate the decision of Islamist parties to stay out of the formal political sphere, thus offering a different perspective on 'pragmatisation' as the ability to maximise one's interests in a given environment. Indeed, pragmatisation and obedience to extant rules in exchange for political inclusion do not necessarily overlap, as Nathan Brown reveals in the case of Kuwait, Jordan, Palestine and Egypt.[21] Brown explains that here Islamist organisations have preferred to protect their credibility as oppositional forces or critics of the ruling elite by staying away from the formal political game, which would have imposed strict limitations on the scope of their anti-establishment critique and possibly co-opted them. Again, this choice is not confined to Islamists, especially in the case of political parties/organisations that operate in authoritarian environments. Looking at the case of Zimbabwe, which is compared against all countries that experienced an authoritarian presidential election between 1990 and 2008, Tavishi Bhasin and Jennifer Gandhi explain that opposition parties often choose electoral boycotts rather than participation to avoid complying with political limitations that they do not agree with or accepting circumstances they do not see as favourable.[22] When it comes to politically unstable contexts – such as those that experienced regime change and subsequently free elections in the MENA region in 2010–11 – or to contexts characterised by competitive authoritarian elections, boycotts may also represent a powerful bargaining chip for political parties to maximise their interests in a new, or quickly changing, environment.[23] In other words, structural and environmental factors seem to be determinant, although not the only ones to be relevant, in the electoral strategy that oppositional forces choose but, while there is a robust scholarship on this topic produced by specialists in the region, only a few scholars have engaged in cross-area comparisons.

The uprisings did not exert a uniform impact on Islamist social and political organisations in the MENA. Far from it, their impact has in fact varied according to the domestic context in which Islamists found themselves and their situation (that is whether they are/were repressed, oppositional, co-opted by the ruling elite or in power). As Volpi and Stein highlight, post-uprising shifts in state–society relations did not affect quietist Salafi organisations in the same way as they affected those Islamists that sought state power.[24] Following this same line of argument, Stein insists that it remains crucial to reject a 'one size fits all' approach to Islamism, also questioning the idea of Islamism as the only electoral and political alternative to the ruling parties available in Muslim-majority societies.[25] Not only is Islamism not the only game in town, but the opening up of the political sphere post-uprising has also forcefully highlighted the increase of competition in the ideational-political market.

This volume brings together chapter contributions that cover a wide range of different types of Islamist social and political organisations that enjoy different relationships to state power, from those aspiring to conquer it (those Volpi and Stein would label as 'statist' or Ewan Stein[26] would call 'pseudo-democratic'), to those (quietist) Salafi forces that have traditionally disengaged but have strategically reconsidered their options, to those that engage in charitable work within civil society and are virtually indifferent to political programmes promoting participation in elections and institutions. Moreover, in terms of ideological variations, this volume spans a broad spectrum of Islamist actors/groupings, ranging from political players that Kamran Bokhari and Farid Senzai label as 'participators' – that is, those forces that accept democracy and see it as compatible with Islam – to 'rejecters' and 'condition-alists' – respectively, who reject or accept democracy but with limitations on, for instance, the extent of women's rights.[27] Amidst these variations, the volume brings together contributions exploring how environmental changes have impacted on the menu of political action available to Islamist actors, and explores the decisions and behaviours of Islamists when confronted with factors such as decreased/increased political competition with other Islamist and non-Islamist political organisations, possibilities for alliance-building, changes in the discursive framing of political choices and access to transnational financial networks.

Themes and chapter contributions

Following on from the above, this volume identifies four trajectories that, broadly speaking, have characterised the evolution of Islamist organisations and politics since the Arab uprisings. These concern first, the transformation of Islamist political parties from parties of the opposition to parties of power (although with diverse fortunes) and the challenges of political and economic governance that this brings with it; second, the pluralisation of domestic Islamist actors and the growth of intra-Islamist competition and conflict; third, the concomitant rise in levels of societal polarisation along 'secular–Islamist' lines in many Arab states and its impact on both Islamist and 'secular' domestic players; and finally, the resurgence of sectarian discourse and conflict in the region, particularly between adherents of Sunni and Shi'a Islam. While these four trajectories are not new, they have arguably acquired new impetus in the wake of the uprisings as a result of the restructuring of institutional and public spheres via constitutional reforms, new and fairer elections, authoritarian retrenchment or liberalisation, and the ongoing competition for regional hegemony, which translates into war and sectarian conflicts. The volume discusses these trajectories in twenty-one chapter contributions grouped into four thematic parts.

Comprising six chapters, Part I of this volume, entitled 'Islamists and issues of political and economic governance', touches on a range of questions pertaining in the broadest sense to Islamist organisations in power, to issues of Islamist governance as well as contention to it. The contributions by Mariz Tadros, Paola Rivetti/Alam Saleh and Truls Hallberg Tønnessen all examine questions of governance, albeit each with a focus on different sets of actors and policy arenas. Exploring the workings of the short-lived Morsi administration, Tadros highlights the challenges it faced in reconciling its doctrinaire positions with the need for compromise and inclusivity during Egypt's early post-transition period. Focusing on the case of Iran, Rivetti and Saleh turn their attention to intra-elite discourses on the rights to political participation post-'Green Movement'. Shunning culturally relativist interpretations, the authors highlight how both progressive and conservative forces draw on 'secular and religious epistemologies' extant in Iran's legal system to advocate an expansion of participatory rights, thus shaping a common ground for negotiating the governance arrangements necessary to guarantee political and institutional continuity after the dramatic polarisation that the repression of the Green Movement created. Moving outside the confines of conventional state structures, Tønnessen, meanwhile, sheds light on the nature of 'rebel governance' by the IS in the territories it controls/controlled in Iraq and Syria, asserting that the group's insistence on being a state was driven as much by ideology as by rivalry with other jihadi–Salafi groupings in the region.

Resistance to governance, in turn, takes centre stage in the chapter by Wanda Krause and Melissa Finn. The authors explore Islamic and Islamist women in Qatar who are active in the charity sector and/or affiliated with organisations such as the Qatari al-Ikhwan al-Muslimun (Muslim Brotherhood, MB), and what they label as their 'refusal' to submit to oppressive policies and the *status quo* through, among other things, day-to-day mobilisation of citizenship. Through their ethnographic study, the authors question conventional conceptions of resistance with their focus on institutionalised and/or organised expressions of contention defined exclusively in opposition to the state. For Krause and Finn expressions of a 'silent', yet resilient, resistance by Islamic/Islamist women were strengthened, in fact, in the wake of the Arab uprisings, and may constitute a significant governance challenge to Qatari rulers in the longer-term.

The last two chapters of this section, by Angela Joya and by Nazlı Bilgili and Hendrik Kraetzschmar, hone in on issues of *economic* governance, and here in particular on the appropriation of, and resistance to, neo-liberal orthodoxy that gained traction in the economic policies of MENA regimes from the 1970s onwards. In her class analysis of the Egyptian MB, Joya contends that the rise to prominence of an *ikhwani* entrepreneurial class during al-Sadat's *infitah* (open door) policies of the 1970s in no small measure explains the group's endorsement of free market principles, which it then sought to implement following the electoral victory of Mohamed Morsi in the 2012 presidential elections. Focusing on the case of Turkey, meanwhile, Bilgili and Kraetzschmar highlight how the neo-liberal economic policies pursued by successive Erdoğan governments since the early 2000s constituted a key source of inspiration for the emergence of an Islamic leftist current, which sought to critique market orthodoxy from within the parameters of Islamic teachings. The two chapters thus problematise the relationship between Islamism and capitalism, highlighting the breadth of positions extant on market-economic policies within Islamism itself and the contention surrounding its adoption. Indeed, whilst Bilgili and Kraetzschmar's chapter demonstrates how capitalism serves as a lever to critique the forces in power, Joya's chapter makes apparent its unquestioned acceptance by mainstream Islamist actors, thus revealing the continuity of orthodox market-economic policies under Islamist rule post-Arab uprisings.

Part II of the volume, entitled 'Islamist and secular party politics' comprises six chapter contributions that examine Islamist parties located in broader multi-party environments where they interact and compete with a range of rival ideological forces. Taking on a relational approach, according to which strategies, interests and choices are the result of complex interactions with a set of diverse players, the chapters examine the Islamists' interplay with the ruling powers (chapters on Morocco, Bahrain), other Islamist forces (Kuwait,

Egypt), and so-called 'secular' political parties (Tunisia, Egypt). Honing in on the cases of Morocco, Egypt, Bahrain and Kuwait, the chapter contributions by Mohammed Masbah, Barbara Zollner, Marc Valeri and Luciano Zaccara, Courtney Freer/Hendrik Kraetzschmar reveal, among others, just how diverse and context-specific the fortunes were of Islamist parties post-2011, with no uniform trend discernible. In some cases, the Arab uprisings and their aftermath facilitated the rise to prominence of Islamist parties, as demonstrated by Masbah in his analysis of the Moroccan PJD, which has not only won successive elections since 2011 but also managed to lead two consecutive coalition governments. For Masbah, this success of the PJD is only partly rooted in its astute electoral outreach and mobilisation, and has much to do with the party's pragmatism towards the monarchy as well as in the formulation of policy. In other cases, meanwhile, the longer-term plight of Islamist parties has been rather less clear-cut, or even progressively worse. Zollner's chapter on Egypt's Islamist party landscape, for instance, highlights how the *coup d'état* of 2013 and the restructuring of the political system under Abdel Fattah al-Sisi heralded a rapid reversal in the electoral/political fortunes of both moderate Islamist and Salafi parties. This development also resonates with the plight of the mainstream Islamist political societies in Bahrain, which, according to Valeri, fell victim to the regime's brutal crackdown during the 2011–12 demonstrations and its skilful attempts at cloaking the protests in a sectarian mantle. This holds true for the most prominent Shi'a Islamist political society, al-Wifaq, whose cadre faced harassment and arrest from 2011 onwards and whose operating licence was finally revoked in 2016, as well as for the country's main Sunni Islamist political societies who in the post-uprising era failed to transform themselves into a credible political force independent of the Palace and its influence. In Kuwait, meanwhile, Zaccara, Freer and Kraetzschmar reveal how the Arab uprisings elsewhere impacted particularly on the country's main Sunni Islamist political associations. The authors assert that, whilst the overall contagion of the Arab uprisings on Kuwaiti politics was limited due to local specificities, a clear link can be discerned between the political/electoral strategies pursued by the country's Islamist political proto-parties/associations and both the experience of (exclusionary) Islamist governance in Egypt under Morsi as well as the ensuing regional crackdown on the MB organisation from 2013 onwards. To ward off threats to their own survival in light of these regional developments, the authors highlight how Sunni Islamist proto-parties/associations sought shelter in the formation of broader cross-ideological alliances as well as in the expression of moderate reform demands that fell well short of calling for regime rupture.

The final two chapter contributions of Part II by Anne Wolf and Hendrik Kraetzschmar/Alam Saleh move the investigative locus away from a focus on Islamist parties to a discussion of the oft-evoked 'secular–Islamist' binary in MENA party politics. Focusing on the cases of Tunisia and Egypt, the two contributions stress that ascribing fixed ideological markers, such as 'Islamist' and/or 'secular', to MENA political parties misrepresents the wide ideological fluidity and policy overlap detectable between the two, particularly on matters pertaining to the role of religion in politics. In the case of Tunisia, for instance, Wolf demonstrates how the allegedly 'secular' Hizb Nida' Tunis (Call of Tunisia Party) is in reality home to a plurality of religious expressions and policy positions that render questionable any such labelling. This view is also replicated in the chapter by Kraetzschmar and Saleh, who reveal that in discourse and policy, most of Egypt's so-called 'secular' parties seek to dismiss the charge of being 'anti-religious'/'anti-Islam'. In both cases then the authors find that conflict between Islamist and non-Islamist political parties is intimately linked to elite competition and survival, and to the struggle around the definition of national identity and the interpretation of national history. Islam seems to be crucial in the political expression and rhetoric of all actors, and the actual contention seems to evolve around the appropriation of it.

Entitled 'Intra-Islamist pluralisation and contention', Part III of this volume explores the diffusion of Islamist players/movements in the post-uprising era and the growing contestation (for votes/ideological high ground) among them. The examination of this theme revolves around four chapters and two levels of analysis. Focusing on single-country cases, the first two chapters look at the case of Tunisian Islamism (Francesco Cavatorta) and Egyptian Salafism (Jérôme Drevon). The two chapters demonstrate how the pluralisation of political actors engaged in national politics has not only strengthened the traditional competition between Salafi and moderate Islamism – whether symbolised by the Egyptian MB or Tunisia's Hizb al-Nahda (Renaissance Party) – but how competition has been on the rise internally as well, between Egyptian and Tunisian Salafi organisations/parties respectively. This intra-Islamist competition – be it among Salafi forces or between Salafis and moderate Islamists – has been multi-dimensional in character, involving electoral and broader political strategies as well as matters of doctrine and political outlook.

Comprising the chapters by Ibrahim Al-Marashi and Katerina Dalacoura, the second level of analysis, in turn, problematises the trajectories of political Islam at the intersection between the national and the transnational. In a nutshell, it reveals the close inter-connect between local and regional-level dynamics and how the two have shaped opportunities for engagement, pluralisation and contention for a plethora of Islamist state and non-state actors in the post-2011 era. Focusing on the local effects of broader regional developments, the chapter by Al-Marashi, for example, reveals just how little influence the region-wide growth in Shiʻa solidarity – particularly in the wake of the civil war in Syria and the rise of the IS – has had on intra-Shiʻa relations within the national setting of Iraq. Indeed, rather than being informed by solidarity and cooperation, Al-Marashi's analysis exposes how conflict and the pursuit of narrow self-interested politics remain the hallmark of interactions between Iraq's principal Shiʻa Islamist parties.

The chapter by Dalacoura, in turn, explores the dialectic effect of national and regional developments on the plight of key exponents of 'third-worldist' (Iran and Hizbullah), 'radical' (al-Qaeda and the IS) and 'moderate' (al-Nahda and al-Ikhwan al-Muslimun) Islamism. In her bird's view account of the international relations of the MENA, Dalacoura contents that each of these strands of Islamism has undergone considerable change since the Arab uprisings of 2010–12. Whilst state-breakdown' and regional conflict precipitated a 'delegitimisation' of third-worldist Islamism and the growth of sectarianism, they also created the necessary opportunities for jihadi–Salafist groupings to make a forceful entry onto the regional political stage through their conquest of large swathes of territory in Iraq, Syria and Libya. The rise to power, meanwhile, of moderately Islamist political players in Egypt and Tunisia has, according to Dalacoura, affected not only the country's foreign policies but the regional balance of power more widely, motivating a reaction on the part of both domestic constituencies and international powers that have considered them as possible threats.

Part IV of this volume, entitled 'The Sunni–Shiʻa divide', finally, tackles the issue of sectarian politics and conflict in the post-uprisings era. Comprising three chapters, it explores the dynamics of Sunni–Shiʻa identity politics in some of the countries most affected by sectarian contention and conflict, including Yemen (Vincent Durac), Syria (Souhaïl Belhadj and Laura Ruiz de Elvira Carrascal) and Iraq (Chérine Chams El-Dine). Sectarianism has been one of the most evident regional dynamics strengthened by the uprisings, notably as a consequence of the growing geopolitical competition between Iran and Saudi Arabia, which overlaps with the broader regional Sunni and Shiʻa camps. The chapters challenge the notion of sectarianism and a simplistic representation of it, and search for the causes of the ongoing confrontation in specific grievances rather than in doctrinal tensions between Sunni and Shiʻa Islam. However, the authors recognise the performative influence that representing the conflict as a sectarian confrontation may have in making it so. In order to tease out this conundrum, all three chapters turn to history and to an in-depth examination of the political relevance of identity politics to the wider population and political elites. The case of Yemen is paradigmatic in this regard, and Durac offers material to reflect on the balance between specific local grievances and their role in driving the Houthi rebellion, and the broader regional sectarian dynamics. The chapter on Syria by Belhadj and Ruiz de

Elvira Carrascal also digs into the history of Syrian nation-building to reveal that sectarianism has always been part of Syrian politics – particularly under Hizb al-Ba'ath al-'Arabi al-Ishtiraki (Arab Socialist Baath Party of Syria) rule – and that the current circumstances have re-signified sectarian identities rather than created them.

This section, however, also makes room for critical voices, demonstrating that anti-sectarian identities and mobilisations have been present in the countries under scrutiny. Belhadj and Ruiz de Elvira Carrascal remind us in this regard that, whilst Syria's present conundrum is steeped in sectarian rivalry and acrimony, identities in the country remain multiple, with the nation and nation-state constituting a key point of reference for many Syrians despite years of sectarian warfare. Looking at the case of Iraq, Chérine Chams El-Dine also finds evidence of anti-sectarian sentiment and behaviour in the Arab Spring-inspired protest cycles that gripped the country between 2011 and 2012 and again from 2015 onwards – a sentiment that survives despite the recent pro-independence vote in Iraqi Kurdistan. This, claims Chams El-Dine, is evident, among others, in the rise to prominence of new politicised actors (youth and ordinary citizens) and discourses which – particularly in the protest cycle of 2015–16 – sought to counter the growth in sectarian politics post-2003 by resorting to slogans and banners that were explicitly secular and nationalist in character.

The concluding chapter, authored by Jillian Schwedler, wraps up this edited volume by proposing a new approach to the study of political Islam. Schwedler puts forward the notion of 'Islamistness' to call for an 'oblique' entry point to the analysis of environments and contexts, rather than of Islamist organisations and/or political parties. While the examination of single political groups is a worthy enterprise when it comes to explaining their evolution or strategic choices, it does not help us overcome 'old' categories of analysis which, in the post-2011 region, ought to be questioned. The insistence on the 'moderate–radical' binary, for instance, may allow scholars to frame an organisation's policy choices, but tends to obscure the complex intersection of values, strategic considerations and ideological genealogies, as well as the varying degrees of 'Islamistness', that inform those choices. Echoing the contributions made by Rivetti /Saleh, Wolf and Kraetzschmar/Saleh in this volume, Schwedler calls, in fact, for going beyond the current binary options that inform scholarship on political Islam (Islamist/secular, pragmatic/ideological, Islamist/non-Islamist), and for making space for nuances and the contemporary presence of Islamist and secular, or non-Islamist, ideational and political forces to explain social phenomena. Consequently, she proposes a shift in focus, moving from an examination of single organisations and groups to an examination of contexts and events. Contextual to her effort of renewing well-established analytical approaches, Schwedler also proposes an innovative categorisation of the chapters included in the volume. Instead of regrouping the chapters according to the trajectory they consider, be it the rise to power of Islamists and the challenge of governance or the Sunni–Shi'a divide, as they do indeed in the book, she identifies other salient categories for reading the collectivity of chapters and the contribution that they make to the 'Islamistness'-centred approach that she advocates.

Notes

1. As highlighted in Joas Wagemakers (2016), 'Revisiting Wiktorowicz: categorising and defining the branches of Salafism', in Francesco Cavatorta and Fabio Merone (eds), *Salafism After the Arab Awakening: Contending with People's Power*. London: Hurst, pp. 7–24.
2. As noted in Chapter 19 on Syria.
3. A very original analysis and account of this historical trajectories, intertwined with elements of introspection and personal biography, is offered by François Burgat (2016), *Comprendre l'islam politique: une trajectoire de recherche sur l'altérité islamiste, 1973–2016*. Paris: La Découverte.
4. Raymond Hinnebusch (2015), 'Change and continuity after the Arab uprising: the consequences of state formation in Arab North African states', *British Journal of Middle Eastern Studies*, 42:1, pp. 12–30, and (2017), 'How Europe contributed to MENA's failing states system and how MENA blowback threatens Europe, in Richard Gillespie and Frédéric Volpi (eds), *Routledge Handbook of Mediterranean Politics*. London: Routledge, pp. 60–71.
5. This volume went to press in the aftermath of the so-called 'independence referendum' in Iraqi Kurdistan on 25 September 2017. While the regional implications of the pro-independence vote are still unclear, the event itself is another testament to the ripple effects of the Arab uprisings on domestic politics, particularly in Syria and Iraq.
6. Gilbert Achcar (2015) 'What happened to the Arab Spring?' *Jacobin*, 17 December, <https://www.jacobinmag.com/2015/12/achchar-arab-spring-tunisia-egypt-isis-isil-assad-syria-revolution/> (last accessed 13 September 2017).
7. Fatim-Zohra El Malki (2017), 'Morocco's Hirak movement: the people versus the Makhzen', *Jadaliyya*, 2 June, <www.jadaliyya.com/pages/index/26645/moroccos-hirak-movement_the-people-versus-the-makhn> (last accessed 13 September 2017).
8. Habibulah Mohamed Lamin (2017), 'Protests grow over police actions in Morocco', *Al-Monitor*, 4 July, <www.al-monitor.com/pulse/originals/2017/07/protest-police-morocco-rif-hoceima-popular-movement.html> (last accessed 14 September 2017) and Maati Monjib (2017), 'The relentless tide of Morocco's Rif protests', *Carnegie Endowment for International Peace*, 21 June, <http://carnegieendowment.org/sada/71331> (last accessed 14 September 2017).
9. Elizabeth R. Nugent (2017), 'Islamists after the "Arab Spring": what's the right research question and comparison group, and why does it matter?', *POMEPS Studies*, 26, <https://pomeps.org/2017/04/27/islamists-after-the-arab-spring-whats-the-right-research-question-and-comparison-group-and-why-does-it-matter/> (last accessed 13 September 2017).
10. Islamist parties are in fact mentioned only once in the whole volume, on page 391, and no dedicated space is allocated to their analysis. See: Richard S. Katz and William J. Crotty (2006) (eds), *Handbook of Party Politics*. London: Sage.

11. Frédéric Volpi and Ewan Stein (2015), 'Islamism and the state after the Arab uprisings: Between people power and state power', *Democratization*, 22:2, pp. 276–93.

12. Simon Bromley (1997), 'Middle Eastern exceptionalism: myth or reality?' in David Potter, David Goldblatt, Margaret Kiloh and Paul Lewis (eds), *Democratization*. Cambridge: Polity Press, pp. 321–44.

13. Anna Grzymala-Busse and Pauline Jones Luong (2002), 'Reconceptualizing the state: lessons from post-communism', *Political Theory*, 30:4, pp. 529–54.

14. As noticed and analysed in Chapter 3 on Iran and Chapter 9 on Egypt.

15. Margit, Tavits and Natalia Letki (2009), 'When left is right: party ideology and policy in post-communist Europe', *American Political Science Review*, 103:4, pp. 555–69.

16. Anna Grzymala-Busse (2002), *Redeeming the Communist Past: The Regeneration of Communist Parties in East Central Europe*. Cambridge: Cambridge University Press, and Diana Morlang (2003), 'Hungary: socialists building capitalism', in Jane Leftwich Curry and Joan Barth Urban (eds). *The Left Transformed in Post-Communist Societies: The Cases from East-Central Europe, Russia and Ukraine*. New York: Rowman & Littlefield, pp. 61–98.

17. Morlang, 'Hungary: socialists building capitalism'.

18. Jane Leftwich Curry (2003), 'Poland's ex-Communists: from pariahs to establishment party', in Jane Leftwich Curry and Joan Barth Urban (eds). *The Left Transformed*, pp. 19–60.

19. Grzymala-Busse, *Redeeming the Communist Past*.

20. Tavits, Letki, 'When left is right'.

21. Nathan J. Brown (2012), *When Victory is Not an Option: Islamist Movements in Arab Politics*. Cornell: Cornell University Press.

22. Tavishi Bhasin and Jennifer Gandhi (2013), 'Timing and targeting of state repression in authoritarian elections', *Electoral Studies*, 32:4, pp. 620–31.

23. Staffan Lindberg explains that this is particularly true when all opposition forces are united in support of the electoral boycott. Staffan I. Lindberg (2006), 'Opposition parties and democratisation in Sub-Saharan Africa', *Journal of Contemporary African Studies*, 24:1, pp. 123–38.

24. Volpi, Stein, 'Islamism and the state after the Arab uprisings'.

25. Ewan Stein (2014), 'Studying Islamism after the Arab Spring', *Mediterranean Politics*, 19:1, pp. 149–52.

26. Ewan Stein (2011), 'An uncivil partnership: Egypt's Jama'a Islamiyya and the state after the Jihad', *Third World Quarterly*, 32:5, pp. 863–81.

27. Kamran Bokhari and Farid Senzai (2013), *Political Islam in the Age of Democratization*. New York: Palgrave Macmillan.

Part I

Islamists and issues of political and economic governance

Chapter 2

Participation not domination: Morsi on an impossible mission?

Mariz Tadros

Much Western literature interpreted the events that led to the overthrow of President Mohamed Morsi in July 2013 as a counter-revolution involving a military conspiracy against a civilian-led government[1] or as a backlash by an illiberal intelligentsia to a political party – Hizb al-Hurriyya wa al-'Adala (Freedom and Justice Party, FJP) – whose religious reference point they found threatening,[2] or as a case of the intransigency of Mubarak's deep state. While each of the above propositions largely singles out one particular actor as responsible for Morsi's ousting, this chapter examines the period leading up to the events of July 2013 through the lens of a relational approach,[3] exploring in depth the circumstances around the negotiations of interests across different stakeholders. Particular attention will hereby be paid to al-Ikhwan al-Muslimun (Muslim Brotherhood, MB) whose political wing, the FJP, and its candidate, Mohamed Morsi, had won elections to parliament and the presidency in 2011–12, and had earlier promised to pursue a policy of *musharka la moughalaba* (participation, not domination) *vis-à-vis* other political forces once they assume power. During his short-lived tenure in office between July 2012 and July 2013, President Morsi faced three critical challenges to enacting such a policy: negotiating the terms of rule in relation to the power structures internal to the MB as a movement and political party (FJP); negotiating the power-sharing claims of the opposition and finally, the limits of reconciling doctrine with inclusivity. To be sure, these challenges were set against the backdrop of a broader struggle of changing political alliances, allegiances and (informal) agreements between the MB and the Supreme Council of Armed Forces (SCAF) in ever-changing political settlements, as well as the role of the deep state particularly with respect to the police force. However, while the latter themes have been addressed profusely in the literature on democratisation in Egypt,[4] there has been more limited scholarship around the challenges of these three unfolding power configurations.

In exploring the negotiation of power relations between the MB and the opposition post-June 2012, this chapter argues that the sites for struggle throughout the Morsi presidency revolved not only around the distribution of cabinet posts and ministerial portfolios (as important as they were) but were also doctrinal in nature, revolving around contending visions of sovereignty, the nature of the social contract, and the political community. This is particularly evident when comparing the political thought of the MB prior to the 2011 Egyptian uprising with that adopted by the group and its affiliate party, the FJP, around the constitution negotiated in 2012 under their leadership. While avoiding a consequentialist approach that suggests that the draft constitution was an enactment of the movement's political thought, this author nonetheless suggests that there are striking resonances between the two that merit careful examination. The constitution did become a litmus test for consensus-building, and it will be argued that its theocratic underpinnings undermined the prospects of reconciling non-Islamists' conceptions of democracy with those of the MB/FJP.

Contending claims for *musharka*

The MB, like other political actors in Egypt, has recognised that engaging in coalition-building necessitates arriving at a common ground with other opposition forces. To this effect, the movement has sought to show that the principles of power-sharing are grounded in its doctrinal and political thought. The jurisprudential principle of *musharka la moughalaba*, emanating from a long process of *fiqh*[5] engagement, was first articulated as the MB's stance in relation to power-sharing in November 2010 prior to the last parliamentary elections under the former president Hosni Mubarak (r.1981–2011). Rashad al-Bayoumi, the Deputy Supreme Guide of the MB, emphasised in an interview with Al Sharq al-Awsat newspaper on 26 February 2011 – a week after the ousting of Mubarak – that the MB is committed to the principle of *musharka* and that 'we don't have any ambitions of leadership or domination'.[6] In March 2011, prior to the constitutional referendum, the MB also affirmed its position of being one of *musharka la moughalaba*, professing that it neither aspired for a majority in parliament nor for the nomination of a presidential candidate. Some believed the MB would retain this stance even after its political wing, the FJP, won a plurality of seats in the parliamentary elections of 2011–12. Shortly thereafter, in June 2012, parliament was dissolved by a SCAF order following a Supreme Constitutional Court (SCC) ruling that had deemed the elections unconstitutional on technical grounds. The same month, the MB/FJP fielded Mohamed Morsi as its candidate for the upcoming presidential elections. Morsi then went on to win the election, becoming Egypt's first democratically elected president. At the time, Morsi's victory was met with celebration by the country's Islamist political parties and factions, and greeted with cautious optimism on the part of many belonging to various non-Islamist social and political forces. By the time Morsi assumed the presidency in the summer of 2012, however, Egyptian society had become deeply polarised between those who believed that the new president was a triumph for Islam and more broadly for the Muslim ummah and that he would bring prosperity for the Egyptian people, and those who believed that the country would now move towards theocracy and a renewed form of authoritarianism. A third constituency of Egyptians in-between the two positions, and widely referred to as the 'lemon squeezers',[7] had put aside their discomfort with the MB's ascent to power, regarding the group as the lesser of the two evils compared to Morsi's rival in the presidential elections, Ahmed Shafiq. Shafiq, who narrowly lost to Morsi in the poll, had been a key minister in the ousted Mubarak regime. The 'lemon squeezers' were willing to give the Islamist-dominated legislature and Morsi the benefit of the doubt and, like the rest of the population, hoped that the MB's assumption to power would mark a new democratic era in the country's history.

As Morsi's presidential victory was premised on a very slim margin of votes, there was a need to complement the political constituency base from below with elite support from above through the formation of a power-sharing administration. And indeed, at the time there were numerous contending political forces internal and external to the MB that had expressed aspirations for participating in the new Morsi government. The power configurations at the time were informed not only by a political will to integrate various political contenders into a broad-based government, but also by political capacity. For one, the extent to which Morsi enjoyed sufficient political autonomy so as to make decisions independently of the MB was from the outset questionable. Ever since the establishment of the FJP in April 2011, its relationship to the MB had been a source of deep contention for those within and outside the movement. There was a faction within the movement that endorsed the idea of a clear separation of roles between *da'wa* (the remit of the MB) and political work (the remit of the party). Such a division of labour never worked so neatly on the ground, however, because leaders held multiple hats in both the MB and the FJP and because the movement's guidance bureau continued to serve as the higher decision-making power on all matters, including those pertaining to the FJP, and because of the monopolisation of power in the hands of key figures such as Khayrat al-Shater.[8] It is argued here that the new president's ability to put into practice *musharka la moughalaba* is likely to have been affected by the tensions between a party in office and a parent movement perceived to be a reference point for all followers of the Muslim Brotherhood. In other words, Morsi may have had to negotiate within the MB the kind of political concessions that he would then be able to make to the opposition. Such a double loop negotiation process (within the presidential office and the movement) may have limited his manoeuvring space. The MB also had its own vested interests in keeping Morsi under check. As Bassem Ezbidi noted in this regard,

> the risk for the Brothers is that the Morsi presidency gradually evolves into an independent centre of power, resting on control of institutions and direct access to other centres of power within the state (such as the military), with the Brotherhood becoming simply a privileged lobby among other lobbies.[9]

In addition to the fear of an independent presidency that would not be accountable to the MB, there were also the high aspirations among the movement's movers and shakers who sought reward for their roles and contributions towards the Brothers' success at the polls by being offered positions in the new government, whether at national, governorate or local levels.[10]

Pressures on Morsi were also compounded by political forces and parties external to the MB who had openly supported Morsi's candidacy and now expected that the pledges the president-elect had made prior to winning office would be kept. These included two core groups: the Salafis and other Islamist political parties and factions on the one hand, and the non-Islamist political opposition, including the youth revolutionary forces, on the other hand. From a realpolitik perspective, Salafis may have been perceived by the MB as the more important ally with whom to exercise *musharka la moughalaba* on account of their political weight on the streets and in parliament, as well as their ideological proximity to the group. Indeed, the Salafis had won a quarter of the seats in the 2011–12 parliament and had a large constituency of dedicated members and followers on the ground. However, the Salafis lacked a unified political leadership, their members bearing allegiance to different leaders, political parties and movements. Such diversity posed challenges for the Salafis in arriving at a common political denominator on all occasions and under all circumstances. Yet in the run-off between Shafiq and Morsi, Salafi parties unanimously endorsed the latter over the former. In return for this electoral support, these Salafi parties expected Morsi to share political power in accordance with their remarkable electoral weight. So for instance, prior to Morsi's announcement of his new government Nader Bakar, the spokesperson for Hizb al-Nour (Party of Light, PL), had indicated that they had put forward the names of highly competent Salafi leaders for 'three or four [ministerial] portfolios'.[11] This is corroborated by a statement made by Nasser Abas, a leading figure in the FJP who, also prior to the formation of the first Morsi government, had stated that the PL requested they be given the ministerial portfolios of education, health, industry and trade.[12] According to political analyst Ali Abd al-'Al, the expectation was that Morsi would assign some leading Salafis a number of prominent cabinet posts, and they were left in shock when he eventually only offered them a single ministerial post, that of Minster of Environment. They promptly rejected the offer.[13]

Following on from this initial blow to Salafi expectations, relations between the presidential office and Egypt's Salafi parties remained rocky throughout the MB's year in power, being marked by episodes of both support and contention.[14] For example, when the MB came under assault from a counter-coalition of non-Islamists in December 2012 for the issuance of a presidential decree that concentrated the legislative, judicial and executive powers in Morsi's hands (see below), a large section of the country's Salafi parties showed solidarity with the president and the movement. This may have given the strategists within the MB the impression that the Salafis would, when push comes to shove, side with the Brothers. However, as became evident in June 2013, Salafi support was by no means a given, when its largest political party, the PL, joined the mass protests by non-Islamist opposition forces against Morsi and his administration. Arguably, one of the key drivers responsible for this move by the PL had to do with the MB's unfulfilled promises of power sharing.[15]

As for Egypt's non-Islamist political parties and movements, meanwhile, the MB perhaps had less reason to respond to their demands for power-sharing than to those expressed by the Salafis at the time. This is because whilst the latter political grouping could evidence a strong constituency of supporters on the ground, that of the non-Islamist political forces was, relatively speaking, much more scattered and considerably smaller. Nonetheless, the basis for the non-Islamist political opposition's claim to inclusion in any MB-led administration can be traced back to the so-called Fairmont Agreement, which was forged in June 2012 prior to Morsi being officially declared the winner of the presidential elections. While run-off elections had been held on 16 and 17 June, the Electoral Commission did not announce the official results until 24 June. In the intervening days,[16] a meeting took place at the Cairene five-star Fairmont Hotel that extended into the late hours of the night. The meeting was attended by leading figures of the MB, including Morsi himself, and a number of representatives from non-Islamist political parties and forces, including among others Hizb Misr al-Qawiyya (Strong Egypt Party, SEP) and leading figures from youth revolutionary forces such as the 6 April Youth Movement's co-founder Ahmed Maher, blogger Wael Ghonim, Shady al-Ghazaly Harb, Wael Khalil and Islam Lotfy, among others.[17] The discussions at the meeting centred around the kind of guarantees (or concessions) the MB was willing to make to the opposition in return for their endorsement of Morsi's candidature against his opponent Shafiq. The conditions that were agreed at the time were as follows: that, if elected, Morsi, upon assuming the presidency, would (1) launch a 'national unity project',[18] (2) form a 'national salvation government' that included representatives from all political forces and be headed by an independent political figure, (3) select a presidential team that reflected Egypt's diverse political arena and (4) ensure a diverse and representative membership on the Constituent Assembly responsible for drafting Egypt's new constitution.[19] In effect what was agreed at the Fairmont Hotel was that non-Islamist political parties and youth coalitions would politically endorse the MB's presidential candidate and mobilise their supporters to this effect, in return for an inclusive political settlement that would be enacted in the event of a Morsi victory. Whereas with the Salafis no *quid pro quo* deal was publicly announced, the terms that were reached at the Fairmont Hotel were made public at a press conference on 22 June 2012. It could be argued that the Fairmont Agreement was of limited political weight since the non-Islamists who signed it had very limited ability to mobilise a constituency in favour of Morsi and because the agreement was largely one intended to block a military candidate from coming to power rather than premised on a genuine partnership. However, the announcement by Jabhat al-Inqadh al-Watani (National Salvation Front, NSF)[20] less than two months after Morsi assumed power that the MB and the new administration had failed to comply with the commitments it made at the Fairmont Hotel contributed to turning what were once partners against the military into opponents bent on holding the incumbent regime to account.[21]

Against this backdrop of growing disillusionment with the MB and the Morsi government, the process of forging the country's new post-uprising constitution was seen as strategically important in influencing the trajectory of the country and the distribution of power in the new body politic. This included the MB itself, whose strategic choices in the constitution-drafting process were guided by both pragmatic power-political considerations as well as by the organisation's own doctrine. Indeed, whilst in no way suggesting doctrine was a key driver on all policy issues, it constitutes an under-studied dimension of the negotiations that shaped the constitution-drafting process. Focusing on the 2012 Constitution, the following pages highlight how the doctrine of *musharka la moughalaba* played into the MB's approach to the new constitutional text.

The constitutional conundrum: the doctrinal limits of musharka

The crafting of a new constitution under President Morsi in 2012 was meant to mark a new social contract between state and people post-Mubarak, and conclude the country's 'transition to democracy'. The new constitution itself was to be drafted by an assembly elected by parliament whose composition was to be inclusive, mirroring the diverse socio-political forces in society. In the end, however, the constitution-drafting process was marred by controversy and a walk-out by non-Islamist forces, who perceived the draft constitution as a strong move towards theocracy. What thus was meant to be based on the principle of *musharka* ultimately turned into an episode of *moughalaba*, with a boycott of the drafting process by most non-Islamist actors/forces and the passage of a draft constitution by an Islamist-dominated Constituent Assembly. It is suggested here that the controversies surrounding the draft constitution and the eventual walk-out by non-Islamist actors was partly the consequence of ideological struggles.

Although Morsi had vowed before assuming office to forge an inclusive government and engage in consensus politics, once elected he sought at any cost to fast-track the formulation of a new constitution, even if it meant compromises in the pursuit of participatory processes. Arguably, this urgency lay in a process that had begun months prior to his assumption of office. On 14 June 2012, the SCC announced the dissolution of the first freely elected post-Mubarak parliament on grounds of its unconstitutionality. In the absence of a parliament, it would effectively mean that the next president of Egypt would have both executive and legislative powers concentrated in his hands, including the right to declare war, for example. This prospect increased the anxiety of some members of the non-Islamist political forces, including leading parties such as al-Hizb al-Misri al-Dimuqrati al-Ijtmaʻi (Egyptian Social Democratic Party, ESDP) and Hizb al-Misriyeen al-Ahrar (Free Egyptians Party, FEP), who were concerned that the next president would be bestowed with near absolute power. Consequently, they conveyed their concerns to the SCAF, which responded on 18 June 2012 – a day after the presidential elections – by issuing a constitutional decree that further buttressed the powers of SCAF at the expense of any future president. The constitutional decree gave SCAF four principal powers: (1) the right to legislate in the absence of parliament; (2) the right to declare war and a state of emergency; (3) control over internal governance of all matters associated with the armed forces and all levels of leadership including its commander, and (4) the power to influence the selection criteria for identifying the members of the Constituent Assembly responsible for the drafting of Egypt's new constitution. On 24 June, Morsi's victory over Shafiq as president was formally announced. From his victory onwards, Morsi was under extreme pressure from all political forces, Islamist and non-Islamists alike, to retrieve the powers that were usurped by SCAF. The only option for him to do so was to annul this constitutional decree once president and to replace it with a new one. On 12 August, Morsi did just that, announcing a new constitutional decree that annulled the one issued by SCAF on 18 June. Morsi also appointed General Abdel Fattah al-Sisi as new Minister of Defence, and side-lined Field Marshall Tantawy, the Commander of the Armed Forces who had presided over the transition phase as head of SCAF. This, however, caused the non-Islamist political forces to turn against Morsi, accusing him of concentrating power in his hands in an absolutist manner via a constitutional decree that he had issued unilaterally. Hence, President Morsi found that the only way in which he could legitimately claim these powers was to have a constitution drawn up that would define and bestow upon him the right to rule, replacing the decrees and counter-decrees that had been unilaterally issued up to that point.[22]

As for the drafting process of the new constitution, whilst there were many points of contention over the composition of the Constituent Assembly as well as the design of the new constitutional text itself, it was doctrinal matters that became a prime source of tension between the MB and its political opponents. Islamist members of the assembly, such as Amany Abou al-Fadl, pointed out, for instance, that there were attempts by the 'liberals' to impose on everyone supra-national frameworks that were antithetical to Islamic Shari'ah, such as United Nations international conventions and treaties, which undermined the negotiation process.[23] Waheed Abdel Meguid – a non-Islamist political analyst and Constituent Assembly member who had initially endorsed the election of Morsi and participated in the Fairmont Agreement but who later withdrew from the assembly – also sheds light on how the process of negotiations got stalled.[24] His account suggests that there was a general sense of goodwill at the beginning of the inauguration of the new Constituent Assembly in 2012. However, Abdel Meguid considers that the question of the relationship between state and religion had from the outset led to the emergence of two camps, a pro-Islamist and a non-Islamist one. This polarisation revolved not only around the balance of powers or matters of policy, but around doctrinal differences that appeared at the time irreconcilable. Constitutional articles around which there was contention (no less than thirty) were thus broad and varied, ranging from matters to do with the scope of powers of the military, the nature of regulation of the press and media, the rights of farmers, workers and children. However, the most contentious matters around which constituent members battled were to do with the relationship between religion and the state.[25] According to Abdel Meguid, the Salafis, supported by the MB, proposed a number of measures that would give the state a more Islamic character, such as making more explicit the jurisprudential sources of governance and increasing the power of al-Azhar to oversee legislation to ensure its compatibility with Islamic Shari'ah. Many non-Islamist political forces, meanwhile, vehemently objected to these proposals, partly on doctrinal grounds. The Muslim Brotherhood decided that rather than take these contentious proposals straight to voting, and therefore jeopardise the image of the Constituent Assembly as inclusive, they would initiate a number of informal mediation sessions. These mediation sessions, according to Abdel Meguid, comprised a small group of members from within the Constituent Assembly, including representatives from the MB, the Salafis, non-Islamist political figures, al-Azhar and the Coptic Orthodox Church. The aim was to try and reach consensus over a wording that would be acceptable to all. According to Abdel Meguid's account, these mediation sessions made only slow progress and were cut-short/jeopardised by the president's decision on 7 November 2012 that the draft constitution had to be completed within less than three weeks.[26] Indeed, Morsi's decision caused consternation among non-Islamist assembly members, who felt that the drafting process was being rushed at the expense of finding a tenable compromise on proposed articles that would further Islamicise the state and its governance. Consequently, on 14 November 2012, eleven Constituent Assembly members from across the political spectrum of non-Islamist parties announced their resignation from the assembly, in addition to all the representatives of the various Christian denominations, who had already resigned.[27]

Ultimately, Abdel Meguid's account of the constitution-drafting process suggests that attempts at engaging in consensual politics around the contentious issue of the relationship between religion and the state through mediation sessions failed because, in the end, there were ideological limits of accommodating *musharka la moughalaba* when these touched on fundamental doctrinal positions espoused by the MB and the Salafis in relation to Islamic governance. Indeed, the constitution that was ultimately drafted, and put to a popular vote, was not only the result of a pragmatic desire by the MB not to lose the Salafis as allies in and outside the Constituent Assembly, but in large measure informed by the political thought of the group itself. As concerns the former, it is important to note that the Salafis had been highly critical and oppositional to the MB on a number of other occasions, including for example the MB's leadership of parliament, accusing Mohamed al-Beltagy of not giving them sufficient opportunity to speak.[28] However, when the constitution drafted during 2012 came under fire, against the backdrop of the withdrawal of the Christian church establishment and non-Islamist forces, the Salafis came out in full and open support of the MB. For example, prominent Salafi Sheikh Yasser al-Borhamy on the website *Ana Salafi* fully endorsed the draft constitution, explaining the strong alignment that existed between the MB and the Salafis in preventing attempts by the 'secularists' to block the deepening of the application of Shari'ah.[29]

The strong influence of the MB's political thought within the 2012 constitution, meanwhile, is manifest first and foremost in the number of glaring similarities between ideas around what is meant by a 'civil state with an Islamic reference', articulated by the group in previous decades, and some of the articles introduced in the draft constitution. Indeed, an examination of the MB's political thought in the decades prior to their assumption of office suggests that the genesis of such articles lay in broader ideas around Islamic governance.[30] While historically a plurality of positions and stances can be found within the MB on issues of governance, pluralism and inclusivity,[31] this plurality of views ultimately did not feature in the discussions around the constitution. Instead, the MB presented a unified position within the Constituent Assembly on matters of Islamic governance. Notable cases in point concern for instance the MB's proposed formulations for Articles 2, 4 and 219 of the draft constitution, all of which combined served first to privilege Shari'ah as God's law over human agency, second, to deepen the purpose and place of Shari'ah as a system of governance and third, to privilege the clergy by giving it oversight over the application of Shari'ah on all legislation passed in parliament. Article 2 of the 1971 Constitution had identified Shari'ah as the principal source of legislation. The fact that the constitution of 1971 spoke of Shari'ah principles as opposed to compliance with Shari'ah jurisprudential laws and regulations gave the Egyptian judiciary a certain scope of flexibility in interpreting what the principles of Shari'ah are. In fact, this wording has historically enabled the SCC to circumvent Shari'ah law and issue progressive judgements.[32] In the constitutional discussions of 2012, non-Islamists proposed that Article 2 of the constitution of 1971 remain unaltered in the new constitution. Whilst the MB consented to retaining Article 2 intact, they did, however, propose the addition of a new article, Article 219, which sought to specify the principal sources of Shari'ah stipulated in Article 2. Article 219 stated that '[t]he principles of Shari'ah include general evidence and foundations, rules and jurisprudence as well as sources accepted by doctrines of Sunni Islam and by the larger community'.[33] Unlike the 1971 Constitution, the proposed Article 219 of the 2012 Constitution thus made it explicit that legislation was meant to be compatible not only with the *principles* of Shari'ah but with the laws as dictated by Islamic jurisprudence. Hence this removed possibilities for flexibility in interpretation and potentially moved the judiciary towards compliance with the laws as required by Islamic jurisprudence in their rulings. It also meant that, if this article was to be applied, any future parliament would have to ensure that all legislation would comply with the precepts and laws stipulated in Islamic jurisprudence. While there is a degree of flexibility and variation between, and within, the different schools of jurisprudence, nevertheless, there are limits. For example, criminal law would have had to comply with the *hudud* precepts.[34]

As drafted, Article 219 of the 2012 Constitution bore strong congruence with the political thinking of Sheikh Yussuf al-Qaradawy. Al-Qaradawy remains revered as a high authority and source of learning within the MB, so much so that he was once nominated to assume the role of Supreme Guide of the group (its highest political leadership).[35] As al-Qaradawy argued:

> The Islamic state is a constitution or legitimate state that has its own constitution to which it refers for governance and a law to refer to, and its constitution is represented in the principles and laws of the Shari'ah as came down in the Qur'an and the Sunna in terms of doctrine, 'badat, ethics and mo'amlat'.[36]

The deepening of the premise of Shari'ah law in governance was also supposed to inscribe the principle of the supremacy of God's inscriptions over human agency. Even if inscribed in writing, it is the sovereignty of God's laws, not the sovereignty of the people, that governs. Again, al-Qaradawy argued that:

> by the Lord of the people, the King of the People, and the God of the people. Neither he [ruler] nor others from among people can cancel these rulings or freeze them. No king, nor president nor parliament, nor government nor revolutionary council nor central committee nor people's conference nor any power on earth can change from the constant [non-changeable] rules of God.[37]

Sallah al-Sawy, a leading MB thinker, had also argued in his writing before the 2011 uprising that the supremacy of Shari'ah over any human-made law makes for a superior political order. He had argued that legislation must be based on God's laws in an absolute way, and to share this sovereignty with the people is *shirk* (to associate partners with Allah, to be a polytheist) and to base the law on the sovereignty of the people, as in Western democracies, is a form of *kufr* (apostasy). A system of democracy is not an end solution but is to be accepted only in the transitional phase, because it is anathema to the full application of God's sovereignty.[38] Al-Sawy further argued that representative legislatures that do not rule in accordance with Shari'ah should have a singular purpose: to pronounce the sovereignty of God in the drafting of legislation. Any legislation that does not comply with Shari'ah should be regarded as null and void. Resistance or opposition to the application of Shari'ah is considered a form of *kufr*.[39]

　　Finally, al-Qaradawy argued that because liberal democratic orders are premised on decision-making by consensus, this sometimes leads to unprincipled decisions being made. Undoubtedly, such reasoning carried important bearings on the functioning of the Constituent Assembly delegated with the responsibility of drawing the 2012 Constitution. In view of opposition from some non-Islamist forces to the proposed deepening of Shari'ah rule in the constitution, it was not surprising that there was resistance from within the MB to the notion of consensus-building as a process of drawing up the new constitution. Indeed, from the perspective of some of the MB's key political thinkers, it is the application of God's law, not what the political community agree, that renders governance legitimate.[40] The fact that Shari'ah is enacted through written laws through a Constitutional Court, for example, as al-Qaradawy and Tawfiq al-Wa 'i (see below) proposed, does not obliterate its religious character.

Article 4 of the draft constitution, meanwhile, had also stirred concern among non-Islamist forces for the establishment of an Islamic theocracy. It stipulated that the opinion of al-Azhar was to be taken in all matters pertaining to Islamic Shari'ah. In view of the necessity of bringing all laws into compliance with Shari'ah, al-Azhar's scope of influence would have been potentially unlimited. Indeed, Article 4 of the constitution had created a supra-elite class that assumed a policing role over the executive, judicial and legislative branches of the state, scrutinising legislation for Shari'ah compliance, in accordance with members' own interpretations. It is ironic that when the MB explained their notion of a 'civil state with an Islamic reference' in their writings prior to the ousting of Mubarak, they had often emphasised that their vision of an Islamic state was not a religious one because of the absence of the meddling of a religious elite in politics. Prominent MB political thinker al-Wa'i had argued, for instance, that one element that makes the Islamic state a 'civil' and not a 'religious' one is that governance is not mediated through the powers of the clergy, but through written legislation in accordance with the principles of the Qur'an and Sunna. Where matters arise that do not have clear rulings, they are to be settled through *shura* (consultation) or the principles accorded in the Qur'an and Sunna. However, the standing of the 'ulama in an Islamic government does not suggest a disconnection from the sources of power. Al-Qaradawy noted in this regard that unlike the clergy in former theocratic Europe, in Islam the concept of men of religion (clergy) is non-existent and that instead there are specialised 'ulama in Islamic matters, and that their responsibility is to provide advice and direction for all Muslims, and the state must create the enabling environment for them to do so.[41] He further contends that, in an Islamic system, the principle of the supremacy of Shari'ah is higher than the supremacy of the law because no law-making legislature can deviate from, or violate, the content of Shari'ah. Accordingly, no institution within the state is empowered to change or delay the implementation of the laws of Shari'ah.[42]

Whilst sponsored by Islamist parties/forces in the Constituent Assembly, the inclusion of both aforementioned articles, 4 and 219, were received with great hostility by a majority of non-Islamist forces, who perceived them as significant moves towards a theocratic system of government. Indeed, no single article contributed more to triggering the withdrawal of non-Islamist members of the Constituent Assembly from the process than the proposed Article 219. So for instance, the Coptic Orthodox representative on the assembly withdrew in November 2012, after internal pressure from Coptic civil society upon its representatives to step down from the Constituent Assembly on account of the proposed content of Article 219. All three main denominational Christian churches in Egypt then issued a joint statement decrying the non-inclusive nature of the constitution and its articles.[43] This then snowballed into a wave of withdrawals including a number of renowned intellectuals, the representative of the April 6 Movement, and representatives of key-non-Islamist political parties.

The trigger for the withdrawal of non-Islamist members from the Constituent Assembly was hence at least in part ideological. Ultimately, when key representatives of different social, political and cultural forces and actors are missing from the Constituent Assembly, this creates a legitimacy deficit. Faced with defectors from the Constituent Assembly, the MB therefore decided to go ahead anyway without them, confident in their mobilisational capacity to win a constitutional referendum, if put to the people. As is now known, the draft constitution passed the referendum vote, garnering the support of 63.8 per cent of those who went to the polls.[44]

The significance of doctrinal *moughalaba*

Doctrinal *moughalaba* does not account for the downfall of the MB. In fact, no single factor or actor has such attributable power, since it is a highly complex constellation of factors that led to the mass uprising of Egyptians in June 2013 and the ensuing military intervention on 3 July. Ultimately, doctrinal *moughalaba*, as witnessed in the constitutional saga, was neither predictable nor inevitable. It was unpredictable because, though the MB's political thought on issues of governance, pluralism and inclusively was profusely disseminated prior to their assumption of office, the change of context could have led to a shift in positions. It was not inevitable that the MB's doctrinal stance would lead to the assumption of a position of *moughalaba* in the constitutional debates since it was also subject to the movement's own bargaining power and that of its allies and opponents.

However, the exercise of *moughalaba* politics on the part of the MB in relation to the constitution is significant on other grounds. First, it contributed, among other factors, to the coalescing of the opposition into a unified counter-movement against the MB. While it is impossible to disentangle the many battles of contestation between the MB and other political forces in Egypt in the period leading up to the 3 July 2013 rupture, the Brothers' doctrinal positions in the constitution-drafting process certainly helped deepen the country's growing polarisation between Islamists and non-Islamists. Indeed, the hardening of stances in relation to the handling of the constitutional debates was mutual. On the one hand, when the MB's Mahmood Ghozlan was asked in December 2012 how he perceived the walk-out of major political factions, he said it did not bother him because the rule of democracy is to go by the majority and not the minority.[45] He also asserted that he saw this walk-out as a form of blackmail: that they either get their way or they walk away, especially since the process had been going on for five months. He believed that the Islamists cared more for the good of the country by remaining committed to the constitution-drafting process, while the others were exploitative and ill-willed towards an Islamist president.

Ahmed Maher, the leader of the April 6 Movement, who pulled out of the Constituent Assembly, meanwhile, criticised the 50–50 principle guiding the composition of the assembly on the basis that there were at least four different political forces in Egypt, not two. According to him, the 50–50 was a cover-up for majoritarian politics and not intended to give equal weight to the plethora of political orientations that have a presence in Egyptian political life.[46] Technically, Morsi did not have a direct political role in informing the process of drawing Egypt's new constitution, since the task was assigned to a 100 member-strong Constituent Assembly. However, he did have the right to veto the constitution by not signing the document. Should he withhold his signature, the constitution would not be put forward to the people for a vote. Its passing through a people's referendum without consensus being achieved among the main political, social and economic forces in the country thus suggests that the policy of *moughalaba* prevailed. Ultimately, this contributed to a mobilisation of factions and political forces and their coalescing into a counter-coalition that would put aside its differences and unite in opposition to the Morsi presidency.

Second, by ignoring the ideological underpinnings paving the way potentially for theocratic constitutionalism, narratives of democratisation in Egypt ran the risk of giving a simplistic account of a country that was in transition, no matter how rocky, before the democratisation process was halted in July 2013. Constitutional theocracy, as defined by Hirschl, has four key elements: (1) adherence to some or all core elements of modern constitutionalism, including distinction between political and religious authority, (2) endorsement of a state religion, (3) the constitutional enshrining of the religion, its texts, directives and interpretations as a (or the) main source of legislation and judicial interpretation of laws – essentially, establishing that laws may not infringe upon injunctions of the state-endorsed religion; and (4) religious bodies carrying more than symbolic weight, and certain judicial oversight powers.[47] While many narratives of Egypt's post-Mubarak era astutely point to the dangers of civilian rule emanating from the military, they seem to overlook the dangers to civilian rule emanating from the institution of a theocratic form of governance. The constitution was one site for the deepening of the legitimacy of religious rule. Against the backdrop of the highly authoritarian nature of the current Egyptian regime in power (as of summer 2018), it is possible to reduce the story of the failure of the transition phase to the ousting of the MB and President Morsi from power. Fahmy and Faruqi, for instance, dedicate a whole volume to examining how 'intellectuals and activists so demonstrably committed to the cause of civil society, freedom and democracy in Egypt – indeed to the very impulses that inspired the 2011 uprising – come to abandon those commitments' [by mobilising against the MB and siding with the military after the ousting of President Morsi from power].[48]

The analysis of events presented here is neither meant to vindicate Egyptian intellectuals or activists nor to vilify the Morsi-led government. Rather, it seeks to highlight that at that critical juncture in Egypt's history (2012–13) the sites for struggle revolved not exclusively around policy choices or balancing different powers, as significant and central as these were, but they were also doctrinal/ideological. The latter made President Morsi's mission of remaining committed to, and implementing, *musharka la moughalaba* even more challenging. By exposing the theocratic underpinnings of the constitution inaugurated in January 2013, the chapter raises questions as to how far the regime had been committed to a civilian and inclusive form of governance in the first place.

Conclusions

The notion of *musharka la moughalaba*, originally conceived in the context of negotiating the terms of participation of the MB in the 2010 parliamentary elections (before they withdrew), was premised on jurisprudential (*fiqh*) grounds for pursuing the politics of participation through power-sharing. In the context of Morsi's assumption of the presidency in July 2012, there were a number of challenges in pursuing this policy. The first challenge was internal, associated with negotiating the sources of presidential power in relation to the FJP and its mother organisation, the MB. The extent to which Morsi enjoyed the power to negotiate power-sharing deals with various stakeholders independently of the MB is highly questionable. Indeed, the expectations and aspirations of MB leaders for a tangible reward after years of repression and mobilisation would have put no small measure of pressure on the prospects and possibilities of sharing power with external claims-making actors. The principle of *musharka la moughalaba* informed the negotiation of the Fairmont Agreement with a wide array of opposition figures and parties prior to Morsi's assumption of the presidency. The agreement was an official one, which stated very clearly that in return for support of Morsi's candidature, the new president would pursue an inclusive governance strategy once in power. Meanwhile, once in power, the

MB claimed that they remained committed to power sharing but that it was the opposition that did not want to share the burden of government.

While of a more informal nature, there also seemed to be a tacit agreement that in return for the Salafis' endorsement of the MB in the presidential elections, they too would be incorporated into a power-sharing governance arrangement. As with the non-Islamist opposition, Salafis also protested the exclusivist hold of the MB on power and yet when the Brothers entered into clashes with the non-Islamist opposition in front of the presidential palace in November 2012, the Salafis showed solidarity with the Brothers. In view of their highly differentiated leadership, ultimately those that rose against the Brothers in June 2013 were driven by an opposition to their policy of *moughalaba la musharka*.

This said, the challenge of *musharka la moughalaba* was not one only of realpolitik nor was it of poor tactical judgement, it was also doctrinal. The political thought of the MB prior to the assumption of power was not a predictor of the ideological or political positions that it would take upon assuming office, given that the power dialectics were highly complex. However, some key political choices, such as those informing certain proposed constitutional provisions, were underpinned, in some part, by the doctrinal position of the MB on matters to do with state, society and governance. Indeed, as highlighted above, there is a glaring resonance between the political thought of the MB on 'a civil state with an Islamic reference' (developed prior to the Egyptian uprising) and Articles 4 and 219 of the constitution promulgated in 2013 under their leadership. While caution is needed to avoid a teleological reading as to how doctrine influences political choices, on the other hand, failure to recognise congruence between a rich and well-developed body of doctrine and the political stances taken may lead to a reductionist analysis of why *musharka* was not pursued at certain critical points in Egypt's post-uprising period, such as that of the drafting of the constitution.

Notes

1. Atef Said (2012), 'The paradox of transition to "democracy" under military rule', *Social Research*, 79:2, pp. 397–434; Michael Makara (2013), 'Coup-proofing, military defection, and the Arab spring', *Democracy and Security*, 9:4, pp. 334–59.
2. Housam Darwisheh (2014), 'Survival, triumph and fall: the political transformation of the Muslim Brotherhood in Egypt' in K. Teik Boo, Vedi R. Hadiz and Yoshihiro Nakanishi (eds), *Between Dissent and Power, the Transformation of Islamist politics in the Middle East and Asia*. New York: Palgrave Macmillan, pp. 108–33.
3. The concept of a relational approach is informed by highlighting the centrality of power relations in political analysis, the importance of recognising the influence of structure and agency and *vice versa*, and the changing configuration of coalitional politics. An example of a relational approach can be found in Sam Hickey (2013), 'Thinking about the politics

of inclusive development: towards a relational approach', *ESID Working Paper*, 1, <www.effective-states.org/wp-content/uploads/working_papers/final-pdfs/esid_wp_01_hickey.pdf> (last accessed 20 June 2017).

4. See Mariz Tadros (2017), 'A political settlements lens onto Egypt's critical junctures and cyclic violence (2011–2014)', *Conflict, Security and Development*, 17:3, pp. 265–86.

5. The word *moughalaba* appears in a hadith in which the Prophet Muhammad PBUH says that 'you will not achieve this [religion] through moughalaba'. The Prophet was using the word *moughalaba* in a derogatory manner to suggest a negative use of power, or use of compulsion or domination. The hadith itself appears in *Al Bayhaqi* 1:359, *Al Haythami* 9:372 and *Albany* (Al Selsela al-sahaha, 4:285). The hadith is considered as a strong one. The explanation of the hadith is available in Fath al-Bary, in which the use of the word *moughalaba* in the hadith is explained as meaning a persistent use of force without resorting to legitimate pathways or licence for the achievement of a goal (Ibn Hagar al-`Askalani, Ahmed, Fath al-Bari bi sharh sahih al-boukhari, undated), *Al Maqtabah al-Salafiyya, Tabet Moheb el Din al-Khateeb*, 1:94).

6. Shaaban Abdel Sattar (2011), 'Na'eb Morshed al-Ikhwan fi misr lel sharq al-awsat: lan naqef amam ikhteyarat al-shaab' [Deputy of the Supreme Guide of the Muslim Brotherhood to Al Sharq al-Awsat [newspaper]: 'we will not oppose the will of the people'] *Al Sharq al-Awsat*, <http://archive.aawsat.com/details.asp?section=4&issueno=11778&article=610029#.WCBQZsnDFv5> (last accessed 10 July 2017).

7. The expression comes from the practice of squeezing lemon on food that one does not like in order to make it sufficiently palatable to consume.

8. Issandr El Amrani (2014), 'The Egyptian Muslim Brotherhood: ready for revolution?' in Are Knudsen and Basem Ezbidi (eds), *Popular Protest in the New Middle East*. London: IB Taurus, pp. 61–90.

9. Ibid., p. 86.

10. Interviews with informants (journalists who have internal access to rank and file within the MB, 2013). On the broader question of the challenges of internal reform and transparency with respect to the allocation of positions of power and resources within the MB, see Ashraf Sherif (2014), 'The Egyptian Muslim Brotherhood's failures, Part 1', *Carnegie Endowment for International Peace*, <http://carnegieendowment.org/files/muslim_brotherhood_failures.pdf> (last accessed 12 June 2015).

11. Tamer Abou Arab (2012), 'Nader Bakar', *Al Masry Al Youm*, 13 July, <www.almasryalyoum.com/news/details/200166> (last accessed 14 January 2017).

12. Hani Al Wazeeri (2012), 'Qiyadi Ikhwani yakshef lel Watan tafaseel al-hokoumah al-jadeeda' [A Muslim Brother reveals to Al Watan the details of the new government], *Al Watan*, 24 July, <www.elwatannews.com/news/details/30429> (last accessed 14 January 2015).

13. Aly Abdel`Al (2013), 'Hawl khelaf al-ikhwan wal salafiyeen fi misr [On the dispute between the Brothers and the Salafis in Egypt], *Dimokratiya*, 49, 27 February, <http://democracy.ahram.org.eg/News/432/%D8%AD%D9%88%D9%84-%D8%AE%D9%84%D8%A7%D9%81-%D8%A7%D9%84%D8%A5%D8%AE%D9%88%D8%A7%D9%86-%D9%88-%D8%A7%D9%84%D8%B3%D9%84%D9%81%D9%8A%D9%8A%D9%86-%D9%81%D9%8A-%D9%85%D8%B5%D8%B1-.aspx > (last accessed 4 January 2017).

14. Ibid for detailed discussion.

15. Stéphane Lacroix, and Ahmed Shalata (2016), 'The rise of revolutionary Salafism in post-Mubarak Egypt', in Bernard Rougier and Stéphanie Lacroix (eds), *Egypt's Revolutions Politics, Religion and Social Movement*. London: Palgrave Macmillan) pp. 176–77.

16. The meeting took place on 21 June 2012.

17. See Hamdy Kandeel (2014), *Ana 'Esht Maretein* [I lived twice] (3rd edn). Cairo: Al-Shorouk Publishing House. See also Anon. (2012), 'Morsi campaign press conference at Fairmont Hotel to discuss latest developments', *Ikhwanweb*, 22 June, p. 527, <www.ikhwanweb.com/article.php?id=30125> (last accessed 16 January 2016).
18. A project that would speak to the general aspirations of all Egyptians.
19. Parliament was responsible as per the constitutional decree of March 2011 to elect a Constituent Assembly whose task it would be to develop a new constitution.
20. A coalition comprised of public figures, intellectuals and a number of political parties established to press for a democratic new social contract in Egypt, founded on the ambitions of the Egyptian revolution. See Kandeel, *Ana 'Esht Maretein*.
21. See for example the account of the spokesperson for the National Front, Hamdy Kandeel, on the statement they issued. See Kandeel, *Ana 'Esht Maretein*, pp. 532–33.
22. Mariz Tadros (2016), *Resistance, Revolt and Gender Justice*. New York: Syracuse University Press.
23. Amany Abou el Fadl (2013), *Min kawaleis al-dustour sir al-siyada al-wataniyya wa al-irada al-dawliyya dakhil dustour misr* [The inside story of the constitution: the secrets of sovereignty and international will in the constitution of Egypt]. Cairo: Nahdet Misr.
24. Waheed Abdel Meguid (2013), *Azmet distour 2012, Tawtheek wa Tahleel* [The crisis of the constitution of 2012: documentation and analysis] (1st edn). Cairo: Publisher unnamed.
25. Ibid.
26. Ibid., p. 117.
27. Ibid., p. 126.
28. Salah el Din Hassan (2012), 'Al Salafiyoon wal Ikhwan . . . goozerehem wa ma`alatihhem' [The Salafis and Brothers . . . their roots and future], in Amar Hassan (ed.), *Ali Wak'i wa Moustaqbal al-harakat al-salafiyya fi misr* [On the reality and future of Salafi movements in Egypt]. Cairo: Marzkaz el Neel, pp. 184–89.
29. 'Janeb min Moltaqa al-ulama wal do'ah kalimat Al Sheikh Yasser Borshami [One part of the forum with the ulama and preachers, Yasser Borhami's speech', *Ana Salfi website* [I am a salafi website], <www.youtube.com/watch?v=_xzsVgwG9-o> (last accessed 8 August 2016).
30. Mariz Tadros (2012), *The Muslim Brotherhood in Contemporary Egypt: Democracy Redefined or Confined?* London: Routledge.
31. Ibid.
32. Clark B. Lombardi and Nathan Brown (2006), 'Do constitutions requiring adherence to Shari'a threaten human rights? How Egypt's constitutional court reconciles Islamic Law with the liberal rule of law', *American University International Law Review*, 21:3, pp. 379–435.
33. Mariam Rizk and Osman El Sharnoubi (2013), 'Egypt's constitution 2012 vs 2013: A comparison', *Al Ahram* online, 12 December, <http://english.ahram.org.eg/NewsContent/1/0/88644/Egypt/0/Egypts-constitution--vs--A-comparison.aspx> (last accessed 10 July 2017).
34. *Hudud* precepts are, according to the Oxford Islamic Studies Online resource: 'Limit or prohibition; pl. *hudud*. A punishment fixed in the Qur'an and hadith for crimes considered to be against the rights of God. The six crimes for which punishments are fixed are theft (amputation of the hand), illicit sexual relations (death by stoning or one hundred lashes), making unproven accusations of illicit sex (eighty lashes), drinking intoxicants (eighty lashes), apostasy (death or banishment), and highway robbery (death). Strict requirements for evidence (including eyewitnesses) have severely limited the application

of *hudud* penalties. Punishment for all other crimes is left to the discretion of the court'.
See Anon. 'Hadd', Oxford Islamic Studies Online, <www.oxfordislamicstudies.com/article/opr/t125/e757> (last accessed 10 July 2017).

35. Evidence of the place Sheikh Yussuf al-Qaradawy wields within the MB can be found on the group's website *Ikhwanweb*, which features an article on his contribution to the Muslim Brotherhood. See Hossam Tamam (2008), 'A reading into Al-Qaradawi–Muslim Brotherhood relation', *Ikhwanweb*, 18 July, <www.ikhwanweb.com/article.php?id=17396> (last accessed 10 July 2017).

36. Yussuf Al-Qaradawy (1997), *Min fiqh al-Dawla fi Al Islam* [From the jurisprudence of the state in Islam] (4th edn). Cairo: Dar el Shorouk, p. 32; in Mariz Tadros (2012), *The Muslim Brotherhood in Contemporary Egypt: Democracy Redefined or Confined?* London: Routledge.

37. Yussuf Al-Qaradawy (2007), Al Din wal Siyasa [Religion and Politics] Cairo: Dar el Shorouk, pp 159–60; in Tadros, *The Muslim Brotherhood*.

38. Salah El Sawy (undated), Al Thawabit wal Moutaghayerat fi maseerat al-`amal al-islami al-mou`aser [The Thawabit and Mutaghayerat in the pathway of contemporary Islamic work]. Sanaa: El Quds for Publishers and Distribution; in Tadros, *The Muslim Brotherhood*.

39. *Kufr* means to associate partners with Allah, to be a polytheist.

40. Al-Qaradawy, *Min fiqh al-Dawla fi Al Islam*, p. 32; in Tadros, *The Muslim Brotherhood*.

41. Ibid., pp. 30–1.

42. Ibid., p. 38.

43. Anon. (2012), 'Egypt's churches withdraw from constituent assembly', Ahram Online, 17 November, <http://english.ahram.org.eg/NewsContent/1/64/58411/Egypt/Politics-/Egypts-churches-withdraw-from-Constituent-Assembly.aspx> (last accessed 3 January 2013).

44. Anon. (2012), 'Egyptian voters back new constitution in referendum', BBC News, 25 December, <www.bbc.co.uk/news/world-middle-east-20842487> (last accessed 10 July 2017).

45. Tadros, *Resistance, Revolt and Gender Justice*.

46. Interview by Robeir el-Fares with Ahmed Maher, leader of the April 6 Movement, December 2012.

47. Ran Hirschl (2008), 'The theocratic challenge to constitution drafting in post-conflict states', *William and Mary Law Review 1179*, 49:4.

48. Daanish Faruqi and Dalia F. Fahmy (eds) (2017), *Egypt and the Contradictions of Liberalism: Illiberal Intelligentsia and the Future of Egyptian Democracy*. London: OneWorld Publications, p. 12.

Chapter 3

Governing after protests: the case for political participation in post-2009 Iran

Paola Rivetti and Alam Saleh

While driving on Bakeri Expressway in Tehran in 2016, one of the two authors' friends, A., recalled a protest during the summer of 2009 when the people of Iran took to the streets, giving form to what has since come to be known as the 'Green Movement'.[1] In June 2009, and four months later, protests took place in several cities across the country against the re-election of Mahmood Ahmadinejad (r.2005–13) as president of the republic, an election that the protesters considered rigged. The 'Green Movement', or the *fitna* (sedition) as it is called by the forces that countered it, constituted the fiercest challenge yet to the stability of the Islamic Republic. What started as a dispute over the election results spiralled, as the months passed by, into a comprehensive confrontation between the opposition and Ahmadinejad's government, with radical fringes aiming their critique at the regime itself.[2] As A. recalled:

> We were in Parkway [an important junction in North Tehran where portraits of martyrs from the Iran–Iraq war are at display], and people were shouting '*Basiji vaghei Hemmat bodo Bakeri*' (the real *bassij* were Hemmat and Bakeri) against the *bassij*[3] that had beaten up our brothers and sisters during the protests. The reality is that if Bakeri and Hemmat were alive, they would protest with us to defend the truth and honour of the Islamic Republic, which they created, and to allow people to protest: how do you think the revolution happened?[4]

This short excerpt of a longer conversation speaks directly to the relevance of the issue of political participation in the Islamic Republic, whose political system synthesises authoritarian and democratic characteristics and subsumes political participation as a fundamental trait of its history and genealogy, thus offering fertile ground to build arguments in favour of expanding it. According to the constitution, in fact, Iranians can participate in national politics in a number of ways, from voting to protesting, all of which are rights included in the fundamental law.[5] These rights are based on values that do not only resonate with the Islamic Republic's historical legacy and revolutionary genesis. They are also religiously legitimised by a specific reading of Shi'ism as a 'theology of discontent' and rebellion, which turns important religious celebrations, such as *Ashura* and *ta'zieh*, into 'theatres of protest'. It is not surprising, therefore, that such religious celebrations have been politicised and utilised to spread revolutionary ideas during the 1970s.[6]

Political participation, and the right to it, are at the core of what Saïd Amir Arjomand defines as 'constitutional politics', namely 'the struggle for the definition of social and political order [which] takes place among groups and organizations whose interests align them behind different principles of order'.[7] In fact, political participation, both as a principle and a right, is contested yet, crucially, mobilised by pro-regime and oppositional[8] forces alike. Invocations supporting the expansion of the public sphere and the right to political participation may come from opposed sides, urging the regime to become more inclusive. Although they may have contrasting goals and different nuances, such invocations can have the similar effect of challenging, to a varying degree, the current *status quo*.

Our contribution explores such challenges. It argues that the right to political participation is a cornerstone of Iran's governance which, echoing Janine Wedel, Cris Shore, Gregory Feldman and Stacy Lathrop,[9] is understood as the ensemble of principles and notions sustaining the procedures and structures that govern the interaction between the state and society. It follows that governance in a hybrid regime, such is the Islamic Republic,[10] is sustained and regulated by ideational devices that transcend authoritarianism and come to terms with 'non-authoritarian notions' such as political participation.

This chapter diverges from the rest of the literature on rights and political freedom in Iran. Broadly speaking, most of the literature focuses on the issue of cultural relativism and Islam versus the universality of rights and secularism, and whether the institutions of the Islamic Republic (the government, the judiciary system, the security forces, etc.) respect the citizens' rights, which come under different labels, be they human rights, women and/or minority rights.[11] Complementary to such perspective, scholarship on Iran has also examined the efforts of progressive and reform-minded groups and individuals critical of the regime to reconcile Islam and different types of rights. Mahmood Monshipouri and Mehdi Zakerian, for example, focus their analysis on the struggle of social actors such as NGOs, student groups and women to accommodate a secular and a religious understanding of human rights.[12]

The authors of this chapter take a different approach. Rather than examine how *ijtihad* (the Islamic interpretation) may be stretched to translate secular liberal rights, we draw on the work of Arzoo Osanloo, Mehran Tamadonfar, Naser Ghorbannia among others, arguing that Iran's legal system is built on both secular and religious epistemologies, and that actors willing to advocate for the expansion of rights may build on either. The concepts of politico-civil rights and democratic participation are inscribed in the history and politics of Iran, and reflected in its hybrid legislation.[13] It follows that the right to political participation is part of a common background that both oppositional and conservative forces share, although differences exist. By examining how it is articulated by different political forces, then, the authors seek to reveal the heterogeneous and contested nature of law-making in Iran, questioning the notion of a Shari'ah-based legislation that is, by nature, unchangeable, or changeable thanks only to religious *ijtihad*.

The analysis at hand focuses on the post-2009 period; that is the period following the tenth presidential election in Iran. This election saw un-precedented political action and radicalised discourses and demands for political participation. Like the Arab uprisings two years later, it produced a suspension of political limitations, offering an opportunity to voice discontent and articulate diverse ideological visions present in society.[14] This moment of exceptionality was followed by an authoritarian backlash, however, and the post-2009 securitisation of the public sphere, along with exclusionary politics and divisions within the elite and the population that ensued from the repression,[15] led public figures from a diverse range of political backgrounds – individuals that the regime regards both as insiders and outsiders – to question the discrepancy between the behaviour of the government and the principles enshrined in the constitution.

The 2009–10 protests were a watershed moment in the history of the Islamic Republic: what governance arrangements were possible after the ruling elite and society had become so polarised as a result of the protests and the ensuing repression by the regime? This chapter shows that the effort to refashion governance after the protests reignited the constitutional debate around the foundation of the Islamic Republic, emphasising its epistemo-logical plurality. Individuals calling for the overcoming of social and political polarisation, in fact, built their claim on both the secular and the religious nature of Iran's governance structure, rather than stressing its religious tenets exclusively. This suggests that in order to explain the 'pragmatic' approach adopted by Islamists in power to governance, and to dilemmas pillared around individual and collective rights, it is necessary to complement theories centred on Islamic moderation, or analyses pivoted on Islamic liberalism, with a richer and multi-sourced understanding of the intersection between politics and religion. Adopting such a broadened perspective, the following pages will first discuss the centrality of demands for political participation and rights in the history of Iran. This is then followed by an analysis of how Iran's legal hybridity has provided a fertile environment for reclaiming political participation as a fundamental right encoded both in history and the law. In a third and final section, the chapter illustrates how both oppositional and pro-regime forces have utilised a common historical background and legal plurality to advance the demand for a more inclusive political environment in the post-2009 era.

The genealogy of the 'right to political participation'

The historical and political background

According to Henry Steiner,[16] while political participation is widely recognised across a broad spectrum of countries as a right, its translation into legal provisions has encountered obstacles that are connected to what he calls the different 'theories of political participation' that dominate in different countries. The principle of political participation grants citizens the right to take part, directly or through representatives, in the conduct of public affairs by voting in elections and by influencing governmental decision-making. The right to political participation itself, therefore, includes different modes of participation. While some, such as the right to vote, go unquestioned in the majority of national polities, others, such as the right to organise protests and voice dissent publicly, may be a matter of political contention at the national and international levels. As will become apparent below, in Iran the right to political participation constitutes a pillar of the dominant political culture, yet also remains a deeply divisive and contested right.

The notion of rights (*hoquq*, sing. *haq*) has consistently featured across the history of modern-day Iran. Constitutional rights, human rights and civil rights are notions around which political participation, mobilisations, reform and claims of legitimacy have revolved. The public memory of historical events is often based on a rights-centred perspective. Such a memory is important because it informs ordinary citizens' understanding of their own history and political agency, becoming relevant to the regime too. Two historical events are of particular importance in the Iranian context: the constitutional and the Islamic revolutions. The constitutional revolution (1905–11) is usually regarded as the event that brought notions such as constitutionalism, political equality and ruler's accountability to Iran. Yadullah Shahibzadeh asserts that this event popularised a democratic language promoting the idea that 'the people' consists of citizens with equal political and civil rights (*mellat*) and encouraged Iranians to think and talk about their society through a new vocabulary pillared around the notion of rights.[17] Fakhreddin Azimi argues that the constitutional revolution incardinated in ordinary Iranians' worldview the idea that the ruler is bound by a legal framework and has to deliver 'decent governance'.[18] The memory of the constitutional revolution is still powerful in today's Iran.[19] Intellectuals and politicians consistently refer to it in order to legitimise their claims about rights and the rule of law.[20] Although such claims have often sprung from the most progressive pockets of the elite, or the so-called reformist factions, the historical memory of the constitutional revolution is also used by conservative political forces. In this case, ideas such as nationalism and the right to self-determination, along with religious democracy, are celebrated. The figure of Sheikh Fazlollah Nouri – a prominent religious scholar who supported constitutionalism but later denounced it as perversion into a Westernised and secular political project – is particularly relevant to the conservative reading of the event, also because Nouri was eventually condemned to death by the more 'liberal' constitutionalist factions.[21]

The memory and legacy of the 1979 revolution too symbolise a struggle for rights for reformist/progressive, conservative and pro-regime forces alike, although differences exist between them. Indeed, while all forces emphasise the role of popular protests in defying the dictatorship of the Shah (*estebdad*), the conservative reading underlines more forcefully the role of Islam as the source of inspiration for such justice-seeking political actions. For example, in a speech to a *bassij* gathering in October 2011, the Supreme Leader Ali Khamenei contextualised the experience of the Islamic revolution in a political and religious effort to attain a superior religious form of *mardomsalari*, or democracy. While he recognised that different political ideologies, from liberalism to socialism, have positive aspects, he argued that Islam is the sum of them all and that the revolution had implemented their positive aspects through Islam. It follows that more than a struggle for rights, liberal freedoms and social justice, the revolution was a struggle for Islam.[22] Reformist and progressive forces, on their part, propose a reading of the revolution emphasising its rights-oriented and justice-seeking nature, often turning celebrations commemorating the revolution into an occasion to reaffirm demands for political inclusion. In a tense political environment, characterised by a steady contention against the conservative forces, during his speech on the twenty-fifth anniversary of the revolution, the reformist ex-president Mohammad Khatami (r.1997–2005) warned the conservatives that ignoring the desire for political participation and inclusion, and perpetuating exclusion of political forces critical of the regime, betray the ideals of the revolution and alienate popular support.[23] A similar argument is suggested by a political advertisement circulated after Hassan Rouhani was elected to the presidency of the republic for the first time in 2013. The advert conveyed a message of national reconciliation and political tolerance after the 2009 crisis and featured excerpts from speeches by prominent political personalities from Iran's history, from Ayatollah Khomeini, the leader of the 1979 revolution and the first Supreme Leader of the Islamic Republic, to the former Prime Minister Mohammad Mossadegh (who nationalised Iran's oil company and was overthrown by a coup orchestrated with the help of the UK in 1953), and Ayatollah Taleqani (a democratic leader during the 1979 revolution), who talk about the right of Iranians to be the 'masters of their own future'.[24] These examples suggest that the right to political participation is relevant to the memory of different political forces in Iran, which use it to both voice criticism of the regime and celebrate it.

Legal hybridity

While historical public memory plays an important role in engendering demands for rights, it is not the only source available to extend demands for more inclusive political participation. In fact, the codification of the law in the post-revolutionary era, despite claiming to return to Islam, is characterised by legal pluralism and references to a number of epistemologies, both secular and religious, which also offer an opportunity to extend such demands.

Arzoo Osanloo explains in this regard that, after the 1979 revolution, a willingness to bridge the structure of the newly established republican state and the ideological underpinnings of Shariʿah could not solve the dilemma of how to administer the new law. As a legal codification became necessary, the leaders of the Islamic Republic decided to administer Shariʿah through the European civil law system, which had been the model of judicial organisation during the previous regime.[25] Additionally, Mehran Tamadonfar notes that the legislation derived from Shariʿah primary sources was developed by scholars who focused on the area of private law and had very little to say about public law or affairs of the state. These private laws traditionally formulated rules that could resolve disputes around sales, contracts and matters of worship, and could not be stretched to include areas such as governance, administration or finance.[26] The irony here is that those supposed to bring down the corrupt, Westernised legal system inherited from pre-1979 Iran, with its corollary of morally corrupted values, contributed to reinforcing it.[27]

It follows that what was made available to the population was a hybrid legal system that includes both Islamic, Shariʿah-based provisions and the secular remnants of the pre-revolutionary regime. This allowed the coexistence of a double legal epistemology, one based on religion and one based on a liberal and secular understanding of rights. Counter-hegemonic discourses or critiques that are pillared around the notion of rights may therefore combine the two. On such basis, Osanloo emphasises in her work that the expansion of women's rights in realms such as divorce or child custody goes beyond any efforts to reconcile Islam and liberalism or expand religious interpretation, as it is usually asserted within scholarship. Rights advocates, in fact, draw on legal hybridity – or what Osanloo terms 'Islamico-civil law' – and often on the secular nature of legal provisions, to make claims to the Islamic republican state and its institutions.[28]

Beyond women's rights, another instance of such legal hybridity is the contested participation of Iran in the secular and liberal international legal order on the matter of human rights. The Islamic Republic has ratified multiple international rights conventions yet, at the same time, these rights regimes face strong and ongoing criticism from the country's political elites. As Iran ratified international conventions and treaties, it had to establish domestic institutions tasked with guaranteeing their implementation and respect.[29] This is the case for example with the Settad-e Hoquq-e Bashar (Iranian High Council for Human Rights, IHCHR), which was established after Iran became a signatory to the International Covenant on Economic, Social and Cultural Rights in 1975.[30]

This council embodies Iran's compliance with international norms, but is also used to denounce the flaws of liberal–secular international law and elevate an Islamic understanding of rights, while countering the accusations of rights violations made against Iran in the international arena. An example of this are the declarations of Mohammad Javad Larijani, secretary of the IHCHR, at the presentation of the fourth report on human rights in Iran authored by United Nations (UN) Special Rapporteur Ahmad Shaheed in 2013. In order to reverse the UN allegations, Larijani accused Western governments of also being violators. As reported by Iran's Press TV, these counter-accusations were echoed by other Iranian experts, who pointed at the repression of anti-austerity protests by European governments as examples of such violations,[31] thus implicitly recognising human rights as a norm worth respecting. In yet another speech, however, Larijani strongly criticised the liberal international norm of human rights itself, along with the UN. In response to accusations of human rights violations, he asserted that those allegations have the sole purpose of justifying the very existence of the UN and, consequently, safeguarding US and European world hegemony, of which the UN are an agent.[32] The Islamic Republic, Larijani argues in the same intervention, built a socio-political system based on Islamic rationality, rather than secular liberal rationality. Yet as discussed in this chapter, its legal system is significantly informed by secular laws.

The celebration of the superiority of Islamic human rights is a common theme. They are seen as more complete and comprehensive because they have a divine and thus infallible meta-foundation, whereas universal human rights have a human origin that is epistemologically flawed. As one deputy of the parliament's Commission for National Security and Foreign Policy (CNSFP) argued: 'universal human rights are materialistically defined, and they consider only the worldly rights of human beings, but Islam considers both: worldly rights and also moral and afterlife rights'.[33] These words are echoed by Morteza Rezaeian, a contributor to the website Hawzah.net – a website established by state-sponsored religious centres in Mashad and Qom providing interpretation (*tafsir*) of the Qur'an[34] – who asserts that:

> [a]ll the articles brought up in the declarations of human rights exclusively refer to the material aspect of human life and there is no sign of human moral rights, while in the school of Islam, the human's social identity is recognised in morality and beliefs, and it holds that moral and ethical rules are rights of spiritual life and are stabilised in the human, and when they are, material rights.[35]

The presence of the double epistemological nature of Iran's law is here evident, and institutions such as the IHCHR have a double function. On the one side, they keep Iran embedded in a secular and liberal international legal order. On the other side, they give Iran's policymakers involved in that very international order a forum to condemn it, while glorifying a nativist–Islamic version of human rights. However, to those willing to condemn the Islamic Republic's human rights record and the state's authoritarian interventions, the IHCHR provides the opportunity to do so on a secular basis, because the Council implicitly recognises the liberal international norm of human rights, exemplifying effectively the institutional and legal hybridity of Iran's governance.

Contending the right to political participation

The challenge from outsiders

As discussed, disputes around the right to political participation are core to domestic politics and law-making in the Islamic Republic, given its history and the opportunities for reclaiming rights provided by its legal hybridity. Additionally, the end of the Iran–Iraq war (1980–8) resulted in the emergence of a less securitised socio-political environment, precipitating the spread of contentious practices and political ideas. Since the end of the war in 1988 in fact, major socio-economic changes have occurred, along with the blooming of limited political plurality. At the elite level, these transformations originated from within the so-called Islamic left since the early 1990s, namely when it was marginalised by rival political factions causing a rethink about its standpoints on a number of issues.[36] As a corollary of elite factionalism, a quasi-institution-alised and routinised network of intellectuals, academics, theologians, jurists, political strategists and journalists associated with the Islamic left – among whom were Abdolkarim Soroush, Abbas Abdi, Said Hajjarian, Akbar Ganji, Mohsen Kadivar, Mohammad Mojtahed Shabestari and others – critically reviewed their previous positions and turned to a rights-friendly, almost liberal, vision of the world.[37] The 1997 election of the reformist Khatami to the presidency catapulted such visions into the wider public sphere, enraging the conservative establishment, which reacted with arrests and repression. Khatami's supporters and like-minded intellectuals were labelled as *gheyr-e khodi*, or outsiders, in order to emphasise that their ideas were alien to the principles of the Islamic Republic and fell outside the constitution. On such basis, the Ayatollah Mesbah Yazdi, a hard-liner, called for 'shutting the mouth' of reformist intellectuals and their supporters.[38] Khatami's two consecutive governments allowed for the emergence of, and gave resonance to, demands for enlarging political inclusion and participation. After Khatami's mandates came to an end and a conservative government under Mahmood Ahmadinejad was elected, these demands survived and, to some extent, were radicalised, creating the necessary social and activist environment for the 'Green Movement' protests.[39]

The role played by legal hybridity in legitimising such demands for political participation and legal reform is well represented by the reliance on liberal and secular rights, as enshrined in international conventions, by the campaign group Yek Milyun Emza bara-ye Laghv-e Qavanin-e Tab'iz Amiz (One Million Signature Campaign, OMSC). The OMSC sought to collect one million signatures in support of granting women equal legal status with men, thus departing from the Islamic principle of complementarity between men and women. For the two years since its establishment in 2006,[40] it endured harsh repression by conservative authorities and security forces. Noushin Ahmadi Khorasani, one of the founders of the campaign, explains that 'the reconcilia-tion of Islam and feminism in the Campaign is the reconciliation of feminism with millions of Muslims who live with their religion, but who do not seek to draw their power, identity, and legitimacy from it'.[41] She continues:

> [t]he fifth generation of 'circumstantial' feminists we see in Iran today are not, by and large, a group that first asks whether or not something is Islamic before deciding what to make of it. They are not anti-Islamic, but they have distanced themselves from struggles over political and religious authority (the Islamic Republic claims both), and they base their activities on their practical demands rather than on concerns about identity or ideology.[42]

Ahmadi Khorasani states that the campaign is not interested in contributing to the project of Islamic feminism either, because it is not 'willing to value ideological correctness over the primary demands of women'.[43] The campaign took inspiration from the Convention on the Elimination of all Forms of Discrimination against Women (CEDAW), which was ratified by the Iranian parliament in 2003 but later rejected by the Guardian Council for its incompatibility with Shari'ah. The resilience of the inspiration provided by the CEDAW is also evident in the statement of the Coalition of Iranian Women's Movement for Voicing their Demands in the Election, which regrouped activists from the OMSC following repression. The coalition detailed its demands to the candidates of the 2009 presidential election, the first one being the ratification of the CEDAW.[44]

Alongside legal hybridity, Iran's revolutionary legacy also provided the *gheyr-e khodi* with the necessary ideological grounds for advancing their criticism of, and demands towards, the regime. One such example concerns the declarations of the two 'accidental leaders' of the 'Green Movement', Mir Hussein Moussavi and Mehdi Karroubi, who despite their participation in the revolution and institutional life of the Islamic Republic, are considered outsiders by the conservative elite in power.[45] They have consistently referred to the national history and revolutionary legacy to justify their demands for change and political participation. For instance, in his statement number 18, Moussavi states:

> [w]e are still standing tall and proud on the first anniversary of the tenth presidential elections despite our whipped body, which endures bruises and imprisonments. Our demands are the same: freedom, social justice and the formation of [legitimate] national governance. We are confident of victory, hoping for the will and support of God, because we have not demanded anything other than the restoration of our national rights … Today, people know those who have trampled on the basic rights of the nation. People are aware of repeated violations of human rights and the lack of human dignity within the judiciary and intelligence division. People are aware of how far the totalitarians have advanced in desecrating common national legacies, especially with regards to fundamental human rights.[46]

Poor respect for the law and the constitution, which is understood as the source of rights, is equated to un-Islamic and anti-revolutionary attitudes. In his statement commemorating the anniversary of the birth of the 'Green Movement', Karroubi asserts that:

> This year we were unfortunately lacking in the [recognition of the] people's rights under the Constitution. Instead, these fundamental rights were replaced by extreme repression through brutal force, which had no regard for the sanctity of life. Despite all this darkness and bitterness,

we still remain hopeful that the train which has been derailed from the foundations of our Constitution, our Revolution and our Imam, will return to its original path; that the wrong-doers repent and, in doing so, pave the way for dialogue and interaction.[47]

He continues:

Who from the beginning [could have] interpreted the assertion of justified demands and the inquiry into [our] votes to be counter to the *velayat-e faqih*?[48] Why, by means of the *velayat-e faqih*, has a hatchet been taken to the very roots of the Constitution and the Islamic Republic, both of which were founded on the people's votes? Why has the authority of the *velayat-e faqih* been so greatly extended? I doubt that so much authority and power were given to the Prophets themselves, or the infallible [Shi'a] Imams. I even doubt that God considers himself to have the right to deal with his servants in the same way [that the Supreme Leader does]! Historically, Shi'a Islam considers criticism of the ruler not only necessary but a requirement based on the Sharia law stipulation that describes advising the leader of Muslims.[49]

Karroubi and Moussavi not only appeal to the revolutionary legacy to legitimise their demands. They also draw on Iran's legal hybridity, given that they discuss the constitution and the rights guaranteed by it as both a worldly and a religious matter. Ironically, Karroubi suggests that the current amount of power vested in the Supreme Leader Khamenei exceeds that of God. They both pledge loyalty to Islam, the revolution and Khomeini, and place those who ordered and carried out the repression of the protests in 2009 outside of the constitution and the revolutionary tradition. In so doing, they seek to reclaim the revolution and its ideals, based on people's democratic rights, somehow reversing the accusation that they are the *gheyr-e khodi*, or outsiders in Iranian politics.

The challenge coming from the insiders

As discussed, the repression of the 2009 protests became a real watershed moment in Iran's contemporary history and *gheyr-e khodis* were not alone in questioning the Supreme Leader Khamenei and the government on their respect of Iranians' rights. In fact, *khodi* people, or the insiders, have been critical too.[50] A substantial blow to the regime came from amidst the martyrs' families. In Iran, the memory of the Iran–Iraq war is perpetuated and reproduced by the daily remembrance of the martyrs or *shahidan* (sing. *shahid*). Not only are the capital Tehran and other minor cities full of murals and portrayals of those who gave their life in the war, but a potent ensemble of museums, mausoleums and civil rituals is tasked with keeping their memory alive. Considering this, the critical stance that some of the family members of well-known martyrs took after the repression in 2009–10 represented a significant challenge for the regime, which had to face disapproval coming from a category of *khodi* par excellence.

As mentioned earlier in the chapter, one slogan chanted during the protests in 2009–10 was '*Basiji vaghei Hemmat bodo Bakeri*',[51] meaning that the real *bassij* were those who gave their life to defend Iran during the war, as the martyrs Mohammad Ebrahim Hemmat and Mehdi Bakeri had done, and not those who repressed their brothers and sisters during the peaceful protests. The Bakeri family is famous in Iran as it gave three young brothers to the struggle first against the Shah and later against Iraq. Hamid Bakeri's daughter Assieh, during a speech at the University of Tehran in the autumn of 2009, declared that '[i]f my father and my uncle were alive today, they would have not tolerated these atrocities carried out in the name of the martyrs by the *bassij* against the people. If they were alive today they would be in prison'.[52] Other family members too reacted to the crackdown on protesters by raising criticism of the regime. Assieh's mother, Hamid Bakeri's widow Fatemeh Amirani, publicly criticised Ali Jafari – the commander of the Islamic Revolutionary Guard Corps (IRGC) whom her husband had commanded during the war – for repressing the protests. In a public letter to Jafari, she described the re-election of Ahmadinejad as a *coup d'état* and warned that the violence against protesters would only cause damage to the regime, which would eventually lose its legitimacy. Confirming that today's *bassij* are different from the *bassij* during the Iran–Iraq war, Amirani also wrote that the asymmetry of power between the Shah's regime and the people was less dramatic than the one in the Islamic Republic today, where one side 'has all the means of power and the other side [the people] [is] without any power'.[53] The sister of the three martyred Bakeri brothers, Zahra, also made her voice heard in a letter to the Iranian authorities, in which she compared imprisonment during the Shah's time and after the revolution. She concluded that, while today family members have no right to talk to lawyers or have information, before the revolution they could even talk to international human rights organisations and denounce unlawful detentions.[54] The Bakeri family paid for their outspoken criticism with arrests and harassment, along with members of other martyrs' families such as the Hemmat family.[55]

Other examples of 'internal criticism' have come from two well-known intellectual figures, namely Mohammad Nourizad and Emad Afrough. Nourizad is a former columnist of the hard-line newspaper *Keyhan* and a film director, while Afrough is a conservative intellectual and former MP. Nourizad, who was imprisoned after his initial criticism of the crackdown, wrote fifteen open letters to Khamenei in which he defended the right of the people to protest and have their criticism answered, not merely repressed: 'I am saying that when it is accepted ... that protesting is people's rights, this protest will not necessarily lead to our downfall. We should understand this not take this right away from people.'[56]

Afrough pushed his criticism so far as to discuss and criticise the rule of the Supreme Leader during an interview on state TV in January 2012. While talking about the notion of *mardomsalari dini* (religious democracy), he emphasised that it is composed of two distinct aspects, namely religious rule and its democratic legitimacy, underlining that religious rule has to be accepted by the people. He then discussed the notion according to which divine and human government are bridged together through a leader, as indicated by the role models of the Imam Ali and Khomeini, and today by Khamenei. During this discussion, however, he declared that 'there must be guarantees [as] the country can't be ruled by one single leader, by one single person'. He added in fact that 'we have to rule considering the people's rights' and called for an active questioning of the rule of the Supreme Leader who has to respond, or else be 'automatically dismissed'.[57]

Criticism came from the security forces as well. Hossein Alaei, a retired IRGC general and a war hero, authored an op-ed published in January 2012 in the newspaper *Etela'at* in which he implicitly compared the current situation in Iran with the one during the Shah's time. He suggested that the Shah and Khamenei might have commonalities when it came to the way they treated political opponents, and referred to the house arrest of dissidents, implicitly talking about Karroubi and Moussavi. The article featured a series of questions such as 'If, instead of placing some [prominent political figures] under house arrest, sending others to exile, and jailing political activists [the Shah] had opened a dialogue with them, would [he] have been forced to flee the country?'[58] The letter sparked debate and criticism of Alaei, against whom sit-ins and open letters were organised and published. He later declared that his op-ed had been misinterpreted.

Like outsiders, insiders too have drawn on secular and religious references to justify demands to extend the right of political participation to dissidents and excluded political figures. Highlighting that being insiders does not necessarily equate with supporting the violent repression of the 'Green Movement' or being anti-democratic, they have in fact referred to the right of the people to protest and to the tenets of a democratic government, invoking principles of legal plurality and discussing historical examples relevant to today's Iranian elite.

Conclusion

Like the Arab uprisings, the 'Green Movement' represented an exceptional juncture in recent history, at which Iranian society was able to express a diverse range of political opinions without significant limitations. However, this moment did not last long and soon violent repression quashed the street protests. What governance is possible after such disruptive/repressive events? As this chapter has sought to illustrate, calls to enlarge political participation have aimed to overcome social and political polarisation, resulting in the strengthening of both the secular and the religious legal-political epistemologies that inform Iran's governance system. Indeed, in line with scholars arguing that the Islamic Republic has paradoxically accelerated a process of secularisation,[59] this chapter has demonstrated how secular and liberal referents have been mobilised in order to reclaim the right to political participation by different categories of citizens and political elites following the 2009–10 repression. As securitisation has threatened to close down the public sphere in the post-2009 era, secular-inspired demands for political inclusion expressed by 'insiders' of the regime have become even more significant in highlighting the plurality of Iran's governance foundations.

While this 'secular' discourse has by no means surpassed Islam as the predominant source of legitimacy for the ruling elite, or as a moral compass in society, this analysis suggests that a number of ideological and linguistic frameworks are at work, articulating the need to strike a 'governance balance' between the regime's security and the right to political participation.

Based on these findings, this chapter calls for a pluralistic approach to the study of the choices that Islamists in power make when it comes to governance, emphasising that the ideological foundations informing governance arrangements are hybrid. Therefore, they offer a diversified epistemological background to building the case for revising governance arrangements beyond Islam, even in contexts that are seemingly rigid, such as that of the Islamic Republic of Iran.

Notes

1. The authors thank the Gerda Henkel Foundation for their grant to support this research. Likewise, they are grateful to the anonymous reviewers, Shirin Saeidi and Hendrik Kraetzschmar for commenting on early drafts of this chapter.
2. Arash Reisinezhad (2015), 'The Iranian Green Movement: fragmented collective action and fragile collective identity', *Iranian Studies*, 48:2, pp. 193–222; Ramin Jahanbegloo (2011), 'The Green movement and the dignity of nonviolence in Iran', *Dissent Magazine*, 28 February, <www.dissentmagazine.org/online_articles/the-green-movement-and-the-dignity-of-nonviolence-in-iran> (last accessed 18 May 2017).

3. The *bassij* (mobilisation) force is a voluntary militia founded by the former Supreme Leader Ruhollah Khomeini in early 1980s to protect the revolution and Iran during the Iran–Iraq war. Today, it depends on the Islamic Revolutionary Guard Corps (IRGC) command. *Bassij* members were widely employed to repress the protests in 2009–10. Here, A. refers to Mohammad Ebrahim Hemmat and Mehdi Bakeri, two members of the *bassij* and military commanders in the Iran–Iraq war, who became war heroes.

4. Interview with A., July 2016, Tehran.

5. Mehran Tamadonfar (2001), 'Islam, law, and political control in contemporary Iran', *Journal for the Scientific Study of Religion*, 40:2, pp. 207–8.

6. Hamid Dabashi (2005), 'Ta'ziyeh as theatre of protest', *The Drama Review*, 49:4, pp. 91–9.

7. Saïd Amir Arjomand (2000), 'Civil society and the rule of law in the constitutional politics of Iran under Khatami', *Social Research*, 67:2, p. 283.

8. The authors use binary contrapositions (pro-regime vs oppositional; conservative/hard-line vs reformist/progressive; insiders vs outsiders) to articulate divisions within both the political elite and, more broadly, among social and political actors. While the authors are aware of the internal diversification of such groups, they deploy this division for analytical purposes.

9. Janine Wedel, Cris Shore, Gregory Feldman and Stacy Lathrop (2005), 'Toward an anthropology of public policy', *Annals of the American Academy of Political and Social Science*, 600:1, pp. 30–51.

10. Pejman Abdolmohammadi and Giampiero Cama (2015), 'Iran as a peculiar hybrid regime: structure and dynamics of the Islamic Republic', *British Journal of Middle Eastern Studies*, 42:4, pp. 558–78.

11. Reza Afshari (2011), *Human Rights in Iran: The Abuse of Cultural Relativism* (2nd edn). Philadelphia: University of Pennsylvania Press; Mahmood Monshipouri (ed.) (2011), *Human Rights in the Middle East*. Basingstoke: Palgrave Macmillan; Ann Elizabeth Mayer (2015), *Islam and Human Rights: Tradition and Politics* (5th edn). Boulder: Westview Press.

12. Mahmood Monshipouri and Mehdi Zakerian (2016), 'The State of Human Rights in Iran', in Mahmood Monshipouri (ed.), *Inside the Islamic Republic: Social Change in post-Khomeini Iran*. London: Hurst, pp. 151–76.

13. On legal pluralism/hybridity see e.g. Latif Tas (2016), *Legal Pluralism in Action: Dispute Resolution and the Kurdish Peace Committee*. London: Routledge; Rebecca Gould (2015), 'Ijtihād against Madhhab: Legal hybridity and the meanings of modernity in early modern Daghestan', *Comparative Studies in Society and History*, 5:1, pp. 35–66.

14. Shabnam Holliday and Paola Rivetti (2016), 'Divided we stand? The heterogeneous political identities of Iran's 2009–2010 uprisings', in Shabnam Holliday and Philip Leech (eds), *Political Identities and Popular Uprisings in the Middle East*. London: Rowman & Littlefield, p. 31.

15. Yasmin Alem writes that since 2009 polls have become increasingly exclusionary because of the potentially destabilising nature of elections. Yasmin Alem (2016), 'Politics, power and prospects for reform', in Daniel Brumberg and Farideh Farhi (eds), *Power and Change in Iran: Politics of Contention and Conciliation*. Bloomington: Indiana University Press, p. 188.

16. Henry J. Steiner (1988), 'Political participation as a human right', *Harvard Human Rights Yearbook*, 1, pp. 77–134.

17. Yadullah Shahibzadeh (2015), *The Iranian Political Language*. Basingstoke: Palgrave Macmillan, p. 19.

18. Fakhreddin Azimi (2008), *Quest for Democracy in Iran: A Century of Struggle against Authoritarian Rule*. Harvard: Harvard University Press, pp. 2–3.
19. Nader Hashemi (2010), 'Religious disputation and democratic constitutionalism: the enduring legacy of the constitutional revolution on the struggle for democracy in Iran', *Constellations*, 17:1, pp. 50–60.
20. For instance, magazines linked to the reformist movement and liberal forces have devoted special issues to the constitutional revolution (see *Goftogu*, 51, 1387/2008). The magazine *Cheshmandaz-e Iran*, close to the nationalist movement, published a series of articles linking the revolution to the Iranian people's quest for democracy. See the double interview published in 1382/2003: 'Sad Sal-e tamrin mardomsalari va mahar-e qodrat. Goftogu ba Doktor Hosein Aftajar (Hundred years of exercising democracy and limitation to power. Conversation with Dr Hosein Aftajar)', *Cheshmandaz-e Iran*, 21, pp. 21–33 and 22, pp. 76–87.
21. Amir Mirfakhraie (2016), 'Phobias, selves and citizens in Iranian textbook', in Hisham Ramadan and Jeff Shantz (eds), *Manufacturing Phobias: The Political Production of Fear in Theory and Practice*. Toronto: University of Toronto Press, p. 88.
22. Video: 'Khamenei: Islamic Republic is democracy, freedom, socialism in its own way' YouTube, 2011, <www.lenziran.com/2011/10/khamenei-islamic-republic-is-democracy-freedomsocialism-in-its-own-terms> (last accessed 15 May 2017).
23. Nazila Fathi (2004), 'President Khatami warns clerics ruling Iran against extremism', *New York Times*, 12 February, <www.nytimes.com/2004/02/12/world/president-khatami-warns-clerics-ruling-iran-against-extremism.html?_r=0> (last accessed 15 May 2017).
24. Video: 'Nosafar', YouTube, 25 November 2013, <www.youtube.com/watch?v=Oj64-2bLq8k> (last accessed 16 May 2017).
25. Arzoo Osanloo (2008), 'Whence the law: the politics of women's rights, regime change, and the vestiges of reform in the Islamic Republic of Iran', *Radical History Review*, 101, pp. 42–58.
26. Tamadonfar, 'Islam, law, and political control in contemporary Iran', pp. 209–10.
27. Naser Ghorbannia (2016), 'The influence of religion on law in the Iranian legal system', in Vernon V. Palmer, Mohamed Y. Mattar and Anna Koppel (eds), *Mixed Legal Systems, East and West*. London: Routledge, pp. 209–12.
28. Ibidem; Arzoo Osanloo (2009), *The Politics of Women's Rights in Iran*. Princeton: Princeton University Press.
29. For the list of ratified treaties see UN Human Rights, Office of the High Commissioner website <http://tbinternet.ohchr.org/_layouts/TreatyBodyExternal/Treaty.aspx?CountryID=81&Lang=EN> (last accessed 15 May 2017).
30. Today, the IHCHR operates within the judiciary system, whose head, Sadegh Larijani, is appointed by the Supreme Leader Khamenei. Sadegh Larijani is the brother of Mohammad Javad Larijani, the secretary of the IHCHR.
31. Saman Kojouri (2013), 'Larijani: UN human rights report financially supported by US, West', *PressTV*, 9 March, <www.dailymotion.com/video/xy2o0p_larijani-un-human-rights-report-financially-supported-by-us-west_news > (last accessed 2 June 2017).
32. Video: 'Mohammad Javad Larijani speech in UNHRC', YouTube, 2012 <www.youtube.com/watch?v=F8BR4FDnmn4> (last accessed 15 May 2017).
33. Interview with a member of the CNSFP, November 2012, Tehran.
34. Babak Rahimi (2008), 'The politics of the Internet in Iran', in Mehdi Semati (ed.), *Media, Culture and Society in Iran: Living with Globalization and the Islamic State*. London: Routledge, p. 43.

35. Morteza Rezaeian (1384/2005), 'Hoquq va siasat: hoquq-e bashar va demukrasi (Rights and politics: human rights and democracy)', Hawzah.net, <www.hawzah.net/fa/magart.html?MagazineID=0&MagazineNumberID=5050&MagazineArticleID=44790> (last accessed 16 May 2017).
36. Mehdi Moslem (2002), *Factional Politics in post-Khomeini Iran*. Syracuse: Syracuse University Press.
37. Eskander Sadeghi-Boroujerdi (2014), *Disenchanting Political Theology in post-Revolutionary Iran: Reform, Religious Intellectualism and the Death of Utopia*. PhD thesis, University of Oxford; Mahmoud Sadri (2001), 'Sacral defense of secularism: the political theologies of Soroush, Shabestari, and Kadivar', *International Journal of Politics, Culture, and Society*, 15:2, pp. 257–70.
38. Asef Bayat (2013), 'The making of post-Islamism in Iran', in Asef Bayat (ed.), *Post-Islamism: The Many Faces of Political Islam*. Oxford: Oxford University Press, pp. 62–3.
39. Paola Rivetti (2017), 'Political activism in Iran: strategies for survival, possibilities for resistance and authoritarianism', *Democratization*, 24:6, pp. 1178–94.
40. Marianne Bøe (2015), *Family Law in Contemporary Iran: Women's Rights Activism and Shari'a*. London: IB Tauris, p. 164.
41. Noushin Ahmadi Khorasani (2009), *Campaign for Equality: The Inside Story*. Women's Learning Partnership, p. 50.
42. Ibid., p. 49.
43. Ibid., p. 50.
44. Anon. (2009), 'The Coalition of Iranian Women states its election demands', *Feminist School*, <www.feministschool.com/english/spip.php?page=print&id_article=290> (last accessed 15 May 2017). Similar demands have been advanced by a women's coalition ahead of the 2017 presidential election. See e.g. 'Motalebat-e bakhshi az fa'alan-e hoze-ye zanan az kandidaha-ye riasat-e joumhori (The demands of a section of activist from the women's field to presidential candidates)', *Emtedad*, 16 Ordibehesht 1396/6 May 2017, <http://emtedad.net/2702--2/> (last accessed 16 May 2017).
45. The Supreme Leader Khamenei accused the two leaders of being against Islam and the Islamic Republic. See video: 'Leader meets with Basijis', 24 October 2010, <http://english.khamenei.ir/news/1370/Leader-Meets-with-Basijis> (last accessed 15 May 2017). Mohammad Javad Larijani echoes Khamenei's words, arguing that the reformists in jail are agitators who did not respect the law. He said that Moussavi and Karroubi participated in a *coup d'état* against the state because, even before results were announced, they claimed victory and called the people to the street to bring down the government. See video: 'Euronews Interview: Larijani on Iran's new democracy', 13 March 2012, <www.youtube.com/watch?v=cwipRsIKlO0&feature=related> (last accessed 15 May 2017).
46. 'Mir Hossein Mousavi's 18th statement', *Khordad 88*, 16 June 2010, <http://khordaad88.com/?p=1691> (last accessed 15 May 2017).
47. 'Complete Statement for the Anniversary of the Birth of the Green Movement', *Khordad 88*, 20 June 2010, <http://khordaad88.com/?p=1696> (last accessed 15 May 2017).
48. The *velayat-e faqih* (guardianship of the jurist) is the core principle justifying the office of the Supreme Leader, who is given the duty of custodianship over the people during the temporary absence of the occulted Imam.
49. 'Complete statement for the anniversary of the birth of the Green movement'.
50. On this, Shirin Saeidi offers insights from the Hizbullah movement in Iran, considered to be the social and political group that is most loyal to the regime. In her work, she

emphasises how notions and definition of rights and self-determination as propagated by the regime are received critically and even reinterpreted by Hizbullahi people. See Shirin Saeidi (2018), 'Iran's Hezbollah and citizenship politics: the surprises of religious legislation in a hybrid regime', in Nils A. Butenschøn and Roel Meijer (eds), *The Middle East in Transition: The Centrality of Citizenship.* Cheltenham: Edward Elgar.

51. See also Anon. (2009), 'Where is your 63 percent?' *The Atlantic,* 18 September, <www.theatlantic.com/daily-dish/archive/2009/09/-where-is-your-63-percent/196378/> (last accessed 15 May 2017).

52. Video: 'Hamid Bakeri's daughter's speech at University of Tehran', YouTube, 2009, <www.youtube.com/watch?v=wn5LReerlmg> (last accessed 15 May 2017).

53. Anon. (2010), 'Widow of renowned Iran commander accuses IRGC head of treason', Radio Free Europe/Radio Liberty, 21 September, <www.rferl.org/content/Widow_Of_Renowned_Iran_Commander_Accuses_IRGC_Head_Of_Treason/2164446.html> (last accessed 15 May 2017).

54. 'Matne kamel-e sargoshadeh Zahra Bakeri, khahare shahidan-e Bakeri, dar pasokh be ehanat-e kodetagaran be khanevade-ye shohada (Full text of the open letter of Zahra Bakeri, Bakeri martyrs' sister, in response to the insulting accusation of *coup d'état* against the family)', *Rah-e sabz,* 15 Shahrivar 1388/6 September 2009, <www.rahesabz.net/story/1195/> (last accessed 15 May 2017).

55. Anon. (2010), 'Plainclothes forces harass families of Iran–Iraq war heroes', *Center for Human Rights in Iran,* 5 October, <www.iranhumanrights.org/2010/10/forces-harass-families/> (last accessed 15 May 2017).

56. Cited in Shadi Moktari (2016), '"This government is neither Islamic nor a republic": Responses to 2009 Postelection crackdown', in Daniel Brumberg and Farideh Farhi (eds). *Power and Change in Iran,* p. 268.

57. Anon. (2012), 'Former Iranian MP Emad Afrough in rare criticism of Khamenei on Iranian TV: "a country cannot be governed by a single leader"', *Memri TV,* 14 January, <www.memritv.org/clip/en/3276.htm> (last accessed 15 May 2017).

58. Golnaz Esfandiari (2012), 'Former senior IRGC commander comes under attack', *Radio Free Europe/Radio Liberty,* 15 January, <www.rferl.org/a/iran_former_irgc_commander_under_attack/24452204.html> (last accessed 15 May 2017).

59. See e.g. Naser Ghobadzadeh (2014), *Religious Secularity: A Theological Challenge to the Islamic State.* New York: Oxford University Press; Yasuyuki Matsunaga (2009), 'The secularization of a Faqih-headed Revolutionary Islamic State of Iran: its mechanisms, processes, and prospects', *Comparative Studies of South Asia, Africa and the Middle East,* 29:3, pp. 468–82.

Chapter 4

The group that wanted to be a state: the 'rebel governance' of the Islamic State

Truls Hallberg Tønnessen

The Arab uprisings of 2010–12 have not only given a number of moderate Islamist actors increased political influence within state institutions and the opportunity to rule for the first time in their history. State collapse and fragmentation of authority in the wake of the 2003 US-led invasion of Iraq and the outbreak of civil war during the Arab uprisings in Syria, Libya and Yemen have enabled various Islamist insurgent groups to become *de facto* rebel rulers over large swathes of territory and populations. Of the insurgent groups in Iraq and Syria, al-Dawla al-Islamiyya (Islamic State, hereafter IS) stands out for the breadth and extent of its rebel governance, and one of the most characteristic features that distinguishes IS – not only from other insurgent groups in Iraq and Syria, but also from al-Qaeda affiliates in other countries – is its consistent insistence on being not only a group, but also a 'state'.[1]

This chapter focuses on the rebel governance of IS, mainly in its strongholds of Iraq and Syria. Through a brief overview of the history of IS and its predecessors, the chapter demonstrates that establishing territorial control and an 'Islamic state' has been a consistent focus and defining characteristic of the group. It also illustrates how the group's insistence on being a state has had important repercussions on its rebel governance. The chapter argues that, although there are other factors such as ideology, one important reason why the group insisted on operating as a state was its rivalry with other rebel groups. Both the establishment of IS and the Caliphate were attempts by the group to establish its political and religious authority in a context where it competed with a range of other insurgent groups and non-state actors.

A history of rebel governance

Establishing both some degree of rebel governance and an Islamic state have been a constant and central focus, and a defining characteristic, not only for

IS, but also for its predecessor, Tanzim al-Qaeda fi Bilad al-Rafidayn (widely known by its English name al-Qaeda in Iraq, AQI), almost since its inception in 1999 when the Jordanian Abu Mus'ab al-Zarqawi (the founder of AQI), established a training camp for fighters hailing from the Levant (al-Sham) in Herat, Afghanistan.[2] According to the central al-Qaeda leader Sayf al-Adl, who helped al-Zarqawi establish his camp and served as al-Qaeda's ambassador to al-Zarqawi in Afghanistan, in Herat he wanted to establish a 'complete social structure (*mujtama' mutakamil*)'.[3] The idea of establishing an Islamic state was in fact central to the ideology of al-Zarqawi himself. In May 2004, commenting on the transfer of sovereignty in Iraq from the US to an interim government led by Ayad Allawi, he said that his aim was to establish a Dawlat al-Qur'an (Qur'an state) in Iraq.[4] In an interview with al-Zarqawi, released posthumously, he stated that the group's aim was the establishment of Dawlat al-Islam (Islamic state) in Iraq and then to spread it to other Muslim countries.[5]

The history of the group also reveals that it consistently sought to establish some degree of territorial control and governance, however elusive, each time it had the opportunity to do so. The following historical overview of the group's rebel governance illustrates how these efforts were attempts by the group to exploit power vacuums and fragmentation of authority.

One of the very first examples of the group's rebel governance can be found almost immediately after the official establishment of al-Zarqawi's group in Iraq, under the name of al-Tawhid wa al-Jihad (Monotheism and Jihad, also known by its Arabic acronym TWJ) in April 2004. Following the US withdrawal from Fallujah after the offensive against the city in April–May 2004, the Sunni Arab insurgents became the *de facto* rulers of Fallujah for some months until Iraqi and Coalition forces retook control of the city in November 2004. In the months between May and November 2004, the *de facto* rulers of Falluja were the city's religious leadership along with the insurgents who aligned in the Majlis Shura al-Mujahidin or Mujahidin Shura Council (MSC).[6] This council was founded in May 2004, shortly after the departure of the US forces. Its leader was Abdullah al-Janabi, who had served as Imam of one of the mosques in the city. Among the insurgent groups who were represented on the council were al-Zarqawi's TWJ, Jaysh Ansar al-Sunna and Jaysh al-Islami fi al-'Iraq (Islamic Army in Iraq). TWJ was represented on the council by Umar Hadid, a native of Fallujah.[7]

According to Abdullah al-Janabi, this council was established partly due to the power vacuum created by the US withdrawal. He claims that it was founded by the inhabitants of Fallujah to preserve the security and to defend the city.[8] Sources from AQI, on the other hand, claim that the MSC was founded by Umar Hadid and that the council was to become a nucleus of an Islamic government in Fallujah by implementing the principle of *al-Hisba* (al-amr bi'al-ma 'ruf wal-nahy 'an al-munkar, or Commanding Right and Forbidding

Wrong) and replacing religious leaders not subscribing to the group's ideology with younger ones that were influenced by Salafism.[9] Abu Azzam, who was the overall Amir for TWJ in Fallujah, described this phase as the second phase of the struggle in Fallujah: the first phase was the military struggle against the US forces, the second was against those who deviated from the right path (*ahl al-zaigh wa al-dalal*) and the 'bats of darkness' (*khafafish al-zalam*).[10]

TWJ sources may have exaggerated the group's influence on the council, but other sources confirm that TWJ controlled several districts in Fallujah, in particular the al-Jolan district. The descriptions of how TWJ attempted to turn these areas into Islamic mini-states are reminiscent of how IS later elevated these local experiments to a national level. Inhabitants who sold or drank alcohol were publicly flogged, women were forced to don full body covering, while movie theatres, music stores and hairdressers were closed or destroyed.[11] TWJ also tried to eradicate the Sufi tradition, which was widespread in Fallujah, and forbade the locals from venerating the graves of Sufi saints.[12] Insurgents were afraid of potential spies and executed civilians under the pretext that they collaborated with the enemy.[13]

There are several other examples of AQI's territorial ambitions prior to the establishment of al-Dawla al-Islamiyya fi al-'Iraq (Islamic State of Iraq, henceforth ISI) in October 2006. Each time it acquired control of a limited territory and its people, ISI tried to found Islamic mini-states in these areas by forcing the inhabitants to follow the group's strict interpretation of Islam and of Shari'ah. For instance, when AQI, together with the insurgent group Ansar al-Sunna, took over the city of Haditha in 2005 – exploiting a power vacuum that had arisen following the withdrawal of US forces from the city – they temporarily established what was described by visiting journalists as a 'Taliban state' where alcohol and 'un-Islamic' music were banned, women forced to cover themselves, and alleged criminals publicly punished.[14] Likewise, when in April 2005 AQI took control of Husaybah, a small town close to the Syrian border in Anbar, it forced women to wear *niqab* and closed music stores.[15] Repeatedly, AQI sought to buttress its control and govern by killing those who opposed al-Qaeda or could represent a threat to its position of power.[16]

These efforts towards territorial control and governance became more pronounced after AQI and several lesser-known insurgent groups announced the establishment of ISI on 15 October 2006. It was announced that the leader of ISI was the previously unknown Abu Umar al-Baghdadi, and its new spokesman urged the Sunni community to pledge allegiance to him as *amir al-mu'mineen* (Commander of the Faithful).[17] Such names and honorary titles signal ISI's territorial, Caliphate ambitions. First of all, by referring to itself as a state (*dawla*) and not an emirate (*imara*) ISI indicated that it had ambitions to expand its territorial hold.[18] Second, *amir al-mu'mineen* is usually an epithet associated with the Caliph. Indeed, the long-term ambitions of ISI were evident in the very first statement the group issued. In it, ISI compared its territory to the first Islamic society established by the Prophet Muhammad in Medina, claiming that they extended Shari'ah over an area that was the same size, if not larger, than the state Muhammad had established in Medina.[19]

Although in 2006 ISI claimed that its 'state' was established in the Iraqi provinces with a considerable Sunni Arab population, in reality the group's control over territory at the time remained elusive and scattered. It was not until 2013–14, in the wake of escalating conflicts in Iraq and Syria, that the group was able to establish continuous territorial control over larger areas and populations. In April 2013 the group proclaimed that it had established a presence in Syria and that its new name would be al-Dawla al-Islamiyya fi al-'Iraq wa al-Sham (Islamic State of Iraq and al-Sham, henceforth ISIS). A year later, on 29 June 2014, the first day of Ramadan, the ISIS spokesman Abu Mohamed al-Adnani announced that the group had changed its name again, this time to IS and that its leader, Abu Bakr al-Baghdadi, was proclaimed the Caliph for all Muslims in the world, not only in Iraq and Syria.[20]

Definitions: rebel governance and Islamic state

What then, if any, are the key characteristics of statehood attributable to IS and to what extent does the group's insistence on being called a 'state' carry repercussions on its rebel governance? To answer these questions, it is first necessary to unpack what is meant by 'rebel governance' and explore whether the activities of IS can be described as such. According to Nelson Kasfir 'rebel governance' can be defined broadly as 'organizing civilians for public purpose'.[21] He also singles out three conditions that must be met for an insurgent group to be defined as engaging in rebel governance, all of which are present in the case of the IS: (1) territorial control, (2) a resident population and (3) violence or the threat thereof.[22] It has been estimated that IS at its territorial highpoint in 2014 controlled somewhere between 12,000 and 35,000 square miles in Iraq and Syria respectively and an estimated population of about between 8 and 10 million people in total.[23]

Offering a more detailed definition of 'rebel governance', and one that is more noticeably in line with conceptions of statehood, Zachariah Mampilly considers it as 'the development of institutions and practices of rule to regulate the social and political life of civilians by an armed group'.[24] This can include most of the functions often associated with states, such as a monopoly of power/force, a judicial structure, taxation, health and an educational system.[25]

As will be illustrated below, IS did at least attempt to provide most of these functions in areas where it had established firm territorial control.

From Mampilly's definition it is clear that the distinction between governance by rebels and by states might be blurred. Indeed, following the tradition of Charles Tilly and Mancur Olson, who see war-making as state-making, there exists a large literature on how rebel governance represents embryonic or *de facto* states that could evolve into more consolidated state-constructions.[26] Some, like Stephen M. Walt, have argued that IS could be seen as an example of such a 'revolutionary state-building organization' that potentially over time could be integrated into the international system, such as the revolutionary regimes established following the French, Russian and Chinese revolutions.[27] Others have pointed to groups like Hizbullah, which over time moderated some of its most extreme views, and became integrated into the political system.[28]

This said, caution is in order to not construe rebel governance with fully fledged statehood and to remain sensitive to the differences that exist between the two. One of the key differences between rebel-ruled and regular states, for instance, is that while the rebels might possess empirical (or internal) sovereignty, they lack the juridical (or external) sovereignty conferred to states through recognition by the international community of sovereign states. Rebel rulers therefore have to operate outside the international system and in a territory where another state retains full sovereign *de jure* rights to exercise violence in order to defend its territory.[29] In the literature on so-called '*quasi-states*' and '*de facto* states' it is usually assumed that these states aim to seek international recognition and sovereignty. Indeed, according to several of the definitions of the concepts, to seek international recognition is one of the main criteria in order to be categorised as a '*quasi*-state'[30] or a '*de facto* state'.[31]

This is where the approach of IS to statehood stands out and is somewhat paradoxical. On the one hand, it presents itself as having, or seeking, several of the trappings of a modern state, with its own bureaucratic structures organised under the auspices of a government,[32] providing public goods to, and taxing, the population living in its territory, having its own flag,[33] its own currency,[34] and even having its own 'anthem' (or *nasheed*, an acapella chant).[35] On the other hand, it is ideologically opposed to the very notions of nationalism and nation states, does not respect internationally recognised borders and thus challenges the very basis of the Westphalian system of sovereign territorial states.[36] Indeed, following the establishment of the Caliphate, IS released a movie claiming to have eradicated the border between Syria and Iraq, and thus dismantling the post-World War I Sykes–Picot order where the colonial powers had divided the Muslims into several smaller states.[37]

In contrast to the Islamic Emirate of Afghanistan established by the Taliban in 1996 – which sought but failed to obtain international recognition from the United Nations[38] – IS has neither sought, nor obtained, international recognition by any state and has not established any embassies elsewhere.[39] Instead, IS claimed that its declaration of the Caliphate abolished the sovereignty and the authority of all other 'emirates, groups, states and organizations', as they were replaced with the authority of the Caliphate.[40] Thus, based on the most widely accepted definition of statehood – the Montevideo Convention of 1933 – IS cannot be defined as a state, as it is lacking willingness or 'capacity to enter into relations with other states'.[41] It does, however, fulfil the other requirements for statehood, including a permanent population, a defined territory and a government.[42]

This status of IS as a non-sovereign entity, operating within two sovereign states (Syria and Iraq), has also had a bearing on the nature of its rebel governance. Through its propaganda, the group has attracted foreign fighters to travel to the actual territory of the Caliphate by depicting it as the realisation of a utopian ideal society. In fact, the group's challenge to the existing order not only attracted many foreigners to travel to the group's territory, but it also precipitated a military offensive by members of the international community seeking to rob the group of its territorial control. Undoubtedly, this international offensive against IS has affected its rebel governance, and this in two fundamental ways. For one, it has impeded its ability to provide basic public goods and services to the population under its control. At the same time, it has precipitated behaviour by IS that is increasingly based on coercion and intimidation in order to suppress any resistance against the group and deter potential spies and collaborates with the US-led international military coalition against IS.[43]

Why did IS want a 'state'?

Why then was it so important for the group to establish and operate as a 'state'-like structure in parts of Iraq and Syria? As illustrated above, the establishment of an Islamic state has been a long-term goal of the group, with this state serving as a nucleus for a new Islamic caliphate centred on Baghdad.[44] In addition, the establishment of both ISI in 2006 and the IS and the Caliphate in 2014 was framed as a religious duty incumbent upon the group. For instance, when the group established ISI in 2006, it used as a legitimation for its right to establish a state the fact that it controlled, and established Shari'ah, in an area that was the same size, if not larger, than the first Islamic state established in Medina.[45] Likewise, when the group announced the establishment of the Caliphate in 2014, its spokesman al-Adnani said that they had a religious obligation to establish a 'state' as they were in a position to do so.[46]

As for the timing for the establishment of the IS and a Caliphate, Will McCants argues – mainly based on an account of the defected Chief Judge of ISI, Abu Sulayman al-Utaybi – that ISI was established on an apocalyptic timetable because al-Zarqawi's successor Abu Ayyub al-Masri believed that the apocalypse was imminent, and that the Caliphate hence had to be established prior to the apocalypse.[47] Brian Fishman, meanwhile, posits that ISI was established mainly following the advice from top al-Qaeda leaders to establish an Islamic state under the leadership of an Iraqi, not a foreigner like the Jordanian Abu Mus'ab al-Zarqawi.[48]

It can, however, also be argued that rebel rivalry constituted a critical factor in the establishment of ISI as well as of the IS and the Caliphate. As mentioned above, ISI was established in October 2006, at a time when there were serious discussions concerning a US withdrawal from Iraq, and ISI leaders repeatedly described the establishment of the group as an attempt to preempt other Sunni actors trying to exploit the power vacuum an eventual withdrawal would create, 'stealing' (in the words of ISI) the fruits of their efforts.[49] Uthman Abd al-Rahman, the official in charge of ISI's Shari'ah Commission, stated in this regard that one of the most important reasons for establishing ISI was to fill the void created by the political, military and security failures of the US and its Iraqi allies.[50] Abu Ayyub al-Masri, meanwhile, claimed that although they had planned the establishment of ISI for a long time, the timing was partly to pre-empt other Sunni actors from declaring the existence of a federal Sunni state in the Sunni Arab-dominated provinces of Iraq.[51] Likewise, the withdrawal of the Syrian regime's forces from northern and eastern parts of Syria in 2012–13 led to a fragmentation of authority, with a host of different rebel groups competing to gain control over these territories and their resources.[52]

Finally, the creation of IS, and especially the pronouncement by the group of a Caliphate, was not only an attempt to exploit its recent military success and momentum after the conquest of Mosul in June 2014. It was also an attempt to outbid other Syrian and Iraqi insurgent groups in attracting foreign and local recruits. The establishment of the Caliphate was especially related to the long-standing competition between IS and the al-Qaeda organisation for a position of hegemony within the broader global jihadi movement.[53] To restore the Caliphate has been a long-term goal not only for groups like al-Qaeda, but for the broader Islamist movement ever since the abolition of the Ottoman Caliphate in 1924.[54] By claiming to have realised this utopian ideal, IS attempted to outbid al-Qaeda and other competing factions and to assert itself as the hegemonic group within the broader jihadi movement.[55] Moreover, by demanding all Muslim organisations, including al-Qaeda, swear allegiance to its newly proclaimed Caliph, IS sought to expand the group's authority to the rest of the Muslim world, thus far beyond its actual territorial control.

A trademark common to all three of the above cases is that the withdrawal – or the potential thereof – of a unifying enemy (US forces, Syrian regime forces, and Iraqi regime forces) from certain territories resulted in fierce competition between different rebel factions for control over those territories. The ensuing fragmentation of authority also led to what Mara Revkin has described as 'competitive sovereignty', with several actors seeking a monopoly of legitimate violence in the same area.[56] As will be illustrated in the following pages, this rivalry and competition to establish a monopoly of violence in rebel-held territories had important repercussions on the rebel governance of the Islamic State.

Repercussions on rebel governance

So why does it matter that IS perceives itself to be a state of some sort? As discussed above, although IS cannot be defined as a 'state' according to internationally recognised conceptions of statehood, its insistence on being a state carries important repercussions on its governance and its behaviour. So for instance, it can be argued that, by laying claim to the monopoly on the *legitimate* use of physical force within a given territory, IS subscribes to a Weberian conception of statehood. Thus, like most states, IS protects its territories militarily from 'external' aggressors/enemies (be they Kurdish, Shi'a-dominated militias, foreign nations involved in the international coalition against IS, other rebel groups or the Syrian and Iraqi regimes). Internally, as well, it polices the territory in order to guarantee that it is governed according to the group's strict interpretation of Shari'ah through its religious police force known as al-Hisba. The group has also established a legal system through its many Shari'ah courts, doling out harsh sentences to those who do not abide by the group's stringent laws.[57]

Apart from a monopoly on violence, IS has also sought to monopolise the delivery of a range of basic services and educational provisions to the residents of the territories it controls. The goal here is to secure local (passive) support by ensuring that the residents are dependent on IS, which constitutes the sole provider of security, order and basic commodities, like bread,[58] petrol and education.[59] Education, in fact, has become organised in, and implemented through, the group's very own Ministry of Education (Diwan al-Ta'leem), which introduced a new curriculum so as to indoctrinate children to become model citizens of this new 'Islamic state'.[60]

Lastly, like any state, IS levies taxes on the population in the territories under its tutelage, mainly through *zakat*, an Islamic tax imposed on Muslims who can afford it, but also on all goods, on agricultural produce, on trucks transiting through IS-controlled territories and cash withdrawals for instance.[61] At least according to the propaganda of the group, this tax is redistributed to poor Muslims living within the groups' territory.[62] A special tax, known as *jizya*, meanwhile, is levied on all Christians living in IS-controlled areas.[63]

Together these aspects of rebel governance are clearly meant to buttress IS's control and legitimacy within the territory it controls as well as its claim to statehood. Arguably, however, they are not only that, but also borne out of rebel rivalry; that is out of a desire to establish the group's authority *vis-à-vis* other rival factions operating within the same territory. In 2006, for instance, ISI sought to establish a monopoly of violence by targeting and intimidating those insurgent groups that did not want to join this new 'state' and swear allegiance to its leader, Abu Umar al-Baghdadi.[64] The group's insistence on being a state enjoying a monopoly of violence clearly constituted a watershed moment in the relationship between ISI and the other Sunni Arab insurgent groups in Iraq. Although there had been skirmishes between AQI and other groups prior to the establishment of ISI, they were by and large bound together in a tactical alliance against their common enemies, the US armed forces and Shi'a militias in Iraq.[65]

However, following the establishment of ISI there was a rapid rise of rebel-on-rebel violence as ISI targeted those rebels who did not accept the authority of the group and its leader, al-Baghdadi.[66] This in turn spurred several insurgents to turn against ISI in order to defend themselves from the group's attack.[67] As Sunni Arabs began to turn against ISI, it forced the group into a negative cycle where its attempts to force the Sunni community not to go against it only increased their willingness to cooperate with the US forces in order to gain protection from ISI attacks. This drew ISI into a spiral of violence against the Sunni community, which turned into such a vortex that in September 2007 the group announced that it would prioritise attacking Sunnis who had turned against them.[68] This dynamic constitutes a clear example of rebel rivalry. Indeed, several studies have found that rebel rivalry tends to increase violence against co-ethnic civilians.[69] Paul Staniland, partly based on the case of ISI, argues that, when an armed group decides to become the hegemonic actor within a larger insurgency, the group may attack the other insurgents in order to eliminate its rivals.[70]

Likewise, there are several reports on how in 2014 IS sought to enforce its authority in the territories occupied by systemically killing prominent and influential leaders who had challenged, or posed a potential challenge to, the group's monopoly of power.[71] In both Raqqa and Mosul, for instance, IS distributed a 'city charter' (*wathiqat al-madina*) which stipulated that councils, associations, political or armed groups other than IS were prohibited.[72] Residents who had escaped from the Mosul area claimed that in the months following its takeover IS had arrested between 20,000 and 25,000 individuals, mainly residents who either had an influential position within Mosul before the arrival of IS in 2014, or did not obey its authority.[73] The insistence on being, and behaving like, a *de facto* state also led IS to pursue a more exclusionary method of governance, particularly *vis-à-vis* other Sunni insurgent groups. Indeed, it neither sought nor accepted offers of cooperation from other Sunni Arab insurgent groups, who have collaborated to a much larger extent with other actors in their rebel governance and have set up joint governing institutions.[74] A case in point is Jabhat al-Nusra (currently part of the organization known as Hay'at Tahrir al-Sham), a group that was initially established by ISI and with the same goal of establishing a Caliphate, yet which adopted a more gradual and conciliatory approach to achieving this goal that placed emphasis on making local allies through cooperation and power-sharing. So for instance, Jabhat al-Nusra was one of the leading groups behind the creation of the various Shari'ah Commissions (al-Hay'a al-Shar'iyya) in Syria's Aleppo and Deir al-Zur, together with other Islamist-leaning insurgent groups.[75] Ultimately, however, the increasingly dominant position of IS in Syria and Iraq, and its proclamation of the Caliphate in 2014, prompted Jabhat al-Nusra to abandon its gradual and inclusivist approach for a more assertive and exclusionary one. For one, this is evident in an audio-recording of Jabhat al-Nusra's Amir, Abu Mohamed al-Julani that was leaked shortly after ISI had established its Caliphate. In it, al-Julani asserted that the time had come to establish an Islamic emirate in the Levant (al-Sham).[76] Poignantly, it is also evident in Jabhat al-Nusra's changed approach to rebel governance post-2014. Whilst prior to 2014, the group had avoided unilateral control of areas in Syria, following the rise of IS in Syria, Jabhat al-Nusra began to assume a more forceful position on the issue of statehood, especially in its stronghold in the Idlib province.[77]

To behave like a state by insisting on seeking a monopoly of violence is, however, a risky gambit for IS. This exclusionary approach, in fact, tends to alienate potential allies and foster resistance and rebellion against IS in the population living in areas that it controls. This was particularly illustrated by the Sunni Arab rebellion against ISI in 2007, which was one of the most important factors explaining why ISI was driven out of the Sunni-dominated province of Anbar in 2007–8. Likewise, since 2014 several reports have highlighted the unpopularity of IS and the local resistance against it, which the group has managed, however, to curtail by violent means.[78] The exclusionary rebel governance of IS stands in contrast to Jabhat al-Nusra's more gradual approach, which seeks cooperation with other Sunni Arab groups instead of claiming to be a state and forcing others to submit to it. This approach to governance is also more in line with recommendations from the al-Qaeda leadership, and the recent territorial losses of IS and with it the likely demise of its Caliphate will likely strengthen this approach to rebel governance.

Conclusion

To establish an Islamic state and engage in some form of rebel governance – defined by IS as the implementation of Shari'ah and the restructuring of the territory based on the principle of *al-Hisba* – has been one of the defining characteristics of the group since its inception. Indeed, it can be argued that the main difference between the rebel governance of IS and that of its predecessors is not 'rebel governance' in itself, but its scope and the group's ability to implement it, given the very different context the various incarnations of the group have operated within.

IS constitutes but one example of how the upheaval and collapse of the old state structures in the aftermath of the Arab uprisings of 2010–12 has enabled various non-state actors to exploit the ensuing political vacuum and fragmentation of authority. The same phenomenon can be observed in several other countries affected by the turmoil generated by the Arab uprisings. It has enabled jihadi insurgent groups in countries like Yemen, Libya and Mali to engage in rebel governance to varying extents.[79] Moreover, the phenomenon is not restricted to jihadi groups, as for instance both Shi'a and Kurdish militias have exploited the political vacuum created in the wake of the shrinking state authority in countries such as Iraq, Syria and Yemen to increase their territorial control.[80] As such, the rise and rebel governance of IS and other jihadi–Salafi groups are primarily a symptom, and not a cause, of a much deeper crisis of weak states in the region.

What is more, the fragmentation of authority in Iraq and Syria has resulted in increased rebel rivalry, with several (insurgent) actors competing to exploit this vacuum and establish a monopoly of violence on the same territory. As argued in this chapter, the establishment both of ISI and of IS and the Caliphate can partly be explained by rebel rivalry, with groups attempting to outbid other insurgent groups, particularly al-Qaeda, in both the global and local contest of recruitment and attention. This illustrates that it is not sufficient to study only the ideology of IS, or similar groups, in order to understand its behaviour. It is also necessary to study the context the group operates within and its relationship to other competing groups. To establish an Islamic state and a Caliphate has been a long-term ambition for IS, yet the actual timing of the establishment was more influenced by intra-rebel dynamics and an attempt to outbid its competitors, primarily al-Qaeda, in the context of state fragmentation and failure.

Notes

1. I refer to the group known as 'The Islamic State' consistently with its own Arabic name (al-Dawla al-Islamiyya) and its self-appellation as a state, and not as Daesh or Da'ish, an abbreviation mainly used by the group's enemies.
2. For a good account of the establishment of this camp see Sayf al-'Adl (2005), 'My experience with Abu Mus'ab al-Zarqawi [Tajribati ma'a Abi Mus'ab al-Zarqawi]', *Muntadayat al-Hikmah*, 23 May, <www.hkmah.net/showthread.php?t=7932> (accessed 23 May 2005). Originally printed in Fu'ad Husayn (2005), *Al-Zarqawi, al-Qaida's Second Generation* [al-Zarqawi, al-jil al-thani li-l-qa'ida] (in Arabic), Beirut: Dar al-Khayyal, pp. 115–42.
3. Bryan Price, Dan Milton, Muhammad al-`Ubaydi and Nelly Lahoud (2014), *The Group That Calls Itself a State: Understanding the Evolution and Challenges of the Islamic State*. West Point: Combatting Terrorism Center, p. 11.
4. Abu Mu'sab al-Zarqawi (2004), 'The legal position on the "Iraqi Karzai" government' [al-mawqif al-shari'i min hukumat Karzai al-'iraq] (in Arabic) speech dated 23 June 2004, printed in 'Complete archive of the addresses and speeches of The Lion of Islam, Shaykh Abu Mus'ab al-Zarqawi', issued by *Shabakat al-Buraq al-Islami*, 10 June 2006, pp. 137–44.
5. Abu Yaman al-Baghdadi, 'Dialogue with Abu Mus'ab al-Zarqawi' [Hiwar ma'a al-shaykh Abu Mus'ab al-Zarqawi] (in Arabic) published by the Media Department of *Tanzim al-Qa'ida fi Bilad al-Rafidayn*, posted on *Minbar al-Tawhid wa'l-Jihad*, <www.tawhed.ws> (accessed 3 October 2011).
6. For more on this see the serial by Nir Rosen (2004), 'Fallujah – inside the resistance', *Asia Times*, July; Roel Mejier (2004), '"Defending our honor", authenticity and the framing of resistance in the Iraqi Sunni town of Falluja', *Etnofoor*, 1&2, pp. 37–8.
7. Sayyid 'Ali al-Husayni (2007), *A Cultural, Political, Ideological and Military Map of the Armed Groups in Iraq* [Qira'a wa tahlil fi kharita al-jama'at al-musallaha fi al-'iraq (thaqafiyan wa siyasiyan wa idiyulujian wa 'askariyan] (in Arabic) p. 99; Mukhtar, Ahmed (2004) 'Falluja afire', *Al-Ahram Weekly*, 7–13 October, <http://weekly.ahram.org.eg/2004/711/re8.htm> (accessed 12 May 2010).
8. Anon. (2004), 'Amir of Fallujah, 'Abdullah al-Janabi speaks in meeting with Iraqi newspaper al-Shahid' [Amir al-Fallujah, 'Abd Allah al-Janabi yaqul fi liqa' ma'a sahifa al-shahid al-'iraqiyya'] (in Arabic), Iraqcenter.net, 2 October, <www.iraqcenter.net> (accessed 19 August 2010).
9. Anon., 'From the biographies of the distinguished martyrs – Nr 12 – Umar Hadid' [min siyar a'lam al-shuhada' – 12 – 'Umar Hadid] (in Arabic) Media Department of *Majlis Shura al-Mujahidin fi'l-'Iraq* via *Muntadayat Shabakat al-Hisbah*, <www.alhesbah.com> (accessed 13 February 2006). For more on the concept of al-Hisba see David Cook (2000), *Commanding Right and Forbidding Wrong in Islamic Thought*. Cambridge: Cambridge University Press.
10. Anon., 'From the Biographies of the Distinguished Martyrs – Nr 36 –Abu Azzam' [min siyar a'lam al-shuhada' – 36 – Abu Azzam] (in Arabic), *al-Furqan Media Establishment* on behalf of Islamic State of Iraq, via *Shabakat al-Akhbar al-'Alamiyya*, <www.w-n-n.net/> (accessed 2 December 2009).
11. Anon. (2004), 'Truths and exaggerations about "the resistance" and terrorism in "the Islamic Republic of Fallujah"' [Haqa'iq wa mubalaghat 'an "al-muqawama" wa al-irhab fi "jumhuriyya al-fallujah al-islamiyya] (in Arabic), *al-Sharq Al-Awsat*, 6 June; Sayyid 'Ali al-Husayni (2007), Qira'a wa tahlil fi kharita al-jama'at al-musallaha fi al-'iraq (thaqafiyan wa siyasiyan wa idiyulujian wa 'askariyan) [A cultural, political, ideological and military map of the armed groups in Iraq]. Al-Maktaba al-'Asriyya Publishers, p. 99. Available at

<http://iraker.dk/v/50.htm> (last accessed 11 July 2017); Hamza Hendawi (2004), 'Fallujah emerging as Islamic mini-state', *Associated Press*, 26 May.

12. Karl Vick (2004), 'Insurgent alliance is fraying in Fallujah', *Washington Post*, 13 October; Nir Rosen (2004), 'Fallujah – inside the resistance, Part 7: radicals in the ashes of democracy', *Asia Times*, 24 July.
13. Anon. (2004), 'Truths and exaggerations about "the resistance" and terrorism'; Remy Ourdan (2004), 'Al-Fallujah, 'Mujahedin Emirate', *Le Monde*, 1 July.
14. Omer Mahdi and Rory Carroll (2005), 'Under US noses, brutal insurgents rule Sunni citadel', *The Guardian*, 22 August.
15. Ellen Knickmeyer (2005), 'Zarqawi followers clash with local Sunnis', *Washington Post*, 29 May; Oliver Poole (2005), 'US delight as Iraqi rebels turn their guns on al-Qa'eda', *Telegraph*, 4 July.
16. See for instance Ned Parker and Mohamed al-Kubacy (2006), 'Arm tribes to fight al-Qaeda, say Sunnis', *The Times*, 13 September; Peter Beaumont (2006), 'Iraqi tribes launch battle to drive al-Qaida out of troubled province', *The Guardian*, 3 October.
17. Anon. (2006), 'Statement of Mujahidin Shura Council on establishment of "Islamic State of Iraq"', *Jihadist Websites, OSC Report*, 15 October, via FBIS.
18. For more on the difference between *dawla* and imara see Will McCants (2015), *The ISIS Apocalypse: The History, Strategy, and Doomsday Vision of the Islamic State*. New York: St.Martin's Press, pp. 9, 15.
19. Anon. 'Statement of Mujahidin Shura Council'.
20. Abu Muhammad al-Adnani (2014), 'This is the promise of Allah', *al-Hayat Media Center*, 19 June.
21. Nelson Kasfir (2015), 'Rebel governance – constructing a field of inquiry: definitions, scope, patterns, order, causes', in Ana Arjona, Nelson Kasfir and Zachariah Mampilly (eds), *Rebel Governance in Civil War*. Cambridge: Cambridge University Press, p. 21.
22. Ibid., p. 21.
23. See for instance Kathy Gilsinan (2014), 'The many ways to map the Islamic "State"', *The Atlantic*, 27 August; Anon. (2017) 'Islamic State and the crisis in Iraq and Syria in maps', *BBC News*, 20 January.
24. Zachariah Mampilly (2014), 'Rebel governance and the Syrian War', *The Project on Middle East Political Science (POMEPS)*, 2 December.
25. Ibid.
26. For a good overview and criticism of this literature see Zachariah Mampilly (2011), *Rebel Rulers: Insurgent Governance and Civilian Life during War*. Cornell: Cornell University Press, pp. 25–40.
27. Stephen M. Walt (2015), 'ISIS as revolutionary state', *Foreign Affairs*, 94:6, pp. 42–51.
28. See for instance Stathys Kalyvas (2015), 'Is ISIS a revolutionary group and if yes, what are the implications?' *Perspectives on Terrorism*, 9:4, pp. 42–7.
29. Mampilly, *Rebel Rulers*, pp. 34–9.
30. Pål Kolstø (2006), 'The sustainability and future of unrecognized quasi-states', *Journal of Peace Research*, 43:6, pp. 723–40.
31. Vincenc Kopeček, Tomáš Hoch and Vladimír Baar (2016), 'De facto states and democracy: the case of Abkhazia', *Bulletin of Geography*, 32, pp. 85–104.
32. In April 2007 it was announced that the Shura Council of ISI had formed a fully fledged cabinet for the Islamic State, including a Minister of Petroleum, Minister of Agriculture and Marine Wealth and a Minister of Health. Anon. (2007), 'Islamic state of Iraq issues video statement announcing formation of New Cabinet', *Jihadist Websites – OSC Summary*, 20 April, via FBIS.

33. For details see McCants, *The ISIS Apocalypse*, pp. 19–22.
34. Anon. (2014), 'The currency of the Khilafah', *Dabiq*, 5, pp. 18–19.
35. Alex Marshall (2014), 'How Isis got its anthem', *The Guardian*, 9 November. For more on the *nasheeds* of the Islamic State see Henrik Gråtrud (2016), 'Islamic state nasheeds as messaging tools', *Studies in Conflict & Terrorism*, 39:12, pp. 1050–70.
36. For more on this see for instance Nielsen, Richard A. (2015), 'Does the Islamic State believe in sovereignty?' *Washington Post*, 6 February.
37. Anon. (2014), 'The end of Sykes–Picot', 29 June, released by al-Hayat Media Center.
38. See for instance Alex van Linschoten and Felix Kuehn (2012), *An Enemy We Created: The Myth of the Taliban-Al Qaeda Merger in Afghanistan*. Oxford: Oxford University Press, p. 171.
39. The Islamic Emirate of Afghanistan was recognized only by Pakistan, Saudi Arabia and the United Arab Emirates. It had ambassadors to Pakistan and Saudi Arabia and an embassy in Pakistan. Pakistan also had an embassy and three consulates in Afghanistan. For details see the biography of Taliban's ambassador to Pakistan Abdul Salam Zaeef (2010), *My Life with the Taliban*. Hurst: London.
40. Abu Muhammad al-Adnani (2014), 'This is the promise of Allah', *al-Hayat Media Center*, 19 June.
41. See Eli Bernstein (2015), 'Is the Islamic State a "state" in international law?' 18 November; Zachary Fillingham (2015), 'Is Islamic state a state?' *Geopolitical Monitor*, 5 August.
42. Ibid.
43. William McCants, Nelson Kasfir and Zachariah Mampilly (2016), 'Experts weigh in (Part 6): is ISIS good at governing?' *Brookings*, 22 March.
44. Anon. (2007), 'Program and constants of the Islamic State of Iraq' [Dawla al-islamiyya al-'iraqiyya (manhaj wa thawabit)] (in Arabic) posted on the jihadi forum known as *World News Network*, 15 March, <www.w-n-n.net/> (last accessed 19 March 2007).
45. Anon., 'Statement of Mujahidin Shura Council'.
46. Abu Muhammad al-Adnani (2014), 'This is the promise of Allah', *al-Hayat Media Center*, 19 June.
47. McCants, *ISIS Apocalypse*, p. 32.
48. Brian Fishman (2011), 'Redefining the Islamic State: the fall and rise of al-Qaeda in Iraq', *New America Foundation*.
49. Brian Fishman (2009), 'Dysfunction and decline: lessons learned from inside al-Qa'ida in Iraq', *CTC Harmony Project*, pp. 4–6; Mohammed M. Hafez (2007), 'al-Qa'ida losing ground in Iraq', *CTC Sentinel*, 1:1, p. 7.
50. Anon. (2007), 'Examining the components of the Islamic State of Iraq, its future and repercussions in the region', *Jihadist Websites – OSC Summary* 15 May, via FBIS.
51. Anon. (2008), 'Audio interview with the Minister of War of the Islamic State', *Jihadist Websites*, 24 October, via FBIS.
52. See for instance Ben Hubbard (2012), 'New order emerges: rebels carve out large enclave in North Syria', *NBC News*, 12 August; Anon. (2012), 'Many rebel-held Syria towns attempt to fill power vacuum', *Los Angeles Times*, 18 August; Portia Walker (2012), 'Rebel fighters build shadow state in Syria's countryside', *The Independent*, 15 May.
53. See for instance Celine Marie I. Novenario (2016), 'Differentiating Al Qaeda and the Islamic State through strategies publicized in jihadist magazines', *Studies in Conflict & Terrorism*, 39:11, pp. 953–67. For more on the relationship between rebel governance and rebel rivalry see e.g. Brynjar Lia (2015), 'Understanding jihadi proto-states', *Perspectives on Terrorism*, 9:4, pp. 31–41.
54. Vernie Liebl (2009), 'The Caliphate', *Middle Eastern Studies*, 45:3, pp. 373–91.

55. Thomas Hegghammer (2014), 'The foreign policy essay: calculated Caliphate', *Lawfare Blog*, 6 July, <www.lawfareblog.com/foreign-policy-essay-calculated-caliphate> (last accessed 10 July 2017).

56. Mara Revkin (2016), 'Does the Islamic state have a "social contract"? Evidence from Iraq and Syria'. Yale University Council on Middle East Studies: Program on Governance and Local Development.

57. See for instance Charles C. Caris and Samuel Reynolds (2014), 'ISIS governance in Syria', *Institute for the Study of War*, pp. 15–17, Waleed Abu al-Khair (2014), 'Al-Qaeda war crimes in Syria: hadd punishment and corpse mutilation', *al-Shorfa*, 11 March; Hadil Aarja (2014), 'ISIS enforces strict religious law in Raqqa', *Al-Monitor*, 21 March, <https://www.al-monitor.com/pulse/security/2014/03/isis-enforces-islamic-law-raqqa-syria.html> (last accessed 16 January 2018).

58. José Ciro Martínez and Brent Eng (2014), 'Islamic State works to win hearts, minds with bread', *Al-Monitor*, 29 July, <https://www.al-monitor.com/pulse/originals/2014/07/islamic-state-bread-subsidies-syria-iraq-terrorism.html> (last accessed 16 January 2018).

59. Barak Barfi and Aaron Y. Zelin (2013), 'Al Qaeda's Syrian strategy', *Syria Deeply*, 15 October; Chris Looney (2013), 'Al-Qaeda's governance strategy in Raqqa', *Syria Comment*, 8 December.

60. For details see especially Jacob Olidort (2016), 'Inside the Caliphate's classroom', *Washington Institute for Near East Policy*.

61. According to one estimate from October 2014, the group could have generated about 30 million USD each month from its territories in Iraq and Syria. See: Jean-Charles Brisard and Damien Martinez (2014), 'Islamic State: the economy-based terrorist funding', *Thomson Reuters Accelus*, October.

62. Laith Alkhouri and Alex Kassirer (2015), 'Governing the Caliphate: the Islamic State picture', *CTC Sentinel*, 8:8, pp. 17–20.

63. See e.g. Alison Tahmizian Meuse (2013), 'In show of supremacy, Syria al-Qaida branch torches church', *Syria Deeply*, 30 October.

64. See e.g. Lydia Khalil (2007), 'Divisions within the Iraqi insurgency', *Terrorism Monitor*, 5:7.

65. See e.g. Mohammed M. Hafez (2007), 'al-Qa'ida Losing ground in Iraq', *CTC Sentinel*, 1:1, p. 7; Brian Fishman (2009), 'Dysfunction and decline: lessons learned from inside al-Qa'ida in Iraq', *CTC Harmony Project*, p. 2; John A. McCary (2009), 'The Anbar awakening: an alliance of incentives', *Washington Quarterly*, 32:1, p. 43.

66. In March 2008 a representative from the insurgent umbrella group Jabhat al-Jihad wa al-Taghyir (Jihad and Change Front) recounts how AQI, following the establishment of ISI, began to target those Sunni insurgent groups that did not acknowledge this new Islamic state because of doubts about its religious legitimacy. This signalled a shift of target from the forces of occupation to other Sunnis. See: Anon. (2008), 'Jihad and change front "answers" on issues, "constants", positions', *Jihadist Websites – OSC Summary*, 22 March, via FBIS. See also Ned Parker (2007), 'Insurgents report a split with Al Qaeda in Iraq', *Los Angeles Times*, 27 March.

67. For instance, in April 2007 the Islamic Army in Iraq publicly accused ISI of killing Sunni insurgents, unarmed Sunnis and religious scholars who dared to speak out against the group. See e.g. Anon. (2007), 'Islamic army in Iraq accuses Al-Qa'ida in Iraq of "transgressing Islamic Law"', *Jihadist Websites – OSC Summary*, 11 April, via FBIS. See also Lydia Khalil (2007), 'Divisions within the Iraqi insurgency', *Terrorism Monitor*, 5:7; Sudarsan Raghavan (2007), 'Sunni factions split with al-Qaeda group', *Washington Post*, 14 April.

68. Anon. (2007), 'Islamic State of Iraq gives priority to targeting Sunnis who turned against state', *Jihadist Websites – OSC Summary*, 6 September.

69. See Claire Metelis (2010), *Inside Insurgency – Violence, Civilians, and Revolutionary Group Behaviour*. New York: New York University Press. See also Kathleen Gallagher Cunningham, Lee Seymour and Kristin Bakke (2012), 'Shirts today, skins tomorrow: the effects of fragmentation on conflict processes in self-determination disputes', *Journal of Conflict Resolution*, 56:1, pp. 67–93.

70. Paul Staniland (2012), 'Between a rock and a hard place: insurgent fratricide, ethnic defection, and the rise of pro-state paramilitaries', *Journal of Conflict Resolution*, 56:1, pp. 16–40.

71. See e.g. Ali Mamouri (2014), 'No end in sight for Islamic State's attack on Iraq', *Al-Monitor*, 21 August, <https://www.al-monitor.com/pulse/fr/originals/2014/08/iraq-sunnis-targeted-by-islamic-state.html> (last accessed 16 January 2018).

72. Anon. (2014), 'Wathqa al-Madina', issued by the Media Office of Wilayat Ninawa, 13 June. See also Adam Taylor (2014), 'The rules in ISIS' new state: amputations for stealing and women to stay indoors', *Washington Post*, 12 June.

73. Mushreq Abbas (2014), 'Can Islamic State keep control of Mosul?' Al-Monitor, 14 November, <https://www.al-monitor.com/pulse/originals/2014/11/iraq-mosul-islamic-state-occupy-lose.html> (last accessed 16 January 2018).

74. For a good overview of the various institutions that were created in the aftermath of regime withdrawal see Adam Baczko, Gilles Dorronsoro and Arthur Quesnay (2013), 'Building a Syrian state in a time of civil war', *Carnegie Endowment for International Peace*, April.

75. Charles Lister (2016), 'Profiling Jabhat al-Nusra', *Brookings*, July, p. 12.

76. Suhaib Anjarini (2014), 'Al-Nusra Front not yet dead as its emir devises "Islamic Emirate of the Levant"', *al-Akhbar*, 12 July.

77. For details see Lister, 'Profiling Jabhat al-Nusra', pp. 35–7.

78. See e.g. Anon. (2014), 'Raqqa activist: "Most citizens have rejected ISIS . . . but are afraid"', *Syria Direct*, 23 January; Mathilde B. Aarseth, 'Resistance in the Caliphate's classrooms', forthcoming.

79. See e.g. Will McCants (2012), 'al-Qaeda is doing nation-building, should we worry?' *Foreign Policy*, 30 April; Brynjar Lia (2015), 'Understanding jihadi proto-states', *Perspectives on Terrorism*, 9:4, pp. 31–41.

80. The pro-independence vote in Iraqi Kurdistan in September 2017 is an example of this.

Chapter 5

Islamic and Islamist women activists in Qatar post-Arab uprisings: implications for the study of refusal and citizenship

Wanda Krause and Melissa Finn

This chapter challenges two widely held views about Middle East and North Africa (MENA) activists mobilised by Islamic principles. First, the authors contest the idea that the activists' grounding in Islam and their pursuit of political change necessarily makes them 'Islamists' and thus that they *ipso facto* seek to contest and/or (re)appropriate the state.[1] The authors also challenge the view that activists' location in states of authoritarian rule invariably reduces the status of such actors to 'subjects', when they might otherwise be citizens. In the first view, Islam is thought to produce particular forms of political agency and, in the second view, authoritarianism is seen to deny other forms of political agency, thus rendering people subjects without political subjectivity. Eva Bellin, for example, argues that resilient or robust authoritarian states in the MENA deploy multiple mechanisms to keep people subdued, such as punishing autonomous political action, bolstering elite hostility to the germination of progressive ideas, or repressing and/or corporatising civil society.[2] The authors agree that these dynamics exist in Qatar, but also that resilient authoritarian arguments do not tell the whole story, nor do they capture the activisms with broad-based impact that are irreverently refusing state control mechanisms. Bellin writes that 'the strength, coherence, and effectiveness of the state's coercive apparatus' determine revolutionary success, failure or non-occurrence.[3] Although activist women in Qatar advanced refusal as a means of political mobilisation before the Arab revolts in 2011, their refusals since 2011 confirm the strategic importance of Qatari Islam-centred women's activism and its unique features for the study of political Islam and citizenship. In the analysis that follows, the authors investigate several ways in which Islamic and Islamist[4] women activists in Qatar obfuscate state attempts to erase minority presence, expand networks and sisterhood, challenge Western state manipulation of

MENA politics, and fill the gaps left by insufficient state provisioning. Some of these actions fit the Qatari state policy agenda and enable the *status quo*, such as the perpetual neglect of state provisions, while others refuse, and therefore subvert, state policy focuses and *status quo* political dynamics. Some of the activists studied are women who embrace Islamic principles to create change, and others are Islamist women activists formally affiliated with the Qatari al-Ikhwan al-Muslimun (Muslim Brotherhood, MB). Although Islamic women activists in the MENA are political subjectivities in exile, or, to put it differently, actors forced into the spaces and politics of marginalisation, social control, discomfort and/or alienation, the authors argue that their mobilisations of citizenship ultimately weaken and undermine the coherence and effectiveness of the state's (and patriarchy's) coercive mechanisms. Many women interviewed have built networks and civil society by defying the disempowerment and perceived illegitimacy imposed on them by others. Pushed to the margins of systems of hierarchical 'powering over', the women studied are invested in personal development, and challenge work environments in order to bolster systems of 'powering for' or 'giving power to' others.

Another view in MENA studies that this chapter challenges is the argument, or allusion, that Arab political agency ebbs and flows depending on the extent to which it expands or shrinks liberal democracy, and that women's agency is centrally state-created and therefore state-deferent.[5] It is suggested that because the Arab world lacks liberal democracy, Arabs are subjects without the claims-making authority, rights and capacities of citizens. Citizenship in the Arab world, as elsewhere, is mobilised by what people do, and is not reducible to membership endowed by the state.[6] There is also a reductionist focus in this literature on prominent moments of political activism or well-known civil society movements as the primary sites of political agency. The authors argue that the expansion of mutual aid, *communitas*, and solidarity[7] – core features of citizenship mobilisation – are enabled by self-proclaimed women activists holding membership in formal social movements, and by people who do not see themselves as explicitly activists, but rather as do-gooders, or what Asef Bayat calls 'non-movements'.[8]

Writings on the Arab uprisings tend to affirm and re-inscribe an '*a priori* landscape of domination and resistance', even though this untenable dichotomisation is not supported by empirical nuance derived from ethnographic or qualitative inquiry.[9] Sherry Ortner has observed that ethnography is a solution to the 'thinness' of the literature on resistance and its 'bizarre' refusal to know, write about and engage the lived worlds of those who resist, including their internal politics, cultural richness and subjectivity.[10] An ethnography, or qualitative study that examines the specificities of the context is, itself, an engagement or mobilisation of epistemological, methodological and cultural refusal.[11]

Islamic and Islamist women activists and their diverse activities give form, weight and evidence to many alternative forms of citizenship mobilisation. Such women are chipping away at oppressive policies and practices of the autocratic regime by finding intelligent ways to keep contacts, building critical political infrastructure and tools for engagement, and expanding hope. Islamic women activists are injecting the political realm with knowledge, capacities and *communitas*: qualities that show responsibility to others, and thus, concomitantly, an expectation that the government responsibly protect in kind.[12]

Citizenship as refusal of the *status quo*

Citizenship in Qatar is given meaning through the collective organisation of Islamic and Islamist women activists, and the non-movements of Muslim women leading deliberate action that is politically salient without having an expressly political design. Given the decades-long entrenchment of theories regarding the resilience of authoritarian structures in the MENA region, the documentation of Muslim women activists' refusing *status quo*s is, in fact, the documentation of an empirically verifiable politics of hope. Such documentation is also epistemological investment in hope, as such, that (when observed and justly attended to), situates, mobilises and advances an entirely different knowledge production politics that underscores the importance of premising theory on nuance, multiple angles and intellectual honesty.

For Carole McGranahan, refusal is differentiated from resistance insofar as resistance often has as its impetus a complex recognition of, and desire to, erase different forms of domination. Refusals, on the other hand, are a politics of troubled consciences that say 'no' to *status quo* conditions and apologies, and that refuse to be aspirational in what are considered the 'right' ways to be aspirational.[13] This distinction fits aptly with leading scholarship on Islamic women's agency.[14] Refusal is the redefining of an outcome, the rejection of anticipated reaction, non-fixedness, building attachments, optimism, indulging in possibility, the embracing of complexity and contradiction, selfless gift-giving, the conferring of privilege and safety, an emphasis on dialogism, equitable exchange, a redirection of levels of engagement, the staking of claims, the negation of status(es), and a generative wilfulness.[15] Whereas resistance can be mobilised by class struggle, refusal involves redirection towards multiple levels of individual and collective engagement that ignore the specific affiliations and identities that keep rights and recognitions in abeyance. Refusals can be generative, strategic or deliberate moves towards practices or communities that may or may not be responding to authority. Private abstentions are not anti-social, they are a new form of social because when known, they galvanise people who can identify with them.[16]

Qatar's Islamic women activists differ from most other Islam-centred individuals and groups studied in this volume because they seek a different kind of power ('power to' and 'power for' rather than 'power over'). Their work provides evidence of a diversification within Islam-focused movements that seeks innovative expressions of the Islamic vision, but this work is not individualist, ideologically parochial or hijacked by neo-liberal rationalisations. On the contrary, they reveal a stronger propensity for collaboration, rather than competition with secular forces. The authors argue that regardless of gender, and regardless of a person's sliding scale position between Islam (do unto others) and Islamism (do unto Muslims), activism *qua* charitable giving of oneself is citizenship mobilisation. Islamic women activists especially perceive a duty to mitigate the impact of economic divides and refuse economic and political power structures as they are. The concept of *tawheed* (the unity of God, or, unity, as such, manifested by divine presence) is concretely expressed in the work of these activists when they collaborate to defend the poor, neglected and disaffected. Since the divine breath is perceived within Islamic circles to be blown into all human beings (secular or religious), and therefore the unity of people helps express the already existent unity of God, collaboration and mutual aid are not just expressions of citizenship-imbuing capacities, they are also expressions of *tawheed* itself. Collaboration, where it exists, is therefore not only a subversion of the inevitable outcome of capitalist social relations in producing systems of deep inequality and inequity, it is the realisation of a divine mandate imposed by *tawheed* as the fundamental force regulating all existence.[17] Unlike other social movements described in this volume that use *tawheed* to separate people on ideological grounds, the solidarity among Islamic women activists in Qatar towards others shows how *tawheed* is used for spiritual, political and economic empowerment.

Further, the Islamist women in this study are not pursuing the ascendancy of an expressly Islamic political framework within the state of Qatar, and therefore they differ from other movements of politically concerned Islamic actors where refusal (or resistance) is often primarily focused on the relationship between citizen and state. Instead, their refusal is local and transnational in nature, and sometimes in participation with the state, as a way to defy other state meddling guided by hope and optimism for the future. Islamic and Islamist women activists want to create change within the state and society for the betterment of the marginalised, and this enables their claims as citizens and blunts their apparently inextricable status as subjects. Middle Eastern women are not passive actors in the public domain demanding recognition from the state or the reinscription of patriarchal social relations.[18] Rather, such activists do their work by side-stepping state provision (ignoring the singular central importance of the state for the delivery of wellbeing) and by building networks that are predominately women only.

Although the women activists' discourse does not explicitly use equal rights language and the women do not explicitly seek to reconfigure the gender relations power imbalance, their mere participation in networks to expand citizenship-building capacities in society, such as *communitas* and giving aid to the severely marginalised, serves to break down significant gendered barriers. Through their participation, they create avenues for women to become empowered and to empower others. Their encroachment on institutions once dominated by men, moreover, helps to expand civil society and support new lines of thinking on post-oil era conservatism.

Whereas resistance implies conscious defiance of and opposition to political or social superiors in an asymmetrical power relationship, Islamic and Islamic women activists reject the idea that open opposition is necessary; they wilfully insist on the possible over what is probable, and reimagine (and reclaim) power motivated by Islamic ideals. The margins of power still wield power. Michel Foucault argues that power must be de-linked from a framework of domination and possession, because power permeates all life and, in its myriad forms, produces new forms of desires, objects, relations and discourses.[19] Colin Gordon argues that Foucault sees power as 'an omnipresent dimension in human relations' because it is 'never a fixed and closed regime, but rather an endless and open strategic game'.[20] Power can be wielded by anyone and, the authors argue, can be reclaimed through refusal. Foucault captures the essence of refusal quite poignantly, even if by implication, when he writes:

> [a]t the very heart of the power relationship, and constantly provoking it, are the recalcitrance of the will and the intransigence of freedom. Rather than speaking of an essential freedom, it would be better to speak of an 'agonism' – of a relationship which is at the same time reciprocal incitation and struggle; less of a face-to-face confrontation which paralyses both sides than a permanent provocation.[21]

In the context of this chapter, therefore, the power of the state is agonistic due to the omnipresent presencing of dissenters; the reality is that power-holders can never crush the will of refusal among an entire mass of people, *in toto*. MENA-region elites do not wield power as an essential freedom, despite the dogged nature of their pursuit or possession of their freedom(s). Rather, their power is confronted by the stubborn refusals and uncooperative challenges of activists, politically engaged actors, or non-conformers to the rules of engagement; people who resolutely pursue their own freedom in their own ways.

Muslim women in the MENA often do not struggle for power as a resistance-focused endgame. Their invincible agonism can be essentialised and insufficiently appreciated by the false dichotomy of resistance or compliance to authorities. A more judicious framing of women's agency in Qatar is captured in the concept of refusal, as counter-hegemonic and *communitas-enabling* powers and subjectivities that germinate in the MENA. Women activists are attentive to the nuances of their own struggle and to the fact that power is not possessed, but rather a process enabled by individuals and groups. Power as process is seen in the dynamics of patriarchy that unfold from the household to the state levels; women recognise the systemic forces that oppress them and act to change the conditions affecting their lives.[22] In this sense, power is not definitively expressed in the concepts 'of powering over' or 'being powered over', but also 'power to' as a generative or productive power to accomplish, 'power with', which invokes a sense of the whole being greater than the sum of the individuals, and 'power from within' as the spiritual strength and uniqueness that resides within us.[23] Women in Qatar also express 'power for', which is understood by the authors as selfless gift-giving and social and political exchange, that turn values about power relations on their heads.[24] Islamic women activists structure civic principles and reform into their activism, and ground their grass-roots mobilisation on basic democratic principles that blunt hierarchies found in other parts of Qatari society.[25]

Jean Bethke Elshtain affirms that the activation of a woman's participatory capability must begin with her immediate concerns.[26] Hence, studies must focus on struggles around such concerns and, indeed, Islamic and Islamist women orient their activism to redress lack and marginalisation *vis-à-vis* resources and rights. The authors make a distinction here between women who champion empowerment by promoting mutual aid, solidarity and *communitas*, fulfilment, self-worth, intellectual growth, the acquisition of skills, and secure wellbeing for Muslims, and Islamic women who champion such things for all members of society.

McGranahan argues that refusal can have active and passive forms: refusal gives citizenship (refusal intends citizenship) and citizenship is given through refusal (citizenship is the outcome of refusal). In our study, we have found that refusal may be an intended driving force behind the mobilisation of mutual aid, *communitas* and solidaristic actions. In most cases, however, Islamic and Islamist women activists in Qatar do not explicitly intend refusal. Rather, the *outcomes of their actions* denote refusal. And these outcomes produce different ontologies of social and political becoming and belonging.[27]

The authors scrutinise three case studies that illustrate the positive roles played by Islamic women activists in citizenship mobilisation, and some of their individual and cumulative actions that garner connections, expand possibilities and transform the rules of social and political engagement in the Qatari political order.[28] The Qatari context did not escape the spirit of the Arab revolts, as assumed by most theorists focused on actions directed at the state, largely because acts of refusal reveal that the focus went beyond the Qatari state itself to the region. Political action in Qatar is not reducible to how actors interact with the state, how the state uses and works through activists to protect or overthrow leaders, strengthen or weaken ties with American allies, or gain or challenge power, as for example in Syria. In the following pages, the authors address some nuances that are missed in these readings of Qatar.

Islamic and Islamist women activists

In the Qatari case, the women interviewed are not part of an Islamic movement or group, nor do they seek to extend power to a particular Islamic ideology. Instead, they reimagine and reclaim power by using Islamic principles to guide their refusal of self and other marginalisation. Their refusals have significant import for the conception of citizenship in the Arab world. Unlike secular feminism, Muslim women activists do not see religion as a private matter,[29] and throughout the interviews[30] most women expressed a dislike of the term 'feminism'. For these women, feminism is synonymous with the emulation of perceived Western values where people pursue liberation from religious and cultural foundations. The term 'Islamic feminism' has gained some popularity and has been employed to describe women's activism within an Islamic parameter that also questions aspects of the traditional Islamic orthodoxy.[31] Isobel Coleman reasons that the heart of Islamic feminism is to push the gates of reasoning on Islamic jurisprudence (*ijtihad*) open, and that 'Islamic feminists are now combing through the centuries of Islamic jurisprudence to highlight the progressive aspects of Islam'.[32]

Directly referencing the Qur'an and Sunna gives Islamic feminists and activists leverage, and arguably comprises the most effective means for the defence of basic human rights to education and access to public places in the Islamic world. This is particularly important in contexts where women's mobility and access is tightly monitored and severely constrained by extremist groups, repressive states or local traditions. The importance of such a tactical methodology takes on added value given that (liberal) secularism is suffering credibility in the Muslim world. Indeed, women activists in Qatar rely on these sources to help women achieve greater control over their lives in areas where cultural perceptions and decision-making tend to perceive the status of women harshly. Since women are most often caught in the crossfire on, or placed in the crosshairs of, criss-crossing identity and morality, women of inter-sectional backgrounds and various class statuses often carefully calculate the risk of being outspoken on issues affecting women's and girls' rights.

Women activists draw upon sources and traditions pithily described by Talal Asad as the Islamic 'discursive tradition'.[33] There is competition in this tradition to develop the most compelling (meta)-narratives by referencing coherent and ongoing traditions linked to specific frameworks or histories built in the corpus of Islamic or Islam-focused scholarship.[34] Through this competition for legitimacy, turning the narrative tradition in particular directions can help secure women's rights. Islamic feminism does not, however, lead necessarily to a liberal movement. It can be entirely illiberal. Many *halaqat* (religious study circles) that the authors attended have leveraged highly valued and esteemed Qur'an and Sunna scripts to argue for greater mobility and rights, and to defend constrictions of women's mobility and rights – all by women for women and all for women's betterment and protection.

Reformist Islamic feminism and non-feminist Muslim women activists and thinkers engage in three distinct kinds of refusal that have implications for our understanding of them and their ability to engage with each other. Islamic and Islamist feminists focus on women's intellectual development by engaging in intellectual refusal where they lean heavily on Islamic scripts, the Sunna and wider traditions and practices that will ensure women's wellbeing and empowerment. Non-feminist Muslim women activists partake in a different kind of refusal, which is to either ideologically engage texts in *halaqat* to protect themselves from the ills of society and to stay bonded (thus building a new world in their own mind's eye), or they refuse to engage the texts entirely, leaning heavily on good works (doing *khayr*) as a means of empowering themselves through action. These three forms of refusal can produce liberal and illiberal outcomes, however, wherein the path charted by one side is considered disempowering or even harmful to the worldview advanced by the other side.

The tendency in current research on political Islam to focus on well-known social movements in fact obscures some of these nuances, as well as the broader trajectories and developments that are emerging organically from the political subjectivity development and citizenship mobilisation of actors on the margins. There are two main focuses of this literature: a first, which examines the perceived backwardness or progressiveness of Islamist groups and organisations (or their pursuit of violence for political ends), and a second, which studies the importance of state-directed Islam-focused political projects, Islamic state formation (or changes in leadership at the state level), and/or the institutionalisation of Islamic law and Islamic social alternatives.[35] The work of Islamic and Islamist Qatari women activists cannot be placed effectively in these boxes, and yet what they are doing has implications for the role of Islam in the public sphere; that is the political life of Islamic societies or the impact of Islam on the political as such. Thus, while many researchers, and Qatari women themselves, tend to be reductionist about women's contributions, seeing them in very limited ways, Islamic and Islamist women activists in Qatar (and elsewhere) are in fact playing a critical role in political change, and in counter-acting (and sometimes appropriating or leveraging) the more ambitious masculine expressions of political Islam. The authors predict that productive social and political transformations in Qatar will result not necessarily from the story of politicised Islamic players, but also from women who are motivated by Islamic principles to do good locally, regionally and internationally (for example, by refusing unequal power relations). Much of their work has transnational impact. Such activists are engaged in the empowerment of others, and the scale of their impact is unmatched because of the funding they receive from public and private donors. Through the avenues of networks and organisations, women enable women, men and young children to achieve basic rights to better living conditions, food and clothing, education and skills training. As one woman asserts, '[w]e are helping more than 2.5 million inside and outside Qatar'.[36]

The impact of women's critically significant work is lost in the prominent, politicised and epistemologically problematic focus on the state and the activism of Islamist men, wherewith women's activism becomes marginalised. Far from being motivated by only piety or practical considerations related to the private realm, and far from being inconsequential to larger political processes and citizenship development, women's actions give momentum to positive developments that other activists have failed to accomplish. Women's pursuit of and drive for change in Qatar have been insufficiently theorised and analysed, and as such, the impact of women's activisms and actual grass-roots transformations remain in abeyance.

Women in Qatar during and post-uprisings

Islamic and Islamist women activists operate in a constraining political context in Qatar. Women working in the public sphere have to network and collaborate with men because, as one Islamist activists put it, 'no one wanted to participate with a woman's organisation'.[37] Such activists are therefore forced to choose between working with organisations that are not women-led, or working from home in their own networks of women. Activists feel that they have to be careful talking about taboo issues such as domestic violence, forced prostitution and other human rights issues such as the trafficking of children as camel jockeys because Qatar is a small and conservative society.[38] When enquiries are made about these issues, many participants and experts simply reply that such issues do 'not exist in Qatar'.[39] Women activists are extremely cautious when discussing these issues because opening up about them might jeopardise their work. As one participant clarified 'everyone knows everyone here'.[40] And another stated, 'the women work so hard, I do not want anything you [the interviewer] write to affect them or what they're doing; they are just doing good from the kindness of their hearts'.[41]

Qatar's (non-elite) women activists do not actively challenge government policies, nor are their initiatives state-led, and all research respondents underscored that there is no women's movement in Qatar. When addressing policies that marginalise women, women in Qatar tend to rely on elite women to push the boundaries of what is acceptable, while navigating tradition and rigid religious interpretations of women's roles. Overt activism by non-elites in this context is ineffective. Islamic women activists in Qatar do not take to the streets in protest. During the uprisings, people took to the streets on only a few occasions, and their numbers in one case comprised barely one hundred men. Protests are banned and, where they arise, are immediately squashed. Analysis of civil society activity through a Western (feminist) lens, moreover, that envisions progress and development through the expansion of liberalism captures a mere fraction of activity that empowers people in Qatar.

In the vast majority of cases, women activists in Qatar are focused on charity fundraising for social justice activism. Many women say that their motivation lies in simply doing *khayr* (good deeds).[42] This is captured by a participant who says, 'I do much more than my post. I feel obliged.'[43] Another woman clarifies that her work is simply for the sake of humanity: 'When you help people, you feel that you are human.'[44] In the latter case, the woman's activism is not about empowering women, but rather all people. In some cases, impact is not aligned necessarily by a specific motivation. One networker clarified that she never intended to partake in activities, but became involved because people in need came to her.[45] Qatari women activists, such as those who give to their societies through charity institutions or charitable infrastructure, are tackling some of the most controversial aspects of their society, often by skirting the state, and this particular form of refusal through quiet circumvention helps them avoid being politicised by state and society. In this chapter, the authors examine three key examples of Islamic and Islamist women's activism in Qatar, and provide a clearer picture of their political contributions during and after the Arab uprisings.

The first form of activism sought to mitigate, in the Qatari context, state and mass attempts to squash Shi'a influence. As a research respondent explained, nine of the twelve Shi'a places of worship or gatherings (*ma'tam*) in Qatar had been closed over a ten-year period without explanation, or due to claimed infrastructure issues.[46] Civil society activities normally held in places of Shi'a worship were suspended. As a result, during the uprisings, 'suitable' imams for *Ashura* were difficult to locate. To our knowledge, to date, nothing has been published on the confinement of religious expression of the Shi'a (who comprise 10 per cent of the population) in Qatar.

During the Arab uprisings, *Ashura* was observed in Al-Hilal district, but otherwise all other religious gathering was non-existent for the occasion. Fear was purposefully created and escalated when a Shi'a leader and two young men, all of whom had purportedly never been to Iran, were deported to Iran for their religious activism. Hence, the Shi'a community encountered great difficulties locating a suitable Imam because of growing fears that Shi'a Imams were gaining increasing influence in Qatar, Bahrain and beyond. Yet during the uprisings, student groups, including a group of Shi'a female students, mobilised themselves in response of the systematic confinement and constraining of Shi'a gatherings. They moved their religious learning circles to private places; and they took these actions even though many others (born and raised in Qatar, but without Qatari passport or formal citizenship membership) had abandoned the gatherings for fear of state action. The activists confirmed that their objective was not to resist the state, but rather to develop their religious learning communally.[47] Wanda Krause identified a repeated fear among several Sunni research respondents that Iran was seeking to overtake Qatar (and the MENA region), and some of the same respondents narrated a highly contestable historic reading of Sunni and Shi'a relations in the region, and particularly in Bahrain, that supported their fears. In her study on the Indian and Pakistani diaspora in the UAE, Neha Vora argues that, although several of her research respondents raised in the UAE also fear that, at some point, they will need to leave their homes, their experience of marginalisation compels them to challenge their non-inclusion.[48] Like the subjects of Vora's analysis, Shi'a women activists' simple acts challenging their non-inclusion are forms of refusal that help constitute them as political agents of change and solidarity.

The second form of activism identified was that of Sunni members of the Qatari MB, or wives of Brotherhood members, who sought to overthrow secular despots in neighbouring countries and/or had affiliation with Islamist groups that joined the uprisings. Sunni women activists offered their support through charity. These women activists exhibit overt referentiality towards the states within the region. The activists' attempts to disrupt authoritarian rule in the MENA has aligned well with the Western states' pursuit of regional power and the overthrow of particular regimes including the al-Assad regime in Syria and the al-Qaddafi regime in Libya.

Opposing the official positions of Saudi Arabia, Bahrain and the UAE, the Qatari state, under Hamad al-Thani, enabled the MB, among others, to send resources to the Syrian opposition. For these Sunni women activists, the concept of 'powering for' means pursuit of change to the MENA governance *status quo*, and not the expansion of a feminist objective. The purpose of their charity fundraising work was to create regional change, and to expand freedoms for Islamists in their countries of citizenship. They enjoyed immense freedom gathering in their homes to pursue religious learning and kinship-building. Although Islamist groups in neighbouring countries such as the UAE segregate themselves according to nationality, the women of this study would gather from different Arab nationalities to study together. The women did not fear reprisal for their activities and pursued a sense of common purpose with distinct peers who shared their larger development and political aspirations.

These acts of refusal by Sunni activists against foreign states were not necessarily designed to support the rise of Islamism, but rather to expand freedoms in home countries such as the freedom of religious expression, the ability to gather communally, and to reverse the debilitating neo-liberal policies and economic marginalisation instituted by corrupt secular rulers. Hence, despite being co-opted into a system by US forces to empower the Syrian resistance, MB-affiliated women's activism facilitates several layers of subversion of Western investment in proxy conflict for greater geopolitical control over the MENA region, such as expanding pan-Arab and pan-Islamic connectedness and identifications intra-nationally and transnationally.

A third form of activism identified was that of Islamic women activists who pursue 'power for' (others) motivated by Islamic objectives. A key form of these activists' efforts included garnering generous endowments and charitable contributions. Qataris frequently give without being referent towards, or dependent on the state; such giving is used to undermine *status quo* conditions faced by the urban and rural *bidoon* poor. *Bidoon* is an Arabic term used to designate those who lack formal citizen's membership. The *bidoon* in Qatar are less empowered to refuse their marginalisation compared to the *bidoon* in the UAE because the latter have, relatively speaking, more power to clamour and build networks of solidarity to mobilise political change, whereas the former in Qatar have not built critical infrastructure for this purpose. Islamic women activists give in charity and heart to the *bidoon* in poor locales, and thus extend help as citizens and non-citizens to marginalised non-citizens. This act of refusal is significant because these women are not targeting Muslim populations, but rather any population in need, nor are they attempting to articulate adherence to an Islamist ideology and thus are not working within the typical Islamist framework of distributing charity in order to recruit for their ideology. Before, during and after the uprisings, a group of women attended to the material needs of *bidoon* youth and children motivated by a sense of religious obligation and the attainment of spiritual succour from giving. A woman who would invest her time in helping sick people who were without healthcare stated, 'I love to help sick people. When you see a smile on the baby or their parents' face, it is precious – it is religion.'[49] A woman who teaches the Qur'an explains that she gives charitably of her time for the sake of God.[50] Another woman acknowledged the great discrepancy between the acts of giving and receiving, and noted that giving is an essential part of Islam. She says she role-models the behaviour she seeks to find in others by promoting giving as an Islamic practice.[51]

Exemplary among these activists was one who played a crucial role in repatriating child jockeys earlier drawn from trafficking rings and the *bidoon*. Pursuing human rights, she noted that her activism 'was centred on the study of Islamic law that dignified and protected human beings and rejected [their] exposure to exploitation'.[52] Significantly, activists working for the plight of the *bidoon* subscribe to, and are motivated by a discourse on progress and development not prominently featured in Western and secular frames about the uprisings and rights-based activism. Many activists perceive the conditions that produced the Arab uprisings to have been fomented by a lack of religious practice and economic disparity. For many research respondents, harkening back to Islamic principles enables their pursuit of equality and political agency: 'I always believe that change starts from the person itself, and all of us should work together to protect Man and maintain mankind's dignity and humanity, which are dignified by Allah in His Holy book.'[53]

For many women interviewed, citizenship is about *participating* in the facilitation of change not in relation to the state, but in relation to oneself because, as one activist put it, collaboration is essential for personal development. As Saba Mahmood has argued, feminist scholarship overemphasises politically subversive forms of agency and has ignored other modalities of agency whose significance is missed 'within the logic of subversion and resignification of hegemonic terms of discourse'.[54] Islam-centred political actions and their significance for any attempt to reconceptualise the meaning of citizenship are similarly not reducible to actions of the state or the work of men. Mahmood argues that this overemphasis results from feminism's teleology of progressive politics on the analytics of power.[55] Such focuses obfuscate or exclude the critically sensitive work of activist women, and their pursuit of noble values and goals that directly or indirectly support the impulse of the uprisings. The inclusion of the activist work of Qatari women moreover helps to interject on traditional assumptions about citizenship that male elites and their actions are the model citizen reference points, and that citizenship, as such, like war, is supposed to contain and transcend woman *qua* woman.[56]

Yet the values of women activists give us clues about what might lie ahead for Qatar. While Islamic and Islamist women's activism may be largely directed at helping others or supporting movements outside Qatar against secular despots, their work productively builds discontent in Qatar and beyond regarding men and leadership. There is a relationship, for example, between women's activisms and refusals of state neglect of people by isolated and communal acts of negation, and women's refusal of men, in private and public spheres, as the primary reference point for power mobilisation.[57] The centrality of the state and men as the hubs of referentiality in action is frequently, though not always, critically undone, unacknowledged, unsupported, or dissented (refused) by Qatari women.[58] Islamic women activists in Qatar are not necessarily in pursuit of validation by the state for their status as citizens or mobilising their action through their status (or lack of it). This is similar to the ways such activists act, not necessarily in pursuit of a raised status *vis-à-vis* men or in relation to their reduced status as women, but rather in leaving status, as such, unacknowledged by making claims *on* (against), *about*, or *for* men (in the name of, or for the sake of one/many men, or on behalf of men).

Islamic women activists make claims by expanding their knowledge, and they advance refusal by peaceful reconciliation with struggle motivated by self-knowledge and collaboration.[59] Several women pointed out that many women pursue education in an effort to acquire freedom from patriarchy entrenched through Salafi thinking and traditions.[60] As one elite female organisational leader confirms, 'there is going to be more women in the market with less qualified men. It goes back to the way men are raised in Qatar. They are more spoiled than women.'[61] Another research respondent quoted a Hadith (saying of Prophet Muhammad) concerning corruption and failure among male leadership, and role reversals in leadership during the end times, saying that politics becomes reprehensible 'when your most evil ones are your princes and when your decision is in the hands of your women.'[62] Challenging the dominant Islamist view that women are incapable in positions of authority and therefore that civilisations will decline in end times (when women take on leadership roles), the research respondent turns the perceived leadership lack on its head: 'men are not acting as men anymore. Now maybe it's a problem of how they are raised, they sleep. Ladies are always fighting for rights, they are so motivated to learn and develop.'[63] She is not concerned with the secular dictators of the Middle East, but rather with the Gulf male rulers. In an interesting study on values in Qatar that influence change in organisations, Saeed Hamid Al Dulaimi and S. Mohd Saaid conclude that masculine aspects were negatively correlated with an affective commitment to change. On the other hand, they state that femininity better correlated with productivity and a readiness to embrace change.[64]

Islamic women activists' refusals add nuance to the study of politically relevant action motivated by the Islamic parameter. They show how Islamic actors work with, or entirely refuse, the state's presence to bring good, and they underscore recent turns in critical citizenship studies. Such activists transform the rigidity of linking citizenship to the state's endowment of formal membership or substantive provisioning, and instead empirically substantiate citizenship as action or what people do. The fascinating Qatari case study differs from those of other MENA societies because it does not fit comfortably into the state resistance/acceptance dichotomy. The impulse of the uprisings has not been perpetuated by direct contestation between societal actors and the Qatari state, but rather through state–societal actor collaboration, overtly and tacitly in ways that support the overthrow of the *status quo* across the Middle East. Women have used also their agency and self-determination to create new opportunities through collaboration that definitively reveal the failings of the state by side-stepping it and filling in the gaps in areas it has neglected.

Conclusion

Through the lens of refusal among Islamic and Islamist women in Qatar it is possible to gain insight into how Muslim women pursue change in ways that differ from their male counterparts. Qatari women seek to transform the *status quo* through quiet circumvention, and they entertain and mobilise their troubled consciences at social injustice by going around the state or taking its official place. Such women exemplify what refusal means in their own context, by pursuing alternative ways to be aspirational that leave the status of authority unacknowledged, by redefining the outcomes of action through redirection, by building attachments between people, by taking up possibilities as a mantra for action, by indulging in optimism, by selflessly giving, by conferring the safety of others and by engaging in dogged wilfulness against all odds. The refusals of Islamic women activists in Qatar to structure the nature of their political subjectivities and mobilisations of citizenship beyond traditional readings of the concept, tied as it is to membership within a given geographical locale by a generous state.

When Islamic and Islamist women are challenging their exclusion and others' exclusions from substantive citizenship by charitably offering provisions that should otherwise be provided by the state, they are engaging in acts of refusal. When such women activists pursue religious freedoms secretly in defiance of the rulings of a leader or dictator in power, they are engaging in acts of refusal as gifts of citizenship.[65] Theorisations of citizenship, political subjectivity in exile and refusal are advanced by the work of women who may not necessarily be subverting state policies, but are indeed putting stress on an unjust *status quo* or reading the *status quo* in ways considered important for their own sense of freedom and emancipation. Although elite women often receive the prominence and attention given to women's participation in Qatar, non-elite Islamic and Islamist women activists are slowly creating openings and enhanced opportunities for women. Certainly, their non-elite class status matters in the approach they choose. Most are unwilling to risk their livelihood, security or position in this Gulf country by pursuing overt forms of resistance. They are not in a position to take overt action. However, social and economic class does not define them as non-risk takers or passive actors, as they do seek ways to disrupt the *status quo*. The uprisings have injected a renewed vigour and importance to activisms that have been quietly unfolding in private in Qatar. One activist noted, for example, that she was previously not permitted to lead a delegation to meet with men abroad on issues covered by her specialisation, or to address sensitive issues with men. Now, she says, authorities have left her alone to pursue her interventions in collaboration with men.

Many women activists in fact feel that men are no longer their equals, and that they have ascended above them; that by merit and education they are more capable of taking on leadership roles. What the future holds for political change in Qatar and the region does not rest merely with men. It is the authors' view that the future is being written by women. It is highly possible, as a result of the efforts of activist women, that politics in the MENA will take a completely new trajectory. Islamic and Islamist women activists are charting new directions as Al Dulaimi and Saaid have identified, in which their femininity correlates with a politics that is less about dominance and compliance, and instead about productivity and a readiness to embrace change.[66] As Mahmood suggests:

> [it is important] that we leave open the possibility that our political and analytical certainties might be transformed in the process of exploring non-liberal movements ... , that the lives of the women ... might have something to teach us beyond what we can learn from the circumscribed social-scientific exercise of understanding and translation.[67]

Indeed, if refusal is written as a feminist project about epistemological engagement with the lived realities of people, including Arab women activists, then one act of refusal and citizenship is to let the Islamic and Islamist women activists speak for themselves, even if from the margins and from a status of influence that is only recently emerging.

Notes

1. Salwa Ismail (2006), *Rethinking Islamist Politics: Culture, the State and Islamism*. London: IB Tauris; Katerina Dalacoura (2001), 'Islamist movements as non-state actors and their relevance to international relations', in Daphné Josselin and William Wallace (eds), *Non-State Actors in World Politics*. London: Palgrave Macmillan, pp. 235–48.
2. Eva Bellin (2004), 'The robustness of authoritarianism in the Middle East: exceptionalism in comparative perspective', *Comparative Politics*, 36:2, pp. 139–57.
3. Ibid., p. 142.
4. In our view, Islamic activists are those activists who are Muslim and who believe that Islamic principles encourage them to do good for all people, and so they act upon them. Islamist activists, on the other hand, are those activists who are Muslim or non-Muslim who champion Islam as a cause itself for the aid of Muslims, and pursue the institutionalisation of an Islamic governance structure with Shari'ah as the guiding framework for law.

5. Pernille Arenfeldt (2012), *Mapping Arab Women's Movements: A Century of Transformations from Within*. Oxford: Oxford University Press.
6. Kathleen B. Jones (1994), 'Identity, action, and locale: thinking about citizenship, civic action and feminism', *Social Politics*, 1:3, pp. 256–70.
7. The importance of mutual aid, solidarity-building, and communitas for citizenship claims-making is grounded prominently in the work of Engin F. Isin. See Engin F. Isin (2009), 'Citizenship in flux: the figure of the activist citizen', *Subjectivity*, 29, pp. 367–88.
8. Asef Bayat (2013), *Life as Politics: How Ordinary People Change the Middle East*. Cairo: American University in Cairo Press.
9. On this point, see Carole McGranahan (2016b), 'Refusal: an introduction', *Cultural Anthropology*, 31:3, p. 320.
10. Sherry Ortner (1995), 'Resistance and the problem of ethnographic refusal', *Comparative Studies in Society and History*, 1, pp. 173–93.
11. Ortner, 'Resistance and the problem of ethnographic refusal'; Carole McGranahan (2016a), 'Refusal and the gift of citizenship', *Cultural Anthropology*, 31:3, pp. 334–41; McGranahan, 'Refusal: an introduction'.
12. Melissa Finn and Bessma Momani (2017), 'Established and emergent political subjectivities in circular human geographies: transnational Arab activists', *Citizenship Studies*, 21:1, pp. 22–43.
13. McGranahan, 'Refusal: an introduction'; McGranahan, 'Refusal and the gift of citizenship'; Lila Abu-Lughod (1990), 'The romance of resistance: tracing transformations of power through Bedouin women', American Ethnologist, 17:1, pp. 41–55.
14. See e.g. Saba Mahmood (2011), *Politics of Piety: The Islamic Revival and the Feminist Subject*. Princeton: Princeton University Press.
15. McGranahan, 'Refusal: an introduction'; McGranahan, 'Refusal and the gift of citizenship'.
16. Ibid and Bayat, *Life as Politics*.
17. Amina Wadud (2006). *Inside the Gender Jihad: Women's Reform in Islam*. London: OneWorld Publications.
18. Sondra Hale (1991), *Gender Politics in Sudan: Islamism, Socialism, and the State*. Boulder: Westview Press, p. 31; Mahmood, *Politics of Piety*, pp. 189–90. See also Chandra Mohanty (1991), 'Under western eyes: feminist scholarship and colonial discourses', in Chandra Mohanty, Anna Russo and Lourdes Torres (eds), *Third World Women and the Politics of Feminism*. Bloomington: Indiana University Press; Leila Ahmed (1992), *Women and Gender in Islam: Historical Roots of a Modern Debate*. New Haven: Yale University Press.
19. Michel Foucault (1978a), *The History of Sexuality*. New York: Pantheon; Michel Foucault (1978b), *An Ethics of Pleasure*. Columbia: Columbia University Press; Mahmood, *Politics of Piety*, p. 17.
20. Colin Gordon (1980), *Power/Knowledge: Selected Interviews and Other Writings by Michel Foucault 1972–1977*. New York: Pantheon, p. 5.
21. Ibid and Michel Foucault (1982), 'The subject and power', *Critical Inquiry*, 8:4, p. 790.
22. Ann Bookman and Sandra Morgen (1988), *Women and the Politics of Empowerment*. Philadelphia: Temple University Press, p. 4.
23. Maxine Molineaux (1985), 'Mobilization without emancipation? Women's interests, the state, and revolution in Nicaragua', *Feminist Studies*, 11:2, pp. 227–54.
24. Wanda Krause (2012), *Civil Society and Women Activists in the Middle East: Islamic and Secular Organizations in Egypt*. London: IB Tauris, p. 104.
25. Ibid.

26. Jean Bethke Elshtain (1994), 'Democracy and the politics of difference', *The Communitarian Network*, 4:2; Rian Voet (1998), 'Citizenship and female participation', in Jet Bussemaker and Rian Voet (eds), *Gender, Participation and Citizenship in The Netherlands*. Aldershot: Ashgate, p. 14.

27. McGranahan, 'Refusal: an introduction'; McGranahan, 'Refusal and the gift of citizenship'.

28. Diane Singerman (1995), *Avenues of Participation: Family, Politics, and the Networks in Urban Quarters of Cairo*. Princeton: Princeton University Press.

29. Azza Karam (2000), 'Democrats without democracy: challenges to women in politics in the Arab world', in Shirin M. Rai (ed.), *International Perspectives on Gender and Democratization*. London: Palgrave Macmillan, pp. 64–82.

30. Relying mostly on qualitative field research, the research methodology includes informal and formal interviews and observations. Very little research has been conducted on the role of women in Qatar and, to our knowledge, to date, none has inquired specifically into the role of Islamic women in Qatar. As Al-Ghanim has noted in her research on Qatar, research on women-related issues are extremely scarce and statistics are purposely vague or missing information. Original data is indispensable in order to uncover citizenship mobilisation and political subjectivity development. The women studied in Qatar encompass Qatari and non-Qatari Islamic and Islamist women activists. Qataris comprise merely 13 per cent of the population of Qatar. People living in Qatar without Qatari nationality are the overwhelming majority, and end up being active contributors to the future directions and development the country is adopting and ultimately will adopt. As a result, studies that explicitly focus on Qataris to understand political change or the contributions of women activists will arrive at skewed results. Interviews were based on formal semi-structured interviews and informal interviews with Qatar-based activists held by Wanda Krause. Formal interview data was collected until June 2013 and informal interview data was collected until 2016. Twenty-six formal semi-structured interviews were held with Qatari and non-Qatari women. While these women come from diverse backgrounds, the vast majority were middle class. Given the sensitivity of the topics of Islamism and the Arab uprisings, informal talks often proved to be more substantive. See Kaltham A. Al-Ghanim (2009), 'Violence against women in Qatari society', *Journal of Middle East Women's Studies*, 5:1, pp. 80–93.

31. Isobel Coleman (2012), *Paradise beneath her Feet: How Women are Transforming the Middle East*. New York: Random House, p. xxiii.

32. Ibid., p. xxiv.

33. Talal Asad (1986), *The Idea of an Anthropology of Islam*. Washington: Georgetown University Center for Contemporary Arab Studies, 14.

34. Ibid.

35. Nemat Guenena and Nadia Wassif (1999), *Unfulfilled Promises: Women's Rights in Egypt*. Cairo: Population Council, p. 2.

36. Interview with Participant 1, March 2012, Doha.

37. Interview with Participant 2, March, 2012, Doha.

38. See also Louay Bahry and Phebe Marr (2005), 'Qatari women: a new generation of leaders?' *Middle East Policy*, 12:2, pp. 104–19.

39. Interview with numerous participants, 2011–13, Doha.

40. Interview with Participant 3, April 2013, Doha.

41. Interview with Participant 4, April 2013, Doha.

42. Interview with numerous participants, 2011–13, Doha.

43. Interview with Participant 5, December 2011, Doha.
44. Interview with Participant 6, February 2012, Doha.
45. Interview with Participant 7, April 2013, Doha.
46. Interview with Participant 8, May 2012, Doha.
47. Interview with Participants 9, 10, 11, May 2012, Doha.
48. Neha Vora (2008), 'Producing diasporas and globalization: Indian middle-class migrants in Dubai', *Anthropological Quarterly*, 81:2, pp. 377–406.
49. Interview with Participant 12, June 2012, Doha.
50. Interview with Participant 13, March 2012, Doha.
51. Interview with Participant 14, February 2012, Doha.
52. Interview with Participant 15, December 2011, Doha.
53. Ibid.
54. Mahmood, *Politics of Piety*, pp. 155.
55. Ibid., p. 9.
56. Jones, 'Identity, action, and locale: thinking about citizenship, civic action and feminism'.
57. Finn and Momani, 'Established and emergent political subjectivities'.
58. McGranahan, 'Refusal: an introduction'; McGranahan, 'Refusal and the gift of citizenship'.
59. Gal Levy (2014), 'Contested citizenship of the Arab Spring and beyond', in Engin F. Isin and Peter Nyers (eds), *The Routledge Handbook of Global Citizenship Studies*. London: Routledge, pp. 23–37.
60. Interview with numerous participants, 2011–13, Doha.
61. Interview with Participant 16, March 2013, Doha.
62. Interview with Participant 17, April 2013, Doha.
63. Ibid.
64. Saeed Hamid Al Dulaimi and S. Mohd Saaid (2012), 'The national values impact on organizational change in public organizations in Qatar', *International Journal of Business and Management*, 7:1, pp. 182–91.
65. McGranahan, 'Refusal: an introduction'; McGranahan, 'Refusal and the gift of citizenship'.
66. Al Dulaimi and Saaid, 'The national values impact on organizational change'.
67. Mahmood, *Politics of Piety*, p. 39.

Chapter 6

Is Islamism accommodating neo-liberalism? The case of Egypt's Muslim Brotherhood

Angela Joya

As in other Arab Spring countries, the Egyptian uprising of 2011, and the subsequent parliamentary and presidential elections, precipitated the rise to power of political Islamists. In the first free and fair lower and upper house elections of 2011–12, the newly created Hizb al-Hurriyya wa al-'Adala (Freedom and Justice Party, FJP)[1] – an al-Ikhwan al-Muslimun (Muslim Brotherhood, MB) affiliate – won significant pluralities of both the vote and seats. A little later, in June 2012, the FJP/MB's presidential candidate, Mohamed Morsi, beat his nearest rival, Ahmed Shafiq, in the second round of voting, thus completing the group's effective domination over the country's executive and legislative institutions.[2]

This chapter is concerned with the economic policy and performance of the MB/FJP during its brief period in power between 2011 and 2013. It argues that, while the Arab uprisings offered new opportunities for political participation and policy formulation to the MB, and its FJP affiliate, their failure to offer a radically progressive vision of the economy contributed in no small measure to their ousting from power. While initially the MB/FJP tried to reconcile with other parts of the ruling class, it appeared their strategy was not supported by Mubarak-era capitalists or the military. To be sure, Islamists have faced a challenging environment and serious dilemmas pertaining to social justice and political rights as well as the economy in the post-uprising period. However, the nature of these dilemmas was context-specific, and so were the range of limited options available to them. Under new political circumstances – and having only recently entered the echelons of power – the MB/FJP not only had to establish its legitimacy in the eyes of the electorate, but also ward off challenges to its hold on power from rival elite groups, most notably from the powerful Supreme Council of the Armed forces (SCAF) as well as from Mubarak-era capitalists.

The chapter is divided into four sections. Section one examines the literature on political Islam and its relationship with the changing global economy. Section two discusses the evolution of the MB in Egypt from 1952 to the period of economic liberalisation in 1991, and examines how the group pursued its economic interests in a context where the main areas of the economy were dominated either by businessmen close to erstwhile president Hosni Mubarak (r.1981–2011) or by the Egyptian military. Section three then analyses the 2011–13 era in which politics was dominated by the MB/FJP and the short-lived Morsi administration.[3] It scrutinises the economic policies adopted by the MB/FJP and the Morsi government and their impact on the Egyptian population. Finally, the chapter concludes by discussing the downfall of the MB/FJP and its implications for the group's businesses and their economic power.

Islamism and neo-liberalism

Influential studies of Islamist movements take the history of Islam as a crucial point of departure[4] and, although they may acknowledge the socio-political contexts of the rise of Islamism, Islam tends to take centre stage as their explanatory tool. As such, they assume the primacy of religious beliefs as the guiding principle of all Muslims who live in a totality called the Muslim world.[5] Likewise, Islamist movements act in ways that express past historical practices which lie at the core of Islam, and which were formed centuries ago. As such, they tend to emphasise the role of ideas and explain Islamic movements' actions as 'an expression of a religious essence abstracted from time, place and social context'.[6] In this chapter, the author intends to shift the focus to the contextual specificity in explaining the actions of Islamist movements, especially in the context of the expansion of capitalist social relations in the Middle East and North Africa (MENA) and beyond.

A number of issues emerge in the study of Islamist movements and capitalism.[7] First, the question emerges as to how to best study political Islam without falling into the trappings of Orientalism whereby groups that fall under political Islam are seen purely through the lens of religion. In their comparative study of political Islam in Indonesia and Malaysia, Vedi R. Hadiz and Boo Taik Khoo trace the source of Islamic politics to struggles over the state and material resources. The degree to which political Islam was integrated into the post-colonial state and economy determined the outcome of Islamic politics in society. In other words, where Islamic forces were integrated into the state, as in the case of Malaysia, they posed less of a threat to the state and dominant class. In Indonesia, meanwhile, where Islamic forces were excluded from politics, tensions between Islamist forces and the state have continued. Hadiz and Khoo suggest that the study of political Islam should not focus solely on religion, but rather on political groups who are seeking power and contesting the state and political economy of a specific society.[8] Doing so goes some way to 'de-sacralising' the MENA region, where most emphasis is placed on religion, by shifting the focus to political struggles and material interests.[9]

Second, the response of political Islam cannot be understood solely as a development situated in the contemporary period. The decline of political Islam can be traced back to the nineteenth century when the modern state began to emerge in places like the Middle East as old trade routes experienced a decline. Islamists who had retained a powerful position as the 'ulama (the Islamic clergy) within pre-modern states began experiencing a loss of power not only over material resources but also over ideology as modern education replaced mosques as an extension of the modern state. This historical decline continued into the twentieth century as nationalist forces succeeded in establishing secular states in the post-colonial period. While in some cases – such as Malaysia – Islamists were integrated into the post-colonial state and economy, in most cases they were excluded and pushed to the periphery. Economic development policies often empowered nationalist capitalists while marginalising the merchants, traders and small businesses who formed the core support base of Islamists. In the latter cases, political Islam retained its relevance through the charitable work pursued by Islamist organisations in society. Moreover, in instances where the post-colonial state was seen as faltering, political Islam tended to re-emerge as a dominant force, sometimes through direct confrontation with the state, as was for instance the case in Syria in 1979–82 when al-Ikhwan al-Muslimun fi Suriyya (Syrian Muslim Brotherhood, SMB) challenged the secular Baathist regime and was subsequently crushed and its leadership exiled. In short, the struggle over the state in the post-colonial period remained a dynamic process between political Islam and secular-nationalist state actors.

Thus, ever since independence from colonial rule Islamists have been competing for power over the state and the economy, while ideologically struggling to remain relevant. In terms of historical evolution, political Islam emerged as a strong opponent to the secular state, overtaking its social welfare functions and challenging its legitimacy. At the same time, political Islam offered a critique of the corruption and failure of the secular state to respond effectively to socio-economic challenges such as poverty, unemployment, housing and health. As such political Islam presented itself as part of the resistance to corrupt rulers and authoritarian states.

In the late 1970s, political Islam experienced a surge in popularity as the rise in global oil prices and the crisis of state capitalism weakened the post-colonial state's legitimacy across the MENA. On the one hand, the oil crises of the 1970s resulted in the delegitimation of economic and secular nationalism, and facilitated new processes of capital accumulation that privileged Islamic economic actors organised through Islamic banks and investment companies.

This shift affected the way political Islamists viewed the global economy and their place within it. On the other hand, domestic struggles between the right and the left resulted in political elites empowering Islamists to defeat leftists. This resulted in the spread of political Islam to professional syndicates and student unions. In the 1980s, the state continued to retreat by cutting budget allocations to social services, which resulted in a vacuum for political Islamists to fill, as happened in the case of Egypt.[10]

The crisis of the secular state in the new millennium offered new openings where Islamists could vie for political power. The strategies adopted by Islamists varied: some pursued power through engaging in the political process while others opted for outright confrontation. After two decades of neo-liberal policies, it was clear that economic liberalisation had further discredited the secular-nationalist state and its ability to respond to the needs of citizens. However, at the same time Islamists had adapted to free market strategies, carving out economic spaces of influence for themselves, particularly in small and medium-sized enterprises and Islamic finance.[11]

Thus, while the period of neo-liberalism represented a political opening for Islamism, it also complicated its ability to present itself as an alternative to the secular capitalist forces that had captured the state since independence. This raises the question of whether Islamism can still be seen as anti-systemic or if it has accommodated itself to the hegemonic system of neo-liberal capitalism. Some scholars argue that, because of their conception of politics, Islamist politics and practices may lend themselves to accommodating the capitalist system: Islamists do not recognise social class, but rather treat society holistically. This leads them to restrict themselves to a moral rather than a socio-economic critique of capitalism.[12] Moreover, both offer protection and respect for private property.

Furthermore, long-standing conflicts over identity in the MENA re-emerged forcefully in the post-1990 period as post-colonial states failed to create a strong sense of national identity. As the promises of citizenship and its associated benefits declined, political Islam filled the gap by reasserting Islamic identity and an Islamic model of state, society and economy. However, Islamists face the challenge of articulating a qualitatively different vision of state and economy that can meet the needs of the Islamic ummah (community) within a capitalist global economy.[13]

States, markets and society in the Muslim world

In Islam, the market is not conceptualised as a self-regulating mechanism that is autonomous from society. Rather, the economy is very much shaped by broader social concerns, such as the welfare or wellbeing of the community, as opposed to merely that of the individual. In contrast to this, capitalist social and economic thought argues that 'Homo economicus must be freed from restrictive or irrelevant social practices in order to get on with the business of generating "utility". (. . .) Homo economicus was secular, materialistic, and ultimately on his or her own'.[14]

Recently, however, scholars have argued that Islamic finance and capitalist free markets are very compatible,[15] and Islamists argue that they can tame capitalism by emphasising morality and social justice (through charity and *zakat*) and by targeting corruption in the sphere of the market. Islamists view the socio-economic structures of capitalism as fundamentally sound, while flaws are attributed to particular individual practices and behaviours, which can be curbed by Islamic morality. Here, the state plays an important role in regulating the markets and thus ensuring social justice and fighting monopolies.

Islamic economic thought expresses preference for small and medium-sized businesses over large-scale industries. The result has been that Islamic thought has not sufficiently debated, or theorised on, how to respond to global economic forces, thus preventing Islamist parties from devising effective Islamic economic policies. Moreover, whilst embracing the free market, the economic policy of Islamists remains burdened with contradictions. So for instance, whilst adopting market-led economic strategies, little serious thought has gone into how to meet goals of social justice as well as meaningful employment.[16] Consequently, they risk alienating their traditional support base, which sees no difference between secular and Islamist profit-maximising business practices.

As it stands, it is not solely Egypt where such problems of marrying the market with ideals of Islamic justice remain a challenge. A number of other countries where Islam plays an influential role in social organisation have moved towards globalisation in an uncertain and pragmatic way, reflecting their fears and unpreparedness to effectively understand, or respond to, the forces of the market. In the post-uprisings MENA, political Islam has adapted to neo-liberalism and free market ideas, sometimes at the expense of its own legitimacy. Thus, while Islamists have adopted variations of Islamic finance as an alternative to 'Western' economic practices, it is not clear that Islamic finance remains shielded from capitalist imperatives of competition, profit maximisation and exploitation.[17] The danger then that Islam may lose its 'doctrinal connection to social justice is a powerful rallying point'.[18]

Egypt's Muslim Brotherhood: Evolution, the state and the struggle for power

Under erstwhile president Gamal Abdel Nasser (r.1956–70), the statist economic focus on large-scale industry marginalised small and medium-size businesses as well as the large landed classes, groups among which the

Brotherhood enjoyed substantial support. In the 1950s, under the influence of Sayyid Qutb – who encouraged a holy war against non-Muslim rulers in Muslim lands – the Brotherhood became the enemy of the post-colonial state, especially after the attempted assassination of Nasser by Islamists. Qutb was executed in 1954 and the group was banned from political activity until 2011, leading to the emigration of many Brothers to the Gulf States. Adapting to these new circumstances, the MB focused its activism at the societal level. It began pursuing informal politics through its charitable work, which facilitated the dissemination of its political message.

With the coming to power of President Anwar al-Sadat (r.1970–81), the MB experienced a turn in its fortunes. To consolidate his power, al-Sadat needed Islamists to defeat the communists and leftists who had dominated state institutions and the ruling al-Ittihad al-Ishtiraki al-ʿArabi (Arab Socialist Union, ASU) since Nasser's rule. He thus took a more lenient stance towards the group, allowing for its re-emergence as a socio-political player in Egyptian politics. By mid-1975, all imprisoned Brothers had been released and many exiled MB cadre returned home. Besides providing an opening to MB cadre for employment in educational and state institutions, such as university campuses and professional syndicates, al-Sadat's economic programme of liberalisation – known as *infitah* (open door) – also paved the way for the organisational and economic rebirth of the MB. *Infitah* eased regulations in order to attract private foreign capital to Egypt and encouraged the import–export trades, which expanded opportunities for small and medium-sized businesses and merchants.

For the MB the consequences of this economic policy were multiple. As *infitah* facilitated the growth of 'importers, financiers, middlemen and profiteers', it resulted in a process of class formation among the ranks of the Brotherhood and their social base.[19] While some took advantage of the opening to engage in economic gains,[20] others established networks with public sector managers to gain contracts. Al-Sadat's restitution of private property also facilitated the revival of Brotherhood landed families, most of whom assumed leadership positions within the group. The group's private hospitals catered to rich clients and its services were of high quality in contrast to the fledgling state hospitals in Egypt. *Infitah* policies also resulted in the emergence of a consolidated middle class affiliated with the MB and engaged in the financial sector. These new Islamic economic actors were labelled as the *infitahi* classes.

One significant inroad by MB members was in the realm of finance, resulting in a clash between the statist faction of the ruling class and the Brotherhood in the mid-1980s. *Infitah* policies had facilitated the rise of informal financial institutions, known as Sharikat Tawzif al-Amwal al-Islamiyya (Islamic Money Management Companies). These Islamic investment companies, linked to the *nouveau riche* rather than to the older, elitist Brotherhood, marked a new era in the economic participation of Brotherhood supporters. Popular among small depositors and workers in the Gulf States, Islamic investment companies amassed billions of Egyptian pounds in savings that were invested in various domestic and international markets. After Hosni Mubarak assumed power in 1981, the rising influence of the MB in the realm of finance came to be increasingly seen by the regime as a direct threat to the state. State banks were starved of savings as depositors opted for Islamic investment companies instead. As global oil prices declined, competition to attract the remittances of workers in the Gulf intensified. Finally, Mubarak enacted a new investment law in April 1988 that put an end to Islamic investment companies, while transferring their capital into the Central Bank of Egypt. Consequently, most of the Islamic investment companies had collapsed by May 1988.

The 1980s also saw the MB expand its influence in the sphere of social services. As state budgets shrank, the state was unable to offer employment to university graduates or continue to provide adequate social services. The Brotherhood took over, offering charity programmes and social services to rural and impoverished urban areas of the country. Eventually, the 1980s witnessed the transformation of the Brotherhood from a religious into a politically active group, which began seriously contesting the state and the economy from this point onwards. The rise in its economic power was reinforced by the group's ideological influence. Using its economic power, the Brotherhood began establishing Islamic publishing houses – the largest being Dar al-Shuruq – which flourished in the 1980s and 1990s.

As Egypt embraced new rounds of economic liberalisation in the 1990s, the opportunities for Brotherhood businesses did not expand as they did for those businessmen and women close to President Mubarak and affiliated with the ruling al-Hizb al-Watani al-Dimuqrati (National Democratic Party, NDP). The Brotherhood watched as public resources were siphoned off by NDP businessmen and state bureaucrats, while the military enjoyed protected markets. The Brotherhood and its members, meanwhile, felt increasingly marginalised in the economic realm dominated by NDP capitalists. Operating under emergency law, which was re-enacted by Mubarak repeatedly throughout the 1980s, 1990s and 2000s, the MB thus concentrated its activities on building its support base by expanding its social services and charity work.[21] As such, the MB filled the vacuum left in social services delivery by a state pursuant of International Monetary Fund (IMF)/Word Bank-induced neo-liberal policies. In 1992, when an earthquake struck the slum areas of Cairo, the MB was first to deliver aid and relief for those affected. Slow in its response to the earthquake, the government, meanwhile, accused the MB of exploiting the disaster for political gains and asked the group to cease all relief work in this case and stop pretending to function like a 'parallel state'.[22] Acknowledging the emergence of the MB as a potent social force, the regime thus sought to curb its societal outreach and charitable activities.

Since the 1980s, the MB has become an ardent believer in the free market. Part of this has to do with the group's economic evolution in the absence of state support, reinforcing its belief in the power of free markets to expand opportunities for wealth creation. However, while promoting the free market, the MB is also aware of the influences of expanded consumerism, unemployment and the social ills that may result from free market economics. To remedy the effects of economic liberalism, the Brotherhood has shifted its approach from charity provision to individual responsibility, spirituality, self-help and voluntarism.[23]

In the 2000s, however, the MB increasingly lost its traditional touch with the population as it concentrated its efforts and aid strategically on winning political office through participation in associational and parliamentary elections. As Emad Siam argues, in the period following the 2011 uprising the Brotherhood changed its tactics of charity provision by offering one-off help during the month of Ramadan to voters in exchange for their votes, thus resorting to clientelistic relations in very obvious ways, a move that alienated the youth wings of the MB.[24] While the official Brotherhood organisation abandoned its traditional social justice roles in favour of seeking political office through new pragmatic ways of reaching the electorate, its previous popular engagement in charity and social services provision was handled by a new type of organisation with greater space for youth political activism.[25] While at odds with the group's older generation of leaders over political strategy and democracy within the group, the Brotherhood's youth played a crucial role in the Egyptian uprising and subsequently in mobilising the vote that secured parliamentary and presidential success for the group's affiliated party, the FJP.

The Muslim Brotherhood, Morsi administration and neo-liberal economic governance

When the MB/FJP took power following the Egyptian uprising of 2011, the country faced serious socio-economic challenges. In February 2012, Egypt was faced with a budget deficit, a balance of payments deficit and depleting foreign reserves. Foreign direct investment levels fell from $13 billion per annum to $8 billion after the uprising. The budget deficit stood at 10 per cent of GDP, and Egypt's foreign reserves declined from $32 billion in February 2011 to $16 billion in February 2012.[26] The government had to rely on its existing reserves for imports, public sector salaries and subsidies. Tourism was also negatively affected by the uprising. To make matters worse, Egypt was downgraded multiple times by the credit ratings agencies, which adversely affected its borrowing capabilities and import activities. These challenges were compounded by the need to absorb 700,000 graduates into the labour market, who were competing for 200,000 jobs prior to the uprising and who were now competing in a context of far worse unemployment.[27]

To deal with these post-uprising socio-economic challenges, the MB/FJP – and from June 2012 onwards, the Morsi administration – effectively had two policy options at their disposal: they could advocate/support the government taking an interventionist role in the economy, or a *laissez-faire* approach. In the end, dominant figures within the MB/FJP, such as Khairat al-Shater and Hassan Malek, supported a *laissez-faire* approach arguing for a 'liberal, market economy with a business-friendly climate'.[28] The economic development policy, which was laid out in the FJP's 2011 electoral programme, was to a large extent informed by these two individuals and others around them.[29] As their businesses expanded, Brotherhood capitalists became increasingly supportive of the neo-liberal ideas that emerged in the late 1970s and early 1980s. A peek into the business life of Brotherhood members reveals the extent of their influence within the economy. Al-Shater and Malek themselves, for instance, own a joint business empire that spans seventy large companies in land reclamation, real estate, construction, clothing, food and furniture and other sectors. Given their vast business interests and networks, the MB, and its affiliate the FJP, 'had a keen interest in reproducing existing patterns of capital accumulation developed under Mubarak'.[30]

Like its Turkish counterpart in the Adalet ve Kalkınma Partisi (Justice and Development Party, also known by its Turkish acronym AKP), the FJP/MB had an interest in promoting small and medium-size components of capital, albeit within the framework of neo-liberalism. While Mubarak had promoted large-scale economic sectors such as communications, construction, agribusiness and energy, it appears the Morsi/MB-led government between 2012–13 promoted medium to small-scale consumer commodities such as for instance furniture, clothing and food. Furthermore, the MB firmly believed that its emphasis on welfare and social justice would reduce the adverse effects of neo-liberalism on society.[31] The group's long-term (twenty-year) economic plans were laid out in the 2012 *Nahda* (Renaissance) Project, which sought to shift Egypt's economy from one based on rentier capitalism to what they coined as 'productive' capitalism. It was hoped that the Renaissance Project, a brainchild of al-Shater, would, if successful, lead to high levels of economic growth, lower levels of unemployment and offer solutions to poverty.[32] Critics saw the Renaissance Project as representing more of a wish list than a real, concrete plan to deal with challenges facing the Egyptian economy and society.

Thus, when the project was declared a failure by the MB/FJP's opponents, the MB/FJP did not dispute this fact.[33]

What then led to this failure of the group's economic strategy? One reason may have been the group and its businessmen's idealistic view of the free market without realising the extent of power struggles that lay under the foundations of free markets. This *naïveté* was obvious in the priorities set out by the Morsi government as well. This said, initially, the Morsi administration attempted to implement a modest version of its free market agenda. Elaborating further on MB/FJP's immediate economic strategy, Ahmed Soliman, the FJP's then Assistant Secretary General, stated in an interview with Fatima al-Saadani on 12 March 2012, that the main goal was to shift the economy from one with an onus on services to one based on production.[34] To this end, the MB/FJP focused on developing agriculture, livestock, industry, energy and mining through the following strategies: (1) rationalising energy subsidies by supporting labour-intensive industries and removing support from energy-intensive industries; (2) improving tax collection; (3) expanding agricultural land area by bringing new land under cultivation; (4) spreading out the revenues from tourism to benefit Upper Egyptians, and (5) encouraging the establishment of Islamic banks alongside existing commercial banks. It is noteworthy though that Soliman cautioned against challenging the legality of privatisation deals that were made under Mubarak in order to ensure protection of private property.[35]

Throughout 2012, meanwhile, many MB/FJP entrepreneurs were forging regional links and promoting their businesses. Their main area of economic focus was hereby small-scale manufacturing, which the MB/FJP hoped to develop in collaboration with Turkey and the Gulf Cooperation Council (GCC) states.[36] Thus, in 2011–12 al-Shater toured Malaysia, Thailand and Turkey, consulting on ways to improve social services and boost the Egyptian economy and deal with other pressing issues such as population density in Cairo, garbage collection and transport.[37] In addition, in April 2012, Hassan Malek, a senior Brotherhood member, launched the Egyptian Business Developmental Association (EBDA) with the aim of promoting the textile and food sectors.[38] Their hope was to open up factories in these sectors and absorb large numbers of Egypt's unemployed workers.[39]

Later on, the Morsi administration came to the realisation that escaping the neo-liberal logic was not as easy as it may have appeared at first. Thus, we notice a shift away from the initial policies of relatively controlled markets to the *status quo* neo-liberal policies of the Mubarak era. It is noteworthy that this later advocacy of the free market became a key pillar of economic policy, as manifest in the government's efforts to secure aid from the IMF and other foreign donors at a lower interest rate, as well as in its endeavours to protect private business and financial markets, cut the budget deficit, increase profits from state land sales, increase the value-added tax (VAT) on local and imported goods and make it easier for small and medium-sized enterprises to lend money to facilitate job creation.[40] While these policies do not particularly reflect a continuation of the *laissez-faire* strategies that were promoted under Mubarak, critics (including some former MB members) point out how the intrinsic marriage of power and capital remained intact under MB/FJP rule.[41] One journalist at the time described the FJP/MB leadership as being 'evangelical in their support of private enterprise, the stock market and full engagement with the global economy'.[42] In an interview with multinational investors, al-Shater also expressed his support for the free market in the following terms: 'We believe in a very, very big role for the private sector.'[43]

As a result of this embrace of a neo-liberal free market strategy, the Morsi administration was perceived by the public as failing to address the issue of socio-economic justice (redistribution). The MB/FJP had argued that social justice goals would be achieved through *zakat* or charity. Yet, in a country where over 25 per cent of the population live under the poverty line, an anti-poverty policy much more effective than *zakat* was needed to tackle the issue as well as gain political legitimacy for the group.[44] Some MB/FJP proposals mentioned in their election programme of 2011 were to increase government revenues by revisiting the price of Egyptian energy exports to Israel, repossessing formerly state-owned lands that were privatised under Mubarak and making *zakat* payments compulsory.[45] These proposals did not, however, offer a radical alternative to neo-liberalism. Instead the MB/FJP opted to go after the Brotherhood's competitors by targeting their wealth, while positioning their own members within state institutions and the economy. Equally importantly, as part of their initial compromise with the Egyptian armed forces, the MB/FJP supported SCAF's Decree no. 4 of 2012, which offered immunity from criminal charges to Mubarak-era capitalists.[46]

Thus, during its year in office (30 June 2012–3 July 2013), the Morsi administration straddled the challenge of bringing its economic policy in line with Islam while also keeping investors calm. As a result, the administration's economic agenda appeared less as a coherent set of policies that would have set Egyptian society and economy on a radically new path, and more as a set of ideas, which continued to reproduce results (unemployment, inequality, wealth disparity) similar to those of the neo-liberal policies of the Mubarak era. A number of contradictions remained at the heart of the MB/FJP administration. While it was claimed that through their Renaissance Project, the MB/FJP government would deal with chronic unemployment, rentierism, corruption and poverty, no plan was put in place to allow for the realisation of these goals. While the initial focus on reviving manufacturing and reducing monopolies may have come across as Keynesian, the Morsi government ultimately shifted its focus to establishing fiscal restraints using typical neo-liberal strategies of reducing subsidies, cutting the public sector wage bill (reform of the bureaucracy) and disciplining the workforce.[47] To be sure, the latter policy shift may reflect not so much the Morsi government's ideological commitment as it reflects the realities of structural power of international financial institutions and existing domestic elites.

While economic challenges remained unresolved, the MB/FJP became more fully consumed by the political struggles of the day. Thus the power struggle between the military and the Brotherhood took centre stage for the group following the parliamentary elections of 2011–12, when the military sought to curtail the growing influence of the Islamists. After the FJP's sweeping win in the 2011–12 parliamentary elections, the MB/FJP demanded that it be given the chance to form a new cabinet. However, the SCAF insisted that its appointed cabinet would remain in power until after the presidential elections on 23–4 May 2012. This move by SCAF prevented the MB/FJP from taking political decisions that may have undermined the interests of the more dominant factions of the ruling class, that is the military and Mubarak-era capitalists. In late March, the MB threatened that it might field a presidential candidate if the FJP was not allowed to form a cabinet immediately. As the military hesitated in meeting this demand, the MB announced the candidacy of al-Shater for the presidency. This increased tensions between the military and the Brotherhood, as the latter was seen to have a strong chance of winning the presidency, which would have placed the Brotherhood in control of the state and significant policy-making power. Soon, fears of a possible coup began circulating. On 14 April 2012, al-Shater was disqualified from running in the presidential elections, leading to the nomination of Morsi as the next-in-line presidential candidate for MB/FJP. The group's focus remained on short-term economic goals rather than long-term economic development strategy.

The demise of the Muslim Brotherhood

The fate of the MB/FJP and the Morsi administration was sealed when the group tried to undermine the interests of the other factions of the ruling class by reorienting the Egyptian economy through alliances with Qatar and Turkey. This move would have marginalised Egypt's main regional backer, Saudi Arabia, but more importantly, it would have reduced the influence of the armed forces and Mubarak-era capitalists in some of the planned new mega-economic projects, such as the Suez Canal expansion and the Red Sea economic zone project.[48] Clearly, the MB/FJP's rise to power was not welcomed by the incumbent capitalists and military elite. The military was more powerful, given its historical legacy with state-building, and enjoyed stronger legitimacy linked to the security of the state, while the MB did not enjoy a similar degree of legitimacy in the eyes of the general public, as the state had for decades associated the group with terrorism and painted it as an enemy of the state. Given this lack of popularity, Morsi was under scrutiny as soon as he assumed power in June 2012. The actions of Morsi and the MB/FJP in the course of their one-year reign further damaged the relationship between the people and the Brotherhood. To begin with, the Brotherhood were seen as power-grabbers rather than power-sharers. Morsi's November 2012 decree, granting him powers over the courts, turned many in the Egyptian judiciary against him. By December 2012, public anger against the MB turned into mass protests by women, Coptic groups and liberals.[49] The media turned against the Brotherhood after the Palace protests of December 2012 when Brotherhood supporters shot a journalist. In short, during its reign, the MB/FJP and Morsi administration alienated the media, the police[50] and the judiciary.

Thus, backed by a popular movement, the military removed the Morsi administration from office in July 2013.[51] The Brotherhood leadership, including al-Shater and Malek, were rounded up on various charges and their assets frozen. Charges against the leadership included corruption and money laundering. To further undermine the influence of the MB/FJP, the military-backed interim government that took over following Morsi's ousting closed down the Brotherhood's medical facilities, schools and community associations. A court ruling banned the MB, ordering its dissolution and confiscating its funds and offices. By late 2013, the group was designated as a 'terrorist organisation'.[52] A year later, in 2014, a court ruling also ordered the dissolution of the FJP.

With the benefit of hindsight, scholars and journalists have compiled a list of weaknesses of the Brotherhood that contributed to its fall from power. To begin with, the MB/FJP did not offer a viable alternative economic programme to that of Mubarak's neo-liberalism. With minor adjustments to limit imports, they retained the broader neo-liberal framework for job creation and growth and thus did not resolve the imbalanced power relationship between labour and capital. Politically, moreover, it is widely agreed that the Brotherhood underestimated the power of competing elites and did not think of power-sharing as an option to stay in power. The Brotherhood did not embark on restructuring the institutions of the state and instead decided to work with the existing institutions, but with its own personnel. This meant that the underlying authoritarian nature of state institutions remained in place. The group was overconfident about the extent of power it had gained through the electoral process and thus underestimated the balance of power *vis-à-vis* other elites and society in general. Also, it did not take the demands of the uprising for social justice, accountability and reform seriously. In short, these failings discredited the group, revealing massive gaps in their economic and political programme.

Conclusion

This chapter contextualised the evolution of the MB within the changing global economic context, as well as within the process of state formation and domestic political struggles in Egypt. As such, it approached the study of the MB through class analysis, highlighting how the group has engaged in political and economic struggles in order to gain power and expand their networks beyond Egypt. It was argued that, given the transformation of the Brotherhood into a faction of the ruling class, the group did not see any contradictions in advocating the neo-liberal policies that had shaped Egypt's political economy since 1991. Comparing the MB/FJP's economic agenda with that of the Mubarak era, Magda Kandil, an economist with the IMF, made the following observation: 'It's very easy to confuse their economic platform with the previous regime: private-led growth, free market economy, scaling down the role of government, empowering the private sector. The big difference is which private sector you are talking about.'[53] Thus, while the group's economic agenda may not appear as outright neo-liberal, because of its call to combat monopolies and regulate markets, the MB/FJP did not necessarily attempt to restructure economic relations but rather wanted to tamper with markets in order to allow more room for Brotherhood-affiliated businesses. This fact was not missed by most Egyptians who were closely observing the MB/FJP's performance after the elections.

From the perspectives of ordinary Egyptians, the group failed to consider the demands of the uprising for social justice, jobs and democracy. The Brotherhood's political decisions had serious repercussions in the economic realm as the MB/FJP failed to formulate a radical critique of neo-liberalism and instead opted to work within it, while promoting virtue and morality. As one journalist argued, for the electorate the group's appeal to religion and identity was insufficient to solve the real problems of poverty, unemployment, housing, education and health.[54]

As the Brotherhood reflects on its political and economic failures, it may serve the group well to reconsider what it overlooked during its time in power: that politics is conducted through compromise and power-sharing with other factions of the ruling class and that those who rule in public office will be held accountable to the electorate. More importantly, the Brotherhood needs to seriously rethink whether the free market is reconcilable with Islamic doctrine in ways that will not undermine the Brotherhood's social base; otherwise, the group will lose its ideological claim to being the party of faith.[55]

The case of the Brotherhood's economic policies raises serious questions about the compatibility of neo-liberalism with the social aspects of Islam that promote social justice and the collective good. For groups like the Brotherhood to recover from their current crisis, they will need not only to reckon with the power of their rivals, but also to fuse economic policies with Islam in ways that can actually deliver radical, progressive alternatives. Otherwise, from the perspective of the population, the Brotherhood is no different than the dictators who served before them.

Notes

1. The FJP was founded on 30 April 2011 by the Muslim Brotherhood leadership to give the latter a chance to engage formally in the post-uprising political arena. During its existence, the party was widely seen as an extended arm of the MB, due to its close interpersonal ties and similarities in policy outlook with the group. It is for this reason that the two will be discussed conjointly in this chapter. The FJP was dissolved by court order on 9 August 2014, following the coming to power of President Abdel Fattah al-Sisi.

2. For a discussion of the election results see e.g. British Broadcasting Corporation (2012), 'Egypt's Islamist parties win elections to Parliament', 21 January, <www.bbc.com/news/world-middle-east-16665748> (last accessed 22 June 2017); David D. Kirckpatrick (2012), 'Named Egypt's winner, Islamist makes history', *New York Times*, 24 June, <www.nytimes.com/2012/06/25/world/middleeast/mohamed-morsi-of-muslim-brotherhood-declared-as-egypts-president.html?mcubz=0> (last accessed 22 June 2017).

3. In July 2013 President Morsi was forced from office by a military *coup d'état*. See: Patrick Kingsley and Martin Chulov (2013), 'Mohamed Morsi ousted in Egypt's second revolution in two years', *The Guardian*, 4 July, <www.theguardian.com/world/2013/jul/03/mohamed-morsi-egypt-second-revolution> (last accessed 22 June 2017).

4. See e.g. John L. Esposito (ed.) (1983), *Voices of Resurgent Islam*. Oxford: Oxford University Press; Gilles Kepel and Yann Richards (eds) (1990), *Intellectuels et militants de l'Islam contemporain*. Paris: Editions du Seuil.

5. Salwa Ismail (2006), *Rethinking Islamist Politics: Culture, the State and Islamism*. London: IB Tauris, pp. 5–7.

6. Joel Beinin (2005), 'Political Islam and the new global economy: the political economy of an Egyptian social movement', *New Centennial Review*, 5:1, p. 112.

7. See Maxim Rodinson (1977), *Islam and Capitalism*. London: Penguin Books; Peter Gran (1998), *Islamic Roots of Capitalism: Egypt 1760–1840*. Syracuse: Syracuse University Press; Charles Tripp (2006), *Islam and the Moral Economy: the Challenge of Capitalism*. Cambridge: Cambridge University Press.

8. Vedi R. Hadiz and Boo Teik Khoo (2011), 'Approaching Islam and politics from political economy: a comparative study of Indonesia and Malaysia', *Pacific Review*, 24:4, pp. 463–85.

9. Sami Zubaida (2011), *Beyond Islam: A New Understanding of the Middle East*. London: IB Tauris, p. 1.

10. On the spread of Islamism and its diversity in the 1980s, see e.g. Ziya Onis (1997), 'The political economy of Islamic resurgence in Turkey: the rise of the Welfare Party in perspective', *Third World Quarterly*, 18:4, pp. 743–66; Asef Bayat (2013), 'Egypt and its unsettled Islamism', in Asef Bayat (ed.) *Post-Islamism: The many Faces of Political Islam*. Oxford: Oxford University Press, pp. 185–239.

11. Fawaz Gerges (2012), 'The new capitalists: Islamists' political economy', *Open Democracy*, 10 May, <www.opendemocracy.net/fawaz-gerges/new-capitalists-islamists-political-economy> (last accessed 22 June 2017).

12. Katerina Dalacoura (2016), 'Islamism and neoliberalism in the aftermath of the 2011 Arab uprisings: the Freedom and Justice Party in Egypt and Nahda in Tunisia', in Emel Akcali (ed.) *Neoliberal Governmentality and the Future of the State in the Middle East and North Africa*. Basingstoke: Palgrave Macmillan. pp. 62–3.

13. Gerges, 'The new capitalists'.

14. Dalacoura, 'Islamism and neoliberalism', pp. 115–16.

15. Olivier Roy (1994), *The Failure of Political Islam*. London: IB Tauris, p. 135.

16. Gerges, 'The new capitalists'.

17. Ibid.

18. Roy, *The Failure*, p. 124.

19. Beinin, 'Political Islam and the new global economy', p. 120.

20. Ibid. By 1980, eight out of the eighteen families who dominated Egypt's private sector belonged to the Brotherhood. Their businesses may have constituted around 40 per cent of private sector enterprises.

21. The Emergency Law was first enacted in 1958 under Gamal Abdel Nasser and remained effective – except for a short period of suspension (1980–81) – during the rule of Anwar al-Sadat and Hosni Mubarak. Emergency legislation under Mubarak was mostly used against Islamists. After the Egyptian uprising of 2011, the law was suspended on 31 May 2012, but was reactivated on 13 June 2012 by the SCAF prior to the 2012 presidential elections. The Emergency Law has enabled state authorities to make thousands of arrests leading to warnings of human rights abuses by Amnesty International. The Law continues to remain in effect under the current Sisi government, see Anon. (2017), 'Egypt's Emergency Law explained', *al-Jazeera*, 11 April <www.aljazeera.com/indepth/features/2017/04/egypt-emergency-law-explained-170410093859268.html> (last accessed 22 June 2017).

22. Carrie R. Wickham (2015), *The Muslim Brotherhood: Evolution of an Islamist Movement*. Princeton: Princeton University Press, pp. 77–8.

23. Mona Atia (2012), '"A way to Paradise": pious neoliberalism, Islam, and faith-based development', *Annals of the Association of American Geographers*, 102:4, p. 822. See also Samuli Schielki (2015), *Egypt in the Future Tense: Hope, Frustration and Ambivalence before and after 2011*. Bloomington: Indiana University Press.

24. Emad Siam (2012), 'The Islamist vs. the Islamic in welfare', *IDS Bulletin*, 4:1, p. 91.

25. It was youth associated with these organisations that participated in the uprising of 25 January 2011 and after, especially through the establishment of Hizb al-Tayyar al-Misri (Egyptian Current Party) and by mobilising the vote in support of Abd al-Mun'im Abu al-Futuh's candidacy for the Egyptian presidency in 2012. See Jeffrey Martini, Dalia Dassa Kaye and Erin York (2012), *The Muslim Brotherhood, Its Youth, and Implications for US Engagement*, Library of Congress: The Rand Corporation.

26. Amira Howeidy (2012), 'Brothers tread cautiously', *Al Ahram Weekly*, 12–18 January, <http://weekly.ahram.org.eg/2012/1080/eg5.htm> (last accessed 20 January 2017).

27. Duncan Green (2011), 'What caused the revolution in Egypt?' *The Guardian*, 17 February, <www.theguardian.com/global-development/poverty-matters/2011/feb/17/what-caused-egyptian-revolution> (last accessed 22 June 2017).

28. At the time, al-Shater was the Brotherhood's deputy Supreme Guide who ran as the MB/FJP candidate in the 2012 presidential elections before being disqualified and replaced by Muhammad Morsi. Mohamed El Dahshan (2012), 'Where will the Muslim Brotherhood

take Egypt's economy?' *Yale Global Online*, 6 February, <http://yaleglobal.yale.edu/content/muslim-brotherhood-take-egypts-economy> (last accessed 22 June 2017); Amr Adly (2014), 'Investigating the Muslim Brotherhood economy', *Tahrir Institute for Middle East Policy*, 7 July, <https://timep.org/commentary/investigating-muslim-brotherhood-economy/> (last accessed 22 June 2017).

29. The FJP Election Program, 2011, p. 8, <http://kurzman.unc.edu/files/2011/06/FJP_2011_English.pdf> (last accessed 8 June 2017).
30. Maha Abdelrahman (2015), *Egypt's Long Revolution: Protest Movements and Uprisings*. London: Routledge, p. 130.
31. Susan Hansen (2012), 'The economic vision of Egypt's Muslim Brotherhood millionaires', *Bloomberg News*, 19 April, <www.bloomberg.com/news/articles/2012-04-19/the-economic-vision-of-egypts-muslim-brotherhood-millionaires> (last accessed 22 June 2017).
32. Farah Halime (2013), 'Egypt's long term economic recovery plan stalls', *New York Times*, 2 May, <www.nytimes.com/2013/05/02/world/middleeast/02iht-m02-egypt-renaissance.html?mcubz=0> (last accessed 22 June 2017).
33. Ibid.
34. Fatima El-Saadani (2012), 'Freedom and Justice Party Assistant Secretary General: the future of Egypt may very well lie with the FJP and its reforms', *Businesstodayegypt*, 12 March <http://businesstodayegypt.com/news/display/article/artId:306/Q-A-with-Ahmed-Soliman/secId:3> (last accessed 22 June 2017).
35. Ibid.
36. Hansen, 'The economic vision'.
37. Amira Howeidy (2012), 'Meet the Brotherhood's enforcer: Khairat El-Shater', *Ahram Online*, 29 March, < http://english.ahram.org.eg/NewsContent/1/64/37993/Egypt/Politics-/Meet-the-Brotherhood%E2%80%99s-enforcer-Khairat-ElShater.aspx> (last accessed 22 June 2017).
38. Nadine Marroushi (2012), 'Senior Brotherhood member launches Egyptian business association', *Egypt Independent*, 26 March.
39. The MB/FJP condemned labour protests and strikes in the post-uprising period. They favoured pursuing policies such as subsidy reform in order to curry favour with the International Financial Institutions and the West.
40. Daria Solovieva (2012), '$4.8 billion IMF loan gives Morsi's Egypt a confidence boost', *International Business Times*, 24 November, <www.ibtimes.com/48-billion-imf-loan-gives-morsis-egypt-confidence-boost-898344>; Ikhwan Web (2012), 'Dr Morsi assures IMF of his party's resolve to boost Egyptian Economy, growth, development', 20 March, <www.ikhwanweb.com/article.php?id=29795> (last accessed 22 June 2017).
41. Hansen, 'The economic vision'.
42. Sherine Abdel Razek (2011), 'Gung ho for capital', *Al Ahram Weekly*, 24–30 November, <http://weekly.ahram.org.eg/2011/1073/fo131.htm> (last accessed 1 December 2012).
43. Abdel Razek, 'Gung ho for capital'.
44. Anon. (2014), 'More than 22 million Egyptians live in poverty: report', *Egyptian Streets*, 13 July, <http://egyptianstreets.com/2014/07/13/more-than-22-million-egyptians-live-in-poverty-report/> (last accessed 22 June 2017); Anon. (2016), '27.8 percent of Egyptian population lives below poverty line: CAPMAS', *Egypt Independent*, 27 July, <www.egyptindependent.com/news/278-percent-egyptian-population-lives-below-poverty-line-capmas> (last accessed 22 June 2017).
45. FJP Election Programme, Parliamentary Elections 2011, <http://kurzman.unc.edu/files/2011/06/FJP_2011_English.pdf> (last accessed 22 June 2017).

46. Al-Markaz al-Misri lil-Huquq al-Iqtisadiyya wal-Ijtima'iyya (2012), *Al Huquq al-Iqtisadiyya wal-Ijtima'iyya fil-Shuhur al-Ula lil-Ra'is Mursi: Ma'at Yawm min Siyasat al-Tajahul wal-Tahmish*, Cairo: ECESR, p. 6.

47. Halime, 'Egypt's long term economic recovery plan stalls'; Hansen, 'The economic vision'; Stephen Glain (2012), 'Egypt's Muslim Brotherhood adopting caution on economic matters' *Washington Post*, 24 January; Anon. (2013), 'Morsi's policies to blame for deepening crisis', *Human and Trade Union Rights News*, 1 July, <www.ituc-csi.org/egypt-morsi-s-policies-to-blame?lang=en> (last accessed 22 June 2017).

48. The main source of conflict between the military and the MB/FJP at the time may have concerned the mega projects – the Suez Canal expansion and the Red Sea economic zone projects – which the military assumed were its areas of influence and not negotiable with the MB/FJP. See Anon. (2013), 'Sisi warns Morsi and Qandil – there will be no title given to land near the Suez', *Misr El Gdida*, 21 March.

49. The urban working class too was unhappy with the decisions of Morsi and the MB/FJP to target their labour unions and bring them under their control. See Peter Hessler (2013), 'Big Brothers: where is the Muslim Brotherhood leading Egypt?' *New Yorker*, 14 January, https://www.newyorker.com/magazine/2013/01/14/big-brothers (last accessed 15 January 2018).

50. The FJP drafted 51 bills with the intention of removing corruption from the police force by increasing oversight as well as downsizing its personnel, instating a maximum and a minimum wage, eliminating monopolies, redistributing public subsidies and easing restrictions on civil society.

51. Also known as *Tamarod* (rebellion), this movement collected 20 million signatures in support of removing President Morsi and his government from power.

52. Preceding this designation, the new army-backed regime had crushed a popular protest that demanded the restoration of Morsi to the presidency. In the course of this crack-down about a thousand protesters were killed and many more injured in a massacre by the military that has become known as the Rabaa massacre.

53. Hansen, 'The economic vision'.

54. Ibrahim El-Houdaiby (2013), 'From prison to palace: the Muslim Brotherhood's challenges and responses in post-Revolution Egypt', *FRIDE Working Paper*, No. 117, February, pp. 10–11.

55. There is also a serious need for internal reform of the group to make more room for diverse voices, especially from among the MB youth. As is well known, the group's other handicap is that most of its leadership has been educated in hard sciences, such as engineering or medicine, and not in the social sciences. Also, having spent many years in prison they have grown to be suspicious of others outside of the group and thus have not developed the skills of fruitful political exchange, and instead have opted for hard and inflexible positions. In so many ways, authoritarian state practices have left a legacy – including within the MB – by shaping the nature of interaction and the perceptions of competing elites as well as those of the broader population.

Chapter 7

A critique from within: the Islamic left in Turkey and the AKP's neo-liberal economics

Nazlı Çağın Bilgili and Hendrik Kraetzschmar

Whilst it was during the first years of the Republic – the 1920s – that the ruling Kemalist elite decided Turkey should follow the Western model of a secular state, it was only much later in the 1980s that an export-oriented, neo-liberal economic model was adopted, ending the state capitalist, protectionist system that had been in place before. Widely embraced, at the time this neo-liberal model received only marginal criticisms from some radical leftist and Islamist groups, among which was Milli Görüş (usually translated as 'National Outlook'), which rejected Westernisation and big industry capitalism. This rejection did not stem, of course, from adherence to Marxist/leftist principles but was driven by the movement's close connect to the small *bourgeoisie* of Anatolia, and its view that small indigenous entrepreneurship was to be empowered as a means to combat the prevalence of Western imperial capital in Turkey, which had kept the country weak and subordinate. Thus, it is only with the rise of Adalet ve Kalkınma Partisi (the Justice and Development Party, also known by its Turkish acronym AKP) – which was established by so-called reformists from within Milli Görüş as the result of an internal split in 2001[1] – that Western-oriented, neo-liberal economics became firmly embedded in the political programme of the Islamist camp.

The AKP itself swept to power in the 2002 parliamentary elections on the heels of a serious financial crisis in 2000–1, that left the country's economy in tatters, leading to massive job losses, a devaluation of the Turkish lira and a staggering rise in inflation and poverty. Punishing the preceding coalition government – and coalition politics more broadly – the Turkish electorate vented their fury at the economic crisis caused by political mismanagement by handing the AKP the first absolute majority in parliament for decades and thus the opportunity of forming a single-party government. Addressing the economic crisis, once formed, the new AKP government pursued a number of policies aimed at recovery. These included strengthening political and economic ties with Western powers, advancing/accelerating EU membership and boosting economic growth through neo-liberal policies, such as the sale of state companies, lower corporate taxes and improved protection of foreign investors.[2] Following IMF-induced austerity and restructuring measures, the AKP eventually succeeded in returning the country to economic stability and growth. Indeed, in the period between 2002 and 2015, Turkey witnessed robust annual growth rates of 4.7 per cent on average.[3]

Internationally, the AKP's neo-liberal turnaround of Turkey's economy was hailed at the time as a big success, whilst domestically it was rewarded with consecutive victories in the 2007, 2011 and 2015 parliamentary elections. Now in its fifteenth consecutive year in power, the AKP has, moreover, not only been able to consolidate power, but also facilitated the enrichment and empowerment of the country's Islamic *bourgeoisie*, which was once marginalised by secular state forces, including the military and the judiciary.

However, this accumulation of power in the hands of the AKP administration, and the pursuit of neo-liberal economic policies, has not remained unchallenged. Indeed, growing criticism of the AKP more widely in society, particularly in the wake of the 2013 Gezi Park protests, has been matched by voices from within the Islamic community, criticising the AKP for its neo-liberal policies and for having forgotten the major teachings of Islam regarding social rights, equality and justice. Most ardent in its criticism of the AKP's neo-liberal politics is hereby the so-called Islamic left,[4] which – albeit small in size – has attracted significant public interest and media attention, particularly for its participation in a series of popular protests, including those at Gezi Park in 2013, but also for two other reasons. First, defining itself as opposition from within, the Islamic left has developed an economic counter-narrative to that of the AKP which sees no contradiction – in Islamic terms – in the pursuit of economic policies based on the principles of neo-liberalism. The Islamic left, meanwhile, critiques the general perception that Islamist politics is inherently rightist and that the Islamic economic model is closer to capitalism than it is to socialism. Second, the Islamic left has been widely viewed as a potential ally of other secular and leftist critics of the AKP, thus raising the hope that the 'Islamists versus secularists' polarisation plaguing Turkish politics can eventually be overcome.

This chapter discusses the Islamic left's criticism of the AKP government's neo-liberal economic policies and the alternative socio-economic and political models it offers. Although attention has already been paid to the religious sources used by the AKP to justify its neo-liberal policies, little has as yet been written on the Islamic left and its theologically founded critique of neo-liberalism. This omission is even more significant because the Islamic left's religion-based criticism of the AKP's policies aligning Islam with neo-liberalism[5] is unique not only in the Turkish context but by regional standards too, as even in the wake of the Arab uprisings of 2010–12 neo-liberalism remained largely an unquestioned economic orthodoxy in the Middle East and North Africa (MENA). Katerina Dalacoura observes, for instance, how the Islamist parties voted into office in post-revolutionary Egypt and Tunisia did not challenge, or transform, the neo-liberal economic structures that had been put in place by Presidents Hasni Mubarak (r.1981–2011) and Zine al-Abidine Ben Ali (r.1987–2011).[6] Indeed, it is remarkable that Islamist-led administrations elected in free and fair elections after the uprisings did not aim to displace neo-liberalism which, during the previous authoritarian era, had led to glaring socio-economic inequalities and the development of a patronage-driven economy benefiting the few.[7] This appears particularly troublesome given that popular demands for social and economic justice were characteristic of the uprisings across the region.

The apparent unwillingness of incoming Islamist-led administrations – which theoretically and historically were expected to be critical of the West and its free market economy – to opt for a radical change in economic policy has been interpreted as a sign that political Islam in the region was moderating and adopting Turkey's AKP as a model of governance.[8] This assertion seems to find confirmation in a public opinion survey conducted by the Turkish Economic and Social Studies Foundation (TESEV) just after the Arab uprisings (19 October–15 December 2011) in sixteen regional states,[9] which revealed that 61 per cent of the respondents agreed that Turkey could act as an economic and political model for other MENA countries. Among those respondents 32 per cent justified their arguments by pointing to the democratic system in Turkey, while 25 per cent argued that its economy was what made Turkey a potential model for other MENA countries.[10]

Whilst outside perceptions of the AKP government thus remained relatively positive, particularly for many of the protesters and activists who had led the Arab uprisings and who sought a new model of governance for post-authoritarian rule, in Turkey itself the AKP had started to face increasing criticism from the early 2010s onwards for its declining performance in both the economic and political spheres. As mentioned above, one such criticism emanated from the rising Islamic left, whose critique of AKP economic politics was couched in theological terms. Drawing on a range of in-depth interviews conducted with representatives of the Islamic left,[11] this chapter spells out the key theological foundations of its criticism of the AKP's neo-liberal economic policies, illustrating that the Islamic left refers mainly to the Qur'an and early Islamic history in its assertion that Islam is on the side of the poor, needy and the oppressed. Moreover, by examining the Islamic left's discourse, this chapter sheds light on the heterogeneity of the Islamic community in Turkey, a country that is frequently, and mistakenly, represented as being torn between strictly 'secular' and 'Islamic' poles.

The AKP's neo-liberalism and its discontent

Since its inception in 1970, Turkey's largest Islamist movement, Milli Görüş, has been represented in Turkish politics by different political parties at different times, given that Islamist parties have repeatedly been closed down by the Constitutional Court for violating the tenets of secularism enshrined in the country's constitution. Once of little significance, these Islamist political parties gradually rose to visibility and prominence during the second half of the 1990s with the emergence of Refah Partisi (Welfare Party, known by its Turkish acronym RP) under the leadership of Necmettin Erbakan. In the 1995 general elections the RP managed to secure a plurality of seats in parliament, which eventually led in 1996 to the formation of an RP-led coalition government headed by Erbakan.[12] The country's secular state elite, and more specifically the army, were highly disturbed by the formation of this first ever Islamist-led administration and ended its term in power by forcing Erbakan, the decades-long-leader of Milli Görüş, to resign as prime minister in 1997.[13] The RP government's inability to survive then led in 2001 to a significant split within Milli Görüş, with the formation of the AKP by younger reform-minded members who sought a clear ideational break with the parent movement. As such, the AKP adopted a fiercely pro-Western and pro-democratic stance that downplayed its Islamist credentials, and that was aimed at broadening the party's support in society, including among the country's liberals. Economically, meanwhile, the AKP moved distinctly to the right of the RP. Indeed, although the economic model proposed by the RP – known as *Just Order* – had not rejected capitalism *per se*, it had remained strongly in favour of a state-regulated market economy within which interest would be forbidden. The AKP, meanwhile, pushed this path towards acceptance of market economic principles within the Islamist movement further yet, by fully embracing neo-liberal and pro-business polices.[14]

When the AKP was voted into office for the first time in 2002, it worked hard to prevent a resurgence of the economic crisis of 2000–1, strictly adhering to the prescriptions demanded by the International Monetary Fund (IMF) and the European Union (EU). Over the following years Turkey then experienced an economic boom, manifest in solid inflation-free growth rates of on average 4.7 per cent and the rise of a new conservative *bourgeoisie*.[15] Known as the second-generation *bourgeoisie* – given that they are latecomers compared to the Istanbul *bourgeoisie* that emerged in the 1960s and 1970s – these Islamic-oriented Anatolian capitalist groups emerged only in the post-1980 period, gaining prominence under AKP rule.[16] In the world of the AKP and this emergent pious *bourgeoisie*, Western-style free-market capitalism and secular politics were not incompatible with Islamic precepts, and hence there was no room for any perceived threats to the Turkish/Muslim way of life from the West.[17] In fact, it was the contradiction between this view and the RP's *Just Order* that had alienated these capitalist groups from the RP and encouraged the emergence of the AKP in 2001.[18] Most members of this new *bourgeoisie* operate in the construction sector, which has come to serve as the locomotive of the AKP's neo-liberalism.[19] Indeed, the AKP's developmental/ economic policies are heavily based on mega-construction projects, such as the construction of a third international airport in Istanbul, a shopping mall in Gezi Park, and a third bridge across the Bosporus. For the AKP – and Recep Tayyip Erdoğan in particular – these projects constituted the hallmark of its legacy and the benchmark of successful developmental policies.

For all its fanfare and international admiration, the AKP's economic agenda and transformation of the Turkish economy did not, however, come without its domestic critics. Indeed, the 2013 Gezi Park protests[20] – the largest anti-government protests Turkey had witnessed under AKP rule – originated as a reaction to the AKP's neo-liberal interventions in the public space and its de-velopmental agenda.[21] As Nilüfer Göle states, 'constructing a shopping mall in the middle of Gezi Park meant private capital's confiscation of a public space, of a park open to all'.[22] When the bulldozers initially gathered around the park, a small group of environmentalists and leftists – which also included members of the Kapitalizmle Mücadele Derneği (Association of Struggle against Capitalism, known as Anti-Capitalist Muslims in short and ACM hereafter) an Islamic leftist group – were the first to react, staging a sit-in at the park. What mobilised the masses[23] thereafter, and led to large-scale anti-government demonstrations, was the perception that the authorities had used excessive violence against the initial protesters and that the government appeared to be ignoring their demands. The demography of the protesters at the time was wide-ranging and cut across Turkish society, comprising mostly urbanites of the coastal cities, the young and the educated.[24]

Although the Gezi Park protest in 2013 against the AKP and its neo-liberal politics was broad-based, bringing millions to the streets, in the ensuing par-liamentary elections of 2015 (June/October) the AKP nevertheless managed to retain power, largely because of its ability to mobilise electoral support from the country's lower-middle classes, as well as the more conservative segments of society, who had labelled the anti-government protesters at Gezi Park as looters and vandals. For some, this ability to maintain electoral support among the lower-middle classes – that is, those benefiting least from the AKP's economic programme – appeared puzzling. A closer reading of the AKP's strategy reveals, however, that the party in government has always been at pains to balance its neo-liberal economic policies with a healthy dose of welfarist policies, particularly for the poor. A case in point concerns, for instance, the establishment of the Housing Development Administration (known by its Turkish acronym TOKİ) which provides affordable housing for lower and middle-income groups on public land. Following the same logic, the AKP government also reformed the country's public health[25] and education systems, making both, as Tim Dorlach argues, more accessible and egalitarian in character.[26] Indeed, although significant inequalities persist, both systems have undoubtedly become more inclusive under AKP rule. As Dorlach furthermore explains, under the AKP 'social security and labour market regulations were retrenched, while social assistance was expanded', meaning 'less welfare protection for workers but [its] expansion for the poor'.[27] Reforms to the social security system thus sought to integrate 'all sections of the population, not only the formally employed but also the informally employed and unemployed'.[28] Although previously official employment was necessary to receive social security, a new law introduced in 2006 meant that henceforth any Turkish citizen could benefit from the social security system irrespective of his/her employment status.

The AKP thus pursues neo-liberal economic policies that simultaneously work to satisfy the needs particularly of the impoverished sections of society, without advancing a return to state welfarism. This is being done by 'institutional diversification and pluralisation of welfare provision in the country', and, as Mine Eder explains, by encouraging 'charity groups' and 'philanthropic associations' to take over 'some state functions or the state subcontracting its welfare provision duties to the private sector'.[29] Scholars working on Turkey's political economy have referred to this balancing of neo-liberal economic policy with social security assistance as 'neoliberalism with a human face',[30] 'social neoliberalism'[31] or 'neoliberal populism'.[32]

A new oppositional pole: the rise of the Islamic left

The so-called 'Islamic left' in its current form is widely associated in Turkish politics with a group of intellectuals and theologians, the most prominent of whom is Ihsan Eliaçık,[33] as well as a number of groupings, including most notably the aforementioned ACM as well as the so-called Emek ve Adalet Platformu (Labour and Justice Platform, LJP hereafter). Collectively, they charge the AKP and its neo-liberal policies for advancing solely the interests of the country's rich and of being indifferent to the plight and rights of the working classes. Although similar criticism has been voiced by various other civil groups and political parties, the Islamic left is unique in the sense that they present their criticism with an explicit Islamic frame of reference.

As regards to the term 'Islamic left' itself, whilst being widely used by outsiders and in the media, it is viewed with scepticism by some, though not all, of those associated with the current. Eliaçık notes in this regard, for instance, that the label would be deemed surprising, and even controversial, by many in Turkey, where Islam is automatically associated with centre-right economic politics.[34] The LJP as well rejects the label 'Islamic left' and being positioned within it. According to them, the left is too didactic and overbearing towards people and this contradicts the LJP's ultimate goal of empowering the people and voicing their demands rather than controlling them.[35] The ACM, meanwhile, appears not to be averse to being identified as 'Islamic left', given that their ideas are leftist ideas based on Islam.[36]

Whilst the Islamic left cites Islam as the main source of its ideas, their understanding of it is ostensibly different from that of the traditional mainstream expressions of Islam prevailing in Turkey. According to one ACM research respondent, for instance, Islam can be interpreted, and hence applied, to real-world politics and society in various ways. Indeed, throughout history humankind has witnessed examples of what it coins as 'positive' and 'negative' interpretations of religious scripture (Qur'an and Sunna), although the latter have ultimately proved dominant. Any readings of Islam that justify oppression, dominance and capitalist profit-driven politics are deemed 'negative' and those emphasising equality, social justice and the rights of the oppressed 'positive'. That negative interpretations of Islam have prevailed in the modern era is, according to the group, linked to the fact that it best serves the interests of the rich and powerful.[37]

According to the Islamic left, historically meanwhile many Muslim scholars and leaders, including the Prophet himself, espoused a 'positive' interpretation of Islam, and hence even though such interpretations appear nowadays new and unusual in the Turkish context,[38] they are in fact merely a resurrection of a proper understanding of Islam. For members of the ACM the sole difference between then and now is that the group nowadays borrows from leftist and Marxist terminology in its economic discourse, using, for instance, terms such as 'social class' and 'exploitation'. Indeed, although the ACM strives to be recognised and included within the Muslim community in Turkey, it appears unwilling to alter the leftist terminology it uses, even though it is aware that this terminology is controversial and considered to be too leftist by many conservative Muslims, particularly in the Anatolian heartland. However, according to ACM research respondents, the use of leftist terminology is inevitable. In fact, *ijtihad*, the interpretation of the Qur'an and the Sunna that provides the legal language of Islam, was completed by Muslim jurists during pre-capitalist times and hence does not reflect upon the problems generated by capitalism. It follows that in the contemporary era, when capitalism poses the greatest threat to social equality and justice, leftist terminology is more appropriate than the Islamic language generated before capitalism.[39]

The appearance of the Islamic left in the Turkish public sphere can be traced back to Ramadan 2011, when a number of young religious people criticising the Islamic community's indifference to existing inequalities in society organised 'modest *iftars*'[40] in public spaces (streets and parks) to protest the 'luxurious' hotel *iftars*[41] that have become increasingly popular among the country's emerging pious *bourgeoisie*. Through these 'modest *iftars*', the Islamic left sought to criticise the extreme consumerism, splendour and extravagance that it felt characterised the lives of the strata of the *bourgeoisie* that had become richer and more powerful on the heels of the AKP's ascendancy to power.

Almost a year later, in 2012, these left-leaning young religious people attracted public attention once more, this time by organising a 1,100 people-strong march from Fatih Mosque to Taksim Square in Istanbul as a part of the celebration of the International Workers' Day (1 May).[42] Led by Eliaçık, organisers of the march named themselves the Kapitalizmle Mücadele Korteji (Cortege of Struggle against Capitalism). Later on, they evolved into the ACM, by which the group is nowadays known. This process of evolution from a cortege into an association involved a series of disengagements due to several disagreements within the Islamic leftist community, and because there were those who did not want to take part in any formal associational activity.

As the preceding narrative made apparent, the Islamic left hence constitutes a heterogeneous current in Turkish politics – although this is not widely recognised by the Turkish public in general – involving several distinct groupings and actors/activists. As well as the ACM, which is relatively popular and well-known, the current comprises the aforementioned LJP which was established in 2011 – thus before the ACM – and which is also an influential group within the Islamic left. One of the major societal issues the LJP advances, concerns the problems facing workers and the homeless. Alongside its engagement in street activism, members of the LJP also regularly organise talks by important thinkers of the current with the aim of furthering the group's intellectual development. In the words of its members, the major distinction between the LJP and ACM is that, unlike the latter, they are not ideological in outlook. Moreover, they argue that, unlike the LJP, the ACM seeks to attract public attention through controversial public acts and symbols. A case in point, according to LJP members, was the ACM's choice of route on the May Day march in 2012, which lead them from Fatih Mosque to Taksim Square, two iconic places in Turkish social life, the former for the pious and the latter for the seculars. 'We also walked on 1 May', LJP members say, 'but we walked with the workers'.[43]

The Islamic left attracted even more public attention as an oppositional actor to the AKP in the wake of Eliaçık's and the ACM's involvement in the 2013 Gezi Park protests. Indeed, the occupation of the park by different societal groups, and the communal life that took place in the park throughout the protests, is interpreted by members of the ACM and Eliaçık[44] – who had their own tents in the park – as a successful example of the oppressed uniting against oppression. For representatives of the ACM this union could, in fact, have acted as a first step in overcoming the growing secular–Islamic polarisation in Turkey.[45]

At the time, public opinion tended to view the protesters in the park as of a mostly secular persuasion. Agreeing with this perception, Eren Erdem – a well-known thinker and established author of the Islamic left and currently an MP of the centre-left Cumhuriyet Halk Partisi (Republican People's Party, also known by its Turkish acronym CHP) – explains that the protesters were in the park to criticise the government not only for planning to cut down trees and build a hotel and mall in their place, but also for interfering in their private lives. To back up his assertion, Erdem points to – in his view – the most popular slogan used during the protests in the park, which was 'cheers, Tayyip' (the first name of Erdoğan).[46] Emrah Çelik, who interviewed the protesters at the time, similarly explains that except for the ACM and a few other religious individuals, the bulk of religious people who supported the protests at the beginning eventually withdrew their support due to the violent methods and secular-leaning slogans used.[47] In these circumstances, Erdem believes that the appearance of the Islamic left in the park was a sign that it was ready to fight for the protection and freedom of different groups and lifestyles within Turkish society.[48] Leftist and secular protesters' gathering around their praying comrades during Friday prayers in the occupied park also raised the hope that the secular–Islamic bifurcation of Turkish politics could be overcome.[49] In his analysis of the Gezi Park protest movement, Çelik corroborates this view, illustrating that hopes for an end to ideological polarisation were widespread among participating university students who criticised the instrumentalisation of ideological binaries and advocated freedom for all people and lifestyles, be they religious or secular.[50]

Societal attempts at overcoming polarised politics were also evident in the *yeryüzü sofraları* (usually translated as 'earth tables'), which were organised by the ACM after the evacuation of the park and attracted a diverse range of attendees from across society, including secular, religious, Turkish, Kurdish, Alevi and Sunni participants. Indeed, when the protesters were pushed out of Gezi Park by the security forces, the ACM adopted two approaches to the pursuit of cross-ideological cooperation that had characterised the Gezi Park spirit: *yeryüzü sofraları* and park forums. As Ramadan 2013 commenced just after the park had been evacuated, the ACM used this occasion as an opportunity to revive its 'moderate *iftars*', this time inviting anyone feeling the 'Gezi Park spirit' and thus targeting an ever more heterogeneous group of attendees. The first such *iftar* table was laid on Istiklal Avenue in Taksim, and proved extremely popular, so much so that its extension to Taksim Square itself was only stopped by police intervention.[51] Although not organised by ACM itself, the park forums, meanwhile, were also strongly supported by the group as arenas of direct democracy. Once forced out of Gezi Park, the protesters decided that every evening they would meet at a different park in Istanbul to exchange ideas for a more democratic, egalitarian and tolerant political system in Turkey.[52] Among ACM members, these park forums raised the hope that they would eventually empower civil society *vis-à-vis* the state and political society (that is the country's principal political parties), the latter of which were thought to have been the key drivers and beneficiaries of societal polarisation. Eventually, these hopes failed to materialise, however, as political parties and party representatives quickly succeeded in establishing themselves as the dominant protagonists at the park forums. For ACM, the Gezi Park events, and particularly the park forums, hence turned out to be a disappointment.[53]

Unlike the ACM, the LJP meanwhile did not participate in the Gezi Park protests as a group/platform. Nonetheless, on the initiative of the LJP, religious people, who called themselves the opposition within the Islamic community, met during the protests in order to discuss the latest developments. They also drafted a statement criticising the government's violent crackdown of the Gezi Park protests, for which they solicited signatures from within the Muslim intelligentsia. The aim was to show that voices critical of the police's excessive use of violence and of the government's obstinacy were existent within the Muslim community too. Although thirty-eight renowned Muslim intellectuals signed the statement, other Muslim intellectuals harshly criticised the document, highlighting the contentious and marginal status the Islamic left enjoys within the Islamic community in Turkey.[54]

The Islamic left's economic and political alternatives to neo-liberalism

As concerns their programmatic outlook, the main goal uniting the disparate forces and thinkers of the Islamic left is the establishment of economic and social justice in the world. And like their secular counterparts, the Islamic left identifies capitalism as the main obstacle to achieving both. In the manifesto of the ACM, for instance, capitalism is defined as 'the enemy of Allah, humanity, nature, the poor, the hungry, the downtrodden'.[55] According to members of the ACM, capitalists are hegemons and they are the reasons behind oppression, injustice and wars in the world.[56] The LJP in its programme mentions more specifically neo-liberalism as the main problem today, defining it as the new ideological form of capitalism that requires eradication.[57]

As mentioned above, unlike the secular left, the Islamic left draws on Qur'anic sayings in its critique of capitalism and its advancement of an alternative economic model based on equality and social justice. The Qur'anic expression *lahu al-mulk* – which is Arabic for 'property belongs to God' – hereby forms the main point of reference of this critique and for the argument that Islam mandates common ownership of the means of production. For representatives of the Islamic left, in fact, belonging to God in religious terms actually means belonging to the public, although Eliaçık in his interview with one of the authors circumscribes this tenet by asserting that it does not pertain to private homes and possessions. According to him, anything that has a surplus value and that generates income – such as for instance land, mines, farms, gardens, vineyards – should belong to society. Eliaçık criticises the pious *bourgeoisie* for their capitalist attitude which he mockingly reads as 'ok, the moon, the sun and the stars belong to God but land is mine, oil is mine'.[58]

Following this interpretation of *lahu al-mulk*, the ACM argues that, on the basis of their labour and contribution to profit generation, factory workers should become shareholders in the companies they work for. They should have access to significant financial information, such as how much profit the company makes and how much their managers earn. In the view of the ACM, Islam is forthright about the rights of workers. They point out a number of Islamic principles on the issue such as, for instance, 'woe to those who give less than due' or 'give the worker his wages before his sweat dries'.[59] As regards these principles, ACM members believe that ownership of the means of production is a critical concern of Islam and they criticise Turkish Islamists for having ignored this religious prescript for decades. Although Turkish Islamism has a history of questioning certain aspects of capitalism – especially before the rise of the AKP – it has been hostile to communism too, which is known to be secular and atheist. Indeed, it is this latter hostility which has arguably prevented the emergence of a more radical criticism of capitalism by many Islamists.[60]

According to the economic model advocated by the Islamic left, then, no segment of society should suffer from economic inequality. In this regard, Eliaçık shows appreciation for the Soviet economic model, which provided all its citizens with basic goods such as jobs, inexpensive housing, free healthcare and education. As he points out, the Soviet model is 'truly appropriate for Islam' in that sense.[61] Erdem, as well, defines Islam as a worldview that defends a classless egalitarian socio-economic structure.[62] However, although Eliaçık, Erdem and others within the Islamic left highlight the detrimental impact of property ownership and a class-based society, they do not propose an economic model that is an exact copy of socialism. The LJP, for instance, asserts that they have a reading group, which seeks to develop an Islamic economic model that is not based on socialism. Moderate in its objectives, the LJP in fact states that complete equality is almost impossible to achieve and hence, rather than aim for revolutionary change of the system, they strive to reduce extant inequalities within the existing order.[63] Eliaçık also makes it clear that he imagines a socio-economic order without private property, yet that this 'is not exactly like socialism either, in the sense that it includes entrepreneurship and private initiative'.[64] Interestingly, Eliaçık confesses that he does not exactly know how such a mixed system comprising certain tenets of each economic model – sharing in socialism and production in capitalism – would look like, let alone how it could be established.[65]

This said, there is another discernible difference between socialism and the economic (and political) model advocated by the Islamic left, and this pertains to the role of the state in politics. As Erdem notes in this regard, for instance '[c]ertainly not in economic terms but in politics, I am liberal in terms of minimising the state'.[66] This quest for a minimal state, in fact, is shared as a political ideal by all actors and groupings of the Islamic left, who view it as a precondition for the maximisation of individual liberties. By 'minimal state' the Islamic left insinuates two things: (1) a state that is kept away from non-political social and religious issues; and (2) a state whose institutions are limited in their involvement in the decision-making process, and that maximises citizens' participation in politics. With regards to the former, for instance, Eliaçık argues that individual basic goods should be available to all, whether that is shelter, access to healthcare, education or a means of earning one's livelihood. However, as for who should be responsible for providing these basic goods, he goes on to argue that the state should get involved only if society cannot manage to deliver protection and a secure life on its own.[67] With regards to the latter conception of a 'minimal state', meanwhile, the Islamic left strives for a more decentralised political system in which the decision-making process functions in a bottom-up manner. The justification for this is found in the Qur'anic expression *la ilaha illa Allah*, meaning 'there is no deity but God' in Arabic. In fact, this verse is commonly referenced by the Islamic left to reject the authority of the state and other institutionalised power-holders. While Erdem suggests that this expression advocates anarchy, given that it asks for the abolition of the state,[68] the ACM's interpretation is less radical, suggesting that it refers to the principle of shared administration where no human being would be given absolute authority over others. Along these lines, members of the ACM argue that parliamentary democracy and its major institution-alised protagonists – political parties – are nothing but tools of control and repression to keep people pacified by giving them the illusion of participating in politics through voting, when in fact their voice does not count. Indeed, by voting, citizens elect 'so-called' representatives whom they mostly do not know in person, and because of this physical/emotional distance between MP and voters, the former feels greater loyalty to the party leadership than to his/her constituents.[69] Moreover, in the view of the ACM, party leaders across the board pursue their own interest, rather than the collective good, caring more about vote shares in elections than the problems and concerns of their voters. Based on these ideas, the ACM rejects any engagement with the country's extant political parties both at the level of individual members and as a group, asserting that such engagement would cost the group its political independence and credibility. It follows that they reject representative parliamentary democracy *per se*, preferring instead the establishment of a plebiscitary democracy, or, if that is not possible, at least greater direct citizen engagement in decision-making processes.[70]

Alongside the Qur'anic term *la ilaha illa Allah*, the other scriptural source of inspiration guiding the political views of the Islamic left concerns the so-called 'Medina Contract', which was written in AD 622 as the constitution of the first Islamic state established by the Prophet and his followers in Medina. The text is widely believed to be an early example of a social contract which, rather than being imposed by the ruler, that is the Prophet, was prepared and signed by both the Prophet and all other members of civil society in Medina. The contract itself is thought to advocate the establishment of a religiously pluralistic state that accepts Muslims and non-Muslims alike as equal members of one nation, the ummah.[71] Taking the Medina Contract as their point of reference, the various actors of the Islamic left all argue that in their calls for equality and justice they do not draw a distinction between Muslims and non-Muslims. Rather they concentrate on one societal distinction: that between the oppressor and the oppressed.[72]

Conclusion

This chapter explored an intellectual/ideological current – the Islamic left – which, although few in numbers, has undoubtedly attracted significant public attention and expressed one of the most fundamental criticisms of the AKP's neo-liberal economic politics to date. Identifying themselves as marginalised actors within the Islamic community, the heterogeneous collection of thinkers and groupings comprising the Islamic left has developed a critique of the

AKP's understanding of Islam with its emphasis only on conservative social values and worshipping practices. Referring to the Qur'an, the Prophet and early Islamic history, the current argues that over time Islam has been distorted to serve the interests of the powerful. Hence, Muslims have come to forget that Islam, by nature, emphasises economic and social justice. Indeed, besides active opposition to the government in street politics and social media, the current is known for its radical perspective on Islamic principles. Interpreting today's mainstream Islamism as a distorted model of Islam, the Islamic left pairs what it refers to as 'true Islam' with leftist arguments and terminology, and argues that Islam in its essence is closer to leftist calls for equality and justice than to conservative and capitalist right-wing politics.

What then is the future of this current in Turkish politics? Whilst difficult to predict, this chapter has revealed a number of challenges the Islamic left will need to overcome, if it is to stand any chance of broadening its societal base. For one, the Islamic left remains highly heterogeneous, with significant inter-personal and policy divisions plaguing the current. So long as these divisions prevail, it is unlikely for the current to gain traction with a broader public. The rejection of institutionalised politics by some, and their reluctance to ally with established political parties, may also prove detrimental to the advancement of their agenda and ultimately of their aim to overcome the secular–Islamic binary in Turkish politics. Lastly, as this chapter illustrated, although the Islamic left is unequivocal in its criticism of the existing neo-liberal economic and political order, it has yet to present a detailed alternative model of society, politics and the economy. Indeed, both in terms of economics and politics the Islamic left has yet to speak with one voice, let alone formulate clear-cut proposals on how a classless political society infused by Islamic scripture would look like.

Notes

1. The founding fathers of the AKP dismissed their Milli Görüş identities, openly stating that they took off their Milli Görüş shirts and called themselves conservative democrats. However, the general perception of the Turkish public has been that the AKP is just another party of the political Islamist movement in Turkey, given that leading figures of the party played significant roles within the movement in the pre-AKP period. See also Ergun Özbudun (2006), 'From political Islam to conservative democracy: the case of the Justice and Development Party in Turkey', *South European Society and Politics*, 11:3, pp. 543–57.
2. Ziya Öniş (2009), 'Beyond the 2001 financial crisis: the political economy of the new phase of neo-liberal restructuring in Turkey', *Review of International Political Economy*, 16:3, pp. 409–32, 423.
3. GDP growth (annual %) Turkey, World Bank Data, <http://data.worldbank.org/indicator/NY.GDP.MKTP.KD.ZG?end=2015&locations=TR&name_desc=false&start=2002> (last accessed 14 March 2017).

4. In this chapter, the term Islamist is specifically used for any groups, political parties or ideas that refer to Islam as a political ideology. All other forces that have an affiliation to Islam, but do not accept it as a political ideology, are labelled *Islamic*. It is due to their open rejection of Islam as a political ideology that Turkey's Islamic left is labelled as such throughout this chapter.

5. For more information on these AKP policies, see Yıldız Atasoy (2009), *Islam's Marriage with Neoliberalism: State Transformation in Turkey*. London: Palgrave Macmillan, pp. 1–31; Nikos Moudouros (2014), 'The "harmonization" of Islam with the neoliberal transformation: the case of Turkey', *Globalizations*, 11:6, pp. 843–57.

6. Katerina Dalacoura (2016), 'Islamism and Neoliberalism in the aftermath of the 2011 uprisings: the Freedom and Justice Party in Egypt and Nahda in Tunisia', in E. *Akcali* (ed.), *Neoliberal Governmentality and the Future of the State in the Middle East and North Africa*. Basingstoke: Palgrave Macmillan, pp. 61–83, 61–2.

7. Koenraad Bogaert (2013), 'Contextualizing the Arab revolts: the politics behind three decades of neoliberalism in the Arab world', *Middle East Critique*, 22:3, pp. 213–34, 223.

8. For more on this discussion, see Aslı Ü. Bali (2011), 'A Turkish model for the Arab Spring?' *Middle East Law and Governance*, 3, pp. 24–42; Alper Y. Dede (2011), 'The Arab uprisings: debating the "Turkish model"', *Insight Turkey*, 13:2, pp. 23–32.

9. Egypt, Jordan, Lebanon, Palestine, Saudi Arabia, Syria, Iran, Iraq, Tunisia, Oman, Bahrain, Qatar, Kuwait, UAE, Yemen and Libya.

10. Mensur Akgün and Sabiha Senyücel Gündoğar (2011), Orta Doğu'da Türkiye Algısı 2011 [The Perception of Turkey in the Middle East 2011]. Istanbul: TESEV Foreign Policy Program, p. 21.

11. The authors conducted a total of twelve semi-structured interviews with members of the Islamic left in December 2014. Research respondents included members of Kapitalizmle Mücadele Derneği (Association of Struggle against Capitalism, known as anti-Capitalist Muslims, ACM) and members of Emek ve Adalet Platformu (Labour and Justice Platform, LJP), a less well-known group. Rather than its activism, the LJP is better known for its intellectual contribution to the movement. İhsan Eliaçık, a theologian who is known to be the intellectual *guru* of the current, and Eren Erdem, a writer recently elected as MP, were also interviewed due to their reputation and intellectual influence on the movement.

12. For more information on the RP, see Ziya Öniş (1997), 'The political economy of Islamic resurgence in Turkey: the rise of the Welfare Party in perspective', *Third World Quarterly*, 18:4, pp. 743–66.

13. For more information on the so-called 'February 28' process and its impact on the Turkish politics, see Umit Cizre-Sakallioglu and Menderes Cinar (2003), 'Turkey 2002: Kemalism, Islamism, and politics in the light of the February 28 process', *South Atlantic Quarterly*, 102: 2/3, pp. 309–32.

14. Ivo Furman (2013), 'Allah, bread and freedom: the anti-capitalist Muslims and the crises of political Islam in Turkey', *Critical Contemporary Culture*, 3:4, <www.criticalcontemporaryculture.org/article-ivo-furman-allah-bread-and-freedom-the-anti-capitalist-muslims-and-the-crises-of-political-islam-in-turkey/> (last accessed 28 August 2016).

15. For more information on the financial policies of the AKP government, see Ziya Öniş (2009), 'Beyond the 2001 financial crisis: the political economy of the new phase of neo-liberal restructuring in Turkey', *Review of International Political Economy*, 16:3, pp. 409–32.

16. Umut Bozkurt (2013), 'Neoliberalism with a human face: making sense of the Justice and Development Party's neoliberal populism in Turkey', *Science and Society*, 77:3, pp. 372–96, 380.

17. Levent Ünsaldı (2013) 'Between neoliberalism and morality: the Muslim conception of development in Turkey', in Gilles Carbonnier et al. (eds), *International Development Policy: Religion and Development*. Basingstoke: Palgrave Macmillan, pp. 144–58.

18. Bozkurt, 'Neoliberalism with a human face', p. 381.

19. Peter Mayo (2013) 'Conservative-neoliberal alliance and popular resistance in Turkey: the uprising in Turkey', in U. B. Gezgin et al. (eds), *The Gezi Revolt: People's Revolutionary Resistance against Neoliberal Capitalism in Turkey*. Brighton: Institute for Education Policy Studies, pp. 310–14, 311, <www.um.edu.mt/library/oar/bitstream/handle/123456789/1483/Conservative-Neoliberal_Alliance_and_Popular_Resistance.pdf?sequence=3&isAllowed=y> (last accessed 28 August 2016).

20. What started as a small and ineffective reaction to Erdoğan's attempt to replace a tiny park at the heart of Istanbul with a late Ottoman revivalist shopping mall turned into a massive country-wide series of protests. For more details on the protests, see Müge İplikçi (2013), '*Biz Orada Mutluyduk*' [We were happy there]. Istanbul: Doğan Kitap; Nilüfer Göle (2013a), 'Gezi – anatomy of a public square movement', *Insight Turkey*, 15:3, pp. 7–14.

21. For more on this discussion, see Cihan Tuğal (2013), 'Occupy Gezi: the limits of Turkey's neoliberal success', *Jadaliyya*, 4 June, <www.jadaliyya.com/pages/index/12009/occupy-gezi_the-limits-of-> (last accessed 28 August 2016); Johm Lovering and Hade Türkmen (2011), 'Bulldozer neo-liberalism in Istanbul: the state-led construction of property markets, and the displacement of the urban poor', *International Planning Studies*, 16:1, pp. 73–96, 78.

22. Nilüfer Göle (2013b), 'Public space democracy', *Eurozine*, 29 July, <www.eurozine.com/articles/2013-07-29-gole-en.html> (last accessed 28 August 2016).

23. It has been reported by the Ministry of Interior that during the Gezi Park protests 2.5 million people were mobilised in 79 out of the country's 81 cities. For more on these figures, see Milliyet (2013), '2.5 milyon insan 79 ilde sokağa indi [2.5 million people hit the streets in 79 provinces]', 23 June, <www.milliyet.com.tr/--milyon-insan-79-ilde-sokaga/gundem/detay/1726600/default.htm> (last accessed 28 August 2016).

24. One of the most prestigious research agencies in Turkey, KONDA, conducted research on the demography of the protesters at Gezi Park and found that the age average of the protesters was twenty-eight. As concerns educational levels, moreover, they found that 42.8 per cent of the protesters were university graduates and another 12.9 per cent to be working on, or having, completed a Master's or a PhD degree. See Anon. (2014), 'Gezi Raporu: Toplumun "Gezi Parkı Olayları" algısı Gezi Parkındakiler kimlerdi?' (The Gezi Report: Society's perception of the Gezi Park events: who were the protesters in the Park?), KONDA Research Agency, 5 June. <http://konda.com.tr/wp-content/uploads/2017/02/KONDA_GeziRaporu2014.pdf> (last accessed 9 May 2017).

25. Simten Cosar and Metin Yegenoglu, 'The neoliberal restructuring of Turkey's social security system', *Monthly Review*, 60:11 <http://monthlyreview.org/2009/04/01/the-neoliberal-restructuringof-turkeys-social-security-system/> (last accessed 30 January 2017).

26. Tim Dorlach (2015), 'The prospects of egalitarian capitalism in the global South: Turkish social neoliberalism in comparative perspective', *Economy and Society*, 44:4, pp. 519–44.

27. Ibid., p. 533.

28. Yonca Özdemir (2015), 'Turkey's Justice and Development Party: an utmost case of neoliberal populism', *ECPR Conference Paper*, 19, <https://ecpr.eu/Filestore/PaperProposal/1afd5880-af7d-4232-a8ca-97da30743db6.pdf> (last accessed 27 August 2016).
29. Mine Eder (2010), 'Retreating state? Political economy of welfare regime change in Turkey', *Middle East Law and Governance*, 2:2, pp. 152–84.
30. Marcie J. Patton (2006), 'The economic policies of Turkey's AKP Government: rabbits from a hat?' *Middle East Journal*, 60:3, pp. 513–36.
31. Dorlach, 'The prospects of egalitarian capitalism in the global south'.
32. Bozkurt, 'Neoliberalism with a human face'.
33. Eliaçık is the most popular and most active figure within the Islamic left. He is also known as the 'intellectual guru' of the current, given that he has been writing and speaking on a radically different understanding of Islam for more than two decades. Besides his activism in the media and on the street, he is also actively involved in gathering young people around his ideas and organising regular meetings with them. Eliaçık has been jailed at different times of Turkish political history because of his ideas and activism.
34. Interview with İhsan Eliaçık, 10 December 2014, Istanbul.
35. Interview with LJP members, 15 December 2014, Istanbul.
36. Interview with ACM members, 12 December 2014, Istanbul.
37. Interview with ACM members, 9 December 2014, Istanbul.
38. As opposed to the general perception, Eren Erdem mentions that this perspective was rather popular in Turkey several decades ago. Between 1960 and 1980, various books on the affinity between Islam and socialism were translated into Turkish. Erdem interprets these two decades as a period 'when Islamists and socialists perceived each other as shield comrades against the official ideology'. Interview with Eren Erdem, 10 December 2014, Istanbul.
39. Interview with ACM members, 9 December 2014, Istanbul.
40. *Iftar* refers to the evening meal that ends the day-long fasting during Ramadan.
41. *Hürriyet Daily News* (2011), 'Luxurious iftars spark Ramadan inequality row', 14 August, <www.hurriyetdailynews.com/default.aspx?pageid=438&n=iftar-protests-call-for-a-debate-on-social-injustice-2011-08-14> (last accessed 7 November 2016).
42. *Hürriyet* (2012), 'Antikapitalist Müslüman Gençler 1 Mayıs'ta [Anti-capitalist young Muslims in 1 May Celebrations]', 1 May, <www.hurriyet.com.tr/antikapitalist-musluman-gencler-1-mayista-20458489> (last accessed 7 November 2016).
43. Interview with LJP members.
44. The general perception in Turkey is that Eliaçık and the ACM are identical in their thinking and that they exclusively act together. However, the interviews conducted as part of this research reveal that there are a number of significant disagreements between the two. While Eliaçık's Islamic reformism constitutes a harsh criticism of AKP voters, the ACM believes that the AKP is to be criticised but that its voters also form part of the oppressed and hence should be attracted to the struggle against the oppressor.
45. Interviews with ACM members, 12 December 2014 and with İhsan Eliaçık, both in Istanbul.
46. The Turkish word for 'cheers' is exclusively used by individuals who consume alcohol and thus the slogan is believed to sarcastically reject the new alcohol consumption regulation that prohibits the sale of alcoholic beverages after 10pm.
47. Emrah Çelik (2015), 'Negotiating religion at the Gezi Park protests', in I. David and K. Toktamış (eds), *Everywhere Taksim: Sowing the Seeds for a New Turkey at Gezi*. Amsterdam: Amsterdam University Press, pp. 215–29, 222–5.

48. Interview with Eren Erdem.
49. *Hürriyet Daily News* (2013), 'First "Friday prayers" in Istanbul's Taksim after clashes', 7 June, <www.hurriyetdailynews.com/first-friday-prayers-in-istanbuls-taksim-after-clashes.aspx?pageID=238&nid=48438> (last accessed 28 August 2016).
50. Çelik, 'Negotiating religion at the Gezi Park protests', p. 229.
51. These were the modest and collectively prepared *iftar* tables, like the ones organised in 2011. Especially the first *iftar* organised on the first day of Ramadan 2013 in Taksim brought together a vast and diverse crowd. For more on this event, see e.g. Fehim Taştekin (2013) 'Turkey's Gezi Park protesters regroup for Ramadan', *Al-Monitor*, 14 July, <www.al-monitor.com/pulse/originals/2013/07/turkey-gezi-park-protesters-observe-ramadan-iftars.html> (last accessed 28 August 2016).
52. For more information on these forums, see e.g. İrem İnceoğlu (2014), 'The Gezi resistance and its aftermath: a radical democratic opportunity?' *Soundings*, 57, pp. 23–34.
53. Interview with ACM members, 13 December 2014, Istanbul.
54. Anon. (2013), 'Dindar aydınlar: Eskiden mazlum olmak zalimin yanında olmamızı gerektirmez (Religious intellectuals: as we were oppressed once does not mean we will be on the side of the oppressor)', *T24 Online Newspaper*, 14 June, <http://t24.com.tr/haber/emek-ve-adalet-platformu-toplumun-taleplerine-kulak-tikayan-siyaset-tarzi-sorun-uretiyor,232015> (last accessed 9 May 2017).
55. Anon. (2014), 'The manifesto of the ACM', in Bayram Koca (ed.), *Türkiye'de İslam ve Sol [Islam and the Left in Turkey]*. Istanbul: Vivo Yayınevi, pp. 452–8.
56. Interview with ACM members, 9 December 2014, Istanbul.
57. Interview.with LJP members.
58. Interview with İhsan Eliaçık.
59. Interview with ACM members, 12 December 2014, Istanbul.
60. Interview with ACM members, 9 December 2014, Istanbul.
61. Interview with İhsan Eliaçık.
62. Interview with Eren Erdem.
63. Interview with LJP members.
64. Interview with İhsan Eliaçık.
65. Ibid.
66. Interview with Eren Erdem.
67. Interview with İhsan Eliaçık.
68. Interview with Eren Erdem.
69. Interview with ACM members, 12 December 2014, Istanbul.
70. Interview with ACM members, 13 December 2014, Istanbul.
71. For more details on the Medina Contract and the type of social and political organisation it established in Medina, see Ali Khan (2006), 'The Medina constitution: understanding Islamic law', <https://ssrn.com/abstract=945458> (last accessed 20 February 2017).
72. Interviews with ACM members, 13 December 2014, and with İhsan Eliaçık, all in Istanbul.

Part II

Islamist and secular party politics

Chapter 8

Rise and endurance: moderate Islamists and electoral politics in the aftermath of the 'Moroccan Spring'

Mohammed Masbah

On 25 November 2011, Morocco held its first parliamentary election after the constitutional reforms that had been initiated by King Mohamed VI in response to the popular protests that had rocked the country in the wake of the Arab uprisings. The moderate Islamist Hizb al-ʿAdala wa al-Tanmiyya (Party of Justice and Development, PJD), which had been in opposition ever since its creation in 1996, received 27 per cent of the votes, winning 107 out of 395 contested parliamentary seats. This victory transformed the PJD into the largest parliamentary party in Morocco by far, and catapulted its Secretary General Abdelilah Benkirane into the post of prime minister (PM) of a coalition government. Five years later, at the election of 7 October 2016, the dominance of the PJD was confirmed by an even more impressive victory than that of 2011, with the PJD obtaining 31.6 per cent of the popular vote and a total of 125 parliamentary seats. Several days later on 11 October 2016, King Mohamed VI charged Benkirane with the formation of his second consecutive administration.[1] In the following five months, however, Benkirane was unable to forge a new coalition government, causing the longest period of political deadlock in the reign of Mohamed VI. Consequently, the king used a controversial reading of Article 47 of the constitution to dismiss Benkirane on 17 March 2017, replacing him with another PJD leader and the former foreign minister Saad Eddine El Othmani. Only a few days later a new PJD-led coalition government was announced, comprising al-Tajammuʿ al-Watani lil-Ahrar (National Rally of Independents, RNI), al-Haraka al-Shaʿbiyya (Popular Movement, PM), al-Ittihad al-Dustouri (Constitutional Union, CU), Hizb al-Taqqadum wa al-Ishtirakiyya (Party of Progress and Socialism, PPS) and al-Ittihad al-Ishtiraki lil-Quwat al-Shaʿbiyya (Union Socialiste des Forces Populaires, USFP). The second consecutive PJD-led coalition government since the Arab uprisings of 2010–12 was hence formed.

The sustained electoral success of a single political party across consecutive elections, and consequently its endurance at the helm of government – in this case of the PJD – is unique in the political history of Morocco. Over the last two decades, the country's traditional political parties have tended to decline in popularity as a result of their participation in government. In contrast, the PJD was able to increase its electoral support between 2011 and 2016, and succeeded in maintaining a position at the helm of government for two consecutive mandates, a feat that has eluded all other political parties during the era of King Mohamed VI.

The PJD also represents a unique case for Islamists in the Arab world. Following the eruption of the Arab uprisings in 2010–11, Islamist political parties ascended to power as a result of the political opening in Egypt, Morocco and Tunisia, yet only a few years later all of them had been removed from office, except in Morocco. Indeed, the PJD is the only Islamist party in the Arab world to have both survived a full term in office, and won subsequent re-election with an increased majority. In Tunisia, for example, Hizb al-Nahda (Renaissance Party) won the 2011 parliamentary elections, but went on to lose the 2014 poll. Similarly, the Egyptian al-Ikhwan al-Muslimun (Muslim Brotherhood, MB) and its affiliate, Hizb al-Hurriyya wa al-'Adala (Freedom and Justice Party, FJP) were overthrown by a military *coup d'état* in 2013 after only one year in power. This renders the PJD an excellent, and unique, case to study the rise to, and endurance in, government by moderate Islamist parties post-2011.

Although much has been written about how and why Islamist forces moderate their ideology and behaviour through political participation,[2] far fewer studies are available on the survival of Islamist forces once they have reached executive power. Focusing on the case of the PJD in Morocco, this chapter aims to explain how Islamist parties rise to power, shed light on the challenges they face as rulers in an authoritarian setting, and explore how, once in government, these challenges affect both the party itself and the wider political setting. The central question addressed in this chapter thus concerns the structural and agency-related factors that explain the Moroccan PJD's rise to power in 2011, as well as its resilience at the helm of government between early 2012 and early 2017.

Drawing on political process and rational choice theories, as well as the literatures on political parties in the Arab world, this chapter argues that the PJD's emergence as a relevant political actor, and its remarkable endurance at the helm of government between 2011 and 2017, can be best explained as a result of three factors. First, its rise and endurance was made possible by the unique circumstances that characterised Moroccan politics in the post-2011 period. As elsewhere in the region, in 2011 the regime had come under significant pressure from the Moroccan street to initiate political reform. To relieve the pressure, the monarchy initiated a series of political reforms that included a new constitution and the organisation of early parliamentary elections, which were relatively free and fair in comparison to previous polls. Whilst pre-2011 the PJD had been allowed to participate in Moroccan politics within proscribed lines,[3] they were able to capitalise on the 2011 political opening by taking advantage of the regime's short-lived crisis in 2011 and, once in power, by carefully navigating the political space between conciliation with the Palace and the retention of independence from it. This strategy enabled the party to avoid being fully co-opted by the Palace while in government, and as such helped it to retain its popularity among constituents and the broader public. Second, the PJD benefited from the prevalence of a fragmented party system, characterised by the declining performance of the main traditional parties including Hizb al-Istiqlal (Independence Party, IP) and the USFP. While the electoral popularity of these parties has declined as a result of the weakness of their party machinery and loss of credibility among their core constituencies, the PJD was able to build and sustain a strong organisational structure and base, as well as taking advantage of the vacuum left by these traditional parties to broaden its electoral appeal.[4] Third, the pragmatism of the PJD is an element contributing to its 'optimal' rational choices. Over the course of the past twenty years, the PJD has learned how to balance between abiding by the political rules established by the monarchy and crafting a political discourse that is able to attract voters. This was based on a strategic calculation that relies on the PJD retaining its loyalty to the king, while at the same time denouncing the hegemony of the regime. It seems that this approach has resonated with many PJD voters, who want to hear a party denouncing corruption within the regime without confronting the monarchy. As Mohamed El Hachimi has observed, the PJD's pragmatism was the result of a long process of learning, which has led the party to moderate its position ideologically, obliging it to accept political participation in an authoritarian political system.[5] Accordingly, through 'rational' and 'calculated' choices, the PJD benefited the most from the 2011 political opening and turned it to its advantage. A pragmatic party, the PJD understands the reality of power politics in Morocco and, at times, has demonstrated its willingness to sacrifice its Islamist philosophy for power-political considerations.[6]

The PJD's rise to power

2011: Transforming the crisis into opportunity

Returning to the first argument presented above, it is suggested here that the ascendancy to power of Morocco's PJD cannot be properly understood without positioning it within the broader political context of 2011. Before

2011, in fact, the PJD leadership was preparing for the prospect of further repression, rather than planning to win a parliamentary election.[7] Yet due to the popular protests that erupted in Morocco in February 2011 – the so-called 'Moroccan Spring' lead by the 20th February Movement[8] – the PJD's fortunes changed dramatically, enabling it ultimately to emerge as the governing party in the post-Spring era. Indeed, while across the region most Arab states responded to the democratic protest movements of 2011 with increased repression, the monarchy in Morocco opted for a different tactic: bowing to the storm. The actions of the monarchy followed a pattern of adapting to public pressure in order to maintain stability and survive.[9] Accordingly, the monarchy was quick to respond to the protests with a series of reform measures. First, it softened its security-oriented approach. So for instance, police repression of the demonstrations was measured and low-level, thereby avoiding an escalation of the protests and allowing the population to vent its anger. Second, the monarchy adopted a series of political reforms to address some of the protesters' demands for greater popular participation. Only three weeks after the protests of 20 February 2011, King Mohamed VI gave a speech at which he promised 'genuine' constitutional reforms.[10] Ratified by popular referendum on 1 July 2011, these constitutional reforms included significant amendments, such as granting greater space for public freedoms, expanding the powers of the government and upgrading parliamentary oversight of the government. By the same token, however, the king retained important powers, such as his role as head of the military and security apparatus and his powers to conduct foreign policy, as well as a largely symbolic maintenance of his title as 'commander of the faithful', granting him religious legitimacy. Nonetheless, the king did agree to delegate some of his former prerogatives to a prime minister to be designated from the largest party in parliament, with the power to appoint ministers, dissolve the lower house of parliament[11] and direct the country's internal affairs.[12] Following the constitutional reforms, the king called for early parliamentary elections, which were held in November 2011 and won by the PJD. That vote was judged by international observers[13] to be more honest and transparent than any previous elections.

Although remarkable in the speed of its ascendance to power, the PJD's path towards governmental responsibility was not straightforward. Moderate Islamists faced both internal and external pressures during the early period of the 'Moroccan Spring' in 2011. Indeed, early on the PJD officially declined to join street protests because it believed that this could risk the trust-building with the monarchy, while at the same time it used the threat of exit from formal politics to enhance its bargaining power *vis-à-vis* the monarchy.[14] Activists who took part in the 20th February Movement, as well as many of the PJD's own rank and file, harshly criticised the PJD leadership at the time for declining to join the protest movement. Even worse, two prominent leaders resigned from the party's political bureau on 19 February 2011 because they refused to obey the party's decision not to join the protests.[15] Several ordinary PJD members followed the same pattern and disobeyed the leadership's instructions, opting to participate in the protests. At the time, the party was on the verge of a major internal split.

To maintain a balance between pressures from street protests and the constraints of being a loyal opposition party, the PJD eventually decided to combine both of them by channelling grievances within the confines of the formal political sphere. By mid-2011, the PJD proposed a 'third way' – based on the premise of a genuine partnership between the monarchy and the PJD – that promised to bring about more far-reaching reforms than those proposed by the Palace without the disruption that might be caused by uncontrolled popular upheaval.[16] This 'third way' approach was then put to the test in March 2011, when the PJD and its allies in civil society launched an initiative called Nida' al-Islah al-Dimuqrati (Call for Democratic Reform, CDR).[17] The creation of this networking structure was motivated by a desire to build an alliance that would project the PJD's influence well beyond the immediate political sphere and into society.[18] It also sought to serve as a structure of coordination between the various affiliates of the PJD – the party itself, Harakat al-Tawhid wa al-Islah (Movement of Unity and Reform, MUR), the PJD's youth and student sections Chabibabte al-'Adala wa al-Tanmiyya (Justice and Development Youth, JDY) and Monadamat al-Tajdid al-Tulabi (Students' Renewal Organisation in Morocco, OREMA), its labour union al-Ittihad al-Watani li-Choghl bi al-Maghrib (National Labour Union in Morocco, UNTM), and its women's forum Muntada al-Zahra' (Azzahrae Forum). This initiative had three main objectives: (1) to establish an alternative political platform for open debate and public deliberation, (2) to work towards peaceful social mobilisation, and (3) to allow for participation without being involved directly in street protests.[19] From March until the November 2011 elections the CDR, led by the PJD, organised hundreds of public meetings all over the country, to a much greater extent than the other formal political parties.[20] According to a PJD leader, this approach bridged the gap between conflicting views within the party, and enabled its leadership to remain consistent *vis-à-vis* both its constituency and the Palace.[21] Indeed, arguably it was this move that saved the PJD from paralysis during the 2011 protests, enabling the party to build up its own resources so as to benefit fully from the political opening provided by the new constitution and the subsequent organisation of relatively free and fair elections.

As for the 2011 parliamentary elections themselves, there are two factors that explain the PJD's relative success in mobilising electoral support. The first factor pertains to the monarchy's permissive attitude towards the PJD during the elections. Because of the crisis triggered by the mass protests of February 2011, the monarchy sought allies among the country's political and social forces in order to ward off the threat posed by the 'Moroccan Spring'. As part of this strategy the monarchy decided not to curb the PJD's activities so as to discourage the party from joining the street protests and retain it within the orbit of pro-regime parties. Instead, the regime focused on controlling the street protests that were already occurring, in which officially the PJD played no part. The second factor, meanwhile, pertains to the PJD's public discourse, which at the time resonated particularly well with the urban middle class; a portion of society that aims for political change without risking stability. Tapping into this sentiment, the PJD's electoral discourse revolved around 'fighting corruption and authoritarianism', whilst preserving the monarchical system of government. Consequently, the PJD fared particularly well among the urban middle classes and more specifically the upper middle class in the big cities such as Rabat, Tangier and Casablanca.

The authorities' relative non-interference during the 2011 parliamentary elections, together with the commitment of the king himself to respect the new constitution, thus to some extent produced the conditions for the subsequent electoral success of the PJD and its rise to power. As will become apparent below, however, these conditions coincided with additional structural factors that facilitated a PJD victory in 2011. These pertain first and foremost to the fragmented nature of Morocco's party system and the weakness of some of its traditional (opposition) parties.

Morocco's fragmented party system

In her monograph on political parties in North Africa, Lise Storm described how the party system in Morocco has historically been fragmented and characterised by ongoing electoral volatility.[22] Since its inception in the 1990s, the PJD has operated in this fragmented party system and benefited from its flaws. In Morocco, political parties are divided between a secular-nationalist camp (IP and USFP) and the so-called 'royal' or 'administrative' parties. The latter include parties such as Hizb al-Asala wa al-Mu'assara (Party of Authenticity and Modernity, PAM), the RNI, CU and PM, all of which are characterised by the lack of a real social basis. As noted by Eva Wegner, the most decisive characteristic of these 'royal' parties is their unconditional support for the king's political initiatives, although the monarchy is not directly associated with any of them.[23] With little grass-roots support to draw upon, for the most part these parties tend to rely on support from the so-called *Makhzen* (the Moroccan establishment) – a nebulous network of actors loyal to the Palace, with the

Ministry of the Interior constituting its backbone – to achieve electoral results. Moreover, they operate mainly in rural areas, which remain marked by high levels of illiteracy, either by buying votes directly or by operating indirectly through the mobilisation of local authorities in favour of certain candidates. The obvious reason behind the creation of royal-rural parties is to counterweigh the growth of nationalist and Islamist parties, whose constituency is mostly urban and middle class.

Although the PJD itself emerged from out of al-Haraka al-Sha'biyya al-Dustouriyya al-Dimuqratiyya (Popular Democratic and Constitutional Movement, PDCM) – a party created in the late 1960s by Abdelkarim Khatib and a politician close to the Palace – its social base differs sharply from that of the administrative parties and overlaps significantly with that of other nationalist parties, and hence its electoral advances in 2011 occurred mostly at their expense, and here particularly at the expense of the leftist USFP. Following the failure of the short-lived USFP-led *gouvernement d'alternance* experiment between 1997 and 2002 by former PM Abderahman Youssoufi, and after the nomination of a technocratic prime minister in 2002, the USFP declined in electoral popularity. The truth is that among the nationalist parties, the USFP lost most from the *alternance* experiment. The reasons behind its decline are (1) related to the USFP's failure at the time to take credit for its policies as a result of the monarchy's appropriation of all positive political developments,[24] and (2) because the competition among its leaders for key positions fatally weakened the party's internal coherence. By 2007, the USFP had lost half of its seats in parliament, its leadership was divided and, above all, it had lost its traditional support base (the urban electorate, trade unions, employees and civil servants). As a result, the USFP electoral base shifted to a constituency similar to that of the administrative/royal parties; that is the rural voters.[25] In the 2016 elections, the USFP and other leftist parties failed to garner seats in large urban districts, except in very few cases, and the seats they won were restricted to three marginal regions out of the twelve regions of the kingdom.[26]

The decline in support for the USFP and other leftist parties among urban middle class citizens in the 2000s benefited the PJD. The PJD advanced electorally in the same areas that used to be strongholds of the left between the 1970s and 1990s and that experienced, from 2002 onwards, a gradual shift in voter allegiances towards the Islamists.[27] Indeed, by 2016 the majority of voters in key cities, such as Casablanca, Mohammedia and Agadir – which constituted traditional strongholds of the left – had shifted in allegiance to the PJD. This shift in voter allegiances towards the PJD was not replicated, however, in the rural areas of the country, where the PJD remains poorly represented in comparison to the royal-rural parties.[28] As highlighted above, this is largely due

to the predominance of the 'royal' or 'administrative' parties in rural constituencies, which are able to hold sway in the countryside by means of electoral
manipulation and their close connection to the *Makhzen*.

Taming the Islamists: the royal recipe

As we have seen, the PJD's rise to power in 2011 occurred within the context of
the new political opportunities opened up by the 'Moroccan Spring' as well as the
country's fragmented party system and the depletion of the traditional political
left. It was also possible, however, due to the monarchy's long-standing policy of
pre-emptive inclusion, which facilitated the electoral entry of the PJD in the first
place and has allowed it to participate in mainstream politics ever since.

As noted by Michael Willis and others, the Moroccan monarchy – much
more so than pre-Spring Tunisia and Algeria – has a long tradition of taming
opposition parties through pre-emptive inclusion within the formal political
sphere.[29] This approach works by allowing the opposition to benefit from
being formally included in mainstream politics without really gaining power,
which remains in the hands of the Palace. The monarchy's calculus is hereby
straightforward: by allowing moderate Islamists to participate in the country's
politics they bind potential challengers into the regime's fold and force them
to play by the rules of the game.[30] As part of this strategy as well, the regime
resorts at times to mild to severe repression to tame opposition parties that it
considers to be a real threat to royal interests.

The regime's approach of pre-emptive inclusion had been pursued by the
previous King Hassan II (r.1962–99), and remains a key feature of the reign
of King Mohamed VI. In the early 1990s, for instance, Hassan II believed that
Morocco was on the brink of a major political crisis as a result of economic
hardship due to consecutive seasons of drought that resulted in a low growth
rate. To relieve pent-up societal pressure, Hassan II launched a constitutional
reform in 1996, and one year later he appointed the former opposition leader
and head of the leftist USFP, Abderahman Youssoufi, to the position of prime
minister. A similar strategy of inclusion was adopted towards the country's
moderate Islamists. By the mid-1990s, the regime had worked to include
(partially) some components of the Islamist family, through the already-extant
PDCM, which in 1998 changed its name to PJD.

The monarchy's approach of dealing with the country's Islamists is based on
the idea of 'peeling' the moderate Islamists away from the 'hardliners'.[31] While
seeking to include moderate Islamists, the monarchy uses repression against
the most radical Islamist forces, such as the so-called 'jihadi–Salifists'. Yet far

from being a black-and-white approach, the coefficient of 'repression-inclusion' varies according to several variables pertaining to the country's Islamists': (1) their level of loyalty to the monarchy, (2) their degree of pragmatism, (3) their level of acceptance of the regime's political rules and (4), the strength of the political party in question. It appears that for the monarchy to date, the PJD is the only Islamist party in Morocco that meets all of these criteria. For example al-'Adl wa al-Ihsan (Justice and Charity Organisation, JCO) possesses the fourth and partially the second. Hizb al-Badil al-Hadari (Civilisational Alternative Party, CAP) and Hizb al-Ummah (Party of the Ummah, PU), partially possess the first three criteria, but their party machine is weak.[32] From the perspective of the regime, it is clear why the PJD appeared as the best option for selective inclusion: it presented itself as a pragmatic Islamist party playing according to the rules of the game with an effective party machine, and above all with professed loyalty to the monarchy.

Despite this, the monarchy's relation with the PJD has not always been smooth. In fact, on occasions the regime has relied on repressive measures to curtail the PJD and to remind it of the regime's red lines. This was evident, for instance, in the aftermath of the 2003 Casablanca terror attacks when the government accused the Islamists of moral responsibility for the atrocity and blamed them for having created a climate enabling the bombings to take place.[33] As a result, the authorities seriously contemplated the dissolution of the PJD, and when this idea was discarded, pressured its leadership to limit the party's participation in the 2003 elections[34] because of fear of an Islamist electoral tide.[35]

Moreover, instead of dissolving the PJD, the Palace opted for a tested recipe to contain it: the creation of loyal parties that would safeguard the fragmented nature of Morocco's party system and ensure that no single political party was able to muster a parliamentary majority. In 2008, Fouad Ali El Himma, a close friend of the king and then-minister delegate of the interior, resigned from the government in order to establish the PAM. A few months later, the PAM obtained more than a third of the 22,000 contested seats in the 2009 local elections. Obviously, the creation of the party was meant to help contain the PJD's electoral rise.[36] In this respect, the establishment of the PAM reflects the monarchy's response to a profound crisis in the Moroccan party landscape; in particular, the difficulties faced by traditional secular parties in maintaining, or renewing, their legitimacy[37] in the eyes of their constituencies and the resulting decline in voter turnout at the expense of a surging PJD.[38]

In the aftermath of the 2011 mass demonstrations, the PAM, meanwhile, lowered its profile following popular accusations that it was polluting the political sphere and subsequent calls for its prohibition. By May 2011, El

Himma had resigned from the party and joined the royal cabinet. Again this played into the hands of the PJD. Since the PAM lost the support of the *Makhzen*, the PJD could easily outperform it in the 2011 elections. Since then, the PAM has been used as a substitute player that the regime calls upon to counterbalance the PJD in the absence of real opposition from the country's traditional secular-nationalist political parties (USFP, IP).

Understanding the PJD's resilience in government

Since its first ascendancy to power in the aftermath of the Moroccan Spring, the PJD has led a full-term coalition government (2011–16) and, after winning re-election in 2016, was able to forge a second broad-based coalition government under its leadership, albeit at a price. Indeed, as highlighted above, the price for remaining at the helm of government was the removal from office of its charismatic leader Abdelilah Benkirane and his replacement with a more pragmatic figure within the PJD, Saad Eddine El Othmani, as well as the relinquishment of key government portfolios to pro-Palace non-partisan technocrats. So, for instance, some of the most important government ministries, such those of the Interior,[39] Foreign Affairs and Education, went to pro-Palace personalities. The PJD, meanwhile, had to make do with lesser ministries, which combined control as little as 6 per cent of the government budget, while ministries held by non-partisan technocrats, the PM and RNI control more than 85 per cent of the budget.[40]

Nevertheless, the PJD's survival as the principal governing party since 2011 is rather unique in the history of Morocco and clearly challenges the premise that participation in government electorally weakens ruling parties as a consequence of their limited ability to enact the reforms demanded by their constituents and/or take adequate credit for those implemented. In the case of the USFP, as we saw, the party's move from opposition to government in 1997 weakened the party machine and divided its leadership, thus precipitating its electoral demise. By contrast, once in government the PJD not only managed its internal conflicts despite the pressures of governing, but ultimately also benefited from its position in power and capitalised electorally on it, as evident in its 2016 performance.

Although its longer-term popularity and success in government under new leadership and in a new coalition are hard to gauge, it is possible to pinpoint a number of agency factors that help explain the PJD's resilience in government between 2011 and 2016. These pertain to the following: (1) the flexibility of the PJD and its balancing act between loyalty to the king and its maintenance of grass-roots support, (2) the 'latent' secularisation of the party due to separation between the party and the religious movement, (3) their relative success in building sustainable cross-ideological alliances with other secular parties, (4) the preservation of the party machine by strictly separating party and government positions, and finally (5) the pursuit of an effective PR campaign.

Pragmatism

The PJD is a model of a pragmatic Islamist party, one which considers political interest as more important than ideology. This is a key factor in understanding the PJD's relative success in government as of 2018. This pragmatism is born out of political necessity in order to survive within the regime setting. The monarchy in Morocco retains control over key state positions, including the Ministry of the Interior, which remain the strongest component of the Moroccan establishment and as Michael Willis reminds us, Morocco represents a case where the progressive transparency of elected institutions does not necessarily equate with meaningful democratisation.[41] This means that any governing party that seeks to successfully advance its political agenda needs to cooperate with the monarchy.

The PJD understands this political reality and has thus proclaimed on many occasions that any genuine reform must be implemented in cooperation with the monarchy and other relevant actors, such as the Ministry of the Interior. The party has also reiterated its loyalty to the monarchy, with Benkirane incessantly 'advertising' his loyalty to the king to the extent that he was accused of being 'more royalist than the king'.[42] Thus, the party's leadership has understood its interest in cooperating with the monarchy to remain in government, since even from its position within government, it does not hold all the power it needs to carry out any major political and economic reforms.[43]

Consequently, the governing PJD has chosen to support most of the king's initiatives for the purpose of normalising its presence within the formal political sphere and building trust with the monarchy.[44] In pursuing this strategy, the PJD has had to make concessions in favour of the Palace. As alluded to earlier, this pragmatism was visible, for instance, during the PJD's management of the political impasse that lasted between November 2016 and March 2017. When Benkirane failed to form a new government, the PJD had the option of refusing to accept the king's dismissal of Benkirane and hence returning to the opposition benches or calling for early elections. In the end, however, the PJD opted to give up its leader and form a weak coalition government that would please the Palace, as a price for remaining at its helm. This pragmatism was also visible after the dismissal of Benkirane in March 2017. Indeed, in his search for coalition partners, the new PJD prime minister, unlike his predecessor, has not shied away from approaching the PAM, thus offering seats at the cabinet table to a party that has been one of the prime rivals of the PJD. Yet another example of PJD pragmatism, this time during the tenure of Benkirane, concerns the PM's willingness to forsake his constitutional prerogative to nominate hundreds of key state positions to the king. Moreover, when the IP withdrew from the first PJD-led coalition government in June 2013, the party ceded several of its cabinet portfolios to technocratic Palace-backed ministers who henceforth controlled strategic positions in government.[45]

Conversely, while remaining loyal to the monarch as head of state and to the monarchy as the unifying institution for the country, the PJD has also criticised the king's entourage several times, although mostly indirectly. The PJD has used metaphors in its media narrative to attack the royal Palace without naming it directly. In an interview with Al-Jazeera journalist Ahmed Mansour in 2012, for instance, Benkirane used the terms of *tamassih wal 'afarit* (crocodiles and ghosts) to explain to Moroccan citizens why he failed to deliver substantial reforms.[46] These terms allude to the Palace and its allies in the administration allegedly trying to undermine PJD efforts to implement the reforms they had set out to undertake. Later the party used another term, *al-tahakum* (hegemony, or control), to denote the same problem. In an interview with *al-Aoual* website in July 2016, Benkirane explicitly implicated the Palace, and more precisely one of the king's closest friends and advisor Fouad Ali El Himma, of being the orchestrator of *al-tahakum*. He even alluded to Mohamed Oufkir – the Minister of the Interior during the reign of Hassan II who plotted the coups in 1971 and 1972 – to argue that the king's entourage might contain some anti-monarchic elements because of their greed for power.[47]

This ambivalent position of professing loyalty to the king, while at the same time criticising his entourage, was an effective political tactic that helped Benkirane and the PJD maintain an 'optimal' balance between remaining on good terms with the monarchy and retaining legitimacy and support from its constituents. In fact, this ambivalence has persisted in other forms as well. The PJD, for instance, has consistently threatened that it could 'un-moderate'.[48] This was clear on several occasions, such as for instance during the campaign to support the constitutional amendments in 2011 when the party announced that it would vote 'no' to the new constitution if it contained provisions against having Islamic references in the charter.[49] This dual position of working within the government and maintaining an oppositional discourse has been a source of contention with the Palace, and might be one reason behind Benkirane's eventual dismissal in 2017. Indeed, according to one source in the Palace, who confided to the *Jeune Afrique* magazine in summer 2016, the king's displeasure with PM Benkirane stemmed in large measure from the fact that the latter was pro-monarchy on weekdays, but an 'opponent at weekends during his meetings within his party'.[50] The tactic of loyalty to the king, while at the same time denouncing *tamassih wal 'afarit* and *al-tahakum,* seems to have been effective in attracting voters who wanted a 'clean' party that denounces the corruption of the regime without risking the stability of the country. As of 2018, it is also evident of course that this strategy came at a price, with relations between the PJD and the Palace being increasingly strained.

'Latent secularisation'

The second factor that might explain the PJD's survival in government is its ideological moderation. Since coming to power, a shift in the PJD's political behaviour has been noticeable. The relatively new pragmatism of Islamist activists has often been interpreted as a tactic to reach power. However, this view neglects the fact that Islamist movements are active agents operating within their own societal contexts.[51] This is evident with regards to the PJD whose Islamist rhetoric has seen a significantly metamorphosis over the years towards 'latent secularisation'. By 'latent secularisation' this author refers to processes in which an Islamist party (1) quits its religious mother organisation, (2) divides its religious activities from its political ones, and (3) explicitly recognises its 'mundane' nature, which means that its political activities are based on rational calculations rather than purely religious objectives. By contrast, the concept of 'moderation' broadly speaking refers to a trajectory in which parties renounce the idea of violence and accept the notion of political participation in mainstream politics. While moderation thus signifies the reverse process of radicalisation, secularisation constitutes the reverse process of 'Islamisation', and refers to movement towards a post-Islamist discourse that revolves around concepts of citizenship as well as cooperation with other secular parties. As such, all secularised Islamist parties are moderate, but not all moderate Islamist parties are secularising.

As for the PJD, the process of 'secularisation' started in the aftermath of the 2003 Casablanca terrorist attacks. During that period, Islamists were under pressure from the regime and in order to maintain their legal recognition, the PJD at the time made a strategic move: separating the party from the social movement that had created it, the MUR. This separation between party and mother organisation was, however, not total; it was rather a division of labour that concerned three sectors: activism, speeches and leadership.[52] Indeed, the PJD and MUR established a complementarity agreement that placed the PJD in charge of the political struggle and representing Islam, whilst leaving the MUR in charge of *da'wa* (preaching) and education.[53] The separation of the MUR and the PJD signalled the end of proselytising and the beginning of politics for the PJD.[54] A decade later, the Tunisian Islamist al-Nahda would emulate the Moroccan model of separation between party and parent movement. In March 2015, al-Nahda invited leaders from the MUR and PJD to discuss the Moroccan model of separation between *da'wa* and politics,[55] and a few months later adopted the same division of labour.[56] As demonstrated by Suveyda Karakaya and A. Kadir Yildirim, the separation between the party and the religious movement was not purely tactical moderation, but rather a strategic separation, and includes ideological moderation. This implies that the PJD shifted its whole ideological platform to a more moderate and mainstream political party to respond to societal changes (economic liberalisation, economic growth, electoral loss and changing voter preferences) and to gain greater popular support.[57]

Since that time, the PJD has arguably been transformed into a quasi-secular political party with an Islamic flavour. A good example of this is seen in the party's positions *vis-à-vis* the permissibility of music festivals. Before 2011, the PJD criticised music festivals as being a tool of moral corruption and a way to distance youth from their Islamic identity.[58] Once in office, meanwhile, the PJD avoided commenting on this issue. Another example concerns the PJD's electoral programmes. For instance, when comparing its electoral programmes of 1997 and 2016, one can easily observe the progressive dilution of its Islamic identity. In 1997, the PJD's Islamic identity was accentuated and was the epicentre of its electoral programme, while by 2016 it became ephemeral and diluted. In the 2016 electoral programme, the PJD explicitly cited that it 'separates between religious and political sphere (...) and that its political praxis is done through political tools which are based on human and relative understanding that is one possibility of reform among others'.[59]

The PJD 'rediscovers' from time to time its Islamic identity to please its constituency, but it does not pursue an 'Islamising' agenda. In fact, during its first term of office the PJD avoided any ideological clash with secular rivals. This could be explained as the result of pragmatic calculations. Because the PJD requires the support of other secular parties to form and sustain a governing coalition, it has learned in due process that it is in the party's interest to avoid ideological quarrels. During its mandate at the helm of government, the PJD rarely commented on ideological matters, such as, for example, the decision by the Ministry of Interior to ban the Burqa in January 2017.[60] As a PJD leader told this author, the party did not want to 'provoke the government formation by creating an ideological contradiction with our secular partners and this is the reason why we did not answer to such provocations'.[61]

In parallel, the PJD managed to build trust with its constituency thanks to its moral credentials. Shortly after its ascendance to power, the PJD updated its ethics procedures and tightened its internal auditing. This self-regulation and discipline allowed the party to keep an eye on its elected officials. The image the party tries to portray of itself is that of a non-corrupt organisation which, unlike the other parties, has resisted the temptations of power because of its strong moral values stemming from its religious grounding. Combined with its Islamic identity, the PJD attracted a portion of conservative segments of society who wanted to vote for a 'clean' party[62] and people of *maakoul* (trustworthiness).

The formation of cross-ideological alliances

Beyond ideological calculations, the PJD also understood that it was to its advantage to maintain strong alliances with other secular parties to avoid isolation and to achieve common objectives.[63] This is because the PJD understands that being in government in Morocco requires coalition partners and does not mean yielding sole power. In June 2016, for instance, a well-known PJD minister told this author that if the party were to gain the absolute majority of seats in the 2016 election, it would still include other parties in a coalition government because it would teach them 'how to control the lust of power and to lift doubts about Islamists' putschist mindset'.[64] This seems to be a strategic decision made by the PJD leadership that goes beyond electoral calculations. Indeed, building alliances with secular parties seems to serve the aim of achieving three objectives: (1) maintaining the PJD's position in government, (2) isolating its main rival, the PAM (and hence the Palace) and (3) sending positive signals to the regime and foreign observers about the PJD's pragmatism and inclusiveness.

The PJD's approach in dealing with secular parties was to avoid ideological quarrels and instead work to build a common language about fighting *al-tahakum* and pushing through political and socio-economic reforms. Hence, in its formation of both the 2012 and the 2017 governments, the PJD has voiced objections to secular parties based not on their ideology, but rather on political considerations. One anecdote is that the PJD complained that the secular parties, such as the PM, USFP, CU and RNI, wanted to enter the government coalition in 2016 at any price. The move was seen by observers as an attempt not only to isolate the PJD within parliament but also to dilute its presence in the government itself by thus forging a broad-based coalition government.[65]

The PJD has also worked to strengthen its alliance with its key secular allies, the PPS and IP. In April 2016, the PJD signed a strategic alliance with the PPS. The alliance implied that both parties would remain in government or go into opposition together.[66] In reality, this move was just symbolic because the PPS needed the PJD more than the other way around, considering the PPS' weakness (twelve seats in the 2011 parliament, half of which lost in 2016). In addition to this, the PJD succeeded, relatively speaking, in isolating its main opponent, the PAM. Between mid-2013 and the end of 2015, the IP was a strong ally of the PAM, before re-allying itself with the PJD (even if, in the end it did not join the government coalition).

The party machine and PR

One of the main factors that might explain the PJD's resilience in government is its ability to maintain a functional party machine and an effective communication strategy. In the 2015 regional and local elections, the PJD swept up almost all large and medium cities,[67] allowing local PJD leaders to deliver services to citizens and maintain constant contact with their constituencies. At the same time, the PJD showed little appetite for accepting key state positions at the national level. These are high-level positions in the bureaucracy that constitute the backbone of the state. Before 2011, the king appointed most of these positions and this was a tool of patronage that the regime used to strengthen the loyalty of incumbent elites. The new constitution of 2011, however, transferred this prerogative to the prime minister, who is now entitled to propose candidates for high-level state positions who are nominated by the king only symbolically. During its first term in government, the PJD avoided proposing its own members to key administrative positions so as not to clash with the Palace, which still maintains *de facto* control of the state administrative machine. This allowed the party to keep its national leadership focused on preserving the party machine and reinforcing its constituencies at the local level without being immersed in the everyday management of the administration.

Moreover, once in government, the PJD has maintained a successful media strategy. Thanks to its presence in different conventional and non-conventional media outlets, the ruling Islamists outperformed other parties on this front. Benkirane's monthly meetings in parliament became popular because they were broadcast live on national television and garnered a wider audience than other politicians in the country. The PJD's website attracts hundreds of thousands of viewers every month and outperforms those of all other parties.[68] The party's presence on social media, meanwhile, is also noticeable. The PJD youth section is active on social media and specifically on Facebook, labelled by its opponents as Kataib PJD (PJD's Facebook Brigades). The PJD's Facebook activists have played a key role in defending their party's achievements in government, while harshly attacking and seeking to discredit the party's opponents. Their criticism was so effective and extensive that it pushed Aziz Akhannouch – the Minister of Agriculture and head of the RNI, a party ruling in coalition with the PJD – to express his concern about the role of PJD youth activists in derailing policy implemented in his ministry.[69]

The PJD's media strategy has allowed it to reach out to the public and widen its influence in society. Social media has also provided a space for direct communication with citizens without passing through state-sponsored or conventional media, which were critical of the PJD. Most importantly, the PJD has used the media to defend itself when it felt that it was under pressure from the *Makhzen*.

Conclusion

As demonstrated above, the PJD was able to survive in government largely due to its pragmatic instinct, which allowed it to transform the 2011 crisis into an opportunity. In a tumultuous political environment, the PJD not only managed to keep its ranks unified and avoid internal schism, but also benefited from a weakened and fragmented political sphere. The Palace's approach of relying on technocrats and its creation of the PAM has led to an unintentional weakening of the traditional parties, such as the USFP. The regime's strategy of countering the Islamists through the PAM backfired after the 2011 protests. The PJD seems to be the main beneficiary of the 'Moroccan Spring', even if it did not participate in the protests. The PJD went through a strategic adaptation and has opted for pragmatic positions rather than ideologically driven ones. Accordingly, the PJD has succeeded in broadening its alliances with other secular parties, keeping in check its main rival (the PAM) and seizing the opportunity of being in office to strengthen the party machine.

This said, the 2017 dismissal of Benkirane and the path charted by the new PJD prime minister will, of course, affect the party. Indeed, thus far the party's achievements have been intimately linked to the charismatic leadership of Benkirane, who enjoys considerable popularity within the party and beyond. Following its 2017 national conference, which resulted in a further demotion of Benkirane with his replacement as party leader, it is likely, however, that the PJD will experience a considerable weakening of its party machine as well as a loss of popular support in future elections.[70]

Beside this internal challenge, the PJD will also face another challenge coming from the Palace. The relation between the two continues to fluctuate between cooperation and non-cooperation. This will probably endure in the near future as the conflict of interests grows. It seems likely that the Palace does not aim to wage an open war against the PJD, but its long-term strategy is to curtail the PJD by diluting its influence in government while preparing the soil for the resurgence of loyal parties such as the PAM and the RNI at the next election. Whether the Palace will eventually succeed with this strategy will be largely down to the ability of the PJD to remain internally cohesive, effective in government and able to retain the loyalty of its electoral support base.

Notes

1. Anon. (2016), 'Morocco's king names PJD chief as new prime minister -party official', Reuters, 11 October, <www.reuters.com/article/us-morocco-election-idUSKCN12A22U> (last accessed 2 February 2017).

2. Several authors have focused on how political participation leads to Islamist moderation. See e.g. Jillian Schwedler (2006), *Faith in Moderation: Islamist Parties in Jordan and Yemen*. Cambridge: Cambridge University Press; Asef Bayat (2007), *Making Islam Democratic: Social Movements and the Post-Islamist*. California: Stanford University Press. Kirdiş Esen (2015), 'Between movement and party: Islamic movements in Morocco and the decision to enter party politics', *Politics, Religion & Ideology*, 16:1, pp. 65–86; Francesco Cavatorta and Fabio Merone (2013), 'Moderation through exclusion? The journey of the Tunisian Ennahda from Fundamentalist to Conservative Party', *Democratization*, 20:5, pp. 857–75.

3. Spiegel Avi (2015), 'Succeeding by surviving: examining the durability of political Islam in Morocco', Brookings Institution, p. 2.

4. Maati Monjib (2016), 'Record gains for Morocco's Islamist party', *Sada Journal, Carnegie Endowment for International Peace*, 27 October, <http://carnegieendowment.org/sada/64968> (last accessed 2 February 2017).

5. Mohamed El Hachimi (2015), 'Democratisation as a learning process: the case of Morocco', *Journal of North African Studies*, 20:5, p. 7.

6. Mohamed Daadaoui (2016), 'In Morocco's election last week, the major Islamist party won again: here's what that means', *Washington Post*, 13 October, <www.washingtonpost.com/news/monkey-cage/wp/2016/10/13/what-moroccos-election-results-tell-us-about-islamist-parties/?utm_term=.0ca6f2089fce> (last accessed 2 February 2017).

7. For instance, in 2010 the Moroccan authorities imprisoned a senior PJD figure for alleged corruption offences in a series of measures aimed at curtailing the electoral potency of the PJD. Surprisingly, he was released on 19 February 2011, one day before the protests planned for 20 February 2011 took place, and was even nominated for a high position in the newly established National Economic and Social Council in a move that was intended to absorb the PJD's wrath and to neutralise it. Interview with a PJD leader, February 2012, Rabat.

8. The 20th February Movement was launched in the aftermath of the popular upheavals that swept the Arab world and had led to the toppling of two dictators in Tunisia and Egypt. It constituted the largest mass demonstrations during the reign of Mohamed VI, mobilising hundreds of thousands of citizens across the country. Unlike elsewhere, during the protests the 20th February Movement did not call for the abolition of the monarchy but instead demanded far-reaching political reforms that would transform the country into a truly constitutional monarchy. For more details see e.g. Adria Lawrence (2016), 'The mixed record of Morocco's February 20 protest movement', *Washington*

Post, 20 February, <www.washingtonpost.com/news/monkey-cage/wp/2016/02/20/the-mixed-record-of-moroccos-february-20-protest-movement/?utm_term=.e384773f6ac3< (last accessed 7 April 2017).

9. Haim Malka (2015), 'Power and authority in Morocco', *Adelphi Series*, 55:452, p. 60.
10. Anon. (2011), 'Morocco announces constitutional reform plan', *The Guardian*, 9 March, <www.theguardian.com/world/2011/mar/09/morocco-constitutional-reform-king> (last accessed 2 February 2017).
11. Anon. (2011), '2011 Moroccan Constitution, Article 104', *Bulletin Officiel*, No. 5964, 30 July, <www.maroc.ma/en/system/files/documents_page/bo_5964bis_fr_3.pdf> (last accessed 2 February 2017).
12. Raphaël Lefèvre (2013), 'Balancing act: Islamism and the monarchy in Morocco', *Journal of North African Studies*, 18:4, p. 626.
13. Anon. (2012), 'Observation of the parliamentary elections in Morocco, 25 November 2011', Council of Europe, 23 January, <http://aceproject.org/ero-en/regions/africa/MA/morocco-final-report-legislative-elections-of-25/view> (last accessed 2 February 2017); Anon. (2011), 'Final report on the 2011 Moroccan parliamentary elections', National Democratic Institute, <www.ndi.org/sites/default/files/Morocco-Final-Election-Report-061812-ENG.pdf> (last accessed 2 February 2017).
14. Matt Buehler (2013) 'The threat to "un-moderate": Moroccan Islamists and the Arab Spring', *Middle East Law and Governance*, 5:3, p. 5.
15. Anon. (2011), 'Interview exclusive avec Mustapha Ramid du PJD: "Je continuerai à soutenir le mouvement du 20 février"', <www.yabiladi.com/articles/details/4668/interview-exclusive-avec-mustapha-ramid.html> (last accessed 2 February 2017); Anon. (2011), 'Ramid wal choubani yastakilan min amanate al-adala wal tanmia [Ramid and Choubani resign from PJD political bureau]', *Hespress*, 19 February, <www.hespress.com/politique/28231.html> (last accessed 2 February 2017).
16. Marina Ottaway (2012), 'Morocco: can the third way succeed?' *Carnegie Endowment for International Peace*, 31 July, <http://carnegieendowment.org/2012/07/31/morocco-can-third-way-succeed-pub-48968> (last accessed 2 February 2017).
17. Anon. (2011), 'al adala wal tanmia wal islah wal tawhid yotlikan mubadara lil islah al-dimoucrati [the PJD and MUR launch an initiative for democratic reform]', *Assabah*, 21 March, <www.maghress.com/assabah/7143> (last accessed 2 February 2017).
18. Mohammed Masbah (2014), 'Morocco's Slow motion reform process: the tug of war between the Palace and the Justice and Development Party', *SWP Comments*, January.
19. Anon. (2011), 'Islamiyun youtlikoun nidaa al-islah al-dimoucrati [Islamists launch the call for democratic reform]', *Hespress*, 18 March, <www.hespress.com/politique/29231.html> (last accessed 2 February 2017).
20. Interview with Mustafa Khalfi, former Minister of Communication (PJD), 20 May 2011, Rabat.
21. Interview with a PJD leader, 21 May 2011, Rabat.
22. Lise Storm (2014), *Party Politics and the Prospects for Democracy in North Africa*. Boulder: Lynne Rienner Publishers.
23. Eva Wegner (2011), *Islamist Opposition in Authoritarian Regimes: The Party of Justice and Development in Morocco*. Syracuse: Syracuse University Press, p. 3.
24. Marina Ottaway and Hamzawy Amr (2007), 'Fighting on two fronts: secular parties in the Arab World', *Carnegie Papers, Middle East Program*, May, p. 10.
25. Maâti Monjib (2011) 'The "democratization" process in Morocco: progress, obstacles, and the impact of the Islamist-Secularist divide', Brookings Institution, August.

26. Stitou Imad (2016), 'Why the left flopped in Morocco's elections', *Sada Journal, Carnegie Endowment*, 22 November, <http://carnegieendowment.org/sada/?fa=66231> (last accessed 12 May 2017).

27. Samir Ben-Layashi (2007), 'Morocco's 2007 elections: a social reading', *Middle East Review of International Affairs*, 11:4, p. 72.

28. Yasmina Abouzzohour, (2017), 'The Persistent Rural Failure of Morocco's Justice and Development Party', *Project on Middle East Political Science*, September, p. 11.

29. Michael J. Willis (2006), 'Containing radicalism through the political process in North Africa', *Mediterranean Politics*, 11:2, p. 144.

30. Driss Maghraoui and Zerhouni Saloua (2014), 'Searching for political normalization: the party of Justice and Development in Morocco', in Quinn Mecham and Julie Chernov Hwang (eds), *Islamist Parties and Political Normalization in the Muslim World*. Philadelphia: University of Pennsylvania Press, p. 117.

31. I owe this idea to Shai Feldman, Director of the Crown Center for Middle East Studies, at the Brandeis University.

32. For example Hizb al-Badil al-Hadari (Party of the Civilizational Alternative) participated in the 2007 elections and obtained merely 16,000, or 0.3 per cent, of the votes and no seats.

33. Ilhem Rachidi (2003), 'Shaken by attacks, Morocco cracks down on militants: tough sentences given to 43 men convicted of May bombings in Casablanca', *Christian Science Monitor*, 27 August, p. 10, <www.csmonitor.com/2003/0827/p10s01-wome.html> (last accessed 2 February 2017).

34. Anon. (2010), 'Moroccan government, Islamist leader in verbal war over Casablanca bombings', *BBC Monitoring Middle East*, 1 October, *ProQuest*. Web (last accessed 2 February, 2017).

35. For instance, the regime vetoed the selection of Mustafa Ramid as head of the PJD's parliamentary block because he was an outspoken leader of the PJD, dismissed some PJD mayors from their positions and, as mentioned earlier, imprisoned one of its leaders in 2010.

36. Fahd Iraqi (2016), 'Fouad Ali El Himma: l'homme-orchestre de Mohammed VI', *Jeune Afrique*, 21 June, <www.jeuneafrique.com/mag/333963/politique/fouad-ali-el-himma-lhomme-orchestre/> (last accessed 2 February 2017).

37. Amel Boubekeur (2009), 'Morocco: the emergence of a new Palace Party', *Carnegie Middle East Centre*, 28 July, <http://carnegie-mec.org/2009/07/28/morocco-emergence-of-new-palace-party-pub-23426> (last accessed 2 February 2017).

38. Ferdinand Eibl (2012), 'The Party of Authenticity and Modernity (PAM): trajectory of a political *deus ex machina*', *Journal of North African Studies*, 17:1, p. 46.

39. For example, the new Minister of Interior Abdelouafi Leftite is not only a loyal servant of the palace, but also an ardent foe of the PJD.

40. Anon. (2017), 'Gouvernement El Othmani: ce qu'il faut retenir du classement des ministères "Budgétivores"', *leseco.ma*, 10 April, <http://leseco.ma/elothmani/56328-gouvernement-el-othmani-ce-qu-il-faut-retenir-du-classement-des-ministeres-budgetivores.html> (last accessed 17 April 2017).

41. Michael J. Willis (2008), 'Islamism, democratization and disillusionment: Morocco's legislative elections of 2007', *St Antony's College, Oxford Research Paper*, No. 1.

42. Ellinor Zeino-Mahmalat (2014), 'Constitutional reform and constitutional reality in Morocco: between monarchical stability and democratic renewal', *KAS International Reports*.

43. Anon. (2016), 'Moroccan parliamentary elections: political parties jockey for power', *Arab Center for Research and Policy Studies.*

44. Saloua Zerhouni (2014), '"Smartness" without vision: the Moroccan regime in the face of acquiescent elites and weak social mobilization', *SWP Comments*, p. 3.

45. Anouar Boukhars (2014), 'Morocco's Islamists: bucking the trend?' *FRIDE, Policy Brief*, No. 182, June, p. 4.

46. Interview of Abdelilah Benkirane with Ahmed Mansour on Al-Jazeera, <www.youtube.com/watch?v=kHSEZWD69uM> (last accessed 2 February 2017).

47. Anon. (2016), 'L'étonnante interview de Abdelilah Benkirane (video)', *HuffPost Maroc*, 4 July, <www.huffpostmaghreb.com/2016/07/04/benkirane-_n_10803372.html> (last accessed 2 February 2017).

48. Buehler, 'The threat to "un-moderate".

49. Anon. (2011), 'Benkirane Yuhadidu bi chan al-harb ala machrou' al-dustour [Benkirane threatens to wage war on the new constitution]', *Hespress*, 12 June, <www.hespress.com/videos/32839.html> (last accessed 2 February 2017).

50. Anon. (2016), 'Maroc: Mohammed VI mécontent à l'encontre d'Abdelilah Benkirane', *Jeune Afrique*, 20 July, <www.jeuneafrique.com/mag/342177/politique/maroc-mohammed-vi-mecontent-a-lencontre-dabdelilah-benkirane/> (last accessed 2 February 2017).

51. Sanae El Mellouki (2015), 'The infusion of Islam into pluralistic politics: the need to explore the Islamist identity beyond ideological boundaries: the case of the Moroccan Party of Justice and Development', *Discourse & Society*, 26:6, p. 663.

52. Hassan Rachik (2014), 'Where Islamists distinguish politics from preaching', *OASIS*, February, p. 43.

53. Vish Sakthivel (2016) 'Justice and Development Party', *Oxford Islamic Studies Online*, <www.oxfordislamicstudies.com/article/opr/t343/e0181> (last accessed 10 February 2016).

54. Ashraf Habib El Sherif (2012), 'Institutional and ideological reconstruction of the Justice and Development Party (PJD): the question of democratic Islamism in Morocco', *Middle East Journal*, 66:4, pp. 660–82.

55. Interview with Amer Larayedh, 1 March 2015, Tunis.

56. Piser Karina (2016), 'Why Ennahda, Tunisia's Islamist Party, shed its "political Islam" label', *World Politics Review*, 20 May, <www.worldpoliticsreview.com/trend-lines/18850/why-ennahda-tunisia-s-islamist-party-shed-its-political-islam-label> (last accessed 2 February 2017).

57. Suveyda Karakaya and Yildirim A. Kadir (2013), 'Islamist moderation in perspective: comparative analysis of the moderation of Islamist and Western Communist parties', *Democratization*, 20:7, p. 1323.

58. Marvine Howe (2005), *Morocco: The Islamist Awakening and Other Challenges*. New York: Oxford University Press, p. 196.

59. Anon. (2016), 'al barnamaj al-intikhabi li hizb al-adala wal tanmia [Electoral programme of the Party of Justice and Development]' pjd.ma, 7 October, p. 9 (in Arabic), <http://pjd.ma/%D8%A7%D9%84%D8%A7%D8%AE%D8%A8%D8%A7%D8%B1/%D9%87%D8%B0%D8%A7-%D9%87%D9%88-%D8%A7%D9%84%D8%A8%D8%B1%D9%8 6%D8%A7%D9%85%D8%AC-%D8%A7%D9%84%D8%A7%D9%86%D8%AA%D8% AE%D8%A7%D8%A8%D9%8A-%D9%84%D8%AD%D8%B2%D8%A8-%D8%A7%D 9%84%D8%B9%D8%AF%D8%A7%D9%84%D8%A9-%D9%88%D8%A7%D9%84%D 8%AA%D9%86%D9%85%D9%8A%D8%A9> (last accessed 2 February 2017).

60. Aida Alami (2017), 'Morocco said to ban sale of burqas, citing security concerns', *New York Times*, 11 January, <www.nytimes.com/2017/01/11/world/africa/morocco-ban-burqa-niqab.html?_r=0> (last accessed 3 February 2017).
61. Interview with a PJD Executive Bureau member, 14 January 2017, Rabat.
62. Angel M. Rabasa, Cheryl Benard, Peter Chalk, C. Christine Fair, Theodore Karasik, Rollie Lal, Ian Lesser and David Thaler (2004), *The Muslim World After 9/11*. Santa Monica, CA RAND Corporation, p. 165.
63. For more details on cross-ideological alliance formation between Islamists and secularists in the Arab world see Janine A. Clark (2006), 'The conditions of Islamist Moderation: unpacking cross-ideological cooperation in Jordan', *International Journal of Middle East Studies*, 38:4, pp. 539–60; Eva Wegner and Miquel Pellicer (2011), 'Left–Islamist opposition cooperation in Morocco', *British Journal of Middle Eastern Studies*, 38:3, pp. 303–22.
64. Interview with prominent PJD leader, 30 June 2016, Rabat.
65. Maati Monjib (2017), 'Lopsided struggle for power in Morocco', *Sada Journal, Carnegie Endowment for International Peace*, 25 January, <http://carnegieendowment.org/sada/67795?lang=en> (last accessed 2 February 2017).
66. Reda Zaireg (2016), 'Le PJD et le PPS renouvellent leur alliance', *HuffPost Maroc*, 18 April, <www.huffpostmaghreb.com/2016/04/18/pjd-pps-alliance_n_9718506.html> (last accessed 2 February 2017).
67. Anon. (2015), 'Au Maroc, les islamistes du PJD progressent dans les grandes villes', *Le Monde*, 7 September, <www.lemonde.fr/international/article/2015/09/07/au-maroc-les-islamistes-du-pjd-progressent-dans-les-grandes-villes_4747718_3210.html> (last accessed 2 February 2017).
68. Anon. (2013), 'Politique: Sur la toile, le PJD écrase tous ses concurrents', medias24.com, 18 June, <www.medias24.com/pdf2006-Le-PJD-domine-largement-la-toile.html> (Last accessed, 18, April 2017).
69. Anon. (2015), 'Maroc: Benkirane-Akhannouch, chambre à part', JeuneAfrique.com, 15 December, <www.jeuneafrique.com/mag/284385/politique/maroc-benkirane-akhan-nouch-chambre-a-part/> (last accessed 2 February 2017).
70. Anon. (2017), 'Saad Eddine El Othmani elected new leader of the PJD', *Morocco World News*, 10 December, <www.moroccoworldnews.com/2017/12/236010/el-othmani-new-leader-pjd/> (last accessed 29 January 2018).

Chapter 9

Does participation lead to moderation? Understanding changes in the Egyptian Islamist parties post-Arab Spring

Barbara Zollner

Is it still important to consider the issue of participation and moderation in post-Spring Egypt? The question of inclusion and moderation was at the heart of debates about the prospect of the 'taming' of Islamist movements and political parties throughout the early 2000s, that is at a time when democratisation seemed to be a possibility, albeit a distant one. In the post-Spring era, which saw the return of an authoritarian regime under President Abdel Fattah al-Sisi, there seems to be little taste for discussing whether there is still scope for the inclusion of Islamists in the political system.

Yet there is good reason to stipulate an ongoing relevance of this topic, particularly when studying Egypt's Islamist parties in the post-Spring setting. First, the change of context, that is from a semi-authoritarian multi-party system under erstwhile president Hosni Mubarak (r.1981–2011) to a democratising system during the Arab uprisings and finally to a much more politically restrictive framework under al-Sisi, allows us to investigate the trajectories of Islamist parties and, in reference to pre-Spring analyses, to appraise their commitment to democratic values.[1] A second reason is related to the fact that there are a range of Islamist parties in post-Spring and post-coup Egyptian politics. Aside from al-Ikhwan al-Muslimun (Muslim Brotherhood, MB) and its subsidiary Hizb al-Hurriyya wa al-'Adala (Freedom and Justice Party, FJP), which were banned following the military coup of 2013, there exists a wide spectrum of religious-based parties, which is, as Marc Lynch rightly remarked, 'uncharted'.[2] When mapping these, one encounters a paradox. Salafi parties, which are ultra-conservative in their religious interpretations and are regarded as fundamentally incompatible with a democratic stance, participated in the first post-coup parliamentary elections of 2015. Many of the so-called moderate Islamist parties, on the other hand, boycotted these elections, thus deliberately excluding themselves from the formal political contest. This brings us to a third reason for why it remains important to engage with the 'participation-moderation' debate. Returning to previous assessments allows us to debate whether the conceptual framework continues to hold traction.[3] Indeed, the post-Spring constellation of Islamist parties provides us with material to reflect on the issue of strategic versus ideological moderation and that of sequencing which, as Jillian Schwedler points out, constitute key aspects of the moderation debate.[4]

The aim of this chapter is to critically examine the 'participation-moderation' thesis and, moreover, to engage in an original analysis of the political trajectories of Islamist parties in post-Spring Egypt. Focusing on those Islamist parties that demonstrated considerable influence in the period of democratic transition, in particular the 2011–12 parliamentary elections as well as the post-coup parliamentary elections of 2015, we can see that Salafi parties chose to participate for strategic reasons, while reformist Islamist parties opted for non-participation. While the 'participation-moderation' thesis remains a good starting point for analysing Islamist movements, this chapter reveals that the model has conceptual limitations with regards to predicting ideological reform.

Pluralisation of Islamist parties in post-Spring Egypt

Egypt saw a sharp increase in new political parties in the post-Spring era. About eighty new parties received their official licence in 2011, with slightly fewer new registrations of Islamist parties compared to those on the secular side.[5] Overall, the spectrum of Islamist parties experienced a pluralisation, when more than thirty were registered in the course of 2011, of whom about twenty took part in the contest for seats in the parliamentary elections of the same year. These included not only the MB-linked FJP, but also so-called reformist Islamist parties that are, for the most part, Brotherhood offshoots such as Hizb Misr al-Qawiyya (Strong Egypt Party/SEP or simply Strong Egypt), Hizb al-Tayyar al-Misri (Egyptian Current Party, ECP) and Hizb al-Wasat (Centre Party/ CP, or simply al-Wasat). Furthermore, the post-Spring transition also saw the first-time formation of Salafi parties, among them the Alexandria/Delta based Hizb al-Nour (Party of Light/PL, or simply al-Nour) and Hizb al-Bina' wa al-Tanmiyya (Building and Development Party, BDP), which represents the official outlet of al-Jama'a al-Islamiyya (Islamic Group, also known simply as IG), as well as subsequent offshoots of these parties, notably Hizb al-Asala (Authenticity Party/AP, also simply al-Asala) and Hizb al-Watan (Homeland Party/HP, also simply al-Watan). Beyond these, Table 9.1 illustrates that a large number of Islamist parties appeared on the formal political scene post-2011. Only a few of them gained seats, but the mere fact that a range of Islamist

Table 9.1 Islamist parties in the post-Spring era

Party name	Legalised/ banned	Theology-based orientation	Political spectrum[6]
Hizb al-ʿAdala al-Ijtimaʿiyya (Social Justice Party)	1993	Socialist	Left
Hizb al-ʿAmal al-Islami al-Misri (Egyptian Islamic Labour Party)	2011	Reformist with socialist tendencies	Left
Hizb al-ʿAmal al-Jadid (New Labour Party)	2011	Reformist with socialist tendencies	Left
Hizb al-Asala (Authenticity Party)	2011	Salafi	Centre-right
Hizb al-Binaʾ wa al-Tanmiyya (Building and Development Party)	2011	Salafi (GI)	Right
Hizb al-Fadila (Virtue Party)	2011	Salafi	Right
Hizb al-Hurriyya wa al-ʿAdala (Freedom and Justice Party)	2011; banned 2013	MB; orthodox tendencies among leadership	Centre-right
Hizb al-Islah al-Misri (Egyptian Reform Party)	not	Orthodox with reformist tendencies	Ultra-right
Hizb al-Islah wa al-Nahda (Reform and Renaissance Party)	2011	Reformist tendencies; remains orthodox on key issues	Centre-left
Hizb al-Islah wa al- al-Tawʿiyya (Reform and Awakening Party)	2011	Socialist	Ultra-left
Al-Hizb al-Islami (Islamic Party)	not	Salafi	Ultra-right
Hizb al-Jihad al-Dimuqrati (Democratic Jihad Party)	2012	Salafi	Centre-right
Hizb Misr al-Fatah (Young Egypt Party)	2011	Socialist	Left
Hizb Misr al-Mustaqbal (Egypt's Future Party)	2011	Reformist with revolutionary tendencies	Left
Hizb al-Muhafidhin (Conservative Party)	2011	Orthodox	Right
Hizb al-Nahda (Renaissance Party)	2011; merged with Hizb al-Wasat in 2013	Reformist with orthodox tendencies	Right
Hizb al-Nasr (Victory Party)	2011	Sufi	
Hizb al-Nour (Light Party)	2011	Salafi (al-Daʿwa al-Salafiyya)	Ultra-right
Hizb al-Raya (Flag Party)	2013	Salafi	Ultra-right
Hizb al-Riyada (Pioneer Party)	2011	Reformist tendencies; remains orthodox on key issues	Centre-left
Hizb al-Shaʿab (People Party)	not		Right
Hizb al-Tahrir al-Misri	2011	Sufi (al-ʿAzamiyya)	
Hizb al-Takaful (Solidarity Party)	2011		Right
Hizb al-Tawhid al-ʿArabi (Arab Unification Party)	2011	Socialist leanings with orthodox tendencies	Left
Hizb al-Umma (Umma Party)	1983	Socialist	Left
Hizb al-Wasat (al-Wasat Party)	2011	Reformist with orthodox tendencies	Centre-left
Hizb al-Watan (Homeland Party)	2012 (offshoot from Hizb an-Nour)	Salafi	Right
Hizb Misr al-Qawiyya (Strong Egypt Party)	2012	Reformist	Centre-left
Hizb Misr al-Thawra	2011	Revolutionary	Ultra-left
Hizb Nahdat Misr (Egypt Renaissance Party)	2011	Reformist with orthodox tendencies	Centre-right
Hizb Shabab Misr (Youth for Egypt)	2005	Reformist with strong orthodox tendencies	Centre-right
Hizb Sout al-Hurriyya (Voice of Egypt)	2011	Sufism	
Hizb al-Tayyar al-Misri (Egyptian Current Party)	2011; merged with Hizb Misr al-Qawiyya in 2014	Reformist	Centre-left

parties aimed for inclusion in the political process shows a shift in their strategic thinking and behaviour insofar as participation in formal processes became a viable option for them, which allowed them to bring forward their political agenda.

Abdel Fattah al-Sisi's ascendance to power in 2013 had a considerable impact on the Egyptian party landscape. Because of changes to electoral laws, the authoritarian shift under al-Sisi has reduced the influence of parties, both locally and nationally.[7] Beyond this, Islamist parties underwent considerable contraction in terms of their presence in the political system. Most obviously, the FJP and its mother organisation the MB were banned in the course of 2013–14. This left a vacuum in Islamist presence, which was only partially filled by Salafi and other reformist parties. In fact, only al-Nour managed to secure seats in the 2015 parliamentary elections, although its presence decreased.[8] Also, a number of Islamist parties folded, partly because of the pressures of regime change and partly because they could mobilise only limited support. Table 9.1 indicates the disappearance of these parties, with notable changes to the reformist field. Not unexpectedly, smaller Islamist parties were pushed to consolidate, merging with parties that held similar political views and often competed for the same constituency. Among them were the ECP, which joined Strong Egypt, and al-Nahda Party, which joined al-Wasat. Following this consolidation, two reformist parties remain meaningful players in the field of Islamist actors: Strong Egypt and al-Wasat. On the other end of the spectrum, meanwhile, we can detect some changes due to intra-organisational tensions which have led to offshoots forming. The case of al-Nour is of note here, whereby Emad Abd al-Ghaffour, one of the founders of the party, moved on to establish al-Watan in late 2012.[9] Yet the increase in numbers due to splits and offshoots is rather marginal, and it is likely that small and medium-sized parties will either disappear or, once again, merge with larger parties. Overall, the post-Spring era presents us with a varied spectrum that will, despite al-Sisi's seemingly anti-Islamist policies, continue to influence Egyptian politics in the years to come.

Ideological moderation of Islamist parties?

The participation of Islamist parties in post-2011 politics demonstrates that it is necessary to distinguish between *strategic* and *ideological* moderation.[10] When applying this differentiation, we can observe three trajectories. First, the case of the FJP shows that participation can have a negative effect on intra-organisational reform. Second, the political decisions and subsequent actions of reformist Islamist parties, such as for instance al-Wasat and Strong

Egypt, are evidence that moderation – particularly ideological and value-based moderation – can lead to non-participation. Finally, whilst remaining dedicated to the electoral process, the trajectory of Salafi parties, among them al-Nour and the BDP, demonstrates that there is evidence of strategic moderation, but little indication of substantial, micro-level ideological reform.

The post-Spring development of the FJP is an example of strategic moderation, which, paradoxically, came at the expense of ideological moderation. Being largely dependent on the directives of the MB leadership, the case of the FJP shows that the opportunities afforded by formal political participation in the post-Mubarak era undercut a rising reformist tendency within the organisation and thus played into the hands of an 'old guard' that had continued to dominate the group's Guidance Council.[11]

What makes the case of the MB confusing is the fact that socio-religiously orthodox and politically conservative members who, for decades, dominated the MB's leading Maktab al-Irshad (Guidance Council), did not show much interest in political participation throughout the Mubarak period, rather focusing on changing Egyptian society by acceding to conservative socio-religious norms. The MB's politics of opposition to the regime at the time was driven by a reformist faction that had gradually built up its strength since the late 1980s.[12] As such, they developed a presence in professional syndicates and, beyond that, attempted to gain seats in parliament either through alliances with other parties, as in the elections of 1984 and 1987, or by running independent candidates, such as in the elections of 1995, 2000, 2005 and 2010.[13]

The formation of al-Wasat in 1996 exposed open rifts between reformists and the MB's conservative leadership. The trigger was an attempt by reformists to formulate a party platform in 1996 with the aim of obtaining legal recognition by state authorities. Not only did the MB leadership see the initiative as a challenge to its authority, but it also rejected ideas in the platform document that suggested equal political rights for women and for minorities. These ideational differences led to an intra-organisational crisis that resulted in the departure of several members, most notably Abu al-Ala al-Madi. He continued to run al-Wasat as an alternative to the MB, albeit gaining legal recognition only in 2011.

In August 2007 reformists and the Guidance Council, this time under the leadership of Mahdi Akif, once again clashed in another party platform debate. At the centre of this crisis was again the formulation of the goals of a future political party, but also the issue of the political rights of non-Muslims and the equal status of women.[14] The tension between reformists and conservatives culminated in the controversy over the succession of Akif. With the election of Mohamed Badi'a, the Guidance Council took a clear stance against Mohamed Habib, the Deputy Murshid, who was sympathetic to reformists.

These events show that, although attempts at reform gained so much ground that they reached the echelons of the MB's executive, reformists failed substantially to change the organisation. It is for this reason that a number of experts who reviewed the level of the MB's ideological moderation, among them Carrie Wickham and Eric Trager, critically remarked that, despite much intra-organisational debate, conservative political-religious attitudes were not sufficiently re-addressed.[15]

The final round of this intra-organisational battle played out in the post-Spring period. It is then that the religiously, socially and politically conservative leadership prepared to participate in formal political processes. The Guidance Council regarded the creation of a political party as a strategic opportunity to influence the transition process. Members of the reformist faction such as Abd al-Mun'im Abu al-Futuh, Islam Lutfi and Mohamed Habib, meanwhile, rejected the step, taking the position that any decisions over the creation of a party, or indeed regarding the status of the MB as a social movement or political foundation, needed to be debated collectively in the Shura Council as the MB's central democratic organ.[16] The Guidance Council fended off this challenge by pressing forward with the establishment of the FJP which thus became a political mouthpiece of the conservative MB leadership. Moreover, by placing an emphasis on organisational cohesion, leading members of the reformist tendency were forced to leave after a short and intense battle over the organisation's direction, while others, among them Issam al-Arayan and Sa'ad Katatny, chose to conform (and were then rewarded with leadership roles in the MB and FJP).[17]

Islam Lutfi, Mohamed al-Qassas, Ahmad Abd al-Gawad, Hani Mahmud, Mohamed Affan, Ibrahim Za'afrani and Mohamed Habib left the MB. A similar fate befell Abu al-Futuh, who pointed out that his expulsion in April 2011, following his announcement that he intended to run as a candidate in the presidential elections of 2012, was not due to his having broken with MB directives at the time but was rather due to his persistent differences with the group's leadership.[18] This deep rift also affected the MB, and by extension, the FJP along generational lines, not least because many young MB activists were ideationally closer to reformist circles. When the conservative leadership attempted to conscript them into the FJP, it triggered a dispute about the right of MB members to support political parties other than the FJP or, as a young female MB activist emphasised, the right not to support any party.[19] The Guidance Council enforced its authority, which led to the departure of a number of MB youth and student leaders. By the end of 2011, there was little intra-organisational contestation to the Guidance Council, which continued to imprint its ideological understandings upon the FJP.

The strategic choice to participate in democratic processes gave the MB the opportunity to pursue a religious vision in negotiations about the constitution of the state and its formal institutions. According to the official MB position, its idea of the state was both civic and Islamic.[20] This relates to the position that legal interpretation and legislative powers of a parliament are allowed in areas where the Qur'an is not explicit or in areas that are not considered part of the Sunni legal consensus. In these terms, the MB ideology shows a degree of temperance, one that allows a state to be defined as Islamic while being at the same time civic. Still, the MB and its subsidiary, the FJP, have retained an ideological vision that remains religiously orthodox and vested in socially conservative concepts. This is particularly obvious on contested issues such as the equal status of women and equal citizenship rights for non-Muslim minorities.[21] The FJP's political success during 2011–13 was seen by the MB leadership as a public validation of its strategic choices. Being the dominant political force, there was no incentive for ideological moderation. Yet this set party and mother organisation on a course of confrontation with the military on the one hand and with other political parties and movements on the other hand.

If the participation-moderation model suggests a sequential development, whereby political inclusion leads to strategic and eventually to ideological reform, the trajectory of reformist parties disproves it. As seen above, in the case of the reformist faction within the MB, ideological moderation took place before the establishment of its parties. The fact that the founding leaders of today's reformist Islamist parties abandoned the MB umbrella is not purely incidental, but indicates that ideological moderation is the result of intra-organisational disputes rather than the outcome of political participation. This holds true for al-Wasat, for instance, whose founding members, notably al-Madi, were forced to leave the MB in 1996.[22] It is also the case with the ECP, which was set up by former MB Youth Leaders, al-Qassas and Abd al-Gawad in June 2011, or for al-Nahda, which was set up by al-Za'frani and was joined shortly after by Habib.[23] Strong Egypt was established by Abu al-Futuh two years after his expulsion and a year after his unsuccessful candidacy in the 2012 presidential elections.[24] Despite losing against the MB's candidate, Mohamed Morsi, Abu al-Futuh was able to present himself as a significant alternative. Moreover, the fact that reformist parties were set up at a time when the MB/FJP dominated the Islamist spectrum indicates that the concept of sequencing is flawed. Competing against the MB/FJP, these new parties had relatively little prospect of immediate success; hence the choice to set up reformist parties was first and foremost driven by ideological contretemps rather than strategic prospects. This point comes through in an interview with al-Qassas of the ECP in November 2011, when he admitted his party was relatively under-represented in rural areas and hence did not field candidates in all districts.[25] Beyond this, as will be set out below, the most important indication that sequencing is not a reliable facet of the participation-moderation model is the fact that most reformist parties decided to boycott the 2015 parliamentary elections. It demonstrates that ideological moderation can lead to a refusal to participate and consequently a rejection of potential political representation for a legislative period.

Because of their background, the aforementioned reformist parties retain a softened version of the *ikhwani* political frames and even take inspiration from the MB's foundational history. This said, they also distance themselves from the MB to an extent that cannot be explained away as a strategic choice, but involves a more fundamental ideational shift towards moderation. Indeed, overall reformist parties show a propensity towards democratic values that sets them apart from the orthodoxy of the MB. Where they differ, however, is the profundity and diffusion of democratic values in their programmes and, beyond this, their social and political leanings.

Al-Wasat, previously also al-Nahda, are perhaps slightly more traditionalist on social issues and politically more centre-right.[26] In its religious interpretation, al-Wasat is inspired by a religiously reformist current that Raymond Baker has described as 'New Islamist'.[27] Furthermore, Wickham notes, reformists acquired political skills by interacting with other contenders who were in opposition to Mubarak's regime.[28] Although al-Wasat underwent fundamental ideological change, there are nevertheless areas where its tendentiously more orthodox views remain tangible. These are, first and foremost, al-Wasat's view that Shari'ah is the principal source of legislation, but also the orthodox position held by the party that parts of Islamic law are divinely defined (however, it is not clear which areas are fixed). The final controversial point touches on gender equality. Although al-Wasat emphasises women's equality, the party retains conservative views on the role of women in family and society. Considering these issues, Wickham therefore voices concerns about al-Wasat's level of ideological moderation.

Strong Egypt, and previously also the ECP, meanwhile, have made a much clearer step towards fully accepting liberal democratic values. Although Ashraf El Sherif is critical of the party's ideological sophistication, it needs to be recognised that Stong Egypt no longer regards an Islamic state or the implementation of Shari'ah as goals.[29] Hence, in the stricter sense, it is no longer an Islamist party, but a 'Muslim democratic party' with centre-left leanings. To illustrate this, Abu al-Futuh stressed that he stands for the protection of individual rights and recognises full gender equality and freedom of religion as core values.[30] Drawing a comparison with parties that draw on Christian values, such as the Christian Democratic Parties in Europe, he argues that there is no reason why religious values should not be at the heart of political convictions. Similar points were made by al-Qassas who, since the merger of the ECP with Strong Egypt, has acted as its Head of Political Communication. He added that there needs to be a separation of religion and state, yet on a personal level religion does matter in politics.[31]

As mentioned above, Strong Egypt and al-Wasat boycotted the post-coup parliamentary elections of 2015. However, their reactions to the coup show fundamental differences in their political positions. Al-Wasat condemned the events of July 2013 and subsequently joined the Anti-Coup Alliance. Despite its conflicts with the MB, it regarded Morsi's presidency as carrying democratic legitimacy and argued that the 2013 Constitution reflected the ideas of a civic state based on Islamic principles.[32] Strong Egypt, on the other hand, had previously expressed support for the mass movement against Morsi's government and, although it objected to the military's intervention, did not give its support to the Anti-Coup Alliance.[33] This shows that they differed on the question of Morsi's legitimacy and the path to transforming Egypt. Still, they agreed that the military coup was a backward step that opened the door to the renewed authoritarianism under al-Sisi. This led them to call for a boycott of the 2014 presidential elections and subsequently of the 2015 parliamentary elections. Despite leaving the Anti-Coup Alliance in August 2014, al-Wasat's rejection of the regime was expressed in much clearer terms in the run-up to the parliamentary elections, openly criticising arbitrary arrests including that of the party leader al-Madi, human rights violations, and, more broadly, questioning the legitimacy of al-Sisi's rule.[34] Strong Egypt's critique was more cautious, voicing particular concerns about constitutional issues, electoral laws and the return of patrimonial politics without attacking the regime directly.[35] In all, both reformist parties take a clear stance against the return of authoritarian politics, a position that is informed by an appreciation of democratic values. This shows that ideological moderation can lead to the rejection of opportunities provided by formal participation.

Salafi parties, meanwhile, reconfirm that a clear distinction is needed between *strategic* moderation and *ideological* moderation.[36] Their participation in pre- and post-coup parliamentary elections is rooted in a strategic calculus that allows them to voice their ultra-conservative socio-religious views and agenda in a public manner. Yet as Jérôme Drevon convincingly shows, neither al-Nour nor the BDP has revised its ideological premises in a substantial manner.[37]

There are a number of Salafi parties, but al-Nour has been the most successful in recent years. Its main influence is in Alexandria and the Delta region, where the loose network of al-Da'wa al-Salafiyya (Salafi Call) has had some impact.[38]

Saudi–Wahhabi principles inform its ideological outlook, as can be seen in the writings of al-Nour leader Yasser Hussein Burhami.[39] Yet intra-organisational tensions over the direction of the party, particularly on what a Salafi party should stand for, emerged in the course of 2012. This led to the departure of Abd al-Ghaffour, who went on to establish the electorally less successful al-Watan Party, in December of the same year.[40] As for al-Nour, it backed protests against Morsi in 2013; yet the party was reluctant to support al-Sisi after the events of July 2013.[41] Leaving all strategic options open, al-Nour neither supported Morsi's return to power nor did it support the military intervention. Al-Nour deliberately hung back from calling for challenges to the transitional government and, subsequently, to al-Sisi's regime. The party thus evaded major arrests and, despite a legal challenge to its status, was able to survive.[42] In the 2014 constitutional referendum, al-Nour urged voters to support the new legal framework, thus indicating a pragmatic and tactical approach to politics. Its strategic calculation became apparent when al-Nour fielded candidates for the 2015 parliamentary elections.[43] Gaining eleven seats, all of them through independent candidacies in the Delta and Cairo, it became the only Islamist party with seats in the House of Representatives. Yet compared to its previous results in 2011–12, the results were rather poor and thus did not fill the void left by the FJP.

The Salafi stance also finds representation in the BDP and al-Asala. While al-Nour has its roots in the Salafi-Wahhabi trend of the Delta region, the BDP is directly linked to the IG which was particularly dominant in Upper Egypt and in poorer areas of Cairo with a dominant Sa'idi population. As a party, the BDP was established in 2011 on the initiative of the IG leadership.[44] Al-Asala is similar to the BDP and, although the party is not directly linked to the IG, it drew members from its circles. Both parties show similarities with al-Nour in their post-Spring political trajectory. The BDP achieved some modest success in the 2011–12 parliamentary poll, winning thirteen seats, while al-Asala secured three seats.[45] In 2013, the BDP and al-Asala joined the Anti-Coup Alliance but, because of tactical manoeuvres similar to those of al-Nour, avoided major repercussions. Still, the post-coup era left the BDP and al-Asala side-lined. Although both parties withdrew from the Anti-Coup Alliance in 2015, they failed to secure any seats in the 2015 parliamentary elections.

As an organisation, the IG was known for its militancy. It was involved in a number of terrorist activities, including the assassination of Anwar al-Sadat and the 1997 Luxor attack, which claimed eighty-seven lives.[46] Subsequently, the organisation underwent a 'deradicalisation' process.[47] Analysing fundamental ideological positions, Roel Meijer shows that the IG applied a dual strategy: on the one hand it justified the use of militancy, but on the other it undertook to build wider social support among ultra-conservative sections of society.[48] It is the latter aspect that remained the strategic focus of the IG in its four central books published in 2004, which articulate to their supporters a renunciation of violence. Yet Drevon critically remarks that despite the recantation of violence, militancy as a political tactic was never formally rejected.[49] In fact, jihad, even in its violent interpretation, continued to be regarded as a strategic option should the context in question call for such action. Although its party, the BDP, formally engages in political participation, the IG retains this position until today. Hence, there remains a distinct question-mark over the ideological moderation of the BDP, with the party so far remaining a clear example of moderation only at the strategic level.[50]

The political ambivalence of Salafi parties evidences the strategic calculus that binds them to political participation. These parties are far from re-evaluating their ideological positions. Although there is an ongoing intra-organisational debate in all three Salafi cases, this does not amount to ideological moderation. Given that al-Sisi's regime appears to tolerate their political participation and, in fact, appears to regard Salafis as an Islamist alternative to the MB that can be held in check because their ultra-orthodox ideas do not find widespread support, there is little incentive for change as there is little internal or external pressure that could trigger the intra-organisational debates that are key to ideological reform.

Conclusion

Does the political participation of Islamist parties lead to moderation? The case of Egypt's Islamist parties in the post-Spring era seems to challenge the 'participation-moderation' model. It suggests that, by including parties in formal political processes, they change not only their political behaviours, but eventually also their ideological frames. Looking at post-Spring Egyptian cases, we can trace a variety of political trajectories among Islamist parties, but none of them actually substantiates the participation-moderation model. As we have seen above, the FJP's development demonstrates that participation in formal politics can undermine ideological reform. Meanwhile, the various Salafi parties participate in elections, but there is little evidence of ideological reform in any of them. Finally, reformist movements have accepted democratic values, but this has led to their boycotting the 2015 parliamentary elections; in short, their ideological moderation led to non-participation.

Still, the paradigm, if used critically and with caution, remains a useful facsimile, perhaps an ideal-type, by which to assess the trajectories of political parties in transition. Egyptian post-Spring developments illustrate that numerous Islamist parties have adapted to the new political setting and as such have shown some level of moderation. As such, strategic moderation is a minimal denominator as it allows Islamist parties, similar to any other legally recognised party, access to pursuing their agenda through formal political institutions. From this point of view, participation has a direct, positive effect, although many of the more influential parties such as the FJP, al-Nour, the BDP and al-Asala have merely participated due to strategic calculations and without engaging in substantial ideological reframing.

While participation has a direct impact on strategic moderation, the Egyptian cases of Islamist parties suggest that ideological moderation is not prompted by political inclusion. When reviewing Islamist parties in the post-coup era, there is no case supporting the 'participation-moderation' thesis, which suggests a direct relationship between political inclusion and ideological moderation. For example, the strategic decision of the MB/FJP to participate in the political system (and effectively to dominate it) undermined the possibility of ideological moderation; the reason for this lies in the fact that there were few incentives for the organisation to change. While there is limited concrete evidence that the MB, and its now irrelevant FJP, have any intention to turn to violence as a strategic option in response to the ban of the MB in 2013, this aspect in itself does not demonstrate ideological moderation in terms of a relative process of accepting democratic principles and values. Salafi parties such as al-Nour, the BDP, al-Asala and al-Watan continue to participate in post-coup politics, but they also show little sign of ideological reform. Their turn to formal politics is mainly driven by a strategic calculus, thereby continuing to consider violent jihad as a potential option should a formal institutional path be blocked. Moreover, their views on the status of non-Muslims and the role of women in society and politics remain firmly guided by ultra-orthodox religious precepts. Only reformist parties show a considerable degree of ideological moderation, although with notable differences between them. As such, al-Wasat remains more on the orthodox side of the reformist spectrum given its positions on Shari'ah. Not altogether successfully, al-Wasat attempts to bridge the gap between traditional Islamic positions and democratic values. Strong Egypt, however, clearly demonstrates a high level of ideological moderation, supporting positions which present an interpretation of Islam that is fully compatible with democratic processes and liberal values. Yet even in the case of Strong Egypt, this ideological moderation is not necessarily the result of political participation, but rather the outcome of reflections triggered by a dispute with the conservative MB leadership. The fact that reformist parties boycotted the 2015 parliamentary elections in protest against the return to an authoritarian regime epitomises that ideological moderation is not the result of participation; on the contrary, non-participation here is the consequence of ideological moderation.

Reformist parties that did engage in ideological moderation, thus undergoing a micro-level transformation that internalised (at least to a considerable extent) democratic principles and values, did not reframe their positions as a result of participation in the political system. In fact, in the case of the reformist Islamist parties, it is apparent that their ideological shifts are the outcome of intra-organisational debates. In the Egyptian cases, these resulted in the departure of reformists from their mother-organisations as ideological differences proved irreconcilable. We can identify several triggers for intra-organisational tensions, both negative and positive factors, which put the given parties under considerable pressure. These include (1) levels of repression and exclusion which, as in the Tunisian case, encourage parties to foster alliances and thus to negotiate with what constituted opponents previously; (2) (relative) political openings which, as in the Egyptian cases, provide new opportunities to participate and to absorb political skills; and/or (3) tensions caused by generational cleavages. In any case, the process of ideological moderation is not triggered by a strategic consideration as there is usually a high cost involved, adversely affecting a party's mobilising capacity and hence its short-term strategic influence. Taken beyond the remit of Egypt's Islamist parties, there is thus certainly reason to substantially reconsider elements of the participation-moderation model, albeit without dismissing the basic concept completely.

Notes

1. A number of Middle East specialists, amongst them notably Schwedler, Wickham, Clark and Dalacoura have made noteworthy contributions. Unfortunately, there is not sufficient room in this chapter to address the discussion over definitions and the subsequent empirical debates. To engage with these issues, see e.g. Jillian Schwedler (2011), 'Can Islamist become moderates? Rethinking the inclusion–moderation hypothesis', *World Politics*, 63:2, pp. 347–76; (2006), *Faith in Moderation: Islamist Parties in Jordan and Jemen*. Cambridge: Cambridge University Press; Carrie Rosefsky Wickham (2004), 'The path to moderation: strategy and learning in the formation of Egypt's Wasat party', *Comparative Politics*, 36:2, pp. 205–28; Carrie Rosefsky Wickham (2013), *The Muslim Brotherhood: Evolution of an Islamist Movement*. Princeton: Princeton University Press; Katerina Dalacoura (2011), *Islamist Terrorism and Democracy in the Middle East*. Cambridge: Cambridge University Press, pp. 123–47.
2. Mark Lynch (2016), 'In uncharted waters: Islamist parties beyond Egypt's Muslim Brotherhood', *Carnegy Endowment for International Peace*, 16 December, <http://carnegieendowment.org/2016/12/16/in-uncharted-waters-islamist-parties-beyond-egypt-s-muslim-brotherhood-pub-66483> (last accessed 11 May 2017).
3. Ashour provides a working-definition, stating that 'moderation is a process of relative change within Islamist movements that is mainly concerned with the attitudes of these movements towards democracy'. Omar Ashour (2009). *The De-Radicalization of Jihadists: Transforming Armed Islamist Movements*. New York: Routledge, p. 6.

4. Schwedler, 'Can Islamists become moderates?' pp. 347–76.
5. Evan Hill (2016), 'Egypt's crowded political arena', Al-Jazeera, 17 November, <www.aljazeera.com/indepth/spotlight/egypt/2011/11/2011111510295463645.html> (last accessed 11 May 2017); Anon. (2014), 'Egyptian political parties and movements', *Carnegie Endowment for International Peace*, 24 February, <http://carnegieendowment.org/2014/02/24/parties-and-movements/h1pm#islamist> (last accessed 11 May 2017).
6. The category is in reference to parties' views on the distribution of wealth and their stance on the economic system. It is well-known that most Islamist parties, including the Muslim Brotherhood, hold conservative views on the political economy. See Janine A. Clark (2004), *Islam, Charity, and Activism: Middle-Class and Social Welfare in Egypt, Jordan and Yemen*. Bloomington: Indiana University Press, pp. 42–81. There is some research on the alliances between Islamists with the left in the pre-Spring period. See Maha Abelrahman (2009), '"With the Islamists? Sometimes. With the state? Never!" Cooperation between the left and Islamists in Egypt', *British Journal of Middle Eastern Studies*, 36:1, pp. 37–54. So far there is no adequate investigation on 'left-wing' Islamist parties, i.e. those that emphasise greater social justice, a regulated capitalist, or even socialist, system in their manifestos. The assessment above is therefore only indicative and based on the experience of the author.
7. Nathan J. Brown (2014), 'Egypt's constitutional cul-de-sac', *Carnegie Endowment for International Peace*, 31 March, <http://carnegieendowment.org/2014/03/31/egypt-s-constitutional-cul-de-sac-pub-55310> (last accessed 11 May 2017). Note: the 2014 Electoral Law (No. 46) stipulates that 2/3 of parliamentary seats are filled through independent candidacies, while only 1/3 is chosen through party-lists. It works to the benefit of local elites and introduces a high degree of patrimonial leverage. It also opens a backdoor to candidates previously affiliated with the ousted Mubarak regime. See Anon. (2015), 'Elections in Egypt: 2015 House of Representatives Elections: frequently asked questions', *International Foundation for Electoral Systems*, 14 October, <www.ifes.org/sites/default/files/2015_ifes_egypt_hor_elections_faq_final.pdf> (last accessed 11 May 2017); Nathan J. Brown and Michele Dunne (2013), 'Egypt's draft constitution rewards the military and Judiciary', Carnegie Endowment for International Peace, 4 December, <http://carnegieendowment.org/2013/12/04/egypt-s-draft-constitution-rewards-military-and-judiciary-pub-53806> (last accessed 11 May 2017). For the text of the 2014 Constitution, see High Elections Committee (2014), 'Constitution of The Arab Republic of Egypt issued in January 2014', January, <www.elections.eg/images/pdfs/laws/Constitution_2014-En.pdf> (last accessed 11 May 2017). The Electoral Law is available at High Elections Committee (2014), 'Law no.46/2014 on the House of Representatives', <www.elections.eg/images/pdfs/laws/HouseOfRepresentatives2014-46_en.pdf> (last accessed 11 May 2017).
8. In the parliamentary elections of 2011/12, al-Nour was run as part of the Islamic Bloc. The party won 107 (of 497 seats). In 2015, it won eleven (of 596 seats).
9. Stéphane Lacroix (2016), 'Egypt's pragmatic Salafis: the politics of Hizb an-Nour', Carnegie Endowment for International Peace, 1 November, <http://carnegieendowment.org/files/CP_287_Lacroix_al_Nour_Party_Final.pdf> (last accessed 11 May 2017), pp. 7–10.
10. According to Schwedler, strategic moderation reflects the acceptance of the institutional side of electoral politics and hence merely describes a tactical decision to take part in formal institutional processes. Ideological moderation goes hand-in-hand with the adoption of democratic principles on the one hand, and liberal values, such as tolerance and the equality of all humans on the other. Schwedler, 'Can Islamist become moderates?' pp. 347–76.

11. Barbara Zollner (2016), 'The Muslim Brotherhood in transition: an analysis of the organisation's mobilising capacity', in Peter Lintl, Christian Thuselt and Christian Wolff (eds), *Religiöse Bewegungen als politische Akteure im Nahen Osten*. Berlin: Nomos, pp.: 43–70; Eric Trager (2011), 'The unbreakable Muslim Brotherhood: grim prospects for a liberal Egypt', *Foreign Affairs* September/October, <www.foreignaffairs.com/articles/north-africa/2011-09-01/unbreakable-muslim-brotherhood?gp=68074%3Ab1d4c9534e7a0d23> (last accessed 5 June 2017).

12. See Carrie Rosefsky Wickham (2002), *Mobilizing Islam: Religion, Activism, and Political Change in Egypt*. New York: Columbia University Press; Mohammed Zahid (2010), *The Muslim Brotherhood and Egypt's Succession Crisis: The Politics of Liberalisation and Reform in the Middle East*. London: IB Tauris; Zollner, 'The Muslim Brotherhood in transition', pp. 43–70.

13. Wickham, *The Muslim Brotherhood: Evolution of an Islamist Movement*; Zahid, *The Muslim Brotherhood and Egypt's Succession Crisis*, pp. 112–15.

14. Interviews with Abd al-Mun'im Abu al-Futuh, 10 July 2010, Cairo, and Kamal El-Helbawi, 9 October 2011, Cairo.

15. Wickham, *The Muslim Brotherhood: Evolution of an Islamist Movement*; Trager, 'The unbreakable Muslim Brotherhood'.

16. Interviews with senior MB member, 15 July 2010, New Cairo, Abd al-Mun'im Abu al-Futuh, 10 July 2010, and Islam Lutfi, 24 October 2011, Cairo.

17. Zollner, 'The Muslim Brotherhood in transition', pp. 43–70.

18. Interview with Abd al-Mun'im Abu al-Futuh, 1 November 2011, Cairo.

19. Interviews with junior MB member, 9 November 2011, Cairo and Muhammad Affan, 25 November 2011, Cairo.

20. Dalia Malek (2012), 'Exclusive interview with Mohamed Morsi: what to expect from the Muslim Brotherhood', *Mic Network*, 24 June, <https://mic.com/articles/380/exclusive-interview-with-mohamed-morsi-what-to-expect-from-the-muslim-brotherhood#.kdckceR1b> (last accessed 11 May 2017).

21. Wickham, *The Muslim Brotherhood: Evolution of an Islamist Movement*; Barbara Zollner (2009), *The Muslim Brotherhood: Hasan al-Hudaybi and Ideology*. Abdingdon: Routledge.

22. Joshua A. Stacher (2002), 'Post-Islamist rumblings in Egypt: the emergence of the Wasat party', *Middle East Journal*, 56:3, pp. 415–22; Wickham, *The Path to Moderation*, pp. 205–28. See also the party's website: 'Hizb al-Wasat: official website', <www.alwasatparty.com/> (last accessed 11 May 2017).

23. Noha El-Hennawy (2011), 'Political freedom, competition drives rifts between Muslim Brotherhood factions', *Egypt Independent*, 24 March, <www.egyptindependent.com/news/political-freedom-competition-drives-rifts-between-muslim-brotherhood-factions-0> (last accessed 11 May 2017).

24. Anon. (2015), 'Strong Egypt Party (Hizb Misr al-Qawiyya)', Tahrir Institute for Middle East Policy, 16 October, <https://timep.org/pem/political-parties/strong-egypt-party/> (last accessed 11 May 2017). See also the party's Facebook page <https://www.facebook.com/pg/MisrAlQawia/about/?ref=page_internal> (last accessed 11 May 2017).

25. Interview with Muhammad al-Qassas, 5 November 2011, Cairo.

26. See al-Wasat Party, 'Hizb al-Wasat: official website'. Also interview with Ibrahim Za'frani, 17 September 2011, Cairo.

27. Raymond Baker (2003), *Islam without Fear: Egypt and the New Islamists*. Cambridge: Harvard University Press.

28. Wickham, *The Path to Moderation*, pp. 205–28.

29. See Strong Egypt Party, 'Hizb Misr al-Qawiyya. Misr Al Qawia Party. Facebook'. Also interviews with Abd al-Mun'im Abu al-Futuh, 1 November 2011, Muhammad al-Qassas, 5 November 2011 and Islam Lutfi, 24 October 2011. Furthermore, see Ashraf El Sherif (2016), 'The Strong Egypt Party: representing a progressive/Democratic Islamist Party?' *Contemporary Islam*, 10/3, pp. 311–31.

30. Interview with Abd al-Mun'im Abu al-Futuh, 1 November 2011.

31. Interview with Muhammad al-Qassas, 5 November 2011.

32. Ghada Atef (2014), 'Wasat Party withdraws from NASL, considers parliamentary elections', 24 August, <http://thecairopost.youm7.com/news/123570/inside_egypt/wasat-party-withdraws-from-nasl-considers-parliamentary-elections-source> (last accessed 11 May 2017). See al-Wasat's declarations of July and August 2013 on Hizb al-Wasat's official website, <www.alwasatparty.com/> (last accessed 2 January 2017).

33. Jayson (2015), 'A sense of belonging: a sympathetic analysis of Egypt', 18 February, <https://asenseofbelonging.org/2015/02/18/strong-egypt-a-party-in-the-middle/> (last accessed 11 May 2017). See Strong Egypt's declarations of July and August 2013, available at Strong Egypt Party, 'Hizb Misr al-Qawiyya. Misr Al Qawia Party. Facebook', <https://www.facebook.com/pg/MisrAlQawia/about/?ref=page_internal> (last accessed 2 January 2017).

34. See al-Wasat's declaration on the election boycott; al-Wasat Party, 'Hizb al-Wasat: official website'.

35. See Strong Egypt's declaration on the election boycott: Strong Egypt Party, 'Hizb Misr al-Qawiyya. Misr Al Qawia Party. Facebook'. See also Anon. (2015), 'Strong Egypt party to boycott upcoming parliamentary elections', *Mada Masr*, 4 February, <www.madamasr.com/en/2015/02/04/news/u/strong-egypt-party-to-boycott-upcoming-parliamentary-elections/> (last accessed 11 May 2017).

36. There are many streams of Salafis. For an overview see Bernard Haykel (2009), 'On the nature of Salafi thought and action', in Roel Meijer (ed.) *Global Salafism: Islam's New Religious Movement*. New York: Columbia University Press, pp. 33–50.

37. Jérôme Drevon (2015), 'The emergence of ex-jihadi political parties in post-Mubarak Egypt', *Middle East Journal*, 69:4, pp. 511–26; Lacroix, 'Egypt's pragmatic Salafis', pp. 7–10.

38. Stéphane Lacroix (2012), *Sheikhs and Politicians: Inside the New Egyptian Salafism*. Doha: Brookings Doha Center, June, <www.brookings.edu/wp-content/uploads/2016/06/Stephane-Lacroix-Policy-Briefing-English.pdf> (last accessed 11 May 2017). See also Anon. (2015), 'an-Nour Party' *Tahrir Institute for Middle East Policy*, 16 October, <https://timep.org/pem/political-parties/an-Nour/> (last accessed 11 May 2017).

39. Lacroix, *Sheikhs and Politicians*.

40. Drevon, 'The emergence of ex-jihadi political parties in post-Murbarak Egypt', pp. 511–26.

41. Lacroix, 'Egypt's pragmatic Salafis', pp. 10–16.

42. Mahmoud Mostafa (2015), 'Court rejects An-Nour party's dissolution', *Daily News Egypt*, 5 July, <www.dailynewsegypt.com/2015/07/05/court-rejects-an-Nour-partys-dissolution (last accessed 11 May 2017).

43. Lacroix, 'Egypt's pragmatic Salafis'.

44. Drevon, 'The emergence of ex-jihadi political parties in post-Murbarak Egypt', pp. 511–26; Lacroix, *Sheikhs and Politicians*.

45. Ibidem.

46. James Troth (2003), 'Islamism in Southern Egypt: a case study of a radical religious movement', *International Journal of Middle East Studies*, 35, pp. 547–72; Roel Meijer

(2009), 'Commanding right and forbidding wrong as a principle of social action: the case of the Egyptian Jama'a al-Islamiyya', in Roel Meijer (ed.) *Global Salafism: Islam's New Religious Movement.* New York: Columbia University Press, pp. 189–220.

47. Ashour, *The De-Radicalization of Jihadists*; Lisa Blaydes and Rubin Lawrence (2008), 'Ideological reorientation and counterterrorism: confronting Militant', *Terrorism and Political Violence*, 20:4, pp. 461–79.

48. Meijer, 'Commanding right and forbidding wrong', pp. 189–220.

49. Drevon, 'The emergence of ex-jihadi political parties in post-Murbarak Egypt', pp. 511–26.

50. Ibid., pp. 511–26.

Chapter 10

Islamist political societies in Bahrain: collateral victims of the 2011 Popular Uprising

Marc Valeri

On 17 July 2016, the High Civil Court of Manama ordered the dissolution of the most important Bahraini political society, the Shi'a Islamist Jam'iyyat al-Wifaq al-Watani al-Islamiyya (Entente – National Accord Islamic Society, or in short al-Wifaq), and the liquidation of its funds.[1] It took place a few weeks after the society's Secretary General, Ali Salman, was sentenced to jail for nine years on charges related to 'promoting forceful change of the regime'[2] and the stripping of citizenship of Bahrain's most prominent Shi'a cleric and al-Wifaq's spiritual leader Isa Qasim. Al-Wifaq's dissolution represents one of the latest developments in a massive crackdown on both secular and Islamist opposition that has taken place in the wake of the popular uprising that started in 2011.

Since 2011, the Kingdom of Bahrain has experienced one of the darkest periods of its history, marked by a structural division of society probably unknown since the 1970s. Drawing on personal interviews and observations conducted in Bahrain, this chapter studies the role of both Sunni and Shi'a legal Islamist societies in the 2011 popular mobilisations and, more generally, the uprising's impact on political Islam in Bahrain. The chapter argues that mainstream pro-regime and opposition legal societies, in particular Islamist ones, have been the biggest losers in post-2011 political developments. The main Shi'a Islamist force (al-Wifaq), which had proposed a conciliatory approach to reform, and which had been transformed by the regime into an institutionalised safety valve since 2006, has never been able to break with its sectarian image in order to broaden its popular support and embody a real cross-sectarian political alternative. It suffered tremendously from its incapacity both to resist the regime's sustained efforts at undermining the society's political role after 2011 and to become a legitimate intermediary between the throne and the more revolutionary Shi'a movements. On the other hand, Sunni Islamist forces, which had maintained unquestioned loyalty to the regime in the 2000s, have proved unable to propose a platform immune from the regime's manipulation since 2011. While the regime, in its strategy to portray the popular uprising as a Shi'a sectarian one, encouraged in 2011 the development of a loyalist encompassing Sunni Islamist platform, the latter only played the temporary part assigned to it by the regime and quickly lost its momentum, being unable to transform into an autonomous, self-sufficient political movement.

The chapter itself is structured as follows. It first provides some background on the legal Sunni and Shi'a Islamist political societies during the first decade of King Hamad bin Isa al-Khalifa (r. 1999-), which can be considered as the Golden Age of political societies in Bahrain, before examining the role they played during the 2011 uprising. It then analyses the implications of these events on the structure and capacity of political mobilisation of these legal Islamist societies. In particular, it will reflect on the marginalisation of the mainstream Sunni Islamist organisations (Muslim Brotherhood and Salafi societies) on the one hand, and the dramatic failure of Shi'a Islamist al-Wifaq's conciliatory approach to reform, on the other hand.

The development of Islamist political societies in the 2000s

Hamad bin Isa came to power in 1999 upon the death of his father and Bahraini ruler Shaikh Isa bin Salman al-Khalifa (r.1961–99). His accession followed on the heels of years of civil unrest widely known in Bahrain as the Intifada, which had been triggered by the combination of a deteriorated economic situation after the fall of oil prices in the 1980s and growing frustration at the lack of political opening since the dissolution of the first parliament in 1975.[3] In order to strengthen the legitimacy of the al-Khalifa dynasty, a National Action Charter, which was to outline the future structure and principles of government, was drafted and put to a popular referendum on 14 February 2001. It was approved by 98.4 per cent of voters. A few days before the vote, to dissipate the reluctance of numerous opposition personalities to support a deliberately ambiguous text on the division of powers and the role of the ruler and royal family in politics, Hamad pronounced the abolition of the 1974 decree on state security measures, the release of all political prisoners and detainees and allowed the return of Bahraini opposition activists after years in forced exile abroad.[4]

Finally, this also manifested in the revival of political pluralism in the kingdom, as Hamad enabled political societies (*jam'iyyat*) to register under the old 1989 general law governing civil social and cultural societies (law no. 21/1989), making Bahrain the first Gulf monarchy to legalise political organisations. In August 2005, a new law on political societies (no.26/2005) was passed. According to it, political societies – which have to register with the Ministry of Justice[5] – must not be linked organisationally or financially to any non-Bahraini organisation and are not allowed to build on any ethnic, linguistic, geographic, gender-based, class-based or sectarian element. Formerly banned political groups, on both pro-regime and opposition sides, quickly mushroomed. Political parties *per se* remain banned but societies, including Sunni and Shi'a Islamist ones, functioned like parties in all but name until 2011.

Of these newly formed societies,[6] the largest and best-organised is the Shi'a Islamist al-Wifaq. Established with the 'aim of gathering all the Shi'a Islamic currents under one banner',[7] al-Wifaq is headed by Ali Salman, a cleric who was one of the leaders of the 1990s' Bahraini Intifada. Its manifesto revolves around the establishment of a constitutional monarchy in Bahrain, in which the cabinet is accountable to an elected unicameral legislature, as well as an end of sectarian discrimination. Many former activists of the Islamic Enlightenment Society, the legal front in Bahrain of Hizb al-Da'wa (Da'wa Party, DP) in the 1970s,[8] either joined the society from the beginning or are closely affiliated to it, such as for instance Isa Qasim, who although not formally a member, is generally considered al-Wifaq's spiritual leader.

The other Shi'a Islamist society founded in 2002 was Jam'iyyat al-'Amal al-Islami (Islamic Action Society, IAS), which is an offshoot of the former al-Jabha al-Islamiyya li-Tahrir al-Bahrayn (Islamic Front for the Liberation of Bahrain, IFLB), founded in exile in 1975. In December 1981 sixty IFLB members were accused of plotting against Bahrain's ruling family. In the 2000s, the IAS, which mainly appealed to the followers of Ayatollah Shirazi in Bahrain, was committed, like al-Wifaq, to the implementation of constitutional reform.[9]

Among the pro-regime societies established in the early 2000s, two referred to themselves as Islamist. Jam'iyyat al-Minbar al-Watani al-Islami (National Islamic Tribune, or in short, al-Minbar) is regarded as the political wing of the Bahraini al-Ikhwan al-Muslimun (Muslim Brotherhood, MB). Active since the creation in 1941 of the first organisation representing its ideas in the country (the Students' Club, renamed the Reform Club in 1948, and the Reform Society in 1980), the MB focused until the early 2000s on charitable and educational work and expressed its disagreement with the positions adopted by Arab nationalists and Shi'a Islamists during the Intifada in the 1990s. Recruiting mainly from among the urban middle class and civil servants, it has secured considerable influence and decision-making positions in a number of public departments, including the education sector.[10] Among its most prominent figures have been members of the ruling family, including former Labour Minister Isa bin Mohamed al-Khalifa, who headed the society for five decades (1963–2013). The other pro-regime Islamist force is al-Asala al-Islamiyya (Islamic Authenticity Society, or in short, al-Asala), which is the political wing of the main Salafi organisation in Bahrain, the Islamic Education Society. The latter – whose members are particularly influential within the Ministries of Justice, Islamic Affairs and Endowments – registered as a society in 1990 and quickly attracted support among poorer and more tribal Sunnis from Muharraq and al-Rifaʻ as well as among naturalised Bahrainis. Some attempts at political rapprochement between the MB, the Salafis and other smaller Sunni religious personalities were conducted in 2002 and 2003 under the initiative of Abd al-Latif al-Mahmood, who had been the founder of a small independent charity called al-Jamʻiyya al-Islamiyya (Islamic Society). An al-Azhar-trained Sunni cleric and University of Bahrain professor of Arabic, al-Mahmood had been one of the leaders of the 1992 petition presented to then Emir Isa by a coalition of opposition figures ranging from leftists to Sunni and Shiʻa Islamists and demanding the restoration of the 1973 National Assembly. However, nothing came out of these attempts to establish bridges between the different Sunni Islamist societies.[11]

Four opposition societies, including the Shiʻa Islamist al-Wifaq and the IAS, coalesced into a cross-ideological coalition to boycott the first parliamentary elections in October 2002. Together they published a list of preconditions that would have to be met to secure their electoral participation, including a revision of the 2002 Constitution in order to give full legislative powers to the elected chamber and a redrawing of electoral constituencies on a fair demographic basis in order to redress the imbalance favouring Sunni villages. Within al-Wifaq, many cadres of the movement favoured electoral participation.[12] The society's hard choice to boycott the poll was primarily motivated by pressure from its electoral base, which was not ready to make compromises on the need for constitutional reform. In contrast, the pro-regime Sunni societies participated in the 2002 elections, with the political wing of the MB winning seven and the Salafi al-Asala six out of forty elective parliamentary seats.

Like most other opposition societies, al-Wifaq decided to register under the new law on political societies in 2005. Within al-Wifaq, this decision led, however, to the secession of some cadres. Together with members of secular societies, who also opposed their society's decision to abide by the new rules determined by the regime, al-Wifaq's deputy Secretary General Hassan Mushaimaʻ and cleric Abd al-Wahab Husayn founded Haraka Haqq – Harakat al-Hurriyya wa al-Dimuqratiyya (Right Movement – Movement for Freedoms and Democracy, or in short Haqq). This unlicensed movement, comprised of a dual Shiʻa–Sunni leadership, actively campaigned for the drafting of a new constitution and favoured recourse to civil disobedience.

The issue of an electoral boycott by the opposition resurfaced again prior to the 2006 elections. Al-Wifaq's boycott of the assembly and its engagement in street activism (mass rallies, petitions for constitutional reform) between 2002 and 2006 had significantly increased its popularity and support within the population. However, none of the demands justifying the 2002 boycott had been met four years later. While Haqq, which enjoyed a wide audience among the underprivileged Shi'a youth, called for a boycott (as they would do in 2010 too), both al-Wifaq and the IAS thus decided to compete in the 2006 elections and to forge a cross-ideological electoral pact with the Arab nationalist Jam'iyyat al-'Amal al-Watani al-Dimuqrati – Wa'd (National Democratic Action Society – Promise, or in short Wa'd), which was repeated in the 2010 elections as well.[13]

The 2006 elections marked the triumph of Islamist electoral politics – both opposition and pro-regime – with Islamist political societies conquering a total of thirty-two seats in the forty-seat Council of Representatives. The MB and the Salafi al-Asala agreed not to present candidates in the same constituencies to maximise the Sunni Islamist vote. This proved beneficial, since they won seven and eight seats respectively. On the opposition side, all of al-Wifaq's candidates – seventeen in total – were elected. However, the decision to participate in the elections also confirmed the legal opposition societies' resignation to a political game that the regime controlled. While their 2002 boycott was driven by an unwillingness to comply with rules that were established unilaterally by the regime, the opposition societies' participation in the 2006 elections ratified their capitulation to the regime's 'rules of the game'.

In 2010, a MB-Salafi deal similar to that of 2006 could not be reached and candidates supported by both al-Minbar and the Salafi al-Asala competed against each other in three constituencies. This had a direct effect on their capacity to defend their 2006 success. Only two MB candidates were elected, and the Salafis secured three seats despite competing in eight constituencies. On the opposition side, the electoral success of al-Wifaq was confirmed, with all its eighteen candidates elected in the first round.

Islamist societies in 2011: bystanders of the popular uprising

At the beginning of February 2011, young Sunni and Shi'a online activists called upon fellow citizens to occupy Manama's Pearl Roundabout for a 'day of rage' on 14 February. The movement was called 'February 14 Youth' to mark the tenth anniversary of the National Charter and what its coordinators – who in their vast majority had no affiliation with existing political societies – viewed as King Hamad's 'new era' of broken promises. A loose umbrella coalition with no formal leadership, the February 14 Youth Coalition, was established to gather all online groups and professional networks who had supported the original call to occupy the Pearl Roundabout. Obviously, a variety of views and demands were represented within the coalition, of which, however, only a very small minority initially supported the overthrow of the monarchy. While 'the bulk of the protesters belonged to the majority Shiʻa population, their demands were not sectarian or religious'.[14] The vast majority were calling for the ousting of incumbent Prime Minister Khalifa bin Salman, the establishment of a constitutional monarchy with a parliament holding legislative power and a government accountable to it, as well as the release of all political prisoners.[15]

Whilst Haqq, along with al-Wafa' movement,[16] openly supported the call for protests from the beginning, contributing to the radicalisation of parts of the Bahraini youth when they issued a joint statement on 7 March 2011 calling for a 'democratic republican system' and founded a 'Coalition for the Republic', they were never able to be in control of the movement. This observation applies even more so to al-Wifaq, which lived through the period reacting to the events instead of leading the action. True, the 18 MPs from al-Wifaq resigned from the Council of Representatives on 27 February, in reaction to the violent clearing of the roundabout ten days earlier. Also, until the military intervention of the Gulf Cooperation Council (GCC) joint force (14 March), al-Wifaq, along with the other legal opposition societies, were in almost daily contact with the Crown Prince in order to discuss ways of addressing the crisis. However, they were never really in a capacity to take leadership over the protest movement. Part of the explanation for this is given by a leading human right activist who asserts:

> Both al-Wifaq and Waʻd were unprepared for the movement and unready to know how it was to evolve … They had no clear strategy. When they were in contact with the Crown Prince to negotiate, the youth in the Pearl chanted 'No dialogue' … The youth was leading the politicians and the [opposition] political societies, not the contrary.[17]

More generally, al-Wifaq's participation in the 2006 and 2010 elections and integration into the political institutions of the state had slowly transformed it into a society of professional politicians, living off politics, and with a conciliatory socio-economic and political agenda towards the regime. If its undisputed successes in the 2006 and 2010 Council of Representatives elections established al-Wifaq as the leading opposition group, its incapacity to change everyday life for Shiʻa since then has seriously weakened its political credibility in the eyes of ordinary citizens and deprived the society of any capacity to embody an alternative to Hamad's regime. The opinion that al-Wifaq's strategy during the 2000s to work for change from inside the system proved 'its inefficiency and is doomed to failure'[18] was shared by many young political activists present on the Pearl Roundabout.

Concomitantly, the regime's deliberate policy to portray the 2011 uprising as a sectarian one – added to the Hamad's regime's long-term strategy to emphasise the sectarian division of society as a means of de-legitimising any non-sectarian opposition – has also had tremendous effects on the country's Sunni Islamist societies. The regime strongly encouraged the emergence of a loyalist Sunni organisation, which was supposed to illustrate, in a mirror-inverted configuration, the Shi'a confessional character of the popular uprising. On 19 February 2011, several Sunni political societies, including the MB (al-Minbar), the Salafi al-Asala and several smaller ones, such as the Sunni nationalist Harakat al-'Adala al-Wataniyya (National Justice Movement Society) and the Nasserist-cum-Islamist al-Wasat al-'Arabi al-Islami (Arab Islamic Centre Society), agreed on the necessity to establish an alternative forum to Pearl Roundabout. They thus announced the formation of a new movement called Tajammu' al-Wahda al-Wataniyya (National Unity Gathering, NUG) with the aim of establishing a vehicle to make the Sunni voice heard and to support 'reform over revolution'.[19] Abd al-Latif al-Mahmood was elected NUG spokesperson. This umbrella organisation led two massive rallies at the biggest Bahraini mosque (al-Fatih Mosque) on 21 February and 2 March. At its first rally, the NUG affirmed 'the legitimacy of the existing regime and considered that the maintenance of stability in the country is not negotiable'.[20] It also emphasised 'the unity of the Bahraini people who share the same grievances, problems and challenges' and 'extend[ed] its hand' to the protesters at the Pearl Roundabout.[21] On 22 February, the NUG leaders were publicly praised by the prime minister and received by the king, who 'hailed the peaceful massive rally paying tribute to all loyal citizens for their patriotic stance and allegiance to their leadership and country in confronting challenges'.[22]

While the NUG, whose creation had been encouraged by the government, was useful to the latter in helping present the popular uprising as sectarian, it insisted that it had 'its own demands', to paraphrase the motto of the second of its rallies (*lan mutallib*), and claimed to represent those 'who have not had anyone to represent them',[23] that is those Sunnis who do not belong to the ruling family. In this narrative, Bahrain is not composed of two, but three political groups: 'the leadership of the country',[24] the Shi'a, conflated with the Pearl Roundabout protesters, and the Sunnis. Abd al-Latif al-Mahmood explained later '[w]e consider there to be three forces: the system (royal family), the Sunnis and the Shi'ites, and political and constitutional reform needs the consent of all of them'.[25]

Unsurprisingly the NUG's strongest attacks were directed against al-Wifaq, which was labelled as sectarian and accused of wanting to introduce *wilayat al-faqih* in Bahrain. But a number of the NUG demands were, interestingly enough, not very different from the ones heard among the legal opposition.

They included calls for substantial social and political reform, in particular that 'authority should be vested in the people in reality and not only as a façade' and that 'fundamental and balanced revisions of the Constitution' should be undertaken 'to ensure people are the sources of authority under the kind custodianship of the King'.[26] The NUG also called for the release of political prisoners, the trial of those responsible for the deaths of protesters since the beginning of the uprising, the increase of salaries in both public and private sectors, solutions to the housing problems, greater independence in the judiciary and an end to corruption. Three meetings between representatives of the seven legal opposition societies (including al-Wifaq) and NUG leaders took place at the beginning of March 2011 – two at Abd al-Latif al-Mahmood's Islamic Society office and one at al-Wifaq's headquarters. At the end of one of these meetings, a general common statement was issued to condemn 'inter-communal clashes that had occurred throughout the day in Bahrain, call[ing] on the people not to confront their fellow citizens and warn[ing] against the dangers of sectarianism'.[27]

At its second rally on 2 March, meanwhile, the NUG's initial demands for political reform were dropped to give way to the affirmation of 'the continued legitimacy of both the existing political regime and the ruling al-Khalifa family under the leadership' of the king, the rejection of the opposition's calls for the resignation of the cabinet, 'which would bring destruction to Bahrain', and calls to take 'all necessary measures' to end demonstrations and to bring to trial the leaders of strikes and demonstrations in public services.[28] This change of tone from the first rally on 21 February was precipitated by the regime's increasing pressure on the NUG leadership, but also by the organisation's ambition to establish itself as a reformist conciliatory third force that set itself apart from the Pearl Roundabout protests, which the NUG portrayed as revolutionary and uncompromising. Communication between the NUG and the legal opposition was finally interrupted by the GCC's military intervention to clear the Roundabout on 14 March. In a press conference held that evening, the NUG accused al-Wifaq of being 'responsible for what was occurring in Bahrain' and, in a thinly veiled allusion to the alleged Iranian connection with al-Wifaq, asserted that 'any intervention from outside [the GCC community] was unacceptable'.[29]

A state of emergency was enacted between 15 March and 1 June. During this period, the NUG leaders had to decide how to make the movement evolve. The extreme variety of irreconcilable ideological roots and political interests among the components of this pro-regime coalition made agreement on a common vision all the more difficult. Three options were on the table: (1) carrying on as a loose umbrella coalition composed of independent political societies (the political wing of the MB, al-Minbar, pushed for this route), (2) turning the

NUG into a charitable society with social goals (this was supported by the Salafi al-Asala) and (3) transforming the NUG into a registered political society. The latter, which was supported by Abd al-Latif al-Mahmood, was opposed by al-Minbar and al-Asala, since Bahraini law does not allow simultaneous membership in two political societies. The leaders of al-Minbar and al-Asala were concerned that the registration of the NUG as a political society would lead some of their members to resign and join the NUG. Following the king's decision on 31 May to organise a National Dialogue to start on 1 July, the NUG felt caught up in a race against time. On 11 June, 69 per cent of the eligible members of the NUG voted for its transformation into a political society.[30] It officially registered as a political society on 28 June 2011. The subsequent election of the new society's Central Committee revealed first serious cracks, as no former members of al-Minbar and al-Asala societies were elected to leadership positions. As a result, al-Minbar and al-Asala leaders felt they had no longer any stake in the NUG project and thus officially withdrew from it. From then onwards, the three societies (al-Minbar, al-Asala and the NUG) became *de facto* political competitors. Tensions between the NUG and other pro-regime societies increased even further following a *Washington Times* interview in August in which the head of the NUG Abd al-Latif al-Mahmood stated that the prime minister 'should stay in office until the crisis is over and then step down'.[31] Many Sunnis, especially among al-Minbar and al-Asala, perceived this position as a *lèse-majesté* offence towards the prime minister, who is extremely popular among loyalists for his role in facilitating the military intervention of the GCC joint force in March 2011.

In the by-elections organised in September 2011, following the resignation from the Council of Representatives of all eighteen MPs from al-Wifaq in February, the NUG announced that it would not participate in order to preserve 'national unity'. The MB and Salafi societies did not present candidates either – due to their lack of preparation and political anchorage in the involved (predominantly Shi'a) constituencies – but instead supported candidates considered to have similar programmes.[32] It comes as little surprise, meanwhile, that the legal opposition boycotted these by-elections. The non-participation of all major political societies led to the election of pro-government deputies officially labelling themselves as 'independent'.

The plight of (Sunni and Shi'a) Islamist societies

As illustrated by the modest electoral results of the MB's affiliate al-Minbar and the Salafis throughout the 2000s, these societies, which have always been unquestionably loyal to the regime, were more dependent on the regime than the reverse and never enjoyed the popular support that their Egyptian or Kuwaiti counterparts did. For the first time in 2011, the hypothesis of a movement gathering all Sunni Islamist currents in Bahrain under one banner – a kind of 'Sunni equivalent of al-Wifaq'[33] – became realistic. In its strategy to portray the Pearl Roundabout popular mobilisation as a Shi'a revolt, the regime undeniably supported and benefited from the emergence of a Sunni coalition in spring 2011. However, the regime's tolerance towards an encompassing movement had to do with the very particular political circumstances of the Arab uprisings. Once the regime perceived that its survival was no longer under threat, the existence of a Sunni Islamist political movement – which would be more than just a tool at the ruling family's disposal in times of crisis, but could play a perennial role, potentially pushing specific Sunni demands or claiming to give the Sunnis an independent voice from the regime – was definitely not to the latter's taste. As a result, by the end of 2011, the NUG had lost its usefulness to the regime and its momentum was already waning.

In January 2012, a new movement called Sahwat al-Fatih (al-Fatih Awakening, or in short al-Fatih), and led by young NUG sympathisers, was created. It organised a rally on 21 February to commemorate the anniversary of the first NUG gathering at al-Fatih Mosque in 2011 but did not invite any NUG leaders.[34] Considered by many observers as 'a brainchild of the Muslim Brotherhood and the Royal Court',[35] in an attempt to weaken the NUG, al-Fatih opposed any dialogue between the regime and al-Wifaq. It described the latter as 'terrorists'[36] and claimed that the priority should be 'deterring vandalism that aims to blackmail the nation for foreign agendas', accusing in particular the United States of using Bahrain for its own regional interests.[37] Al-Fatih faded away in the summer of 2012 as quickly as it had emerged a few months before, but it had fulfilled a double political role. Not only did it confirm, and exacerbate in the eyes of many Sunni Islamists, the existential crisis of the NUG, which had started materialising in June 2011 following the break with al-Minbar and al-Asala, who had been founding members of the NUG coalition. But even more so, by illustrating the radicalisation of some Sunni groups to the point that they rejected the possibility of a negotiation between the regime and the legal opposition, al-Fatih enabled the regime to present itself as torn between two uncompromising sectarian components of society and exonerate itself from the responsibility of the National Dialogue's failure. This said, the regime's ongoing strategy to locate the Sunni–Shi'a divide at the centre of the political arena ultimately backfired, paving the way for the emergence of a jihadi–Salafi current. This current finds its roots in a sectarian (virtually exclusively Sunni)[38] recruitment policy – and the conveyance of anti-Shi'a propaganda – within the regime's very security services[39] and openly professes sympathy for the Islamic State, encouraging young Bahrainis to join the latter.[40]

The results of the November 2014 elections for the Council of Representatives illustrated the popular disenchantment with Sunni Islamist political societies, perceived as unable to fulfil the expectations raised in 2011 of being a platform to convey particular (Sunni) demands to the regime. Two months before the elections, the government announced a redrawing of electoral constituency boundaries, intended to 'hinder the chances of Sunni Islamists . . . in favor of tribal independents. The districts of several current Islamist MPs . . . were even combined to force direct electoral face-offs among sitting Sunni legislators'.[41] This constituted a blatant illustration of the reluctance of the regime to have a parliament controlled by Islamists (either Shi'a or Sunni) and of its strategy of favouring pragmatic businessmen and tribal leaders ready to support the regime's policies. In addition to this, following Riyadh's decision to label the MB a 'terrorist' organisation in March 2014, the Bahraini regime was under increasing pressure from its Saudi and UAE allies to limit Sunni Islamists' influence at home, despite the close connection of the regime with the Bahraini Salafi and MB offshoots.

While the MB and the NUG agreed not to present candidates competing in the same constituencies, this deal could not be reached with al-Asala. As a result, the MB and the Salafis went head to head in three constituencies (in one of them, the NUG even presented a candidate). Together these factors explain why Sunni Islamist societies suffered a terrible setback in favour of self-styled 'independent' candidates. While the MB's al-Minbar presented seven candidates and won one seat only, the Salafi al-Asala managed to win three seats out of six candidates it had presented.[42] The results were even more disastrous for the NUG, which presented seven candidates, all of whom were defeated in the first round of the elections.[43]

In the meantime among the opposition, al-Wifaq had been struggling to balance the pressure from the street and the necessity to keep its privileged access to the Crown Prince and the royal family. Many al-Wifaq cadres – particularly concerned by the increasing difficulty to balance the society's moderate wing, which favours a return to normal (that is the 'not-so-bad' pre-2011 period) and the more radical wing, which shared many of the demands of the February 14 Youth Coalition and regards 2011 as a breaking point in Bahrain's history – already expressed worry about a potential implosion of the society. In addition to several unlicensed opposition societies – including al-Wafa' and Haqq, whose leaders had been sentenced to life in prison and who called for a boycott of the elections, as they had done since 2002 – five legal opposition associations, including al-Wifaq and the

IAS, confirmed in October 2014 their decision to boycott the poll. This was decided despite the strong pressures to participate emanating from Western embassies – in particular the UK, which allegedly threatened to stop all contacts with al-Wifaq and hold it accountable for the political deadlock – and from the regime, which had been threatening to ban the society's activities since July 2014.[44] Despite these threats, however, the decision by al-Wifaq to boycott the poll was in the end rather straightforward and accompanied only by few dissenting voices from within. As explained by a cadre of the society supporting the boycott, 'participation would have ratified the society's capitulation to the terrible conditions imposed by the regime since 2011 and would have been perceived as a treason *vis-à-vis* the Shi'a street and the 4,000 political prisoners remaining in jail'.[45]

Conclusion

The chapter of reform opened in 1999 by King Hamad led to the channelling of popular discontent through the legal opposition and a defusing of societal tensions for several years. When the Shi'a Islamist political society al-Wifaq decided to participate in the 2006 parliamentary elections, the goal was to establish a clear demarcation with the illegal opposition. While the latter was directly challenging the monarchical order (through an overtly republican project, such as for example by the unlicensed Shi'a Islamist al-Wafa' movement) or unwilling to play the game and participate in elections (such as for example the cross-sectarian Haqq), al-Wifaq decided to accept the rules of the game in return for representation in parliament and – although limited – some influence over the policy-making process. However, by 2011, al-Wifaq's institutionalisation and failure to change the political system from within had already contributed to an increase in the ranks of opposition activists convinced that a more radical strategy was necessary to achieve meaningful political reforms. After 2011, this class of professional Shi'a politicians, whose legitimacy was based on years in exile, had tremendously suffered from an incapacity both to resist the regime's efforts at undermining their political role, and to represent a legitimate intermediary between the throne and the Bahraini street. In addition, al-Wifaq has been deeply affected by its leaders' experience of harassment and arrests by the regime since 2011. Al-Wifaq's 2014 electoral boycott and its denunciation by foreign embassies – including the UK, which appeared more interested in maintaining an authoritarian order conducive to business deals than in condemning the suppression of most basic human rights by a non-democratic regime – were taken by the Bahraini government as a go-ahead to carry out a widespread crackdown on the legal opposition. With al-Wifaq's dissolution in 2016 and its Secretary General Ali Salman in jail since December 2014, there is almost nothing left of the largest political society under Hamad five years after the popular uprising. In a bitter mirror image of the political situation in the 1990s, many of the society's cadres who are not in jail are in exile and definitely not in a capacity, in the short term, to revive Bahraini Shi'a politics from its ashes.

Among the Sunni Islamists, meanwhile, the picture is no less bleak. As observed by Justin Gengler, 'Sunni nationalism is not a phenomenon the Bahraini state is eager to see, and even much less become institutionalised in the form of organised political societies'.[46] True, Sunni Islamists were extremely useful to the regime in 2011 and 2012, in presenting a pro-ruling family front to stand up against what was abusively denounced as a Shi'a coup attempt. However, as illustrated by the terrible blow suffered by the three main Sunni Islamist societies (Muslim Brotherhood, Salafis, NUG) in the 2014 elections, they have been unable to propose a sustainable post-2011 Sunni Islamist platform immune from the regime's manipulation. Instead, the entrenchment of a jihadi–Salafi current in the country may become the not-so-unexpected legacy of the regime's sectarian strategy that it will have to deal with in the years to come.

Notes

1. Anon. (2016), 'High court dissolves Al Wefaq', *Bahrain News Agency*, 17 July, <http://bna. bh/portal/en/news/736177?date=2016-07-17> (last accessed 28 February 2017).
2. Additional charges included publicly inciting hatred, inciting disobedience, and demeaning public institutions. In December 2016, the Court of Appeal upheld this sentence.
3. Munira Fakhro (1997), 'The uprising in Bahrain: an assessment', in Gary Sick and Lawrence G. Potter (eds), *The Persian Gulf at the Millennium: Essays in Politics, Economy, Security, and Religion*. New York: St. Martin's Press, pp. 167–88.
4. Katja Niethammer (2006), 'Voices in Parliament, debates in *Majalis*, and banners on streets: avenues of political participation in Bahrain', *EUI Working Papers* No. 27, Florence: Robert Schuman Centre for Advanced Studies, p. 4.
5. Including the existing ones, all non-political civil societies register under the Ministry of Social Affairs.
6. Beyond Islamist movements, opposition and pro-regime secular societies were formed. Former exiled leaders of the clandestine Arab Nationalist Jabhat al-Sha'biyya li-Tahrir al-Bahrayn (Popular Front for the Liberation of Bahrain) created Wa'd (Promise) in 2005. The society boycotted the 2002 Council of Representatives elections, but participated in 2006 (with one Wa'd-supported candidate elected). The second new society, Jam'iyyat al-Minbar al-Dimuqrati al-Taqaddumi (Progressive Democratic Tribune Society, PDTS), was founded in 2002 by returning exiles from the clandestine Marxist–Leninist National Liberation Front of Bahrain. The PDTS presented candidates in the first parliamentary

election in 2002 and won three seats. Among the pro-regime side, the most prominent non-Islamist society has been the liberal Jam'iyyat Mithaq al-'Amal al-Watani (National Action Charter Society), comprising businessmen of both sects. The society won three seats in the Council of Representatives in 2002.

7. Laurence Louër (2008), *Transnational Shia Politics: Religious and Political Networks in the Gulf*. London: Hurst, p. 238.

8. Hizb al-Da'wa (Call Party), founded in Najaf (Iraq) in the late 1950s, became one of the major opposition parties to the Iraqi Ba'athist regime.

9. International Crisis Group (2005), 'Bahrain's sectarian challenge', *Middle East Report*, 40, p. 15.

10. Ghassan al-Shihabi (2014), 'Al-Ikhwan al-Muslimun fi-l-Bahrain. Tahulat al-'Aqud al-Sab'a' [The Muslim Brotherhood in Bahrain. The seven decades' Transformations], in *Al-Ikhwan al-Muslimun fi-l-Khalij* [The Muslim Brotherhood in the Gulf]. Dubai: Al-Mesbar Studies and Research Centre, p. 163. According to leaked US diplomatic cables, 'it is rumoured that the Royal Court and the Islamic banking sector bankroll' the society. See Anon. (2008), 'A field guide to Bahraini political parties', *Wikileaks, Cable from US Embassy in Bahrain* (08MANAMA592_a), 4 September, <http://wikileaks.velotype.nl/cable/2008/09/08MANAMA592.html> (last accessed 12 May 2017).

11. Ghassan al-Shihabi (n.d.), 'Ma al-Ladhi Yaqliq al-Sunna?' [What worries the Sunna?], *Gulf Center for Development Policies*, <www.gulfpolicies.com/index.php?%20option=com_content&view=article&id=609:2012-01-06-06-25-44&catid=51:2011-04-09-07-47-31&Itemid=364> (last accessed 28 February 2017).

12. Louër, *Transnational Shia Politics*, p. 286.

13. Although Isa Qasim viewed any cooperation with secular forces with disapproval, the leadership of both societies agreed to pursue this electoral cooperation, which revolved primarily around an agreement not to compete against one another at the district-level. This cross-ideological alliance probably traces its origin to the shared experience of forced exile in the 1990s by the leadership of both organisations and by the well-known longstanding personal entente between al-Wifaq and Wa'd's Secretarys General, Ali Salman and Ibrahim Sharif.

14. International Crisis Group (2011), 'Popular protests in North Africa and the Middle East (III): the Bahrain Revolt', *Middle East/North Africa Report*, 105, 6 April, p. 6.

15. Ibid., p. 6.

16. Tayyar al-Wafa' al-Islami (Islamic Loyalty Current, or in short al-Wafa') was founded in 2009 by Abd al-Wahab Husayn. This unlicensed association officially believes in *wilayat al-faqih* (literally, 'government of the Islamic jurists' principles).

17. Interview, 21 September 2011, Manama.

18. Interview, 20 September 2011, Manama.

19. Interview with a NUG cadre, 9 December 2015, Manama.

20. Anon. (2011), *Bahrain Independent Commission for Inquiry Report*, 10 December, p. 87, <www.bici.org.bh/BICIreportEN.pdf> (last accessed 28 February 2017).

21. Ibid., p. 87.

22. Anon. (2011), 'HM King Hamad receives organisers of national unity rally', *Bahrain News Agency*, 22 February, <www.bna.bh/portal/en/news/448039?date=2011-02-22> (last accessed 28 February 2017).

23. Nancy A. Youssef (2011), 'Huge Bahraini counter-protest reflects rising sectarian strife', *McClatchy Newspapers*, 21 February, <www.mcclatchydc.com/news/nation-world/world/article24612922.html> (last accessed 28 February 2017).

24. Bahrain Independent Commission for Inquiry Report, p. 87.
25. Andrew Hammond (2011), 'Bahraini Sunni says opposition must change leader', *Reuters*, 28 May, <www.reuters.com/article/us-bahrain-cleric-interview-idUSTRE74R 18Q20110528> (last accessed 28 February 2017).
26. Bahrain Independent Commission for Inquiry Report, p. 87.
27. Ibid., p. 129.
28. Ibid., pp. 102–3.
29. Ibid., p. 135.
30. Habib Toumi (2011), 'Bahrain's national unity rally turns into a political society', *Gulf News*, 11 June, <http://gulfnews.com/news/gulf/bahrain/bahrain-s-national-unity-rally-turns-into-political-society-1.820262> (last accessed 12 May 2017).
31. Ben Birnbaum (2011), 'Top Sunni: PM should mull quitting after the crisis', *Washington Times*, 18 August, <www.washingtontimes.com/news/2011/aug/18/leading-bahraini-sunni-prime-minister-should-resig/> (last accessed 28 February 2017).
32. Malik Abd Allah (2011), 'La Jama'iyyat Siyasiyyat Mu'thira fi al-Intikhabat al-Takmiliyya' [No major political societies in the by-elections], *al-Wasat*, 20 August, <www.alwasatnews.com/news/584318.html> (last accessed 28 February 2017).
33. Hasan T. al-Hasan (2015), 'Sectarianism meets the Arab Spring: TGONU, a broad-based Sunni movement emerges in Bahrain', *Arabian Humanities*, 4, <https://cy.revues.org/2807> (last accessed 28 February 2017).
34. Ibid.
35. Interview with a NUG cadre, 9 December 2015, Manama. See also al-Hasan, 'Sectarianism meets the Arab Spring'.
36. al-Hasan, 'Sectarianism meets the Arab Spring'.
37. Andrew Hammond (2012), 'Bahrain Sunnis warn government over dialogue at rally', *Reuters*, 22 February, <http://uk.reuters.com/article/uk-bahrain-protest-talks-idUKTRE 81L0XK20120222> (last accessed 28 February 2017).
38. Laurence Louër (2013), 'Sectarianism and coup-proofing strategies in Bahrain', *Journal of Strategic Studies*, 36:2, p. 246.
39. Ala'a Shehabi (2014), 'Why is Bahrain outsourcing extremism?' *Foreign Policy*, 29 October, <http://foreignpolicy.com/2014/10/29/why-is-bahrain-outsourcing-extremism/> (last accessed 28 February 2017).
40. Noor Mattar (2014), 'Bahrain's Shia Muslims tense as politicians and preachers pledge allegiance to ISIS', *Global Voices*, 24 July, <https://globalvoices.org/2014/07/24/bah-rians-shia-muslims-tense-as-politicians-and-preachers-pledge-allegiance-to-isis/> (last accessed 28 February 2017).
41. Justin Gengler (2014), 'Electoral rules (and threats) cure Bahrain's sectarian parliament', *The Monkey Cage*, 1 December, <www.washingtonpost.com/blogs/monkey-cage/wp/2014/12/01/electoral-rules-and-threats-cure-bahrains-sectarian-parliament/> (last accessed 28 February 2017).
42. Hassan al-Madhub (2014), 'Barlaman 2014: 4 Maqa'id Faqat li-l-Assala wa-l-Minbar' [Parliament 2014: 4 Seats only for al-Assala and al-Minbar], *al-Wasat*, 1 December, <www.alwasatnews.com/news/940913.html> (last accessed 28 February 2017).
43. Hassan al-Madhub (2014), 'Tajammu' al-Wahda Yafshal fi Isal Jami' Murashahih al-Sab'a li-l-Barlaman' [Unity gathering fails to lead its seven candidates to parliament], *al-Wasat*, 24 November, <www.alwasatnews.com/news/938813.html> (last accessed 28 February 2017).

44. Farishta Saeed (2014), 'Bahrain asks court to suspend main opposition bloc's activities', Reuters, 20 July, <www.reuters.com/article/us-bahrain-politics-alwefaq-idUSKBN0F-P0NZ20140720> (last accessed 28 February 2017).
45. Figures published by Freedom House. Also interview with an al-Wifaq cadre, 22 November 2014, Manama.
46. Gengler, 'Electoral rules (and threats)'.

Chapter 11

Kuwait's Islamist proto-parties and the Arab uprisings: between opposition, pragmatism and the pursuit of cross-ideological cooperation

Luciano Zaccara, Courtney Freer and Hendrik Kraetzschmar

Introduction

This chapter is concerned with Kuwait's so-called Islamist proto-parties,[1] and their evolution and responses to the Arab uprisings of 2010–12. Despite the absence of a political parties law, the Kuwaiti government has tolerated the presence of proto-parties and their involvement in legislative, municipal and associational elections since the country gained independence in 1961. Today, numerous such proto-parties operate openly in Kuwaiti politics and represent populist-leftist, national-liberal and Islamist ideological currents.[2] Comprising both Sunni and Shi'a denominations, some Islamist groupings/proto-parties even predate the official creation of the Kuwaiti state. Since the re-establishment of al-Sabah rule after the liberation of Kuwait from Iraqi occupation in 1991, Islamists, both as members of proto-parties and as independents, have been consistently represented in parliament. The most active and well-organised Islamist proto-party has been the mainstream Sunni al-Harakat al-Dustouriyya al-Islamiyya (Islamic Constitutional Movement/ICM, referred to here by its Arabic acronym Hadas), which functions as the political arm of al-Ikhwan al-Muslimun fi al-Kuwait (Kuwaiti Muslim Brotherhood, KMB).[3] Other Islamist proto-parties, such as the Salafi al-Tajammu' al-Islami al-Salafi (Salafi Islamic Gathering, SIG), al-Haraka al-Salafiyya (Salafi Movement, SM) and Hizb al-Ummah (Ummah Party, UP) as well as the Shi'a-based al-Tahaluf al-Watani al-Islami (National Islamic Alliance, NIA) and Tajammu' al-'Adala wa al-Salam (Justice and Peace Assembly, JPA), have also tended to be represented in recent legislatures. Since the 1990s, many of these Islamist proto-parties have alternated between opposing and supporting the government, depending on strategic calculus, domestic political circumstance and regional dynamics. Since the mid-2000s, however, and especially since 2005–6, the two Sunni Islamist proto-parties traditionally known for their close ties to the Kuwaiti government – Hadas and the SIG – have become more visibly oppositional in their approach to the al-Sabah government and its policies, while the Shi'a-based NIA has become increasingly pro-government in outlook.

Over the past decade, the oppositional stances taken by Hadas, the SIG and others – together with mounting (and previously unseen) tribal resistance to the implementation of increasingly restrictive government policies, limiting political participation of independent societal actors – has contributed to an almost permanent deadlock in parliament between government and opposition. Indeed, parliament was dissolved an impressive seven times between 2005 and 2016 alone, largely due to persistent opposition challenges in that body. While Hadas and the various Salafi proto-parties, combined within the 'Islamic bloc', held on average ten to twelve seats in the assemblies elected between 1992 and 2009, this figure reached twenty-two to twenty-five after the February 2012 election – which had followed on the heels of a series of domestic protests in 2011 and the stunning electoral successes of Islamist parties elsewhere in the region – providing this assembly with its strongest Islamist presence ever. For the Kuwaiti government, these electoral gains certainly represented a serious challenge, given that by then a majority of Sunni Islamist proto-parties had become firmly associated with the broader political opposition. The subsequent dissolution of parliament at the hands of the Constitutional Court four months later led to the reinstatement of the largely loyalist assembly that had been elected in 2009. Since restoration of the previous assembly was so controversial, consecutive elections were called in December 2012 and again in July 2013 amidst massive street demonstrations inspired by the Arab uprisings elsewhere.

Notably, following the opposition's success in the February 2012 polls, the government unilaterally imposed a new electoral law that granted each citizen only one vote (each had previously had four) in a measure that members of the opposition assumed was aimed at harming organised proto-parties. As a result, Hadas, alongside other Islamist and secular portions of the opposition, boycotted the elections of December 2012 and July 2013, and only returned to the electoral fold in the November 2016 polls.[4]

As this chapter demonstrates, during their period outside parliament, the principal Sunni Islamist proto-parties, including Hadas and the SIG, resorted to a strategy of cooperation with other (secular) members of the political opposition, partaking in non-institutionalised forms of collective action, such as demonstrations and protests, in order to effect change. Indeed, it was in this environment that Sunni Islamists – perhaps having seen the pitfalls of Islamists going it alone elsewhere in the region – ramped up their cooperation with other strands of the political opposition. As Shadi Hamid observes, such a strategy of forming broad-based coalitions has been used elsewhere in the face of increased government restrictions, as it 'offers protection against government crackdowns, making it harder for regimes to portray Islamists as extremists or terrorists. In one sense, working with other, more "liberal" and "respected" political forces gives Islamists the political cover they need'.[5]

That Hadas and the main Salafi proto-parties have come to increasingly work with other oppositional forces also reflects their understanding of regional dynamics. Indeed, following the ousting of President Mohamed Morsi in July 2013 and the worsening crackdown on affiliates of al-Ikhwan al-Muslimun (Muslim Brotherhood, MB) in Egypt, Saudi Arabia and the UAE, as well as the regional turmoil resulting from ongoing civil war in Syria, cooperation with other proto-parties and a focus on gradual progress towards political reforms have become key pillars in the Islamists' strategic repertoire to avoid falling victim to the regime's red lines and to secure their own political survival. This is also evident in the decision taken by Kuwait's major Islamist proto-parties to end their electoral boycott in November 2016, which demonstrates their acknowledgement of the limits of a protest movement and their willingness to use a more gradualist strategy to effect political reform, working *through* the political system rather than trying to expose its flaws by remaining outside it through election boycotts.

The institutional context

Kuwait's political system, as enshrined in the 1962 Constitution, combines monarchical rule with representative politics. According to Article 4 of the 1962 Constitution, the Kuwaiti political system is a 'hereditary Emirate, the succession to which shall be in the descendants of the late Mubarak al-Sabah'.[6] The constitution further stipulates the creation of a unicameral legislature[7] – the 65-seat Majlis al-Ummah (National Assembly)[8] – to be elected every four years by universal adult suffrage. Until 2005, this suffrage was restricted to male Kuwaiti citizens, but has since been broadened to include full suffrage rights for female citizens as well.[9] Elections to the National Assembly have been held since 1963, although rarely at regular intervals, with the assembly having been dissolved on numerous occasions by the Amir or the Amir-appointed Constitutional Court. Though the constitution requires that new polls be scheduled within two months of the dissolution of parliament, the Amir-mandated dissolutions in 1976 and 1986 were exceptions to this rule and led to years of governance without parliament (1976–81 and 1986–92).

Unlike elsewhere in the Middle East and North Africa (MENA), elections in Kuwait have been formally held on a non-partisan basis, given that in its current form the Kuwaiti constitution does not mandate the legislation of a political parties law. Indeed, although it enshrines some basic democratic rights, including those to establish (non-political) associations (Art. 43) and freedom of assembly (Art. 44), neither the constitution nor its explanatory memorandum stipulate the passage of legislation that would regulate the licensing and operations of the country's proto-parties.[10] According to Luai Allarakia and others, the government's unwillingness to legislate on the matter must be regarded as part and parcel of a broader divide-and-rule strategy to keep the political landscape fragmented and its constituent proto-parties weakly institutionalised and non-threatening to al-Sabah rule.[11] Combined with the presence of electoral rules based on individual candidacies, a society that remains largely circumspect of the idea of 'political parties' and one in which familial, denominational and tribal considerations weigh heavily in voter choices, this legislative framework in fact produces electoral contests that remain dominated by political entrepreneurship and legislatures featuring a majority of MPs unaffiliated to any proto-party.[12]

Two consequences flow from this situation. First, it has prevented the emergence of strong and disciplined proto-parties/blocs in parliament, and thus of a viable rival centre of power to the Amir and his government. Second, it has turned electoral contests into rent-seeking endeavours, whereby candidates/MPs not linked to ideologically motivated Islamist proto-parties seek to extract beneficial resources from the state for their constituents in return for support of the government and its legislative agenda. In Kuwait, MPs engaged in such behaviour are known as 'service' MPs, and their presence in parliamentary politics has been vital to ensure the passage of government legislation.[13]

The spectre of Islamist proto-parties before the Arab uprisings

Representing the diverse range of ideological tendencies in the country, Kuwaiti politics today features proto-parties with populist-leftist, national-liberal as well as Sunni and Shi'a Islamist dispositions. The development of these political tendencies throughout the twentieth century was aided by the arrival of large numbers of Arab migrants, mainly from Egypt and Palestine, who came to the Emirate where they were granted substantial freedom to spread these ideologies, especially in the first decades of the existence of the Kuwaiti state.[14] Over the course of the 1960s and 1970s in particular, Sunni Islamist trends – both mainstream and Salafi – benefited from the patronage of a government that considered Islamism a bulwark against the more politically dangerous leftist and Arab nationalist currents, and indigenous proto-parties/groupings were founded in Kuwait representing both ideologies. Indeed, as expanded upon by Zoltan Pall and others, it is during this period that the Kuwaiti government commenced courting Sunni Islamist forces, including most notably the KMB-affiliated charitable association Jam'iyyat al-Islah al-Ijtima'i (Social Reform Association, hereafter Islah), as well as the Salafi movement, whose entry into formal politics it actively encouraged. For one this was done, of course, to 'counterbalance' the country's Arab nationalist forces and their growing domestic popularity, yet it also served the government to stoke intra-Islamist competition and hence to keep the KMB in check.[15]

Following the decline of Arab nationalist and leftist political parties in the MENA region, as a consequence of the Arab defeat in the 1967 Arab–Israeli war and the geopolitical shifts that occurred after the Islamic revolution of Iran in 1979, Islamist movements, especially the KMB, used their good ties with the government to advance their platforms, penetrating Kuwait's economic and political elites.[16]

As mentioned above, the Islamist political landscape in Kuwait is made up of both Sunni and Shi'a proto-parties and groupings, with the former comprising the mainstream Islamist KMB/Hadas as well as several Salafi proto-parties/ associations. Among the collection of Sunni Islamist forces, in fact, the KMB and its political wing Hadas, can be considered by far the most prominent in terms of popularity and organisational muscle. The KMB itself was founded as a branch of the Egyptian MB nearly a decade before Kuwaiti independence, in 1952, with the establishment of a charitable association, Jam'iyyat al-Irshad al-Islamiyya (Islamic Guidance Society, henceforth Irshad).[17] At the time, Irshad pledged to espouse Hassan al-Banna's ideology by spreading Islamic culture and countering secular and Western influences among the new generations of Kuwaitis.[18] The KMB, as represented by Irshad, was heavily influenced by its Egyptian counterpart, primarily in its organisational set-up and arrangement of networking and *da'wa* activities. The arrival of large numbers of Egyptian teachers and other officials associated with the MB in Kuwait during Gamal Abdel Nasser's (r.1956–70) crackdown on the movement aided in spreading the Brotherhood's ideology.[19] Certainly, with many of these educated immigrants involved in the understaffed education sector, they were able to gain support from the grassroots by spreading their ideas to a new generation of Kuwaiti students.

Following independence, Irshad, which had struggled to gain a Kuwaiti following, was rebranded as Jam'iyyat al-Islah al-Ijtima'i (Social Reform Association, hereafter Islah) and expanded its activities.[20] Several members of the association ran as candidates in Kuwait's first parliamentary elections of 1963, albeit formally as independents. Only one of them was elected, however, with other KMB/Islah-affiliated candidates losing their contests largely due to the prevalence of Arab nationalist sentiment within Kuwaiti society.[21] In the subsequent parliamentary election of 1967 Islah's sole affiliated candidate was elected,[22] but it was only in 1981 that the association resolved to partake in elections officially with its own slate of candidates, rather than through the support of loosely affiliated candidacies. Although it had initially been argued that the group's entry into electoral politics would be a deviation from the mission of *da'wa* and incremental progress towards the ideal Islamic state, as envisaged by al-Banna, the KMB/Islah nevertheless resolved to run, winning several seats in the 1981 and 1985 parliamentary elections. At the time, the KMB/Islah benefited from a slowdown in popular support for Arab nationalists, while also enjoying representation in cabinet due to the group's continued cordial relationship with the Amir and his government. After the Amir invoked the suspension of parliament in 1986, following continued attacks on ministers from the largely oppositional legislature, new polls were not called, leading to years of rule in the absence of an elected parliament.[23]

Following the end of the Iran–Iraq war in 1988, which had been cited as one reason for the suspension of electoral politics,[24] the KMB/Islah joined in the establishment of a cross-ideological alliance entitled al-Harakat al-Dustouriyya (Constitutional Movement, CM). Founded in 1989 by a collection of former parliamentarians, proto-parties and other societal forces, the CM pressed for a range of constitutional reforms, including the restoration of parliamentary life. However, although formally party to the CM, the KMB/Islah remained circumspect about some of the more radical reform demands put forward by members of the alliance, and discouraged its members from participating in protest rallies and demonstrations. According to scholarly accounts, the KMB/Islah did so in order to avoid unsettling the perks it had obtained over the years from its close ties with the authorities, thus setting a precedent for the association's approach to government in the decades to come.[25] Indeed, as shall become apparent below, even when in opposition during the 2000s, the KMB and its political affiliate Hadas chose to practise restraint, espousing a political strategy of engagement with, and acceptance of, the established political order, rather than one driven by a rejectionist and/or radical reformist agenda.

Amidst the CM's advocacy for restoring an elected parliament – and government attempts to quell precisely these demands by offering the creation of a partially elected (fifty elected and twenty-five Amiri appointees) consultative assembly charged with studying 'the advisability and feasibility of a restoration of parliament'[26] – the Iraqi invasion of Kuwait took place in 1990. Some documents, in fact, suggest that erstwhile Iraqi president Saddam Hussein (r.1979–2003) overestimated popular discontent within Kuwait to such an extent that he thought Kuwaitis would welcome his rule. Instead, under occupation, KMB/Islah members took a lead in organising civil resistance and supplying assistance to citizens, showing their support for the ruling elite, who were exiled during the occupation, while also gaining more followers from Kuwaitis who remained inside the country.[27]

After the liberation of Kuwait from Iraqi occupation in 1991, a younger cadre from within the KMB pressed ahead with the establishment of an independent political wing, Hadas, to organise electoral campaigns once parliament was restored.[28] Following its creation and during the early post-liberation period, Hadas and the KMB more broadly were afforded relative freedom in pursuing their local political agenda, particularly once the KMB had formally cut its ties to the international Brotherhood organisation, which had objected to American-led efforts to liberate Kuwait from Iraqi occupation.[29] The KMB's social arm, Islah, meanwhile, remains in operation as a separate association and manages grass-roots outreach and the group's charitable work.

In the early 1990s, Hadas focused its electoral and parliamentary agenda predominantly on religious matters, presenting itself as a socially conservative proto-party that advocated an Islamisation of Kuwaiti politics and society through constitutional means. As such, Hadas actively promoted a revision to Article 2 of the 1962 Constitution with a view to enshrining Shari'ah as the sole source of all legislation, as well as a conservative social agenda on women's rights, taxation and education. As the 2000s progressed, however, Hadas softened its approach, moving from an emphasis on religious doctrine and societal reform to one focused on political reform.[30] Arguably, this shift in priorities was in large measure a consequence of Hadas' growing involvement in parliamentary life and the nitty-gritty of everyday politics, as well as its interaction with political forces espousing fundamentally different conceptions of what Kuwaiti society should look like. As Badr al-Nashi, who led Hadas between 2003 and 2009, explained:

> I also believe that participating in the legislature has increased ICM's [Hadas] interest in issues of political reform and development. Previously we focused more on general issues of morality and societal reform, but now we focus on specific issues such as educational reform, employment, the economy and political issues such as electoral redistricting and reforming laws on publications and political parties.[31]

Alongside Hadas, the Sunni Islamist political landscape comprises a plurality of Salafi groupings/associations and proto-parties. The first such grouping to emerge was al-Jam'iyyat al-Salafiyya (Salafi Group/Gathering, SG) which was established in the mid-1960s as an extension of the broader Saudi-linked movement featuring prominent Salafi figures such as Ajeel al-Nashmi, Mosaa'd al-Abdul Jader and Khalid al-Khadir. As was the case for other proto-parties/associations at that time, the arrival of Arab immigrants contributed significantly to the emergence of the SG. Although the SG never revealed its organisational structure or membership base, it is known to feature a Shura Council responsible for the formulation of the group's policies, and to restrict membership to those who regularly attend lectures and camps. Program-matically, the SG espouses the establishment of an Islamic state through legitimate channels, including constitutional methods and without resorting to violence.[32]

In 1981, SG members succeeded in the establishment of a registered charitable association – Jam'iyyat Ihya' al-Turath al-Islami (Revival of the Islamic Heritage Society, RIHS) – thus enabling the Salafi current to officially engage in social activities, collect *zakat* and tap into state funding.[33] As alluded to above, the creation of the RIHS was, in fact, sponsored by the ruling family as a means to foster a pluralisation of the Islamist political scene and as a counter-balance to the KMB and its growing influence in Kuwaiti politics.[34] Although denied by the SG leadership at the time, the RIHS is widely considered as the group's 'official social front',[35] engaged in charitable work as well as in *da'wa*. Moreover, considerable internal contention not withstanding, from its inception the SG became politically active, expanding its presence in labour and student unions,[36] where it competed against KMB activists, as well as in national politics. Indeed, in 1981 the SG became the first Salafi grouping in the Islamic world to sponsor two candidates for parliamentary elections, both of whom succeeded in winning a seat.[37]

The Iraqi occupation and subsequent liberation of Kuwait in 1991 led to significant divisions within the SG. While a more 'activist' branch of the SG, under the leadership of Egyptian-born cleric Abdul Rahman Abdul Khaliq, opposed the presence of American troops on the Arabian Peninsula during the liberation of Kuwait and advocated the legitimacy of Salafi political engagement, others, influenced by a traditional purist (and largely apolitical/quietist) interpretation of Salafism, felt compelled to support the ruler's decision to involve American troops, regardless of their own opinions about it. Forming a majority within the SG, this branch thus gathered those who believed in the necessity of absolute obedience to the incumbent regime, and who sought to focus their work in parliament on the advancement of a full Islamisation of Kuwaiti law and politics.[38] Dominant within the SG, in the early post-liberation era adherents of this purist/quietist conception of politics, pushed ahead with the creation of a political wing, first under the banner of al-Tajammu' al-Islami

(Islamic Gathering, IG) and thereafter under that of al-Tajammu' al-Islami al-Sha'abi (Islamic Popular Gathering, IPG). In 2000, the proto-party yet again changed its name and was henceforth known as SIG.[39] As Pall suggests, at the time, the formation of the SIG, as well as that of its predecessors, was driven not so much by a desire to 'implement a coherent political vision or agenda', but by a need to protect *da'wa* from 'external threats', most notably from forces with 'liberal–secular' leanings, and to prevent a marginalisation of the Salafi current in Kuwaiti politics.[40]

As mandated by its purist outlook, throughout the 1990s, the IG/IPG and its MPs pursued an agenda focused on Islamising society and politics, introducing a host of draft laws ranging from the establishment of a Saudi-style Public Authority for the Propagation of Virtue and Prevention of Vice, to gender segregation in public schools and the introduction of mandatory *zakat* for all companies working in Kuwait. Whilst most of these law proposals were defeated, some, such as the prohibition of co-education in public schools, did make it onto the statute books.[41]

Triggered by internal rifts within the SG/IPG, in 1996 an activist Salafi group, the Salafi Movement (SM), emerged on the Kuwaiti Salafi scene. Led by Abdul Rahman Abdul Khaliq, the SM united activist Salafis who opposed the ongoing alliance between Kuwait and the United States and were outspoken in their demands for political reforms. Indeed, unlike the purist IPG/SIG and its focus on Islamic morality, the SM advocated early on a range of political reforms that in many ways resembled those expressed by Hadas and non-Islamist proto-parties, including calls for increased parliamentary powers, electoral reform and the introduction of a political parties law. These populist demands enabled the SM to attract many voters from within the country's tribal population who supported political reform but whose conservative religious views prevented them from endorsing any of the more liberal proto-parties. Although the SM never developed a sophisticated institutional structure, it nevertheless managed to win representation in all parliaments between 1996 and 2006.[42]

Possibly due to internal clashes over the future direction of the SM, one of its key figures and a prominent Shari'ah scholar, Hakim al-Mutairi, decided in 2005 to leave the proto-party to create the Ummah Party, the first such grouping in fact to call itself a proper 'political party'.[43] Since its creation, the UP has distinguished itself in its unrelenting and uncompromising 'call for the sovereignty of the people as expressed in the power of the national assembly to decide who should form the government'.[44] Moreover, although very different from traditional quietist Salafi groups that eschew political opposition, the UP does maintain a solid Islamist agenda, advocating the eventual establishment of an Islamic State, the implementation of Shari'ah in all aspects of life, and the elimination of foreign military presence in the Gulf.[45] Nevertheless, the UP remains most outspoken in its defence of Kuwaitis' right to select, and hold to account, their government, as well as the right to form political parties within the framework of a multi-party system. In this respect, the UP contrasts with the positions of the purist Salafis, whose political agenda remains far more conservative, and of Hadas, whose pragmatism has allowed it to work alongside the government, rather than merely challenge it. The UP did not participate in the 2006 parliamentary elections due to the proto-party's belief that the electoral process was corrupt, but then participated in the 2008 elections, yet failed to gain any seats.[46] Following the 2008 elections, the UP boycotted all subsequent polls until those held in November 2016.

As is evident from the above, since the 1990s the Salafi movement in Kuwaiti politics has become increasingly fragmented, being marked by ideological divisions between purists and activists and a concomitant splintering into several proto-parties with either pro-government or oppositional leanings.[47] This state of within-group fragmentation is further reinforced by the preponderance of independent Salafi candidates and MPs, whose decision calculus to stand for elected office outside any of the extant Salafi proto-parties is testimony to the latter's limited popularity and societal embeddedness.

Nevertheless, despite these internal divisions and fractures, Salafi MPs across the various proto-parties, as well as some of their independent counterparts, have at times worked closely together in parliament, joining in the various Islamist parliamentary blocs that were created throughout the 2000s to push for an Islamically oriented legislative agenda. A case in point concerns the 2003–6 legislative term, during which MPs from the SIG and SM, as well as independent Salafis, joined forces with Hadas in an 'Islamic bloc', collaborating amongst others on legislation to reform the country's electoral law (2006), as well as against an extension of voting rights to women (2005).

Kuwait's political landscape, finally, also features a Shi'a Islamist current that – like its Salafi counterpart – remains fragmented into several competing proto-parties.[48] Some, though not all, of these Shi'a Islamist proto-parties officially follow the teachings and leadership of Ayatollah Ruhollah Khomeini and his successor, Ali Khamenei, in Iran, which is why domestically they have been under pressure to reaffirm their loyalty to the al-Sabah ruling family, and to the Kuwaiti state more generally, by taking pro-government positions within the National Assembly.

At present, Kuwait's Shi'a Islamists are mainly organised through the NIA and JPA, which operate in the Kuwaiti body politic alongside a range of lesser Shi'a Islamist proto-parties.[49] The NIA, which in its current incarnation was established in 1998, is widely considered the most influential Shi'a Islamist proto-party in the country, tracing its roots to Hizbullah of Kuwait, which first emerged in the aftermath of the Iranian revolution of 1979. Following the liberation of Kuwait in 1990, numerous Shi'a Islamist groupings, including members of Hizbullah of Kuwait,[50] had banded together under the banner of al-'Itilaf al-Watani al-Islami (Islamic National Coalition, INC) to contest the 1992 elections.[51] By 1998 this coalition all but ceased to exist, however, due to numerous defections, and the creation of the NIA by 'hard-line' members of the INC. The NIA is ideologically proximate to Teheran, following the teachings of Ali Khamenei and subscribing to the dogma of *wilayat al-faqih* (jurist's guardianship).[52] Since its creation, the NIA has trodden a fine line in domestic politics, oscillating between pro-Iranian and oppositional stances and outspoken support for al-Sabah rule. Following the Imad Mughniyeh mourning crisis of 2008, the NIA and its deputies have emerged as firm allies of the government and its agenda.[53]

Created in 2004, the JPA constitutes the second most prominent Shi'a Islamist proto-party/grouping active in Kuwaiti politics. Comprising mostly followers of the Shirazi school of thought in Shi'a Islam, the JPA presents itself as a moderate counterpart to the NIA and holds a clear pro-governmental stance, granting the group a reputation of providing a reliable vote base for the government within parliament.[54] Overall, the JPG has enjoyed very low levels of representation in the legislatures of 2003, 2006, 2009, 2012 and 2013.[55]

Thus constituted, it is apparent that the field of Islamist proto-parties is vast, comprising numerous Shi'a and Sunni Islamist forces. As we have seen, despite contention, cooperation among the various Sunni Islamist forces in elections and parliament has been widespread. And, as will become apparent in the following pages, so has that between Sunni Islamists and secular proto-parties and groupings. Cooperation between Sunni and Shi'a Islamist proto-parties, meanwhile, has been more elusive, due not solely to ideological and doctrinal differences, but, in recent years, primarily due to the common alignment of Shi'a proto-parties with government policies, while Sunni proto-parties have increasingly adopted an oppositional stance in and outside parliament.

Islamist proto-parties and oppositional politics pre-Arab Uprisings

When the popular uprisings swept across the MENA in 2010–11 – with millions of people taking to the streets calling for far-reaching socio-political change – Islamist proto-parties, including most notably Hadas, the SIG, SM and UP, alongside their secular counterparts and other civil society groupings, had already been engaged in a longer-term campaign focused on institutional reform and the fight against corruption. Gaining traction in the wake of the emergence of Harakat Nabiha Khamsa ('We Want Five' movement) in 2006,[56] this campaign played out on the streets as well as in the National Assembly, where MPs across the ideological divide proved increasingly willing (though not always able) to set aside their ideological differences and work together towards common constitutional reform objectives as well as in holding government ministers to account through interpellations.[57]

Harakat Nabiha Khamsa (also known as the 'Orange Movement') was itself a bottom-up youth-led movement that brought together reform-minded Kuwaitis who had grown frustrated with the poor state of political life in the country. Organising a series of demonstrations, the movement demanded most notably a reduction of electoral districts from twenty-five to five, hoping this change would help diminish the likelihood of gerrymandering and vote buying, as well as reducing the importance of family, clan and tribal affiliations in future elections.[58] Unseen since the days of the Constitutional Movement in 1989, at the time Harakat Nabiha Khamsa not only attracted many Kuwaiti citizens to its cause, but managed to solicit the support of a majority bloc of twenty-nine MPs in the 2003–6 legislature, comprising deputies from across the ideological divide.[59] Supporting Harakat Nabiha Khamsa's electoral reform demands, several of its deputies, in fact, joined in the street demonstrations that rocked the capital in 2006, including MPs from Hadas, which became a major player in the movement, alongside secular members of the opposition.[60] Other (independent) Salafi MPs, meanwhile, remained more circumspect in the movement's goals, primarily because many of its tribal supporters feared the proposed electroral reform would diminish their political clout.[61]

To spread their message, Harakat Nabiha Khamsa supporters organised several demonstrations throughout the spring and summer of 2006, even entering parliament to place leaflets about their cause on the desks of cabinet ministers. Ultimately, 'the intensity of the movement forced the emir's hand'.[62] The government first offered to reduce the number of districts from twenty-five to ten instead of five, as demanded by the movement.[63] Voting with their feet, this 'compromise' proposal led, however, to additional demonstrations outside parliament, which ultimately turned violent and, in turn, spurred more street protests and louder calls for political reform.[64]

Following this display of popular outrage, the Amir, Sheikh Sabah al-Sabah, called for the dissolution of parliament and new elections. The ensuing June 2006 poll (the first in which women were granted the right to vote) was a success for the opposition, which had formed a broad-based electoral alliance around the issue of political reform and collectively garnered a majority of thirty-five of the fifty elective parliamentary seats. Of the main Islamist proto-parties contesting the elections, Hadas won six seats, the SIG and NIA each two and the JPA one.[65] Following on from this electoral success, the opposition was able to push through a law reducing the number of electoral districts to five, as had been demanded by Harakat Nabiha Khamsa. Throughout the remainder of this opposition-dominated legislature (2006–8) and again during the 2008–9 and 2009–12 legislatures, opposition contention with the government remained strong, although levels of cross-ideological coordination between Islamist and liberal MPs became increasingly shaky, largely due to deep-seated suspicion by liberal MPs of the socio-political agenda of their Islamist counterparts. Indeed, whilst the opposition had lost its majorities in the 2008 and 2009 legislatures, parliament remained unruly with Islamist opposition MPs from Hadas and others continuing in their collaborative efforts at pressuring the government on political reforms and in interpellating cabinet members suspected of corruption. In both of these legislatures, in fact, opposition MPs made significant strides in holding government to account by managing to interpellate Nasser Bin Mohamed al-Sabah, the prime minister (PM) at the time. Although the PM was not removed from office until 2011, these interpellations nevertheless constituted a significant departure from parliamentary practice, as hitherto no PM had ever been subjected to any such questioning.[66]

In the years immediately leading up to the Arab uprisings then, Kuwaiti politics had not only experienced growing opposition contention in and outside parliament and calls for major political reform, but also the emergence of a cross-ideological reform movement, albeit limited and short-lived, that in many ways resembled that of the protests that were to sweep the country in the 2011–13 period, and in which Islamist proto-parties were to play a key role.

Islamist proto-parties and the Arab uprisings

When the popular uprisings swept across the Arab world in 2010–12, Kuwaiti politics had thus already experienced a sustained period of heightened contention, pitting a cross-section of the country's opposition, including most notably the KMB/Hadas and (activist) Salafi proto-parties, as well as national-liberal forces, against the government and its supporters in parliament. Although very much driven by local circumstance and concerns, however, this contention received further impetus in the wake of the Arab uprisings, renewing a spirit of cross-ideological opposition cooperation and activism that had been on the wane since its heyday of the Harakat Nabiha Khamsa protests. As before the Arab uprisings, the key bones of contention for civil society activists, opposition MPs and proto-parties, including those of the Islamist current, remained widespread government corruption, which became primarily associated with PM Nasser al-Sabah, and political reform. Indeed, unlike elsewhere in the region, Kuwait's opposition and the mass rallies held throughout the 2011–13 period, never called for a rupture with the extant al-Sabah regime, but merely for a range of political reforms that would see Kuwait transform into a constitutional monarchy.[67]

In April 2011, amidst growing calls for PM Nasser al-Sabah to stand down and the submission of several petitions by liberal and Shi'a MPs to question key government ministers, the cabinet resigned.[68] Whilst the Amir replaced some of its members, the new cabinet remained led by PM Nasser al-Sabah, whose position had become increasingly untenable in the eyes of the opposition. Low-level protests against the government, mostly by youth since March 2011, then escalated in the fall of 2011, after it had transpired that the PM might have been implicated in the payment of bribes to pro-government MPs.[69] Outraged by the prevalence of rampant corruption and perceived government inefficiency, a cross-ideological collection of Kuwaiti youth, civil activists and MPs from secular as well as Islamist proto-parties (including Hadas), demanded yet again major constitutional reforms, most notably that the PM be elected by parliament rather than appointed by the Amir. Remarkably, these political reform demands also gained traction among some purist pro-government Salafis, who had initially 'opposed the revolutions [but] revised their stance after the brutal crackdowns of protestors in Libya and Syria'.[70] Continued protests then ultimately led to the government's resignation, including that of PM Nasser al-Sabah, and the Amir's decision to dissolve parliament prematurely in December 2011 and schedule fresh elections.[71]

Beyond the Kuwaiti street, the period of 2011–16 was also marked by renewed cross-ideological coordination between proto-parties at the electoral and parliamentary levels. When in February 2012 new elections were called, opposition candidates and proto-parties across the political divide campaigned fiercely around shared demands for political reform and an end to corruption. In the short-lived February 2012 legislature, meanwhile, proto-parties and independent MPs belonging to the country's populist-leftist, liberal and Sunni Islamist currents/proto-parties forged a loose opposition bloc – the so-called Kutlat al-Aghlabiyya ('majority bloc') – against the government and its supporters in parliament, pressing for the very same demands.[72] Indeed, the February 2012 elections and their outcome are noteworthy for two reasons: first, because for the first time since 2006, they produced a legislature dominated by opposition MPs, of which deputies belonging to the Sunni Islamist current – including representatives/affiliates of Hadas and the SIG – constituted a clear plurality with twenty-one seats.[73] With Sunni Islamist forces dominant in the new assembly, their influence in fact became quickly apparent, with Islamist MPs driving the parliamentary agenda, calling for the interpellation of cabinet ministers and the tabling of numerous laws, the most notorious of which sought to impose the death penalty for blasphemy and for insulting the Prophet and his wives.[74] Second, and related to the former, the February 2012 elections are noteworthy because their outcomes are so closely aligned with developments elsewhere in the immediate post-uprising era, with Sunni Islamist parties – including both Brotherhood and Salafi currents – making significant gains in a series of uniquely free and fair elections across the MENA region.

As is now widely known, the tenure of the February legislature came to an abrupt end in June 2012, when the country's Constitutional Court declared it unconstitutional on the grounds that the previous (2009) assembly's dissolution had been illegal, ordering the latter's reinstatement.[75] Amidst popular outrage at the decision, the opposition again forced the Amir's hand by forging a broad-based front entitled al-Jabha al-Wataniyya li-Himayat al-Dustour (National Front for the Protection of the Constitution), which comprised deputies from the 'majority bloc' as well as numerous civil society groups which protested against the reinstatement of the 2009 assembly. In November 2012, the cabinet finally resigned, and the Amir called for fresh elections to be held in December 2012, this time, however, under the 'one-person-one vote' electoral system that had been rushed through by government against stiff opposition protestations.[76] As a result, and in the spirit of ongoing cross-ideological cooperation, Hadas, jointly with most of the country's opposition proto-parties/groupings – the UP, the populist Kutlat al-Amal al-Sha'abi (Popular Action Bloc, PAB), the liberal Kutlat al-'Amal al-Wataniyya (National Action Bloc, NAB) and al-Minbar al-Dimuqrati al-Kuwaiti (Democratic Forum of Kuwait, DFK) as well as the large tribes of the Awazem, Mutairi and Ajman – decided to boycott any polls held under the new electoral law, which they considered unconstitutional.[77] Within the SIG, meanwhile, the Arab uprisings more broadly, and the opposition's call for an election boycott more specifically, had led to serious internal turmoil and fragmentation. Indeed, while some of its members supported the boycott, others sought to reassert their pro-government outlook by putting forward candidates for the December 2012 poll.[78] On the Shi'a Islamist side, lastly, the largest of its proto-parties – the NIA – decided not to participate in the electoral boycott called for by the opposition, opting instead to put forward candidates in the December 2012 elections. In line with its pro-government outlook, it is widely assumed that the NIA's decision to forgo the boycott was driven largely by its desire to reaffirm loyalty to the regime in light of the Bahraini uprising and crackdown on its Shi'a Islamist forces.[79]

Following the decision to boycott elections, Hadas partook in mass rallies against the new electoral law and, after the December 2012 polls, against the newly elected legislature. Working alongside other secular proto-parties and groupings hereby provided Hadas and activist Salafi proto-parties with the political cover needed to ensure that they would not be targeted individually. This said, throughout the 2012–13 protest cycle, Hadas and its parent organisation, the KMB, never crossed the government's red lines of permissible opposition, by advocating political reforms that fell well short of rupture.[80] As such, the KMB/Hadas appear to have pursued a double-edged strategy, partaking in street protests to rack up pressure on the regime, but also retaining its position of a pragmatic Islamist force that accepts al-Sabah rule and is willing to operate within the confines of the existing order.

The maintenance of a pragmatic political, rather than religious, agenda in the 2012–16 period, focused on matters of political reform, also transpires from Hadas' decision to sign on to an opposition document in 2013, spelling out wider-ranging constitutional reforms. Adopted by a cross-section of liberal-nationalist and Islamist political forces and activists, the document called for the establishment of 'a full parliamentary system, with a stronger legislature, independent judiciary and revised criminal code'.[81] As Courtney Freer noted in this regard, the willingness of Hadas, but also of other activist Salafis, to espouse a platform exclusively focused on attaining limited political reforms, constituted a significant departure from its long-standing objectives of Islamising politics and society and turning Shari'ah into the sole source of all legislation.[82]

Alongside a growing preparedness to collaborate with secular opposition forces, this show of pragmatism by Kuwait's Sunni Islamist proto-parties and associations during the early post-uprising period is in all likelihood the result of a combination of factors. For one, it is likely to have been shaped by the long-standing ties that existed particularly between KMB/Hadas and the government, and that have influenced the proto-party's acceptance of al-Sabah legitimacy and rule. More immediately, moreover, this pragmatism might also have been part of a deliberate strategy to ward off growing domestic and regional antagonism towards the broader MB movement. Indeed, whilst in late 2012 some pro-government MPs had launched a campaign with the slogan 'loyalty to the homeland, enmity to the Brotherhood' to discredit those protesters linked to the KMB/Hadas, accusing them of looking to replicate the MB's (electoral) successes in Egypt as a model for Kuwait, by 2013 the tide had fully turned against the broader MB movement with the ousting of President

Mohamed Morsi.[83] Whilst strongly critiquing the ousting of Morsi and the plight of the MB in Egypt,[84] the KMB/Hadas did not, however, radicalise in the wake of a clamp-down on the wider MB movement, but instead maintained its position of a pragmatic force in Kuwaiti politics that remained pro-monarchy in outlook and limited in its domestic reform demands.

Pragmatism again also prevailed in the decision taken by Hadas, and other forces within the broader opposition, to end their election boycott and re-enter the arena of institutional politics in the wake of the November 2016 parliamentary elections. Again, these elections were called for early, with some asserting that this was purposefully orchestrated by the regime to prevent the opposition from organising an effective election campaign. Be this as it may, Hadas' decision to re-enter the electoral fray followed on the heels of a heated internal debate on the matter, with those maintaining that reform could only be adequately affected through parliament narrowly winning an internal vote over those that sought a continuation of the boycott.[85]

The elections themselves, held in November 2016, proved that neither Hadas, nor the Sunni Islamist current more broadly, had lost much popular appeal, despite years of extra-parliamentary opposition and work. Indeed, various Salafi candidates and those sponsored by Hadas/KMB, won nearly half of the twenty-four opposition deputies elected, thus constituting yet again a clear plurality of members within the parliamentary opposition.[86] According to Giorgio Cafiero, Hadas' pragmatism in emphasising the need for political reform ahead of any Islamisation of society allowed it to widen its appeal, thus contributing to its electoral success.[87]

The 2016 elections, lastly, also hone in on yet another reality pertaining to the politics of Kuwaiti Sunni Islamist proto-parties in the post-uprisings era; namely that despite the aggregate success of Sunni Islamist candidates at the polls, the Salafi political landscape remains fragmented into numerous proto-parties and independent candidacies/deputies. Indeed, whereas Hadas managed to remain unified throughout the tumultuous post-uprising years – from the street demonstration in 2011–13 to its return to the electoral fold – for the Salafi current the uprisings not only brought about ongoing fragmentation, but a significant realignment within one of its key proto-parties, the SIG. As alluded to above, in 2011–12 the pro-government/purist SIG experienced a fundamental internal schism, with the emergence of reform advocates who partook in anti-government protests and the 2012 electoral boycott alongside Hadas, national-liberal and populist-leftist proto-parties as well as other civil forces. For Pall, the emergence of this reformist trend within purist Salafism, and its alignment with the country's opposition, were largely fuelled by both domestic (a growth in the oppositional stances taken by Salafis with tribal background) and regional (the Syrian civil war and the growth in sectarian politics) developments, and are likely to result in a strengthening of activist Salafi proto-parties/forces at the expense of their quietist pro-government counterparts, which have hitherto been dominant in the Salafi political scene.[88]

Conclusion

Exploring the evolution of Islamist proto-parties in Kuwait, this chapter revealed that in the aftermath of the Arab uprisings their behaviour was guided mostly by pragmatism, albeit with different outcomes. As we have seen, within the Sunni Islamist political current this pragmatism was manifest in a focus by most proto-parties on political reform (and not rupture) as well as a willingness to set aside ideological differences and work closely with liberal-national and populist-leftist forces in driving this reform agenda forward. It was also evident to some extent in the downplaying of their traditional social/religious agenda, although, of course, its pursuit was never entirely abandoned, as evident in the legislative initiatives put forward by some of the Salafi proto-parties during the post-uprising period. Within the principal Shi'a Islamist constituency, meanwhile, pragmatism, as espoused by the NIA, was manifest in the proto-party's steadfast show of loyalty to, and support for, the government and its policies in light of growing regional sectarian tensions and the crackdown on Shi'a (Islamist) forces and activists in Bahrain.

Reminiscent of the 2005–6 period, cross-ideological cooperation to advance political reforms thus once again earmarked the nature of oppositional politics in and outside parliament in the years following the Arab uprisings. Indeed, it provided not only the opposition with greater muscle to press for constitutional reforms, but also with political cover for the country's principal Islamist proto-parties in the face of growing region-wide anti-MB sentiment, particularly from 2013 onwards.

Whether these collaborative endeavours between Islamist and secular opposition will survive in the *longue durée* and entice the al-Sabah regime to accede to the opposition's long-standing reform demands remains, however, far from certain. For one, the euphoria of the Arab uprisings has long since made way for an authoritarian re-entrenchment in many parts of the MENA, with governments no longer showing any appetite for liberalising reforms, and with Arab societies growing increasingly weary of the turmoil and conflict the uprisings have brought about. In this climate, the Amir and the Kuwaiti government may well feel little inclination to succumb to any reform pressures at home from civil/political society. More significantly, there remain serious question-marks over the sustainability and scope of such cross-ideological cooperation among Kuwaiti proto-parties. With suspicion running deep within the liberal-national current about the ulterior motives of Islamist proto-parties, such cooperation remains prone to friction and breakdown. Moreover, so long as fundamental differences remain between the country's various ideological currents on matters of religion and state, cooperation is likely to remain shallow, and directed towards procedural change, rather than more comprehensively towards a multiplicity of questions pertaining to the future identity of the Kuwaiti polity. In fact, so long as Islamist proto-parties show little willingness in principle to modify their long-term goal of Islamising Kuwaiti society and politics, the pragmatism alluded to above cannot, and should not be construed as policy moderation.

Notes

1. Following Hendrik Kraetzschmar's work on the subject, the term 'proto'-parties is used here to denote the numerous named political forces nowadays operating in Kuwaiti politics and to signal their status as non-legalised, yet tolerated, parties-in-waiting. See Hendrik Kraetzschmar (2018), 'In the shadow of legality: proto-parties and participatory politics in the Emirate of Kuwait', in Lise Storm and Francesco Cavatorta (eds) *Political Parties in the Arab World: Continuity and Change*. Edinburgh: Edinburgh University Press, p. 232.
2. For a comprehensive account of the spectrum of proto-parties operating in Kuwaiti politics, see Kraetzschmar, 'In the shadow of legality', pp. 237–9.
3. Hadas is widely regarded as the most organised proto-party in the country, featuring established governing structures and procedures to elect its leadership. See Nathan J. Brown (2007), 'Pushing towards party politics? Kuwait's Islamic constitutional movement', Carnegie Papers No. 79, *Carnegie Endowment for International Peace*, < http://carnegieen-dowment.org/files/cp79_brown_kuwait_final.pdf> (last accessed 20 July 2017).
4. See also: Michael Herb (2013), 'Kuwait's endless elections: the opposition in retreat', *Project on Middle East Democracy* POMED, <http://pomed.org/wp-content/uploads/POMED-Policy-Brief-Herb-Sep-2013.pdf> (last accessed 20 July 2017).
5. Shadi Hamid (2014), *Temptations of Power: Islamists and Illiberal Democracy in a New Middle East*. New York: Oxford University Press, p. 51.
6. Article 4 of the 1962 Kuwaiti Constitution (reinstated in 1992 following the liberation of Kuwait from Iraqi occupation), <www.pm.gov.kw/kuwait-constitution.aspx> (last accessed 20 July 2017).
7. Article 51 of the Kuwaiti constitution states that 'legislative power is vested in the Amir and the National Assembly', thus providing the assembly with the powers to scrutinise and approve/reject government bills as well as propose laws. The National Assembly also has the right to question ministers and the prime minister (Articles 99 and 100), granting it the most wide-ranging powers among legislatures in the Arab world and a relatively extensive level of control over the executive. See 1962 Kuwaiti Constitution.
8. Fifty of 65 legislative seats are filled through direct plural elections. The remaining 15 seats are taken up by cabinet members, who sit in parliament as *ex officio* MPs. Michael Herb

(2009), 'Kuwait: obstacles to parliamentary politics', in Joshua Teitelbaum (ed.), *Political Liberalisation in the Persian Gulf*. London: Hurst, p. 135.

9. Hassan M. Fattah (2005), 'Kuwait grants political rights to its women', *New York Times*, 17 May, <www.nytimes.com/2005/05/17/world/middleeast/kuwait-grants-political-rights-to-its-women.html> (last accessed 20 July 2017).

10. Kraetzschmar, 'In the shadow of legality', pp. 234–5.

11. Luai Allarakia, 'Rent Distribution as an epiphenomenon of regime type: economic voting in Kuwait's 23th and 13th National Assembly', Unpublished paper.

12. Kraetzschmar, 'In the shadow of legality', pp. 243–5.

13. See e.g. Ghanim Alnajjar (2000), 'The challenges facing Kuwaiti democracy', *Middle East Journal*, 54:2, pp. 250.

14. Falah Abdullah Al-Mdaires (2010), *Islamic Extremism in Kuwait: From the Muslim Brotherhood to al-Qaeda and other Islamist Political Groups*. London and New York: Routledge, p. 10.

15. Zoltan Pall (2018), 'Do Salafi parties represent a contradiction in terms? The development and fragmentation of Kuwait Salafi Islamic Group', in Lise Storm and Francesco Cavatorta (eds) *Political Parties in the Arab World: Continuity and Change*. Edinburgh: Edinburgh University Press, pp. 104–5.

16. Zoltan Pall (2014), 'Kuwaiti Salafism and its growing influence in the Levant', *Carnegie Endowment for International Peace*, <http://carnegieendowment.org/2014/05/07/kuwaiti-salafism-and-its-growing-influence-in-levant-pub-55514> (last accessed 1 December 2016).

17. The KMB itself remains an illegal entity in Kuwait, with Irshad and later Islah constituting the sole 'legal manifestation' of the group. See Brown, 'Pushing towards party politics?' p. 5.

18. Al-Mdaires, *Islamic Extremism in Kuwait*, pp. 11–12.

19. Brown, 'Pushing towards party politics?'.

20. Al-Mdaires, *Islamic Extremism in Kuwait*, p. 19.

21. Ibid., p. 20.

22. Michael Herb, Kuwait Politics Database: Elections, <www.kuwaitpolitics.org/%D8%A7%D9%84%D8%A7%D9%86%D8%AA%D8%AE%D8%A8%D8%A7%D8%AA/> (last accessed 28 July 2017).

23. Nicolas Gavrielides (1987), 'Tribal democracy: the anatomy of parliamentary elections in Kuwait', in Linda L. Layne (ed.), *Elections in the Middle East: Implications of Recent Trends*. Boulder, CO and London: Westview Press, p. 183.

24. Ibid.

25. Al-Mdaires, *Islamic Extremism in Kuwait*, p. 21.

26. Carrie R. Wickham (2015), *The Muslim Brotherhood: Evolution of an Islamist Movement*. Princeton: Princeton University Press, p. 201.

27. Al-Mdaires, *Islamic Extremism in Kuwait*, p. 21.

28. Kraetzschmar, 'In the shadow of legality', p. 237.

29. Nathan J. Brown and Scott Williamson (2013), 'Kuwait's Muslim Brotherhood under pressure', *Foreign Policy*, 20 November, <http://foreignpolicy.com/2013/11/20/kuwaits-muslim-brotherhood-under-pressure/> (last accessed 21 July 2017).

30. The political agenda of Hadas includes calls for the creation of an elected PM, an enlargement of parliament and changes to its bylaws, the legalisation of political parties and electoral reform. See Nathan J. Brown and Amr Hamzawy (2010), *Between Religion and Politics*. Carnegie Endowment for International Peace, pp. 126–27; Brown, 'Pushing towards party politics?' pp. 11–12.

31. Amr Hamzawy (2008), 'Interview with Dr. Badr Al Nashi, president of Kuwait's Islamic Constitutional Movement (ICM)', *Carnegie Endowment for International Peace*, <http:// carnegieendowment.org/sada/20913 > (last accessed 15 February 2017).
32. Al-Mdaires, *Islamic Extremism in Kuwait*, pp. 33–4.
33. Carine Lahoud (2008), 'Koweït: Salafismes et rapport au pouvoir'', in Bernard Rougier (ed.), *Qu'est-ce que le salafisme?* Paris: Presses Universitaires de France, pp. 123–35.
34. Pall, 'Do Salafi parties represent a contradiction in terms?' p. 105.
35. Al-Mdaires, *Islamic Extremism in Kuwait*, pp. 34.
36. As elsewhere in the region, the Kuwaiti Salafi movement has experienced serious internal divisions throughout its existence on the issue of electoral participation and the establishment of a political party, with prominent Salafi ulema arguing that so doing would fragment the Islamic ummah. For a detailed discussion of these internal debates see Pall, 'Do Salafi parties represent a contradiction in terms?' and Pall 'Kuwaiti Salafism and its growing influence in the Levant'.
37. Zoltan Pall (2015), 'Kuwaiti Salafism after the Arab uprisings: the reconfiguration of the power balance', *Middle East Insight* No. 124, 15 April p. 1, <https://mei.nus.edu.sg/ themes/site_themes/agile_records/images/uploads/Download_Insight_124_Pall. pdf> (last accessed 20 July 2017); Al-Mdaires, *Islamic Extremism in Kuwait*, p. 35.
38. Pall, 'Kuwaiti Salafism and its growing influence in the Levant', pp. 8–10.
39. Al-Mdaires, *Islamic Extremism in Kuwait*, pp. 45–9.
40. Pall, 'Do Salafi parties represent a contradiction in terms?' p. 101.
41. Ibid., pp. 47–9.
42. Bjorn Olav Utvik (2014), 'The Ikhwanization of the Salafis: piety in the politics of Egypt and Kuwait', *Middle East Critique*, 23:1, p. 23; Pall, 'Kuwaiti Salafism and its growing influence in the Levant', p. 11; al-Mdaires, *Islamic Extremism in Kuwait*, pp. 56–8.
43. Utvik, 'The Ikhwanization of the Salafis', p. 20.
44. Ibid., p. 22.
45. Al-Mdaires, *Islamic Extremism in Kuwait*, pp. 67–8.
46. Michael Herb, Kuwait politics database – individuals and groups, <www.kuwaitpolitics.or g/%D8%A7%D9%84%D8%A7%D9%81%D8%B1%D8%A7%D8%AF-%D9%88-%D8 %A7%D9%84%D9%85%D8%AC%D9%85%D9%88%D8%B9%D8%A7%D8%AA/> (last accessed 28 July 2017).
47. Apart from those internal divisions/splits mentioned here, the SIG experienced further defections and the formation of rival groupings/proto-parties in 2003 with the formation of Tajammu' Thawabit al-Ummah (Gathering for the Umma's Principles) and in 2010, when several of its members left the proto-party and joined the opposition. See Pall, 'Do Salafi parties represent a contradiction in terms?', pp. 110–14.
48. The percentage of adherents to Shi'a Islam in the Kuwaiti population stands, according to a Pew Research Centre report, at about 20 to 25 per cent. See Pew Research Centre (2009), *Mapping the Global Muslim Population: A Report on the Size and Distribution of the World's Muslim Population*, p. 40, <www.pewforum.org/files/2009/10/Shiarange.pdf> (last accessed 20 July 2017).
49. For a fuller account of the Shi'a Islamist proto-parties scene, see Hamad H. Albloshi (2016), 'Sectarianism and the Arab Spring: the case of Kuwaiti Shi'a', *Muslim World*, 106, p. 110.
50. Ibid., p. 112.
51. There is a discrepancy in the figure of candidates and seats obtained by the INC-NIA in the 1992 elections. While Michael Herb's database mentions one candidate and seat obtained, al-Mdaires states the INC-NIA obtained two seats, with four candidates running. See al-Mdaires, *Islamic Extremism in Kuwait*, pp. 97–8.

52. Albloshi, 'Sectarianism and the Arab Spring', p. 112.
53. For more on this crisis and its effects in NIA-regime relations see al-Mdaires, *Islamic Extremism in Kuwait*, pp. 100–1.
54. Laurence Louër (2008), *Transnational Shia Politics: Religion and Political Networks in the Gulf*. New York: Columbia University Press, p. 126, cited in Albloshi, Sectarianism and the Arab Spring', p. 111.
55. Herb, Kuwait Politics Database – Shi'i Islamists, <www.kuwaitpolitics.org/pg3.htm> (last accessed 28 July 2017).
56. Gregory F. Gause III (2013), '"Nabiha 5": A Kuwaiti youth movement for political reform', *AUB Issam Fares Institute for Public Policy and International Affairs*, Background Paper.
57. According to Nathan J. Brown, the period prior to 2005 saw little effective coordination amongst (opposition) MPs mostly because of 'a weak party system hampered parliament's ability to act coherently in support of a positive agenda'. Nathan J. Brown, (2009), 'Kuwait's Islamic constitutional movement: a model or a warning for democratic Islamism?', in M. A. Mohamed Saleh (ed.), *Interpreting Islamic Political Parties*. New York: Palgrave, p. 122. Early on in the 2006 legislature, meanwhile, opposition cooperation was far more widespread with MPs from different proto-parties and blocs coordinating their positions more closely in the production of draft legislation. See Brown, 'Pushing towards party politics?' p. 18.
58. Gause, '"Nabiha 5"', pp. 6–8.
59. Al-Mdaires, *Islamic Extremism in Kuwait*, p. 222.
60. Brown, 'Pushing toward party politics?' p. 9.
61. Steve L. Monroe (2012), 'Salafis in Parliament: democratic attitudes and party politics in the Gulf', *Middle East Journal*, 66:3, pp. 412–13.
62. Mary Ann Tétreault (2006), 'Kuwait's annus mirabilis', *Middle East Report Online*, 7 September, <www.merip.org/mero/mero090706> (last accessed 20 July 2017).
63. Paul Salem (2007), 'Kuwait: politics in a participatory emirate', *Carnegie Papers*, Carnegie Middle East Centre p. 6.
64. Tétreault, 'Kuwait's annus mirabilis'.
65. Abdul Reda Assiri (2007), 'The 2006 parliamentary election in Kuwait: a new age in political participation', *Digest of Middle East Studies*, 16:2, p. 35.
66. Doron Shultziner and Mary Ann Tétreault (2012), 'Representation and democratic progress in Kuwait', *Representation*, 48:3, p. 287.
67. Anon. (date unknown), 'Kuwait's deepening political turmoil', *International Institute for Strategic Studies*, <www.iiss.org/en/iiss-middleeastarabic/latesttranslations/kuwaits-s-deepening-s-political-s-turmoil> (last accessed 28 July 2017); David Hearst (2012), 'Kuwait's protests remind us of the Arab Spring's true spirit', *The Guardian*, 2 November, <www.theguardian.com/commentisfree/2012/nov/02/kuwait-protests-arab-spring> (last accessed 28 July 2017).
68. Anon. (2011), 'Government of Kuwait hands in its resignation', *The National*, 1 April, <www.thenational.ae/world/mena/government-of-kuwait-hands-in-its-resignation-1.427164> (last accessed 29 July 2017).
69. Camilla Hall (2011), 'Kuwait tense as corruption row boils over', *Financial Times*, 23 November, <www.ft.com/content/f51de8c0-15be-11e1-8db8-00144feabdc0> (last accessed 28 July 2017).
70. Pall, 'Kuwaiti Salafism after the uprising', p. 2.
71. Anon. (2011), 'Emir of Kuwait dissolves parliament', *BBC News*, 6 December, <www.bbc.co.uk/news/world-16053422> (last accessed 28 July 2017).
72. See e.g. Herb, 'Kuwait's endless elections'.

73. Together opposition MPs held thirty-four of the fifty elective parliamentary seats. See Gwenn Okruhlik (2012), 'The identity politics of Kuwait's elections', *Foreign Policy*, 8 February, <http://foreignpolicy.com/2012/02/08/the-identity-politics-of-kuwaits-election/> (last accessed 28 July 2017).

74. See e.g. Haifa Zaaiter (2012), 'Islamists take firm grip on Kuwaiti politics', *Al-Monitor*, 11 May, <www.al-monitor.com/pulse/ar/politics/2012/05/islamists-take-advantage-amid-ri.html#ixzz4avjAZCTr> (last accessed 28 July 2017); Azzaman (2012), 'Kuwait ruling family faces impasse with parliament', *Al-Monitor*, 2 November, <www.al-monitor.com/pulse/politics/2012/10/after-demonstrations-successive-parliaments-kuwait-at-impasse.html> (last accessed 28 July 2017).

75. Habib Toumi (2012), 'Kuwait court annuls 2012 legislative elections, reinstates former parliament', Gulf News, 14 June, <http://gulfnews.com/news/gulf/kuwait/kuwait-court-annuls-2012-legislative-elections-reinstates-former-parliament-1.1038246> (last accessed 28 July 2017).

76. For more information on the new electoral law, see 'Kuwait Majles Al-Ommah (National Assembly)', *Inter-Parliamentary Union Database*, <www.ipu.org/parline-e/reports/2171_B.htm> (last accessed 28 July 2017).

77. See Anon. (2012), 'Most political groups boycotting polls', Ahram online, 29 November, <http://english.ahram.org.eg/NewsPrint/59470.aspx> (last accessed 1 December 2016).

78. Pall, 'Do Salafi parties represent a contradiction in terms?' p. 113.

79. Informal conversation by one of the authors with members of Hadas, Kuwait City, November 2014. See also Smith Kristin Diwan (2014), '"Boycott" elections distill Kuwait's divisions', *Atlantic Council*, 4 December, <www.atlanticcouncil.org/blogs/menasource/boycott-elections-distill-kuwait-s-divisions> (last accessed 27 July 2017).

80. Shultziner and Tétreault, 'Representation and democratic progress in Kuwait', p. 288.

81. Anon. (2014), 'Kuwait's opposition: a reawakening', *The Economist*, 17 April, <www.economist.com/blogs/pomegranate/2014/04/kuwaits-opposition>, quoted in Courtney Freer (2015) 'The rise of pragmatic Islamism in Kuwait's post-Spring opposition movement', *Rethinking Political Islam Series*, Brookings Institution, p. 13.

82. Ibid, p. 13.

83. Following the ousting of Morsi, the Kuwaiti press and politicians harshly criticised the KMB and Hadas, accusing it amongst others of 'plotting a coup against the Kuwait government' and warning against 'the Brotherhood's infiltration of sensitive government ministries, which could be used to spread its influence at the expense of the state'. See Nathan J. Brown and Scott Williamson (2013), 'Kuwait's Muslim Brotherhood under pressure', *Carnegie Endowment for International Peace*, 20 November, <http://carnegieendowment.org/2013/11/20/kuwait-s-muslim-brotherhood-under-pressure-pub-53670> (last accessed 28 July 2017).

84. Ibid.

85. Pall, 'Do Salafi parties represent a contradiction in terms?' pp. 115–16.

86. Anon. (2016), 'Kuwait's Islamist-dominated opposition wins near-majority in snap elections', *Deutsche Welle*, 27 November, <www.dw.com/en/kuwaits-islamist-dominated-opposition-wins-near-majority-in-snap-elections/a-36540834> (last accessed 28 July 2017).

87. Giorgi Cafiero (2017), 'Kuwait's pragmatic Islamists', *Middle East Institute*, 8 February, <www.mei.edu/content/article/kuwait-s-pragmatic-islamists> (last accessed 28 July 2017).

88. Pall, 'Kuwaiti Salafism after the uprising', pp. 4–5, 11.

Chapter 12

Secular forms of politicised Islam in Tunisia: the Constitutional Democratic Rally and Nida' Tunis

Anne Wolf

One of the byproducts of the 2010–11 Arab uprisings and the subsequent ascent of Islamist political parties in Egypt, Libya, Tunisia and Morocco was the re-emergence of Western orientalist binaries, especially the pitting of 'secularists' against 'Islamists', and a focus on the perceived polarisation between the two. Much of the scholarship that has appeared since then has tried to better understand political Islam and its various manifestations in the Arab world.[1] The 'secular', by contrast, has received much less attention, presumably because it is perceived as closer to the Western way of life and, at first sight, its meaning might appear to some almost self-explanatory. This chapter is part of an effort to balance this research bias by focusing on two parties in Tunisia that are commonly perceived in the West as showcases of 'secular' party politics: (1) Hizb al-Tajammu' al-Dustouri al-Dimuqrati (Constitutional Democratic Rally, widely known by its French acronym RCD): the quasi-*parti unique* under the former president Zine el-Abidine Ben Ali (r.1987–2011), which was dissolved by court order shortly after his ousting in January 2011 but the networks of which have remained active ever since; and (2) Hizb Nida' Tunis (Call for Tunisia), which was founded in 2012 under the premise of regrouping various political forces to counter the perceived political dominance of Hizb al-Nahda (Renaissance Party, henceforth simply al-Nahda).

The RCD and Nida' Tunis are central to understanding the characteristics of the 'secular' and secularity in Tunisia as well as the rise of legal and institutional Islamism following the 2010–12 uprisings – a trend that has sometimes been framed in opposition to Tunisia's supposed secular legacy, but that also occurred within a variety of so-called 'secular' forces. This chapter demonstrates that, in stark contrast to their secular image, both the RCD and Nida' Tunis have been home to a plurality of religious expressions and varying levels of religiosity/ secularity and that thus there is no dichotomy between the 'secular' and the 'religious' in Tunisia. Indeed, among Nida' Tunis members the place of Islam in the socio-political realm has been a key subject of controversy, alongside their relationship to al-Nahda – a tendency that was also highly visible within the RCD. Domestic and regional events have shaped internal party struggles over the role of Islam. Significantly, these have generational, geographic and social class connotations, which this chapter will discuss in more detail. As for the RCD and Nida' Tunis conflictual relationship with al-Nahda, they are only secondarily related to issues of national identity and religion. In fact, they are primarily a result of elite competition over economic and political resources. Indeed, Islam has been key to the political identity of both the RCD and Nida' Tunis; their contentions with al-Nahda have centred on the appropriation and 'correct' interpretation of religion. To underline this point, this author proposes the notion of 'secular forms of politicised Islam', which encapsulates the organic relationship between the 'religious' and 'secular' that is a reality in Tunisia as in many other countries in the region. It applies to a variety of non-Islamist actors commonly perceived as 'secular' – and who sometimes even identify as such – but who habitually employ religion in their speeches and party programmes.

The chapter first introduces the conceptual foundations of this research and then discusses historic processes of secularisation in Tunisia. It subsequently focuses on the role of Islam within the RCD, arguing that its president, Ben Ali, embarked on a path of desecularisation to respond to a surge in popular religious sentiments – a dynamic that also swayed the inner circles of the ruling party. The following section, detailing the case of Nida' Tunis, demonstrates that the role of religion remains a contentious topic among its different party factions. This author argues that the opening up of the political sphere and competition with al-Nahda have democratised religious practice and politics – a process that has reinforced the importance of Islam even in the most secular corners of Nida' Tunis.[2]

Secular forms of politicised Islam

For any scholar attempting to apprehend 'secular' politics in the Middle East and North Africa (MENA) it is first necessary to scrutinise the historic roots of 'the secular', which underlie many misconceptions of the term's contemporary use in relation to the region. The birth of 'the secular' and 'secularism' is closely linked to the emergence of modern nation states in the West, where they helped to end conflicts between competing religious sects by proposing a political system separate from religious denominations. As a process occurring alongside vast industrial and technological innovations, secularism became associated with the gradual 'modernisation' of society, while religion and myth were denounced as the antipode to 'progress'. However, in reality the place of religion in politics and society varies in secular Western countries. As Talal Asad noted, in France both the state and citizens are secular; in contrast, the British state is linked to the Church but its citizens are mainly non-religious, and in the US the state is secular but citizens are mainly religious.[3] In light of this persistent coexistence of religious and secular realms, he proposes:

> The secular … is neither continuous with the religious that supposedly proceeded it (that is, it is not the latest phase of a sacred origin) nor a simple break from it (that is, it is not the opposite, an essence that excludes the sacred). I take the secular to be a concept that brings together certain behaviours, knowledges, and sensibilities in modern life … in certain respects 'the secular' obviously overlaps with 'the religious'.[4]

Key tasks of the present research are to uncover the main characteristics of 'the secular' and 'secularism' in the RCD and Nida' Tunis and how they relate to and overlap with 'the religious'. This is facilitated by a number of important studies of 'the secular' and 'secularism'. Significantly, Hussein Ali Agrama found that, in Egypt, 'secularism itself increasingly blurs together religion and politics', a trend rooted in 'deeper indeterminacies at the very foundation of secular power'.[5] This chapter also draws on José Casanova's pre-eminent study, which disentangles three distinct processes of secularisation: (1) the decline of religious beliefs, (2) the privatisation of religion and (3) the differentiation of the secular spheres (state, science, economy) from religious institutions.[6] It also benefits from Michael Willis' singular research on political parties in the Maghreb, which traces the central features of their inner workings and *raison d'être*. Willis highlights the role of the *zaïm* (a single dominant leader) and the nature of a party's ties to the state's main powerbrokers as key factors behind its political orientation – more so than ideological divisions.[7]

Willis warns against the fallacy of viewing party politics in the Arab world through the lens of Western ideologies. In many ways, the 'barren ideological construct' of 'secularists against Islamists'[8] reflects an orientalist attempt to codify political dynamics in the region in a manner easily intelligible to Westerners. Alternative propositions – for example, viewing Tunisia's contemporary power struggles as contentious politics between democrats and non-democrats[9] – have received little attention. This is presumably in part because many Westerners – who tend to equate 'secular' with 'liberal' – find some secular parties' lack of democratic traditions confusing. In contrast, the 'secularists against Islamists' paradigm resembles the pitting of Western modernisation forces against the religious establishment in the eighteenth and nineteenth centuries, with the superiority of the secular often implicit. Yet in contrast to the Western secularism that emerged as a tool to end violent conflict, secularisation and Westernisation processes in the Arab world were mainly imposed by colonial powers and a Westernised elite. Therefore, the colours and shapes of the secular in the Arab world are often distinct from their Western manifestations. For example, while in the West secularisation and modernisation are frequently seen as concurrent processes (to the extent that the terms are often used interchangeably), in the MENA a range of socio-political forces have framed religion as compatible with modernisation, or even as a prerequisite to it. This includes some political parties commonly perceived in the West as 'secular', and whose activists sometimes self-identify as such but habitually use religious terminology in their party platforms and during speeches – a dynamic conceptualised as secular forms of politicised Islam.

Indeed, in the MENA, political parties often avoid the 'secular' label since it tends to be associated with atheism and moral decay. Instead, many use terms such as 'leftist', 'social-democrat' or 'Marxist' to express their political leanings.[10] The French legacy in Tunisia is of such importance that, in author interviews, some former members of the RCD alongside Nida' Tunis activists – especially at the elite level – described their ideological inclination as *laïque*. Yet in the vast majority of cases this characterisation did not imply that they advocated for a strict separation between religion and the state along the lines of France's *laïcité*. To better understand the particularities of the secular and Islamic dimensions within the RCD and Nida' Tunis, it is instructive to discuss briefly the historical dynamics of secularisation in Tunisia.

The many faces of secularisation

In author interviews, Nida' Tunis and ex-RCD members typically argued that Tunisia's nineteenth- and twentieth-century reformist movement constituted the forerunner of contemporary secular politics. Back then, state officials introduced innovations in sectors ranging from the military to education, and in socio-political and legal realms. While some occurred under pressure from French Protectorate officials, many were instigated independently by Tunisians, some of whom are now commemorated in statues, street names and textbooks. One of these is Kheireddine Pasha al-Tunisi, who created the Sadiki College in 1875, which taught the modern sciences alongside traditional subjects such as Qur'anic studies. Other Tunisian reformers included Shaykh Mahmood Qabadu, the spiritual guide of Tunisia's prestigious Bardo military school, who in the mid-nineteenth century called for the reintroduction of the sciences into education and asked students to translate European textbooks featuring modern subjects into Arabic.[11] However, his legacy has received little commemoration – arguably in part because his ties to the religious establishment run counter to post-independence state discourse, which frames clerics as counter-modernisation forces.

Though some religious scholars such as Shaykh Qabadu called for wide-ranging innovations,[12] many – particularly from the Zaytouna establishment, Tunisia's historic centre of Islamic learning and education – remained resistant to the kind of modernisation propagated by the state elites. In some cases, this was because of deeply entrenched religious convictions; but many clerics, alongside wide sectors of the population, also opposed reforms because they associated them with Western meddling in domestic affairs. In the words of scholar Kenneth Perkins, they 'feared that the door allowing European penetration of Tunisia, once opened, could never be closed'.[13] This was particularly the case because as early as the mid-nineteenth century – several decades before the French Protectorate was established over Tunisia in 1881 – European products came to jeopardise local economic structures and the many people relying upon them. This process was particularly visible in the souk and in southern and central Tunisia, where people were both incapable of competing with Western traders and cut off from potentially lucrative deals with them. Evidently, nineteenth-century modernisation processes were 'multi-dimensional'; whereas for some they meant 'progress', for many they entailed socio-economic marginalisation.[14]

The nationalist independence movement, organised around Hizb al-Hurr al-Dustouri al-Jadid (New Constitutional Liberal Party, also known as Neo-Destour), reflected the different sensitivities of the Tunisian people. Its president, Habib Bourguiba, hailed from the coastal town of Monastir and was educated at the prestigious Sadiki College. In contrast, its vice president, Salah Ben Youssef, grew up in a small town in the southern province of Djerba and was close to the Zaytouna establishment. While some of their socio-political susceptibilities varied, accounts that describe Bourguiba and Ben Youssef as part of a wider clash between 'a modernising liberal elite' and 'conservative forces'[15] are caricatured. For example, Hedi Baccouche – a former prime minister and close advisor of Bourguiba, who also knew Ben Youssef – stressed in front of the author that Bourguiba was very well versed in Islamic studies and entertained ties to the Zaytouna establishment.[16] Moreover, Bourguiba initially promoted conservative stances on issues such as gender policies, although he later reversed some of them.[17]

In the 1940s and early 1950s, frictions mounted between Bourguiba and Ben Youssef, who both wanted to lead the struggle for independence. Bourguiba was closer to French culture and willing to discuss the option of internal autonomy, whereas Ben Youssef immediately demanded full independence and sought to strengthen Tunisia's arabophone heritage. France's support of Bourguiba's leadership bolstered his sway, and Ben Youssef was gradually forced to seek self-exile. Yet Ben Youssef's support base within Tunisia remained substantial, particularly in the centre and south, as well as in some Tunis neighbourhoods.[18] Following independence in 1956, Bourguiba launched wide-ranging secularisation reforms, dismantling Zaytouna University and establishing a modern education sector. Bourguiba's reforms were partially driven by his desire to modernise Tunisia, yet he also sought to marginalise the constituency of Ben Youssef – a process that culminated in Bourguiba personally ordering Ben Youssef's assassination in August 1961 in Frankfurt, Germany.[19]

In subsequent years Bourguiba reinforced his secularisation programme, which focused on establishing boundaries between the state and religious institutions. It also promoted the privatisation of certain aspects of religious life, especially Islamic education. Yet religion never disappeared from the public sphere. Islam remained the official state religion and a source of legislation next to more secular laws. For example, Tunisia's renowned Personal Status Code promoted Western-style women's rights, but confirmed the status of the man as the head of the family and enshrined unequal inheritance rights, among others. Moreover, in his speeches and policy programmes, Bourguiba frequently referred to Islamic precepts and even criticised the Turkish state for its *laïcité*.[20] Such secular forms of politicised Islam illustrate that Bourguiba did not intend to abolish religion and privatise it altogether. Rather, he envisioned that the secular and the religious coexisted and complemented one another.

Bourguiba's top-down secularisation reforms did not translate into a decline in religious beliefs, however. Indeed, Mark Tessler found a rise in personal piety in the late 1960s and the early 1970s,[21] possibly in part because some portions of society felt alienated by his reforms – a tendency that highlights the organic relation between the secular and the religious in Tunisia. The Neo-Destour party – Bourguiba's quasi-*parti unique*, renamed in 1964 Hizb al-Ishtiraki al-Dustouri (Socialist Destourian Party, also known by its French acronym PSD) – accommodated this ambivalence through what Clement Henry Moore identified as the 'elasticity of the party's principles'. It allowed its members to have 'diverse views' – provided they did not challenge the authority of its uncontested *zaïm*, of course.[22] Thus, in contrast to its secular image, the PSD was also home to an 'Islamo-Destourian' faction, which sought to revive Tunisia's Islamic heritage from within the state structures.[23] It was particularly present in Tunisia's provinces, which remained largely immune to the influence that Western codes of conduct and dress codes had come to yield over the PSD in the capital and the Sahel, the coastal belt to the east. Beginning in the late 1960s, however, some religious portions of society also organised outside official state structures. They founded the secretive al-Jama'a al-Islamiyya (Islamic Group, IG), which in 1979 became Harakat al-Ittijah al-Islami (Islamic Tendency Movement, also known by its French acronym MTI) and focused on issues of morality and socio-economic deprivation. MTI activists quickly rose to become Bourguiba's main political opponents. Alongside other forces, they plotted to overthrow the ageing and increasingly senile president in 1987; yet Bourguiba's Prime Minister Ben Ali, who had devised his own coup, forestalled them. On 7 November 1987, Ben Ali deposed the president in a bloodless *oup d'état*, henceforth discontinuing his secularisation programme.

Ben Ali's RCD: desecularisation

Contrary to the common perception that Ben Ali and his RCD – which emerged out of a renaming of the PSD – 'continued the tradition of secular politics in Tunisia',[24] Tunisia's new president in fact embarked upon a process of gradual desecularisation. The RCD's *zaïm* personally launched top-down re-Islamisation campaigns, which the party's countrywide branches were central to implementing. During religious holidays, for example, local RCD offices were tasked with organising festivities and distributing gifts to the poor. On a more institutional level, soon after taking power, Ben Ali re-elevated the status of the Zaytouna to that of a university, although it had lost much of the significance it had enjoyed before independence. The new president also established a Supreme Islamic Council and a Ministry of Religious Affairs. In 2003, he created a pompous mosque in the wealthy Carthage suburb, which he named after himself and attended with his family during holidays to pray.

While some interpreted Ben Ali's desecularisation policies as a way 'to co-opt the popularity of religious sentiments in Tunisia',[25] it is questionable as to whether they were solely motivated by a desire to bolster his power. Indeed, although most were secular-leaning, some of Ben Ali's own family members were religiously observant, which interviews and documents suggest was not a pure masquerade.[26] This included his son-in-law, Sakher al-Materi, a leading figure within the RCD[27] who sought to spearhead Islamic finance and launched the religious Radio Zaytouna. Irrespective of the intentions behind the regime's re-Islamisation policies, they became a reality for many Tunisians, especially in the years immediately after Ben Ali's ascent to power. The support Shaykh Abderrahman Khelif – a former Imam of the renowned Uqba ibn Nafi Mosque in Kairouan – expressed for Ben Ali and his RCD is a case in point. Under Bourguiba, Shaykh Khelif was dismissed as an Imam after opposing the shooting of an American film inside the walls of the mosque. When Ben Ali took power, however, Shaykh Khelif was keen to join politics and even came to head the RCD electoral list during general elections in 1989. He explained:

> For almost thirty years, Islam and the men of religion were excluded and marginalised. The political change of 7 November rectified this situation. It gave back to Islam its natural place in society and the state. The current government has a Minister for Religious Affairs, a Superior Islamic Council was established, the Zitouna University is progressively becoming what it should never have ceased to be: a place of education and legitimation of Islamic faith and culture ... All this means that things are now evolving in a positive way. My presence on an RCD list means that I take this evolution into account and that I support it.[28]

Shaykh Khelif was not the only cleric to join the RCD. Indeed, many research participants affirmed that Ben Ali opened up the party to observant Muslims, who believed that the new president fought for their rights and the revival of Tunisia's Arabo-Islamic heritage. Other political tendencies also integrated into the RCD. 'Baathists, leftists, nationalists, even Islamists integrated the Rally', explained one former party member, evaluating that this broad set-up was one of the main reasons for the RCD's disintegration in later years.[29] The Islamo-Destourian tendency within the RCD became particularly strong within the central and southern provinces, where Bourguiba's secularisation programme had remained limited in sway and big family clans dominated political life. One former RCD leader from Gafsa affirmed that, in the south, 'some family clans sympathise with religious themes [and] family topics'. He suggested that 'these religious roots ... reflect in part the roots of Hizb al-Nahda',[30] which emerged out of the renaming of the MTI in 1988 and constituted the regime's most fervent opposition. Yet not all observant Muslims supported the 'political position of Hizb al-Nahda', which was particularly popular among the youth, so some of them joined the RCD.[31] When referring to al-Nahda's 'political position', the research participant alluded to the primacy its members supposedly bestowed on Islamic law. Some activists of al-Nahda's more scripturalist wing indeed desired the establishment of some kind of Islamic state at that time, but others favoured a more flexible interpretation of religious texts and early on called for multi-party rule, encompassing also leftist forces.[32] Thus, while there were ideological differences between al-Nahda members and the RCD, there were also common interfaces. Both the more pragmatic al-Nahda members and the RCD's Islamo-Destourian wing called for an increased role for religion without challenging the foundations of the state.

The sharp political reservations many RCD activists harboured against al-Nahda, including from the Islamo-Destourian wing, must be understood in a context in which state officials stoked fears that its followers would pursue 'extremist' policies if elected. They affirmed that al-Nahda constituted a danger to national unity and security, and brutally cracked down on the movement. Implicitly, such rhetoric helped to reinforce the RCD's own supposed commitment to a 'moderate' Islam. Many observant Muslims who decided to join the RCD affirmed in front of the author that Ben Ali defended the 'right' Islam and protected Tunisia from 'extremists'.[33] Many alleged that al-Nahda members followed the political goals of the international al-Ikhwan al-Muslimun (Muslim Brotherhood, MB) and were hence unpatriotic. They typically denounced al-Nahda's desire to conflate religion with politics, seemingly oblivious of the RCD's own politicised forms of Islam – a trend that highlights the power of rhetoric in gaining religious legitimacy. Indeed, in an attempt to counter the persistent sway of al-Nahda, state authorities were particularly careful to monitor and control religious discourses, especially in places of worship – traditionally the centre of the Islamists' recruitment efforts. Among others, officials in the Ministry of Religious Affairs wrote the content of sermons to be held in mosques. Provincial governors, usually with close ties to the ruling party, proposed Imams, who were then appointed by the Ministry of Interior.[34] Clearly, the regime's politicised expressions of Islam evolved around the appropriation and promotion of the 'right' Islam, alongside the use of physical and symbolic violence against its religious contenders.

The exact nature of this Islam remained contested, however, including within the inner circles of the RCD. This was particularly the case from the 2000s onwards, when 'new Islamic veils'[35] emerged in Tunisia (alongside many other countries). These headscarves, which were particularly popular among youthful women, did not necessarily signify adherence to the MB or one of its regional offshoots, but reflected wider social, cultural and aesthetic sensitivities. This included a reinterpretation of 'the modern' as compatible with religious practice and belief.[36] Ben Ali initially interpreted the increasing presence of the Islamic veil – previously worn almost exclusively by al-Nahda supporters – as a threat to his religious authority, and responded by reinforcing anti-*hijab* laws. Yet such policies were criticised by religious corners of his own constituencies – particularly in the centre and south and in popular Tunis neighbourhoods, where new veils had become popular among young women. In these locations, many grass-roots RCD followers denounced the crackdown on *hijab* wearers as a violation of Ben Ali's stated commitment to promoting Islam. In contrast, the more francophone elite of the RCD – mostly in the northern suburbs of Tunis and the Sahel – often played a key role in enforcing anti-*hijab* policies, including during sensitive periods such as Ramadan.[37] This illustrates the great extent to which the level of religiosity or secularity differed among RCD members depending on factors such as social class, age and locality. If Tunisia's contemporary political landscape is often seen through the lens of 'Islamists versus secularists', the RCD itself was a platform in which battles over the role of Islam in society and politics were fought; its activists came in many different colours and shapes, and varying levels of religiosity and secularity.

Nida' Tunis' brand of Islam

Friction between different RCD constituencies heightened during the 2010–11 uprisings, which launched a wider restructuring process of the religious political scene in Tunisia. Many RCD officials framed their opposition to the protests, which culminated in the overthrow of Ben Ali, through a religious lens. During author interviews, some denounced Mohamed Tarek Bouazizi, whose self-immolation sparked the countrywide protests, and said he should not be celebrated as a martyr because suicide is prohibited in Islam – statements many RCD grass-roots activists, who often joined the protests, fiercely denounced.[38] RCD figureheads also sought to bolster the regime's religious and symbolic authority by praising Ben Ali's religious objectives and *avant-garde* policies; these discourses were spread through the regime's omnipresent media organs, including *Le Renouveau*, the RCD's daily publication.[39] During the unrest, *Le Renouveau* also called upon Imams to 'attend training sessions to improve their performance and the quality of their work' and to 'adapt the religious discourse to the concerns and expectations of Tunisians'.[40] By staging a commitment to religious renewal and reforms, RCD officials sought to contain internal criticism over Ben Ali's religious credentials at a time when his overall legitimacy was quickly crumbling.

Frictions between rival RCD trends further intensified following Ben Ali's ousting on 14 January 2011. In author interviews, some former party activists blamed the RCD's 'Islamist elements' for Ben Ali's fall and the subsequent dissolution of the RCD, in complete denial that a range of non-Islamist activists were a central force behind the protest movement. In part, their denunciation of the Islamo-Destourian faction as 'Islamists' results from a restructuring of the political scene that took place after the uprisings. This restructuring saw some RCD individuals alongside prominent family clans from the Islamo-Destourian wing (mostly in central and southern Tunisia) join al-Nahda, a development some interpreted as evidence that they had never been truly loyal to Ben Ali. However, some Islamo-Destourian activists also became members of Nida' Tunis, which absorbed a particularly high number of former RCD members. Some of them joined Nida' Tunis because they believed the party was best placed to defend their socio-economic interests, or because they did not support al-Nahda's political platform, even though they were close to its socio-cultural premises. As a consequence of such restructuring, the religious divisions between Nida' Tunis and al-Nahda have become blurred in the provinces and at the local level. Sofien, a former RCD youth leader from the Sidi Bouzid governorate in central Tunisia who is close to Nida' Tunis, told the author:

> We are witnessing a new generation of parties which are not based on ideological differences ... Instead this new generation of parties is based on programmes. Their programmes need to be followed and they have to reflect that we are living in an Arab and Islamic country.[41]

For Sofien, the differences between Nida' Tunis and al-Nahda are rooted in the concrete policies their leaders pursue but are not ideological, as both parties act within the framework of Tunisia's Arabo-Islamic heritage. So, from a religious point of view, Sofien did not distinguish between the followers of al-Nahda and Nida' Tunis. While this might at first seem counterintuitive, in the provinces many common Islamic traditions (such as women covering their hair) are practised by al-Nahda and Nida' Tunis followers alike. By contrast, it would be unthinkable for female Nida' Tunis leaders, who typically hail from the capital or the Sahel, to wear the headscarf, a practice strongly associated at a national level with al-Nahda women.

Even though the secularism of Nida' Tunis' political figureheads is more pronounced in the capital, its characteristics and particularities have markedly evolved in the years since the party's creation. Nida' Tunis emerged out of a perceived need to regroup a range of non-Islamist actors to counter the political dominance of al-Nahda, which emerged as the biggest electoral force in the October 2011 Constituent Assembly election. Nida' Tunis includes leftists, labour unionists and women's rights activists alongside many former RCD members. Like previous RCD officials, Nida' Tunis leaders positioned themselves as the 'moderate' alternative to al-Nahda, which they denounced as 'extremist'. They stressed al-Nahda's supposed links to the MB, in contrast to Nida' Tunis' roots in the eighteenth-century Tunisian reformist movement. Such a stance was attractive to a range of people, particularly after the assassination of two political opposition figures by religious radicals in 2013, events that Nida' Tunis blamed on the al-Nahda-led Troika government. The assassinations evoked a major popular outcry, as well as the withdrawal of dozens of lawmakers from the Constituent Assembly.[42] Nida' Tunis activists, capitalising on the popular outrage, intensified their anti-al-Nahda rhetoric to bolster their political sway. They also stressed their commitment to 'modern' values, including women's rights, alleging that al-Nahda was pursuing a 'retrograde' agenda. However, the fact that Nida' Tunis officials failed to promote many of its female activists to key party posts exposed the gap between its stated values and actual practices.[43] Initially, therefore, anti-Islamism remained the strongest glue holding the party's diverse membership together.

However, once the Troika had resigned and a national unity government was created, Nida' Tunis' leaders revisited their ideological underpinnings and increasingly came to stress their own Islamic values and roots. During the 2014 election campaign, many observers noticed that the only party officials who seemingly did not stop talking about Islam hailed from Nida' Tunis.[44] In part, this was certainly a strategic considerations, particularly a fear of being considered too *laïque* or even atheist – an appearance that had disfavoured their secular counterparts during the 2011 ballots.[45] However, it also reflected an internal search for the party's own religious identity, especially once its focus on anti-Islamism became politically unsustainable.

Three key dynamics led many Nida' Tunis leaders gradually to distance themselves from the anti-al-Nahda label and to embrace politicised forms of Islam. First, al-Nahda leaders' persistent focus on reconciliation and compromise, which rendered many accusations of them being 'extremists' obsolete; second, the eruption of religious violence under the national unity government, which demonstrated that insecurity and political instability were not tied to al-Nahda's rule; and third – and most importantly – Nida' Tunis' coalition government with al-Nahda, alongside some smaller parties, which was created following the October 2014 parliamentary elections out of a need to ensure a stable parliamentary majority. Nida' Tunis' decision to enter into a coalition with al-Nahda led to an outcry among its most secular corners. It reinforced frictions among rival leaders within Nida' Tunis that culminated in a major internal party split when Mohsen Marzouk, a leftist figurehead, left the party in December 2015.[46] Yet some leftists and women's rights activists decided to remain loyal to Nida' Tunis. In front of the author, one leftist lawmaker said: 'Hizb al-Nahda … is a religious party, but it changed, it started to change. I am actually not sure if [Hizb al-Nahda] is really changing or if it just pretends to'.[47] While many leftists and secular women's rights activists remained confused about their coalition with al-Nahda – their previous arch-enemy – Nida' Tunis' RCD constituency was comparatively compromising towards the Islamists. This is because, in contrast to the far left, al-Nahda leaders sought reconciliation with members of the former ruling party and supported their reintegration into politics – a tendency that highlights the complexity of Tunisia's emerging political landscape, which cannot be grasped through the 'Islamist versus secularists' paradigm. Post-uprising political alliances and coalitions are driven by various factors. While some of these are ideological and religious, they are usually forged on the basis of shared strategic interests, party leaders' priorities and social and regional affiliations.

Conclusion

As Nida' Tunis figureheads sought to move beyond their anti-Islamism to focus on their own religious underpinnings, they re-established ties with the Zaytouna University and stressed their adherence to the Maliki school of Islam, historically the most influential Islamic jurisprudence in Tunisia. Moreover, the secular-leaning media regularly distributes pictures of Nida' Tunis leaders praying and visiting mosques to prop up their religious and symbolic capital. Beji Caid Essebsi, the founder of Nida' Tunis who was elected president in 2014, even published a book entitled *Tunisia: Democracy in the Land of Islam* in December 2016, which is dedicated to advocating the compatibility of Islam and democracy – also a key concern of al-Nahda since the 1990s. In an interview with this author, Mohamed Ghariani – the RCD's last Secretary General, who joined Nida' Tunis after the uprisings before integrating a competitor party, Mubadara (Initiative) – explained:

> Islam is different [from Christianity]. The West managed to separate religion from politics. In the Muslim world, this is difficult. I am in favour of reforming Islam and I prefer to encourage political currents that accept change [and] make efforts to reform their ideological and religious ideas. I consider Hizb al-Nahda in this context.[48]

Ghariani clearly seeks to portray himself as a conciliatory figure between al-Nahda and former RCD officials. Whether based on actual convictions or strategic considerations, Ghariani's statement illustrates the extent to which a variety of political forces have sought not only political but also religious reconciliation after the uprisings. As a consequence, the Islamic underpinnings of Nida' Tunis and al-Nahda are progressively converging on not only the local but also the national level. This has become even more the case since al-Nahda's party congress in May 2016, when its officials abandoned the Islamist label to become 'Muslim democrats'.[49] Al-Nahda officials also sought to prop up their religious capital by framing their movement as part of Tunisia's early nineteenth and twentieth-century reformist movement – just like RCD and Nida' Tunis leaders. In their competition for religious authority and legitimacy, both al-Nahda and Nida' Tunis leaders are increasingly adapting their policies to the religious sensitivities and concerns of the people, portraying themselves as centrist and modern religious forces. As a result, Nida' Tunis' use of religious discourse and religious-inspired policy has not merely become more acceptable – it has become a political priority. Ultimately, the 2010–12 uprisings not only diversified the political and religious landscapes in Tunisia but also democratised religious practice and politics.

Notes

1. See e.g. Robin Wright (ed.) (2012), *The Islamists Are Coming: Who They Really Are*. Herndon: United States Institute of Peace Press; Tariq Ramadan (2012), *Islam and the Arab Awakening*. New York: Oxford University Press; George Joffé (ed.) (2012), *Islamist Radicalisation in North Africa: Politics and Process*. London: Routledge; Francesco Cavatorta and Fabio Merone (eds) (2015), *Salafism after the Arab Awakening*. London: Hurst.

2. The data for this chapter were gathered through interviews and archival research was carried out in Tunisia between February 2012 and September 2016, as part of a book project on political Islam and a doctoral thesis about CDR networks. Together, these projects helped to uncover some of the contradictions inherent in the 'secularists versus Islamists' paradigm in Tunisia.

3. Talal Asad (2003), *Formations of the Secular: Christianity, Islam, Modernity*. Stanford: Stanford University Press, p. 2.

4. Ibid., p. 25.

5. Hussein Ali Agrama (2010), 'Secularism, sovereignty, indeterminacy: is Egypt a secular or a religious state?' *Comparative Studies in Society and History*, 52:3, p. 495.

6. José Casanova (2002), 'Rethinking secularization: a global comparative perspective', *Hedgehog Review*, 8:1/2, pp. 7–22.

7. Michael J. Willis (2002), 'Political parties in the Maghrib: the illusion of significance?' *Journal of North African Studies*, 7:2, pp. 1–22.

8. This expression was borrowed from Tariq Ramadan (2012), 'Waiting for an Arab Spring of ideas', *New York Times*, 30 September.

9. The notion of democrats versus non-democrats was brought up regularly during author interviews with civil society activists and members of Tunisia's Hizb al-Mu'tammar min ajl al-Jamhuriyya (Congress for the Republic Party), including with former President Moncef Marzouki, May 2015, Tunis.

10. John L. Esposito (1998), *Rethinking Islam and Secularism*, ARDA Paper Series, <www.thearda.com/rrh/papers/guidingpapers/esposito.pdf> (last accessed 4 December 2016).

11. Mohamed El-Tahir El-Mesawi (2008), 'Muslim reformist action in nineteenth-century Tunisia', *American Journal of Islamic Social Sciences*, 25:2, p. 51.

12. Another example is Shaykh Mohamed Al-Tahir Ibn Ashur (1879–1973), who called for the reopening of *ijtihad*; that is, the interpretation and independent reasoning of Islamic law.

13. Kenneth J. Perkins (2008), *A History of Modern Tunisia*. Cambridge: Cambridge University Press, p. 24.

14. See for details: Anne Wolf (2017), *Political Islam in Tunisia: The History of Ennahda*. New York: Oxford University Press.

15. Mounira M. Charrad and Allyson B. Goeken, 'Continuity or change: family law and family structure in Tunisia', in Yaw Oheneba-Sakyi and Baffour K. Takyi (eds), *African Families at the Turn of the 21st Century*. Westport, CT: Praeger, p. 30.

16. Interview with Hedi Baccouche, September 2015, Tunis.

17. Among others, Bourguiba initially voiced reservations about Tahar Haddad, who advocated for more women's rights through Islamic precepts. For details, see Wolf, *Political Islam in Tunisia*.

18. The March 1956 Constituent Assembly elections revealed that, even following Independence, Ben Youssef's support remained significant. Voter abstention rates reached 71 per cent in Djerba, his hometown, and 41 per cent in Tunis. For details see Perkins, *A History of Modern Tunisia*, p. 131.

19. Yadh Ben Achour (1979), 'Islam perdu, Islam retrouve', *Annuaire de l'Afrique du Nord*, p. 68.

20. For details see Lofti Hajji (2011), *Bourguiba et l'Islam: le Politique et le Religieux*. Tunis: Sud Editions, p. 31.

21. For details, see Mark A. Tessler (1980), 'Political change and the Islamic revival in Tunisia', *Maghreb Review*, 5:1, pp. 8–19.

22. Clement Henry Moore (1965), *Tunisia since Independence: The Dynamics of One-Part Government*. Berkeley: University of California Press, pp. 106–7.

23. This term was borrowed from Michel Camau and Vincent Geisser (2003), *Le Syndrome Autoritaire: Politique en Tunisie de Bourguiba à Ben Ali*. Paris: Presses de Sciences Po, p. 276.

24. Angel M. Rabasa, Cheryl Benard, Peter Chalk, C. Christian Fair, Theodore Karasik, Rollie Lal, Ian Lesser and David Thaler (2004), *The Muslim World After 9/11*. Santa Monica, CA: RAND Corporation, p. 157.

25. Anon. (2005), 'The dichotomy of Islam in Tunisia', *Wikileaks, Cable from US Embassy* (05TUNIS2420), 29 November, <https://wikileaks.org/plusd/cables/05TUNIS2564_a.html> (last accessed 9 June 2017).

26. Interview with a friend of Sakher el-Materi's family, October 2016, Tunis. For more details, see also Anon. (2009), 'Tunisia: Dinner with Sakher El Materi', *Wikileaks, Cable from US Embassy* (09TUNIS516), 27 July, <https://wikileaks.org/plusd/cables/09TUNIS516_a.html> (last accessed 9 December 2016).

27. In the late 2000s, al-Materi became a member of the CDR Central Committee and an MP.

28. Anon. (1989), 'Interview avec Cheikh Abderrahman Khelif', *Réalités*, 189, 31 March–6 April.

29. Interview with Abderrazak Souileh, June 2016, Gafsa.

30. Interview with Sofien, June 2016, Sidi Bouzid governorate.

31. Interview with Gley Kaabachi, June 2016, Gafsa.

32. For details, see Wolf, *Political Islam in Tunisia*.

33. Interview with Mehdi, September 2015, Tunis-Bab Souika. For a comparative perspective, see Rikke Hostrup Haugbølle (2015), 'New expressions of Islam in Tunisia: an ethnographic approach', *Journal of North African Studies*, 20:3, pp. 319–35.

34. See for details Anne Wolf, *Political Islam in Tunisia*.

35. Mohamed Kerrou (2010), *Hijâb: Nouveaux Voiles et Espaces Publics*. Tunis: Cérès éditions.

36. Ibid.

37. Anon. (2006), 'Tunisian government cracks down on Hijab', *Wikileaks, Cable from US Embassy* (06TUNIS2565_a), 13 October, <https://wikileaks.org/plusd/cables/06TUNIS2565_a.html> (last accessed 9 December 2016).

38. Several CDR officials reiterated this during author interviews. See also Anne Wolf (2017), '"Dégage RCD!" The rise of internal dissent in Ben Ali's constitutional democratic rally and the Tunisian uprisings', *Mediterranean Politics*, published online, 7 February.

39. Anon. (2011), 'Rationaliser le discours religieux, consacrer les nobles valeurs de l'Islam', *Le Renouveau*, 13 January.

40. Ibid.

41. Interview with Sofien, June 2016, Sidi Bouzid governorate.
42. For details, see Anne Wolf (2014), 'Can secular parties lead the new Tunisia?' *Carnegie Endowment for International Peace*, April 2014, <http://carnegieendowment.org/2014/04/30/can-secular-parties-lead-new-tunisia-pub-55438> (last accessed 12 May 2017).
43. For example, during interviews in the Nida' Tunis headquarters, the author struggled to meet female party members because the vast majority of its leaders were men.
44. This impression was repeatedly voiced during interviews and confirmed by the author's own observations.
45. For details, see Wolf, 'Can secular parties lead the new Tunisia?'.
46. The split was also driven by leadership struggles within Nida' Tunis, which pitted a clan led by Essebsi's son, Hafedh, against political rivals who denounced his ascent as undemocratic and nepotistic.
47. Interview with Mohamed Anour Adhar, May 2016, Bardo.
48. Interview with Mohammed Ghariani, May 2016, Tunis.
49. See e.g. Ibish, Hussein (2016), '"Islamism is dead!" Long live Muslim democrats', *New York Times*, 2 June.

Chapter 13

Political parties and secular–Islamist polarisation in post-Mubarak Egypt

Hendrik Kraetzschmar and Alam Saleh

This chapter is concerned with the polarisation that gripped Egyptian politics in the period following the Tahrir uprising of 2011 and the *coup d'état* of 3 July 2013 which led to the ousting of the country's first directly elected post-uprising president Mohamed Morsi.[1] Whilst this polarisation took on many shapes, involving contentious episodes between revolutionaries and *felool*,[2] between establishment politicians and advocates of radical structural reform, as well as between leftist, nationalist and liberal forces,[3] its most talked-about dynamic concerned the discursive and physical battles fought out between the country's so-called 'secular' and 'Islamist' forces.[4] Indeed, the growth in secular–Islamist polarisation – particularly with the coming to power of al-Ikhwan al-Muslimun (Muslim Brotherhood, MB) in 2012 – has become one of the more pertinent prisms through which local protagonists and outside observers have sought to evaluate this early post-uprising period.[5] Unfortunately, for the most part this was done by means of a rather uncritical usage of labels such as 'secular' and/or 'Islamist', and by treating secularism and Islamism as discrete ideological frames.

Drawing on a range of interviews conducted with party elites,[6] this chapter casts a critical eye on the secular–Islamist binary in early post-uprising Egyptian party politics. With a focus on the country's secular parties, it scrutinises their discourses and policies during the 2011–13 period, juxtaposing the two and assessing them within the context of an alleged secular–Islamist polarisation. Two inter-related scholarly debates will hereby form the theoretical point of departure. The first debate concerns the legacy of secular–Islamist rivalries in Egyptian (party) politics, dating back to the al-Sadat presidency (r.1970–81), and more recent efforts at cross-ideological cooperation between representa-tives of leftist, liberal and Islamist political currents. Gaining traction in the early 2000s, a handful of academics in Egypt and elsewhere in the region have studied the rising occurrence of such cross-ideological initiatives, critically unpacking the depth and purpose of such collaboration as well as their propensity to overcome decades-old ideological divisions in favour of joint opposition activism against authoritarian incumbency. Whilst cautiously optimistic about its occurrence, in the Egyptian case much of this work pre-2011 revealed such cross-ideological cooperation to be mostly short-termist and tactical in nature, involving few attempts at policy accommodation and compromise, let alone the development of a common political vision among the collaborating parties. The academic tenor at the time thus appeared to be broadly sceptical about the implications of such collaboration for future ideological accommodation and unity of purpose in the eventuality of regime change.[7] Regrettably, since the Arab uprisings, this nascent literature has seen little further advancement, and to date a retrospection of the impact of such cross-ideological collaborative endeavours in light of the Egyptian uprising and its aftermath remains lacking.

Connected to the first is the second academic literature of relevance here which revolves around the antipode to cross-ideological cooperation: that of ideological polarisation. Following Piero Stanig, polarisation, as it pertains to party elites, is here conceptualised as the distance in policy positions from the political centre, however defined.[8] For the analysis at hand, the political centre of the pre-2013 party system is identified as the estimated mid-point between the two most extreme political parties on a two-dimensional progressive–conservative socio–cultural and left–right economic scale. As highlighted above, numerous commentators and scholars of Egyptian politics have characterised the period between the ousting of Mubarak and the July 2013 *coup d'état* as highly polarised, with elite contention revolving primarily around secular and Islamist ideological poles. However, this representation of Egyptian politics is being increasingly challenged by scholars who question bounded conceptualisations of ideology that (1) fail to recognise the cross-fertilisation between, and fluidity of, ideological currents in Egypt and (2) are evoked and reproduced by protagonists on the ground for instrumental power-political purposes.[9] As Sune Haugbølle notes in this regard, scholars of the Arab world 'have tended to separate Islamist and secular positions too neatly'.[10] It follows that what is needed is a far more critical engagement with, and deconstruction of, the 'secular–Islamist' binary as well as clarification of what we mean by polarisation in the Egyptian context.

Feeding into both the aforementioned debates, in the case of Egypt this chapter makes the following assertion: elite polarisation as it takes place at the discursive level is not necessarily a sanguine reflection of the factual ideological/policy distances extant between political parties. As will become apparent below, in the Egyptian case, elite discourse at the back end of June 2013 was highly polarised, evoking a bifurcation of the party landscape into a secular camp and an Islamist camp marked by near irreconcilable differences. This discourse sits at unease, however, with some of the realities on the ground, which present a party landscape in which differences in policy positions – particularly with regards to the role of religion in the public realm and on the economy – were far less clear-cut than the secular–Islamist binary makes one believe, and which saw the emergence of several parties that identified themselves as post- or cross-ideological.

When it comes to the study of party politics, evidence from Egypt thus suggests that, whilst elite polarisation can be *substantive* – that is, it can revolve around policy distances – it may also be *strategic*, that is, it can be deployed rhetorically by party officials for power-political considerations/gains, and that the two do not necessarily go hand in hand. As regards the Egyptian case, it is apparent, in fact, that this distinction has been insufficiently drawn in most (scholarly) accounts of the elite polarisation that gripped domestic politics in the 2011–13 period, thus precipitating an imagery of the Egyptian party landscape in the early post-Mubarak era that is incomplete at the least and distorted at worst.

The Tahrir spirit, the Morsi presidency and the politics of polarisation

When mass demonstrations swept Egyptian autocrat Hosni Mubarak (r.1981–2011) from power in early 2011, there were as yet few signs that the transitional months following his ousting and the election of a new parliament and president in 2011–12 would be characterised by high levels of elite polarisation. Indeed, the uprising in Egypt, as elsewhere in the region, was marked not only by the hope of millions of citizens that decades of authoritarianism would make way for a just and democratic order, but by a unique spirit of unity and respect among the different political forces in Egyptian politics.[11] As we now know, this Tahrir spirit was short-lived – driven as it was by a shared desire to see the back of Mubarak – and quickly unravelled into growing animosity and conflict between the various forces vying for power in the 'new' Egypt, most notably of course between the MB and its affiliate, Hizb al-Hurriyya wa al-'Adala (Freedom and Justice Party, FJP)[12] and the secular political opposition, comprising both old and new forces on the party political scene. As detrimental as it ultimately proved to be to the prospects for democratic change, the fact that Egypt's revolutionary moment unravelled so quickly into acrimony and conflict following the successful ousting of Mubarak should not come as a surprise. Indeed, a close reading of pre-uprising Egyptian politics, particularly following the *infitah* (open door) policies introduced by al-Sadat,[13] reveals a protracted history of hostility and rivalry between secular and Islamist opposition groupings/parties. While the regime was intent on keeping the opposition divided, the secular opposition was driven largely by suspicion of the MB's political project. It particularly questioned the Islamists' claim of being committed to pluralism and democracy, and feared its superior capacity for societal outreach and electoral mobilisation.[14] Placing a gun theatrically on his desk in an interview with one of the authors in the early 2000s, one leading leftist politician asserted that he kept it for the purpose of deterring MB members from visiting party premises, thus vividly illustrating the scale of hostility and intolerance extant particularly in leftist quarters towards the group.[15]

As it turns out, during the Mubarak era (and beyond) this legacy of mutual suspicion and intolerance proved too persuasive to eventually yield to a spirit of broad-based opposition collaboration and accommodation, and this despite the various cross-ideological initiatives between leftist, liberal, nationalist and Islamist activists that had gained traction from the mid-1990s onwards.[16] Several factors may account for the failure of such cross-ideological cooperation to lay the foundation for fostering inter-elite trust and for bridging extant ideological/policy divisions. As Maha Abdelrahman highlighted, first, in most instances these collaborative episodes occurred outside the realm of formal politics, revolving around informal networks of activists and groupings rather than institutionalised parties and party elites, many of whom retained deep-seated resentments against one another, particularly among the older guards. Added to this can be the short-termist/strategic nature of much of this collaboration, which militated against the possibility of longer-term consensus-building and was often premised on the retention of high levels of independence and decision-making autonomy among the collaborating actors.[17] In this Egypt's experience in cross-ideological cooperation contrasts with that of Tunisia, where collaborative endeavours such as the 18 October Collectif were set up by ideologically diverse parties and civil society organisations with the explicit aim of reaching consensus on a post-Ben Ali political settlement, which survived in an authoritarian setting for five years. Indeed, whilst failing to expedite President Ben Ali's downfall, the Collectif arguably played an important (yet certainly not the only) role in setting the scene for the inter-elite accommodation reached in the 2011–12 Constituent Assembly, thus paving the way for the successful conclusion of the country's transition phase.[18] As concerns Egypt, meanwhile, Ellen Lust rightly predicted that the short-termist and strategic nature of past cross-ideological cooperation would render multi-issue coalitions between secular and Islamist groupings vastly more difficult to sustain, particularly once the stakes of removing Mubarak from office were replaced by the need to formulate a new post-Mubarak democratic order.[19] With little trust and social capital developed between political elites, and virtually no legacy of cross-ideological accommodation on substantive issues – let alone on a common vision for Egypt[20] – to build on, the chances for consensus on the country's future political identity thus seemed bleak.

That this eventuality became reality is now widely known. Indeed, once the dust had settled on the Tahrir uprising, relations between secular and Islamist political parties quickly descended into rivalry and acrimony, with the secular opposition decrying among others the 'power grab' and exclusionary style of governance by the MB and its FJP affiliate, and the Morsi administration in turn charging the secular opposition with subverting a democratically elected government, stirring chaos and plotting the president's downfall.[21] Several contentious episodes during the initial Supreme Council of the Armed Forces (SCAF)-led transition (February 2011–June 2012) and throughout the short-lived Morsi presidency (June 2012–July 2013) fuelled this polarisation, which eventually culminated in mass demonstrations against MB/FJP rule and the ousting of Morsi by the armed forces in July 2013. During the SCAF period the key bones of contention, resulting in a wave of (at times violent) protests and counter-protests, revolved primarily around the question of whether parliamentary/presidential elections should precede or follow the drafting of a new constitution and whether SCAF should issue a set of supra-constitutional principles, guiding the ensuing constitution-drafting process. Whilst the MB and its allies supported the SCAF transition plan of elections first and fiercely opposed the issuing of such a set of principles, its rivals from the secular opposition took the reverse stance, demanding the constitution be drafted before the scheduling of elections and, once this was voted down in the May 2011 constitutional referendum, unsuccessfully lobbied SCAF for the adoption of such supra-constitutional principles.[22] During the Morsi presidency, meanwhile, the bifurcation of the post-uprising political scene into proponents and opponents of the MB/FJP garnered further pace, particularly in the aftermath of the president's constitutional declaration in November 2012[23] and throughout the constitution-drafting process. Decried by his opponents as an illegitimate power grab, the former resulted in the formation of Jabhat al-Inqadh al-Watani (National Salvation Front, NSF), which comprised a broad collection of leftist, liberal and conservative parties as well as prominent public figures, and which from then on became the lead institutionalised expression of opposition to the Morsi government.[24] Secular–Islamist trenches were further deepened by the alleged unwillingness of President Morsi to form an inclusive administration, as well as around contention over the composition, content and drafting process of Egypt's first democratic constitution. At the time, most representatives of the secular opposition critiqued not only the lack of diversity in the 100-member Constituent Assembly tasked with drafting the new constitution, but the

Islamist character of the draft charter and the manner in which it was rushed through ratification by Morsi. Consequently, numerous representatives of opposition parties, the Coptic Church and other Christian denominations, as well as of revolutionary groups and professional syndicates, walked out of the Constituent Assembly and called for a rejection of the draft constitution in the ensuing referendum.[25]

With moderate voices drowned out in an increasingly acrimonious showdown between proponents and opponents of Morsi and his government, the scene was hence set for the ultimate collapse of the transition to democracy and a return to military rule.

Party elites and the polarisation discourse

How then did this polarisation of Egyptian politics play out at the discursive level? What were the discursive practices used in the accounts given by secular party elites of the political conflict unfolding between proponents and opponents of the MB/FJP and the Morsi government? Honing in on the 2012–13 period, several common traits can be detected in the discursive practices deployed by secular party elites for the purpose of self-description and the 'labelling' of the other; that is the MB/FJP and its allies. These included the evocation of an 'us-versus-them' binary that emphasised the positive properties/actions of oneself and derided those of the others, and which was clearly aimed at undermining the legitimacy of the Morsi government and the country's Islamist parties more broadly. To this end as well, secular party elites also drew on the discursive practices of 'categorisation' and 'distancing'. Categorisation, as elaborated upon by Mohammed Eissa, refers to the 'grouping of entities into larger categories',[26] which usually carry negative/ideological connotations and are deployed for the purpose of creating stereotypes and to stigmatise the other.[27] Distancing, as coined by the authors, in turn, relates to the self-positioning of individual parties on a party political spectrum and contains two types of speech acts: those that emphasise (ideological) distance over extant policy congruence/convergence as well as conversely those that emphasise (ideological) proximity at the expense of policy distance. Both types of distancing were evident in the Egyptian case.

As will become apparent below, in the Egyptian case the discourse deployed by secular party elites at the back end of the Morsi presidency was very much a reflection of, and shaped/constrained by, the broader societal givens in the country as well as the more immediate political context. Indeed, both the prevalence of a deep-seated religiosity and conservatism in Egyptian society[28] as well as the ascendancy to power of the MB/FJP and its governance since 2012 circumscribed the narrative of secular party elites, particularly in regards to their self-positioning within the nascent party system and their assessment of the culprits of elite polarisation. When it comes to an assessment by secular party elites of Egyptian party politics and the Morsi presidency, for instance, the tenor was unequivocal: ideological polarisation was a reality and was seen as being stoked by the MB/FJP and other Islamist parties to discredit the secular opposition in the eyes of a largely devout voting population. This was apparent, according to these elite accounts, in the evocation by Morsi and the MB/FJP of 'us-versus-them', 'good-versus-evil' narratives that drew on sharp binaries between 'believers' and 'non-believers', the 'devout' and the 'infidel', between those who are 'with' and those who are 'anti-Shari'ah' and/or those who practise Islam as opposed to secularists or atheists, who have abandoned their faith.[29] For some secular party elites, in fact, the use of such rhetorical binaries constituted nothing less than an attempt by Morsi and the MB/FJP to present its opponents as operating outside the bounds of the Egyptian mainstream and to cloak normal politics in a religious mantle for electioneering purposes.[30]

As a means of retorting to such alleged depictions by the MB/FJP and its allies many secular party elites deployed two rhetorical devices. First, they reiterated a mantra that, as Marina Ottaway and Amr Hamzawy have highlighted,[31] hawks back to the Mubarak era, arguing that their parties are in fact not secular in the sense of being anti-religious, but 'civil' parties that are neither anti-Islamic nor opposed to the country's religious heritage and identity.[32] Illustrative of such counter-exclamations is the introspection of one Hizb al-Karama (Dignity Party, henceforth referred to as Karama) official, who stated that secularism was alien to Egypt and that:

> the Nasserite party is a national party with leftist leanings. The term left is a bit problematic. If by left I mean 'classes' and 'social justice', then the Karama party is a leftist party in that sense. If you mean left as adhering to communism, then we are not leftists. We are not a liberal party in the Western liberal sense. We are not a secular party in the Western secular understanding.[33]

Following a slightly different line of reasoning, other secular party elites, meanwhile, asserted they took no issue with the term secularism *per se*, and were in fact happy to label their party as such, but felt that within the Egyptian context the term had acquired such negative connotations that its use constituted an electoral liability, particularly in the countryside. This is why, so went the argument, they would refrain from using the term.[34]

Second, and concomitant to the latter, several secular party representatives also pointed to their use of religious symbols and slogans in public discourse – particularly during election campaigns – for the dual purpose of countering allegations of being anti-religious and as a means of mobilising electoral support.[35] As one leading Hizb al-Tajammu' al-Taqaddumi al-Wahdawi (National Progressive Unionist Party, also known as al-Tajammu') official explained when asked about his party's use of religious slogans: 'we don't like to use religion, except when we have to against our adversaries, especially in the rural areas.'[36] Taking such discursive practices even further, during the 2011–13 period al-Sayyed al-Badawi, the leader of the centre-right Hizb al-Wafd al-Jadid (New Wafd Party, NWP), single-handedly removed the cross from the party's logo and proclaimed in public that the party was not anti-Shari'ah but in fact Islamic.[37] Whilst many in the party decried al-Badawi's move at the time as unilateral and as contravening the party's long-standing advocacy of the Coptic minority, it was thought that he had done so strategically to take the NWP out of the firing line of the Islamists and to woo devout voters into the party's electoral fold.[38]

Labelling and the evocation of an 'us-versus-them' binary, meanwhile, were not only restricted to the sacred, but also conjured up by secular party elites through the use of derogatory worldly labels aimed at delegitimising the Morsi administration and the Islamist current more broadly. The most common adversarial images evoked hereby included the notions of 'authoritarianism', 'violence', 'brotherhoodisation' and 'transnationalism'. Indeed, without fail, secular party elites would depict Morsi and his government as exclusionary and authoritarian in character as well as working against the national interest, and the Islamist current more broadly as 'anti-progressive', 'anti-democratic' and comprised of 'fanatics' and/or former 'terrorists'.[39] Within this imagery comparisons between the MB/FJP and the previous al-Hizb al-Watani al-Dimuqrati (National Democratic Party, NDP) regime were drawn, and representatives of the government and the broader Islamist current presented as undermining, rather than advancing, the goals of the Tahrir uprising.

Beyond the use of such adversarial imagery aimed at placing the MB/FJP outside the bounds of the revolutionary mainstream, most of the secular party elites interviewed also resorted to rhetorical categorisation and distancing in their assessments of the evolving post-uprising party landscape in Egypt. Hawking back to orientalist accounts of political Islam,[40] it is possible to detect a tendency in the narratives of secular party elites to present Egypt's diverse range of Islamist parties as a single undifferentiated grouping, thus reinforcing an imagery of Egyptian politics marked by clear ideological binaries. In this narrative Salafi parties, the FJP, other reformist parties, such as Hizb al-Wasat (Centre Party, CP), and parties widely referred to nowadays as 'Muslim democrat' – such as for instance Hizb Misr al-Qawiyya (Strong Egypt Party, SEP) and Hizb al-Tayyar al-Misri (Egyptian Current Party, ECP)[41] – were all grouped together, with respondents refusing/failing to acknowledge the significant differences in policy positions/ideology that exist between this heterodox group of parties.[42] Several respondents, in fact, derided the SEP and its leader Abdel Mone'm Abu al-Fotouh, as well as the ECP, as mere MB 'split-offs' or as just one of the 'faces of the MB', thus negating the ideological distance that had developed between the two and the MB, as well as the latter's autonomy from the group.[43] Representative of such rhetorical categorisation are the statements made, for instance, by an al-Tajammu' official who purported that 'Morsi rules in the name of God and political Islam and all groups, even those who disagree with him inside political Islam, belong to the current that is ruling Egypt',[44] adding that '[n] ow, all liberal parties that are non-religious are the true opposition'.[45] When comparing Egypt's Salafi parties to the MB, meanwhile, leading Hizb al-Islah wa al-Tanmiyyah – Misruna (Reform and Development Misruna Party, RDMP) and NWP officials also summarily grouped the two together,[46] with the NWP representative asserting that 'the main idea that Shari'ah be applied and Islam rule is an idea that unites them all'.[47]

Although more subtly, the creation of ideological binaries through rhetorical categorisation also permeates to some extent the self-positioning of secular parties on the nascent post-uprising party scene. Coined as distancing above, two trends can hereby be detected: a first, pertaining to speech acts that expose a propensity by the respondent to either (1) overstate the (ideological) distance between his/her party and those deemed to belong to the Islamist camp, or (2) position their party exclusively within the realm of fellow secular parties on the economic left–right spectrum, thus drawing little to no reference to parties classed as Islamist. In this latter scenario, any references to Islamist parties, in fact, were for the most part drawn only upon the explicit encouragement by the authors.

The second observable trend, in turn, concerns narratives that – often concomitantly to the first – contain a propensity by the respondent to downplay/understate extant (ideological/policy) distances between so-called 'liberal' and 'leftist' parties within the secular camp. Examples of both sets of rhetorical distancing abound, yet are particularly noteworthy with regards to economic policy positions. In conversations with the authors, officials from Hizb al-Mo'tammar al-Misri (Egyptian Conference Party, henceforth referred to as al-Mo'tammar) and Hizb al-Misriyeen al-Ahrar (Free Egyptians Party, FEP), for instance, would exclusively position themselves within the spectrum of 'secular' parties although, according to expert opinion, on economic policy there is considerable programmatic overlap between the two and the Islamist FJP.[48] The same is evident with regards to the self-positioning of party elites from al-Hizb al-Misri al-Dimuqrati al-Ijtma'i (Egyptian Social Democratic Party, ESDP), who purported the party was closest to Hizb al-Tahaluf al-Shaabi al-Ishtiraki (Socialist Popular Alliance Party, SPAP) on economic issues, and who made no reference to economically proximate Islamist parties, such as for instance the SEP or ECP.[49] Sharing the ESDP's centrist economic outlook, arguably in fact, both of these parties are far more proximate to the ESDP than the socialist-oriented SPAP.[50]

Two tentative conclusions might be drawn from these practices of rhetorical distancing. First, it suggests that at the time broader 'ideological' trench thinking by secular party elites seems to have precluded a more nuanced/ accurate self-positioning of their parties on the full post-uprising party spectrum; one that would have mandated a more benign confrontation with the programmes of Islamist parties. Second, and following from the above, it suggests that rhetorical distancing as a speech act by secular party elites tells us more about the nature of polarised politics in Egypt at the time, than about actual policy distances between its constituent parties.

Rhetorically, secular party elites thus deployed a range of discursive practices aimed at delegitimising Morsi and his government and at drawing out (ideological) distances between those in opposition to Morsi/the MB/FJP and representatives of the Islamist camp. In so doing, their narratives reinforced an imagery of Egyptian politics at the back end of June 2013 as one being shaped primarily by secular–Islamist polarisation. However, as will become apparent in the following pages, this depiction of Egyptian (party) politics under Morsi is difficult to sustain once the investigative spotlight is moved from speech acts to policy positions, which reveal a party system that is far less ideologically clear-cut than the polarisation narrative makes one believe.

Beyond the secular–Islamist binary

As in life, modern-day politics is never a clear-cut 'black or white' affair, but messy, ambiguous and complex. In Egypt this applies as much to the dynamics of the Tahrir uprising and its eventual demise, as to the party political scene that emerged following Mubarak's ousting. Indeed, whilst marked by growing rhetorical polarisation between allegedly secular and Islamist political elites, closer inspection of this party political scene reveals a level of ideological fluidity and ambiguity that muddies secular–Islamist binaries and renders problematic any narratives subscribing to such a depiction of Egyptian politics. Several observations inform this latter characterisation of Egyptian party politics in the 2011–13 period, two of which will be expanded upon here. They pertain first to secular party positions on the role of religion in public life and on economic policy, and second to the emergence of several parties whose composition and programmatic self-positioning fall outside simple secular and/or Islamist categorisations.[51]

Party positions on Shari'ah[52] and its application in public life are one area that obfuscates clear secular–Islamist binaries in Egyptian party politics. As Michael Hannah astutely observed on the matter '[i]n terms of their approach to sharia and the role of religion in public life, even avowedly secular parties have bowed to the current realities of Egyptian society and ceded the fight over the inclusion of Islamic law'.[53] Indeed, for many secular party elites the question is not one of whether or not Shari'ah should be applied – and hence whether Islamic teachings should remain entirely outside the realm of public life as 'assertive' forms of secularism would mandate[54] – but which teachings should apply and who should carry the authority to decide which interpretations and precepts be adopted and enforced. So for instance, whilst secular parties have called for a ban on religious parties,[55] and have voiced their objections to prescribing Shari'ah as sole source of legislation, to the adoption of *hudud* in the criminal code and to the involvement of religious authorities (e.g. al-Azhar) in matters of governance,[56] this should not be read as an outright rejection of Shari'ah in all aspects of public life. When it comes to other areas of Egyptian law and politics in fact – such as for instance with regards to views on Article 2 of the 1971, 2012/13 and 2014 Constitutions or on personal status matters and Islamic *sukuk*[57] – many secular parties appear to postulate positions that deviate from the strictures of a clear separation of religion and state/politics. As Tarek Masoud and others have highlighted, for example, most secular parties have expressed their support for the retention of Article 2 of the 1971 and subsequent Constitutions, which prescribes Shari'ah as a principal source of legislation.[58] Certainly, in part this support constitutes a reflection of the societal stigma associated with 'Western' secularism. For several secular party elites, moreover, it is informed by an interpretation of Shari'ah that is minimal in application, with its strictures being considered more as an ethical frame of reference guiding politics than as a set of religious prescripts that require strict adherence.[59] In this, of course, secular parties differ from some of their Islamist counterparts, who regard Article 2 as a mandate to ensure all legislation is fully Shari'ah-compliant.[60] Be this as it may, the important point here is that, by endorsing Article 2, secular parties have come out in favour of a conception of statehood and politics that is bounded by a religious canon, minimal as this may be.

This is also evident in other areas of primary legislation, such as those governing personal status matters (marriage, divorce, adoption and inheritance) and the economy. As concerns personal status matters, for instance, most secular party elites take little issue with the extant *status quo* that is governed by legal pluralism and religious prescripts.[61] Whilst some have challenged the exclusionary remit of the current law – which applies exclusively to the three Abrahamic faiths and thus leaves in legal limbo members of minority denominations such as the Baha'i – party representatives from the NWP, al-Tajammu', al-Mo'tammar, Karama, ESDP and Hizb Ghad al-Thawra (Revolution's Tomorrow Party, RTP) all expressed little opposition in principle to the current *status quo* and its enshrinement in Article 3 of the 2012/13 Constitution.[62] As one high-ranking Karama executive explained '[p]ersonal status law, in my opinion, must remain under the purview of Islam and the Qur'an and what is there scripturally. We believe that what is specified there should be abided by.'[63] This point of view also resonates within al-Tajammu', as is evident in the following remarks made by one of its top officials: 'we can never agree to a Muslim [woman] marrying a Christian [man] and all of this nonsense. They can, however, practice their freedom of faith and their social life within the parameters of their religion.'[64] Whether these positions on personal status matters are expressions of conviction politics or driven instrumentally by electoral calculi is, of course, hard to ascertain and it may well be a combination of the two. Of note in the context of this research is this, however: by accepting aspects of Shari'ah as part of the corpus of Egyptian law, secular parties advocate not only a blurring of boundaries between religion, state and politics, but with it conceptions of citizenship and personal liberties that are discriminatory and unequal in nature, mostly with regards to the rights of women and minority denominations.[65]

On economic policy as well, the positions of secular parties are not as clear-cut as the polarising rhetoric may make them appear. An illustrative case in point concerns the introduction by the Morsi administration of a law on Shari'ah-compliant bonds (Islamic *sukuk*) in the Spring 2013, with which the government sought to shore up its credentials of managing Egypt's fledging economy, as well as put 'a more "Islamic" stamp'[66] on the country's finance sector.[67] Reviewing the Shura Council debate of the draft law, and conversations with research respondents on the issue, two points become apparent. First, the stiffest opposition to the law did not come – as one might have expected – from the handful of secular opposition representatives in the Shura Council, but from religious scholars affiliated to al-Azhar[68] and Salafi lawmakers 'who protested [against the law] both on nit-picking religious grounds and due to nationalist fears that *sukuk* might become a back-door route to selling off Egyptian state assets to foreigners';[69] and second, several secular politicians viewed the proposed law overall benignly, treating Islamic *sukuk* as simply yet another form of 'investment choice',[70] and voicing concerns more about specific details of the law than regarding its Islamic underpinnings.[71]

In the realm of policy-making then, it is apparent that the 2011–13 period in Egyptian party politics was never marked by razor-sharp secular–Islamist fault lines. What we encounter instead below the veneer of elite polarisation is a nascent party landscape that was characterised not only by a lack of programmatic distinctiveness and fluidity, but also by the absence of parties with an unequivocal secularising policy agenda. This observation holds true, in fact, not only for those parties traditionally classed as secular or secularist (such as e.g. the FEP, ESDP, SPAP or al-Tajammu'), but also for a new brand of political parties that emerged in the aftermath of the Tahrir uprising and whose very *raison d'être* has been premised on the idea of bridging Egypt's ideological divide. These include most prominently some of the country's nascent 'youth' parties, such as Hizb al-'Adl (Justice Party, JP) or the ECP, both of which were established by revolutionary youth from diverse ideological backgrounds, and with the explicit aim of positioning themselves outside the secular–Islamist binary. Whilst the JP sought to position itself as a centrist party, advocating a 'third way' between Islamism and liberalism in domestic politics,[72] the ECP cast itself as a 'post-ideological' force which, in the words of one of its representatives, during its existence prescribed to a 'combination of ideologies, and not specifically to one particular ideology'.[73] Although in the end of little electoral relevance – largely due to a combination of internal disunity, lack of programmatic clarity and heightened elite polarisation – the existence of these and other such parties is of note as they constitute concrete attempts at inter-ideological accommodation and programmatic consensus-building and as such may well have provided a blueprint for broader-based societal agreement on a new political settlement for Egypt.

Conclusion

As this chapter has sought to demonstrate, depicting Egyptian party politics in the early post-uprising period through the lens of elite polarisation and/or secular–Islamist contention is problematic on two accounts. For one, there is a real danger of oversimplification wherever narratives fail to look beyond the adversarial rhetoric deployed by secular and Islamist party elites, particularly during the Morsi presidency. As we saw, this rhetoric – as ferocious and antagonistic as it was – masked in many ways an emergent party landscape that on substantive issues was characterised by far greater ideological fluidity/flexibility than insinuated by the polarising prism and one in which compromise on substantive issues might well have been possible. Indeed, below the veneer of rhetorical polarisation, we encounter secular policy positions that, whilst disparate, were often far closer to those of their Islamist counterparts than the party elites would have one believe. It follows that at the time elite polarisation was in all likelihood driven at least as much by power-political calculi as by insurmountable policy differences.

Second, such lenses are not only overtly reductionist, but they are also misleading, particularly when it comes to the labelling of parties as secular and/or Islamist. As the authors have sought to demonstrate, the portrayal of Egypt's parties as secular is problematic not only in light of their positions on the role of religion in public life, but also because they run counter to the self-depiction of party leaders, many of whom object to being labelled as such. A cursory look at Egypt's vicinity, in fact, highlights the broader significance of this finding, as here as well we encounter parties branded as 'secular', while they espouse policy positions that cannot be classed as such. Indeed, as Anne Wolf and Mohammed Masbah have shown, in Tunisia and Morocco very few, if any, of the extant political parties advocate a complete separation of the sacred from worldly politics, and rejection of the label 'secular' remains widespread.[74]

Be it in Egypt or elsewhere in the region, it is apparent then that drawing parties onto a secular–religious/Islamist policy axis is of highly questionable utility and that in so doing we run the risk of downplaying the complexities and singularities of regional party systems and the positioning of parties therein. Not only this, but as Elizabeth Shakman Hurd has pointed out, in Western policy circles such labels are frequently stigmatised/orientalised, with 'secularism' being associated with 'good' (democracy and rights) and 'Islamist' with 'bad' ('irrational, threatening') politics.[75] This of course, presents a gross misrepresentation of Egyptian/regional (party) politics that ought to be avoided and, as far as the authors are concerned, is best accomplished by moving away from the use of secular/Islamist labels altogether.

Notes

1. The authors thank the Gerda Henkel Foundation for their grant to support the fieldwork conducted for this research in Egypt.
2. The Arabic term *felool* means 'remnants' and is widely used in Egypt and the literature to designate members of the ousted Mubarak regime as well as counter-revolutionary forces.
3. See e.g. Juan Cole (2014), 'The real Egyptian divide is between Tahrir self-government and authoritarians of all stripes', *Informed Comment Blog*, 14 May, <www.juancole.com/2014/05/egyptian-government-authoritarians.html> (last accessed 5 May 2017); Esam Al-Amin (2013), 'Egypt's political map: clearing the fog', *Counterpunch*, 8 February, <www.counterpunch.org/2013/02/08/egypts-political-map-clearing-the-fog/> (last accessed 5 May 2017).
4. See e.g. Noha El-Hennawy (2012), 'Islamist-secular rift threatens Egypt's emerging democracy', *Egypt Independent*, 2 June, <www.egyptindependent.com/news/islamist-secular-rift-threatens-egypts-emerging-democracy> (last accessed 5 May 2017); Kal B. Khalid (2011), 'Secularists and Islamists in the Maghreb: the dangers of polarisation', *tunisialive*, 7 December 2011, <www.tunisia-live.net/2011/12/07/secularists-and-islamists-in-the-maghreb-the-dangers-of-polarisation> (last accessed 5 May 2017).

5. See e.g. Ingmar Weber, Venkata R. K. Garimella and Akka Batayneh (2013), 'Secular vs. Islamist polarisation in Egypt on Twitter', in proceedings of the 2013 *IEEE/ACM International Conference on Advances in Social Networks Analysis and Mining*, pp. 290–7; Hussein A. Agrama (2012), 'Reflections on secularism, democracy and politics in Egypt', *American Ethnologist*, 39:1, p. 27.

6. As part of this research a total of twenty-four semi-structured interviews were conducted with party officials, covering the breadth of ideological currents operating in Egyptian politics at the time. Most of the interviews involved two sessions, the first conducted prior to 3 July 2013 and the second in its aftermath.

7. See e.g. Maha Abdelrahman (2009), '"With the Islamists? – Sometimes. With the state? – Never!" Cooperation between the left and Islamists in Egypt', *British Journal of Middle Eastern Studies*, 36:1, pp. 37–54; Jillian Schwedler and Janine A. Clark (2006), 'Islamist-Leftists *Cooperation* in the Arab World', *ISIM Review*, 18, pp. 10–11; Francesco Cavatorta and Azzam Elananza (2008), 'Political opposition in civil society: an analysis of the interactions of secular and religious associations in Algeria and Jordan', *Government and Opposition*, 43:4, pp. 561–78.

8. The authors acknowledge the distinction made in the literature between societal/popular and elite polarisation, whereby the former relates to a scenario where society/the electorate is starkly divided on policy issues and/or along partisan/ideological lines. In this chapter, the focus is exclusively on elite polarisation at the level of political parties and not with wider societal polarisation, although it recognises the interlinkages between the two. See Piero Stanig (2011), 'Measuring political polarisation in comparative perspective', paper presented at APSA Conference, Seattle.

9. See e.g. Charles Hirschkind (2012), 'Beyond the secular and religious: an intellectual genealogy of Tahrir Square', *American Ethnologist*, 39:1, pp. 44–8; Sune Haugbølle (2012), 'Reflections on ideology after the Arab uprisings', *Jadaliyya*, 21 March, <www.jadaliyya.com/pages/index/4764/reflections-on-ideology-after-the-arab-uprisings> (last accessed 5 May 2017); Hamid Dabashi (2012), 'False Islamist–secular divide in Egypt is a wedge in hopes for preserving democracy', *Al Jazeera*, 9 December.

10. Haugbølle, 'Reflections on ideology'.

11. Emad El-Din Shahin (2012), 'The Egyptian Revolution: the power of mass mobilization and the spirit of Tahrir Square', *Journal of the Middle East and Africa*, 3:1, pp. 46–69.

12. The FJP was created by MB cadre to represent the political branch of the grouping. It was legalised in April 2011, and went on to win a plurality of seats in the 2011–12 lower and upper houses of parliament elections. Following the ousting of Morsi in 2013 the party was banned and the MB designated a terrorist organisation.

13. As part of *infitah*, al-Sadat opened the political space for the first time since President Gamal Abdel Nasser (1954–70) to a limited number of political parties and permitted the hitherto suppressed MB to re-emerge as a tolerated socio-political player in Egyptian politics. See Maye Kassem (2005), *Egyptian Politics: The Dynamics of Authoritarian Rule*. Boulder: Lynne Rienner Publishers.

14. Abdelrahman, '"With the Islamists? – Sometimes"', pp. 41–2.

15. Interview with Hizb al-Tajammu' al-Taqaddumi al-Wahdawi (National Progressive Unionist Party) official (Cairo, 21 and 22 August 2000).

16. For examples of such cooperation consult e.g. Abdelrahman, '"With the Islamists? – Sometimes".

17. Ibid., pp. 41–2, 44–6.

18. Rikke H. Haugbølle and Francesco Cavatorta (2011), 'Will the real Tunisian opposition please stand up? Opposition coordination failures under authoritarian constraints', in Hendrik J. Kraetzschmar (ed.) *The Dynamics of Opposition Cooperation in the Arab World: Contentious Politics in Times of Change*. Abingdon and New York: Routledge, pp. 39–58.

19. Ellen Lust (2011) 'Opposition cooperation and uprisings in the Arab world', in Hendrik J. Kraetzschmar (ed.) *The Dynamics of Opposition Cooperation in the Arab World: Contentious Politics in Times of Change*. Abingdon and New York: Routledge, pp. 185–96.

20. Tarek Masoud (2011), 'Liberty, democracy, and discord in Egypt', *Washington Quarterly*, 34:4, p. 117.

21. Anon. (2013), 'Translation: President Mohamed Morsi's address to the nation', *Atlantic Council*, 28 June, <www.atlanticcouncil.org/blogs/menasource/translation-president-mohamed-morsi-s-address-to-the-nation> (last accessed 5 May 2017).

22. For a full analysis of this period and the contentious episodes mentioned here see e.g. Emile Hokayem and Hebatalla Taha (eds) (2015), *Egypt after the Spring: Revolt and Reaction*. Adelphi Series 55.

23. Amongst others, this constitutional declaration placed the president and his decision-making authority above the law and any other institutions of the state. It also prescribed that neither the sitting Shura Council (upper house of parliament) nor the Constituent Assembly could be dissolved by any other authority, thus pre-empting their possible dissolution by the Egyptian judiciary. In the event, Morsi withdrew the declaration in December 2012 amid widespread opposition and political turmoil. See Bassem Sabry (2012), 'Absolute power: Morsi decree stuns Egyptians', *Al-Monitor*, 22 November, <www.al-monitor.com/pulse/originals/2012/al-monitor/morsi-decree-constitution-power.html> (last accessed 5 May 2017).

24. BBC Monitoring (2017), 'Profile: Egypt's National Salvation Front', *BBC*, 10 December, <www.bbc.co.uk/news/world-middle-east-20667661> (last accessed 5 May 2017).

25. Heba Fahmy (2012), 'Wave of walkouts leave Constituent Assembly in Islamists' hands', *Egypt Independent*, 21 November, <www.egyptindependent.com/news/wave-walkouts-leaves-constituent-assembly-islamists-hands> (last accessed 5 May 2017).

26. Mohammed M. Eissa (2014), 'Polarised discourse in the news', *Procedia – Social and Behavioural Sciences*, 134, p. 82.

27. Eissa, 'Polarised discourse in the news', pp. 70–91.

28. According to the 2012 World Value Survey, for instance, 94.1 per cent of respondents in Egypt asserted that religion was 'very important' in their lives. See World Value Survey, Online Data Analysis, <www.worldvaluessurvey.org/WVSOnline.jsp> (last accessed 5 May 2017).

29. Interviews with al-Tajammu' (22 June 2013, Cairo), SPAP (17 June 2013, Cairo), Hizb al-Gabha al-Demuqrati (Democratic Front Party/DFP, 17 June 2013, Cairo), Karama (22 June 2013, Cairo) and al-Mo'tammar (18 June 2013, Cairo) officials.

30. Interviews with al-Tajammu', SPAP, Karama and RDMP (16 June 2013, Cairo) officials.

31. Marina Ottaway and Amr Hamzawy (2009), 'Fighting on two Fronts: secular parties in the Arab world', in Marina Ottaway and Amr Hamzawy (eds), *Getting to Pluralism: Political Actors in the Arab World*. Carnegie Endowment for International Peace, pp. 41–5.

32. Interviews with Al-Tajammu' Karama and Hizb Ghad al-Thawra (Revolution's Tomorrow Party/RTP) officials, 19 June 2013, Cairo.

33. Interview with Karama officials.

34. Interviews with RDMP, DFP (17 June 2013, Cairo), ESDP (official no 2, 20 June 2013, Cairo) and SPAP officials. For an account of Egyptian views on 'secularism' in the

post-Spring era see also Neil MacFarquhar (2011), 'After revolt, Egyptians try to shape new politics', *New York Times*, 18 March.

35. Interviews with ESDP (official no. 1, 27 November 2013, Cairo), al-Tajammu' and NWP (15 June 2013, Cairo) officials.

36. Interview with al-Tajammu' official.

37. Interview with NWP official. See also Amina El-Fekki (2015), 'Al-Wafd Party leader sacks opponents in peak of internal crisis: Secretary General Fouad Badrawi and six supporting members dismissed Friday', *Daily News Egypt*, 30 May.

38. Interview with a NWP official.

39. Interviews with SPAP, ESDP (official no. 2), ECP (15 June 2013, Cairo), RDMP, al-Tajammu', NWP and DFP officials.

40. Luisa Gandolfo (2015), 'From authoritarian to free state: balancing faith and politics in Tunisia', *Mediterranean Quarterly*, 26, p. 13.

41. The ECP merged with SEP in 2014. See Barbara Zollner's contribution in this volume.

42. For an account of intra-'Islamist' policy/ideological differences, particularly on the issue of *Shari'ah*, see Eman Ragab (2012), 'Islamic political parties in Egypt', *IPR – Cairo Policy Brief 2*, Netherlands-Flemish Institute in Cairo; Zollner in this volume.

43. Interviews with al-Tajammu', SPAP, DFP, Karama and al-Mo'tammar officials. See also El Ashraf Sherif (2016), 'The Strong Egypt Party: representing a progressive/democratic Islamist party?' *Contemporary Islam*, 10/3, pp. 311–31.

44. Interview with al-Tajammu' official.

45. Ibid.

46. Interviews with NWP and RDMP officials.

47. Ibid.

48. May Elsayyad and Shima'a Hanafy (2013), 'Voting Islamist or voting secular? An empirical analysis of voting outcomes in "Arab Spring" Egypt', Working Paper 2013-01, *Max Planck Institute for Tax Law and Public Finance*, <ftp://ftp.repec.org/opt/ReDIF/RePEc/mpi/wpaper/TAX-MPG-RPS-2013-01.pdf> (last accessed 5 May 2017); Nader Habibi (2012), 'The economic agendas and expected economic policies of Islamists in Egypt and Tunisia', *Middle East Brief*, 67, p. 5; Jacopo Carbonari (2011), 'Mapping Egypt's political parties', *The Arabist*, 13 November, <https://arabist.net/blog/2011/11/13/mapping-egypts-political-parties.html> (last accessed 5 May 2017).

49. For a discussion of the SEP's economic platform see also El Sherif, 'The Strong Egypt Party', p. 7.

50. For an overview of the party programmes of the ESDP, SEP, ECP and SPAP see e.g. the information provided by Egypt Election Watch (2011), 'Parties and movements', *Jadaliyya and Ahram Online*, <www.jadaliyya.com/pages/contributors/43055> (last accessed 5 May 2017). See also Carbonari 'Mapping Egypt's political parties'.

51. Other aspects of party political behaviour during the 2011–13 period that transpired from interviews with party elites and that suggest the secular-Islamist binary was less razor-sharp than the polarisation narrative would make one believe include (1) numerous reported episodes of collaboration between Salafi parties and the secular opposition on pieces of (MB/FJP-sponsored) legislation in the Shura Council, for example on the protest and judiciary laws, (2) the willingess of some secular party elites to contemplate entering into formal coalitions with some, though not all, Islamist political parties in the event of new elections and (3) the verious attempts at mediation undertaken by al-Nour, the NWP and RTP to overcome the growing political crisis between the Morsi government and the NSF.

52. Following Arafa, Shari'ah is here understood to refer broadly to 'the Islamic way of doing things' including 'private practice, ethics and public law'. Mohamed A. Arafa (2012), 'President Morsi's Egypt Arab Spring: does Egypt Will continue to be a civil state or under the umbrella of Islamic (Sharie'a) law and Islamism', *US-China Law Review*, 9:6, p. 5.

53. Michael W. Hannah (2015), 'Egypt's non-Islamist parties', in Hokayem and Taha (eds) *Egypt after the Spring*, p. 107.

54. Assertive secularism as defined by Kuru 'aims to exclude religion from the public sphere', as opposed to passive secularism. 'which tolerates public visibility of religion'. See Ahmed T. Kuru (2007), 'Passive and assertive secularism: historical conditions, ideological struggles, and state policies toward religion' *World Politics*, 59:4, pp. 568–94.

55. Interviews with SPAP, Karama and al-Tajammu' officials.

56. On all these issues, the MB/FJP and Salafi parties have called for a sharpening of provisions, turning Shari'ah into the sole source of legislation, replacing the term 'principles' with 'rulings' in Article 2 of the constitution and demanding a greater political role for al-Azhar. See Arafa, 'President Mursi's Egypt', pp. 10–12. Also interview with FEP official, 20 June 2013, Cairo.

57. Islamic *sukuk* refers to Shari'ah-compliant bonds, which are 'structured in such a way as to generate returns to investors without infringing Islamic law' that prohibits *riba* or interest'. FT Lexicon, 'Definition of Sukuk (Islamic bonds)', <http://lexicon.ft.com/Term?term=sukuk-(Islamic-bonds)> (last accessed 5 May 2017).

58. See Masoud, 'Liberty, democracy, and discord in Egypt', p. 124; Mohamed Elagati, Nouran Ahmed and Mahmoud Bayoumi (2015), 'Citizenship on the discourse of Egyptian political parties', *EUSpring* Working Paper 6, June; Hannah, 'Egypt's non-Islamist parties', p. 113. Also interviews with ESDP and Karama officials.

59. Interviews with Karama and al-Mo'tammar officials. See also Moataz el Fegiery (2013), 'The "new Liberals": can Egypt's civil opposition save the Revolution?' *FRIDE Policy Brief*, 155, p. 3.

60. Egypt Election Watch, 'Parties and movements', *Jadaliyya and Ahram Online*.

61. Whilst most areas of Egyptian law were 'secularised' in the nineteenth century, personal status matters have remained infused/guided by Shari'ah, and here particularly by the Hanafi School in Sunni Islam. As of today, legal pluralism thus prevails in personal status matters, with regular courts drawing on either Shari'ah rulings or the religious laws of the other recognised Abrahamic faiths (Christianity and Judaism) when adjudicating on such matters. See Nathan Brown (2012), 'Egypt and Islamic Shari'a: a guide for the perplexed', *Carnegie Endowment for International Peace*, <http://carnegieendowment.org/2012/05/15/egypt-and-islamic-sharia-guide-for-perplexed-pub-48119> (last accessed 5 May 2017).

62. First devised in 2012, Article 3 of the 2012/13 and 2014 Constitutions elevated the practice of legal pluralism into a constitutional principle, stipulating that 'The principles of Christian and Jewish Sharia of Egyptian Christians and Jews are the main source of legislation that regulate their respective personal status, religious affairs, and selection of spiritual leaders'. See: Egyptian State Information Service, 'The Constitution of the Arab Republic of Egypt 2014' <www.sis.gov.eg/Newvr/Dustor-en001.pdf> (last accessed 4 July 2017); World Intellectual Property Organisation (WIPO), 'The Constitution of the Arab Republic of Egypt 2012' <www.wipo.int/edocs/lexdocs/laws/en/eg/eg047en.pdf> (last accessed 4 July 2017). Interviews with NWP, SPAP, Karama, TRP and al-Mo'tammar officials. See also Elagati *et al.*, 'Citizenship on the discourse of Egyptian political parties'.

63. Interview with Karama official.

64. Interview with al-Tajammu' official.

65. Elagati *et al.*, 'Citizenship on the discourse of Egyptian political parties'. On discrimination against women in Egyptian divorce law, governed by Shari'ah, see e.g. Human Rights Watch (2004), 'Divorced from justice: women's unequal access to divorce in Egypt', Report, 16:8, p. 19.

66. Anon. (2013), 'Sukuk it and see', *The Economist*, 19 April, <www.economist.com/blogs/pomegranate/2013/04/egypt-finance> (last accessed 5 May 2017).

67. See e.g. David Mikhael (2013), 'Implications of Egypt's Sukuk law', *Atlantic Council News Analysis*, 4 April, <www.atlanticcouncil.org/blogs/menasource/implications-of-egypts-sukuk-law> (last accessed 5 May 2017).

68. See e.g. Maggie Hyde (2013), 'Government struggles to get a sukuk law on the books', *Egypt Independent*, 18 January <www.egyptindependent.com/news/government-struggles-get-sukuk-law-books> (last accessed 5 May 2017).

69. Ibid.

70. Ibid.

71. Interview with FEP official, 20 June 2013, Cairo.

72. See e.g. Abdel-Rahman Hussein (2011), 'Egypt's centrists seek to overcome Islamist-secular divide', *Egypt Independent* 26 August <www.egyptindependent.com/news/egypt%E2%80%99s-centrists-seek-overcome-islamist-secular-divide> (last accessed 5 May 2017); Anon. (2011), 'Egypt election: Al-Adl party', *The Cairo Review of Global Affairs*, 12 November <www.thecairoreview.com/tahrir-forum/egypt-election-al-adl-party/> (last accessed 5 May 2017).

73. Interview with ECP official.

74. See contribution by Anne Wolf in this volume. See also Mohammed Masbah (2014), 'Islamist and secular forces in Morocco: not a zero-sum game', *SWP Comments 51*, German Institute for International and Security Affairs, November <www.files.ethz.ch/isn/186120/2014C51_msb.pdf>.

75. Elizabeth Shakman Hurd (2011) 'Guestview: misrepresenting Egypt – the Mubarak myth of "secular" vs "Islamic"', Reuters, 14 February, <http://blogs.reuters.com/faithworld/2011/02/14/guestview-misrepresenting-egypt-the-mubarak-myth-of-secular-vs-islamic/> (last accessed 5 May 2017).

Part III

Intra-Islamist pluralisation and contention

Chapter 14

The complexity of Tunisian Islamism: conflicts and rivalries over the role of religion in politics

Francesco Cavatorta

The fall of the Ben Ali regime in 2011 quickly, and surprisingly, gave way to a process of transition to democracy that, at least from an institutional perspective, is a success, particularly when compared to post-uprisings developments elsewhere in the region. While there is much criticism of the way in which the transition has taken place,[1] there is no doubt that significant institutional progress has been made. Since 2011 Tunisia has enjoyed two rounds of free and fair legislative elections and one round of competitive presidential elections, approved a new constitutional text enshrining individual freedoms and boasts a very lively and plural civil society. In short, the country has successfully transformed into a liberal democracy. The opening up of the political system immediately showed two rather surprising trends. First, it became readily apparent that Islamism was particularly strong. Very few expected, for instance, that Hizb al-Nahda (Renaissance Party, henceforth al-Nahda) would so quickly reorganise, enthuse voters and win the 2011 elections for the Constituent Assembly. Second, it became apparent that al-Nahda was not the only Islamist actor on the political scene and was in fact unable to monopolise the Islamist camp because of the challenge from jihadi–Salafism. Following on from this, the majority of works on Tunisian Islamism have since focused on al-Nahda and its role in the institutional success of the transition, accounting for the party's strategy, behaviour and ideological change during the transitional period.[2] A number of scholars then focused on the rise of jihadi–Salafism, a relative novelty for the country and a potential threat to the success of democratisation, in its organisational form of Ansar al-Shariʿah (Defenders of Shariʿah).[3]

This chapter asserts, meanwhile, that the whole post-revolutionary camp in Tunisia should not be reduced to al-Nahda and Ansar al-Shariʿah because the collapse of the regime and the political developments that occurred during the transition allowed a number of Islamist actors to enjoy the opportunities that the new political system offered. Thus, one ought to take into account the divisions within al-Nahda, the presence of different strands of Salafism, the violent splinters emerging from the failure of Ansar al-Shariʻah as a social project, and the work of unaffiliated civil society groups promoting an autonomous practice of Islamism.

Explaining the plurality of post-revolutionary Islamism in Tunisia, this chapter suggests that its different manifestations are not simply the product of the conflicts within the Islamist camp that came to a head with the transition to democracy, but also the outcome of long-standing differences about the role Islam should play in politics and society. The roots of such differences can be traced back in the history of Tunisia.

Al-Nahda: from Islamist party to the party of Muslim democrats?

Before the transition to democracy in 2011–12 there was an academic and policy-making consensus that the only Islamist movement of any note who could have an impact on Tunisian politics was al-Nahda. Since the 1970s the movement/ party had occupied a prominent role in Tunisian politics, albeit from a position of illegality. Notably, its leader Rachid Ghannouchi was also believed to be the only Islamist personality of note given his role in the party and his standing as a respected Muslim intellectual. Thus, soon after the departure of President Zine el-Abidine Ben Ali (r.1987–2011) and the return of Ghannouchi from exile to Tunisia to participate in the construction of a new political system, the focus of observers and the public was almost entirely on al-Nahda, its leader and the choices he would make. By 2018, it is fair to acknowledge that one of the most significant changes that the Tunisian transition brought about is the transformation of the Islamist party al-Nahda into a pillar of a new liberal democratic system. Whereas large sectors of Tunisian society, and many within the international community, believed at the outset of the transition process that the party would use democratic mechanisms instrumentally to impose its vision of society on the whole of the country,[4] the party strived instead to become a consensual political player and sought to compromise with other parties to avoiding being excluded from the game of democratic politics. Thus, it accepted the need to play what Amel Boubekeur termed 'bargained competition'[5] despite its relative strength compared to other parties, and become an integral part of the newly emergent political system. This entailed significant political and ideological compromises that departed from the original ideology of the movement. As Kasper Ly Netterstrøm maintains, 'the new constitution is in stark contradiction with Ennahda's original Islamist ideology'.[6]

For some, this departure is the product of the natural evolution of a movement that was never as radical and ideologically inflexible as others in the region.[7] For others, it is the product of ideological discussions taking place over time within a changing political environment both in Tunisia and in the wider Middle East and North Africa (MENA) where the rise of extremely violent groups was perceived by al-Nahda as the hijacking of what Islamism should stand for.[8] Others still tended to dismiss the role of ideological rethinking as post-facto justification of a strategic decision taken because of organisational necessities, namely to preserve the movement from returning to the days when it was banned and repressed.[9] Irrespective of the reasons that led to the compromise, and the benefits it had for the success of the Tunisian transition, the party is now fully integrated and a reliable member of the current political system. Furthermore, at the tenth congress of the party in May 2016, the leadership put forth, and pushed through, a motion that the party would become autonomous from its parent movement. In the words of Ghannouchi, al-Nahda 'can finally be a political party focusing on its political agenda and economic vision rather than a social movement fighting against repression and dictatorship'.[10] The rationale for this decision is that there is no longer the need for political Islamism in Tunisia given that no one now needs to defend and protect religion because the state refrains from imposing a secular vision on society. In fact the ideological neutrality of the state ensures that the faithful can follow their religious principles and there is therefore no need for a party that would stand between them and the state to protect their right to practise religion as they wish in daily life. It follows that the party can abandon the label 'Islamist' and become the party of Muslim democrats according to Ghannouchi.[11] Thus, the separation between da'wa (proselytising) and politics is now both complete and official. The party can now focus on what matters to citizens – the economy or foreign affairs for example – while the social movement can continue its social activism, promoting specific religious practices in society. The overarching objective is to promote an Islamist 'sub-culture' that is officially disconnected from political institutional representation, but instrumental to electoral success.

In fairness, it should be noted that the change in direction the party formalised in 2016 was already evident in earlier years. It follows that the loss of 'revolutionary spirit' and radicalism, with the abandonment of references to anything Islamist including Shari'ah, possibly contributed to the lack of appeal of the party among young people. The youth had only known the repression of the later Ben Ali years and had formed their views on Islamism through the internet and TV channels, given the impossibility for al-Nahda to participate in public life in any form during the 1990s, 2000s and 2010s.[12] Fabio Merone explains convincingly that the political project of al-Nahda after the transition was to make sure that the social constituency it largely represented – a conservative and petty *bourgeois* middle class with very little interest in revolutionary and ideological politics – could finally be integrated into the political system and share, in some ways, the spoils and benefits of being included in the state and in the running of the country from which it had been excluded since independence.[13] This objective is what made the compromise with the nationalist-secular sectors of society possible, and the democratic game could then regulate this compromise to mutual satisfaction by excluding the proponents of radical political, social and economic change.

In any case, this momentous change is far from representing the complete transformation, or the end, of Islamism in Tunisia. In fact, the multiple voices of Islamism that emerged forcefully after the transition to democracy retain their significance, suggesting that the decision the party leadership took is widely contested both internally and in the broader Islamist camp. This puts to rest the notion that Islamist challenges to the current structures of power are no longer an issue given the conversion of al-Nahda to democratic politics and the pre-eminence of individual rights. If anything, the evolution of al-Nahda and its decision to separate the movement and the party has exposed further its internal fault lines and motivated its external Islamist challengers.

Since its inception, al-Nahda has functioned according to the principle of democratic centralism that other highly ideological political parties across the globe have adopted. This principle simply means that the leadership and the members can have heated internal discussions about ideological direction and strategy, but once a decision is made to follow a certain path all will conform despite their initial opposition. Thus, dissent is managed internally and a united front is presented to the outside world. The presence of a charismatic leader, as in the case of Ghannouchi for al-Nahda, allows for democratic centralism to operate even more efficiently because the leader is able to hold together the different factions. However, democratic centralism does not safeguard against splits when different positions and opposing beliefs cannot be reconciled. As Rory McCarthy highlights, different trends within the party have learned different lessons from their personal engagement within al-Nahda.[14] Leaders in exile have seemed more interested in reconciliation and getting into office once the transition began, while those who remained in Tunisia during the dictatorship shunned party politics because of repression and began to think about civil activism as the realm in which Islamist messages could be propagated. In addition, al-Nahda is also divided between an older generation of leaders who experienced all phases of the movement from its inception and a younger generation whose ideological references and personal experiences are different. In the party therefore there is at times an uneasy coexistence, for instance, between what one might call genuine Muslim democrats like Abdel

Fattah Mourou and members close to Salafi thinking. Splits have affected the party in the past and as Susan Waltz noted even in 1986:

> [s]ince 1981, MTI leadership has seized every available opportunity to affirm democracy as the framework within which they would work to advance their goals, but there is apparent within the MTI today an openly anti-democratic wing, impatient with the homage to democracy paid by its leadership.[15]

The MTI[16] eventually split, with a minority going on to found a more militant group and the rest transforming the group into al-Nahda.

Thus, while the tenth congress formalised the distinction between movement and party, this decision did not have the support of the whole membership. This might not be problematic *per se*, given that the principle of democratic centralism remains strong, but indicates that there is no consensus over the supposed end of Islamism and the turn to Muslim democracy because for many ordinary members this represents a considerable, and potentially unacceptable, departure from the original objectives of their engagement. In fact, there is very little to nothing, they would contend, that is Islamist in either the political system or al-Nahda. It is for this reason, as Netterstrøm observes,[17] that party members had to be convinced by the leadership of the necessity of compromise and ultimate change. While this effort to convince militants was broadly successful, it has also encountered failures. Giving up on the core principles of Islamism, and in particular references to Shariʿah in legislation and the constitution, has been particularly difficult for many members, and this might explain in part the poorer electoral results in the 2014 legislative elections compared to the ones held in 2011. Ultimately though, as Ghannouchi states, over '80 per cent of the delegates at the Congress voted in favour of the formal shift',[18] implicitly approving the radical change in the party's direction. In short, al-Nahda is far from its origins when, as Lewis B. Ware notes citing the review *Peuples Méditer-ranéens*, the movement strived for:

> [t]he resurrection of the Tunisian Islamic personality; the renewal of Islamic thought in the light of fundamental religious principles; the recovery for the people of the right to self-determination; the reconstruction of Islamic life on a humane basis and a redistribution of wealth according to Islamic practices; and lastly, the making of a contribution to the resurrection of a civilisational and political Islamic entity on the Maghreb, Arab and global levels so as to save people from injustice and international hegemony.[19]

The majority of members and followers have accepted the new direction, but a minority does not, making the strategic evolution of al-Nahda problematic because it liberates a political space that other political movements can occupy in the name of reviving Islamism. Thus, the party's decision has significant repercussions on the broader field of Tunisian Islamism.

Salafi parties

When it comes to rival Islamist political parties, al-Nahda has so far not suffered greatly electorally from their activism and participation. However, it is important to briefly discuss their role, strategies and political positions to highlight the multi-faceted nature of Islamism as a whole. The political parties competing for the Islamist vote with al-Nahda in the new Tunisia are all part of what can be called the Salafi galaxy. As will be detailed later in the chapter, the greatest threat to al-Nahda within the Islamist camp following the revolution came from the jihadi–Salafi movement Ansar al-Shari'ah, but Salafism is a complex phenomenon and its 'political' trend established a number of parties that have attempted to offer a more radical and purer vision of Islamism than al-Nahda.

The political tendency of Salafism, when it comes to the relationship between politics and faith, is ideologically close to the thinking of al-Ikhwan al-Muslimun (Muslim Brotherhood, MB) in the early days. 'Politicos' recognise that Salafism should not organise itself into parties or movements, because this would simply encourage divisions in the community of the faithful. However, they argue that creating political parties and competing in elections, where possible, is a necessity in modern nation states, if 'religion' is not to be defeated and relegated to the private sphere by liberals and Muslim Brothers who have accepted both democracy and liberalism. Politicos in Tunisia follow the same line of thinking, and after coming back from exile or being freed from prison they set up political parties to defend Salafi positions and ideas, namely the necessity to install an Islamic state ruled through Shari'ah. In this respect, they challenge the notion of liberal democracy and argue that its procedural mechanisms and processes are only permissible insofar as they do not generate decisions that go against God's laws. In short, democratic sovereignty cannot belong to the people when it allows them to pass legislation that goes against God's will. Saving the injunctions of Islam from unrestrained popular sovereignty thus permits politicos to argue in favour of creating political parties. As mentioned above, in Tunisian elections they have so far performed very poorly and do not enjoy much support in society because their ideological positions are considered to be extremely regressive, conservative and out of tune with Tunisian modernity. Among the demands of one of the Salafi parties, Jabhat al-Islah (Reform Front), for instance are the abolition of the egalitarian personal status legislation and the creation of a *hisba*-style police force to crack down on anti-Islamic behaviour. These stances pit them against al-Nahda, which is accused of abandoning its earlier commitment to precisely these kinds of policies of Islamisation.[20] The turn of Ghannouchi's party to Muslim democracy and the relegation of Islamism to social activism outside of political institutions have led to internal grumblings, and the Salafi parties might be able to reap electoral benefits from the disenchantment of al-Nahda members and constituents. It follows that the Islamist electoral offer in Tunisia is still present, although Salafi parties also have a difficult time attracting young members in part because their open rejection of the use of political violence to achieve regime change is not attractive to radicalised young people.

Another political party that was legalised in the aftermath of the revolution is the pan-Islamic movement Hizb al-Tahrir (Liberation Party). While its national chapters in the Arab world operate underground, the Tunisian chapter manages to operate in stops and starts – despite attempts at banning it for good – to promote its core objectives, namely the return of the Caliphate and the implementation of Shari'ah. This vision differs from the one that other Salafi parties propose, insofar as Hizb al-Tahrir struggles for the creation of a politically united ummah, taking in all Muslim lands. In Tunisia, it naturally opposes al-Nahda, not only because it accuses the party of having abandoned Islamism, but also because al-Nahda accepts the nation-state as the supreme political entity within which politics is conducted. For Ghannouchi the modern nation-state is here to stay and is not a temporary and contingent entity, while for Hizb al-Tahrir the goal of Islamists should be to go beyond the nation-state and re-establish the Caliphate as the sole political authority. The party has a very limited following in Tunisia and has recently been at loggerheads with the security services and the presidency, which are seeking a judicial order to ban the party because its extremism constitutes a threat to the state.[21] It should be highlighted that Hizb al-Tahrir also opposes al-Nahda's acceptance of market economics. The party published the following statement regarding the country's socio-economic situation:

> [t]he failure in solving the problems of the people from the side of the consecutive governments does not come from the weakness in material potential and capabilities as they have portrayed it to us. Rather, its cause is the capitalist system perched over our chests. It represents the basis of the disease, the source of distress and house of corruption and those who cause corruption. In addition to being in opposition to the pure Shari'ah of Allah which by itself is enough to bring the anger of Allah upon us.[22]

In short, political alternatives to al-Nahda exist within institutional politics. Although they are quite weak at the moment because of their limited appeal to the wider electorate and the pressure they are under from state security despite their legal status, the abandonment of Islamism on the part of al-Nahda might provide them with the opportunity to attract militants and voters feeling betrayed by Ghannouchi's choices.

Jihadi–Salafism: Ansar al-Shari'ah and its challenge to al-Nahda

Outside of party politics, there exist in Tunisia other forms of Islamism that challenge the prominent role of al-Nahda in its social movement form. While jihadi–Salafism is no longer as central to political debates in Tunisia as it was in the immediate post-revolutionary period, it is a phenomenon worth reassessing and exploring because it provides the opportunity to discuss the legacy it has left and to understand its potential future impact.

The emergence of Salafism as a powerful social and political force in Tunisia was not necessarily a surprise for observers of the country, given that the trend had been present since independence. While it remained the preserve of a very small minority, Salafism or Salafi tendencies existed from the start within the Islamist movement from which al-Nahda saw the light of day. As mentioned above, in the late 1980s some members of the MTI left the movement to found a more militant group, which, through armed struggle, had the objective of overthrowing the regime. The sudden opening of the political system in 2010–11 allowed this trend to re-emerge and occupy the public space. Post-uprising Salafism in Tunisia took on overtly jihadi undertones, employing the symbols and language of international jihad. The objective was to push through muscular bottom-up social activism for the creation of a genuine Islamic state ruled by a strict interpretation of Shari'ah.[23] Crucially, Tunisian jihadi–Salafists by and large did not subscribe to the widespread use of violence to install an Islamic state. Rhetorically, the main organisational representative of the movement – Ansar al-Shari'ah – argued that its activism would not target the nascent democratic structures because the revolution had conferred legitimacy on the new political order. In the post-revolutionary context violence was to be avoided because there were alternatives to armed struggle to spread the message of Islam and the movement took advantage of the liberal nature of the political system to organise and recruit. As long as the state respected the organisation's right to operate, there would be no call for jihad against the democratically elected government. However, Ansar al-Shari'ah militants were involved in a number of high-profile violent acts,[24] leading the major political parties to discuss the idea of banning it to save the transition. Ansar al-Shari'ah therefore operated in plain sight from 2011 until August 2013, but it was then banned and labelled a terrorist organisation. What matters most though in the rise of jihadi–Salafism is how it mobilised many ordinary young citizens through a radical, uncompromising and literal interpretation of what Islam required of them and of the authorities. This type of mobilisation stood in sharp contrast to the appeasing and moderate discourse employed by al-Nahda and the small Salafi parties that were happy to compete in the new democratic system. The continuation of the revolution through street politics in opposition to the system being built excited many young people for whom the revolution had not yet finished. While Ghannouchi and the al-Nahda leadership were busy finding a compromise that would allow their party to become a central player in the transition, and therefore avoid a return to the political margins of society, other forms of Islamist engagement took hold where the centrist, appeasing and pro-democracy discourse of al-Nahda found no echo. The 2011 electoral victory allowed al-Nahda's leadership to negotiate and compromise from a position of relative strength, but, at the same time, this detracted attention from the fact that almost 50 per cent of Tunisians did not go to the polls and that many of them, and in particular the youth, were finding discussions about the creation of a liberal democratic system a betrayal of the revolutionary struggle.[25] As it became apparent with the rise of jihadi–Salafism, many of these young people subscribed to a political project that was, in their eyes, genuinely revolution-ary, clear in its objectives and in tune with what many of them had 'learned' through satellite television and the internet during the 2000s.

There was therefore a significant disconnect in political discourse and strategy between al-Nahda and Ansar al-Shari'ah. The young jihadi–Salafis had contempt for the efforts of the al-Nahda leadership to be part of a political system that they saw as a continuation of past social and economic practices with a democratic veneer. They also had very little knowledge of, and respect for, al-Nahda leaders because the party had been cut off from Tunisia and in particular from Tunisian youth for a long time. Ansar al-Shari'ah's ideological references, its strategies and recruitment pool were entirely different from those of al-Nahda. In terms of ideological references for its political project al-Nahda was, and still is, linked to the modernist reformism of the MB, but with a much greater focus on religious reformists from the Maghreb.

Thus, Ghannouchi and the leadership have incorporated the work of Malek Bennabi on the compatibility between democracy and Islam, and the work of Mohamed Ben Achour on Tunisian Islam's singularity and openness.[26] These ideological references are in sharp contrast with the ones espoused by the Ansar al-Shari'ah leadership. Forged in foreign jihads and in complete disaccord with the institutional strategies of the MB, the Ansar al-Shari'ah leadership relied on scholars like Sayyid Qutb to argue against liberalism, Mohamed al-Maqdisi to argue against democracy and for the necessity of *da'wa* as jihad, and al-Qaeda-linked intellectuals like Abdullah Azzam. In terms of strategies, al-Nahda looked for the validation of its role as a pillar of the new Tunisia and compromised all of its radical stances in the name of acceptance in the system.[27] Ansar al-Shari'ah for its part promoted revolutionary change from below and employed aggressive *da'wa* to gain traction in society and held the political system, parties and the leadership of the country in contempt because they represented the opposite of revolutionary zeal and were the spokespeople of a generation and a social class Ansar al-Shari'ah held responsible for the poor state of Tunisia.[28] In terms of recruitment, Ansar al-Shari'ah had its strongholds in disenfranchised areas of urban centres where there are very few social services, few job prospects and a higher incidence of criminality. Most members of the group were young, with little to no prior engagement in politics or social activism before the revolution, but who had individually come across Salafi literature during the later years of the Ben Ali regime.[29] For its part al-Nahda has an older membership and is popular with a conservative middle class marginalised under both Habib Bourguiba (r.1956–87) and Ben Ali.[30]

Although initially al-Nahda saw the emerging Salafists and the young people swelling their ranks as potential allies and voters in their quest for affirmation in the new political system, the party's leadership was never comfortable with their presence and actions because they fundamentally undermined the party's project to create a political system where it would not face once again the repression of the state. The Salafists' actions and discourse attracted not only social opprobrium, which al-Nahda wanted to avoid in order to prevent the discrediting of Islamism *tout court*, but also created a tense climate that, according to the leadership, would inevitably invite repression as it had occurred in the past. Ghannouchi and the leadership of al-Nahda feared that such repression would target all Islamists and by the summer of 2013 the party, in government at the time, decided that it would outlaw the largest Salafist organisation and side decisively in defence of the nascent democratic system.

As mentioned above, the ideological, political and strategic conflict between al-Nahda and Ansar al-Shari'ah over the best course to ensure the realisation of the Islamic state is not a novelty in the Tunisian Islamist landscape and finds echoes in the split within the MTI in the late 1980s. What is, however, novel in the contemporary struggle between the two is that much like al-Nahda, the jihadi–Salafist movement had its internal divisions, which came to a head when the movement was banned in the summer of 2013. Many within Ansar al-Shari'ah believed that the Tunisian experience of jihadi–Salafism was an entirely new one because mobilisation along jihadi–Salafi lines had never occurred in a pluralist political and social context before. Jihadi–Salafism had always been forged in opposition to au-thoritarian leaders or in international armed struggles through the category of anti-imperialism, such as the war in Iraq against US occupation. Tunisia was a different experience, insofar as for over two years since the 2011 revolution an avowedly jihadi–Salafi movement was allowed to carry out its activities, propagate its beliefs, hold its annual congress and be present in both the media and the public space without much hindrance from the state or the police authorities. This horrified a considerable number of ordinary Tunisians, but the freedom of expression and the freedom to organise had also a profound influence on the Ansar al-Shari'ah leadership and its members because they had the opportunity to 'practise' what a number of jihadi–Salafi sheikhs, and al-Maqdisi in particular, had theorised. Like other jihadi–Salafists, al-Maqdisi had been disturbed by the sectarian violence perpetuated by the jihadi movement in Iraq and had argued that, when given the possibility, jihad should be equated to *da'wa*. In short, if jihadi–Salafist ideas about how to organise society politically and behave individually were free to circulate, members of the movement should be engaged in *da'wa* as their jihad.[31] This meant that violence was not a necessary part of jihadi–Salafism but a fall-back instrument of struggle for when the ideas of the movement could not be propagated and discussed.

Life after Ansar al-Shari'ah

Despite its political and analytical significance, it should be noted that jihadi–Salafism did not occupy the whole Salafi scene in Tunisia. In line with Quintan Wiktorowicz's categorisation of Salafi movements[32] – the jihadis, the politicos and the quietists – all these tendencies also emerged in Tunisia following the uprising. This is not to argue that such tendencies did not exist under authoritarianism, but they became visible and important socio-political actors only after the revolution. The quietist tendency of Salafism, meanwhile, has always been the dominant one across the MENA, but it seemed on the back foot in Tunisia after the revolution, when engagement in politics and social activism through the creation of political parties and associations was seen as indispensable in defending and promoting the faith. This rush towards the politicisation of Salafism did not characterise only Tunisia, but could be seen in Egypt and Yemen very clearly, as well as in Jordan and Morocco.[33] The challenges of the Arab uprisings had a profound impact on Salafi sheikhs and scholars who had quite suddenly to contend with the rise of 'people power' and had to devise strategies to respond to it. Engagement rather than withdrawal towards doctrinal studies seemed to be the way forward for Salafism. This, however, changed quite rapidly because political space, except in Tunisia, closed down as rapidly as it had opened up and the descent into civil conflict in many countries demonstrated that *fitna* was indeed a real and considerable danger. Quietist Salafism therefore, with its emphasis on doctrinal studies and disengagement from parties and associations perceived to be divisive, has made a comeback. Tunisia has not been immune to it, and the political disappointment with the transition as well as the choice of violence of many within Ansar al-Shari'ah has made quietist Salafism again appealing because one can live one's religiosity undisturbed from the state in today's Tunisia. It is for this reason that quietist sheikhs are occupied with building places of doctrinal religious learning, such as the Shari'ah University in Tunis. Through these activities they connect with a tradition of individual civil engagement that traces back to the later Ben Ali years when quietist Salafism was tolerated, and even encouraged, as an antidote to radicalism. This is because quietist Salafism does not challenge political rule and focuses instead on personal religious growth away from politics. This tradition of civil society activism is linked to the growth of Qur'anic schools for example, a phenomenon that had begun under Ben Ali and is now more widespread as religious Tunisians seek a 'safe' space to practise and live their faith free from the interference of politics and the violence of ideological conflicts.[34] Salafi quietist tendencies have become more relevant in the aftermath of the banning of Ansar al-Shari'ah because many of its militants decided to abandon their revolutionary engagement and fall back on the traditional positions of Salafism, namely refraining from challenging political authority.

Other former Ansar al-Shari'ah militants, meanwhile, have chosen the path of political violence and moved on to join pre-existing terrorist groups outside the country, or set up new ones. Many of these former members were already much more committed to the idea of armed struggle against the local infidels as the only and just way to impose an Islamic state. For them, Ansar al-Shari'ah was a sort of cover they could employ to begin organising embryonic armed groups that, when ready, would genuinely take up the fight against the *taghout* (tyrant) regime because democracy and liberalism were just as bad as the previous authoritarian Ben Ali regime. These jihadi–Salafis took the role of violence very seriously and, as mentioned, were involved in political assassinations and other violent episodes that plagued the Tunisian transition from 2011 until the summer of 2013.[35] Once Ansar al-Shari'ah was disbanded, they went on to commit terrorist atrocities inside Tunisia or joined international jihadi networks in Iraq, Syria and Libya.[36]

The divisions within the Salafi movement are an important part of the complex story of Tunisian Islamism because they suggest again how the surrounding environment is in constant tension with ideological beliefs and while at times the environment shapes how groups and individuals react, at other times fixed ideological positions shape the surrounding environment.

Conclusion

As Luisa Gandolfo convincingly states, 'the use of the collective "Islamists" fails to acknowledge the ideological nuances among the groups'[37] and the analysis of the so-called Islamist camp in Tunisia confirms it. Despite being a small and homogeneous country, all forms of Islamism are present post-2011 in the country, illustrating the necessity to understand their complexity. It would, however, be erroneous to believe that the complexity of Tunisian Islamism is the product of the uprising and the transition to democracy that followed. While both events have had an impact on the restructuring of the Islamist camp and have set off new avenues for ideological debate and strategic decision-making, many of the fault lines we see today are the product of long-standing divisions that have periodically resurfaced in Tunisian history. The abandonment of the Islamist label on the part of al-Nahda is a momentous shift for the movement and its leadership and for parties that have chosen to play the democratic institutional game elsewhere in the region, but this does not suggest the end of Islamist politics in Tunisia and elsewhere. The Islamist offer is varied, and channelling faith into politics remains important for ordinary citizens. How they will do so will determine not only the real success of the Tunisian transition, but also the future direction of the region.

Notes

1. Nadia Marzouki (2015), 'Tunisia's rotten compromise', *MERIP on-line*, 10 July, <www.merip.org/mero/mero071015> (last accessed 12 May 2017).
2. See e.g. Monica Marks (2014), 'Convince, coerce or compromise? Ennahda's approach to Tunisia's constitution', Brookings Doha Center Analysis Paper, pp. 3–30; Larbi Sadiki (2014), 'The Tunisian elections: towards an Arab democratic transition', *Middle East Institute*, October, <www.mideasti.org/content/article/tunisian-elections-toward-arab-democratic-transition> (last accessed 12 May 2017).
3. See e.g. Stefano Torelli, Fabio Merone and Francesco Cavatorta (2012), 'Salafism in Tunisia: challenges and opportunities for democratization', *Middle East Policy*, 19, pp. 140–54; Anne Wolf and Raphaël Lefèvre (2012), 'The demon or the demonized? Deconstructing Salafism in Tunisia', *Open Democracy*, 5 June, <www.opendemocracy.net/anne-wolf-raphael-lefevre/demon-or-demonized-deconstructing-"salafism"-in-tunisia> (last accessed 12 May 2017).
4. Kmar Bendana (2012), 'Le parti Ennahdha à l'épreuve du pouvoir en Tunisie', *Confluences Méditerranée*, 82, pp. 189–204.
5. Amel Boubekeur (2016), 'Islamists, secularists and old regime elites in Tunisia: bargained competition', *Mediterranean Politics*, 21:1, pp. 107–27.

6. Kasper Ly Netterstrøm (2015), 'The Islamists' compromise in Tunisia', *Journal of Democracy*, 26:4, pp. 11–124.

7. Alaya Allani (2009), 'The Islamists in Tunisia between confrontation and participation: 1980–2006', *Journal of North African Studies* 14:2, pp. 257–72.

8. Francesco Cavatorta and Fabio Merone (2015), 'Post-Islamism, ideological evolution and la tunisianité of the Tunisian Islamist party al-Nahda', *Journal of Political Ideologies*, 20:1, pp. 27–42.

9. Netterstrøm, 'The Islamists' compromise'.

10. Rachid Ghannouchi (2016), 'From political Islam to muslim democracy: the Ennahda party and the future of Tunisia', *Foreign Affairs*, 95, pp. 58–67.

11. Ibid.

12. Rikke Hostrup Haugbølle (2013), 'Rethinking the role of the media in the Tunisian uprising' in Nouri Gana (ed.) *The Making of the Tunisian Revolution*. Edinburgh: Edinburgh University Press.

13. Fabio Merone (2015), 'Enduring class struggle in Tunisia: the fight for identity beyond political Islam', *British Journal of Middle Eastern Studies*, 42:1, pp. 74–87.

14. Rory McCarthy (2016), 'How Tunisia's Ennahda party turned from its Islamist roots', *Washington Post*, 23 May, <www.washingtonpost.com/news/monkey-cage/wp/2016/05/23/how-tunisias-ennahda-party-turned-from-their-islamist-roots/> (last accessed 12 May 2017).

15. Susan Waltz (1986), 'Islamist appeal in Tunisia', *Middle East Journal*, 40:4, pp. 651–70.

16. MTI is the French acronym for Harakat al-Ittijah al-Islami (Movement of Islamic Tendency). The MTI was renamed al-Nahda in 1989.

17. Netterstrøm, 'The Islamists' compromise'.

18. Ghannouchi, 'From political Islam'.

19. Lewis B. Ware (1985), 'The role of the Tunisian military in the post-Bourguiba era', *Middle East Journal* 39:1, p. 28.

20. Torelli *et al.*, 'Salafism in Tunisia'.

21. Anon. (2016), 'Tunisia calls for ban on Hizb ut-Tahrir', *Arab News*, 8 September, <www.arabnews.com/node/981606/middle-east> (last accessed 12 May 2017).

22. The statement was published on 6 May 2016. It is available in English at: <www.hizb-ut-tahrir.info/en/index.php/leaflet/tunisia/10508.html> (last accessed 12 May 2017).

23. Torelli, 'Salafism in Tunisia'.

24. The attack on the US embassy in 2012 and the assassination of two prominent left-wing politicians were the most notable incidents.

25. Monica Marks (2013), 'Youth politics and Tunisian Salafism: understanding the jihadi current', *Mediterranean Politics*, 18:1, pp. 104–11.

26. Ghannouchi, 'From political Islam to Muslim democracy'; Cavatorta and Merone, 'Post-Islamism'.

27. Francesco Cavatorta and Fabio Merone (2013), 'Moderation through exclusion? The journey of the Tunisian *Ennahda* from fundamentalist to conservative party', *Democratization*, 20:5, pp. 857–75.

28. Francesco Cavatorta and Fabio Merone (2013), 'Salafist movement and Sheikh-ism in the Tunisian democratic transition', *Middle East Law and Governance*, 5:2, pp. 308–30.

29. Olfa Lamloum and Mohamed Ali Ben Zina (eds) (2016), *Les Jeunes de Douar Hicharet d'Ettahdem: Une Enquete Sociologique*. Paris: Arabesque.

30. Fabio Merone and Damiano Facci (2015), 'The new Islamic middle class and the struggle for hegemony in Tunisia', *Afriche e Orienti*, 1:2, pp. 56–69.

31. Joas Wagemakers (2012), *A Quietist Jihadi: The Ideology and Influence of Abu Muhammad al-Maqdisi*. Cambridge: Cambridge University Press.
32. Quintan Wiktorowicz (2006), 'Anatomy of the Salafi movement', *Studies in Conflict and Terrorism*, 29:3, pp. 207–39.
33. Francesco Cavatorta and Fabio Merone (eds) (2017), *Salafism after the Awakening: Contending with People's Power*. London: Hurst.
34. Rikke Hostrup Haugbølle and Francesco Cavatorta (2012), 'Beyond Ghannouchi: Islamism and social change in Tunisia', *Middle East Report*, 262, pp. 20–5.
35. For an in-depth analysis of the internal workings of Ansar al-Shari'ah see Fabio Merone (2016), 'Between social contention and Takfirism: the evolution of the jihadi–Salifi movement in Tunisia', *Mediterranean Politics*, 22:1, pp. 71–90.
36. Georges Fahmi and Hamza Meddeb (2015), 'Market for Jihad: radicalization in Tunisia', *Carnegie Middle East Center*, October, pp. 3–20, <http://carnegieendowment.org/files/CMEC_55_FahmiMeddeb_Tunisia_final_oct.pdf> (last accessed 12 May 2017).
37. Luisa Gandolfo (2015), 'From authoritarian to free state: balancing faith and politics in Tunisia', *Mediterranean Quarterly*, 26:4, p. 13.

Chapter 15

The reconfiguration of the Egyptian Islamist Social Movement Family after two political transitions

Jérôme Drevon

The 2010–12 Arab uprisings have helped to refine existing understandings of Islamist groups' evolution.[1] New opportunities to participate in free and fair political processes have presented a unique chance to re-examine previously covered issues ranging from their decision and strategy-making processes[2] to the study of their constituencies.[3] Moreover, the electoral successes of a few Islamist groups affiliated with al-Ikhwan al-Muslimun (Muslim Brotherhood, MB) and their subsequent endorsement of governmental responsibilities have generated important empirical and theoretical discussions of their pragmatism[4] and inspired noticeable calls for innovative methodological approaches including cross-country[5] and micro-level studies.[6]

Although new studies have substantially enriched existing analyses of Islamist groups and movements, post-2011 research has frequently exposed two biases: (1) the study of political opportunities as electoral processes only and (2) a primary focus on Islamist groups' elites and factions. The prevailing study of Islamist groups' decision and strategy-making in consideration of their interpretations of new electoral means to reach political power and mobilise their constituencies has generated very detailed case studies that often overlook non-electoral political opportunities and remain centred on these groups' leaders and prominent factions. However, the Arab uprisings have also generated non-parliamentary political opportunities and facilitated the emergence of new repertoires of protest for Islamist and non-Islamist movements alike, whose consequences have not been fully analysed. Furthermore, whilst Islamist elites' positions and factional divergences need to be fully deciphered, Islamist movements cannot be solely understood through the positions of their leaders without comprehending how they are simultaneously influenced and constrained by the reactions of their members and their broader *milieu*.

This chapter accordingly develops a relational approach to the reconfiguration of the Egyptian Islamist Social Movement Family (SMF hereafter), which is defined as a 'nationally based, historical configuration of movements that – though they have different specific goals, immediate fields of struggle and strategic preferences – share a common worldview, have organisational overlaps, and occasionally ally for joint campaigns',[7] after 2011 and the 2013 July military coup. This relational approach focuses on intra and inter-movement interactions and their consequences, with the premise that Islamist groups' ideological and behavioural evolution should be analysed conjointly. These groups indeed share common ideational and organisational resources and overlapping constituencies, which suggests that their respective choices and associated outcomes influence their decisions over time. However, existing research has primarily examined the impact of these groups' interactions with non-Islamist actors[8] and paradoxically overlooked cross-Islamist interactions.[9]

This chapter argues that the 2011 Egyptian uprising and the 2013 military coup have destabilised the Egyptian Islamist SMF in contrasting ways. The liberalisation of the political process after 2011 stimulated the institutionalisation of loosely organised movements, challenged the organisational cohesion of established Islamist groups, and empowered Islamist constituencies through the development of new repertoires of contention. The subsequent removal of President Mohamed Morsi (r.2011–13) from the MB marginalised established Islamist groups, challenged their organisational control over their constituencies and impeded the development of political alternatives to armed violence.

A relational approach to the Egyptian Islamist Social Movement Family

Academic research on Islamist movements has long investigated the impact of repression and political participation on their ideological and behavioural evolution. This corpus posits that Islamist movements accommodate political liberalisation with political participation, while exclusionary and reactive repression can spark their militarisation.[10] The decisions of MB-affiliated movements to participate in electoral processes in Egypt, Jordan and Yemen have accordingly been rationalised by the necessity to protect their preaching activities and sustain the Islamisation of society by providing legal cover and non-Islamist allies in civil society.[11] The prevailing consensus on the consequences of political participation underlined in the so-called 'inclusion-moderation' thesis additionally states that electoral participation can moderate these groups' ideological leanings, although ideological moderation is less applicable with regards to several issues associated with Islamic law.[12]

The Arab uprisings have generated new studies examining Islamist groups' performance in power, their electoral constituencies and their comparative political choices across cases. However, two important biases still characterise the study of Islamist politics after the Arab uprisings. The first bias pertains to these studies' understandings of post-2011 political opportunities. Generally defined in social movement studies as the 'features of regimes and institutions that facilitate or inhibit a political actor's collective action and [. . .] changes in those features',[13] political opportunities include political participation, although they are not limited to parliamentary access to state institutions. Yet most post-Arab uprising studies have extensively analysed Islamist groups' political and governmental participation without thoroughly covering the development of new repertoires of contention,[14] including street demonstrations and organised forms of activism, and their consequences. But new repertoires of contention can influence Islamist groups' internal cohesion and decisions beyond the electoral calculus.

The second noticeable bias of post-2011 studies is elitism. Although there are exceptions,[15] research on Islamist politics has often relied extensively on Islamist elites and prominent factions and their disputes to explain Islamist groups' political decisions after 2011. For example, the Egyptian MB's internal factionalism and contest for power between the *da'wa* faction, the pragmatic conservatives and the reformist youths have provided critical information on the group's decision-making processes and diverging preferences following the January uprising.[16] While the elite and factional perspectives are essential, focusing exclusively on them tends to isolate these groups from their members and constituencies and overlooks additional internal and external dynamics. These analyses are therefore less convincing in explaining the impact of new repertoires of contention on Islamist groups' positions and the influence of these groups' constituencies on their leaders. Analysing only Islamist elites generates top-down explanations that can only be partial from a social movement perspective.

Several pre- and post-2011 uprising studies have indeed already suggested that Islamist groups' internal and external relational patterns yield considerable influence on their leaders and members. For instance, the Egyptian MB's participation in professional and student syndicates has shaped their members' political views on non-Islamist actors and generated important moderating cognitive processes,[17] while cooperation between the MB and non-Islamist political parties has generated limited ideological changes in Jordan.[18] More importantly, a rich political ethnography of the Moroccan Islamist SMF substantiates that, in contrast to prevailing assumptions, Islamist sympathisers do not follow their leaders blindly but make informed choices based on their interests, identities and preferences.[19] By focusing on the dynamic ideational market constituted by the Islamist SMF, this author contends that Islamist movements have to be responsive to the expectations of their followers if they want to maintain their popularity. Moreover, considering that Islamist groups share valuable resources and constituencies, their respective decisions are naturally influenced by each other's choices and their associated outcomes. Islamist groups therefore cannot be studied individually without considering general patterns of interactions with their *milieu* and broader SMF.

The present chapter similarly adopts a relational understanding of the Islamist SMF after the 2011 uprising and the July 2013 military coup. Relational approaches are rooted in broader theoretical academic debates in relational sociology and social movement studies.[20] In contrast with 'substantialist' studies dedicated to single actors,[21] relational approaches contend that social movements cannot be studied in a vacuum but should be analysed relationally with their environments. An actor's ideational and behavioural evolution is indeed shaped by relational patterns of interactions with interdependent allies, contenders and *milieu*. For example, inter-organisational ties regulate social movement organisations' strategic actions and choices and can stimulate the adoption of similar forms of contention.[22]

Relational approaches to social movement studies examine social movements from a multi-level perspective, explaining how different types of political opportunities at the macro-level are constructed, interpreted and mediated by meso-level organisational dynamics and micro-level developments. While drawing on the theoretical tools and concepts of social movement theory, relational approaches investigate more specifically the constraints and opportunities inherent in a social movement's internal and external relational patterns of interactions, arguing that the structure of different types of relationships determines the diffusion of information, resources and repertoires that cannot necessarily be understood by focusing on a single social movement actor.

The decision to examine the Egyptian Islamist SMF instead of a single Islamist actor is justified by this chapter's relational approach. Focusing on the broader Islamist SMF in Egypt facilitates the study of the impact of various types of political opportunities on patterns of interaction inside and across Islamist actors as well as with non-Islamist actors. This perspective therefore keeps its distance from elite-centred analyses in order to examine how Islamist groups have been divergently affected internally and externally by post-2011 environmental developments.

The multi-dimensional impact of the 2011 uprising

In January 2011, unprecedented demonstrations destabilised the Egyptian authoritarian regime and sparked the downfall of its president, Hosni Mubarak (r.1981–2011).[23] These demonstrations paved the way for an opening of political opportunities that objectively altered Egypt's political configuration as well as social actors' subjective understanding of available modes of mobilisation. New constitutional provisions temporarily broadened political participation and bolstered freedom of assembly and demonstration between January 2011 and June 2013.

The main observable impact of the January uprising is the unparalleled development of the institutional and organisational components of the Islamist SMF. Before 2011, the Islamist SMF was forcibly disjointed by Egypt's political system. The assassination of President Anwar al-Sadat (r.1970–81) by armed Salafis in 1981 catalysed the separate development of the MB, the Salafis and the proponents of violence by imposing the choice of confined approaches to political action, which were associated with specific mobilisation and socialisation processes that limited internal interactions inside the Islamist SMF.[24] The MB endorsed political participation in professional and student syndicates and presented candidates in legislative elections.[25] Mainstream Salafis favoured informal modes of mobilisation and distanced themselves from the proponents of armed violence in order to avoid state repression. Finally, unaffiliated and 'new' Islamists and personalities engaged the public sphere independently.[26]

After 2011, pre-2011 dividing lines quickly eroded. Non MB-affiliated movements joined the political process, including many Salafis[27] and ex-jihadis.[28] Independent Salafi preachers and institutions formed the new Majlis Shura al-'Ulama (Council of the Scholars),[29] while al-Azhar scholars defended its independence,[30] and a plurality of formal and informal groups emerged from the middle class *salafiyocosta* (the Salafis of Costa Coffee) to the more radical Ansar al-Shari'ah (Supporters of Islamic Law), al-Haraka al-Islamiyya li Tatbiq shar' Allah (Islamic Movement for the Application of Islamic Law), and Tulab al-Shari'ah (Students of Islamic Law). An unprecedented Islamist organisational diversity materialised in only a few months.

Organisational pluralism unfolded in parallel with the growth of new repertoires of contention. Broadly defined as 'the ways that people act together in pursuit of shared interests',[31] post-2011 repertoires of contention ranged from electoral participation, public street protests, sit-ins and assemblies to an array of private activities. While single repertoires used to be associated primarily with specific actors before 2011, most Islamists subsequently diversified their approaches to political action. For example, political protests used to be circumscribed to an educated minority or workers affiliated with trade unions before 2011, with the exception of several wider protest movements organised on foreign policy issues (the war in Iraq and Palestine).[32] In turn, Islamists scarcely socialised publicly with one another before the uprising. The post-2011 political configuration was therefore an unprecedented opportunity for the Islamist trend to attend public demonstrations organised in defence of wide issues ranging from Egypt's Islamic identity and Islamic law to the Syrian jihad and bearded army and police officers. The new public sphere facilitated the intermingling of internal components of the Islamist SMF and further blurred pre-2011 dividing lines.

The new competitive Islamist market presented more opportunities and choices than ever before to Islamist constituencies, which virtually affected all Islamist actors. Islamist groups' organisational challenges differed. The MB's strong organisational cohesion and hierarchical norms, rationalised in an authoritarian environment by the necessity to survive state repression, were contested by the younger generation's demanding a bigger share of responsibility and say in the group's decision-making processes.[33] Unusual disputes regarding the group's political positions on the post-2011 setting sparked the departure of leading MB members, including the prominent reformist Abdel Mone'm Abu al-Fotouh, and the creation of new splinter political parties such as Misr al-Qawiyya (Strong Egypt Party, SEP) and al-Tayyar al-Misri (Egyptian Current Party, ECP) which recruited younger MB members and leading reformists. According to the author's extensive field research, Muslim Brothers with more conservative outlooks conversely participated in Islamist public protests and became closer to Salafi-leaning Islamists on the ground and effectively distanced themselves from younger reformist MB members. The MB was therefore torn on both sides of the spectrum by political liberalisation. These new dividing lines, which partially reflected social and geographic internal divisions, mean that the group's conflicting political positions cannot be analysed solely as an elite intra-MB conflict.

The Salafis initially attempted to follow an opposite direction towards greater organisational cohesion. Since the loose organisational structures and mobilising processes characterising pre-2011 Salafism proved unsuited to party politics, several Salafi political parties were created in order to capitalise on political liberalisation and promote their agenda. The most successful party, Hizb al-Nour (Party of Light, PL), used the pre-existing mobilising structures of the Alexandria-based al-Da'wa al-Salafiyya (Salafi Call), while Cairo-based Hizb al-Fadila (Virtue Party, VP) and Hizb al-Asala (Authenticity Party, AP) faced vigorous organisational challenges informed by the absence of similar pre-existing structures and pre-2011 divisions.[34] The PL, the most organised Salafi political party, faced a notable predicament: its religious leanings became increasingly popular in society but political realism imposed a postponement of unadulterated religious demands in the political sphere. Moreover, the absence of established and legitimate organisational structures akin to those of the MB and the internal competitiveness of the Islamist SMF signified that the group's voters could not necessarily be considered secure and loyal in the long run.

The Salafi loose cannon Hazem Abu Ismail is a manifestation of the diversification of the Islamist SMF and its competitive ideational market. A television religious preacher who was supported by the MB in the 2005 legislative elections, Abu Ismail exploited the expansion of the Salafi revolutionary *milieu* to position himself as its leading figure.[35] Revolutionary Salafism, which combines a Salafi heritage with revolutionary repertoires, mobilised unaffiliated youths on the margins of Salafi party politics and Salafi jihadism around the idea that Islamic law should be implemented immediately.[36] As an emerging social movement, revolutionary Salafism aggregated young Egyptians who were socialised individually, in small groups or institutions, with different Salafi tendencies before 2011. After the uprising, they united and converged around a shared Islamic revolutionary platform according to field research. Revolutionary Salafism epitomises the hybridisation of repertoires of contention associated primarily with secular movements in the 2000s, including street protests, and a Salafi outlook. At the same time, loose modes of organisation and mobilisation implied that no structured group managed to claim a monopoly on this *milieu*, and that populism prevailed. Abu Ismail's popularity among Salafi revolutionaries is easily explained by his firm political positions and astute public performance, which reinforced his popularity from Salafi–jihadi sympathisers to MB members.

Islamist competition inside the post-2011 newly diversified SMF generated two contradictory outcomes for Islamist political parties, contextualised by the expectations of a demanding Islamist constituency versus the requirements of political realism. On the one hand, the development of a competitive ideational market – noticeably marked by rising Salafi forces – reinforced assertively religious references and demands, from a description of the constitutional referendum in March 2011 as an early Islamic expedition[37] to subsequent calls for the Islamisation of the constitution. Street support of the Islamist SMF and public calls for the immediate application of Islamic law pressured Islamist parties to endorse wider religious claims, and the MB – which had softened its position on the application of Islamic law in Egypt before 2011 – felt particularly pressured to accept these new religious constitutional demands. This development does not necessarily reflect a long-entrenched ideological commitment, as is sometimes claimed.[38] Political support for religious law and Egypt's religious identity[39] is a direct outcome of outbidding processes affecting the newly competitive Islamist SMF. On the other hand, party politics imposed some level of pragmatism. For example, many Salafi political parties, including the PL and the political party formed by the ex-jihadis of al-Jama'a al-Islamiyya, Hizb al-Bina' wa al-Tanmiyya (Building and Development Party, BDP) refused to endorse the zealous candidacy of Hazem Abu Ismail in the 2012 presidential elections and recognised that political realism should prevail considering the circumstances, according to personal interviews. Senior members of the PL leadership further upheld the primacy of politics when they split and created a new political party, Hizb al-Watan (Homeland Party, HP), in response to the Salafi Call's religious sheikhs' control over the party's political strategy.[40] The contradictions and tensions between religious dogmatism, stemming from their constituencies' pressure in support of Islamic law, and political realism, informed by the requirements of party politics, thus became apparent within the Islamist SMF before the July 2013 military coup.

Finally, the diversification of the Islamist SMF informed ideational developments on domestic and international issues from a social movement perspective. At a domestic level, the Islamist SMF broadly endorsed the political process despite pre-2011 contentions over Islam and its incompatibility with democracy.[41] The development of a credible political alternative to preaching and violence legitimised political participation in the eyes of most Salafis who had formerly considered party politics akin to apostasy. Extensive field research also suggests that a majority of young Salafi–jihadis supported the candidature of Hazem Abu Ismail, to the dismay of some jihadi–Salafi scholars, such as Abu Mohamed al-Maqdisi, who rebutted Abu Ismail's candidacy on his online mouthpiece *Minbar Tawheed wa al-Jihad*. The legitimisation of political participation is hence not solely a choice imposed by Islamist elites on their followers. Indeed, the reverse may well be the case, with Islamist elites being pressured to accept political participation by their constituencies on the ground.

While the Egyptian Islamist SMF broadly rejected the resort to armed violence after the uprising, a simultaneous legitimisation of violence in another Muslim country crystallised. The repression of the Syrian uprising by the regime gradually justified the use of violence against Syrian armed forces in the public sphere. In Cairo, Syrian-led demonstrations were backed by Egyptian Salafis of all persuasions, whose legitimisation of armed violence became consensual within the Islamist SMF. Pre-2011 opposition to armed violence in Muslim countries dissipated in Syria, long before President Morsi and Salafi political parties' participation in a massive conference in support of the Syrian jihad in June 2013. As in the legitimisation of party politics, support for armed violence in Syria was not necessarily elite-led.

Competition inside a plural ideational market, the development of new repertoires of contention, and the contradictions and tensions between political idealism and realism, have considerably altered the making of the Egyptian Islamist SMF after 2011. Beyond stereotypical portrayal as blind followers of their political leaders and religious sheikhs, Islamist constituencies challenged Islamist actors and used post-2011 political opportunities to contest the latter's monopoly over the ideological making and repertoires of contention endorsed by the Islamist SMF. This development was nonetheless interrupted by the July 2013 military coup, which suddenly ended Egypt's democratic experiment.

The repercussions of the 2013 military coup

Opposition to President Morsi escalated in Spring 2013 and climaxed on 30 June, when mass protests organised throughout the country demanded his resignation. On 3 July, an army-led coalition suspended the Egyptian constitution and removed Morsi from power. In the next few months, thousands of Egyptians were killed during the violent dismantlement of the sit-ins organised by opponents to the military coup in the Rabaa and Nahda squares and tens of thousands were arrested and detained in atrocious conditions.[42] The military authorities terminated Egypt's democratic experiment and restored a militarised and brutal version of Hosni Mubarak's regime.

The post-2013 political configuration was formerly unknown to the Egyptian Islamist SMF. Previous authoritarian regimes – with the possible exception of Nasser's brutal repression of the MB in the 1950s and 1960s – always manifested some level of tolerance for some of the activities of the Islamist SMF,[43] even when they were repressing specific Islamist groups and their members. Egypt's new autocrat Abdel Fattah al-Sisi conversely decided to asphyxiate the Islamist SMF with an unparallelled level of repression that affected the entire Islamist spectrum and its constituencies. Although the regime officially claimed that it was only fighting terrorism, every Islamist actor was affected in specific ways.

The main target was the MB. Along with the classification of the group as a terrorist organisation, the MB's first- and second-tier leaders were arrested or had to quickly depart the country. The Brotherhood was virtually decimated on the ground as a structured group and the hierarchical norms that previously characterised its organisational structures vanished. In the absence of the organisational cohesion and consensual deliberation that previously typified the MB's approach to political action, younger MB members have become increasingly active in the streets of the country and have gradually pushed for a confrontational approach to the military authorities that the MB's old guard has been both reluctant to endorse and unable to prevent.[44]

Smaller Salafi political parties and institutions have attempted to eschew state repression by endorsing a lower profile that substantially contrasts with their pre-2013 public pre-eminence. Many mainstream Salafi preachers associated with the Majlis Shura al-'Ulama, who had become vocal after 2011, left the country. Moreover, although most Salafi political parties supportive of the MB had joined al-Tahaluf al-Watani li-Da'm al-Shari'ah (National Alliance in Support of Legitimacy) in favour of the reinstatement of President Morsi, they never crossed the new regime's red lines by attacking the president or the army, nor did they obtain any noticeable political concession from it. The main backlash to Egyptian Salafism, meanwhile, stems from the regime's exploitation of religion in the public sphere and associated insistence that religious extremism, more than political repression, caused the wave of violence witnessed after 2013. The regime has accordingly called for a religious revolution and promoted an unprecedented ban of traditionalist Islamic scholarship associated with Salafism, control over Egypt's mosque networks, and a monopolisation of the Friday sermons against independent Salafi preachers.

Against this post-2013 political backdrop, the main Salafi political party, the PL, has faced a unique predicament. Whilst the party, in contrast to all major Salafi actors, was used by the military when it supported the coup, regime-led charges against Salafism inevitably affected its subsequent political orientation. The PL has consequently muted its pre-2013 religious constitutional demands and strived to defend its existence as a non-religious party with an Islamic frame of reference only in order to thwart public calls for the application of a general ban on religious political parties. The PL's inconsistent political positions, combined with the public backlash against political Islam on the one hand and a feeling of betrayal by Islamist constituencies on the other, contextualise its post-2013 unique electoral losses. Whereas Alexandria-based Salafis managed mostly to eschew repression after 1981, when they distanced themselves from the proponents of violence,[45] the post-2013 backslash against the Islamist SMF prevented a similar development owing to the new regime's strategy of delegitimising Islamist political actors *in toto*.

The most challenging developments, however, have occurred on the ground, among Islamist constituencies. In contrast to pre-2013 developments, political repression (rather than a competitive Islamist SMF) has reinforced the marginalisation of organised Islamist groups in the streets of the country. Unprecedented waves of arrests, combined with a unique degree of repression and isolation of Islamist political parties, have hindered the development of a political alternative in the Islamist SMF. The younger generation sympathetic to the latter has therefore taken the lead by engaging in street protests around the country's universities and in specific neighbourhoods. Moreover, the spiral of violence has fuelled the legitimisation of armed conflict in the absence of a political solution. According to many personal testimonies,[46] violence has been paradoxically perceived as less risky than non-violent forms of resistance, considering that the high personal risks taken during public marches contrast with the lower chances of being caught while participating in clandestine armed actions.

Although small skirmishes occurred only on an irregular basis before July 2013, armed attacks against various types of targets have significantly escalated since. Violence covers an array of repertoires ranging from the use of hand grenades in hit-and-run attacks against the security forces to more sophisticated selective assassinations and car bomb attacks. This diversity suggests the existence of various groups and networks with access to diverging logistics and military expertise.

The most notable of such armed attacks have taken place on the Sinai Peninsula and are attributed to the Ansar Bayt al-Maqdis group (Partisans of the Holy Place/Jerusalem), later renamed Wilayyat Saina' (Sinai Province, WS hereafter). The WS formally emerged after the 2011 uprising, although its origins can be traced back to the early 2000s. The group's inception is rooted in the peculiar socio-political conditions of the region and its antagonistic relations with the Egyptian state.[47] Armed militancy in the Sinai Peninsula emerged in response to economic and political marginalisation combined with harsh state repression. The growing use of violence by the WS after 2013 was primarily the result of the state's iron fist approach after the removal of Morsi.

Two additional patterns characterise the violence perpetuated from within the Islamist SMF in mainland Egypt after 2013. The first pattern is defined by the absence of military expertise and its targets (the security forces, broadly defined). These attacks are characterised primarily by the use of light weaponry against army checkpoints, police stations and members of the security forces. Limited logistics and military experience suggest that the perpetrators of these attacks are not formally affiliated with violent networks or groups. Indeed, these attacks are probably conducted by local groups of friends and acquaintances, considering the risks involved. Some of the low-level attacks have been self-attributed to al-'Iqab al-Thawri (Revolutionary Punishment), although this designation appears to be a generic name used by unaffiliated or loosely connected individuals.

The second pattern refers to professional and selective armed attacks committed against prominent targets. High-ranking individuals affiliated with the security forces, the Ministry of Interior and the judiciary have been executed by unknown networks and groups. These attacks reveal a higher degree of professional expertise that significantly contrasts with those perpetrated by previously unaffiliated individuals. They range from the assassination of General Mohamed Said in January 2014 and Egypt's state prosecutor Hisham Barakat in June 2015, to failed attempts against the Minister of Interior.

The proliferation of low-level armed contention, combined with the marginalisation of virtually all organised Islamist groups, constitute two complementary facets of post-2013 Egypt. Such complementary developments are, in fact, commonly traced in social movement studies. Indeed, scholars of contentious politics have long asserted that armed violence tends to emerge on the periphery of mainstream social movements at the end of cycles of protest, when the 'prevailing behaviour of the movement families [are] more confrontational and the political culture polarised'.[48] Moreover, the inability of mainstream Islamist groups such as the MB to provide a credible political alternative and influence their members and sympathisers on the ground has fuelled the narrative that violence is the sole response to state repression. The Egyptian regime has triggered a self-fulfilling prophecy: designating established Islamist groups as terrorist entities has effectively marginalised them, radicalised their members and obstructed the development of non-violent political alternatives.

Conclusion

Charting the evolution of the Egyptian Islamist SMF since 2011 constitutes an important contribution to current understandings of Islamist politics after the Arab uprisings. While most studies in the field have chosen to revisit the 'inclusion-moderation' thesis or investigate Islamist groups' electoral constituencies, this chapter has sought to show that it is equally important to examine the Islamist SMF more generally as well as the emergence of new repertoires of contention among its supporters. This focus substantiates that, beyond the calculus of Islamist elites, new relational patterns of interactions inside the Islamist SMF altered its organisational making and shaped new ideational developments that cannot be solely comprehended by a top-down logic. Far from being blind followers of theirs groups and sheikhs, Islamist supporters contested established hierarchies and ideas and developed new forms of political activism. In turn, established and newly created Islamist groups had to adapt to the expectations of their sympathisers and be answerable to their demands. Unfortunately, the July 2013 military coup abruptly terminated this new experiment.

The military coup and its repercussions on the Islamist SMF, meanwhile, constitute a textbook case study of social movement radicalisation. A brutal authoritarian regime crushes a broad social movement, dismantles its organisational structures, prevents the development of a non-violent political opposition, and eventually bolsters the proponents of armed violence. The articulation of a radical theology of violence cannot be studied as the manifestation of a violent Islamist essence. In Egypt, in fact, it was largely a response to an unprecedented wave of repression obstructing any non-violent political alternative.

If/once the al-Sisi regime realises that the mainstream Islamist opposition has to be reintegrated into domestic politics, the main challenge of the Islamist SMF and organised Islamist groups will be the presentation of a viable alternative and the integration of its younger constituencies, who are not likely to submit to their leaders unconditionally and accept not being fully part of these groups' decision-making processes.

Notes

1. Research for this chapter was supported by a scholarship from the Swiss National Science Foundation (SNSF).
2. Nathan J. Brown (2012), *When Victory is not an Option: Islamist Movements in Arab Politics*. Ithaca: Cornell University Press; Shadi Hamid (2014), *Temptations of Power: Islamists and Illiberal Democracy in a New Middle East*. New York: Oxford University Press; Jérôme Drevon (2015), 'The emergence of ex-jihadi political parties in post-Mubarak Egypt', *Middle East Journal*, 69:4, pp. 511–26.
3. Melani Cammett and Pauline Jones Luong (2014), 'Is there an Islamist political advantage?' *Annual Review of Political Science*, 17, pp. 187–206; Laurence Deschamps-Laporte (2014), 'From the mosque to the polls: the emergence of the Al Nour party in post-Arab Spring Egypt', *New Middle Eastern Studies*, 4, pp. 1–21.; Neil Ketchley and Michael Biggs (2017), 'The educational contexts of Islamist activism: elite students and religious institutions in Egypt', *Mobilization*, 22:1, pp. 57–76.
4. Joyelyne Cesari (2014), *The Awakening of Muslim Democracy: Religion, Modernity, and the State*. Cambridge: Cambridge University Press; Shadi Hamid (2016), *Islamic Exceptionalism: How the Struggle Over Islam Is Reshaping the World*. New York: St. Martin's Press; Halil Ibrahim Yenigün (2016), 'The political and theological boundaries of Islamist moderation after the Arab Spring', *Third World Quarterly*, 37:12, pp. 2304–21.
5. Jason Brownlee, Tarek E. Masoud and Andrew Reynolds (2014), *The Arab Spring: Pathways of Repression and Reform*. New York: Oxford University Press; John Chalcraft (2016), 'The Arab uprisings of 2011 in historical perspective', in Amal Ghazal and Jens Hanssen (eds), *The Oxford Handbook of Contemporary Middle-Eastern and North African History*. New York: Oxford University Press; Steven Heydemann, 'Explaining the Arab uprisings: transformations in comparative perspective', *Mediterranean Politics*, 21:1, pp. 192–204.
6. Wendy Pearlman (2013), 'Emotions and the microfoundations of the Arab Uprisings', *Perspectives on Politics*, 11:2, pp. 387–409; Jillian Schwedler (2015), 'Comparative politics and the Arab uprisings', *Middle East Law and Governance*, 7:1, pp. 141–52; Ahmad Akhlaq (2016), 'The ties that bind and blind: embeddedness and radicalisation of youth in one Islamist organisation in Pakistan', *Journal of Development Studies*, 52:1, pp. 5–21.
7. Donatella della Porta and Dieter Rucht (1995), 'Left-Libertarian movements in context: a comparison of Italy and West Germany, 1965–1990', in J. Craig Jenkins (ed.), *The Politics of Social Protest: Comparative Perspectives on States and Social Movements*. Minneapolis: University of Minnesota Press, pp. 229–72. See also Jérôme Drevon (2017), 'The constrained institutionalization of diverging Islamist strategies: the Jihadis, the Muslim Brotherhood, and the Salafis between two aborted Egyptian revolutions', *Mediterranean Politics*, 22:1, pp. 1–19.

8. See e.g. Carry R. Wickham (2002), *Mobilizing Islam: Religion, Activism and Political Change in Egypt*. New York: Columbia University Press; Janine A. Clark (2006), 'The conditions of Islamist moderation: unpacking cross-ideological cooperation in Jordan', *International Journal of Middle East Studies*, 38:4, pp. 539–60; Maha Abdelrahman (2009), '"With the Islamists? – Sometimes. With the State? – Never!": Cooperation between the left and Islamists in Egypt', *British Journal of Middle Eastern Studies*, 36:1, pp. 37–54; Eva Wegner and Miquel Pellicer (2011), 'Left–Islamist opposition cooperation in Morocco', *British Journal of Middle Eastern Studies*, 38:3, pp. 303–22.

9. Notable exceptions include Avi Max Spiegel (2015), *Young Islam: The New Politics of Religion in Morocco and the Arab World*. Princeton: Princeton University Press.

10. François Burgat (2002), *L'islamisme en Face*. La Découverte; Mohamed Hafez (2003), *Why Muslims Rebel: Repression and Resistance in the Islamic World*. Boulder, CO: Lynne Rienner Publishers.

11. Lisa Blaydes (2010), *Elections and Distributive Politics in Mubarak's Egypt*. Cambridge: Cambridge University Press; Jillian Schwedler (2013), 'Islamists in power? Inclusion, moderation and the Arab uprisings', *Middle East Development Journal*, 5:1, 1350006; Carrie R. Wickham (2013), *The Muslim Brotherhood: Evolution of an Islamist Movement*. Princeton: Princeton University Press; Hamid, *Temptations of Power*.

12. Janine Clark (2004), *Islam, Charity, and Activism: Middle-Class Networks and Social Welfare in Egypt, Jordan, and Yemen*. Bloomington: Indiana University Press; Clark, 'The conditions of Islamist moderation'; Carrie R. Wickham (2004), 'The path to moderation: strategy and learning in the formation of Egypt's Wasat party', *Comparative Politics*, 36:2, pp. 205–28; Wickham, *The Muslim Brotherhood*; Jillian Schwedler (2006), *Faith in Moderation: Islamist Parties in Jordan and Yemen*. Cambridge: Cambridge University Press; Brown, *When Victory When Victory is not an Option*; Cesari, *The Awakening of Muslim Democracy*.

13. Sidney Tarrow and Charles Tilly (2009), 'Contentious politics and social movements', in Carles Boix and Susan C. Stokes (eds), *The Oxford Handbook of Comparative Politics*. New York: Oxford University Press, p. 440.

14. An exception being Chalcraft, 'The Arab uprisings'.

15. Francesco Cavatorta and Fabio Merone (2013), 'Moderation through exclusion?: The journey of the Tunisian Ennahda from fundamentalist to conservative party', *Democratization*, 20:5, pp. 857–75; Spiegel, *Young Islam*; Chalcraft, 'The Arab uprisings'; Biggs and Ketchley, 'The educational contexts'; al-Anani, Khalil (2016), *Inside the Muslim Brotherhood: Religion, Identity, and Politics*. New York: Oxford University Press.

16. Wichham, *The Muslim Brotherhood*. See also Ibrahim El Hudaybi (2012), 'Islamism in and after Egypt's revolution', in Bahgat Korany and Rabab El-Mahdi (eds), *The Arab Spring in Egypt: Revolution and Beyond*. New York: Oxford University Press; Khalil Al-Anani (2015), 'Upended path: the rise and fall of Egypt's Muslim Brotherhood', *Middle East Journal*, 69:4, pp. 527–43.

17. Wickham, *Mobilizing Islam*; Wickham, *The Muslim Brotherhood*.

18. Clark, 'The conditions of Islamist moderation'.

19. Spiegel, *Young Islam*.

20. Mustafa Emirbayer (1997), 'Manifesto for a relational sociology', *American Journal of Sociology*, 103:2, pp. 281–317; Nick Crossley (2010), *Towards Relational Sociology*. London: Routledge; Pierpaolo Donati (2010), *Relational Sociology: A New Paradigm for the Social Sciences*. London: Routledge.

21. Emirbayer, 'Manifesto', p. 282.

22. Jennifer Hadden (2015), *Networks in Contention*. Cambridge: Cambridge University Press.

23. Jeroen Gunning and Ilan Zvi Baron (2014), *Why Occupy a Square? People, Protests and Movements in the Egyptian Revolution*. New York: Oxford University Press.

24. Drevon, 'The constrained institutionalization of diverging Islamist Strategies'.

25. Wickham, *Mobilizing Islam*.

26. Raymond Baker (2009), *Islam without Fear: Egypt and the New Islamists*. Cambridge MA: Harvard University Press.

27. Khalil Al-Anani (2012), 'Islamist parties post-Arab Spring', *Mediterranean Politics*,17:3, pp. 466–72.

28. Drevon, 'The emergence of ex-jihadi political parties'.

29. Faid Abdullah (2014), 'al-salafiyyun fi misr: min shari'a al-fatwa ila shari'a al-intikhabat' [The Salafis in Egypt: from the legitimacy of the fatwa to the legitimacy of the elections], in Bashir Musa and Abd al-Mawla Iz al-Din (eds), *al-dhahira al-salafiyya al-ta'adudiyya al-tandhimiyya wal-siyasiya* [The Salafi Phenomenon: organisational and political diversity]. Doha: Markaz al-Jazeera lil-Dirasat, pp. 49–74.

30. Nathan Brown (2011), 'Post-revolutionary al-Azhar', *Carnegie Endowment for International Peace*, 3 October, <http://carnegieendowment.org/2011/10/03/post-revolutionary-al-azhar-pub-45655> (last accessed 12 May 2017).

31. Charles Tilly (1995), *Popular Contention in Great Britain, 1758–1834*. Cambridge MA: Harvard University Press, p. 41; See also Donatella della Porta (2013), 'Repertoires of contention', in Doug McAdam (ed.) *The Wiley-Blackwell Encyclopaedia of Social and Political Movements*. Malden: Blackwell.

32. Reem Abou-El-Fadl (2012), 'The road to Jerusalem through Tahrir Square: anti-Zionism and Palestine in the 2011 Egyptian revolution', *Journal of Palestine Studies*, 41:2, pp. 6–26; Gunning and Baron, *Why Occupy a Square?*

33. Drevon, 'The constrained institutionalization of diverging Islamist strategies'.

34. Richard Gauvain (2011), 'Be careful what you wish for: spotlight on Egypt's Muslim Brotherhood and Salafi organizations after the uprising', *Political Theology*, 12:2, pp. 173–79; Stéphane Lacroix (2012), *Sheikhs and Politicians: Inside the New Egyptian Salafism*. Doha: Brookings Doha Center.

35. Faid, 'al-salafiyyun fi misr'.

36. Stéphane Lacroix and Ahmad Chalala (2015), 'Le Salafisme Révolutionnaire dans l'Égypte post-Moubarak', in Bernard Rougier and Stéphane Lacroix (eds), *L'Égypte en Révolutions*. Paris: Presses Universitaires de France (PUF).

37. Mohamed Hussein Yaqub, a prominent salafi preacher, described the outcomes as *ghazwa al-sanadiq* (expedition of the ballot boxes), as if the positive outcome of the referendum indicated a critical Islamist victory.

38. Eric Trager (2016), *Arab Fall: How the Muslim Brotherhood Won and Lost Egypt in 891 Days*. Washington DC: Georgetown University Press.

39. Patrick Haenni (2015), 'Les causes d'un échec', in Bernard Rougier and Stéphane Lacroix (eds), *L'Égypte en Révolutions*. Paris: Presses Universitaires de France (PUF).

40. Stéphane Lacroix (2016), 'Egypt's pragmatic Salafis: the politics of Hizb al-Nour', *Carnegie Endowment for International Peace*, 1 November, <http://carnegieendowment.org/2016/11/01/egypt-s-pragmatic-salafis-politics-of-hizb-al-nour-pub-64902> (last accessed 12 May 2017).

41. Drevon, 'The constrained institutionalization of diverging Islamist strategies'.

42. Amnesty International (2016), 'Egypt: "Officially you do not exist – disappeared and tortured in the name of counter-terrorism', 13 July, <www.amnesty.org/en/documents/mde12/4368/2016/en/> (last accessed 12 May 2017).

43. Wickham, *Mobilizing Islam*.
44. Abdalrahman Ayyash (2015), 'The Brotherhood's post-pacifist approach', *Sada Journal, Carnegie Endowmnent for Interational Peace*, 9 July, <http://carnegieendowment.org/sada/?fa=60665> (last accessed 12 May 2017).
45. Drevon, 'The constrained institutionalization of diverging Islamist strategies'.
46. Including this researcher's personal interviews with young Egyptians, which were corroborated by journalists on the ground.
47. Muhannad Sabry (2005), *Sinai: Egypt's Linchpin, Gaza's Lifeline, Israel's Nightmare*. Cairo: American University Press.
48. Donatella della Porta (1995), *Social Movements, Political Violence, and the State: A Comparative Analysis of Italy and Germany*. Cambridge: Cambridge University Press.

Chapter 16

Iraq's Shi'a Islamists after the uprisings: the impact of intra-sectarian tensions and relations with Iran

Ibrahim Al-Marashi

While Iraq cannot be considered as one of the so-called 'Arab Spring' states *per se*, it is nevertheless apparent that the 2011 uprisings have had a significant impact on Iraq's predominant Shi'a Islamist political parties: Hizb al-Da'wa al-Islamiyya (Da'wa Party, DP), al-Majlis al-A'ala li-Thawra al-Islamiyya fi al-'Iraq (Supreme Council of the Islamic Revolution in Iraq, SCIRI) and al-Tayyar al-Sadri (Sadrist Movement). The collapse of the state in neighbouring Syria and its descent into civil war in the wake of the uprisings created the context for the emergence of al-Dawla al-Islamiyya fi al-'Iraq wa al-Sham (Islamic State of Iraq and Syria, ISIS) in 2014, which in turn prompted these Iraqi Shi'a Islamist parties to rally their constituencies in defence of the nation. However, the emergence of a common foe in the shape of ISIS neither resulted in the creation of a unified political front among these parties nor consensus over their respective relationships with Tehran. Indeed, despite the emergence of a pan-Shi'a identity across the region after the 2011 uprisings, and the common threat posed by the rise of ISIS, conflicts persist among the Shi'a Islamist parties/elites in Iraq and Iran, where the pursuit of narrow self-interest and political survival continues to trump intra-sectarian solidarity and cooperation.

This chapter focuses on three dominant Iraqi Shi'a Islamist political parties, the DP, the SCIRI and the Sadrist Movement. All three of the parties can be classed as Shi'a Islamist, as all have articulated a future vision of Iraq that reflects the Shi'a majority status and demographic weight in the country and advocates a defining role for Islam in the constitution to ensure Iraq's Islamic identity and character. Yet despite similar Islamist agendas and a shared sectarian affiliation, the interest-driven aims of Shi'a politicians in the post-2003 electoral environment have lead to ongoing fragmentation rather than unity. In fact, this chapter posits that, since the Iranian Revolution of

1979, ongoing rivalries among Iraq's Shi'a Islamist parties demonstrate that they have primarily sought dominance within the national setting against rival domestic Shi'a groups, and autonomy in their position *vis-à-vis* Tehran, all the while enjoying the financial and military largesse of the Islamic Republic. Dispelling the widely inferred 'Shi'a crescent' narrative with regards to Iraqi politics, it reveals that the context of the Arab uprisings has precipitated further fragmentation and conflict among the three Shi'a Islamist parties, as manifest (1) during the 2011–12 wave of anti-government protests, (2) the contested 2014 formation of a third al-Maliki government in the shadow of the ISIS threat and (3) the resurgence of service delivery and anti-corruption protests from 2015 onwards.

Contesting notions of the 'Shi'a Crescent'

In the aftermath of the 2003 US-led invasion of Iraq, Jordan's King Abdullah II alluded to the spectre of a 'Shi'a Crescent' spreading from a resurgent Iran, a newly assertive Shi'a Iraq, to Allawi Shi'a-controlled Syria, and finally to a Hizbullah-dominated Lebanon.[1] Sectarianism as a concept has gained renewed prominence following the Arab uprisings as the causative dynamic behind conflicts in Bahrain, Syria, Yemen and Iraq, framed as part of a 'sectarian Cold War'. Such analytical frames are often embedded in an assumption that sectarian conflict can be attributed to tensions raging since time immemorial as an irreconcilable Sunni–Shi'a conflict, explained away by the 'ancient ethnic hatred' trope. When metaphors such as the 'Shi'a Crescent' or 'sectarian Cold War' are invoked, they tend to describe sects as social units that are historically continuous and primordial, rather than as a reaction, and mobilisation strategy, to unique political crises in certain states. Representative of academic work that evokes this sectarian bipolarity is, for instance, Geneive Abdo's *The New Sectarianism* and Khalil F. Osman's *Sectarianism in Iraq*, both of which posit that 'primordial sectarian affiliations' lie at the heart of the conflict in Iraq.[2]

Countering this line of analysis, a literature has emerged that questions the notion of sectarianism itself, and problematises extant tensions between the Arab Shi'a and Iran, as well as intra-Shi'a conflicts within national setting such as Iraq. So for instance, Vali Nasr's work, *The Shi'a Revival*, examines the ramifications of a Shi'a-led government in Iraq on regional dynamics.[3] Despite the suggestion in the title, Nasr does not argue that a 'Shi'a International' exists between Iran and its Shi'a Arab allies. Rather he acknowledges the differences that exist among the region's Shi'a communities. He argues that the regional Arab Sunni *status quo* was upset by the overthrow of Saddam Hussein in 2003, and demonstrates how certain states, such as Saudi Arabia and Jordan, perceive this change as a seismic shift that upset the balance of power in favour of Iran. F. Gregory Gause, in his piece 'Beyond sectarianism', argues as well that sectarian rationales alone are insufficient to explain the post-2011 regional crisis in the Middle East, and focuses instead on an Iranian–Saudi proxy conflict based on rational balance-of-power calculations.[4] Finally, these readings of regional politics also resonate with Graham Fuller and Rend Rahim Francke's work, *The Arab Shi'a*, which examines the intellectual origins of the pan-Shi'a construct. The authors argue that the Shi'a in both the Arab world and Iran since the Iranian revolution of 1979 tend to be portrayed within Western and Middle Eastern policy circles and the mainstream media as a homogeneous, monolithic sect, ignoring differences within this community in each country, such as for instance the distinction between religious and secular Shi'a, the disparity between well-educated, middle-class Shi'a and the poorer segments of this community, urban versus rural divides, and most often ignored, the national differences between Shi'ism in Iraq, Kuwait and Lebanon, or the widely theologically divergent Shi'a sects in Syria and Yemen.[5]

Prominent scholars devoted to the study of Shi'ism, meanwhile, also tend to argue against Shi'a homogeneity within the broader region as well within Iraq. Yitzhak Nakash's *The Shi'is of Iraq*, for instance, provides a history of this community until 1958, highlighting the cultural distinctions that emerged between them and their co-religionists in Iran.[6] Faleh A. Jabar also provides a history of the Iraqi Shi'a until the 2003 war, demonstrating divisions along political, religious and social lines, challenging the oft-perceived homogeneity of this community.[7]

Taking this more critical reading of sectarianism and Shi'a politics in the Middle East as a point of departure, this chapter examines Iraqi politics since the Arab uprisings of 2010–12, highlighting the pluralisation of, and ongoing fragmentation among, Shi'a Islamist parties and the concomitant growth in intra-Shi'a Islamist competition and contention within Iraq and bilaterally with Iran, a neighbour that enjoys a paramount influence over internal Iraqi affairs.

The emergence of Iraq's Shi'a Islamist parties

Of the three Shi'a Islamist parties under scrutiny here, the DP emerged first in the 1960s to mobilise the Iraqi Shi'a, providing a religious alternative at the time to secular parties, such as al-Hizb al-Shuyu'i al-'Iraqi (Iraqi Communist Party, ICP) and Hizb al-Ba'ath al-'Arabi al-Ishtiraki fi al-'Iraq (Arab Socialist Baath Party of Iraq, or simply Baath party), both of which had begun to make inroads into this community. Following the Baathist *coup d'état* of 1968 and the ascendancy to power of Saddam Hussein in 1979, the DP was banned, allegedly for being complicit in a failed assassination attempt against Tariq Aziz, then Iraqi deputy prime minister.[8] From then onwards the party operated clandestinely, while most of its leadership sought refuge in Iran, Syria and the UK.

Throughout the 1980s, whilst underground and in exile, the DP retained relations with the Islamic Republic of Iran. In fact, at the time the Iranian regime actively encouraged the DP to join an Iraqi Shi'a umbrella organisation, SCIRI, which had been forged in 1982 under the leadership of exiled Iraqi cleric Mohamed Baqir al-Hakim. Sponsored by Iran, SCIRI served as a means for the Iranian leadership to unite and control Iraqi Shi'a factions, as well as a government in exile that would assume control of Iraq after Saddam Hussein's expected demise during Iran's early military successes in the Iran–Iraq war (1980–8). Having initially joined SCIRI, the DP later withdrew, however, due to its apprehensions about Iranian control over the organisation, and its refusal to acknowledge the legitimacy of the *wilayat al-faqih* (rule of the theological jurist), a post held by Ayatollah Khomeini and which fused Shi'a religious authority with the highest executive political authority in Iran.[9] The DP's attempts to distance itself from SCIRI and Iran represents an open manifestation of tensions between an Iraqi Shi'a group resisting Iranian influence, even at a point where the party was weak and outlawed and its leadership exiled.

Alongside the DP and SCIRI, within Baathist Iraq itself, the following three grand ayatollahs emerged as spiritual leaders of the country's Shi'a community: Abul-Qassim al-Khoe'i, his successor Ali al-Sistani, and Mohamed Sadiq al-Sadr. Al-Sadr, who had a wide following among the inhabitants in the east Baghdad district known as Saddam City, was killed in February 1999, allegedly at the hands of Iraq's security forces for his incendiary sermons. His surviving son, Muqtada went into hiding and would later emerge as a pivotal force in Iraqi Shi'a politics.[10] All three clerics remained separate from the exiled Shi'a Islamist parties in order to survive in Baathist Iraq. Both al-Sadr and his son leveraged this distance to present themselves as leaders free of foreign (that is Iranian) control and steadfast in guiding Iraq's Shi'a during Baathist rule.

Muqtada al-Sadr re-emerged from hiding after the 2003 regime change, founding the Sadrist Movement, a political organisation that sought to represent the marginalised lower and less-integrated social classes among the Shi'a community. As such al-Sadr created a movement that fused sect and socio-economic status, and sought to cultivate its image as an indigenous Iraqi nationalist and anti-American one, transcending the sectarian divide, and one that developed from within the nation, as opposed to the exiled Shi'a parties. While al-Sadr was still too young to elevate himself to his father's status as a learned religious scholar, he proved himself as a shrewd political tactician, elevating himself from relative obscurity in 2003 to developing a cult of personality and Shi'a sub-culture that has emerged as a fixture in Iraq's politics ever since.[11]

Whilst the DP, SCIRI and the Sadrist Movement can all be classed as 'Islamist' parties for the reasons highlighted above, it is important to note that none of them ever sought the establishment of an Iranian-style Islamic system of government. Al-Sadr, for instance, had called for the establishment of an Islamic republic in Iraq shortly after the fall of Saddam Hussein in 2003, yet insinuated that he disagreed with the Iranian notion of *wilayat al-faqih*, and did not wish its implementation in Iraq.[12] Since the 1980s, the DP, as well, had expressed its reservations about the notion of clerical authority as exercised within the Islamic Republic.[13] Even SCIRI, which has depended on Iranian support since its creation, did not advocate the establishment of an Iranian-style Islamic Republic in Iraq post-2003, when the party shifted its allegiance from Ayatollah Khamenei to Ayatollah al-Sistani in 2007, as a means of cultivating an Iraqi nationalist image.[14] What is more, given that from 2003 onwards the USA had become the paramount authority in Iraq, and given its commitment to creating a successful democracy that would serve as a beacon for the rest of the region, the three parties and the leadership in Tehran realised that it would have been impossible to create an Iranian-style state even if they had wanted to, and that Iraq's other ethno-sectarian and secular communities would have been opposed to it. Rather, the electoral process set up under American aegis would be sufficient for these Shi'a Islamist parties to assume power, given the Shi'a demographic majority in Iraq.

The introduction of electoral politics after the fall of Saddam Hussein in 2003 thus spurred the DP, SCIRI, the Sadrist Movement and other smaller Shi'a (Islamist) parties to enter into a complex game of alignment and rivalry in the new political system based on power-political considerations. Iraq's first post-2003 plural elections took place in January 2005 for the 275-member Council of Representatives, tasked with drafting a new constitution as well as the formation of a transitional government. This and subsequent elections featured a proportional electoral system based on party lists rather than individual candidacies.

In the 2005 elections the DP, SCIRI and candidates loyal to al-Sadr formed an electoral alliance, al-I'tilaf al-'Iraqi al-Muwahhad (United Iraqi Alliance, UIA), under whose umbrella they managed to secure a plurality of the votes and seats in parliament.[15] At the level of governance, meanwhile, Iraqi politics started to mimic Lebanon's consociational system, in which administrative posts were allocated not on merit or qualification but primarily on the basis of a politician's ethno-sectarian background. This was done so as to give the appearance of a balanced and inclusive government that represented the nation's diversity. The allocation of executive posts benefited the former exiled Shi'a Islamists, as the political consensus among the dominant parties, both Shi'a Islamist and Kurdish, was that since the UIA had secured a plurality of the votes, it should determine who was to form the transitional government. Ibrahim al-Ja'fari of the DP was thus duly chosen as prime minister (r.2005–6), an arrangement deemed acceptable to both the US and Iran. Although al-Ja'fari was a Shi'a Islamist, the DP itself remained sufficiently distant from Iran at the time to allay US concerns, whilst Iran was able to leverage SCIRI, a key party in the transitional government, to advance its goals. The principal party representing the country's Kurdish community, meanwhile, Yekîtiya Nishtimane ya Kurdistanê (Patriotic Union of Kurdistan, PUK), was awarded the presidency, whilst the position of speaker of parliament went to a representative of the Sunni community. Other key posts in the transitional government, meanwhile, were allocated to Shi'a Islamists, including the posts of vice president and Ministry of Interior, which went to representatives of SCIRI, as well as the ministries of Health and Transport, which went to politicians loyal to Muqtada al-Sadr. Since then, this consociational arrangement has evolved as a political norm in Iraq, and this despite the fact that the new Iraqi constitution, ratified in 2005, does not explicitly stipulate that the prime minister must be Shi'a, the president Kurdish, and the speaker of parliament an Arab Sunni. Indeed, in subsequent elections, Shi'a Islamists would seek to leverage the benefits of the consociational arrangement that governs the distribution of executive posts, allowing these parties the opportunity to expand their patronage network, for example, by offering supporters local development projects or jobs in the ministries or in the security forces controlled by the Ministry of Interior.

Following the ratification of the new Iraqi constitution and a second UIA electoral victory in the December 2005 parliamentary elections, Nouri al-Maliki, a DP member, was chosen as the country's first post-transition prime minister. During his first term in office from 2006 to 2010, al-Maliki was widely accused of seeking to centralise power in his own hands, and installing an authoritarian system of government in a country increasingly divided by sectarian factionalism and civil war. It is in this period also that tensions broke out between members and parties/groupings of the governing UIA coalition, ultimately leading to its break up. In August 2007 a skirmish broke out between members of SCIRI and the Sadrist militia, the Mahdi Army, during the pilgrimage in Karbala, leading to a two-day street battle. Al-Maliki faulted the Mahdi Army for starting the incident and ordered government forces to crack down on the militia, a force that had challenged his centralising drive.[16] The final break between al-Maliki and the Sadrists then occurred when the PM sought to break the power of the Mahdi Army, ordering the military to attack them in Basra and Baghdad in 2008, with fighting ending after Iranian mediation.[17] Al-Maliki thus proved to Iraqis that he would combat his fellow Shiʿa and forgo an alliance with them to restore domestic security, enhancing his nationalist credentials.

Taking advantage of this momentum, al-Maliki sought re-election as PM in the ensuing parliamentary election of 2010 by putting together an entirely new electoral alliance, Dawlat al-Qanun (State of Law). Although his ticket included DP members, the new name was designed to appeal to a more nationalist strand among the Shiʿa, as well as Sunnis and secularists. SCIRI, meanwhile, had also rebranded itself as al-Majlis al-Aʿala al-Islami al-ʿIraqi (Islamic Supreme Council of Iraq or ISCI), indicating that it sought to distance itself from its origins in Iran during Khomeini's project to export the Islamic revolution, and also to adopt a more nationalist-sounding name.

Al-Maliki sought to rebrand himself and his alliance as Iraqi nationalist, first to rival the secularly oriented al-Haraka al-Wataniyya al-ʿIraqiyya (Iraqi National Movement, also known as al-ʿIraqiyya), an electoral alliance led by Iyad Allawi, a Shiʿa and former Baathist with close ties to Saudi Arabia, and second to distance himself from ISCI and the Sadrist Movement, which were already alienated by his policies during his first term in office. Iran in turn encouraged ISCI to make amends with the Sadrists and form a new combined electoral list entitled al-Iʾtilaf al-Watani al-ʿIraqi (Iraqi National Alliance, INA).

The breakup of the UIA and the fragmentation of the Shiʿa Islamist political current into two principal parties/alliances in the 2010 elections made it possible for Allawi's al-ʿIraqiyya to secure a plurality of ninety-one seats in the new parliament, whilst al-Maliki's State of Law alliance came second with eighty-nine seats, and the INA third with seventy seats (thirty-nine to the Sadrists, and seventeen to ISCI).[18] As the Iraqi constitution stipulated that the largest parliamentary party/bloc should be charged with the formation of a government, the odds were initially stacked in favour of Allawi and his secular al-ʿIraqiyya alliance. However, to prevent this scenario from materialising, and thus for Allawi – who was deemed close to Saudi Arabia – to become PM, Iran encouraged the two rival Shiʿa Islamist parties to reconcile their differences, realign as a majority bloc in parliament and hence form the next government. The INA and State of Law subsequently forged a majority bloc in parliament, even though ISCI and the Sadrists did not want to see al-Maliki renewed as PM. Precipitating a new crisis between the two parties, the ISCI and the Sadrists were in fact adamant in their rejection of al-Maliki, whilst al-Maliki himself showed no sign that he intended to make way for an alternative candidate. Iran finally summoned the two parties/alliances to Tehran for negotiations. The Sadrists, under Iranian urging, broke ranks and agreed to support al-Maliki's second term in office, essentially leaving the rest of the Shiʿa alliance with little choice but to allow al-Maliki to remain.[19] At the time Iran was thus able to prevent a Saudi-linked candidate from assuming the prime ministership, yet this fragile Iraqi Shi'a Islamist alliance broke down soon after, as shall become apparent below.

In sum, plural politics in post-2003 Iraq initially witnessed a short period of Shi'a Islamist cooperation in the form of the UIA, but this electoral alliance soon broke down after the formation of Iraq's first government in 2006. Despite Iran's efforts at fostering Shi'a unity, differences between the leaders of each party resulted not only in tensions within the alliance between the major three parties, but also in armed confrontation. A shared Shi'a Islamist identity was thus not sufficient to get the parties to cooperate after 2006, particularly in the lead up to the 2010 elections, ultimately costing all three parties an electoral defeat. Following the 2010 elections, the only instance when these same-sect parties united was to prevent Allawi's bloc from forming a new government but, as we saw, this cooperation was also short-lived. By the time the Arab uprisings broke out in 2010–11, Iraq's three principal Shi'a Islamist parties were thus bitterly divided, not least on how to respond to the ensuing regional instability.

Iraqi Shi'a plurality following the 2011 uprisings

Extant tensions between the ruling coalition of ISCI, the Sadrist Movement and al-Maliki's State of Law prior to 2011 were further compounded by the onset of the Arab uprisings of 2010–12. Inspired by the popular uprisings in neighbouring states, Iraqis themselves took to the street in 2011, not for a change of regime, but to demand improved public services and governance. The government's failure to meet the demands of the protestors led to the emergence of a renewed protest movement in 2015, a movement that the Sadrists sought to embrace as a tool in their rivalry with al-Maliki's State of Law and ISCI. In the meanwhile, security concerns had grown for Iraqi Shi'a due to the emergence of the Islamic State of Iraq (ISI, also known as al-Qaeda in Iraq), which later became the al-Dawla al-Islamiyya fi al-'Iraq wa al-Sham (ISIS). Both pursued an aggressive anti-Shi'a politics and the seizure of Mosul in 2014 by al-Dawla al-Islamiyya's (Islamic State, IS) precipitated a crisis in leadership among Iraq's Shi'a Islamist parties.

To demonstrate the effect of the uprisings on the Shi'a Islamists, the following pages examine three contentious episodes that emerged following 2011, highlighting ongoing tensions between Iraq's three main Shi'a parties: (1) the Shi'a parties' response to the Arab uprisings, (2) the elections of 2014 and the resignation of PM al-Maliki, and (3) the Sadrists and the anti-government protests beginning in 2015.

Pan-Shi'ism as a response to the Arab uprisings

Taking inspiration from the uprisings in Tunisia and Egypt, Iraqis took to the streets in February 2011 in what was deemed as 'Iraq's Day of Rage'. Protests erupted in the capital Baghdad and the cities of Falluja and Ramadi, in the Anbar governorate, Mosul in the Nineveh governorate, and Hawija, near Kirkuk, with demonstrators demanding reliable public services and an end to rampant corruption, nepotism and unemployment.[20] At the time, PM al-Maliki ordered security forces to suppress the protests without addressing their root causes, thus leaving societal tensions simmering. In January 2013 protests broke out once more in the same cities, launched by disenfranchised Iraqi Arab Sunnis in response to al-Maliki's crackdown of prominent politicians from their community.

Al-Maliki blamed the Arab Sunni demonstrations of 2013 on Turkey, Saudi Arabia and Qatar, who had been the chief backers of the rebellion in Syria. In terms of linkages between Iraq and Syria following the uprisings, Iraqi Arab Sunni protesters had been emboldened by what they perceived as an Arab Sunni uprising against the Alawite Shi'a government in Syria. One Iraqi protester, for instance, expressed sentiments that internalised the notion of a 'Shi'a Crescent', asserting:

> [b]oth our governments are very close to Tehran, and both of us oppose Iranian plans in the region. Iran wants to turn Baghdad and Damascus into its provinces and form a Shi'a axis stretching from Tehran to the Mediterranean Sea.[21]

Protesters invoked the pejorative term 'Safavid' to describe al-Maliki's government, a reference to the Turco-Persian dynasty that converted Iran to Shi'ism wholesale in the 1500s and later contested the Ottoman Empire for control over Iraq, while others carried posters of then Turkish PM Recep Tayyip Erdoğan, who had been an early supporter of the Arab Spring protests in Egypt, Libya and Syria.[22] Al-Maliki sought to take advantage of these developments and rally Iraq's Shi'a population by stoking the fear that disenfranchised Iraqi Arab Sunnis had sought out support from the former Iraqi Baathists and ISIS based in Syria, as well as receiving aid from Turkey, Saudi Arabia and Qatar. While al-Maliki sought to cultivate a nationalist image prior to the 2010 elections, by 2013 he used sectarian fears to rally his constituents and mobilise against his rivals.

One of the effects of the uprisings was that al-Maliki and other Shi'a Islamist parties could invoke an emergent pan-Shi'a imaginary as a response. What is striking about this is the fact that prior to the Syrian and Yemeni conflicts after 2011, Iraqi Twelver Shi'a rarely thought of Syrian Alawites or Yemeni

Zaydis as fellow Shi'a.[23] Indeed, in the Iraqi Twelver Shi'a imagination, Bashar al-Assad's government and the Alawites of Syria became 'Shi'a' by sheer virtue of buying into the narrative that Damascus was under attack from anti-Shi'a Salafis.[24] They disregarded the near past, when from 2004 onwards al-Assad had allowed foreign Salafi jihadists (precursors of ISIS) to cross from Syria into Iraq, thus enabling most of the sectarian killing against their community during the Iraqi civil war.[25] Along with this trend, the Saudi air campaign in Yemen against the Zaydi Houthi movement created an Iraqi Shi'a solidarity with the Houthi community.[26]

However, while the Syrian civil war and the conflict in Yemen allowed for a rekindling of pan-sectarian identities, this identity was not embraced by all Iraqi Shi'a, or Sunnis for that matter, who saw through the veneer of such opportunistic discourses and expressions of solidarity. Indeed, if anything, this resurgent pan-Shi'ism represents an illustrative case of what Marina Calculli calls the 'securitisation of identities'; that is, a transnational social process utilised by political elites to mobilise constituencies that serve as a proxy for direct military confrontation.[27] This process reconciles discursively the dissonance between Shi'a actors that invoke a pan-Shi'a imaginary, whether it is Iran or Iraq's Shi'a Islamists, even if they pursue policies that undermine sectarian unity. In this regard Iran and Iraq's Shi'a Islamist parties securitised a Shi'a identity in the aftermath of the uprisings in order to bolster their own domestic as well as transnational legitimacy. They did so, however, while it was clear that pan-Shi'ism was not their principal driver for domestic/regional policy choices, which remained dictated by real political concerns and power-political rivalries.

In the Iraqi context, in fact, pan-Shi'a imaginaries are evoked primarily by Shi'a Islamist parties to enhance their mobilisation potential, while these parties pursue policy choices that often fly in the face of Shi'a unity in Iraq and/or across the region. For example, given his pre-existing tensions with al-Maliki, al-Sadr expressed solidarity with the Arab Sunni protests, highlighting ongoing fissures among the Shi'a Islamist political parties. He even appropriated the language of the Arab Spring, labelling the Anbar protests as 'Iraq's Arab Spring'.[28]

For Iraqi Sunnis to believe al-Sadr was an Iraqi nationalist who put nation before sect would have amounted to nothing less than a miracle, of course, given that some within his militia had been implicated in some of the worst sectarian killings that took place between 2006 to 2008. Al-Sadr's embrace of the Sunni protesters then served as his attempt to distance himself from the sectarian bloodletting of the past, as well as from the entrenched Iraqi political elite. This tactic in 2013 would ultimately foreshadow al-Sadr's embrace of the politics of protest in 2015–16, another episode of intra-Shi'a conflict.

On 23 April 2013 clashes between security forces and protesters in the town of Hawija broke out, leading to fifty deaths. Further armed clashes followed between the Iraqi security forces and Arab Sunni protesters. After the Hawija incident ISIS's bombing campaign reached a level unprecedented since the height of sectarian conflict between 2006 and 2008, with terror attacks being carried out against religious centres, security forces' headquarters and checkpoints, crowded markets, and politicians, affecting both Shiʻa and Sunni districts. At the time, al-Maliki blamed Iraq's Arab Sunnis for enabling ISIS to conduct these attacks. The worsening security situation, however, did not affect al-Maliki's political prospects, and perhaps in fact strengthened his base, as he invoked the new pan-Shiʻi narrative in the run-up to the 2014 elections.

The elections of 2014 and the resignation of al-Maliki

Despite heightened sectarian conflict and fears, when the 2014 parliamentary elections were called there were no cohesive ethnic or sectarian coalitions to speak of. ISCI and Sadrists' rivalry with al-Maliki continued, and both parties failed to join the PM's State of Law alliance. ISCI ran in the elections under al-Muwatin (Citizen) alliance and the Sadrists ran separately as part of Kutlat al-Ahrar (Liberal Bloc) alliance. Indeed, not only had the grand Shiʻa Islamist coalition (UIA) broken down by 2010, but Iraq had since witnessed further pluralisation of the Shiʻa political field with the emergence of several smaller Shiʻa Islamist parties. Most notably, these included Hizb al-Islah (Reform Party), formed after Ibrahim al-Jaʻafari split from the DP, Hizb al-Fadila (Virtue Party), a rival to the Sadrists, and the Munadhamat al-Badr (Badr Organisation), which had split off from ISCI, and allied with its rival, al-Maliki's State of Law alliance.

As mentioned above, divisions among the core Shiʻa Islamist parties can be traced back to disagreements over the re-election of al-Maliki as PM for a second term in 2010. In the lead-up to the 2014 parliamentary elections, Shiʻa parties thus simply sought to maximise the number of votes/seats for their respective electoral lists, upon which they would then argue that its politicians be awarded the most important cabinet positions and ministries based on their popularity. The formation of coalitions would be negotiated after the elections, rather than before. Thus, by 2014 a shared Shiʻa identity no longer provided sufficient glue to unite Shiʻa Islamist parties at the political and electoral levels, instead fostering fierce competition for votes and political posts among its constituent parties. It is for these reasons, and because of the consociational arrangement that had governed Iraqi politics since 2005, that the formation of broad electoral alliances lost traction with Shiʻa Islamist parties.

In the 2014 elections themselves al-Maliki's State of Law alliance won the most seats, ninety-two, while the Sadrist Movement and the ISCI came in second and third, winning thirty-four and twenty-nine seats respectively. Theoretically, the three Shi'a parties thus were in a position to form a coalition government with the help of a number of the smaller Shi'a parties. This scenario, however, did not materialise, with al-Maliki's persona becoming yet again a key bone of contention between the key Shi'a Islamist parties. Whilst al-Maliki argued that winning most seats had granted him a national mandate to run for a third time as PM, the Sadrists and ISCI were adamantly opposed. Another post-election stalemate akin to 2010 thus emerged, centred on the personality of al-Maliki, leaving Iraq without the necessary leadership to coordinate a national response to the ISIS incursion into Iraq and its seizure of the country's second largest city of Mosul as well as several urban centres along the Tigris and Euphrates in the summer of 2014. This incursion, and particularly the fall of Mosul under al-Maliki's watch, gave ISCI and the Sadrist Movement further impetus to deny the PM a third term, blaming his policies for alienating Arab Sunnis, who, they asserted, either actively abetted or passively supported, the ISIS invasion. The two Shi'a Islamist parties, and even some members from within the DP itself, thus joined Kurdish and Arab Sunni politicians calling for al-Maliki's resignation. Ayatollah al-Sistani also called for al-Maliki to step down (albeit subtly, in a Friday sermon), and so did the Iranian government.[29] Pressure for his resignation also came from the Obama administration in the US, which made military aid contingent on finding a less divisive candidate to head a new government.

Consequently, the Iraqi Shi'a political parties, in addition to Iran, dropped support for al-Maliki as PM, rallying instead behind Haidar al-Abadi, who appeared a less divisive and polarising figure within the DP. In response, al-Maliki mobilised the elite special forces, the Golden Division, a unit he had established as his own 'praetorian guard', and for a few days rumours of a coup abounded, in response to what had been essentially an Iraqi Shi'a and Iranian vote of no confidence. In the end, al-Maliki did not resort to force in order to secure a third term in office but rather relinquished power, calculating that Iraq's political structure could allow for his eventual political comeback.[30]

Once al-Abadi had become prime minister in 2014, with the support of disparate Shi'a political parties, a new government was formed in which the Shi'a Islamists once again reaped the benefits of key ministerial posts. The actual allocation process is opaque as it is negotiated beyond public scrutiny, and it is difficult to ascertain why, despite securing more votes than ISCI, the latter secured the all-important Oil Ministry, as well as that of Transportation, while the Sadrists secured the 'lesser' ministries of Housing, and Industry.[31] In terms of other executive posts, the Sadrist Baha al-'Araji was made one of three deputy prime ministers, a largely ceremonial post. Thus, al-Sadr had little stake in the new government in terms of powerful ministerial portfolios, which would explain his later embrace of the 2015 protesters' demands to dissolve the cabinet and replace it with a technocratic one.

The Sadrists and the anti-government protests

Finally, inter-Shi'a divisions are apparent in the wake of the service delivery protests that swept Iraq in 2015–16. Indeed, whilst the Sadrist Movement and ISCI had jointly opposed al-Maliki's third term in office in 2014, they would break over the issue of government accountability and corruption during the protests.

In August 2015 sustained mass protests erupted in Baghdad's Tahrir Square, Basra in the South, and the predominantly Shi'a heartland towns of Najaf, Karbala and Hilla. Protesters demanded an end to corruption and improved public services, particularly in the delivery of electricity, and the sectarian quotas that hindered efficient governance.[32] Although the demonstrations began as a popular uprising, al-Sadr took the lead in galvanising the protest movement against the al-Abadi government. He had earlier embraced the politics of street protest in 2013, seeking to appear as a grass-roots Shi'a and Iraqi nationalist leader who stood above the fray of partisan Shi'a politics. In February 2016, he continued to cultivate this image, as he convened a rally in Baghdad's Tahrir Square, mobilising crowds to pressure the PM to follow through with anti-corruption reforms.[33] To increase the pressure, he then called on protesters to stage a sit-in outside of the Green Zone, the location of Iraq's key state institutions and where most of Iraq's politicians reside.

Al-Sadr pressured the PM to accede to his demand for the creation of a technocratic non-partisan cabinet that would tackle government corruption and improve public services. Apparently giving in to this pressure, in April 2016 al-Abadi presented a list of technocrat candidates to form a new Iraqi cabinet, including new ministers for electricity, finance, oil and water where corruption in these ministries affected daily public services. None of the candidates on this list came from the major political parties, but were nominated for their technical expertise. However, a technocratic cabinet would have entailed the resignation of career politicians, many of whom were Shi'a politicians. For example, the ISCI party member, Adil Abd al-Mahdi who was Minister of Oil, was to be replaced by a Kurdish technocrat. In response to this measure, Ammar al-Hakim, the ISCI leader, responded 'if we have a totally technocratic cabinet, then PM al-Abadi must be a non-partisan technocrat or PM al-Abadi must go'.[34] ISCI rebuked its co-religionist by demanding that the PM should resign given his connections to the DP. The resistance al-Abadi faced from career politicians was symptomatic of the entrenchment of a new post-2003 political elite, including Shi'a Islamists, who had benefited from the new political system. Politicians from the Sadrist Movement, meanwhile, held thirty-four seats in parliament, but al-Sadr ordered his MPs to boycott any future sessions until his call for a technocratic cabinet was heeded.

The deadlock benefited al-Sadr's political standing and granted him a political victory, despite the Iraqi parliament's failure to approve a technocratic cabinet. Al-Sadr clearly challenged the power of the al-Abadi government, which at its helm comprised the two Shi'a political parties, the DP and the ISCI, precipitating an intra-Shi'a conflict among his rivals.[35] From a power calculus perspective, the Sadrist strategy during the 2015–16 protests had a more cynical motive for pressuring al-Abadi to introduce a technocratic cabinet. In order to respond to protesters' demands in August 2015, al-Abadi had already dissolved the three positions of deputy prime minister, thus depriving the Sadrist Movement of its one post in the cabinet, albeit a weak and largely ceremonial one.[36] It appears that al-Sadr was willing to relinquish his party's hold on the remaining ministries of Housing and Industry, given that his Shi'a rivals in government would lose far more powerful posts in the event of the establishment of a technocratic government.

What is more, al-Sadr's strategy had been to assert himself as an Iraqi Shi'a nationalist, independent of Iranian influence (despite engaging with Iran in the past, such as after the contested 2010 elections). Indeed, the protests offered al-Sadr a means to undermine Iran's objective to unite the various Iraqi Shi'a parties, with the caveat that they formed a united front to augment Iran's influence in Iraq. This anti-Iranian sentiment was demonstrated by the protesters who chanted against the Islamic Republic's influence in Iraq and Tehran's support of the 'corrupt' Shi'a incumbent elite, particularly the DP and ISCI politicians. Ahmad Abd al-Hussein, a leader of the protests working alongside the Sadrists, used Facebook to articulate this sentiment, stating that 'Iran's insistence on embracing corrupt thugs and thieves, desperately defending them, assisting them during crises and covering up for their disastrous corruption and failure will drive Iraqis to hate Iran, if it continues to sponsor these thugs'.[37]

The consociational arrangement of dividing executive posts among the country's diverse ethno-religious communities was meant to ensure that the majority Iraqi Shi'a would never again be ruled by an oppressive Sunni minority. In the event, however, al-Sadr, himself a Shi'a, challenged this system, demonstrating that analysing Iraq's politics as a simple conflict between Shi'a versus Sunni is reductive at best. Iran's policy after 2014 of fostering Shi'a unity in Iraq deprived al-Sadr of asserting his own presence on the Iraqi political landscape, and thus he embraced a protest movement that has proved to stoke intra-Shi'a conflict in the government.

Conclusion

After the US-led invasion of Iraq in 2003, a pluralisation of Shi'a domestic Islamist actors took place in the new Iraqi body politic, resulting in intra-Shi'a Islamist competition within Iraq and bilaterally with Iran, a neighbour that enjoys a paramount influence over internal Iraqi affairs. This chapter examined why same-sect political parties aligned with, or rivalled, each other in this environment, focusing in particular on the rationale behind the behavior of different Shi'a Islamist parties in key moments of post-2011 Iraqi politics: the immediate street protests in 2011 and then 2013, the crisis surrounding al-Maliki's premiership in 2014, and the anti-government protests of 2015–16. Problematising the evolution of identity politics in the country, it sought to show how sectarianism is used by Iraqi Shi'a political actors to craft political and societal discourses and practices. As such, the chapter illustrated that, despite widespread assumptions and fears in both the region and internationally of a cohesive Shi'a regional bloc emerging in the region after 2003 and 2014, shared sectarian affiliation did not serve as a basis to unify Iraqi Shi'a Islamist political parties and elites. In fact, as we saw, even the ISIS invasion of northern Iraq in 2014 failed to produce a 'rally around-the-flag' effect among Iraq's Shi'a Islamist political actors.

Arguably, since the 2010–12 Arab uprisings a greater pan-Shi'a narrative has developed around the notion of 'a securitisation of Shi'a identity'. This Iraqi Shi'a narrative should not be reduced, however, to an essentialist reading of an alliance based on reasserting Shi'a dominance in the region, but rather as a means for Iraqi Shi'a political parties to legitimise power within their national setting. By virtue of a shared identity, Iraqi Shi'a can form connections with Iran, and *vice versa*, but this relationship is shifting, informed by political bargaining and competition among themselves and with Tehran. Indeed, before and after the Arab uprisings, Iraqi Shi'a Islamist elites have contested power and formed shifting alliances, due to influences ranging from domestic opportunity structures to the role of opportunities posed by external actors, such as Iran. Based on this past precedent, and with tensions likely to continue unabated in Iraq in the near future between the Shi'a Islamist parties, ISIS remnants and other Arab Sunni and Kurdish parties, conflict and policy divisions are likely to prevail over the sense of Shi'a unity in the foreseeable future.

Notes

1. Waleed Hazbun (2010), 'US Policy and the geopolitics of insecurity in the Arab world', *Geopolitics*, 15:2, p. 254.
2. Genevieve Abdo (2016), *The New Sectarianism: The Arab Uprisings and the Rebirth of the Shi'a-Sunni Divide*. New York: Oxford University Press; Khalil F. Osman (2015), *Sectarianism in Iraq: The Making of State and Nation since 1920*. London and New York: Routledge.

3. Vali Nasr (2006), *The Shia Revival: How Conflicts Within Islam Will Shape the Future*. New York: WW Norton.

4. Gregory F. Gause III, (2014), 'Beyond sectarianism: the new Middle East Cold War', Brookings Doha Center, 11, July.

5. Graham Fuller and Rend Rahim Francke (1999), *The Arab Shi'a: The Forgotten Muslims*. New York: St. Martin's Press.

6. Yitzhak Nakash (1995), *The Shi'is of Iraq*. Princeton: Princeton University Press.

7. Faleh A. Jabar (2003), *The Shi'ite Movement in Iraq*. London: Saqi Books.

8. Phebe Marr and Ibrahim Al-Marashi (2017), *The Modern History of Iraq*. Boulder: Westview Press, p. 137.

9. Jabar, *The Shi'ite Movement in Iraq*, pp. 250–8.

10. Ibrahim Al-Marashi (2013), 'Sadrabilia: the visual narrative of Muqtada Al-Sadr's Islamist politics and insurgency in Iraq', in Sune Haugobolle and Christianne Gruber (eds), *Rhetoric of the Image: Visual Culture in Modern Muslim Contexts*. Bloomington: Indiana University Press, p. 149.

11. Ibid., pp. 147–51.

12. Muhsin Al-Nuri Al-Musawi (2004), *Al-Sayyid Muqtada Al-Sadr, sadr al-'Iraq al-thalith: Ahdafahu, muwaqifahu, mashru'ahu* [Muqtada al-Sadr, the third Sadr of Iraq: his goals, his positions, his project]. Baghdad: Markaz Wali Allah.

13. Rodger Shanahan (2004), 'Shi'a political development in Iraq: the case of the Islamic Da'wa Party', *Third World Quarterly*, 25:5, p. 947.

14. Anon. (2014), 'Ayatollah Sistani's role in post-Saddam Iraq: interview with Fadel Reda Al-Kifaee', *Musings on Iraq*, 10 February, <http://musingsoniraq.blogspot.com/2014/02/ayatollah-sistanis-role-in-post-saddam.html> (last accessed 12 May 2017).

15. Marr and Al-Marashi, *The Modern History of Iraq*, p. 227.

16. Ibid., p. 244.

17. Ibid., p. 254.

18. Ibid., pp. 271–2.

19. Ibid., pp. 273–4.

20. Ahmed K. Al-Rawi (2014), 'The Arab Spring and online protests in Iraq', *International Journal of Communication*, 8, p. 918.

21. International Crisis Group (ICG) (2013), 'Syria's metastasizing conflicts', *Middle East Report*, 143, 27 June, p. 12.

22. Ali Abel Sadah (2013), 'Ahmed Al-'Alwani: Za'im radikali lisunna al-Anbar' ['Ahmed Al-'Alwani: radical leader of the Sunnis of al-Anbar'], *Al-Monitor*, 1 October, <www.al-monitor.com/pulse/ar/originals/2013/10/iraq-sunni-leader-incitement-shiites.html#ixzz3lfzebHmg> (last accessed 12 May 2017).

23. Omar al-Jaffal (2014), 'Al-huthiyyun yahzun bihtimam shi'a al-'iraq' ['Yemen's Houthis draw the attention of Shi'a in Iraqi'], *Al-Monitor*, 16 October, <www.al-monitor.com/pulse/ar/originals/2014/10/iraq-shiite-support-yemen-houthis.html#ixzz3lfGLmeZE> (last accessed 12 May 2017).

24. Ali Mamouri (2014), 'Khatar al-tashaddud al-salafi yuwahhid al-shi'a' ['The danger of Salafist militancy unites the Shi'a'], *Al-Monitor*, 1 October, <www.al-monitor.com/pulse/ar/originals/2014/10/shiite-pan-identity-threat-islamic-state-iran.html> (last accessed 12 May 2017).

25. Peter Neumann (2014), 'Suspects into collaborators', *London Review of Books*, 36:7, 3 April, pp. 19–21.

26. Adnan Abu Zeed (2015) 'Al-intima al-taifi yuhaddid al-muwaqif al-iraqiyya min "asifa al-hazm"' ['Sectarian affiliations reveals Iraqi positions on "Decisive storm"'], *Al-Monitor*,

14 April, <www.al-monitor.com/pulse/ar/originals/2015/04/iraq-sunni-shiite-positions-operation-decisive-storm-yemen.html> (last accessed 12 May 2017).

27. Marina Calculli (2016), 'Middle East security: conflict and securitization of identities', in Louisa Fawcett (ed), *International Relations of the Middle East*. Oxford: Oxford University Press, pp. 219–35.

28. Ali Abel Sadah (2013), 'Muqtada al-Sadr: nida akhir ila maliki ba'ad al-silsila tafjirat Baghdad' ['Muqtada al-Sadr: ultimatum to Maliki after a chain of Bagdad explosions'], *Al-Monitor*, 29 May, <www.al-monitor.com/pulse/ar/originals/2013/05/sadr-maliki-iraq-warning.html#ixzz3lg5wYkUj> (last accessed 12 May 2017).

29. Ali Mamouri (2014), 'Kayf najaha al-sistani biizaha Maliki' ['How did Sistani succeed in ousting Maliki?'], *Al-Monitor*, 20 August, <www.al-monitor.com/pulse/ar/originals/2014/08/iraq-sistani-democratic-ways-successors-maliki.html#ixzz3lgLdUFfl> (last accessed 12 May 2017).

30. Mohammed A. Salih (2016), 'Hal wakhatat al-Maliki lil-'awda tra'is al-hakuma' ['Is al-Maliki planning a return to head the government'], *Al-Monitor*, 3 August, <www.al-monitor.com/pulse/ar/originals/2016/08/iraq-nouri-maliki-visit-kurds-prime-minister.html> (last accessed 12 May 2017).

31. Economist Intelligence Unit (2015), *Country Report Iraq*. London: Economist Intelligence Unit, November, p. 17.

32. Marr and Al-Marashi, *The Modern History of Iraq*, p. 306.

33. Ibid.

34. Mehdi Al-Katib (2016), 'Inside Baghdad: the current state of play', *Open Democracy*, 5 April, <www.opendemocracy.net/arab-awakening/mehdi-al-katib/inside-baghdad-current-state-of-play> (last accessed 12 May 2017).

35. Ibrahim Al-Marashi (2016), 'Sadr's challenge to Iraq's sectarian politics', Al-Jazeera, 21 April, <www.aljazeera.com/indepth/opinion/2016/04/sadr-challenge-iraq-sectarian-politics-160421072216275.html> (last accessed 12 May 2017).

36. Anon. (2015), 'Iraq's Prime Minister slashes Cabinet by one-third', Al-Jazeera, 16 August, <www.aLJPazeera.com/news/2015/08/iraq-prime-minister-slashes-cabinet-150816191005577.html> (last accessed 12 May 2017).

37. Ali Mamouri 'Al-sadriyyun yahtafun dhud Iran dakhil al-mantaqa al-khadra' ['The Sadrists protest against Iran in the Green Zone'], *Al-Monitor*, 12 May, <www.al-monitor.com/pulse/ar/originals/2016/05/sadrist-stances-iraqi-shiites-opposing-iranianpolicy.html> (last accessed 12 May 2017).

Chapter 17

The impact of Islamist trajectories on the international relations of the post-2011 Middle East

Katerina Dalacoura

This chapter interprets the 'international relations of the Middle East' as the complex web of linkages that criss-cross the region and embed it in world politics. They include the foreign policies of states, but also of non-state actors, and the foreign policies of regional states but also of major outside powers involved in the region, mainly the United States and Russia. The international relations of the Middle East are not, however, only about actors' decisions and their implementation: they also encompass shifting relations, connections, alliances and balances of power. These shifting connections and balances are determined by material, political and military factors but also by ideas, ideologies, and abstract values such as 'recognition' and 'legitimacy'.[1]

This chapter, however, does not deal with the international relations of the Middle East in their totality but only to the extent they have been shaped by the different trajectories (or trends) that can be observed within Islamist movements and ideologies in the region since the uprisings of 2011. It must, therefore, at its outset identify and outline these trajectories. This is no easy task, given that 'Islam' is woven into the fabric of Middle Eastern politics in a variety of ways: even secular movements and political actors make reference to it as a set of cultural idioms or as a marker of identity. This is not unique to the Muslim-majority societies of the Middle East, but what is particular is that the region contains quite a number of movements, peaceful and violent, with an explicitly Islamist agenda. It is these movements, not the role of 'Islam' in general, that this chapter investigates.

Specifically, the chapter will focus on those Islamist movements that rose to prominence or changed significantly as a result of the 2011 uprisings and, at the same time, had an impact on the international relations of the region. The author will hence not be concentrating, for example, on the Kuwaiti or Algerian Islamist movements, which are important in themselves but were not changed significantly by the uprisings, or on the Moroccan Islamists or the Egyptian Salafis whose political fortunes were shaped by the 2011 uprisings but who did not impact the international relations of the region directly. Moreover, this author defines governments such as Iran, Saudi Arabia or Egypt under President Mohamed Morsi (r.2012–13) as Islamist actors but examines their foreign policies only insofar as they pursue Islamist objectives.

This chapter argues that there have been three major strands within Islamism in the Middle East since 2011 and that each was affected significantly by the uprisings of that year (this is what the word 'trajectories' in the title refers to). The first is constituted by the historically pre-existing, more 'established' Islamism, pursuing a 'third-worldist' or anti-imperialist agenda, associated with Iran and Hizbullah, which in the 2000s had defined itself as 'the resistance' against Israel and the West. This Islamist strand experienced a change in its fortunes and regional standing following the 2011 revolt against Bashar al-Assad and the decision by Hizbullah and Iran to take his regime's side in the Syrian civil war that followed. The second strand includes (but is not exclusively confined to) the moderate al-Ikhwan al-Muslimun (Muslim Brotherhood, MB) and al-Nahda (Renaissance) movements in Egypt and Tunisia, which rose to political power through elections following the overthrow of the Mubarak and Ben Ali regimes and then lost power through a military coup or loss of public support. These moderate movements shaped the international relations of the region either directly, by changing Egypt's and Tunisia's foreign policies, or indirectly, by contributing to a shift in regional balances of power. The third trend comprises radical Islamist movements such as al-Dawla al-Islamiyya (Islamic State, IS) and al-Qaeda, and others, which emerged, or re-emerged, as a result of the Syrian civil war and continuing internal division in Iraq, the security vacuum in the Sinai Peninsula in Egypt, and, even more seriously, in Libya after the fall of the al-Qaddafi regime following the 2011 uprising. The chapter covers each of these in turn in its three sections, outlines their impact and concludes by assessing their collective effect on the region and its future. The author notes that the regional conflicts that have erupted as a result of the 2011 uprisings have connections with, and in some cases have been fed by, pre-existing ones, such as the internal conflict in Iraq, the Israeli–Palestinian conflict, the Kurdish conflict and many others. This chapter touches on these only insofar as they are relevant to its argument.

The de-legitimation of 'third-worldist' Islamism and the growth of sectarianism

During the 2000s, one of the two core confrontations that characterised the international relations of the Middle East was between a 'pro-Western' camp, comprising Israel, Egypt, Saudi Arabia and Turkey and a loose coalition of state and non-state actors, led by Iran and joined by Hizbullah, Hamas and others.

Despite the presence of secular actors, such as the Baathist Syrian regime, the latter camp was partly associated with and, indeed, driven by, an Islamist ideology of a third-worldist, anti-imperialist kind symbolised above all by Hizbullah. The group presented itself as the heart of the resistance against Israel and the West in the Middle East. It had emerged in 2000 as the sole (Arab) entity that had 'defeated' Israel, in that it had forced the Israeli government to withdraw most of its armed forces from southern Lebanon after a lengthy conflict. The anti-Western camp's agenda was popular in the Arab world and beyond, particularly after the brief Lebanon war of 2006 which confirmed, in the eyes of some, Hizbullah's ability to withstand the might of Israel. Hizbullah had been closely associated with Iran since its inception. Iran also supported Hamas, particularly after it took over control of Gaza in 2007.[2] In the years after the US invasion of Iraq in 2003, the government in Baghdad also aligned itself loosely with Tehran. Confrontations between Hamas and Israel, in particular in December 2008–January 2009, in which Hamas was supported by Iran and Hizbullah, confirmed Hamas' centrality, symbolic and military, to the anti-Western camp. The 'nuclear issue' – the charge, or suspicion, by the West and the international community more generally that Iran was on track to build nuclear weapons – was part and parcel of this struggle between Iran and the West.[3]

This situation changed significantly with the eruption of the Syrian crisis following the popular rebellion against the al-Assad regime in 2011. The people's insurrection turned into a civil war in Syria, pitting the regime against an array of forces, from moderate to extremist, mostly Sunni Islamist: from the Syrian al-Ikhwan al-Muslimun to Jabhat al-Nusra, an affiliate of al-Qaeda, and IS, an indirect product of al-Qaeda in Iraq which had been defeated there after 2006.[4] Iran and Hizbullah were sucked into the Syrian crisis by their decision to support the al-Assad regime militarily. Hizbullah in particular became increasingly involved in a conventional conflict, gaining considerable experience in this type of warfare.[5] This has strengthened the movement in material terms, but has severely diminished its standing and damaged the legitimacy it had previously enjoyed in the Arab world. From the hero of the Arab world against Israel it has come to be seen, at least by some, as an ally of the butchers of Damascus.[6] Hizbullah's loss of the moral high ground as proud resistance to the universal Israeli enemy was underlined by the fact that Israel looked unfavourably on the loss of control by al-Assad, thereby belonging in some way to the same 'side' as Hizbullah.

The main consequence of this development has been the gradual identification of Hizbullah and Iran with a sectarian (Shi'a) as opposed to an Islamist, third-worldist and anti-imperialist agenda. Iran's and Hizbullah's support of the al-Assad regime has come to be seen as support for their fellow Shi'a (specifically Alawites, the Shi'a offshoot from which many of the al-Assad regime personnel are drawn) against Syria's Sunnis. The changing fortunes of Hamas are evidence of this 'sectarianisation'. The Hamas leadership, and in particular Khaled Mashal, had been sheltered by the al-Assad regime in Damascus for years, but following the start of the crisis in Syria in 2011 left for Egypt and then Qatar. The reasons for this decision were complex, but a key element was that, partly as a result of their MB antecedents, Hamas found themselves unable to side with al-Assad in an increasingly sectarian-tinged confrontation. Hamas' decision strained its relationship with Iran, which only started to partially mend in 2014.[7]

The implications of the change in this Islamist strand from a third-worldist, anti-imperialist agenda towards a more sectarian one have been profound for the international relations of the Middle East. The Syrian civil war has triggered a regional clash between the supporters of al-Assad (Iran, Hizbullah) and his opponents (Turkey, Qatar, Saudi Arabia) which has, in turn, acquired a sectarian colouring.[8] The Barack Obama (r.2009–17) administration's attempt to extricate the United States from the Middle East,[9] and the growing assertiveness of Saudi Arabia at a regional level, contributed to the transformation of the confrontation between 'pro-Western' and 'third-wordlist' camps into a 'Sunni–Shi'a' one led by Saudi Arabia and Iran respectively. The confrontation is the latest incarnation of a historical enmity between the two countries that goes back to the establishment of the Islamic Republic following the Iranian revolution of 1979 and the twin ideological and geopolitical challenge it posed to Saudi–Wahhabi Islam and the Saudi monarchy. In the Middle East environment defined by the 2011 rebellions, the renewed Saudi–Iranian antagonism has tangible and pernicious implications in many parts of the region. One example is Yemen, where the Saudi–Iranian clash, with its Sunni–Shi'a hue, has been super-imposed on and exacerbated a complex set of internal conflicts that erupted into violence following the domestic changes in 2011–12.[10] Bahrain is another example where a Shi'a uprising against the Sunni regime provoked a Saudi intervention in 2011, partly because of the conviction that it was instigated by Iran.[11]

Since the rise of IS in 2014, a further shift may be occurring in regional balances, with potential implications for the 'third-worldist' camp. IS has increasingly drawn the United States and the West into the Syrian civil war but it is also a threat to the al-Assad regime and, by implication, to Iran and Hizbullah, as well as Russia, which supports their side (through direct military intervention since September 2015).[12] This may lead to a convergence between the al-Assad regime and parts of the opposition as they focus on a common enemy. The Iran nuclear deal of 2015 between Tehran and the five permanent members of the UN Security Council plus Germany did not tackle the Syria crisis but may play an enabling role, should other conditions permit an agreement in Syria in the future.[13] Such an agreement can potentially attenuate the conflicts between Iran, Hizbullah and the West and between Iran and Turkey[14] – though not necessarily between Iran and Saudi Arabia, which has deep ideological and geopolitical roots and has now acquired a strong sectarian dimension – with significant regional implications, including for the position of Israel.

The rise and fall of moderate Islam

The 2011 uprisings led to rapid and dramatic changes in the fortunes of moderate Islamist movements in the Middle East. The overthrow of Presidents Hosni Mubarak (r.1981–2011) and Zine el-Abidine Ben Ali (r.1987–2011) in Egypt and Tunisia respectively was the result of a popular uprising (in the case of Egypt also backed by the military) with inchoate demands. However, in both cases, mainly because of their superior organisation and their implicit promise of social justice, the Islamist MB and al-Nahda were able to benefit from the electoral contests that followed the fall of the regimes.[15] In 2011–12, the MB affiliate Hizb al-Hurriyya wa al-'Adala (Freedom and Justice Party, FJP) won a plurality of seats in both houses of the Egyptian parliament, and in June 2012 Mohamed Morsi, a Muslim Brotherhood leader, became president of Egypt. Similarly, in Tunisia, al-Nahda, by then transformed into a registered political party, became the largest participant in a coalition government in 2012–13 that included secular and leftist parties. Neither in Egypt nor in Tunisia, however, did this rise of the moderate Islamist groups to power end well for them.[16] Morsi was overthrown by a military coup in July 2013, but this was on the back of a tremendous turnaround in popular opinion against the Brotherhood, which mismanaged power and showed itself incompetent and unable to work with others (though, to be fair, others were also unwilling to work with them). Al-Nahda, meanwhile, was able to form coalition governments in Tunisia, but its popularity suffered anyway because of its own mistakes and the difficult situation that it faced in political, economic and security terms. The result was the loss of its plurality in the parliamentary elections of October 2014. In other settings, such as Jordan, Morocco and Kuwait, the situation of moderate Islamist movements also changed as a result of the 2011 uprisings but in less direct and clear-cut ways.[17] In places where 'hot' wars broke out, in Syria and Libya, the Muslim Brotherhood and other moderate groups became marginalised as extremists gained ground.

The fluctuating fortunes of moderate Islamist movements shaped the international relations of the Middle East directly through the changes that the MB and al-Nahda effected in Egyptian and Tunisian foreign policies. The overthrow of Mubarak unsettled regional and Western actors, with Saudi Arabia in particular accusing the United States of 'abandoning' Mubarak. It also caused uncertainty in Israel, which feared the implications of the regime's fall for Gaza. The military-controlled transitional regime that replaced Mubarak did not signal a major change of direction in foreign policy but this did occur, to an extent, with Morsi's arrival in the presidency. Although they did not have full control of the reins of power or foreign policy, the MB steered Egypt to a closer relationship with Qatar and Turkey. Their presence in government also further alienated Saudi Arabia, because of the latter's historical and ideological antipathy towards the Brotherhood. The arrival of the Brotherhood in the seat of Egyptian power also boosted Hamas in neighbouring Gaza which, as we saw, had been weakened by the crisis of its relations with the Iran camp. This caused further alarm in Israel and has had implications for the situation in Sinai, to be discussed below.[18] Finally, Brotherhood control had implications for Egypt's relationship with the United States, which scrambled to establish a *modus vivendi* with the Morsi administration.[19]

The changes Tunisia experienced in its foreign policy and positioning in the Middle East had some parallels with Egypt, though Tunisia is a smaller actor with a different and distinct foreign policy history. The participation of al-Nahda as the major partner in the coalition government that replaced Ben Ali led to partial changes in Tunisia's external relations and position. The presence of the centrist (in Islamist terms) al-Nahda in government did not affect Tunisia's Western orientation and it continued being supported by the West and international financial institutions. However, regional relations saw some modification. While Nahda was in the ascendant, Qatar supported and began investing in the country, while Saudi Arabia kept its distance, again because of its historical and ideological antipathy towards the dominant party.[20] Turkey also became a key supporter of Tunisia, because of the close relations and affinity between the Adalet ve Kalkınma Partisi (Justice and Development Party, also known by its Turkish acronym AKP) and al-Nahda. When the government changed in Tunisia and al-Nahda lost its principal role, first in February 2013 with the resignation of the Hamadi Jebali government and then in October 2014 with the electoral victory of the secularist Hizb Nida' Tunis (Call of Tunisia), a recalibration of Tunisia's regional relations took place, with Qatar and Turkey receding in prominence.[21]

The changing fortunes of moderate Islamist movements also had a broader impact on the international relations of the region. The rise of the MB in Egypt – and, secondarily, of al-Nahda in Tunisia – alarmed Saudi Arabia, which saw the political model they represented as antagonistic to its own. It thus redoubled its efforts to combat the MB, not just in those two countries but also across the region; taking dramatic action in June 2017 against Qatar because of its support for the MB. Saudi success in doing so entailed greater legitimacy in the region for its model of government or Islamism as opposed to a 'Muslim Brotherhood' model, which entailed a more politicised role for

Islam. However, it also contained a danger for Saudi Arabia, in that it opened a second front in its regional policy, alongside the one with Iran. The military coup against Morsi in July 2013 caused a rift between the new president Abdel Fattah al-Sisi and Turkey, and tension between Turkey and Saudi Arabia. Relations between the latter two had improved by 2015 (though they deteriorated again during the Qatar crisis, as Turkey supported Qatar against Saudi Arabia), but the coldness between Egypt and Turkey was more long-standing, with diplomatic relations severed following the expulsion of the Turkish ambassador from Cairo in November 2013.[22]

The fall of the Brotherhood in Egypt and the decline of the political fortunes of al-Nahda in Tunisia also affected the regional standing of Qatar and Turkey, which had staked their regional policy to a considerable extent on the ascendance of the two movements. The blow was particularly hard for Turkey, whose appeal and popularity in the Middle East had soared in the period immediately after the 2010–12 Arab uprisings. Finally, as already suggested, Hamas had been boosted by the support of the Morsi government but, conversely, it suffered as a result of its overthrow.[23] The Gaza blockade, which had been eased between 2012 and 2013, was tightened again with the arrival of the al-Sisi government in July 2013 as it reverted to closer collaboration with Israel. The changing standing of Hamas as a result of domestic developments in Egypt affected its relationship with Iran, as we saw in the previous section.

The growth of Islamist extremism

The third way in which the 2011 uprisings shaped Islamism in the Middle East region was in strengthening extremist movements. Like the electoral successes of moderate Islamist groups in Egypt and Tunisia, this was not a direct product of popular demands or preferences. On the contrary, the millions who were mobilised to overthrow repressive regimes in the region did not call for an Islamic system or show support for extremist Islamist ideas, and it would be fair to say that the rebellions indicated a marginalisation of such ideas. Rather than the product of popular choice, the upsurge in extremism in the post-2011 Middle East was the result of the vacuum of power that was created by the breakdown of state institutions, as popular uprisings in some cases caused insurrection and civil war. This development had two epicentres (which eventually became inter-connected) in the Fertile Crescent and North Africa. The impact of this upsurge in extremism was felt far and wide in the region and beyond, with Yemen and the Gulf Cooperation Council (GCC) countries, Europe and even the United States, suffering attacks directed or inspired by al-Qaeda and IS. It also had some, albeit indirect, implications for the situation in Afghanistan where the Taliban insurgency is continuing.[24]

The eruption of violence in Syria in 2011 stoked the coals of conflict in Iraq, which had hardly died down after the bloody decade that followed the US invasion of 2003. During that time, chaos and bloodshed had enabled the birth of al-Qaeda in Iraq, a 'franchise' of al-Qaeda, which had employed vicious violent tactics in support of the Sunnis of Iraq. The group was crushed in the period after 2006, as we saw, but elements of it re-emerged a few years later, in the form of IS, as a result of the sectarian policies of the al-Maliki government and Iraqi Shi'a majoritarianism in general. IS found some support among the disillusioned Sunni minority and former Baathists populated its ranks.[25] It gained control of the city of Mosul in June 2014 and other significant parts of Iraq. From there it spread to Syria where it secured territory centred on the city of Raqqa. The deepening of the civil war in Syria led to the sidelining of moderates such as the Syrian MB and the proliferation of extremist groups, alongside IS, the most significant of which was Jabhat al-Nusra (al-Qaeda's 'franchise' in Syria from 2012 until it cut ties with it in 2016).[26] All of them, including their opponents – led by the al-Assad regime – purveyed an extreme brutality but the IS 'brand' was particularly dependent on a twisted and vicious image that contributed to its appeal abroad and 'pull' of jihadists from Europe, the Middle East, Central and Southern Asia and the Caucasus.[27]

The upsurge in Islamist extremism in the Fertile Crescent caused it to spill over into North Africa, where it was fed by the breakdown of authority. In the Sinai Peninsula, a combination of local Bedouin discontent and Islamist infiltration from outside had caused violence and instability since the early 2000s, and even earlier. When the Egyptian government's control over Sinai diminished after the overthrow of Mubarak, the pre-existing situation was exacerbated, leading to the emergence of the radical Islamist group Ansar Bayt al-Maqdis (Partisans of the Holy Place/Jerusalem). It pledged allegiance to IS in 2014 and continued to wreak havoc against the Egyptian army and security forces, even extending its activities to Cairo.[28]

Competition between IS and al-Qaeda in North Africa fuelled violence and pushed them to ever greater extremes. 'Al-Qaeda in the Maghreb' had had a presence in Algeria since the 2000s[29] and the arrival of IS caused friction. Al-Qaeda has links with the militant al-Shabaab group in Somalia, with the latter pledging allegiance to it in 2012. IS expanded into Libya, taking advantage of the chaos there to take over the city of Sirte in the East.[30] The overthrow of the al-Qaddafi regime in October 2011 had caused the breakdown of state institutions (already atrophic because they had been deliberately undermined for decades by the regime). The result was the collapse of authority, the spread of militias and weapon proliferation within Libya and beyond. The chaos in Libya affected the whole of North Africa and the Sahel, already destabilised by the conflict in Mali (in which al-Qaeda is involved) and the rise of Boko Haram in Nigeria. Boko Haram joined IS in 2015 but then broke away and rivalry between them ensued.[31] Algeria, which had not experienced an uprising in 2011 or any significant change as a result, suffered terrorist attacks against the In Amenas gas plant in January 2013. The consequences for Tunisia were even more serious. Its internal Islamist terrorism problem, which had predated 2011, was aggravated as some Tunisians who had pledged allegiance to IS and insurgents from Libya in the south carried out attacks on its territory against tourists and Tunisian citizens.[32]

The upsurge in Islamist extremism has reconfigured the international relations of the Middle East in multiple ways, many of which are difficult to make out because the situation is still unfolding.[33] Jordan and Lebanon have received multiple waves of refugees, with implications for their resources, stability and security. Turkey has been drawn into the Syrian crisis on its doorstep, both unwillingly and as a result of its foreign policy objectives and choices. The number of refugees it has received is the largest in the region but constitutes a much smaller proportion of its population compared to Jordan and Lebanon. Turkey's involvement grew because of its active pursuit of the overthrow of the al-Assad regime, from as early as 2011–12. As the crisis unfolded, its reasons for intervening became more urgent: the emergence of a Kurdish enclave in Syria where a significant organised armed group, the Yekîneyên Parastina Gel (People's Protection Units, also known by its Kurdish acronym YPG), with close links to the Partiya Karkerên Kurdistanê (Kurdistan Worker's Party, widely known by its Kurdish acronym PKK), became the dominant force and alarmed Ankara.[34] The emergence of IS in Iraq and Syria worried Turkey, but its primary focus and enemy remained the YPG.[35] In August 2016, following the failed coup attempt against it in July 2015, the AKP government was able to overcome the military's objections and intervene in Syria militarily in a more direct way.

IS's strategy is to provoke retaliation from its enemies by carrying out extreme attacks against them, to create a sense of crisis and mobilise support in its favour.[36] It did this in Turkey, Jordan, and, further afield, in Egypt, France, Belgium, Russia and the United States. The result has been a concentration of effort against IS in its stronghold in Iraq and Syria that has reduced its territory and weakened it militarily. IS, and other extremist groups such as Jabhat al-Nusra, is not everyone's primary enemy, however. Saudi Arabia and Qatar are primarily concerned to defeat al-Assad, not IS.[37] The same applies to Turkey, but it may currently be changing, as the threat from IS is growing. Turkey's intervention in Northern Syria in late 2016 attempted to also deal with this conundrum. Similarly, on the opposing side, Iran, Hizbullah and Russia are concerned with al-Assad's survival, not the elimination of IS. This does not bode well for the containment of extremism in the Fertile Crescent and beyond. As pointed out by the International Crisis Group, enmity between Middle Eastern states is so profound at present that 'regional powers worry less about extremists than about their rivals, or even quietly indulge these groups as proxies'.[38]

In North Africa, we can observe a similar pattern of various regional and global actors being drawn into local conflicts because of the rise of Islamist extremism. The situation in Sinai is causing concern in Israel. In February 2015, 21 Egyptian Copts were kidnapped and beheaded by IS in Libya. In March 2016 Tunisia suffered an attack from IS along its southern border with Libya. Both of these attacks caused retaliation, particularly from Egypt. Western powers, and particularly the United States, have been increasingly concerned with the turmoil and fragmentation of authority in Libya, which have allowed IS to gain a foothold. NATO intervention enabled the fall of al-Qaddafi but Western powers withdrew after the event. They have returned in support of the internationally recognised government of Libya, hounding IS from its basis in Sirte with a bombing campaign in the course of 2016 and ensuring that only some elements of it remained in place in Libya in 2017.

Conclusion

The 2011 uprisings, and the conflicts they gave rise to, have had a significant impact on Islamist movements and ideologies in the Middle East which, in turn, have transformed the international relations of the region. The foreign policies of state and non-state actors have been altered, the standing and identities of these actors have been influenced and region-wide alliances and balances of power have been changed. The Middle East continues to be embedded firmly within global economic structures and to be the focus of the attention of global powers and interests in political and security terms: what happens there reverberates far beyond its boundaries. As a result, outside powers have been sucked back into the Middle East and are becoming increasingly involved in its conflicts once again. This, in turn, has impacted on regional policies and balances.

This chapter has argued that there are three major 'Islamist' trends or strands in the Middle East whose trajectories have been changed by the 2011 uprisings and the conflicts that derived from them, with significant implications for the international relations of the region. The first consists of a more 'established' revolutionary, 'third-worldist' and anti-imperialist Islamism, sponsored by Iran and centred on Hizbullah. The focus of this constellation of Islamist actors has shifted, in effect, from Israel to Syria. This has meant that the rivalry between the Iran-centred and Western-centred camps that has defined the region since the 2000s, if not before, has taken a different form. The main confrontation is now between an Iran-led and a Saudi-led camp, with the result that the ideological dimension of the confrontation has been attenuated and the sectarian one (with everything that it obscures and skews) has been strengthened. The emergence of extremism in the shape of IS in Iraq and Syria in 2014, and the nuclear deal with Iran sponsored by the Obama administration in 2015, could have lead to the toning down of the rivalry between the West, specifically the United States, and Iran (though this now seems to have dissipated with the arrival of Donald Trump in the White House). The extent to which this will have an impact on the Iran–Saudi relationship more broadly is not clear, however, given the profound and multi-faceted antagonism between them.

The second important strand in the Middle East region whose trajectory has been affected by the 2011 uprisings and subsequent conflicts is moderate Islam. The political fortunes of the MB in Egypt and al-Nahda in Tunisia appeared to improve following the uprisings but then declined equally dramatically. The rise and fall of moderate Islam changed Egyptian and (less so) Tunisian foreign policies. It affected the region-wide confrontation between Iran and Saudi Arabia directly, through the changing position of Hamas, and also in many indirect ways. It refashioned relationships and balances within the 'anti-Iran' camp, so to speak, creating tension between Saudi Arabia, Turkey and Qatar. Turkish and Qatari support for the MB in Egypt and Saudi support for the Sisi regime that overthrew it caused bad blood between these powers, which also find themselves supporting different groups in the anti-al-Assad coalition in Syria.

Finally, the rise of extremism in the form of a continuing al-Qaeda insurgency and the new phenomenon of IS has heightened chaos and instability in the region by hardening conflict and increasing the cost of compromise. The rise of extremism has changed relations and identities and reinforced sectarianism in the region as a whole. It has also led to rebalancing, though in the current situation of turmoil future patterns are difficult to discern. Defeating Islamist extremism is not necessarily the priority for all the parties intervening in Syria and Libya but they may in the end achieve its defeat or containment. IS, after all, has no powerful allies or sponsors and its strategy of provoking over-reaction seems to have become self-defeating. The rise of extremism has drawn the West, and specifically the United States, back into the region and Russian support of al-Assad has placed the two powers on opposing sides in the Syrian civil war. This may change if the United States and Russia perceive a convergence of interests in Syria but the course of their relationship – and its potential impact on the Middle East – are particularly difficult to predict under the Donald Trump administration, whose policies in Syria have not yet crystalised.

Notes

1. It is not the place here to explore the relationship between material and ideational factors in the international relations of the Middle East. Suffice to say that my analysis treats them as interdependent and mutually constituted, as the conclusion of the chapter will make clear.
2. Naim Qassem (2010), *Hizbullah: The Story from Within*. London: Saqi.

3. International Crisis Group (2014), 'Iran and the P5+1: solving the nuclear Rubik's cube', *Report No. 152*, 9 May, <www.crisisgroup.org/middle-east-north-africa/gulf-and-arabian-peninsula/iran/iran-and-p5-1-solving-nuclear-rubik-s-cube> (last accessed 5 September 2016).
4. Audrey Kurth Cronin (2015), 'IS is not a terrorist group', *Foreign Affairs*, March/April, <www.foreignaffairs.com/articles/middle-east/isis-not-terrorist-group> (last accessed 5 September 2016).
5. Nicholas Blanford (2013), 'The battle for Qusayr: how the Syrian regime and Hizballah tipped the balance', *Combating Terrorism Center at West Point*, 27 August, <www.ctc.usma.edu/posts/the-battle-for-qusayr-how-the-syrian-regime-and-hizb-allah-tipped-the-balance> (last accessed 1 September 2016).
6. Katerina Dalacoura (2013), 'Iran's diplomacy shows a recognition of its decline', *Financial Times*, 20 October, <www.ft.com/cms/s/0/036170e6-374b-11e3-9603-00144feab7de.html> (last accessed 1 September 2016). This interpretation is contested. See for example the argument of Akram Belkaïd (2016), 'Maghreb still supports Assad', *Le Monde Diplomatique* (English edn), 4 April, <https://mondediplo.com/2016/04/05maghreb> (last accessed 30 August 2016) that Hizbullah remains popular in North Africa because it is supporting al-Assad (an observation that indicates that sectarianism is not dominant in public opinion in these countries). Contrast this to Marie Kostrz (2016), 'Hizbullah's mission in Syria', *Le Monde Diplomatique* (English edn), 4 April, <https://mondediplo.com/2016/04/07hizbullah> (last accessed 5 September 2016), who highlights tensions and doubts between the supporters of Hizbullah in Lebanon about the group's intervention in Syria.
7. Harriet Sherwood (2014), 'Hamas and Iran rebuild ties three years after falling out over Syria', *The Guardian*, 9 January, <www.theguardian.com/world/2014/jan/09/hamas-iran-rebuild-ties-falling-out-syria> (last accessed 1 September 2016).
8. Daniel Byman (2014), 'Sectarianism afflicts the new Middle East', *Survival*, 56:1, pp. 79–100.
9. Andreas Krieg (2016), 'Externalizing the burden of war: the Obama Doctrine and US foreign policy in the Middle East', *International Affairs*, 92:1, pp. 97–113; Daniel Serwer (2016), 'Recalculating US policy in the Middle East', *Middle East Institute*, April, <www.mei.edu/sites/default/files/publications/Serwer.pdf> (last accessed 1 September 2016).
10. Stacey Philbrick Yadav and Sheila Carapico (2014), 'Yemen in Turmoil: the breakdown of the GCC Initiative', *Middle East Report*, 273, pp. 2–6; International Crisis Group (2016) 'Yemen: is peace possible?' 9 February, <www.crisisgroup.org/middle-east-north-africa/gulf-and-arabian-peninsula/yemen/yemen-peace-possible> (last accessed 23 November 2016).
11. Jane Kinninmont (2012), 'Bahrain: beyond the impasse', *Chatham House*, June, <www.chathamhouse.org/sites/files/chathamhouse/public/Research/Middle%20East/pr0612kinninmont.pdf> (last accessed 23 November 2016).
12. Paul Salem (2015), 'Putin comes to Syria: causes and consequences', *Middle East Institute*, 21 September, <www.mei.edu/content/at/putin-comes-syria-contexts-and-consequences> (last accessed 30 August 2016).
13. The Donald Trump administration, which came into office in January 2017 in the US, has expressed opposition to the Iran deal but it is too soon to make an assessment about this at the time of writing (November 2016). It is also impossible at this stage to judge whether the Trump administration would be open or not in the future to a deal with al-Assad.
14. Gareth Porter (2016), 'Turkey and Iran reach agreement on conditions for Syria peace', *Truthout*, 18 August, <www.truth-out.org/news/item/37291-turkey-and-iran-reach-agreement-on-conditions-for-syria-peace> (last accessed 1 September 2016).

15. Quinn Mecham (2014) 'Islamist movements', in Marc Lynch (ed.), *The Arab Uprisings Explained: New Contentious Politics in the Middle East*. New York: Columbia University Press, pp. 169–82. Also see Tarek Masoud (2014), *Counting Islam: Religion, Class and Elections in Egypt*. Cambridge: Cambridge University Press.

16. Katerina Dalacoura (2016), 'Islamism and neoliberalism in the aftermath of the 2011 uprisings: the Freedom and Justice Party in Egypt and Nahda in Tunisia', in Emel Akçalı (ed.), *Neoliberal Governmentability and the Future of the State in the Middle East and North Africa*. Basingstoke, Hampshire and New York: Palgrave Macmillan, pp. 61–83.

17. For an in-depth discussion of the plight of moderate Islamist forces in Kuwait and Morocco, see the contributions to this volume by Luciano Zaccara, Courtney Freer, Hendrik Kraetzschmar, and Mohammed Masbah.

18. Amichai Magen (2015), 'Comparative assessment of Israel's foreign policy response to the "Arab Spring"', *Journal of European Integration*, 37:1, <http://portal.idc.ac.il/Faculty Publication.Publication?PublicationID=2960&FacultyUserName=YW1pY2hhaW0=> (last accessed 5 October 2016).

19. Marc Lynch (2015), 'Obama and the Middle East: rightsizing the US role', 9 October, *Carnegie Endowment for International Peace*, <http://carnegieendowment.org/2015/10/09/obama-and-middle-east-rightsizing-u.s.-role-pub-61582> (last accessed 5 October 2016).

20. Kristina Kausch (2013), 'Foreign funding in post-revolution Tunisia', *FRIDE*, 20 May, <http://fride.org/download/WP_Tunisia.pdf> (last accessed 1 September 2016): 16–17). On Qatar's foreign policy, see: Lina Khatib (2013), 'Qatar's foreign policy: the limits of pragmatism', *International Affairs*, 89:2, pp. 417–31, <https://fsi.stanford.edu/sites/default/files/INTA89_2_10_Khatib.pdf> (last accessed 5 October 2016).

21. Sebastian Sons and Inken Wiese (2015), 'The engagement of Gulf States in Egypt and Tunisia since 2011', *DGAPAnalyse*, No. 9, October, <https://kops.uni-konstanz.de/bitstream/handle/123456789/33148/Sons_0-317350.pdf?sequence=3> (last accessed 5 October 2016); Youssef Cherif (2015), 'Tunisia's foreign policy: a delicate balance', *Atlantic Council*, 23 March, <www.atlanticcouncil.org/blogs/menasource/tunisia-s-foreign-policy-a-delicate-balance> (last accessed 23 November 2016).

22. London School of Economics Middle East Center Report (2016), 'The AKP and Turkish foreign policy in the Middle East', *Collected Paper*, 5, April, <http://eprints.lse.ac.uk/66139/1/Kaya_AKPForeignPolicy_2016.pdf> (last accessed 5 October 2016).

23. Benedetta Berti (2015), 'Hamas hedging its bets in the region', *Cairo Review of Global Affairs*, 18 September, <www.thecairoreview.com/tahrir-forum/hamas-hedging-its-bets-in-in-the-region/> (last accessed 30 August 2016); Benedetta Berti and Zack Gold (2015), 'Hamas nears the breaking point', *Foreign Affairs*, 18 February, <www.foreignaffairs.com/articles/egypt/2015-02-18/hamas-nears-breaking-point> (last accessed 5 September 2016).

24. Anon. (2016), 'Exploiting disorder: Al-Qaeda and the Islamic State', *International Crisis Group* 14 March, <www.crisisgroup.org/global/exploiting-disorder-al-qaeda-and-islamic-state> (last accessed 2 September 2016) pp. 21–2.

25. Ibid., pp. 15–19.

26. Erika Soloman (2016) 'Al-Nusra's break from al-Qaeda seen as a strategic move', *Financial Times*, 30 July, <https://next.ft.com/content/4eda41ba-5665-11e6-9f70-badea1b336d4> (last accessed 2 September 2016); Raphael Lefèvre (2015), 'Islamism within a civil war: the Syrian Muslim Brotherhood's struggle for survival', *Brookings, Rethinking Political Islam Series*, Working Paper, August, <www.brookings.edu/wp-content/uploads/2016/07/Syria_Lefevre-FINALE.pdf> (last accessed 23 November 2016).

27. Terrence McCoy (2014), 'ISIS, beheadings and the success of horrifying violence', *Washington Post*, 13 June, <www.washingtonpost.com/news/morning-mix/wp/2014/

06/13/isis-beheadings-and-the-success-of-horrifying-violence/> (last accessed 5 October 2016).

28. Daveed Gartenstein-Ross (2015), 'Ansar Bayt Al-Maqdis' oath of allegiance to the Islamic State', *Wikistrat*, February, <http://wikistrat.wpengine.netdna-cdn.com/wp-content/uploads/2015/02/Ansar-Bayt-Al-Maqdis-Oath-of-Allegiance-to-the-Islamic-State-Wikistrat-Report.pdf> (last accessed 1 September 2016); Tom Wilson (2016), 'Egypt, Hamas and Islamic State's Sinai Province', *Henry Jackson Society*, October, <http://henryjacksonsociety.org/wp-content/uploads/2016/10/Egypt-Hamas-and-Islamic-States-Sinai-Province.pdf> (last accessed 23, 2016).

29. Katerina Dalacoura (2011), *Islamist Terrorism and Democracy in the Middle East.* Cambridge: Cambridge University Press, pp. 53–5.

30. Sam Jones and Heba Saleh (2016), 'FT Big Read: IS in Libya: stoking conflict', *Financial Times*, 20 March, <www.ft.com/cms/s/0/c06fb0d6-e1f7-11e5-8d9b-e88a2a889797.html#axzz4JgbHzILb> (last accessed 5 September 2016).

31. Maggie Fick (2016), 'Boko Haram dispute with Isis bursts into the open', *Financial Times*, 5 August, < https://www.ft.com/content/bed19ac2-5a61-11e6-8d05-4eaa66292c32> (last accessed 2 September 2016).

32. Anon. (2016) 'Jihadist violence in Tunisia: the urgent need for a national strategy', *International Crisis Group* Brief No. 50, 22 June, <www.crisisgroup.org/middle-east-north-africa/north-africa/tunisia/jihadist-violence-tunisia-urgent-need-national-strategy> (last accessed 23 November 2016).

33. The growth of extremism has also fostered a spirit of intolerance in the region and contributed to the decline of liberalism. See e.g. Borzou Daragahi (2015), 'FT Big Read: Middle East, taking liberties', *Financial Times*, 6 May, <www.ft.com/cms/s/0/91774db6-f300-11e4-a979-00144feab7de.html#axzz4Jf8xRSlA> (last accessed 1 September 2016).

34. Middle East Centre (2016), *Rojava at 4: Examining the Experiment in Western Kurdistan, Workshop Proceedings*, London School of Economics, <http://eprints.lse.ac.uk/67515/1/Rojavaat4.pdf> (last accessed 10 September 2016).

35. While in 2016–17 this caused considerable strain between Turkey and the US, which saw the Kurds as an ally against IS, the pro-independence Kurdish referendum in Iraqi Kurdistan may change this state of affairs prompting a rapprochment. See e.g. Amberin Zaman (2017), 'What's next after Kurdish independence vote?' *Al-Monitor*, 25 September, <www.al-monitor.com/pulse/originals/2017/09/iraq-kurdistan-region-independence-barzani-turkey-syria-iran.html> (last accessed 26 September 2017). For a background on US-Turkey strained relations, see e.g. Henri Barkey (2016), 'Syria's dark shadow over US-Turkey relations', *Turkish Policy Quarterly*, 7 March, <http://turkishpolicy.com/article/782/syrias-dark-shadow-over-us-turkey-relations> (last accessed 1 September 2016).

36. David Gardner (2015), 'The hideous dialectic of IS savagery', *Financial Times*, 19 February, <www.ft.com/cms/s/0/de2135f6-b772-11e4-981d-00144feab7de.html> (last accessed 1 September 2016). In contrast, al-Qaeda's strategy is becoming more pragmatic, more cautious 'about killing Muslims' and 'sensitive to local norms and popular opinion'. Anon. 'Exploiting disorder', p. 25.

37. This may be changing, however. In December 2015, Saudi Arabia announced a coalition of Islamic countries 'against terrorism'. See Noah Browning and John Irish (2015), 'Saudi Arabia announces 34-state Islamic military alliance against terrorism', Reuters, 15 December, <www.reuters.com/article/us-saudi-security-idUSKBN0TX2PG20151215> (last accessed 1 September 2016).

38. Anon. 'Exploiting disorder', p. 6.

Part IV
The Sunni–Shi'a divide

Chapter 18

Islamism in Yemen: from Ansar Allah to al-Qaeda in the Arabian Peninsula

Vincent Durac

On 21 September 2014, fighters belonging to the Houthi movement, also known as Ansar Allah, entered the Yemeni capital Sana'a, setting off a chain of events that led to the overthrow of the internationally recognised government of Abd Rabbo Mansour Hadi, civil war and ultimately military intervention in Yemen by an alliance of states led by Saudi Arabia with the objective of defeating the Houthis and restoring the political *status quo ante*. The war in Yemen has been read variously in terms of a sectarian civil war in which the Houthis – a Zaydi Shi'a movement – are engaged in conflict with representatives of the majority Sunni Muslim population of the country, or, alternatively, as another front in the regional conflict between Saudi Arabia and Iran. According to this latter reading, the Houthis function as Iranian proxies while the Saudi-led intervention is designed to restore the power of its local allies in Yemen and limit, if not eliminate, the influence of Iran in the country. This chapter will argue that, notwithstanding the significance of religio-political cleavages in Yemeni political life or that of the direct entry of regional actors into Yemeni affairs, the conflict flows inexorably not from inherent sectarian tensions at either the national or regional levels. Rather, it flows from the dysfunctionality of the post-2011 transitional process, with roots further back in the quasi-authoritarian regime of Ali Abdullah Saleh, which dominated the politics of Yemen from 1990 to 2011.

The chapter will first explore the origins of the Houthi movement, its rise to prominence and its ideological underpinnings. It will then examine the complex relationship between the Houthis and other political actors in Yemen, especially other 'Islamic' actors such as al-Tajammu' al-Yamani lil-Islah (Yemeni Congress for Reform Party, henceforth referred to as al-Islah), Salafi elements and the radical Islamists of Tanzim al-Qaeda fi Jazirat al-'Arab (al-Qaeda in the Arabian Peninsula, AQAP). Finally, the chapter will locate the ongoing conflict in Yemen in the context of what is often represented as a broader regional tension between Sunni and Shi'a Islam with a view to exploring the extent to which it constitutes an expression of specifically Yemeni grievances rather than another aspect of a regional sectarian conflict.

The Houthi movement: origins, ideology and objectives

The Houthi movement has its origins in Saada governorate in northwest Yemen. Saada is the heartland of Zaydi Islam whose adherents comprise some 35–40 per cent of the overall population of the country, most of the rest following the Shafi'i school of Sunni Islam. Zaydism differs in significant ways from the Twelver Shi'ism practised in Iran, Iraq and Lebanon. Zaydism emerged in the eighth century AD among early Muslims who believed that Ali was the rightful successor to Prophet Muhammad in the spiritual and temporal leadership of the Muslim community. The Zaydis emerged from disagreement among Shi'a communities as to which descendant of Ali should be considered Imam. Unlike the majority, Zaydis consider Zayd bin Ali, a grandson of Ali's son Hussein, to be the fifth Imam and became known as 'Fivers' or Zaydis as a result. Thus, for Zaydis, the spiritual leader of the Muslims must be a sayyid or Hashemite[1] – a descendant of the Prophet through the line of Ali and Fatima – and that leader – the Imam – should also be the leader of the state. Zaydism took root in Mesopotamia and Central Asia in AD 740 but gradually moved south, where it reached Yemen.[2] Zaydism differs in significant ways from Sunni Islam on the question of leadership of the community. However, in other respects Zaydi practices are closer to those of Sunnis than they are to the Twelver Shi'ism practised by the majority of Shi'as worldwide. Zaydis represent themselves as a fifth school of thought within Islamic jurisprudence rather than as a branch of Shi'ism. Historically, Zaydis have not sought to propagate their beliefs, nor does Zaydi doctrine embrace the *wilayat-al-faqih* (the rule of the jurisconsult), as promoted by Ayatollah Khomeini and which lies at the heart of political system in Iran. Unlike Iranian Twelver Shi'ism, Zaydism has moved away from the notion of rule by an Imam, and contemporary Zaydis are not subordinate to a clerical hierarchy.[3] As Christopher Boucek notes, Zaydism is frequently viewed as a Sunni school of Shi'ism and Shafi'ism as a Shi'a school of Sunnism.[4]

The Houthi movement emerged from a broader Zaydi revivalist trend in Saada in response to a number of factors. Religious considerations constituted an important driver of that revival. However, a range of broader socio-economic and political factors were also significant. These included the widespread perception of the marginalisation of the region by the central government in Sana'a; the increasing rapprochement of the regime with

Sunni elements and the concomitant increase in the promotion of Sunni and Salafi Islam in the governorate; and changes in the character of Zaydi society in Saada.

Saada has long been remote from control and penetration by the government in Sana'a. During the civil war that followed the overthrow of the imamate in 1962, it became a refuge for supporters of the imamate who resisted anti-imamate revolutionary forces. Saada only joined the Yemen Arab Republic (YAR) following a treaty of reconciliation in 1970.[5] Saada is among Yemen's poorest regions and receives little by way of government services. The post-1962 period also witnessed important changes in Zaydi society in Saada, which had traditionally been divided between those who claimed descent from the Prophet Muhammad through Ali and the rest of the community. The former were known by the honorific title of *sayyid* and were a privileged and educated class. However, post-1962 regimes, although nominally Zaydi, condemned their social aloofness and promoted a mainstream Sunnism that narrowed the gap between Zaydis and Shafi'is further, such that many Zaydis no longer defined themselves specifically as Shi'a. The consequent 'crisis within Zaydism' was exacerbated by regime promotion of Salafi ideology in the northern highlands and in Saada itself, which provoked a Zaydi backlash. This process saw the introduction of so-called 'scientific institutes'; that is, religious schools that propagated the Wahhabi version of Islam adhered to in neighbouring Saudi Arabia.

The growing ideological challenge confronting Zaydism in Saada prompted the development of a Zaydi revivalist movement. Elite Zaydis took advantage of the political pluralism of the newly unified Yemen to establish Hizb al-Haqq (Truth Party, henceforth referred to as al-Haqq) as an expression of Zaydi interests in response to Wahhabi encroachment. One of these was Badr al-Din al-Houthi, a prominent Zaydi scholar. While al-Haqq was established to counter increasing Wahhabi influence, it also constituted an attempt to obtain political recognition and largesse from the regime. But, as an elite party, disinclined towards mass political participation, it held little appeal for an increasingly activist younger generation of northern Zaydis.[6]

When prominent Zaydi scholars linked to al-Haqq declared that the ruler, or Imam, no longer needed to be a Hashemite, Badr al-Din al-Houthi and other Saada-based scholars split from it. His son, Hussein al-Houthi, together with others, created a network of associations, sports clubs and summer camps that came to be known as Muntada al-Shabab al-Mu'min (Believing Youth). Believing Youth was rooted in the assertion of the material, political and spiritual needs of Saada. Until the late 1990s, both al-Haqq and Believing Youth received some support from the regime in Sana'a in its attempts to counterbalance the increased influence of Wahhabism and al-Islah, particularly during the legislative elections of 1997, by which time al-Islah had joined the political opposition.[7]

By the 2000s, Believing Youth had begun to lose momentum. Ultimately, events at the global level, and responses to them in Saada, led to outright conflict between the regime and the movement. In the aftermath of the attacks of 11 September 2001, the Yemeni President Saleh (r.1990–2012) entered into greater levels of cooperation with the United States, becoming an ally in the so-called 'war on terror'. However, closer ties with the US provoked criticism within Yemen both from Salafi elements and from Zaydi revivalists. On 17 January 2002, Hussein al-Houthi gave a talk in Marran, his home village in Saada, in which he called on his compatriots to fight against an American hegemony that weighed more heavily every day on the Arab and Muslim world and to repeat at meetings after Friday prayers the slogan: 'Allahu akbar, al-mawt li Amrika, al-mawt li-Isra'il, al-la'na'ala-l-yahud, al-nasr li-l-Islam' ('God is great, death to America, death to Israel, a curse upon the Jews, glory to Islam'). In January 2003, as Saleh passed through Saada on his way to Mecca, the slogan was repeated in his presence and relations between al-Houthi and the regime deteriorated further. After the failure of attempts to reconcile the two sides, as well as continuing demonstrations including one in the Grand Mosque in Sana'a, the government sought to secure al-Houthi's arrest. This led to the outbreak of open hostilities between the two sides.[8] Between 2004 and 2010, the two sides engaged in violent conflict on six separate occasions. Despite the subsequent characterisation of the conflict between the Houthis and the regime as sectarian in nature, each outbreak of fighting stemmed from different causes. The sixth and final round of conflict broke out in 2009. By November 2009, the conflict had assumed a regional dimension as Saudi Arabia directly entered the fighting to establish a demilitarised zone on the Yemeni side to defend against future attacks on Saudi soil. Direct Saudi involvement reflected the broader support offered by Gulf Cooperation Council (GCC) countries to the Yemeni regime while a number of Sunni Arab states lobbied the US to encourage its support for the military action.[9] A February 2010 truce brought the sixth round to an end without any conclusive resolution of the underlying conflict between the Houthis and the regime.

The Sunni Islamist spectrum in Yemen

The Sunni Islamist movement in Yemen has its origins in the 1940s when Yemenis from both North and South were first exposed to the ideology of al-Ikhwan al-Muslimun (Muslim Brotherhood, MB) in Cairo and Beirut. A Muslim Brotherhood movement was established in North Yemen in the 1960s but it had little input into formal political life.[10] By the 1980s a Brotherhood-influenced 'Islamic Front' had developed considerable influence within the ruling al-Mo'tamar al-Sha'abi al-'Aam (General People's Congress, GPC) in the YAR. However, in the broader context of the weakness of representative institutions within the country, this functioned neither as a party nor as a broad-based social movement.[11] The creation of a multi-party political system in the new Republic of Yemen, which emerged from the unification of the YAR and the People's Democratic Republic of Yemen (PDRY) in 1990, prompted debate within Islamist circles regarding the appropriateness of organising and competing in a party system. While many rejected the notion, the Muslim Brotherhood trend, already active in such political institutions as existed in the pre-unification North, joined with Salafis prepared to engage in party-building and with significant tribal figures, such as Sheikh Abdullah al-Ahmar, to create al-Islah.[12] Following the first multi-party elections in the new republic, held in 1993, al-Islah entered into coalition with Saleh's GPC. However, the electoral success of the GPC in elections held in 1997 meant that the GPC was no longer reliant on al-Islah for support and assumed an increasingly authoritarian character. This led some in al-Islah, particularly, its Muslim Brotherhood component, to begin to move towards a more democratic orientation. Saleh's success in the first presidential elections in 1999, with more than 96 per cent of the vote, and followed by the adoption of a series of constitutional amendments that increased his powers, hastened al-Islah's move into outright opposition. In 2002, the party joined a cross-ideological alliance called Ahzab al-Liqa' al-Mushtarak (Joint Meeting Parties, henceforth JMP) with the shared aim of challenging an increasingly authoritarian regime.[13]

In contrast to the activism of those involved in al-Islah, the Salafi trend in Yemen has historically been characterised by its quietism. Indeed, Laurent Bonnefoy suggests that the denunciation of political participation has marked the rhetoric of Yemeni Salafis more than in other national contexts.[14] Membership of political parties was seen as a kind of corruption leading to *hizbiyya* (factionalism). Thus, Yemeni Salafis also criticised democracy, elections and any kind of organisation that implied any kind of loyalty other than to God. However, despite apparently implacable opposition to political involvement, an association called al-Hikma (Wisdom) was created in 1992 by former students at the Dar al-Hadith Study Centre in Dammaj, which, initially confined to benevolent activities, was gradually drawn into political activities.[15] Nonetheless, prior to the 2011 uprising, no Salafi leader expressly supported the establishment of a political party.

Yemen's jihadist groups, meanwhile, also reject multi-party politics and democracy but have adopted very different means towards the achievement of their objectives from those of the Salafis. Jihadism in Yemen has its origins in the return of fighters from the anti-Soviet Afghan jihad in the early 1990s. During this period, the so-called Afghan Arabs shared hostility towards the socialists of the former PDRY with the Saleh regime and acted as regime proxies during the short-lived civil war of 1994. A precursor to al-Qaeda, the Aden-Abyan army was established in the late 1990s and was linked to an attack in 2000 on the US warship, USS Cole, which was docked off Aden harbour. In June 2009, AQAP was formed from a merger of the Saudi and Yemeni branches of al-Qaeda and was considered by the US as the most dangerous branch of the group. Its influence within Yemen was, nonetheless, limited at this point.[16]

Yemeni Islamism, the uprising and the transitional process

The political situation in Yemen was transformed utterly with the outbreak of countrywide protests against the Saleh regime in early 2011. The protests were led by young people, while established political actors initially adopted a cautious approach. The JMP response to the protests was designed to signal its position as 'loyal opposition', with reformist rather than revolutionary objectives.[17] However, by 20 February, the JMP announced an end to dialogue with the ruling GPC as it continued to attack protesters. On the same day, the Houthi movement announced that it would cooperate with the protesters in the organisation of protests in a number of governorates. Increasing regime violence in the face of an expanding protest movement led to significant defections from its support base. Following a massacre in Sana'a of demonstrators leaving Friday prayers on 18 March 2011, a number of members of parliament in Saleh's GPC resigned, as did approximately half of the country's ambassadors. The most significant defection was that of General Ali Mohsen, who had played a prominent role in the wars in Saada. His defection to the protest movement was a reflection of his opposition to the widely anticipated succession to the presidency of Ahmad Saleh, Ali Abdullah's son, who was being groomed for the role. Although widely mistrusted, his defection provided the protesters with protection from regime forces. The embattled regime was further weakened with the withdrawal of support by the al-Ahmar family.[18]

The instability in the country and the threat of outright civil war prompted the intervention of external actors, in the form of the GCC, with Saudi Arabia taking the lead. The GCC initiated talks in Riyadh between the various factions in order to end the crisis. These negotiations led to what became known as the GCC Initiative, which Saleh eventually signed in November 2011 having initially signalled his willingness to agree to the deal as early as April. The GCC Initiative contained a number of controversial proposals. The GPC and the

JMP were signatories to the deal, which provided not for the replacement of Saleh's ruling party in government but for power-sharing between the two. Saleh was to step down as president in favour of his deputy, Abd Rabbo Mansour Hadi, but retain his position as head of the GPC.

However, the GCC Initiative excluded the youth protesters who had initiated the uprising from any share of power, as well as the Houthis and southern separatists. Controversially, the deal provided for a grant of immunity for Saleh and his family from prosecution for 'politically motivated' crimes other than terrorist offences. The first phase of the transition process ended with the success of Hadi in presidential elections that took place in February 2012 in which, in accordance with the terms of the GCC deal, he was the only candidate.

The transitional arrangements envisaged by the GCC Initiative were seen very differently by the youth protesters and by Islamist actors. The concession of immunity to Saleh and his associates led protesters to target the JMP for its complicity in the deal. Members of the Houthi movement, who had cooperated with other elements in the protest movement, including al-Islah, began to bring weapons to protest meetings as those collaborative relationships began to disintegrate.[19]

However, the key terms of the deal greatly increased al-Islah's power. As the largest and best-organised member of the JMP alliance, now sharing government with the GPC, al-Islah was in a position to shape the opposition half of the transitional government. The GCC deal also guaranteed al-Islah a significant role in the second phase of the transitional process, which was dominated by a National Dialogue Conference (NDC). The GCC Initiative envisaged that the NDC would address a series of intractable problems facing the country by bringing together a diverse set of participants, and would do so within a six-month period. These included the drafting of a new constitution, the southern issue,[20] the situation in Saada, promoting progress towards a democratic system, and sustainable economic development. To minimise some of the complexities of the negotiation process, President Hadi appointed a sixteen-member technical preparatory committee with representatives from across the political spectrum, including the youth and civil society movements that had emerged during the uprising. This committee drafted a twenty-point plan of confidence-building measures to be implemented before the NDC began its work. Its work was undermined, however, when Hadi, with the support of the JMP, launched the NDC without implementing the plan. Youth and civil society representatives on the preparatory committee resigned and removed their representation from the NDC. The main factions of the Southern Movement also withdrew from the NDC, to be replaced by representatives of other southern factions with little support on the ground.[21]

The dramatic shift in the political landscape also prompted significant developments within Yemen's Salafi movement. For many quietist Salafis the region-wide uprisings brought chaos and benefited the enemies of Islam. However, some prominent leaders began to rethink their loyalty to Saleh as the 'Imam of the Muslims', as protests accelerated a pre-existing trend towards politicisation. Many Salafi activists participated in the uprising through small-scale informal organisations. This led to the establishment of Rabitat al-Nahda wa al-Taghyir (League of Revival and Change, LRC) to guide these associations at the national level. This was followed in turn by the formation of Ittihad Rashad (Rashad Union) in March 2012. The Rashad Union distanced itself from al-Islah's 'lack of orthodoxy' and emphasised its origins as one of the rare new parties that were not linked to long-established political actors in the country.[22] It was allowed to join the NDC as a new party with five seats and exercised a rightward influence in committee sessions by working with al-Islah.[23]

On 21 January 2014, the final NDC document, with almost 1,800 recommendations, was accepted in a plenary session with further agreement that Hadi would remain in office until a new president was elected. However, the negotiations were bedevilled by profound disagreement over the southern issue and proposals for a federal structure for the country. In September 2013, Hadi appointed another committee to explore this question. After months of negotiation, there was agreement that Yemen should become a federal state with greater local autonomy and control devolved to the regions. But, consensus on how much power should be devolved, or how many regions would constitute the new federal Yemen, was harder to secure. The southern representatives sought a division into just two regions – North and South – which suggested a return to the pre-unification situation. Others preferred a division into four, five or six regions. Following the conclusion of the NDC, Hadi announced that there would be a six-region federal structure – four regions in the North and two in the South – in spite of the fact that such a proposal had already been suggested and rejected. Hadi's plan was similarly rejected by southern representatives but also by the Houthis who believed that the plan deprived Saada of resources and access to the sea.

Throughout this period, while Houthi political representatives took part in the transitional process, their fighters continued to expand their territorial control. Having secured control of Saada during the course of the 2011 uprising, they moved south. The short-lived alliance with their old adversaries, al-Islah, Ali Mohsen and the al-Ahmar family, began to fray. Clashes within the NDC between the Houthis and al-Islah were matched by the outbreak of armed conflict between militias allied to each group. By January 2014, battles raged across the north of the country from the border with Saudi Arabia to the gates of Sana'a.[24] As the economy entered rapid decline, Hadi introduced a cut in fuel subsidies in order to secure financial aid from the IMF and the World Bank. The protests that ensued gave the Houthis the excuse to enter and take control of the capital Sana'a.[25]

The Houthi seizure of Sana'a was made possible in part by a stunning shift in political dynamics. In its initial phases, former president Ali Abdullah Saleh and his supporters accepted the transitional process, on the assumption that his continued leadership of the GPC would allow him to maintain influence in public life. However, as Hadi gradually moved with international support to exclude Saleh and his family from positions of influence, this position changed. By 2014, an utterly unexpected reconfiguration of forces had developed as Saleh and the Houthis entered into an alliance of convenience based on their newly shared opponents: Hadi, al-Islah and Ali Mohsen. The Houthi expansion was greatly aided by the cooperation, or at least non-resistance, of forces loyal to the former president.

Following the seizure of the capital, Yemen's main political parties signed a Peace and National Partnership Agreement (PNPA) that could have put the transition back on track. It mandated the formation of a new inclusive government, the withdrawal of Houthi fighters from the territories they had gained and a review of the issue of state structure. However, neither the government nor the Houthis honoured their commitments. Instead, the latter set up a shadow government to oversee ministries and, ostensibly, to fight corruption. When Hadi tried to push through a federalism scheme to which they were opposed and which was in clear violation of the PNPA, they arrested a presidential advisor and surrounded the presidential palace. Hadi and his government resigned in January 2015. In a further provocation, the Houthis appointed a 'revolutionary council' by 'constitutional announcement' in February and marched south towards Aden to which Hadi had fled and where he had retracted his resignation and re-established his government.[26] At this point the conflict was internationalised, as Saudi Arabia, with the support of nine other states, launched an air attack on Houthi military positions with the stated objective of restoring the Hadi government and reversing the Houthi advance.[27]

The ensuing political instability provided an opening for radical Islamists. While the outbreak of the uprising in 2011 had taken AQAP by surprise, it took advantage of the breakdown of regime control to entrench itself in the southern governorates of Abyan and Shabwa and declared several towns to be 'Islamic emirates'. It also 'rebranded' itself Ansar al-Shari'ah (Partisans of Islamic Law) in an attempt to dilute the negative connotations of the global al-Qaeda brand.[28] By March 2015, al-Dawla al-Islamiyya (Islamic State, IS) had emerged on the scene with four coordinated suicide attacks on mosques in

Sana'a frequented by Houthis. Both AQAP and IS have benefited from state collapse and the opportunity to present themselves as better alternatives to the state in providing services, from Houthi expansionism and the preoccupation of regional states with the threat of Iran, and from a war economy, which has allowed AQAP, in particular, to increase its resources through bank raids, the control of seaports and smuggling.[29]

Conflict in Yemen: sectarian war or regional rivalry by proxy?

The ongoing conflict in Yemen is complex and multi-dimensional in its origins and character. However, it is frequently seen in simplistic terms. At the domestic level, the conflict is represented as a battle between the Zaydi Shi'ism of the Houthis and their Sunni Muslim adversaries. Sectarianism also informs the rationalisation of the war as a front in a broader regional rivalry between Saudi Arabia and Iran. In this version of events, the Saudi intervention is designed to prevent its most populous neighbour from falling into the hands of a Hizbullah-type movement sponsored by Iran.

The charge of sectarianism has been frequently voiced by Yemeni regimes, both before and after the uprising. In particular, the suggestion is made that the Houthis, despite protestations to the contrary, reject the republican *status quo* and seek to restore the imamate. For the Hadi government, Saudi Arabia and its GCC allies, the Houthis constitute a radicalised Zaydi movement with a political leadership tied to, and directed by, Iran. Fear of Iranian influence is deepened by statements made by some Iranian politicians in praise of the Houthis. However, the suggestion that the conflict in Yemen is primarily sectarian in nature and that it constitutes another 'front' in a broader regional (and also fundamentally sectarian) struggle between Saudi Arabia and Iran is simplistic and belies both history and current realities.

As has been seen, the Houthi movement emerged as a vehicle of Zaydi revivalism in Saada, but also as a response to its marginalisation by the central state and its economic underdevelopment by successive regimes in Sana'a. Furthermore, the argument that the conflict is, in essence, Shi'a *versus* Sunni Islam overstates the differences between them, while ignoring the profound differences between Zaydism and the Twelver Shi'ism of Iran, for whom the Houthis are purported proxies. The 'sectarian' argument overlooks the fact that the Saleh regime has sought, at various points and for political gain, to co-opt the Houthis as well as to crush them, as, at various points, he sought to manipulate Sunni Islamism, in the form of al-Islah and AQAP, in order to secure party and personal advantage. This instrumental approach is evident in the extremely unlikely alliance that developed during the transitional phase between the Houthis and their former adversaries in the GPC. But profound differences persist between the two sides. Many of Saleh's supporters identify themselves as members of a centrist, non-religious party, and remain extremely wary of what they regard as religious radicals who have opened the door to sectarianism in Yemen and unnecessarily provoked conflict by their rash actions. Many Houthi, in turn, find it impossible to trust Saleh or his supporters and hold him responsible for the killing of their founder, Hussein al-Houthi.[30]

The argument that the conflict has an underlying sectarian character at the domestic level is also undermined by analysis of the complexity of the forces arrayed against the Houthi–Saleh 'alliance'. This constitutes an essentially incoherent mix of Sunni Islamists, including AQAP and IS, a diverse mix of southern separatists, as well as what is left of the internationally recognised government. The Islamists include al-Islah, a party that has participated in the political system since 1990 and that has cooperated in opposition with secular and Zaydi parties in the JMP since 2002. Furthermore, al-Islah cooperated with the Houthis in 2011 during the course of the uprising. The anti-Houthi forces also include the violent Islamists of AQAP and IS. Southern separatists are internally divided along several fault lines – on whether to push for immediate independence along regional lines – and there are important divides between fighters from different governorates of the South, and along religious lines between Islamists and non-Islamists in the Southern Movement.[31]

Equally simplistic is the argument that Yemen's war is little more than a proxy for a broader Saudi–Iran contest. The Saudi interest in Yemen has been consistent over the decades. However, Saudi policy has been anything but consistent, while Iranian involvement in Yemen is greatly overstated and largely opportunistic in nature. Saudi policy towards Yemen has traditionally been directed more by the desire to contain Yemen's chaos than as 'a theatre for regional competition'.[32] Indeed, while Saudi Arabia has a long-standing set of strategic interests in Yemen, it has pursued a variety of strategies in its assertion of those interests. During the civil war that followed the overthrow of the Zaydi imamate in 1962, the Saudis supported anti-revolutionary Zaydi forces against Arab nationalist republicans backed by their then regional rival, Nasserist Egypt. During the 1980s, the Saudis became a direct patron of the Yemeni government as well as military and tribal leaders, paying them a monthly stipend for most of the first thirty years of Saleh's rule. However, when Saleh backed Saddam Hussein following Iraq's invasion of Kuwait in 1990, ties with Saleh were cut and an estimated one million Yemeni migrants deported from Saudi Arabia.[33] Four years later, and in part as a response to this, Saudi Arabia supported southern secessionists in the short-lived civil war of 1994; a decision that had little to do with sectarian or religious motivation and everything with teaching a former ally a lesson. The instrumental character of its policy towards Yemen is reflected in the fact that, in spite of its subsequent intervention to address Houthi expansionism, it was suspected that the Saudi regime was happy to see the Houthis and al-Islah weaken each other during the early days of the current conflict.[34] This is not least because of lingering Saudi hostility towards the broader Muslim Brotherhood movement, of which al-Islah is an offshoot.

The Saudi-led intervention undoubtedly reflects concern about deepening Iranian involvement on its southern border. However, it is also related to domestic power calculations. The military intervention followed the death of King Abdullah in January 2015, the accession of Salman to the Saudi throne, and his appointment of his son, Mohamed ibn Salman, to the positions of Crown Prince and Minister of Defence. Thus the war's outcome is linked also to the fortunes of the ruling family at a time of transition in Saudi Arabia itself.

Iranian involvement in Yemen, in turn, is less significant and even less driven by sectarian motivations. As with the Saudis, historically Iran has pursued an instrumental foreign policy in Yemen tied not to religion but to perceptions of where regime interests lay. Prior to the 1979 revolution, the Shah's regime cooperated with Riyadh in backing the imamate in the north of Yemen. After 1979, the YAR maintained close relations with Saddam Hussein's Iraq and supported it during the Iran–Iraq war. However, subsequently relations between Saleh and Tehran became more cordial – in 1986 he met with the then Iranian Foreign Minister to express support for Iran's right to pursue a nuclear programme.[35] Relations began to sour as Saleh accused Iran of providing the Houthis with support. Nonetheless, Saleh never supplied definitive proof of this and cables revealed by WikiLeaks suggest that the US embassy was unconvinced of the merit of the claims.[36] After 2011, and again after 2014, it was widely suspected that the Iranians had increased the level of support to the Houthis. However, the evidence is anecdotal and unclear.[37]

Conclusion

While the conflict in Yemen undoubtedly has sectarian overtones and has indeed drawn in regional actors, it is primarily a reflection of the failures of the transitional process that followed the 2011 uprising. Almost from the outset, there was a failure to address the political, economic and regional grievances that underpinned the uprising. The intervention of external actors in early 2011 and the GCC Initiative that followed resulted in an agreement that guaranteed the survival of political elites but failed to establish an inclusive government. Neither was a transitional justice system put in place, nor were any of those accused of human rights violations brought to justice.[38] The GCC Initiative paid lip service to the demands of protesters – for example, Saleh was forced to leave the presidential office – but the structures of his regime were maintained and the position of many of those closest to him were protected through immunity from prosecution. As president, Hadi, who was elected in what was a plebiscite rather than a competitive electoral process, lacked legitimacy and compounded this through mismanagement of key issues, especially the question of the federal structure of the country. Throughout the transitional period, levels of violence and instability increased, as did socio-economic distress. The NDC process was flawed from the outset. It was intended to promote a national conversation about Yemen's future political organisation. However, from the beginning marginalised groups and civil society representatives complained that the process did not translate into more transparent or accountable government.[39] Stacey Philbrick Yadav has argued that at every stage in the NDC planning process, inclusivity was scuttled in favour of the embedded interests of established partisan, military and tribal figures, while more Yemenis died during this phase of the transitional process than during the 2011 uprising.[40] The willingness of the Southern Movement and of the Houthis to participate was overestimated and the failure to agree on the future structure of the country undermined much of its potential achievement. By 2014, the Houthis struck a chord with segments of society extending beyond their own members simply because it stood up to a regime that was seen as incompetent and corrupt.[41] The expansion of the Houthis was in part due to their ability to capitalise on popular disenchantment with the condition of Yemeni society in the transitional period. While to a limited extent narrow sectarian difference informs the conflict at both domestic and regional levels, it is better understood, therefore, as an expression of the failure of the transitional process in Yemen after 2011.

Notes

1. Not all Yemeni Hashemites are Zaydi, some are Sunni. However, in the context of the Houthi movement, the term is often used to refer to Zaydis who claim to be descendants of the Prophet Muhammad.
2. International Crisis Group (2009), 'Yemen: defusing the Saada time bomb', *Middle East Report*, 86, p. 2.
3. Barak Salmoni, Bryce Loidolt, and Madeleine Wells (2010), *Regime and Periphery in Northern Yemen: The Huthi Phenomenon*. Santa Monica, California: The RAND Corporation, pp. 65–7.
4. Christopher Boucek (2010), 'War in Saada: from local insurrection to national challenge', *Carnegie Middle East Paper*, 110, April.
5. Samy Dorlian (2011), 'The Sa'ada War in Yemen: between politics and sectarianism', *Muslim World*, 101:2, p. 183.

6. Ibid., pp. 94–5.
7. Ibid., p. 183. As discussed in more detail below, Hizb al-Islah, which was established in 1990 following unification, comprises the Muslim Brotherhood, Salafi and tribal elements.
8. Ibid., p. 185.
9. Ibid., p. 188; Boucek, 'War in Saada', p. 9.
10. Stacey Philbrick Yadav (2013), *Islamists and the State: Legitimacy and Institutions in Yemen and Lebanon*. London: IB Tauris.
11. Stacey Philbrick Yadav (2015), 'Yemen's Muslim Brotherhood and the perils of powersharing', Working Paper, Rethinking Political Islam series. Washington: Brookings Institution.
12. Yadav, *Islamists and the State*, p. 26; Yadav, 'Yemen's Muslim Brotherhood', p. 3. Note that until his death in 2007, Sheikh Abdullah al-Ahmar, paramount chief of the Hashid tribal confederation in Yemen to which the president's own Sanhan tribe belonged, was a key ally of Saleh's. On his death, his sons occupied key roles in Yemeni public life.
13. For more on this see Michelle Browers (2007), 'Origins and architects of Yemen's Joint Meeting Parties', *International Journal of Middle East Studies*, 39:4, pp. 565–86; Vincent Durac (2011), 'The Joint Meetings Party and the politics of opposition in Yemen', *British Journal of Middle Eastern Studies*, 38:3, pp. 343–65.
14. Laurent Bonnefoy (2011), *Salafism in Yemen: Transnationalism and Religious Identity*. London: Hurst, p. 61.
15. Laurent Bonnefoy (2011), *Salafism in Yemen: Transnationalism and Religious Identity*. London: Hurst, pp. 61–5.
16. International Crisis Group (2017), 'Yemen's Al-Qaeda: expanding the base', *Middle East and North Africa Report*, 174, p. 4, <www.crisisgroup.org/middle-east-north-africa/gulf-and-arabian-peninsula/yemen/174-yemen-s-al-qaeda-expanding-base> (last accessed 13 June 2017).
17. Yadav, 'Yemen's Muslim Brotherhood', p. 6.
18. Letta Taylor (2011), 'Yemen's hijacked revolution: new protests pushed aside by old rivalries in Sanaa', *Foreign Affairs*, 26 September.
19. Yadav, 'Yemen's Muslim Brotherhood', p. 7.
20. Yemen's Southern Movement was established in 2007 as an expression of frustrations at the marginalisation of the south following the short-lived civil war of 1994. Over time, it has developed into a loose coalition of groups with the broad objective of southern autonomy or independence. See Thanos Petouris (2016), 'Understanding the role of the "Southern Question" in Yemen's war', *Muftah*, 25 July, <http://muftah.org/southern-question-yemen-war/#.WJnzDUJXL8s> (last accessed 12 May 2017).
21. Maged Al-Madhaji (2016), 'How Yemen's post-2011 transitional phase ended in war', *Sana'a Center for Strategic Studies*, May, <http://sanaacenter.org/files/how_yemens_post_2011_transitional_phase_ended_in_war_en.pdf> (last accessed 12 May 2017).
22. Laurent Bonnefoy and Judit Kuschnitizki (2015), 'Salafis and the "Arab Spring" in Yemen: progressive politicization and resilient Quietism', *Arabian Humanities*, 4.
23. Yadav, 'Yemen's Muslim Brotherhood' p. 8.
24. Anon. (2014), 'The Huthis: from Saada to Sanaa', *International Crisis Group Middle East Report*, 154, p. 3.
25. Peter Salisbury (2016), 'Yemen and the Saudi-Iranian "Cold War"', *Chatham House*, 18 February, p. 20.
26. Anon. (2016), 'Yemen: is peace possible', *International Crisis Group Middle East Report*, 167, p. 3.

27. Dan Roberts and Kareem Shaheen (2015), 'Saudi Arabia launches Yemen air strikes as alliance builds against Houthi rebels', *The Guardian*, 26 March, <https://www.theguardian.com/world/2015/mar/26/saudi-arabia-begins-airstrikes-against-houthi-in-yemen> (last accessed 15 June 2017).

28. Elizabeth Kendall (2014), 'Al-Qa'ida and Islamic State In Yemen: a battle for local audiences', in Simon Staffell and Akil N. Awan (eds), *Jihadism Transformed: Al-Qaeda and Islamic State's Global Battle of Ideas*. London: Hurst, p. 94.

29. International Crisis Group (2017), 'Yemen's Al-Qaeda', pp. 10–7.

30. Anon., 'Yemen: is peace possible?' pp. 7–9.

31. Ibid., pp. 12–13.

32. Maria-Louise Clausen (2015), 'Understanding the crisis in Yemen: evaluating competing narratives', *International Spectator*, 50:3, p. 20.

33. Salisbury, 'Yemen and the Saudi-Iranian "Cold War"', pp. 3–4.

34. Anon., 'Yemen: is peace possible?' p. 7.

35. Mahjoob Zweiri (2016), 'Iran and political dynamism in the Arab World: the case of Yemen', *Digest of Middle East Studies*, 25:1, p 11.

36. Thomas Juneau (2016), 'Iran's policy towards the Houthis in Yemen: a limited return on a modest investment', *International Affairs*, 92:3, p. 656.

37. Ibid., p. 658.

38. Gabriele vom Bruck (2014), 'The Houthi advance on Yemen's capital', *Le Monde Diplomatique*, 28 October.

39. Salisbury, 'Yemen and the Saudi–Iranian "Cold War"', p. 14.

40. Stacey Philbrick Yadav (2015), 'The "Yemen Model" as a failure of political imagination', *International Journal of Middle East Studies*, 47:1, pp. 144–7.

41. Sarah Phillips (2013), 'Tracing the cracks in Yemen's system', in David McMurray and Amanda Ufheil-Somers (eds), *The Arab Revolts: Dispatches on Militant Democracy in the Middle East*. Bloomington and Indianapolis: Indiana University Press, p. 141.

Chapter 19

Sectarianism and civil conflict in Syria: reconfigurations of a reluctant issue

Souhaïl Belhadj and Laura Ruiz de Elvira

As most journalists and researchers have observed,[1] the Syrian uprising, which initially relied on a unified (cross-confessional, cross-ethnic and cross-provincial) popular base, has now become an 'overtly sectarian conflict'.[2] The initial revolutionary slogan *wahed wahed wahed, al-sha'ab al-suri wahed* ('one, one, one, the Syrian people are one'), highlights how the early opposition to Bashar al-Assad's regime organised and framed its protest action. However, this 'magical moment' of unity did not last long. The Baathist regime, which purports to be multi-confessional and multi-ethnic, has favoured from 2011 a sectarian radicalisation of the conflict.[3] Moreover, the growing military support provided to the Syrian regime by its Shi'a allies, namely Iran and the Lebanese Hizbullah, arguably exacerbated the confrontation between the country's Sunni majority – a community that represents more than 75 per cent of the Syrian population – and the Shi'a minority to which the Syrian president belongs.[4] These elements partly explain why radical Sunni Islamist groups, such as Jabhat al-Nusra (Nusra Front), later called Jabhat Fateh al-Sham (Front for the Victory in the Levant), and al-Dawla al-Islamiyya (Islamic State, IS) have gradually become stronger and more influential than the Free Syrian Army (FSA, the military wing of the National Coalition for Syrian Revolutionary and Opposition Forces)[5] and al-Ikhwan al-Muslimun fi Suriyya (the Syrian Muslim Brotherhood, SMB), a political movement that also controls some factions of the FSA. The uprising in Syria has hence not only led to the pluralisation of domestic Islamist actors and to the growth of intra-Islamist competition and conflict – as can be observed in other countries of the Middle East and North Africa (MENA) – but also to the resurgence of a Sunni–Shi'a sectarian discourse and conflict, turning Syria into one of its epicentres in the region. In theory, this polarisation of the Syrian conflict along sectarian lines could have entailed both a rapid decline of the regime – due to its increasing reliance on its community of reference (Alawite/Shi'a) – and the partition of Syria into several 'statelets' following the ethnic and religious distribution of the country's population. Yet the former has not collapsed and the country has not yet completely imploded to become a mosaic of independent communities and territories.

Against this background, this chapter aims to tackle the very complex issue of sectarianism – understood here as the politicisation of 'collective identities' in Syria based on ethnic, religious, clan, tribal and/or family affiliations – and to explore how this phenomenon and the current conflict are shaping and reconfiguring one another.[6] To do so, it is necessary to look back at history. The first section of the chapter therefore reviews the evolution of sectarianism in the country from the Ottoman period onwards. This is followed by an analysis of the reconfigurations of the sectarian issue since the beginning of the Syrian uprising in March 2011. The third section, finally, highlights the limits of the sectarian prism to understanding both Syria's current conflict and contemporary political identity.

Diachronic in approach, this chapter reveals that sectarianism has always been part of Syrian politics, particularly during the Baathist era. Indeed, since 1963 the Baathist regime has supervised and managed society in an authoritarian manner through sectarianism. Examples of such sectarian politics include the co-optation of certain minorities within the Baath party, the government and the state-controlled press, the selection of mostly Alawites and Sunnis for key positions in the intelligence services, the armed forces and the Baath national security office (with an over-representation of the Alawites if their demographic weight is taken into account), as well as the preferential treatment of Christian organisations within the country's civil society.[7] Moreover, it can be argued that the Baathist regime managed to remain in power over the past four decades partly thanks to its strategy of developing and advocating the idea of a unified national Syrian society/identity, while at the same time preserving and manipulating its denominational and ethnic cleavages. This said, unlike in Lebanon, sectarianism was never institutionalised in the country, and the Syrian national identity is not inherently a denominational-sectarian one. Likewise, it can be argued that although sectarianism matters strongly today – insofar as it plays a role in the Syrian conflict and in the political and social dynamics that have led to it – it is not the only key prism through which one can understand the evolution of the war taking place in the country. Indeed, even though sectarianism has represented an important factor of radicalisation and fragmentation since 2011, the Syrian national identity and the nation-state still remain the main point of reference for most actors involved in the conflict. This means that national and sectarian identities are paradoxically not mutually exclusive in the Syrian context, where efforts to build a national state and a national community have always gone hand in hand with the use of sectarianism to achieve and/or stay in power.

Nevertheless, most, though not all, analyses on Syria conceptualise the Syrian state and society in sectarian terms, with ethno-religious identities being treated as surpassing all other socio-economic/political cleavages and, hence, as a principal driver shaping national politics.[8] This chapter aims to provide a different entry point into Syrian politics, integrating the question of sectarianism into a wider reflection on the relationship between social structures, political mobilisation and national identity. In so doing, the authors seek to move beyond the idea that sectarianism is principally and solely a tool in the hands of political elites, authoritarian leaders and armed groups to annihilate their enemies, highlighting instead that sectarianism has historically never been the only, let alone the most efficient, tool for political mobilisation in Syria. While sectarianism has been, and remains, a significant component in Syrian politics and society, it is not the founding principle of the construction of the Syrian state or of Syrian national identity. However, in times of crisis the influence of sectarianism naturally increases, since the structure of the state and the regime cannot be totally disconnected from the cleavages and divisions that structure Syrian society.

Sectarianism in Syria before 2011

Throughout the modern history of Syria, all ruling parties – be they the Ottomans (1516–1920), the French (1920–46) or the post-independence governments (1946–63) and the Syrian Hizb al-Ba'ath al-'Arabi al-Ishtiraki (Arab Socialist Baath Party of Syria or simply the Syrian Baath Party, SBP – 1963 to present) – have imposed their rule over the country on the basis of existing ethno-religious divides between communities. This sectarian management of Syrian society contributed to the exacerbation of existing societal conflicts that had their origin in regional, family, confessional and corporatist antagonisms.[9] However, before 2011 and despite the existence of these various ethno-religious communities, sectarianism had never been turned into an explicit principle of government. Indeed, a national consensus that transcends sectarianism and other social divides seems to have been progressively built up since the Ottoman era. Of particular relevance in enhancing the latter was the institution-building process that started during the French mandate, and had at its core the notion of establishing national institutions and a national sense of belonging.

The Ottoman Empire (1299–1923) imposed and religiously legitimised the *millet* system in order to rule over heterogeneous territories covering the Greater Syria (Bilad al-Sham), with populations 'belonging to different faiths'.[10] This system was based on the official recognition of religious communities as well as of their rights, and was characterised by different regulations for each in matters such as taxation, legal personal status and legal collective representation.[11] The Greek Orthodox, Armenian and Jewish communities hence had wide-ranging freedom to order their communal affairs under the authority of their religious hierarchies.[12] The sectarian potential of this *millet* system – understood in terms of conflict and political mobilisation – remained limited until the mid-nineteenth century.[13] Yet religious tensions across the Bilad al-Sham, mainly between Muslims and Christians (e.g. Aleppo in 1850, Nablus in 1856, Zahleh in 1860 between Druzes and Maronites) were present during the era of Ottoman modernisation (*Tanzimat*, 1839–76), resulting in the reform of the *millet*. These tensions eventually culminated in the massacre of thousands of Christians in Damascus in 1860. Scholars assume that, while seeking to establish legal and social equality between all Ottoman affiliates[14] – that is between Muslims and non-Muslims – the *Tanzimat* were detrimental to Muslims and their privileges, and consequently created resentment and a perception of social downgrading, triggering animosity against other communities (notably the Christians, who were perceived as a group with societal privileges). Hence, instead of leading to the establishment of an 'Ottoman affiliation' (citizenship) beyond traditional collective affiliations (ethnicity, religion, tribes, clans, families) as envisioned by the rulers of the Empire, the reform of the *millet* system led to sectarian polarisation. The implementation of the *Tanzimat* was also affected by international politics and the growing influence of France and Great Britain over the Ottoman Empire. Both these European powers, in fact, responded to growing sectarian polarisation by protecting the privileges and the separate status of non-Muslims.[15]

When in 1920 the French imposed their mandate over the territory that roughly constitutes present-day Syria and Lebanon, they ruled it with a sectarian understanding of the old *millet*, and back-paddled on the *Tanzimat* reforms. In other words, the French concentrated their efforts on dividing 'Syria's communities religiously',[16] while extending the old *millet* system. Two statelets were thus established in 1922, one in the coastal region, where the Alawite community was historically anchored, and a second in the southern region, historically populated by the Druze. The Alawites and the Druze, as Muslim communities of Syria, had never been separately recognised as *millets*, but because of their geographical concentration in certain areas, the French reorganisation of the territory reinforced their autonomy through both geographical and legal means. Hence their capacity to make political claims was strengthened. The Alawites, for instance, obtained from the French a low taxation regime and financial support; and certain local leaders supported the idea of an Alawite nation and sought to convert their autonomy into real independence.[17] In addition, two districts were established in the al-Jazira region (the northeast of Syria) and in Alexandretta (the northwest), inhabited mostly by Kurds and Turkmen respectively.

A clear discontinuity between the Ottoman period and the French mandate can hence be noted. The latter tried to transform extant religious communities (*millet*) into autonomous minorities within the framework of a 'secular state-form of the nation-state',[18] a state that was theoretically governed by Syrian elites, but effectively ruled by the French. This contradictory state-building project failed in the end because the various communities never spoke with one voice. They were themselves structured according to internal divisions, be they based on their urban or rural origins (Alawites and Christians), their religious denominations (Christians), their tribal affiliations (Alawites), their clan structure (Druze), or their political beliefs.[19] Consequently, there was never sufficient support for either the establishment of territorial/administrative autonomy for Syria's minorities under French control and within the borders of a unified territorial state, or for territorial separatism (*infisaliyya*). Although the separatist project was able to mobilise many Alawites and Druze in the 1920s, it never succeeded to galvanise a political majority within the two communities. Thus, thanks to the Franco-Syrian Treaty of Independence signed in 1936, the Druze and Alawite 'states' were incorporated into the new-born Syrian Republic. This was preceded by mass mobilisations among both communities in support of Syrian unity.[20]

According to the Syrian nationalist leaders at the time, the main political challenge of this mandatory period was precisely to form a 'national majority', that is to find in each ethno-religious minority a majority in favour of the 'unity project'. In concrete terms, this project was carried out through modern institutions such as political parties/groupings (the National Bloc for instance, a coalition of parties hostile to the French presence in Syria created in 1928), various youth organisations (e.g. the Nationalist Youth or the boy scouts), professional organisations (the Higher Council of Trade Unions) and, to a lesser extent, through the paramilitary wing of youth organisations and the Syrian army.[21] Thus, despite French efforts to implement a policy based on 'the creation of distinct and separate mandatory regimes'[22] within the same country (extending the old *millet* system to Alawite and Druze communities and assigning territories to those new *millets*), new types of political associations emerged throughout the 1930s and 1940s in towns and villages across Syria. Cutting across ethno-religious lines and infused by a nationalist Syrian ideology, these associations ultimately paved the way for the unification of Syria and the attainment of full independence in 1946.

Once independence was obtained, a nominally republican democratic regime was established. Democratic rules based on parliamentarism were applied during short intervals between several phases of dictatorship. In fact, at that time Syria went through a period of political instability (seven *coup d'états* took place between 1949 and 1970) mainly nurtured by elite factionalism grounded in long-standing social antagonisms. The unitary impetus that had been created by the nationalist movement during the French mandate – an impetus that was in itself relatively inter-ethnic, inter-religious and inter-class – hence lost part of its vigour. Indeed, elite factionalism influenced Syrian politics since the first years of independence, most notably *within* and *between* the newly established government, the armed forces and the emerging leftist political parties, that is al-Hizb al-Shuyu'i al-Suri (Syrian Communist Party), the Baathists and later the Nasserites. This factionalism was certainly partly structured by sectarian-based interests, as revealed by the over-representation of Christians and Alawites in al-Hizb al-Suri al-Qawmi al-Ijtima'i (Syrian Social Nationalist Party, SSNP), the strong Sunni character of the Nasserite movement and the attempted *coup d'état* in 1966 by a group of Druze officers, led by the Druze Colonel Salim Hatum. However, the factionalist groups that politically superseded others were not built on religious or ethnic homogeneity. Hafez al-Assad, for instance, an Alawite army officer and Baath member, forged interpersonal relations and formed political alliances – so-called *cliques* – with political activists, members of parliament and army officers belonging to different ethno-religious groups. Al-Assad particularly leant on Sunni Baathist fellows such as the lawyer Abd al-Halim Khaddam and the army officer Mustafa Tlass, who also were army officers, in order to eliminate a rival *clique* within the party and eventually lead the military coup that brought him to power in 1970.

The feasibility and occurrence of such mixed ethnic and religious *cliques* in post-independence Syrian politics is most probably a result of the fact that since the end of the Ottoman Empire, and even more so during the French mandate, marginalised minorities such as the Alawite, Druze and Ismaili, as well as the poor Sunni peasantry, gradually ceased to operate as enclosed, inward-looking social groups, and many of their members became increasingly active in politics. Driven mainly by ideological considerations, but also as a potential path to social mobility and access to power, members of these ethno-religious minorities thus progressively came to dominate key political parties (such as the Baath) as well as the armed forces, which not only facilitated the formation of mixed ethnic and religious *cliques*, but eventually also their rise to the highest offices in the country.

When the SBP took power in 1963, its leadership promised to build a state in which ethnic and religious marginalised minorities (mainly Alawite, Druze and Ismaili, since the Christian minority was more socially integrated than the others) would not only be protected but also integrated into the structures of power. This integration was to be achieved through the intermediation of the SBP itself. One of the SBP's functions was indeed to select, via internal elections, leadership cadres – that is the leading members of branches and sub-branches of the party, the army, national trade unions and professional federations, and youth, student and cultural organisations under the Baath umbrella – from among Syria's different religious and ethnic communities. As representatives of the ruling SBP, many cadres from these minority communities eventually emerged in top leadership positions (including the country's presidency, government ministries, parliament) at the helm of public enterprises, as well as heads of governorate and local administrations.[23]

Although the SBP had asserted that the selection of top party, government and other leadership roles would be based exclusively on political experience and expertise, it is evident that religion, family background and region of origin (for example, Hauran was a Baathist bastion) played a significant role in this process. So, for instance, even though the Alawite minority has never held a majority within the decision-making bodies of the SBP (the Central Committee and the Regional Command, which supervise the activities of state institutions), it was, and still remains, overrepresented in comparison to its demographic weight and compared to the Christian minority (which had a similar demographic weight in the 1960s). This is largely due to the fact that the SBP was dominated by Alawite and Sunni military and intelligence officers who, after they had won factional struggles within the Baath and the army in the 1960s, had purged Nasserist, Druze and Ismaili officers from the forces. These Alawite and Sunni officers remain today at the top of the state institutions and still operate within the same logic, a logic that has gradually established a complex confessional power balance based on the cross-sectarian alliance between Alawite and Sunni officers.[24]

This elite-level power-sharing arrangement between the country's Sunni majority and the Alawites, which is the biggest minority in Syria, has not only encouraged the security elite to work together and maintain its cohesion, but ultimately also contributed to relative regime stability between the 1970s and 2000s. Indeed, the Baath regime has demonstrated an ability to remain in power and consolidate its position, as shown by the orchestrated political succession from Hafez al-Assad to his son Bashar in 2000. Another example of this ability dates back to the political crisis and sectarian violence that resulted from the conflict between the regime and the Sunni Islamist opposition (1979–82). The sectarian dimension of this confrontation was more significant than the two previous contentious episodes in 1964 and 1973, when the SMB, the main Islamist opposition force, challenged the authority of the Baathist regime. Beyond contesting the political hegemony of the Baath party, the SMB intended to break 'the tyranny of a minority in power', arguing that most of the key positions in the state apparatus, particularly within the intelligence services, had fallen to the Alawite community. Three years of violent clashes culminated in the Hama massacre (1982),[25] when the regime crushed the Islamist insurgents and the inhabitants of the city using air strikes, mortar fire and numerous other abuses. Alawite military officers and soldiers were heavily involved in the massacre as members of the army special forces and intelligence commandos. Furthermore, 400 Sunni officers were suspended from the army during the crisis after being accused of being sympathisers of the SMB. This said, however, from the beginning numerous senior Sunni army officers were actively involved in the fight against the Islamist opposition and the surge in Hama. Such loyalty to the regime was also evident among senior Sunni state officials, rendering it problematic to interpret the conflict as a polarised sectarian struggle.

When Bashar al-Assad rose to power in 2000, he sought to reinforce extant collaborative ties between the most influential Sunni and Alawite members of the security and political elite.[26] Meanwhile, in order to gain broader popular support and enlarge his legitimacy beyond the security apparatus, the new president sought to forge a new national consensus based on political and economic liberalisation. This led, in the short term, to the co-optation of Syria's business elite,[27] Sunni religious leaders[28] and representatives of the associational sector, such as the leaders of Christian and Sunni charitable associations, into the regime's orbit.[29] By 2011 this support was not sufficiently broad, however, to protect the regime from the largest and most violent contestation it has faced since 1963.

In sum, like the Ottomans and the French rulers, the SBP – which has always legitimised itself both as a Syrian nationalist and a pan-Arab force – failed to establish a political system characterised by democratic power-sharing arrangements between the various national ethno-religious communities. Instead, over the past fifty years, the Baath has predominantly imposed its political hegemony on society by means of sectarian-driven divide-and-rule and co-optation strategies. Indeed, while not formally institutionalised through a confessional system as in neighbouring Lebanon, Syria's ethno-religious identities have nonetheless been significant, because they were relevant to elites' access to state institutions, representing therefore a resource for social mobility. Consequently, in Baathist Syria, sectarianism can be considered as a significant, yet not unique or decisive, element through which social structures, social mobility and political mobilisation relate.[30]

Sectarianism and the civil conflict in Syria

As noted in the introduction, when the Syrian uprising erupted in March 2011, in the context of the so-called Arab Spring, mobilisation against al-Assad's regime was initially organised along cross-confessional, cross-ethnic, cross-provincial and cross-class lines. Indeed, popular protests took place across the country, including in old rural Baathist strongholds such as Deraa,[31] also called the 'Cradle of the Revolution', coastal rich loyal cities such as Lattakia, inner medium-size urban localities like Deir ez-Zor and

Homs, and urban peripheries such as Douma and Daraya in the Damascus
governorate. Likewise, although most of the protesters were Sunni Arab,
demonstrations were also organised in Kurdish, Christian and Ismaili
(mainly in the town of Salamiye) areas and neighbourhoods. Expressions
of solidarity were also extended by the dissenters across the country to all
regions targeted by the army and the security forces because of their activism.
This was manifest, for instance, in the numerous songs and slogans chanted
during rallies organised in 2011 and 2012,[32] such as for instance 'I am with
Syria', 'Homs in solidarity with Deraa' or 'From Qameshli to Hawran, the
Syrian people won't be humiliated'. According to several testimonies, even
some Palestinians born in Syria (re)discovered their Syrian identity in the
midst of the turmoil.[33] For several months, the will of playing an active role
in the struggle for a free and all-encompassing Syria thus became the main
driving force for, and the frame of reference of, the protesters. 'Dignity',
'freedom' and 'social justice' were the catchwords of this unprecedented
popular mobilisation against the al-Assad regime.

Openly challenged by large segments of Syrian society for the first time since
the Hama massacre, the al-Assad regime, meanwhile, responded to this popular
uprising by portraying the protests as a foreign conspiracy and as *fitna* (civil
conflict) orchestrated by unknown armed saboteurs, Islamists and terrorists
that the army should exterminate. Posters warning of sectarian strife were hung
up in the streets, while state media aired staged footage of arms being found in
Deraa's main mosque and warned that a sit-in in the city of Homs on 18 April
2011 was an attempt to erect a mini-caliphate.[34] At the same time, rumours
about Sunni protesters threatening Alawites started spreading throughout the
country to the point that many elderly women within the Alawite community
became afraid of leaving their houses, neighbourhoods or villages.[35] The slogan
'Christians to Beirut, Alawites to the grave', which according to unconfirmed
reports was launched by peaceful demonstrators,[36] was the most eloquent of
these expressions. In addition, al-Assad presented a narrative that depicted
his so-called 'secular' Baathist regime as the sole guarantor of national unity
and multi-sectarian harmony. This narrative was, moreover, reinforced by
symbolic decisions taken *ad hoc*, such as the appointment for the first time
in the Baathist era of a Christian military officer, General Dawoud Rajha, as
Minister of Defence.[37]

As in the pre-2011 era, sectarianism and the stoking of denominational
fears and antagonisms, particularly among the country's minorities, thus
became a way to ensure loyalty towards the regime and, therefore, an effective
political tool of governance. This instrumentalisation of intra-state ethno-
religious identities had two objectives.[38] On the one hand, it was meant to
consolidate the regime's national, regional and international support base since
it presented itself, from the very beginning, as engaged in a fight against Sunni

terrorism. For instance, after a suicide car bomb exploded in June 2012 next to the Sayyida Zeinab Shiʻa shrine in the suburbs of Damascus, and by surfing on its regional Shiʻa allies rhetoric on the need for protection of the Shiʻa holy places, the regime was able to attract thousands of Shiʻa militiamen from Iran, Iraq and Lebanon into its fighting forces.[39] For Hizbullah's militants, fighting in Syria thus became a 'sacred defence' (*difaʻa mouqaddas*) and a 'defence of the holy places' (*difaʻa al-maqamat*).

On the other hand, this strategy was meant to weaken the opposition and its capacity for mass mobilisation, by fragmenting it and dissuading the country's minorities from participating in anti-regime protests. By strengthening identity politics, the regime succeeded in undermining the opposition's claim to legitimacy, since the protesters were no longer able to pretend to be the expression of a unified national movement. Al-Assad and his high-ranking intelligence officers thus intentionally fanned the flames of sectarian radicalisation of the conflict; a conflict they thought they could more easily win than a cross-confessional one. Arguably, the Christians were not going to support the opposition if they perceived it as mainly Sunni and highly influenced by the SMB. The same logic applied to the Druze community, which was furthermore divided and did not feel strong enough to protect parts of the country other than Soueida, its region of origin. As for the Alawites, they would certainly not reject al-Assad and his regime if they believed that their survival as a minority, and their privileged access to power, was at stake should the Baath regime fall.

At the end of the day, the ambivalence between the promotion of a secular Syria, as officially endorsed by the Baath since its foundation in the 1940s, and the regime's *de facto* sectarian policies, together with the selective brutality of the regime's armed henchmen – known as the *shabiha*,[40] who are mainly, but not exclusively, members of the Alawite minority – helped reinforce sectarian dynamics within the different groups of the opposition. Moreover, the increasing military and economic support provided to the Syrian regime by its Shiʻa allies – mainly Iran and the Lebanese Hizbullah, but also Iraqi and Afghan militias – arguably further exacerbated the confrontation between the country's Sunni majority and its Shiʻa minority, of which the Syrian president is a member.

As Zakaria Taha notes, in such a context of political crisis, and in the midst of a destabilised Near Middle East, Syrian oppositional movements organising along 'primordial affiliations'[41] – that is, religious, ethnic, tribal or regional-based cleavages – started to appear from the end of 2011 onwards.[42] The Encûmena Niştimanî ya Kurdî li Sûriyê (Kurdish National Council), the Partiya Yekîtiya Demokrat (Democratic Union Party, also known by its Kurdish acronym, PYD), the Turkman Bloc and the Syrian Tribal Council are just few such examples. At the military level, the above-mentioned elements also partly explain why jihadist Sunni Islamist groups, such as Jabhat al-Nusra and IS, gradually gained strength and became more influential than the more heterogeneous FSA, which is nowadays almost insignificant beyond the Idlib and Hawran regions. Indeed, from 2012 onwards foreign fighters started pouring into the country and joining these two jihadi groups, while sectarian killings and creeping fundamentalism within the ranks of the armed opposition multiplied. The loss of faith in the West (that is, the US and EU) due to the absence of a meaningful intervention, as well as increasing financial support from the Arab Gulf states, such as Saudi Arabia and Qatar, are likely to have also contributed to these dynamics of radicalisation within the opposition; dynamics that were rooted at the local level in pre-existing sectarian tensions and that started to arise in some regions over the summer of 2011. The initial moment of national opposition unity thus gradually eroded.

Against this backdrop, hatred, resentment and sectarian prejudices and beliefs have inevitably developed among both pro-regime and anti-regime supporters. As explained by a former staff member of a Syrian humanitarian association based in Gaziantep (Turkey) and today employed by an international NGO, sectarianism constitutes nowadays one of the biggest problems in Syria. 'People hate Alawites', he says. To demonstrate this, he recalls the mistrust of his colleagues and subordinates when, in early 2016, he decided to hire a young Alawite woman who happened to be the best applicant for the job that his organisation had offered.[43] This testimony, despite its episodical nature, mirrors a diffused opinion, and suggests that sectarian-motivated resentment against the 'Alawite dictator' runs deep among many Syrians. These feelings extend today to the whole Alawite community, and have become frequent even among well-educated people.

Such feelings of resentment and hatred often go hand in hand with a sense of being victims of injustice, exclusion and sectarian discrimination. This was evident among the members of a medium-size humanitarian organisation that works remotely from Gaziantep (Turkey) in Damascus' besieged areas. During a biographical interview conducted in 2014, one of the workers, a forty-year-old Sunni woman, recalled being discriminated against before 2011 'only because I wore a scarf', whereas Alawites would be 'respected'.[44] The same perception was also discernible in her twenty-year-old Sunni colleague's words, with whom another interview of the same type was conducted the same day:

> Today there are more and more hate against [sic], I mean everybody against everybody. Alawites against Sunnis, Sunnis against Alawites … Christians being afraid also … Well, for me, the people who suffered the most were Muslims, so Muslims are hurt. You know, like inside inside of us, we think like 'why?', 'why isn't anyone supporting us, just because we're Muslims?' So … for me as a Muslim, when I see someone who is for instance Shi'a, Alawite or Christian … I feel like, I don't know, like 'why did

you not support me?' Or 'why is it okay for me to be killed?'... if a Christian
dies everyone will be 'Oh, Christians die!'... While hundreds and hundreds
of Muslims are being killed every day[.][45]

However, mistrust and resentment against the 'other' are never unidirectional,
as the story of Mohamed – whom the authors met and talked to informally in
2014 – illustrates. Before 2011, Mohamed, a volunteer in a Syrian humanitarian
association in Tripoli (Lebanon), was a civil servant and a member of the
SBP. Despite living a comfortable life, when the protests started in Homs he
decided to go and see the demonstrations for himself. He recalls how one day
he saw a young Syrian climbing twelve metres high to destroy a portrait of
Bashar al-Assad during a demonstration. This defiant action struck a chord of
admiration, and he started seeing the protests as something new, bringing some
hope for change. He decided to get involved in the relief sector in Homs, daring
for the first time to raise his voice, while still working as a civil servant. He was
then denounced by his Alawite neighbours, allegedly 'only because' he is Sunni,
and he was imprisoned for four months. After being released, he was jailed a
second time and then set free again. When he learned that he was sought again
by the security services, he decided to leave Syria with his family and headed to
Tripoli, where he has lived since 2014. When asked if he will ever return to his
village once the war is over, Mohamed responds that he could not stand living
side by side with those who denounced him; that is his Alawite neighbours.[46]

As these three fieldwork anecdotes suggest, sectarian resentment currently
runs deep among Syrians, both those inside Syria and those living in Syrian
refugee communities abroad. Indeed, while many of the inhabitants and
armed fighters coming from the rebel regions identify their oppressors and
persecutors as being mostly Alawite and/or Shi'a, most Alawites, in turn, 'recall
centuries of discrimination and persecution at the hands of distant rulers and
urban elites, often drawn from the surrounding Sunni majority'.[47] As for the
Christian and Druze communities, they are sometimes accused of siding with
the regime, a positioning that results mainly from their fear of political Islam.
In sum, in the new configuration emerging from the war, all communities tend
to perceive and portray themselves as (old and/or new) victims of sectarian
discrimination, thereby nourishing a vicious circle in which revenge and hatred
are hard to fight against.

Beyond sectarianism

Seven years into the civil war, the growing polarisation of the Syrian conflict and
society along sectarian lines could arguably have precipitated the collapse of
al-Assad's regime, due to its increasingly narrow (military and financial) reliance

on its own community. Likewise, as some observers asserted in 2013, this polarisation could have also led to an institutionalised partition of the country into several statelets, partly modifying the ethnic and religious distribution of Syria's population (a Kurdish northeast, an Alawite Damascus–Homs–Lattakia axis under al-Assad's control, a Sunni Arab northwest). However, as of 2018 this scenario had not yet materialised and the Syrian nation still exists and remains the main point of reference for most actors involved in the conflict.[48] At the political and military levels, indeed, only the jihadist groups, characterised by a strong presence of foreign fighters, and some Kurdish elements, openly call into question the Syrian national borders and the integrity of the nation-state. As for the majority of the population and civil society, it is possible to observe a rising feeling and display of patriotism since 2011, as the frequent use of the independence flag and evocation of national heroic figures demonstrate. In the post-2011 Syrian context nationalism and sectarian identity are hence still not mutually exclusive.

This raises two important questions: Why do the ideas of the Syrian homeland (*al-watan*) and Syrian national identity still survive? And how can one explain this resilience? According to the authors, this can be interpreted as a sign that, although sectarianism matters and plays a radicalising role, it is not the only lens through which one should understand the evolution of the war taking place in the country. Some elements can be highlighted here. First, as in the past, it is impossible to clearly identify unified claims emerging from the different Syrian ethno-religious communities. This suggests that the politicised confessional polarisation (that is, sectarianism) remains constrained by the internal divisions that exist within each community which, instead of being homogeneous societal groups, are strongly composite. In fact, as shown in the first section of this chapter, the history of Syria since the nineteenth century is one of gradual social and political stratification of the ethnic and religious minorities within the process of nation state-building. This stratification has been accompanied by an increasing complexity of the social structures within these communities, which in turn favours the heterogeneity and differentiation within them. This also applies to the religious majority in Syria, the Sunni community, which is characterised by a high degree of internal heterogeneity. Arguably this heterogeneity is visible not only through the various class, local, tribal and civic identities that cross-cut sectarianism in the country and compete with it,[49] but also through the geographical distribution of the Syrian communities across the national territory.[50] This diversity partly explains the opposed stands taken by the Sunni population *vis-à-vis* the uprising, and is particularly discernible in the current Sunni armed opposition groups (FSA, Jabhat Fateh al-Sham, Ahrar al-Sham and many others). These latter defend different interests and competing visions of society, within which the place assigned to the minorities varies from one case to another. These visions may range from positions close to secularism (asking for the separation of religion from state), Islamism (promoting the construction of both an Islamic state and an Islamic society) and jihadi–Salifism (rejecting democracy, marginalising other Muslim sects and, in the case of the Islamic State, exterminating non-Muslim minorities).[51]

This means that the factional dynamics that fragment the military opposition and have partly prevented it from capitalising on its military gains against the Syrian regime, are not fuelled by a sectarian conflict of an ethno-religious nature as was the case in mid-nineteenth century Syria. Indeed, armed opposition groups are relatively homogeneous in their ethnic and religious composition since they are mostly composed of Sunnis. It is rather the contradictory interests of the regional and international actors supporting the opposition (Turkey, Saudi Arabia, Qatar and the US), their changing strategies (see, for instance, the ambiguous role played by Turkey) and the complexity of the multiple alliances (for example the evolving relations between the US, Russia and Iran) that nourish the above-mentioned factional dynamics within these groups. Likewise, within the Sunni-dominated institutions created by the political opposition, such as the National Coalition for Syrian Revolutionary and Opposition Forces, significant fractures exist based on different divides (exiled versus internal opposition, historical versus new forces, secular versus religious groups, leftist versus conservative, in favour of or against militarisation),[52] which are not related to sectarianism.

Finally, interviews and other empirical material[53] suggest that it is the 'Syrian homeland' (*watan*) more than the state (*dawla*) or the 'Syrian Arab Republic' that the Syrians, beyond their community affiliations, identify most with. In this context, the identity of individuals in Syria may still be (strongly) linked to the sense of belonging to an ethno-religious community, yet not exclusively so. Contrary to what the legitimisation narratives produced by the leaders of the regime during past decades may say, a feeling of national identity, which can neither be simply reduced to a blend of ethno-religious affiliations nor to the Syrian Baathist state, still exists. This feeling can admittedly translate into different visions of the legitimate political order that should prevail in the country, and also lead to competing conceptualisations of what the Syrian nation is and what it should look like, but does not result in alternative national projects (except in the jihadist and Kurdish cases). As Thomas Pierret observes, the idea of the Syrian nation has therefore not only not disappeared but may even have been reinforced during the war.[54]

The work done since 2011 by many Syrian civil society associations and networks, both inside and outside the country, has been fundamental in promoting the idea of an all-encompassing, non-sectarian Syria, thereby preserving what they consider to be the 'Syrian identity'. As a 35-year-old interviewee noted during one focus group:

> We aim to build 'national' associations that promote a certain idea of the future Syria. In this sense, we have diversified our activities that originally aimed at providing humanitarian assistance and now also include

the rehabilitation of schools, the training of young adults, etc. Thus, by meeting the multiple needs of various social and religious groups, we develop and deepen our relations with 'all' the Syrian society.[55]

Symptomatically, when asked why they are involved in such organisations and activities, young Syrian activists who work today in exile often refer to a duty towards their country. The expressions 'giving back to my country', 'building up the country', 'national duty' or 'service' to the country are frequently evoked.[56]

Conclusion

'The [1975–90 civil] war in Lebanon is now over. Sectarianism is not', writes Ussama Makdissi about the country of the cedars.[57] The war in Syria is not over yet but, as in Lebanon, sectarianism is an exacerbating factor of social conflicts, especially since the nineteenth century when it gradually started to amalgamate with political culture. However, unlike in Lebanon, sectarianism in Syria is not institutionalised and hence, it does not serve as a founding principle of the political system: power-sharing arrangements and ethno-religious pluralism are indeed not linked to a political pact between the different communities.

That said, as this chapter has sought to demonstrate, sectarianism has always been politically present in Syria through informal and tacit mechanisms in all institutions (local administration, government, parliament, the presidency of the Republic, security apparatus, the directorate of the SBP, etc.). Extant scholarly research has sufficiently documented that during both Hafez and Bashar al-Assad's rule there has been a permanent contradiction between a discourse based on multi-confessionalism (or confessional neutrality) on the one hand, and sectarian practices on the other. This had the effect of creating a balance of power dominated by an elite formed by Alawites and Sunnis. Yet as today's civil war demonstrates, this balance has always been extremely delicate and has created tensions resulting in contradictory outcomes.

Despite this, as this chapter discussed, sectarianism cannot, and should not, be considered the main driving force of social and political conflict in the country. Even if the sectarianisation of the Syrian uprising reveals the limitations and the failure of the Baathist national project, the conflict has also exposed the resilience of both the Syrian nation and national identity. Looking back at Syrian history and its major crises, it becomes clear that the country is not fundamentally a denominational or sectarian one and that, despite continuous fragmentation dynamics, national identity has always prevailed. This results from the fact that, as an 'imagined community'[58] the Syrian national construction[59] is to some extent a success.[60]

Notes

1. Rita Sfeir (2012), 'Syrian crisis is primarily political, not sectarian', *Al-Nahar*, <www.al-monitor.com/pulse/fa/contents/articles/security/01/02/two-internationalcenters-prepar.html> (last accessed 8 September 2017); Thomas Pierret (2013), 'The reluctant sectarianism of foreign states in the Syrian conflict', United States Institute of Peace, Peace Brief n° 162; Fouad Ajami, (2012), *The Syrian Rebellion*. Stanford: Hoover Institution Press, Stanford University.
2. Jasser Zuhdi (2014) 'Sectarian conflict in Syria', *Prism*, 4, pp. 59–67, <http://cco.ndu.edu/Portals/96/Documents/prism/prism_4-syria/PRISM-Syrial-Supplemental.pdf> (last accessed 8 September 2017); Patrick Cockburn (2012), 'All the evidence points to sectarian civil war in Syria, but no ones wants to admit it', *The Independent*, 12 February, <www.independent.co.uk/voices/commentators/patrick-cockburn-all-the-evidence-points-to-sectarian-civil-war-in-syria-but-no-one-wants-to-admit-6785682.html> (last accessed 8 September 2017); Kadri Gursel (2012), 'Syria faces threat of "Lebanonization"', *Al-Monitor*, 1 March, www.al-monitor.com/pulse/tr/politics/2012/03/from-greater-syria-to-greater-le.html (last accessed 8 September 2017).
3. Raymond Hinnebusch (2012), 'Syria: from "authoritarian upgrading'" to revolution?', *International Affairs*, 88, pp. 95–113.
4. Alawites are considered a branch of Shi'a Islam.
5. The National Coalition for Syrian Revolutionary and Opposition Forces, established in Qatar in November 2012, is the main oppositional political body to Bashar al-Assad's regime.
6. This chapter draws on previous research conducted on the Syrian regime and societal dynamics carried out between 2003 and 2011 by the two authors. Regarding the post-2011 period, during which access to Syria has become extremely dangerous, the analysis is based on semi-structured and biographical interviews carried on in Turkey and Lebanon between 2013 and 2016 as well as on empirical material (videos, reports and testimonies) found on the Internet.
7. On this subject see Laura Ruiz de Elvira (2015), 'Christian charities in Bachar al-Assad's Syria: a comparative analysis', in Leif Stenberg and Christa Salamandra (eds), *Syria from Reform to Revolt Volume 2: Culture, Religion and Society*. New York: Syracuse University Press, 2015.
8. Nikolaos van Dam (1996), *The Struggle for Power in Syria: Politics and Society under Asad and the Ba'th Party*, London: IB Tauris; Milton Jacob Esman and Itamar Rabinovich (1988), *Ethnicity, Pluralism, and the State in the Middle East*. Ithaca and London: Cornell University Press; Michael Kerr and Craig Larkin (eds) (2015), *The Alawis of Syria: War, Faith and Politics in the Levant*. London: Hurst; Itamar Rabinovich (1972), *Syria under the Ba'th 1963–1966: The Army–Party Symbiosis*. Jerusalem: Israel Universities Press; John Devlin F. (1983), *Syria: Modern State in an Ancient Land*. Boulder: Westview Press; Daniel Pipes (1992), *Greater Syria: The History of an Ambition*. New York: Oxford University Press; Michel Seurat (1989), *L'État de barbarie*. Paris: Éditions du Seuil, pp. 84–99; Fabrice Balanche (2006), 'Les Alaouites: une secte au pouvoir', *Outre-Terre*, 2 :14, pp. 73–4; Mahmud Faksh (1984), 'The Alawi community of Syria: a new dominant political force', *Middle Eastern Studies*, 2:20, pp. 133–53. Notable exceptions include Hanna Batatu (1999), *Syria's Peasantry, the Descendants of Its Lesser Rural Notables and Their Politics*. Princeton: Princeton University Press; Alasdair Drysdale (1981), 'The Syrian political elite, 1966–1976: a spatial and social analysis', *Middle Eastern Studies*, 1:17, pp. 3–30; Volker Perthes (1995), *The Political Economy*

of Syria under Asad. London: IB Tauris; Souhail Belhadj (2013), *La Syrie de Bashar al-Asad: Anatomie d'un régime autoritaire*. Paris: Belin.

9. Batatu, *Syria's Peasantry, the Descendants of Its Lesser Rural Notables*; Belhadj, *La Syrie de Bashar al-Asad*.

10. Benjamin White (2007), 'The nation-state form and the emergence of "minorities" in Syria', *Studies in Ethnicity and Nationalism*, 1:7, pp. 64–85.

11. The *millet* system may be defined as a political organisation that granted to non-Muslims the right to organise themselves into communities possessing certain delegated powers under their own ecclesiastical heads. See Kamel S. Abu Jaber (1967), 'The millet system in the nineteenth-century Ottoman Empire', *The Muslim World*, 57, 212–23.

12. Bruce Masters (2001), *Christians and Jews in the Ottoman Arab World: The Roots of Sectarianism*. Cambridge: Cambridge University Press.

13. Jean Paul Pascual (1980), 'La Syrie à l'époque ottomane (le XIXème siècle)', in André Raymond (ed.), *La Syrie d'aujourd'hui*. Paris: Publications du CNRS, pp. 31–53; Masters, *Christians and Jews in the Ottoman Arab World*; White, 'The nation-state form and the emergence of "minorities" in Syria'; James A. Reilly (2012), 'Ottoman Syria: social history through an urban lens', *History Compass*, 1:10, pp. 70–80.

14. Derya Bayir (2016), *Minorities and Nationalism in Turkish Law*. New York: Routledge.

15. Caesar E. Farah (2000), *The Politics of Interventionism in Ottoman Lebanon, 1830–1861*. London: IB Tauris.

16. White, 'The nation-state form and the emergence of "minorities" in Syria'.

17. Philip S. Khoury (1987), *Syria and the French Mandate: The Politics of Arab Nationalism, 1920–1945*. Princeton: Princeton University Press.

18. Benjamin White (2011), *The Emergence of Minorities in the Middle East: The Politics of Community in French Mandate Syria*. Edinburgh: Edinburgh University Press, p. 44.

19. Ibid; Aslam Farouk-Alli (2014), 'Sectarianism in Alawi Syria: exploring the paradoxes of politics and religion', *Journal of Muslim Minority Affairs*, 3:34, pp. 207–26.

20. Khoury, *Syria and the French Mandate*.

21. Ibid.

22. Ibid., p. 5.

23. Raymond Hinnebusch (2001), *Syria: Revolution from above*. New York: Routledge, 2001; Batatu, *Syria's Peasantry, the Descendants of Its Lesser Rural Notables*.

24. Souhail Belhadj (2014), 'L'appareil sécuritaire syrien, socle d'un régime mine par la guerre civile', *Confluences Méditerranée*, 2:89, pp. 15–27.

25. Ismael Quiades (2009), 'The Hamah massacre, February 1982', *Online Encyclopedia of Mass Violence*. Available at <www.sciencespo.fr/mass-violence-war-massacre-resistance/en/document/hamah-massacre-february-1982> (last accessed 20 November 2017).

26. Belhadj, *La Syrie de Bashar al-Asad*.

27. Bassam Haddad (2011), *Business Networks in Syria: The Political Economy of Authoritarian Resilience*. Stanford: Stanford University Press.

28. Thomas Pierret (2013), *Religion and State in Syria: The Sunni Ulama from Coup to Revolution*. Cambridge: Cambridge University Press, 2013; Paolo Pinto (2011), '"Oh Syria, God protects you": Islam as cultural idiom under Bashar al-Asad', *Middle East Critique*, 2:20, pp. 189–205.

29. Ruiz de Elvira, 'Christian charities in Bachar al-Assad's Syria'; Laura Ruiz de Elvira and Tina Zintl (2014), 'The end of the Ba'thist social contract in Bashar al-Asad's Syria: reading socio-political transformations through charities and broader benevolent activism', *International Journal of Middle East Studies*, 46:2, pp. 329–49.

30. Jessica Piombo (2009), *Institutions, Ethnicity, and Political Mobilization in South Africa*. Basingstoke: Palgrave Macmillan; Frederik Barth (1998), *Ethnic Groups and Boundaries: The Social Organization of Culture Difference*. Long Grove, IL: Waveland Press.

31. Belhadj, *La Syrie de Bashar al-Asad*, p. 436.

32. See Burgat François *et al.* (2013), 'La puissance politique des slogans de la révolution', in François Burgat and Bruno Paoli (eds), *Pas de Printemps pour la Syrie: Les clés pour comprendre les acteurs et les défis de la crise (2011–2013)*. Paris: La Découverte, pp. 185–95; Simon Dubois (2013), 'Les chants se révoltent', in François Burgat and Bruno Paoli (ed.), *Pas de Printemps pour la Syrie: Les clés pour comprendre les acteurs et les défis de la crise (2011–2013)*. Paris: La Découverte, pp. 196–200. For a good compilation of these slogans and songs see also the website: 'The creative memory of the Syrian Revolution', <www.creativememory.org/?lang=en> (last accessed 8 September 2017).

33. Informal conversations with two Palestinian brothers born in Damascus, 2011.

34. Peter Harling and Sarah Birke (2012), 'Beyond the fall of the Syrian Regime', *MERIP*, 24.

35. Informal conversation with an Alawite journalist whose family lives in rural Homs (June 2012).

36. The slogan has never been recorded in any of the numerous videos of protests available on the Internet. This suggests that if this slogan was ever shouted by protesters, then it was very unusual circumstance.

37. Zakaria Taha (2016), 'La construction nationale syrienne face aux dynamiques identitaires et communautaires', in Anna Bozzo and Pierre Jean Luizard (eds), *Vers un nouveau Moyen Orient? États arabes en crise: Entre logiques de division et société civiles*. Roma: Roma TrE-Press, p. 140.

38. Raymond Hinnebusch (2016), 'The sectarianization of the Middle East: transnational identity wars and competitive interference', paper presented at the workshop 'Transnational diffusion and cooperation in the Middle East and North Africa', held 8–9 June in Hamburg (Germany).

39. Jean Pierre Filiu (2013), 'La bataille de la fin des temps en Syrie', *Souria Houria*, 9 June, <http://souriahouria.com/la-bataille-de-la-fin-des-temps-en-syrie-par-jean-pierre-filiu/> (last accessed 8 September 2017).

40. The term *shabiha* first appeared in the 1980s in 'the home village of the Asad family, Qardaha, where individuals belonging to the extended Asad family where known to act extra-judicially, operating large-scale smuggling operations and generally intimidating the inhabitants of the coastal region'. Kheder Khaddour (2015), 'The Alawite dilemma (Homs 2012)', in Friederike Stolleis (ed.), *Playing the Sectarian Card: Identities and Affiliations of Local Communities in Syria*. Beirut: Friedrich-Ebert-Stiftung, <http://library.fes.de/pdf-files/bueros/beirut/12320.pdf> (last accessed 8 September 2017). Since 2011, *shabiha* has designated any 'armed paramilitary group or militia with links to the army, the secret service or the Baath Party' (ibid.). The *shabiha* are, for instance, accused of being implicated in the Houla massacre, which occurred in May 2012 and resulted in the killing of 108 people.

41. Elisabeth Picard (2006), 'Les liens primordiaux, vecteurs de dynamique politique', in Elisabeth Picard (ed.), *La Politique dans le monde arabe*. Paris: Armand Colin, pp. 55–77.

42. Taha, 'La construction nationale syrienne face aux dynamiques identitaires et communautaires', p. 130.

43. Informal conversation, June 2016, Gaziantep.

44. Interview, May 2014, Gaziantep.

45. Interview, May 2014, Gaziantep.

46. Interview, June 2014, Tripoli.
47. International Crisis Group (2012), 'Syria's mutating conflict', *Middle East Report*, nº 128.
48. Thomas Pierret (2016), 'Syrie: état sans nation ou nation sans état ?' in Anna Bozzo and Pierre Jean Luizard (ed.), *Vers un nouveau Moyen Orient? États arabes en crise: Entre logiques de division et société civiles*. Roma: Roma TrE-Press, p. 182.
49. Hinnebusch, 'The sectarianization of the Middle East'.
50. A partition of the country would hence be very difficult to achieve today on the demographic basis of ethno-religious communities. This is mainly due to the fact that since the post-independence period, and especially with the acceleration of urban development, the Syrian population has become greatly intermixed. In the region of Latakia, for example, the historical stronghold of the Alawite community, 650,000 non-Alawite, including 340,000 Sunnis, live among 1.8 million Alawites. See Youssef Courbage (2012), 'Ce que la démographie nous dit du conflit syrien', Slate.fr, October, <www.slate.fr/story/62969/syrie-guerre-demographie-minorites> (last accessed 8 September 2017). In sum, apart from the Druze and the Kurds, Syria's ethno-religious communities are not as geographically enclosed as they were in the past.
51. Stanford University (2016), 'Mapping militant organizations: Syria', <http://web.stanford.edu/group/mappingmilitants/cgi-bin/groups> (last accessed 8 September 2017); Saskia Baas (2016), 'Syria's armed opposition: a spotlight on the moderates', *Small Arms Survey*, Dispatch No. 5, January, <www.smallarmssurvey.org/fileadmin/docs/R-SANA/SANA-Dispatch5-Syria-armed-opposition.pdf> (last accessed 8 September 2017).
52. Ignacio Alvarez-Ossorio (2016), *Siria: Revolución, sectarismo y yihad*. Madrid: La Catarata.
53. These include, amongst others, a follow up of videos, social media conversations, and narratives of the Syrian National Coalition.
54. Pierret, 'Syrie: État sans nation ou nation sans état ?' p. 182.
55. Focus group with Syrian NGO leaders based in Gaziantep: Shafak, This is my life and Network for Supporting Palestinian Camps (December 2015).
56. Interviews with members of a Syrian association based in Gaziantep and in Lebanon (June 2014 and June 2016).
57. Ussama Makdissi (2000), *The Culture of Sectarianism: Community, History, and Violence in Nineteenth-Century Ottoman Lebanon*. Berkeley and Los Angeles: University of California Press.
58. Benedict Anderson (1991), *Imagined Communities: Reflections on the Origin and Spread of Nationalism*. London: Verso.
59. Stéphane Valter (2002), *La construction nationale syrienne: Légitimation de la nature communautaire du pouvoir par le discours historique*. Paris: CNRS éditions.
60. Pierret, 'Syrie: État sans nation ou nation sans état ?' p. 182.

Chapter 20

Out of the ashes: the rise of an anti-sectarian discourse in post-2011 Iraq

Chérine Chams El-Dine

Following the popular uprisings that swept across the Arab world in 2010–11, most of the studies exploring these momentous expressions of people's power have focused on Egypt, Tunisia, Libya, Yemen, and to a lesser extent, Syria and Bahrain. Iraq, meanwhile, has seemed to fall outside the limelight of scholarly interest even though throughout 2011 here too demonstrations erupted in numerous provinces and cities over multiple issues, including corruption, insecurity, poor services and political reform. At the time, the Iraqi government under Prime Minister Nouri al-Maliki (r.2006–14) deployed heavy-handed tactics to squash the protests. Galvanised from outside institutional politics by a cross-section of ordinary citizens and youth, neither Shi'a nor Sunni Islamist parties and movements took part in the popular protests of 2011. Indeed, they considered the protests as targeting them and opposing their rule, thus, they rather tried to thwart the popular movement. Receiving neither coverage in the local media nor support from any foreign state, both popular mobilisation and repression at the time went relatively unnoticed. Meanwhile, another major cycle of protest erupted at the end of July 2015, with demonstrators denouncing the sectarian and corrupt nature of the current political system.

Many scholars have argued that sectarianism took an increasingly ominous role in the wake of the Arab uprisings, especially in the Gulf Cooperation Council (GCC) states, where nervous Sunni rulers (particularly in Bahrain and Saudi Arabia) felt threatened and tried to consolidate their power in the face of popular protests led by Shi'a and other groups long prevented from fully participating in political/public life.[1] In Iraq, the post-2011 situation, meanwhile, presented itself differently, insofar as here it had been Shi'a Islamist parties that had tightened their grip on power since the fall of Saddam Hussein (r.1979–2003) in 2003, with al-Maliki's rule becoming increasingly authoritarian since the departure of the American armed forces in 2011.

This chapter argues that the 2011 Iraqi protests gave birth to a larger anti-sectarian protest movement that, culminating in 2015–16, called for political reforms and better living conditions, and questioned the legitimacy of the incumbent Shi'a Islamist parties that tried to stifle the movement using intimidation, repression and the spreading of false rumours. As will become apparent below, in fact, this movement challenged the very foundations of the post-2003 political order in Iraq, which revolved around institutionalised sectarian and other communal identities used by the so-called 'political entrepreneurs' to create constituencies and rally popular support, instead of bridging the divide between the country's Shi'a and Sunni communities.[2] To this day, this order is marked by the empowerment of political actors (mostly exiled politicians under the former Baathist regime) whose obsession with sect-centric politics corresponded with American interests in – and conception of – a new Iraq. As Haddad asserted, this obsession of the Iraqi opposition in exile – which came to power after the fall of Saddam Hussein – with ethno-sectarian identities shaped, or at least reinforced, American views on Iraq.[3] Thus, the post-2003 nation-building process consolidated subnational identities, and created a power structure reproducing sectarianism and bringing about a totally dysfunctional and corrupt administrative order.

Drawing on a range of primary sources,[4] the chapter provides first an overview of the 2011 uprising in Iraq and its demise, before focusing on the emergence of new contentious actors and their anti-sectarian discourse through an analysis of the slogans and banners of the 2015–16 protest movement – the largest popular movement hitherto challenging the post-2003 political order in Iraq.

2011, the forgotten uprising

Concomitant to the onset of popular protests across the Arab world, Iraqi mass demonstrations erupted in February 2011, culminating on 25 February in the so-called 'Iraqi day of rage', when demonstrations attracting thousands of Iraqis were held in around sixty towns and cities across sixteen out of eighteen Iraqi provinces to denounce corruption, price hikes and unemployment.[5] Slogans used by protesters such as 'enough silence', 'enough patience' and 'down to a democracy that transforms bad to worse' clearly expressed widespread dissatisfaction with governmental impotence and an incapacity of state institutions to improve the daily life of Iraqi citizens in a relatively rich country. The explicitly national character of the protest movement that took place in Shi'a and Sunni provinces – and also included the Iraqi Kurdish provinces of Irbil and Sulaymaniyah – was set against a sectarian discourse that had dominated Iraqi politics since 2003.

Like many of the other uprisings that shook the Arab world in 2011, the Iraqi protest movement was youth-led and fashioned by ordinary people, marked by the absence of established political parties (either Shi'a or Sunni) and largely peaceful. Moreover, this movement, like its Arab uprising counterparts, was leaderless and non-hierarchical in character, developing around networked forms of organisation that relied heavily on non-traditional means of mobilisation.[6] These means included, for instance, a number of Facebook groups/pages that mobilised for, and supported, the 2011 protests, such as the 'the Great Iraqi Revolution', 'the Iraqi Revolution of 25 February', 'Support the Iraqi Youth Uprising', and 'the Free Iraqis' Revolution' pages. Typically these Facebook pages would post news, communiqués (issued by the organising movements), photos and videos of protests taking place all over Iraq, as well as of demonstrations held in other countries in solidarity with the Iraqi people.[7]

One of the most important figures of the 2011 protest movement is the Iraqi journalist Uday al-Zaidi, the leader of al-Haraka al-Sha'biyya li-Inqaz al-'Iraq (Popular Movement to Save Iraq),[8] which is a popular, youth-led organisation. Uday and his brothers Durgham[9] and Muntadhir (famed for throwing a shoe at President George W. Bush in December 2008) founded this movement and were among the main instigators of the protests all over Iraq. Other movements and coalitions emerged as well and organised/coordinated the demonstrations and sit-ins in various provinces, such as for instance Harakat Tahrir al-Janub (Movement to Liberate the South), al-Jabha al-Sha'biyya li-Inqaz Karkuk (Popular Front to Save Kirkuk), al-Rabita al-Wataniyya li-Shuyukh 'Asha'ir al-Janub wal-Furat al-Awsat (National Organisation of Tribal Leaders of the South and the Central Euphrates), I'tilaf al-Khamis wal-'Ishrin min Shabat (25 February Coalition) and al-Thawra al-'Iraqiyya al-Kubra (Great Iraqi Revolution).[10] Importantly, all of these movements were cross-sectarian in composition and representative of different groups in Iraqi society – including tribal leaders and students – from all over Iraq, as clearly implied by these movements' names. Meanwhile, other civil society activists affiliated with established labour unions, women's groups, such as for example Munadhamat Huriyyat al-Mar'a fi al-'Iraq (Organisation of Women's Freedom in Iraq), and members of al-Hizb al-Shiyu'i al-'Iraqi (Iraqi Communist Party, ICP) got involved too.[11] The rallies' locations and times were transmitted via Facebook or written on paper currency and circulated for those without access to social media networks.

Protests typically took place after Friday prayers and were themed around particular issues, such as for instance the 'Friday of the Imprisoned' (18 March 2011), demanding the release of thousands of Iraqi political prisoners, the 'Friday of Salvation' (9 April 2011), calling for an unconditional departure of the United States occupying forces,[12] or the 'Friday of Retribution' (7 June 2011), asking for the resignation of the al-Maliki government[13] and the formation of a transitional government of technocrats.[14] Other demands voiced by the protest movement ranged from calls for the abolition of a sect-based quota system in formal politics, an end to Iranian interference in Iraqi affairs, to demands for the improvement of basic services and for the creation of more public sector jobs. At the time, observers criticised the heterogeneous nature of the protesters' demands as too disparate to actually achieve anything, making the whole movement prone to fracturing and fragmentation.[15]

Some analysts, meanwhile, maintained that the 2011 demonstrations in Iraq remained narrowly circumscribed due to the consociational nature of political power that entailed popular mobilisation within sub-state groups and prevented other parts of the population from joining in, leaving the political regime essentially untouched.[16] While partially true, this reading overlooks the range of tactics used by the al-Maliki government and its Shi'a allies to squash the protests. Security forces violently dispersed protesters, and government-backed armed thugs infiltrated the demonstrations, injuring and sexually molesting peaceful protesters.[17] Several demonstrators were shot dead during violent clashes with security forces that used live ammunition. Journalists covering the protests were threatened, attacked, their equipment confiscated/destroyed, and some of them were detained. TV stations' offices were raided by security forces to prevent further broadcasting of the demonstrations.[18] As part of the government's anti-protest campaign, media outlets – which are generally controlled by political parties belonging to the ruling coalition – were instructed not to cover the protests in order to stifle the movement. The United States, meanwhile, seemingly permitted the use of violence by the Iraqi security forces and turned a blind eye to protesters' demands. According to some observers, American helicopters flew over and monitored the protests, which was considered a sign of support for the Iraqi government's repressive measures.[19] Thus, keeping Iraq's stability following the withdrawal of the United States armed forces from Iraq[20] seemed to have been a priority for the American administration at the expense of the protesters' reformist demands/aspirations.

Warnings against demonstrations were issued by the al-Maliki government through meetings with sheikhs and notables, in which they threatened to kill and arrest anyone participating in the protests. Government vehicles with loudspeakers also drove through Baghdad's main streets, calling residents to refrain from participating in the protests. In a blatant effort to delegitimise the protest organisers and its participants, al-Maliki accused them of being remnants of the erstwhile Hizb al-Ba'ath al-'Arabi al-Ishtiraki fi al-'Iraq (Arab Socialist Baath Party of Iraq), or the Baath regime. To justify these allegations, elements close to the government infiltrated the protests, distributed photographs of the former Iraqi president Saddam Hussein and raised slogans glorifying the Baath party – as witnessed by local journalists.[21]

Meanwhile, some government-friendly Shi'a clerics and political forces warned against the exploitation of demonstrations by those described as 'Saddamists', 'Baathists' and 'extremists', and told their followers to stay away. While Ayatollah Ali al-Sistani – Iraq's most pre-eminent *marja'* (religious source of emulation) – affirmed Iraqis' right to peaceful protest, he expressed his concerns regarding the possible manipulation of the protests by groups he described as 'enemies of the Iraqi people'. According to him this could turn the demonstrations from a peaceful process of dissent into a confrontation with the Iraqi authorities and a chaotic situation.[22] As for Muqtada al-Sadr, leader of al-Tayyar al-Sadri (Sadrist Movement), he called for the postponement of the protests in order to give the government a period of grace to improve its performance and public services.[23] Thus, neither al-Sistani nor al-Sadr backed the protesters' demands or endeavours. On the contrary, al-Sistani's statement and al-Sadr's call for a grace period saved the al-Maliki government and indirectly led to the demise of the protest movement by the summer of 2011.

In their analysis of the effect of repression on protest movements' strategies and fate, Mounia Bennani-Chraïbi and Olivier Fillieule concluded that it largely depends on the degree of cohesion and organisational structure of the groups, the amount of public sympathy with, and interest in, their cause, and the international support they enjoy. In this context they noted that when confronted with harsh repression, or unfavourable conditions, protest movements may disappear but are likely to transform themselves into 'abeyance structures' which constitute potential reservoirs for future popular mobilisation.[24] Thus, whilst the regime's severe crackdown on the demonstrations, its anti-protests propaganda backed by Shi'a clerics, scorching summertime temperatures and the lack of media coverage and foreign support caused the protest movement to fade away by the end of the summer of 2011, abeyance or latent structures remained in place.[25]

Although the wave of nation-wide anti-government demonstrations had died down by mid-2011 – and did not develop the same intensity and scale of the uprisings taking place elsewhere in the region – they had seriously questioned the sectarian nature of Iraqi politics and paved the way for subsequent protests. Indeed, despite the period of time separating the two waves of popular protests, some similarities exist between the 2011 and subsequent 2015–16 Iraqi protest movements, especially regarding their national/non-sectarian character and tools of mobilisation. These similarities coincide, however, with noticeable differences in the composition of those forces participating in the 2015–16 protests as well as the evolving structure and longevity of the protest movement, as shall be discussed in the following section.

The 2015–16 uprising: a movement in progress

The second major wave of popular protests rocking Iraqi politics post-2011 commenced on 16 July 2015 in the southern oil-rich province of Basra, when people spontaneously took to the streets to denounce poor public services, especially power outages during extreme summer heat largely exceeding 50°C.

The demonstrators burned tyres to disrupt traffic on the main roads, stormed and burned the headquarters of al-Majlis al-A'la al-Islami al-'Iraqi (Islamic Supreme Council of Iraq or ISCI), one of the governing Shi'a Islamist political parties, and of the Basra city council, office of governor Majid al-Nasrawi. Confrontations between protesters and security forces led to the death of one demonstrator and two others were injured.[26]

The protest movement then spread to other Iraqi provinces – aside from the Kurdish provinces and the territories under the control of the so-called al-Dawla al-Islamiyya (Islamic State, IS) – and reached Baghdad's Tahrir Square on 31 July 2015, when civil society activists called for a popular mobilisation through social media networks. As in 2011, the latter offered Iraqis, especially the youth, a relatively uncensored space to present their views, thus quickly emerging as a prime channel to challenge the *status quo* and organise dissent. Besides rallying against poor public services, this time the protests also turned into an expression of popular anger against rampant corruption and abuse of power by top officials that cost Iraq dearly in its war against IS.[27] Despite the specificity of each province, four key demands thus united the protesters in 2015–16: (1) improving public services, (2) fighting corruption and holding corrupted officials to account, (3) reforming the judiciary and the security sector, and (4) reforming the political system with a view to abolishing the sectarian quota system, also locally known as *mahassah*.[28]

The protests themselves gained momentum during the first week of August 2015 when Ayatollah Ali al-Sistani backed protesters' demands and urged newly installed PM Haider al-Abadi – in charge since September 2014 – to 'rebel against corruption and sectarianism', to 'take bold measures in order to fight corruption, and to sack incompetent officials regardless of their party affiliation or sectarian/ethnic background'.[29] Traditionally inclined to preserve political stability, the *marja'* thus adopted a fundamentally different stance towards the protest movement compared to 2011, pushing al-Abadi to implement drastic reforms that could satisfy popular demands. Moreover, on 20 August 2015, in a written statement from his office in response to questions from the Agence France-Presse, al-Sistani warned that Iraq could be 'dragged to partition' if reforms were not properly carried out by the government.[30] The reason for al-Sistani's intervention this time around is likely to have resided in his fears that a political vacuum would then be filled by more radical political forces and Shi'a pro-Iranian militias involved in the fight against IS.

The following pages will present a profile of the key actors involved in the 2015–16 protests – to explain the demographic and evolving composition of the protest movement – and provide an analysis of the protests' emblematic slogans. The latter analysis will shed light on the rise of an anti-sectarian discourse during the 2015–16 protests that challenged and rejected the sect-centric rhetoric and policies of the incumbent political elites.

Anatomy of the protest movement: new actors and potential divisions

Although widely considered *sha'biyya* (popular) – given that the bulk of the protesters were non-partisan Iraqi citizens who simply rejected the corrupt ethno-sectarian political system and the ruling (Shi'a) elites dominating the political scene since 2003 – several formal and informal groupings took part in the 2015–16 protests. Spearheading the protests was the so-called al-Tayyar al-Madani[31] (Civil Current), whose core was composed of independent secular civil society activists, academics, intellectuals, media professionals and artists. The ICP and some of its allies within al-Tahaluf al-Madani al-Dimuqrati (Civil Democratic Alliance), a secular electoral coalition formed before the 2014 Iraqi parliamentary elections that included Hizb al-Watani al-Dimuqrati (National Democratic Party), Hizb al-Ummah (Nation Party) and Hizb al-Sha'ab (People's Party), meanwhile constituted the largest partisan/established political forces present in the protests. Some ICP members, in fact, were deemed to have been among the driving forces behind the protests,[32] playing an active role in the coordination of protest slogans and demands across Iraqi provinces.[33] Thus the protests were largely cross-sectarian in composition, involving Iraqis from every walk of life: ordinary citizens, intellectuals, civil society activists, and a few established secular political forces with a non-sectarian membership base.

As in 2011, most Sunni and Shi'a Islamist parties and movements refrained from participating in the popular mobilisation of 2015–16, except for the Shi'a Sadrist Movement, which joined *en masse* the protests in February 2016 and 'Asa'ib Ahl al-Haq (League of the Righteous), an armed scission of the Sadrist Movement, which briefly took part in the protests. Indeed, unlike in much of the rest of the Arab world, where Islamist movements took part in anti-regime protests in 2011, Iraq's principal Islamist parties belonged to the governing coalition and were thus not active partners in the protest movement. On the contrary, having then been at the receiving end of the protesters' fury, they were largely anti-protest and sought to undermine them. As one prominent ICP figure asserted, Shi'a Islamist parties and movements 'considered the protests as targeting and opposing them, thus, many of them have tried to stop or thwart the movement'.[34] Thus, Shi'a political forces launched a propaganda campaign to counter the protests and render them less credible, claiming for instance that the uprising was merely 'an external plot to undermine the political process and secularise Iraq'.[35] They moreover accused the activists of being *mulhidin* (atheists) and Baathists,[36] thus seeking to delegitimise their movement and demands in the eyes of the wider populace. By late August 2015, activists and journalists were attacked in the provinces of Basra, Najaf and Babil. According to these activists it was Islamist parties belonging to the Shi'a ruling bloc – namely al-Maliki's wing of the ruling Hizb al-Da'wa al-Islamiyya (Da'wa Party, DP)[37] and Ammar al-Hakim's ISCI – which had sent their henchmen within the security services, or their militias, to intimidate activists and to scare off and discourage protesters.[38] However, these allegations are entirely based on the activists' testimonies and accounts of these incidents, and nothing has been proven to date to verify these claims. Another instance, meanwhile, occurred in Basra when unidentified armed men stormed a sit-in tent, injured two protesters and distributed leaflets threatening demonstrators.[39] Similarly, men in civilian clothes – claiming to be intelligence officers – abducted and beat demonstrators on numerous occasions following August 2015. On 18 September, for instance, three activists on their way out of a demonstration in Baghdad's Tahrir Square were grabbed and carried off (blindfolded) in a pick-up. They were beaten, interrogated separately and released after signing a pledge not to demonstrate again. The activists were threatened with abduction, torture and death if they spoke to the media.[40]

It is evident from the above then that the ruling Shi'a political forces sought to resist demands for change at all costs, resorting to violent repression in an attempt to quell the mass protests. Given Muqtada al-Sadr's participation in the protests from February 2016 onwards, it is also clear, moreover, that the Shi'a political elites were divided on the issue.[41] Whilst al-Maliki's wing of the ruling DP and the ISCI opposed the protest movement and considered it a threat on their hold on power, the Sadrist Movement and its allies supported it, with al-Sadr calling his followers to join the popular demonstrations.[42]

By proclaiming himself *ra'yi al-islah*, or godfather of the reform and the anti-corruption movement, al-Sadr called for massive protests in support of al-Abadi's endeavour to nominate a 'technocratic' government from February 2016 onwards. Al-Sadr's initiatives/calls for mobilisation were usually coordinated with al-Tayyar al-Madani, or in support of al-Tayyar's initial calls for demonstrations. However, the Sadrist Movement and al-Sadr himself had gradually appeared to be the key drivers of the protest movement, largely owing to the large number of the movement's followers and its strong organisational structure.

It is interesting to note in this context, that al-Sadr himself had made a considerable effort to change his reputation as a radical, rebel and firebrand after his return from exile in Iran in 2011. In doing so, he tried to forge a new image as *tha'ir dhida al-zulm wa al-fasad* (rebel against injustice and corruption) for himself. Thus, in a public gesture underpinning his anti-corruption credentials he referred two former cabinet ministers belonging to the al-Ahrar bloc[43] (his own political bloc in parliament) at the end of February 2016 to the Integrity Commission, which is in charge of investigating corruption cases.[44] As part of this transformation, al-Sadr finally also sought to cast himself in his discourse as a nationalist and populist public figure who objected to Iraq's growing sectarian politics, although of course his own popularity remained very much linked to the spiritual legacies of his father and uncle, two prominent Shi'a clerics.[45] Thus, his main audience and followers remain to be found among the Shi'a community who not only revere him for the religious heritage he represents, but also for his capacity to voice and channel their political discontent and to transform it into political power on the ground. By backing the protest movement of 2015–16, and by trying to distance himself from the leaders of other Shi'a Islamist political parties, al-Sadr undoubtedly pursued his own political agenda. Indeed by throwing his weight behind the anti-government protests, he seems willing to forfeit his political bloc's presence in the current government in exchange for maintaining his role as a leader of the anti-corruption and reform movement. In other words, rather than seeking imminent political gains, al-Sadr appears to have focused on bolstering his personal status as a national/unifying politician and his movement's position in Iraqi politics. Accordingly he has positioned himself as a key actor to be reckoned with in future political arrangements/alliances in order to effectively compete in the 2018 parliamentary elections.

On 18 March 2016, al-Sadr called his followers to stage a sit-in at the gates of Baghdad's Green Zone, which houses Iraqi government institutions and foreign embassies. Then, following weeks of political turmoil and in an unprecedented show of force, al-Sadr spearheaded and launched the protesters' breach of the Green Zone on 30 April. On the one hand, this was a tactical move by al-Sadr to put pressure on Iraqi lawmakers to approve al-Abadi's allegedly technocratic government. On the other hand, it constituted a clever ploy to demonstrate his ability to gather and control crowds who respond to his calls, and to hold the Green Zone – the country's centre of power – at his mercy.[46]

As mentioned above, the other Shi'a Islamist force participating in the 2015–16 protest movement, besides the Sadrist Movement, was 'Asa'ib Ahl al-Haq. The League is a pro-Iranian armed scission of the Sadrist Movement – involved in the Iraqi forces' fight against IS – that aims for the establishment of a Shi'a Islamic government in Iraq and Shari'ah (Islamic law) throughout the country. For the most part, members of 'Asa'ib Ahl al-Haq partook sporadically in the popular mobilisation in order to strengthen the League's political position as one of the main Shi'a militias. Generally known as being critical of the al-Abadi government, it called for the replacement of the current parliamentary system with a presidential one, which could give pro-Iranian political forces and militias a better chance to control the Iraqi political system.[47] Its demands did not have much echo within the broader protest movement, however, and its participation in the protests gradually waned.

Overall the participation of the Sadrist Movement, and more broadly of Islamist forces, in the 2015–16 protests proved to be rather problematic. This is evident in the debate among secular civil society activists at the time – the initial instigators of the demonstrations – on the identity of the protest movement. While some activists highlighted the secular character of the protests and considered any partnership with Islamists (including Sadrists) a potential threat to the movement, other important figures within al-Tayyar al-Madani believed that identity had no place in this debate and emphasised instead the national character of the protesters' demands. This second group of activists aimed at enlarging the uprising's popular base by consolidating their alliance with pro-reform Islamist forces. This they sought to achieve, first by capitalising on al-Sistani's support of the protests in order to rally modest Shi'a who were generally weary about the uprising's overall secular slogans. They moreover multiplied visits and meetings with al-Sistani's representatives in Najaf and, from November 2015 onwards, also with Muqtada al-Sadr himself. At the time, some members of al-Tayyar al-Madani believed that an alliance with the Sadrist Movement was conceivable and beneficial to the protesters' cause, given the latter's popular base among the Shi'a population and its leader's pro-reform and anti-corruption stances.[48] Moreover, it was felt that al-Sadr's militias would be able to help protect the demonstrators, who – as demonstrated above – were constantly being attacked by thugs/militiamen of those Islamist parties in power.[49] This approach, was however, not uniformly shared within al-Tayyar al-Madani, with some of its secular activists refusing any coordination with Islamist political forces.[50]

Apart from two big rallies calling for a reform of the electoral process to avoid facilitating the return of the same 'corrupt' political elites to power, by February and March 2017 the protest momentum conspicuously slowed down. This could be at least partially explained by the popular fatigue after almost two years of protests, as well as by the (military) mobilisation against IS, which was widely seen by Iraqis across the board as a priority and as an urgent national security concern.

In sum, the involvement of the Sadrists in the 2015–16 protests certainly enlarged its popular base and thus its capacity to exert pressure on the Shi'a Islamist forces in power. At the same time, however, it also divided the movement's secular constituents, particularly al-Tayyar al-Madani, and changed at least the image, if not the identity, of the protests. As the Sadrists were much more visible, they stole the limelight from the initial instigators of the protest movement, though surprisingly – as shall become apparent below – its cross-sectarian essence and discourse remained alive.

The uprising through its slogans: the rise of an anti-sectarian discourse

Like the 2011 protests in Iraq and across other Arab states, the 2015–16 protest movement relied heavily on social media networks to organise rallies and circulate slogans, news items and videos. In fact, Iraqis have never been so creative in criticising their political leaders or denouncing their poor living conditions. As part of the protests, they designed cartoons, created sarcastic slogans and produced videos that were circulated on social media to express their understanding of the political situation outside the bounds of sectarian/communally based identities.

Two emblematic slogans have marked the protests and emphasised the protesters' fight against corruption and sectarianism. These were: 'bism al-din baguna al-haramiyya' (in the name of religion we were robbed by the looters) and 'hashd[51] dhida al-irhab wa hashd dhida al-fasad' (a popular mobilisation against terrorism and another one against corruption). Through these and other slogans protesters sought to reject not only high-level corruption, but also the instrumentalisation of religion prevalent since 2003 to control power and wealth.

By far some of the most poignant anti-sectarian slogans were produced in the mostly Shi'a provinces of Basra, Najaf and Karbala, where slogans circulated such as 'ma'an li mukafahat tujjar al-din wa mukafahat al-suraq wa tujjar al-dam wa kul man irtada al-'imama al-bayda' wal sawda' min ajl al-sulta wal mal' (let us come together in order to fight the merchants of religion and blood, to fight the looters and all those wearing a white or black turban[52] in order to control power and wealth), or 'al-mutajirun bism 'Ali aswa' min man harabuh' (those trading in the name of Ali are worse than those who fought against him). By referring to Ali ibn Abi Talib, the Shi'a-revered Imam, the latter slogan specifically targeted those Islamist parties in power that used Shi'a sectarian identity/ideology to rally communal support and accumulate wealth. Other slogans, meanwhile, expressed the demonstrators' anger with Shi'a Islamist officials and their sectarian politics, such as '555 bidaya li 'Iraq jadid yahkumuhu al-ta'ifiyun' (the electoral list 555[53] inaugurated the rule of sectarian politicians in a new Iraq), or 'ma nrid wahid multahi, nrid wahid yastahi' (we do not want a bearded/Islamist official, we want one who has shame). In the same vein, a cartoon that circulated in the streets of Basra represented the incumbent parties as an enormous octopus, with each of its tentacles embodying one of Iraq's major problems such as corruption, clientelism, crime and unemployment. Judging by this and other cartoons/banners, the protesters thus clearly drew strong links between corruption, sectarianism and the rise of IS, which (by their banners) appear to have been considered as two sides of the same coin. Many demonstrators, meanwhile, called for a *dawla madaniyya* (a secular state) and a reform of the political system to put an end to the post-2003 ethno-sectarian quota system, thus directly questioning the legitimacy of the current ruling Shi'a elites. Moreover, the slogan 'Tehran barra barra, Karbala' tibqa hurra' (Tehran out, out, Karbala will become free), chanted in the streets of Karbala, revealed the national, and to an extent even nationalistic, essence of the movement. Sectarian or ethnic slogans have been remarkably absent during the protests and only Iraqi flags have been raised. Besides the movement's nationalist fervour, this anti-Iranian sentiment could also be associated with

Iran's earlier support for some Shiʻa political leaders, a fact that linked Iran and these leaders in the popular imagination/mind. The activists have also sought to defy anti-reform forces, who had bet on the rapid decline of the movement, with slogans proving its resilience such as 'jumaʻa wara jumaʻa, al-fasid nittalaʻuh' (Friday[54] after Friday, the corrupt will be kicked out).

Another symbolic slogan reflecting one of the main characteristics of the protests is 'la qiyada kulluna mutadhahirun' (no leadership – we are all protesters). This slogan clearly underlines both the strength and weakness of the movement and raises the issue of its own survival. The fact that it was leaderless and not monopolised by any of the well-established political forces clearly constituted a major incentive for Iraqis from all walks of life regardless of their political affiliation to take part in the protests, thus making them a proper moment of popular dissent. In each province *tansiqiyyat* (organisational committees) were formed to harmonise slogans and ensure the peaceful character of the protests. During the initial months of the protest cycle, the organisation of demonstrations across the country remained horizontal, without any centralised coordination between provinces. With time passing, however, some of the most involved activists became aware that the lack of a centralised leadership – in order to coordinate the protests' slogans and demands and to negotiate on behalf of the protesters with the Iraqi government – had weakened their capacity of action and their ability to impose needed reforms. After the end of 2015, coordination meetings between *tansiqiyyat* did then take place more frequently within each province and across provinces. Thus a few steps were taken towards the 'transformation of the uprising into a more homogeneous organisational and political structure, while preserving its diversity'.[55] If ultimately successful, this is the only strategy that could sustain the protest movement, make its demands more vocal and strengthen its bargaining power *vis-à-vis* the regime.

Thus, through banners and slogans chanted in the streets or circulated on social media, Iraqis expressed their anger during the protests of 2015–16. As evidenced in their demands and slogans, these protests formed a unique moment in recent Iraqi history: a moment that rejected not only corruption and bad governance, but also the sectarian logic that had come to define post-2003 domestic politics.

Conclusion

In all the Arab uprisings the calls for a change of leadership were largely of a secular not of a religious inspiration/aspiration. Thus, despite the participation of some Islamist political forces in the uprisings, religious agendas and slogans were noticeably absent.[56] On this basis, the Iraqi protest movement that was forged concomitantly to the Arab uprisings in 2011, and then again in 2015–16, is perfectly in line with the logic and essence of this Arab wave of popular mobilisations. Indeed, the 2015–16 protest movement created a positive dynamic with the rise of an anti-sectarian discourse and of new actors who mobilised for almost two years and formulated their demands largely outside the bounds of the sectarian or communally based identity politics and rhetoric that have been at the heart of the Shi'a Islamist ruling establishment ever since it took power in 2003–4.

So far the protest movement has been considered a reformist and not a revolutionary one. Its main figures believe that a change within the regime and not the change of regime is needed. The Iraqi protests are thus an example of what Asef Bayat[57] called 'Arab refo-lutions', a term he used to describe the 2010–12 Arab uprisings. According to Bayat, these revolutionary movements 'enjoy enormous social power, but lack administrative authorities; they garner remarkable hegemony but do not actually rule', and they 'want to push for reforms in, and through the institutions of the incumbent states'.[58]

To date, the Iraqi protest movement faces two main challenges, namely (1) ensuring the unity and cohesion of al-Tayyar al-Madani, whose parameters, alliances, and strategies are ill-defined, making it prone to internal division, and (2) transforming this popular momentum into a coordinated central decision-making structure that could represent voices of dissent, sustain pressure and produce change. Otherwise it will fade away like all 'refo-lutions' that carry the perils of 'counter-revolutionary restoration',[59] especially in the Iraqi context where non-sectarian voices have very limited opportunities to survive and rally support.

Notes

1. Lawrence G. Potter (2013), *Sectarian Politics in the Persian Gulf*. London: Hurst, p. 1.
2. Harith Hasan al-Qarawee (2014), 'Iraq's sectarian crisis: a legacy of exclusion', *Carnegie Endowment for International Peace*, 23 April, <http://carnegieendowment.org/2014/04/23/iraq-s-sectarian-crisis-legacy-of-exclusion-pub-55372> (last accessed 8 September 2016).
3. Fanar Haddad (2016), 'Shia-centric state building and Sunni rejection in post-2003 Iraq', *Carnegie Endowment for International Peace*, 7 January, pp. 8–13, <http://carnegieendowment.org/2016/01/07/shia-centric-state-building-and-sunni-rejection-in-post-2003-iraq-pub-62408> (last accessed 8 September 2016).
4. The author conducted interviews with Iraqi activists who participated in the 2011 and 2015–16 protests, and collected first-hand material (slogans, cartoons, and videos) that were circulated on social media.
5. Serene Assir (2012), 'Iraq: the forgotten uprising lives on', *Al-Akhbar*, 28 February, <http://english.al-akhbar.com/content/iraq-forgotten-uprising-lives> (last accessed 7 September 2016).

6. Rashid Khalidi (2012), 'Preliminary historical observations on the Arab revolutions of 2011', in Bassam Haddad, Rosie Bsheer and Ziad Abu-Rish (eds), *The Dawn of the Arab Uprisings*. London: Pluto Press, 2012, pp. 9–16.

7. Ahmed K. Al-Rawi (2014), 'The Arab Spring and online protests in Iraq', *International Journal of Communication*, 8, pp. 924–29.

8. The Popular Movement to Save Iraq faded away with the demise of the 2011 protests. Other organising structures emerged during the 2015–16 protests.

9. Both Uday and Durgham al-Zaidi were harassed, assaulted and detained by the Iraqi authorities, as vocal organisers of the protests.

10. Ali Issa (2015), *Against all Odds: Voices of Popular Struggle in Iraq*. Washington, DC: Tadween Publishing, pp. 40–1.

11. Ibid., p. 6.

12. Sit-ins were set up in front of the US military bases all over Iraq.

13. The government tried to contain dissatisfaction in order to abort the protests: al-Maliki announced a grace period (of 100 days) to improve his government's performance, promised to cut high officials' salaries, to create jobs and to address the problem of basic food items scarcity and rising prices. The so-called 'Friday of Retribution' corresponded to the end of al-Maliki's grace period to address the protesters' demands. Thus the call for a sit-in on 7 June 2011 expressed a broadly held sentiment among Iraqis that the government's promises had not been met.

14. Issa, *Against all Odds: Voices of Popular Struggle in Iraq*, pp. 13–23.

15. Assir, 'Iraq: the forgotten uprising lives on'.

16. Eberhard Kienle (2015), 'Popular contestation, regime transformation and state formation', in Eberhard Kienle and Nadine Sika (eds), *The Arab Uprisings: Transforming and Challenging State Power*. London: IB Tauris, pp. 141–2.

17. Human Rights Watch (2012), 'Iraq: intensifying crackdown on free speech, protests', *World Report*, 22 January, <www.hrw.org/news/2012/01/22/iraq-intensifying-crack-down-free-speech-protests> (last accessed 9 September 2016).

18. Amnesty International, 'Days of rage: protests and repression in Iraq', *Amnesty International Report*, 12 April, <www.amnesty.org/en/documents/MDE14/020/2011/en/> (last accessed 7 September 2016).

19. Zeinab Saleh (2011), 'Revolutionaries under occupation', *Jadaliyya*, 30 April, <http://bit.ly/1SQa36f> (last accessed 8 September 2016).

20. The withdrawal of US military forces from Iraq was completed on 18 December 2011.

21. Kheder Abbas Atwan (2012), 'The political regime in Iraq between reform and legitimacy: an analytic perceptive on the 2011 protests', *Arab Center for Research and Policy Studies Research Papers*, 16 January, pp. 17–8, <http://english.dohainstitute.org/release/db281bc3-5eaf-419e-a59f-3d7a612231df> (last accessed 8 September 2016).

22. Ibid.

23. Ibid.

24. Mounia Bennani-Chraïbi and Olivier Fillieule (2003), 'Exit, voice, loyalty et bien d'autres choses', in Mounia Bennani-Chraïbi and Olivier Fillieule (eds), *Résistances et protestations dans les sociétés musulmanes*. Paris: Presses de Sciences Po, pp. 90–101.

25. At the end of 2012, protests against perceived discrimination of Sunnis were sparked first in restive al-Anbar, then spread to Nineveh, Salah al-Din and Sunni parts of Baghdad. In the following weeks, tens of thousands of Sunnis took to the streets to express their frustrations, blocking the main trade route to Jordan and Syria. Despite the fact that some of the protesters' demands reflected common grievances among Iraqis (such as security and services), the protests have only taken place in predominantly Sunni

areas; they have been portrayed by the authorities as 'Sunni protests', and some of their slogans were considered sectarian and did not replicate the 2011 dynamics. See e.g. Fanar Haddad (2013), 'Can a Sunni Spring turn into an Iraqi Spring?' *Foreign Policy*, 7 January, <http://foreignpolicy.com/2013/01/07/can-a-sunni-spring-turn-into-an-iraqi-spring/> (last accessed 8 September 2016).

26. Anon. (2015), 'Lajnat al-Basra al-Amniya: Maqtal Mutadhahir wa Isabat Ithnayn bi Tadhahura Ihtijajiya Shamal al-Muhafadha' [Basra's Security Committee: one demonstrator died and another injured during a protest in the north of the province], *Al-Sumaria*, 17 July, <http://bit.ly/2kZaz9Y> (last accessed 7 September 2016); Anon. (2015). 'Mutadhahirun fil Basra Yamna'un Artal Sharikat al-Naft min al-Murur Ihtijajan 'ala Inqita' al-Kahruba' [Demonstrators in Basra blocked the way of oil companies' convoys to protest against power cuts], *Iraq News Agency*, 17 July, <http://bit.ly/1PVGlbl> (last accessed 7 September 2016).

27. IS controlled large swathes of land in the Western and Northern Iraqi provinces during summer 2014. Most of the occupied territories have since been liberated by Iraqi forces, including the city of Mosul (Iraq's second biggest city).

28. Author's account based on the demonstrators' slogans and demands.

29. Usama Mahdi (2015), 'Al-Sistani lil 'Abadi: Tamarrad 'ala al-Fasad wal Ta'ifiyya' [Sistani called on Abadi to rebel against corruption and sectarianism], *Elaph*, 7 August, <http://elaph.com/Web/News/2015/8/1029542.html> (last accessed 8 September 2016).

30. Anon. (2015), 'Sistani: Iraq could face partition without reform', *Al-Arabiya*, 21 August, <http://english.alarabiya.net/en/News/middle-east/2015/08/21/Iraq-could-face-partition-without-reform.html> (last accessed 8 September 2016).

31. *Madani* could be translated either as 'civil' or 'secular', which have different implications. This linguistic confusion is reflected in the disagreement among the activists on the meaning of '*madani*'; and thus on the parameters and strategies of the protest movement. In other words, who should be included or excluded in the movement became a source of division and friction within al-Tayyar al-Madani itself.

32. The leading figure of al-Tayyar al-Madani, and one of the main instigators of the protest movement, is Jassim al-Helfi who is a senior official of the ICP and member of its political bureau. Al-Helfi, along with his close friend Ahmed Abdel Hussein (an Iraqi writer and independent activist), is the most prominent figure of al-Tayyar al-Madani and its connecting link with the Islamist forces (i.e. the Sadrists and Ayatollah al-Sistani).

33. Skype interview with an Iraqi academic and activist, 23 January 2016.

34. Skype interview with a prominent figure of the ICP, 24 January 2016.

35. Omar al-Jaffal (2015), 'Al-ihtijaj wal Islah fil 'Iraq' [Uprising and Reform in Iraq], *Al-Safir al-Arabi*, 10 September, <http://arabi.assafir.com/article.asp?aid=3411&refsite=arabi&reftype=home&refzone=slider> (last accessed 7 September 2016).

36. Ibid.

37. Hizb al-Da'wa al-Islamiyya is divided between those who are loyal to the former PM Nouri al-Maliki and those loyal to the current PM Haider al-Abadi. Some intelligence and security units are still loyal to al-Maliki, who is also said to be in control of a part of al-Hashd al-Shaabi militias (the popular mobilisation forces).

38. These statements are based on activists' testimonies and accounts of the incidents on Facebook.

39. Al-Jaffal, 'Al-ihtijaj wal Islah fil 'Iraq' [Uprising and reform in Iraq].

40. Anon. (2015), 'Iraq: protesters beaten, abducted', *Human Rights Watch*, 23 October, <www.hrw.org/news/2015/10/23/iraq-protesters-beaten-abducted> (last accessed 8 September 2016).

41. On the divisions plaguing the Shi'a political establishment at the time see also Ibrahim Al-Marashi's contribution to this volume.

42. Anon. (2014), 'Mutahadith: Muqtada al-Sadr Yad'u Atba'uh lil Indimam li Ihtijajat fi Baghdad Yawm al-Juma'a' [Spokesperson: Muqtada al-Sadr calls his followers to join the Friday protest in Baghdad], Reuters, 24 August, <http://ara.reuters.com/article/topNews/idARAKCN0QT0YP20150824> (last accessed 8 September 2016).

43. Al-Sadr is the spiritual leader of the al-Ahrar bloc. Thus the latter is considered a part of the Sadrist Movement.

44. Al-Sadr's official statement, 28 February 2016, <http://jawabna.com/index.php/permalink /8755.html?print&output_type=txt&output_type=txt> (last accessed 7 September 2016).

45. Respectively Mohamed Sadiq al-Sadr and Mohamed Baqir al-Sadr, who were both senior Shi'a clerics executed by Saddam Hussein.

46. Mohammed Salih (2016), 'Muqtada al-Sadr, the most powerful man in Iraqi Politics?', Al-Monitor, 13 May, <www.al-monitor.com/pulse/originals/2016/05/iraq-shiite-cleric-muqtada-al-sadr-change-politics.html>(last accessed 9 September 2016).

47. Harith Hasan (2015), 'Aba'ad al-Ihtijajat al-Ijtima'iya fil 'Iraq wa Mo'tayat al-Khilaf al-Shi'i' [Dimensions of the social mobilization in Iraq and the Or of the Shi'ite Disagreement], Al Jazeera Center for Studies, 17 August, <http://studies.aljazeera.net/reports/2015/08/2 01581712320835237.htm> (last accessed 9 September 2016).

48. Harith Hasan (2015), 'Al-hirak al-'Iraqi fil Janub: al-Dinamiyyat wal Ma'alat' [The Iraqi uprising in the south: its dynamics and fate], Al Jazeera Center for Studies, 19 November, <http://studies.aljazeera.net/reports/2015/11/2015111911921892441.htm> (last accessed 9 September 2016).

49. Omar al-Jaffal (2016), 'Al-Sadriyun wal Hirak al-Ijtima'i. Mararat al-Khuzlan fil 'Iraq' [The Sadrists and the Protest Movement: the bitterness of disillusion in Iraq], al-Safir al-Arabi, 1 July, <http://arabi.assafir.com/Article/5102> (last accessed 7 September 2016).

50. Skype interview with an Iraqi academic and activist, 23 January 2016.

51. Hashd refers to the popular mobilisation forces (known as al-Hashd al-Sha'abi) fighting IS, with the Iraqi security forces, in Northern and Western Iraq.

52. Sunni clerics wear a white turban and Shi'a clerics wear a black one.

53. '555' was the electoral list of al-I'tilaf al-'Iraqi al-Muwahhad (United Iraqi Alliance, UIA) during the 2005 parliamentary elections. The list gathered the major Shi'a parties and movements including the Sadrists and won more than 40 per cent of the seats in parliament.

54. This is referring to the weekly Friday protest.

55. Skype interview with a prominent figure of the ICP, 24 January 2016.

56. Potter, Sectarian Politics in the Persian Gulf, pp. 18–19.

57. Asef Bayat (2012), 'Paradoxes of Arab refo-lutions', in Bassam Haddad, Rosie Bsheer and Ziad Abu-Rish (eds), The Dawn of the Arab Uprisings. London: Pluto Press, pp. 30–1.

58. Ibid.

59. Ibid., p. 32.

Part V

Conclusion

Chapter 21

Conclusion: new directions in the study of Islamist politics

Jillian Schwedler

The Arab uprisings were undoubtedly a seminal development for Middle East politics. Few states were left untouched, even if only seven experienced revolutionary levels of mobilisation. Besides these challenges to authoritarian regimes across the region, Islamist groups behaved in ways that were sometimes surprising and unprecedented given the established literature on Islamist political participation. Much of that work, as discussed in greater detail below, focused on the experiences and strategies of particular Islamist movements as the uprisings unfolded.

But the uprisings were fascinating in part because the most established Islamist political parties in the region, long fixtures in oppositional politics, were among the latecomers to many of the populist opposition movements that characterised the early uprisings. At the same time, other Islamist groups that had long eschewed active engagement in national politics were quick to jump into the fray. The patterns of interactions between Islamist and secular and leftist groups were maintained in some instances but took new forms (of both cooperation and isolation) in others.

Several years after the uprisings began in late 2010, it is now possible to discern some new patterns of Islamist politics in the region. As with all revolutionary moments, it takes a bit of dust settling to determine what has changed and what continuities remain. To be sure, the conflicts are continuing in many countries, with the outcome of even 'settled' cases like Tunisia and Egypt uncertain in the medium, let alone the long term. This collection explores these ruptures and continuities, bringing forth detailed studies of individual cases with solidly comparative insights. In this concluding chapter, I first outline some contours in scholarly studies of Islamist politics before and after the uprisings. Then I examine the individual chapters of this volume in order to highlight the originality of their contributions, both theoretical and empirical, and how they contribute to the innovation in the study of Islamist politics. I cluster them differently to the way they are organised in the volume in order to bring additional insights and innovations to the fore.

Categories and concepts

For much of the 2000s, scholarly analyses of Islamist groups have been organised around a common set of concepts and hypotheses, often relating to the processes of moderation and radicalisation. Following the events of 11 September 2001 and the global spread of militant extremism by groups like al-Qaeda, Boko Haram, and al-Dawla al-Islamiyya (Islamic State, IS), one set of scholars tracked their attention on the rise of jihadi groups and the use of political violence, while another followed the activities and evolution of groups that eschewed violence and sought to work within existing political systems, regardless of regime efforts to control and limit their influence. This divide led to a flourishing of two nearly distinct sets of literature, one focusing on moderate Islamist movements and another on extremist Islamists (especially jihadism and terrorism). While this common-sense distinction may be useful for gaining analytic traction on certain questions, the near ubiquity of the moderate–radical divide in the literature ultimately limited the insights produced by even the best scholars.

Scholars have never entirely agreed on precise definitions for core concepts such as moderate and radical, but the most common themes and debates of the literature were nevertheless largely built around this binary. Even critiques of one or another of those literatures often did little more than add new categories, while preserving the focus on clustering various groups and offering adjectives that classified them in various ways. This approach fairly consistently located Islamist groups as the object of study, with groups categorised based on their beliefs and practices with regard to participation in the existing political system. Some of the chapters in this volume follow this model. Thus, al-Ikhwan al-Muslimun (Muslim Brotherhood, MB) groups were largely clustered together as one type of group characterised as moderate, pragmatic or integrationist. These movements all broadly followed the teachings of founder Hassan al-Banna, even as they varied significantly in the ways in which they engaged the regime and other political actors in their local settings. They were therefore also set against another cluster, Salafi groups, who were characterised as inspired by the teachings of other founding thinkers, and as engaging – or not engaging – with regimes and other political actors in strikingly different patterns. The focal point of analysis, therefore, was most often a classic comparative analysis seeking to explain variations in trajectory and behaviour between different groups or clusters of groups. While there were some notable exceptions,[1] many of the books and articles of the past two decades were studies of individual groups or of small-n comparisons of two or three Islamist movements or parties.

What got left out of many of these analyses were the diverse ways in which Islam or political Islam was a part of the broader field of politics in ways that did not map easily onto distinct groups or movements. That is, the question of Islamist politics is about not only Islamist groups and their individual (if divergent) trajectories, but also about many ways that people discuss and feel the role of Islam in their lives, in the political realm as well as elsewhere, public and private. The values and ideas that people understand to be connected with Islam find traction in a wide range of realms that we would recognise as political: social relations, economic structures and practices, and informal interactions saturated in power relations even as they stand outside of the formal sphere of politics. I am not referring here to personal piety, although many scholars have elegantly made the case that even this realm is highly political.[2] Rather, I am thinking about the ways in which people connect ideas and values that they associate with their religious beliefs to a range of practices and processes that scholars easily recognise as the realm of the political.

Although the term is a bit awkward, we can imagine this sphere as one of 'Islamistness', which invokes degrees of association or attachment across multiple fields rather than a binary distinction between what is and is not Islamist.[3] The fact that the concept is awkward is part of the reason that it can actually be intellectually productive, in that it continuously reminds us that as a category it does not work unproblematically even as it does aim to capture aspects of Islamist politics that are lost or neglected in movement-centred studies. Thinking about the dynamics and degree of Islamistness can help us to evaluate the importance of particular ideas or debates to policies, affiliations, affect, identity and alliances, without treating those debates as relevant only to those labelled Islamist.

The objective should be to move beyond the ways in which our conventional categories of actors fail to capture the complex and changing role of ideas and beliefs in shaping the region's politics. We can think about the Islamistness of particular spheres or discourses, waxing and waning over time, unevenly saturated in different social spheres or fields of politics. We would move away from attention to the 'ideological' commitments of different groups, as if those ideas were fixed and stood outside of time. We might also strive to recognise more directly in our work the ways in which differing degrees of commitment to Islamistness shape political practices and alliances, and identify the moments when those commitments are subsumed by other political logics. The point is not whether an individual or group is or is not an Islamist, is or is not a member of a particular group, and so on. Islamistness might be about the combination of a number of different logics, which are mobilised and utilised to structure our understandings of the worlds around us.[4] It is not an either/or proposition, but a complex of ideas and practices that help to make sense of the world.

To move beyond the focus on groups, we also might de-centre movements rather than abandoning the study of them, so they are not necessarily the object of our analyses. Instead of a study of the evolution of the MB in Egypt, for example, one might explore a sphere of activity and then see when, where, and how various Islamist actors (attached to groups or not) emerge into our analyses. In my current work on protests in Jordan, instead of studying the protests that the Jabhat al-'Amal al-Islami (Islamic Action Front, IAF) organises or in which it participates, I locate protests themselves as the object of study, ethnographically examining particular locales of protest activities. In many of these, the IAF and other Islamists emerge as participants in that sphere of activity. The protests around the Kaluti mosque in West Amman, for example, often include large numbers of IAF, MB, and unaffiliated Islamist participants and are thus frequently characterised as 'predominantly Islamist' in character. But as confrontations with general police (Amn al-Amm, the Public Security Directorate) or the gendarmerie riot police (*darak*) approach, virtually all Islamists have exited the scene, leaving only a small number of leftists and secular activists, who stay on to push the envelope with the security agencies. Viewing those protesters as 'predominantly Islamist' may be an accurate descriptor for the moment when the crowds are largest, but not at the (more crucial) moment of confrontation with security forces. Even though I have studied Jordan's mainstream Islamist movements for more than twenty years, this dynamic did not become fully evident to me until I began to study the protests writ large; as a result, I gained unexpected insights about the Islamist movement that I had not recognised while I was studying the movement *per se*. By focusing on broader realms of politics, rather than groups themselves, we can more accurately recognise the degrees of Islamistness across multiple social, political and economic spheres of activity and practice.

Another example might be to examine disaster relief activities. Rather than asking what Islamists are doing in the aftermath of disasters when state actors seem incapable of mounting a rapid response, one might study a particular location or site in need of relief, and then discern the extent to which the various responses need to be understood in terms of degrees of Islamistness. To make this more concrete, rather than asking whether Islamists were or were not early responders, we might notice that medical professionals who identify as Islamist organise relief efforts, but that the initiatives did not emerge from the formal groups or parties themselves. Or, perhaps, the presence of individuals with so-called Islamist affiliations may have no immediate bearing on the work being undertaken. This sort of approach also helps to untangle apparently empirical issues as to who is and is not an Islamist. As Carrie Wickham noted in her early study of the Egyptian MB,[5] the question of membership is not easily ascertained: Of the many people who occasionally attend MB events, and even of those who share substantial portions of the movement's positions, many are not 'members' of the organisation. But then how are we to think of those grey zones? An attention to the 'edges' of movements is another way to bring forth the insights that can be gained from a focus on Islamistness rather than on the evolution of groups themselves. It is not that we should not study groups or movements, but that a shift in focus can advance our theories and knowledge of Islamist politics by bringing new practices and degrees of Islamistness to light.

The contributions to this volume do not, of course, adopt the awkward concept of 'Islamistness' that I am suggesting here. Nor am I advocating that they should do so. But the spirit of this awkward concept is prominently represented in this excellent set of contributions. Each of the authors aims to think through the implications of the Arab uprisings and their effects on various spheres of activity readily identifiable as one of Islamist politics. But each is also doing precisely the work that takes us out of, and beyond, the focus on individual group or party life-cycles and genealogies. The theoretical and empirical work here is rich, indeed.

New insights on mainstream Islamist parties

Scholars should not entirely abandon the study of individual Islamist groups, particularly as many continue to be central to contentious politics in the post-uprising Middle East. Branches of the MB, for example, are still functioning legally in some countries while outlawed and subject to severe repression in others. In all cases, they continue to be consequential political actors, even if it is because regimes in places like Egypt, the UAE and Saudi Arabia are attempting to crush them. Careful and close study of these movements and their trajectories still find a central place in the analyses of Islamist politics, and careful studies with rich empirical detail will always be welcome additions to the literature. This collection contains several such noteworthy contributions.

In Chapter 5, for example, Angela Joya explores the economic policy of the MB in Egypt from 2011 until the July 2013 coup ousted it from power. She argues that the group failed in part because it did not offer a radically progressive economic vision, certainly not one that differed significantly enough from the *status quo* commitment to neo-liberal economic projects that flourished during the Mubarak era. Besides failing to present their own vision, other non-Islamist groups also proved unwilling to work with them, in large part due to the MB's unwillingness to reach out to other groups. In Joya's narrower focus on economic policy, she brings forth new insights concerning one particular realm of power relations – that of economic policy – that has received far too little attention in the broader literature on the uprisings in general and on the period during which the MB held some governing authority in Egypt in particular. Because so much of the explanation for the uprisings across the region concerns structural economic conditions, the extent to which the MB reproduced many of the policies of the Mubarak era contributes significantly to our understanding of what has and has not changed. While many analyses emphasise the Morsi period as one of a temporary disruption between an earlier authoritarian and the later one, Joya's analysis draws attention two surprising continuities between Mubarak and Brotherhood rule.

In Chapter 7, Truls Hallberg Tønnessen also turns his attention away from a linear study of a single movement – in this case the Islamic State – to a realm of practical policy-making and practice. When the IS came to control territory in Syria and Iraq, for example, precisely how did it work to realise control not only over those territories? What techniques of quotidian governance did they employ, and how much did those differ from earlier practices of governance? Tønnessen provides a fine-grained analysis of the micro-processes of incipient governance, beginning with the early days of al-Zarqawi's al-Tawhid wa al-Jihad group (founded in 2004), and continuing to the Islamic State's capture and control of broader swaths of territory. This fascinating discussion of differing narratives among groups – particularly concerning who founded what when, and who was responsible for filling the vacuum of the missing state (in Iraq) – contributes to the growing literature on rebel governance. Tønnessen's careful empirical details, like those in the rest of this volume, also contribute significantly to our overall knowledge of the practices of these movements.

In Chapter 8, Mohammed Masbah examines Morocco's Hizb al-'Adala wa al-Tanmiyya (Party of Justice and Development, PJD) after the uprisings, and its unique history (in Morocco) of sustained electoral success and endurance at the helm of government. He asks why this Islamist political party was the only one in that region to ascend to power post-uprisings, and remain in power. Drawing on, but ultimately moving beyond, the inclusion-moderation hypothesis, Masbah builds a framework of analysis that identifies three factors explaining the rise of an Islamist party to power and, perhaps most crucially, why the Moroccan regime has (as of this writing) allowed it to happen. His answer, which focuses on Morocco's unique political context in the post-uprising period, particularly the weakness of other political parties, reminds us that the pragmatism of an Islamist group will always be contingent on the domestic political context, perhaps even more than on any group's stated ideological commitments. The Moroccan case is often treated as one in which an existing regime successfully manoeuvred to deflate growing populist opposition. But Masbah's analysis brings forth quite profound political changes in both the political scene and in the Islamist movement. While the narrative goes that the existing regime has successfully deflated possible threats to its rule, transformations within the Islamist party explain why it does not challenge monarchical rule *per se*.

A broader sphere for Islamist politics

Just as many Islamist parties remain prominent actors in the region, both in power and in opposition, they do not exist in isolation of a diverse range of other political forces. A number of contributors to this volume have examined Islamist movements in careful detail, while also seeking to locate their studies of individual movements within a broader sphere of Islamist political engagement. The focus becomes less the evolution and characteristics of a particular movement than the engagements of various groups and trends within a broader political arena.

In Chapter 9, for example, Barbara Zollner engages with the inclusion-moderation hypothesis to assess changes in Egyptian Islamist parties after the uprisings. But she moves beyond many other analyses of Egyptian Islamists by attending to the wide range of Islamist-oriented parties that emerged post-2011, even if most failed to make a significant mark on the political scene, or even survive. These diverse groups are seldom even mentioned in many studies of Egypt's Islamist trends, presumably because they 'failed' to make a mark on the political scene. But Zollner reminds us that the spear of Islamist politics, even those seeking to engage directly with the regime, is not limited to the larger and seemingly more successful parties, such as those built on the foundations of the MB. Rather, across the region we have for more than a decade seen multiple smaller and alternative Islamist groups emerge to try to compete in the public political realm. Some of these have received a moderate amount of attention, such as Hizb al-Wasat (Centre Party/CP, or simply al-Wasat) in Egypt,[6] but most have been treated merely as a footnote and not integrated, as Zollner has done here, into a substantive understanding of the full realm of Islamist politics. Only by broadening our purview, as this chapter illustrates, can we seek to gain new traction on important questions such as that of sequencing, which became central to the inclusion-moderation hypothesis and the question of ideological versus strategic or pragmatic moderation.[7]

Marc Valeri takes a similar approach in Chapter 10, urging us to examine Islamist politics through a lens that captures a broader range of activities and organisations. In his study of Bahrain – a case that has received little systematic attention – he argues that both pro-regime and opposition mainstream political societies, particularly those that are Islamist in orientation, were the biggest losers of post-uprising politics. Mainstream political societies were marginalised, even as they worked tirelessly to demonstrate their commitment to an open pluralist system, and to reiterate that they did not want to monopolise power. The Shi'a Islamist Jam'iyyat al-Wifaq al-Watani al-Islamiyya (Entente – National Accord Islamic Society, or in short al-Wifaq), for example, went out of its way to demonstrate that it embraced a conciliatory approach to political reform and not a desire to overthrow the regime. But this conciliatory approach proved also to be a failure. Valeri illustrates that when regimes do not see anything to gain by broadening the realm of political participation, they are more than willing and able to simply shut everything down. Bahrain survived its massive cross-sectarian uprising only with outside assistance, but it has repressed all manner of domestic opposition on its own subsequently. The numerous and diverse political societies examined by Valeri have been almost entirely neglected in the scholarly literature, so this chapter is an important corrective empirically, while also building an approach that locates Islamist actors in a wider sphere of Islamist political opposition.

In Chapter 14, Francesco Cavatorta examines post-uprising Tunisia through a lens that complicates conventional portrayals of the field of Islamist politics there as being divided between the mainstream Hizb al-Nahda (Renaissance Party, henceforth al-Nahda), on the one hand, and Salafists on the other. Al-Nahda is like most political parties in that it has several distinct trends internally, some of which have had connections with Ben Ali's regime. Salafists in Tunisia likewise do not make up a unified or homogeneous field. Beyond those divisions, numerous unaffiliated groups in civil society also advocate for various Islamist practices, reflecting a wide range of perspectives concerning the appropriate role of Islam in the political sphere. Like others who adopt such an approach, the analytic framework seeks to understand the complexities of a broader field of Islamist politics rather than the evolution of a single group.

In Chapter 15, Jérôme Drevon rightfully notes that studies of Islamist movements often emphasise the strategies and actions of elite actors, and particularly their participation in elections. Instead, his study of the broader political field of Islamist groups includes formal political parties but also a wider range of groups and movements that invoke Islam to varying degrees and in diverse ways. This relational approach aims to reveal how these movements evolved since the uprisings, but it does not focus on a single group so much as bringing to light how interactions across and within various Islamist groups shaped their ideational commitments, as well as their repertoire of political actions. Drevon insists that a single party's evolution cannot be fully understood in isolation of other movements within the political field. He emphasises the shifting repertoires of contention that shape the debates and interactions among these diverse groups, concluding that the post-uprising period broadened repertoires of contention and encouraged the constituents of various Islamist groups to challenge the existing hierarchies and monopolisation of the elites to develop new forms of activism and political engagement.

In Chapter 16, Ibrahim Al-Marashi examines multiple Shi'a Islamist parties in Iraq and the competition and tensions between them. Although Iraqi politics is the focal point, Al-Marashi moves beyond a nation-centric frame to examine the impact of Shi'a politics elsewhere on the various movements in Iraq. In particular, he identifies how Iraqi groups have struggled to balance their reliance on Iran for support with their desire for autonomy, all the while competing domestically for dominance. The US-led invasion of 2003 also affected the contours of Islamist politics inside Iraq, escalating intra-Shi'a competition as the stakes of the political game increased with the introduction of the confessional electoral system. The emergence of IS in Iraq did not result in intra-sectarian cooperation, as one might imagine, because the individual parties continued their 'pursuit of narrow self-interest and political survival'.[8]

Finally, in Chapter 19, Souhaïl Belhadj and Laura Ruiz de Elvira also decentre Islamist movements in their study of the dynamics of the conflict in Syria. The regime has advanced a 'sectarian radicalisation of the conflict',[9] they argue, particularly given its increasing reliance on Shi'a allies including Iran and Hizbullah. Such reliance created a ripe field for Sunni extremist groups to gain a foothold in opposition to a seemingly sectarian regime. As a result, the Syrian conflict evolved from its original cross-sectarian and peaceful dynamic into a bloody protracted war, increasingly shaped by the politicisation of sectarian identities, exaserbated by the intervention of outside actors with political agendas that do not resonate with those who participated in the early months of Syria's uprisings.

De-centring Islamist movements

As suggested above, the scholarly literature on Islamist politics has advanced to the point that the range and scope of the studies of individual Islamist groups and political parties are substantive enough to enable us to make new forms of comparative analysis fruitful. The literatures on social movements and political parties, as noted above, prioritise certain kinds of questions. These questions include, but are not limited to, how particular groups or parties form, the characteristics of their leadership and constituencies, how they seek to gain new members, their activities, goals, and ideologies, and – most crucially – how they evolve over time. These are great and important questions, and I am not advocating that we should abandon them entirely. We still have much to learn about Islamist parties themselves, particularly if we turn our attention away from elites and electoral competition and examine micro practices and internal dynamics. Not all studies of Islamist politics conform to the 'life-cycle' model central to social movement studies and studies of political parties, of course, but a very large proportion of them do.[10]

Among the most exciting innovations in this volume are analyses that adopt what might be called a relational approach, rather than a movement-centric approach emphasising the evolution of a single group. The focal point of the analysis is the changing political context and its effects on movement strategies and trajectories, but always with multiple actors engaging with other actors in specific locales within the broader political realm.

In Chapter 2, for example, Mariz Tadros asks whether Mohamed Morsi faced an impossible mission in 2012–13. In addition to leading a new political party into the highest offices of governance, among his greatest challenges was the need to unify his own party. Scholars have long noted that the Egyptian MB, like all branches of the organisation, has diverse trends internal to it – a feature common to virtually every political or social organisation globally. But the challenges for Morsi were compounded with the MB's success in the parliamentary and presidential elections of 2011–12. Tadros' relational approach explores Morsi's challenges in uniting a party in which he was not previously among the dominant leaders. But he was also challenged by the need to determine what kinds of relations the party would establish with various other groups in the opposition, including more conservative Islamist parties. Morsi thus needed to lead internal party debates aimed at reconciling MB doctrine with democratic inclusivity, a tall challenge. As the party took power, it lacked internal consensus on the scope of what core concepts such as *musharaka* should entail in practice. Disagreements on such practical and strategic matters such as bureaucratic function (staffing cabinet posts and managing ministerial portfolios) were played out along with contending visions within the party around concepts such as sovereignty, the nature of the social contract, and the political community. Tadros locates Hizb al-Hurriyya wa al-'Adala (Freedom and Justice Party, FJP) at the centre of her analysis, but rather than presenting a study of a party-as-actor moving from opposition into power, she brings forth a broader field of actors, internal and external to the party, and their contending visions and expectations about what holding power could and should mean – including the need to keep Morsi in check. Significantly, these contentious debates also entailed the need to contend with the Salafi political groups, which brought different claims into the public sphere about the appropriate role of Islam. The boycott of the constitution-drafting process by non-Islamists cemented the widespread perception of Islamist homogeneity, even as those internal tensions escalated. But the July 2013 coup nearly erased these complex tensions and interactions, removing the possibility of a post-Islamist moment as a subsequent crackdown served to unify the MB as an opposition under attack.

In Chapter 6, Wanda Krause and Melissa Finn also utilise a relational approach that broadens the arena of attention from distinct Islamist groups to other actors. Their study focuses on women activists in Qatar after the uprisings who utilise Islam as a referent but who do not fit into the conventional analytic categories of either Islamist or non-Islamist. Indeed, Krause and Finn contest the idea that these activists' grounding in Islam necessarily makes them Islamist at all. Even more, these women's political activism is not oriented in a manner that suggests that their ultimate aspiration is to challenge or appropriate the state. They enact instead a form of political agency that at its core rejects the notion that repressive regimes reduce them to subjects who are either disciplined or repressed. Of course, repression exists, but the resilient authoritarian arguments so common in portions of the literature before and after the uprisings fail to address the many ways in which these women (and other actors) are routinely and 'irreverently refusing state control mechanisms'.[11] While aspects of these women's activism might be argued to support the *status quo* (by pursuing actions that fit the regime's own agenda, even if the regime is not doing the actual work), others clearly subvert state priorities, advancing their own agendas. This relational approach brings into focus a messier arena of political actors and debates about Islam, some of which would be classified as independent Islamists or not as Islamist at all, while others are affiliated with the Qatari MB. Even as these women activists are marginalised (as female subjects), they actively mobilise the citizen-subjectivities in ways the regime does not appreciate. They are non-movements, in Bayat's sense, and refuse to be aspirational in the ways that the regime – and other Islamists – would prefer. Most significantly, they are adamant in their refusal to accept the existing economic and political power structures. While they do not employ the categories of rights and citizenship, their actions nonetheless relate to the capacities of an empowered citizenry within society, including for women and other marginalised sectors.

Similarly in Chapter 11, Luciano Zaccara, Courtney Freer and Hendrik Kraetzschmar turn their attention to a broader field of 'proto-parties' in Kuwait: a wide range of organisations that function as parties in the absence of a law that legalises political parties. These proto-parties are diverse, including Shi'a and Sunni denominations, Salafi groups and groups with leftist, liberal and nationalist orientations. These groups explored other means of effecting political change, notably through cooperation across ideological lines in elections and parliament as well as in pressing claims through protests and demonstrations. They follow these practices from the decades before the uprisings to afterward, with the uprisings creating momentum in the cooperation that had already been established in previous decades. The post-uprising context did lead to some internal divisions within certain groups, as their membership struggled with whether to boycott elections or reassert a pro-regime stance. But pragmatism overwhelmingly prevailed, as a coalition of groups across the ideological spectrum ultimately re-engaged with the parliamentary system and ended their boycott.

In Chapter 18, Vincent Durac examines the rise of the nominally Shi'a Houthi movement in post-uprising Yemen. He argues that while sectarianism has taken root in the country in unprecedented ways, the 'Islamist' dimension of the current civil war cannot be reduced to sectarian tensions or even to the Saudi–Iranian tensions that are tainting the conflict. The war in Yemen resulted from long-standing political rivalries and, in particular, the practices of the political regime of Ali Abdullah Saleh dating back decades. While Durac does not deny the importance of religio-political rivalries, he decentres the 'Islamist' dimension of the war – notably the supposed Sunni–Shi'a rivalry embodied in the Saudi–Iranian struggle for power in the region. The war is not a religious conflict, he argues, but a conventional political struggle between rival centres of power both inside and outside Yemen. At the same time, however, those politics have unquestionably elevated sectarian tensions in Yemen, which are certain to resonate well beyond the end of the conflict – which is sadly not in sight.

Beyond 'Islamist' as a category

Finally, several of the contributions to this volume move beyond the focal point of movements and groups entirely. They explore the complex ways in which ideas and practices work to constitute each other in political arenas in which a range of Islamist ideas make up only a portion of the ideas in circulation. It is not only the case that the binary between the Islamist and non-Islamist is complicated, but that there is complexity and fluidity about what even counts as an Islamist idea or practice.

In Chapter 3, for example, Paola Rivetti and Adam Saleh leverage the insight that Iran's legal system is built on multiple secular and religious epistemologies to explore how ideas shape politics and *vice versa*. They note that while a wide range of actors advance political visions and arguments that adopt a 'rights' discourse in calling for expanded political participation, their interventions move from strikingly different epistemological foundations. The result is that conservative and progressive forces alike view political participation as a right, but not for the same reasons. Rivetti and Saleh anchor their insights in a careful examination of the articulation of political demands in Iran over time. The 'legal hybridity' that has emerged in the Islamic Republic has many roots in the constitutional period of the early twentieth century. During the intervening decades, the diverse languages of politics have allowed for the emergence of a perhaps surprisingly strong discourse on the right to political participation. Oppositional and pro-regime forces have used this common historical background to advocate for an inclusive political environment, even if the particularities of those visions might differ. The analysis thus offers a kind of genealogy of the emergence of a rights discourse in Iran, and one that could not appropriately be understood as one in tension between Islamist and secular epistemologies. Contentious debates therefore move across these different epistemologies, just as they cross conventional boundaries inside and outside of the regime. That is, the ideological or ideational foundations of rights discourse in Iran today are in fact quite hybrid, rather than homogeneous. Analytically distinct categories of 'theocratic' and 'secular' foundations have failed to capture the complexity of those articulations of rights about political participation.

In Chapter 4, Nazlı Çağın Bilgili and Hendrik Kraetzschmar also complicate categories of what even counts as Islamist. They build on the notion of an Islamic left to bring forth complex strains of Islamic thought and practice that have unsettled notions of Islamist thinking as either moderate and pragmatic or conservative and radical. That is, like Rivetti and Saleh, they bring into our view a range of debates that are obscured when we think in terms of the Islamist and non-Islamist. For example, neo-liberal economic policies have been incorporated into the political thinking of many Islamist movements despite criticisms from both other Islamist voices and leftist voices, perhaps better characterised as more secular. Discourses about economics here draw again from multiple epistemological foundations that may appear incongruent but in practice find enough overlap to be mutually supporting. The challenges to those economic ideas, however, likewise move from different epistemological foundations, even as the emergent critique settles on notions of justice and equality. Like the debate about the right of political participation in Iran, both the defence of neo-liberal economic policies and challenges to those policies draw on understandings of Islamist thought as they do on more secularly anchored debates about individual rights. Critiques of the repression of the Gezi Park protests in Istanbul should not be understood merely as coming from opposition or anti-regime voices. Rather, many criticisms also came from alternative Islamist voices, ones that emphasise problems with the regime's neo-liberal policies, the neglected Islamic teachings about justice, equality and social rights – especially critiques emanating from the 'Islamic left'.

In Chapter 12, Anne Wolf also extends her analysis of post-uprising politics in Tunisia by bringing two supposedly 'secular' parties into the discussion of the characteristics of the broader political field of contestation. While many studies describe that field as one populated by political parties that can be readily identified as either secular or Islamist, Wolf demonstrates that two parties frequently classified as secular – Hizb al-Tajammu' al-Dustouri al-Dimuqrati (Constitutional Democracy Rally, also known by its French acronym RCD) and Hizb Nida' Tunis (Call for Tunisia) – have become 'home to a plurality of religious expressions and varying levels of religiosity/secularity'.[12] Tensions about various parties have less to do with questions of religion or identity than they do with the conventional dynamics of elite political competition. Ben Ali himself played a role in 'de-secularlisation' during his rule, both as a political strategy of deflating opposition and because some members of his family were devout and called for a role for religion in politics. Political groups evolved over the years in response to changing political circumstances and as the stakes of the field of competition allowed for greater possibilities of engaging and obtaining political power.

In Chapter 13, Hendrik Kraetzschmar and Alam Saleh also examine the shifting dynamics of political groups across the ideological spectrum, focusing on post-Mubarak Egypt and the rise of polarisation. Secular rivalries date to the al-Sadat era, with shifting alliances and tensions over the decades between Islamists and groups with other political orientations. Unlike in Kuwait, Egypt's political field has been one in which cooperation between Islamists and leftists has been only fleeting, with longer-term dynamics better characterised as tense. But Kraetzschmar and Saleh direct our attention away from formal rhetoric, illustrating that discursive tensions are not necessarily congruent with the substantive reality of political positions and platforms. That is, in a field of political competition in which multiple parties are competing, secular and religious parties alike have incentives to portray the other as positioned at the extreme other end of the political spectrum. This 'us-versus-them' strategy sees groups exaggerate ideological distance or congruence for strategic purposes. Even more significantly, many secular or civil parties make use of religious symbolism and slogans in their public discourse. Rhetorical categorisation becomes a political strategy to portray the 'other' as outside of the norm. The post-uprising political field was, at least in 2012–13, in fact characterised by 'far greater ideological fluidity/flexibility' than the rhetoric of a wide range of political actors across the ideological spectrum would lead one to recognise. The analytic framework here provides a clear means of understanding exaggerated polarisation even as actual policy positions are in greater proximity.

Chérine Chams El-Dine focuses her attention on the emergence of an anti-sectarian discourse in Iraq since the uprisings. In Chapter 20, she argues that this new discourse explicitly critiqued the incumbent Shi'a Islamist political parties, which actively sought 'to stifle the movement using intimidation, repression and the spreading of false rumors'.[13] Contra conventional wisdom, Iraq did have an uprising in 2011, but it did not escalate due to lack of international support, repression by the regime and scorching summer temperatures. But it set the stage for another wave of protests, which materialised in 2015–16. El-Dine does not merely document these often-ignored protests, but she illustrates the changed repertoire of the protesters – utilising cartoons, videos and creative slogans – and in particular the effort to forge anti-sectarianism. Some of the slogans emphasised the exploitation of religious symbols and rhetoric by the regime, and others invoked corruption and economic exploitation.

In Chapter 17, Katerina Dalacoura turns our attention to the international relations of the Middle East post-uprisings, asking how the field of Islamist politics has evolved as a result of shifts in aspects of international relations concerning the connections, alliances, balances of power among actors and states. But she extends her inquiry beyond economic, political, and military dimensions to the ideational realm of ideas and values, including notions of 'recognition' and 'legitimacy'. Prior to the uprisings, she argues that Islamist movements across the region had largely positioned themselves in opposition to the 'pro-Western' camp comprised of Israel, Egypt, Saudi Arabia and Turkey. Although varied, much Islamist thought could be described as 'third-worldist, 'anti-imperialist', resisting not only foreign intervention into the region but the regimes propped up by foreign support. But as sectarianism has spread, common causes between groups like Hizbullah and Hamas became strained. Hamas leader Khaled Mishal, for example, no longer found Damascus a hospitable environment, finding refuge first in Egypt but then later in Qatar. Whereas sectarianism was used by a certain political elite to foment tensions and resentments, those ideas have taken hold and now characterise much of the regional and international relations of Middle East politics. The decline or defeat of moderate Islamist opposition movements across the region has likewise affected broader regional politics, where IS is now a major political actor even as it sees its strength in Syria and Iraq challenged. Saudi Arabia and Qatar have taken very different positions on moderate groups like the Muslim Brotherhood branches, and this has impacted domestic politics across the region. Truly regional in scope, Dalacoura's contribution highlights the inter-connections in terms of strategies and commitments as well as the realm of ideas and values, demonstrating that no single-country focus on Islamists could possibly offer a complete picture of the field of Islamist politics.

Conclusion

The contributions to this volume build on the strength of the existing literature on Islamist politics while also exploring new theoretical frameworks that suggest promising directions and new modes of gaining analytic traction. The post-uprising Middle East and North Africa is one in which Islamist actors are continuing to be centrally relevant, not only for their successes but also because strong regimes have focused so much attention on repressing certain Islamist groups and voices. Those very regimes, however, often deploy their own modes of Islamist discourse in their quest to legitimate their repressive and sometimes monstrous regimes. The contributions to this volume demonstrate that rather than moving beyond Islamist politics, we as a scholarly community would do well to innovate and experiment with our analytic frameworks in order to find new means of identifying and understanding the complex ways in which practices of politics shape and are shaped by a wide range ideational and epistemological frameworks that give form to the political arena.

Notes

1. Some sweeping studies aimed to examine political Islam writ large, as one might consider the rise and decline of Arab nationalism. See, for example, Olivier Roy and Carol Volk (2008), *The Failure of Political Islam*, Cambridge, MA: Harvard University Press. One of the most important voices to push beyond the study of Islamist groups was Asef Bayat, who emphasises the evolution of thinking about Islam and politics and the emergence of new modes that do not fit the 'Islamist' model. He adopts the term 'post-Islamism', suggesting a temporal movement beyond the primacy of groups as the repositories of Islamist-inflected political visions, to something else. See Asef Bayat (2007), *Making Islam Democratic: Social Movements and the Post-Islamic Turn*. Stanford: Stanford University Press and Asef Bayat (2013) (ed.), *Post-Islamism: The Changing Face of Political Islam*. Oxford: Oxford University Press.
2. Saba Mahmood (2004), *The Politics of Piety: The Islamic Revival and the Feminist Subject*. Princeton: Princeton University Press.
3. Some of these ideas were first explored in this short memo: Jillian Schwedler (2016) 'Why "Islamism" does not help us understand the Middle East', in *Evolving Methodologies in the Study of Islamism*, POMEPS Studies 17.
4. I am grateful to Paola Rivetti for drawing out this question of multiple logics.
5. Carrie R. Wickham (2002), *Mobilizing Islam: Religion, Activism, and Political Change in Egypt*. Ithaca, NY: Cornell University Press.
6. See e.g. Carrie R. Wickham (2004), 'The path to moderation: strategy and learning in the formation of Egypt's Wasat party', *Comparative Politics*, 1, pp. 205–28 or Joshua A. Stacher (2002), 'Post-Islamist rumblings in Egypt: the emergence of the Wasat party', *Middle East Journal*, 1, pp. 415–32.
7. I provide a survey of this particular question in my review article: Jillian Schwedler (2011), 'Can Islamists become Moderates? Rethinking the inclusion-moderation hypothesis', *World Politics*, 63:2, pp. 347–76.
8. See Ibrahim al-Marashi's contribution to this volume, p, 274.
9. See Souhaïl Belhadj and Laura Ruiz de Elvira's contribution to this volume, p. 322.
10. I include in this category my book on Islamist political parties in Jordan and Yemen, which adopted a highly conventional variation-finding research design. It examines the evolution and trajectory of two separate Islamist parties, both built on the foundation of local branches of the MB, with an eye toward identifying similarities and differences in those trajectories. The resulting contribution is one that leveraged differences between the two parties to generate hypotheses aimed at explaining that variation. See Jillian Schwedler (2006), *Faith in Moderation: Islamist Parties in Jordan and Yemen*. New York: Cambridge University Press.
11. See Wanda Krause and Melissa Finn's contribution in this volume, pp. 70–89.
12. See Anne Wolf's contribution in this volume, pp. 205–21.
13. See Chérine Chams El-Dine contribution in this volume, pp. 341–56.

Index